Microsoft Works 3 for Windows By Example

Craig Hadden

Adapted from Works 2 for Windows By Example
by Suzie Wynn-Jones

Webster & Associates

Microsoft Works 3 for Windows By Example
Craig Hadden

Webster & Associates
Unit 2, Allambie Grove Business Park
25 Frenchs Forest Rd, Frenchs Forest
NSW Australia 2086
Phone: (02) 975 1466
Fax: (02) 452 3493
ACN: 001646 180

Notice of Liability:

The information in this book is distributed on an "As is" basis, without warranty. While every precaution has been taken in the preparation of this book, neither the author nor Webster & Associates shall have any liability to any person or entity with respect to any liability, loss, or damage caused or alleged to be caused directly or indirectly by the instructions contained in this book or by the computer software and hardware products described therein.

Trademarks:

Throughout this book, trademarked names are used. Rather than put a trademark symbol in every occurrence of a trademarked name, we are using the names only in an editorial fashion and to the benefit of the trademark owner, with no intention of infringement of the trademark. Where those designations appear in this book, the designations have been printed in initial caps.

Published 1994

ISBN: 0 86398 050 4

Printed and bound in Australia

Works 3 By Example

This book adopts a visual approach to learning computer software. Each chapter describes and illustrates a number of related concepts, primarily through the use of screen shots and diagrams combined with short concise explanations.

While conventional computer books lean towards providing extensive textual explanations, *Microsoft Works 3 for Windows By Example* takes a far more visual approach—pictures literally show you what to do, and the text is a clear, concise commentary. Learning becomes easier, because the book familiarizes you with the look and feel of your software. Learning also becomes faster, since there are no long-winded passages.

To reinforce the learning process, we have included 13 self-paced exercises, liberally sprinkled with screen shots. The first page(s) of each exercise briefly describe the exercise in step form. The following pages provide more detailed instructions with illustrations and explanations, guiding you through the exercise, expanding each step in simple terms.

Acknowledgments

The author wishes to acknowledge and thank the effort and dedication of the following people:

Tony Webster

Jenny Hamilton

Contents

Chapter 23: Including Spreadsheets in a Word Processor Document

Chapter 24: Including Charts in a Word Processor Document

Chapter 25: Including Databases in a Word Processor Document

Chapter 26: Using WorksWizards and AutoStart Templates

Exercise Section

Introduction

Microsoft Works is an integrated package which is used extensively in business and educational areas. Recent estimates suggest that more than two million people worldwide use Microsoft Works.

With the rising popularity of Microsoft Windows and the graphical operating environment that it creates, a Windows version of Works was made available.

Introduction to Works for Windows

The Windows version retains many of the features which have made Works so popular in the DOS version, while incorporating Windows functions allowing added flexibility and ease of use.

If you are new to Works, you will find Works for Windows easy to learn and use. If you are an experienced user of Works under DOS, you will find the transition to the Windows environment enjoyable and rewarding.

Works for Windows is an integrated package which is made up of four main tools. These tools are a word processor, a spreadsheet, a database, and a communications package. Each of these can be used on its own to manipulate documents of various kinds. The uses of each tool are outlined below.

Word Processor

A word processor is a writing tool which enables you to manipulate characters—letters or digits—on the screen. A word processor can be used to compose letters, papers, and documents in Works for Windows.

Spreadsheet

A spreadsheet is a table of columns and rows. Words (called labels), numbers (called values), and formulas are inserted into the spreadsheet. These are used to calculate things such as budgets and invoices.

Database

A database is a collection of information organized so the information in the database can easily be found and manipulated when needed.

Communications package

A communications package enables you to send and receive information using the telephone line using your computer and a device called a modem.

Integrating the Works for Windows application

The tools in Works for Windows are designed to work together. For example, information from the database can be brought into a word processor document when you need to send a number of copies of the one letter to a number of people.

Another example of integrating data in Works for Windows is to insert a chart into a word processor document. The chart would represent figures in a Works for Windows spreadsheet file. This information can also be linked, which means that when the information changes in the spreadsheet, these changes will be reflected in the word processor document automatically!

Works for Windows incorporates MSDraw, a dedicated graphics package. This allows you to create freehand drawings and insert clipart, which can be imported back into the Word Processor program.

These, and many other features of Works for Windows, are covered in this book.

Windows

Text-based systems

Traditionally, IBM and compatible personal computers have operated on what is called a "text-based" level. DOS itself is a typical text-based program.

In a text-based operating environment, such as that which is created by DOS, commands to the computer are typed in through the keyboard and appear on the screen as alphabetic and numeric characters. The computer communicates with its users by displaying messages and data on the screen; also in alphabetic and numeric form.

Under DOS, if a program is to have any graphical characteristics, these features would have to be created by the program itself.

One result of this limitation is that DOS-based programs require more disk and memory space. Each program has to contain its own commands for using and controlling graphics.

Another result, is that each DOS-based program, because it designs its own graphics, has a unique appearance. This uniqueness makes each program more difficult to learn. It also makes the mastery of one program of little, or no, help in the learning of another.

The Windows graphical user interface

The Windows program creates a graphics-based working environment on your computer called a *graphical user interface* (GUI). In Windows, commands are selected by positioning the mouse pointer over graphical pictures or symbols rather than by typing them in through the keyboard.

There are many advantages to using Windows. All programs written for use with Windows conform to a standard "look and feel." The way commands are entered, the way the screen is organized, and the way programs are manipulated remain standard throughout a wide range of Windows applications.

Under Windows, each application program can concentrate on serving its specialized purpose, while such details as command menus, screen colors, the handling of peripheral devices (printers, monitors, etc.), and the allocation of memory, are left to Windows itself.

Because many aspects of Windows applications are handled by Windows itself, the appearance, and function, of most Windows programs have much in common. Windows applications can be learned and mastered more quickly. The usual confusion that one often faces when switching between programs is minimized in Windows, because there are fewer differences to overcome.

For a more detailed account of the advantages of using Windows, consult your Windows user's manual.

Command menus and dialog boxes

Windows uses a standardized set of on-screen methods to obtain information from its users. It is one of the advantages of Windows, that all Windows applications, including Works, use the same type of input media.

Command menus

Windows uses a device known as a "menu" to accept commands from its users. Figure Intro-1 shows the top of the Works editing screen.

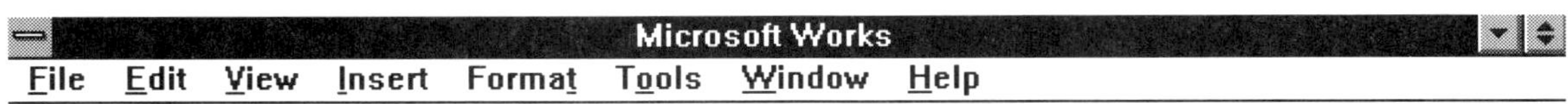

Figure Intro-1. *The menu bar consists of a list of menu titles below the title bar at the top of the Works editing screen.*

The list of words below the title bar is called the menu bar. The menu bar contains the titles of each of the available menus. To view the commands available in a given menu, click the left mouse button once on the menu's title in the menu bar.

As illustrated in Figure Intro-2, a menu consists of a menu title above a list of menu commands. To select a command from a menu, position the mouse pointer over the desired command and click the button once.

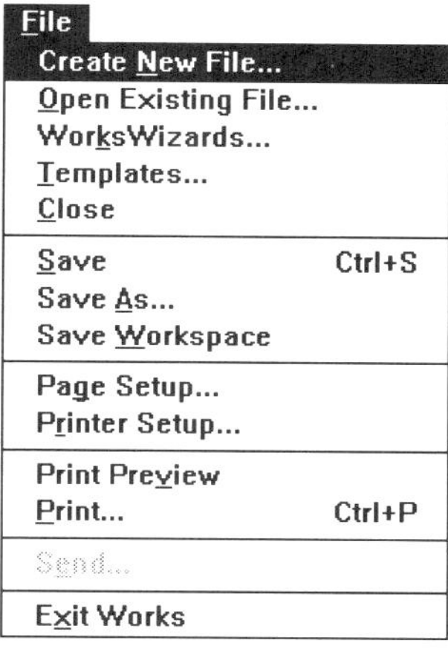

Figure Intro-2. *In Windows programs, a menu consists of a menu title, in this case the word "File," above a list of menu commands. The menu shown here is the* ***File*** *menu from Works.*

A quicker way of selecting a command from a menu is to click, and hold, the mouse button over the desired menu title and—while keeping the mouse button depressed—drag the mouse pointer to the desired command. The command will become selected when the mouse button is released.

In this book, menu titles are always stated in bold-faced type and menu commands are always shown in italics. Thus the command highlighted in Figure Intro-3 would be referred to as the *Tabs* command in the **Format** menu.

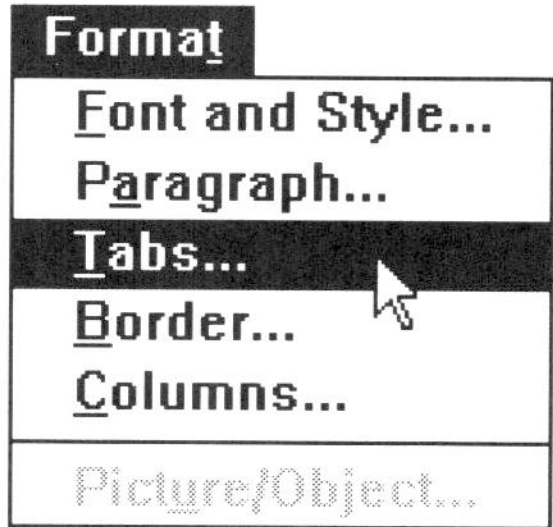

Figure Intro-3. *In this figure, the Tabs command is highlighted in the* ***Format*** *menu.*

Dialog boxes

Sometimes you are required to provide more information before a selected command can be done. To allow this information to be entered, Windows has features known as dialog boxes. Special devices, called input media, appear within dialog boxes to allow you to enter information as easily as possible.

In Works, dialog boxes appear when a menu command with an ellipsis is selected. In Figure Intro-3, for example, you know that a dialog box will appear when *Tabs* is selected.

Figure Intro-4 shows a dialog box that contains examples of the major input media found within dialog boxes.

In this book, all elements within dialog boxes are shown in italics. This makes it easier for you, the reader, to understand the information being presented.

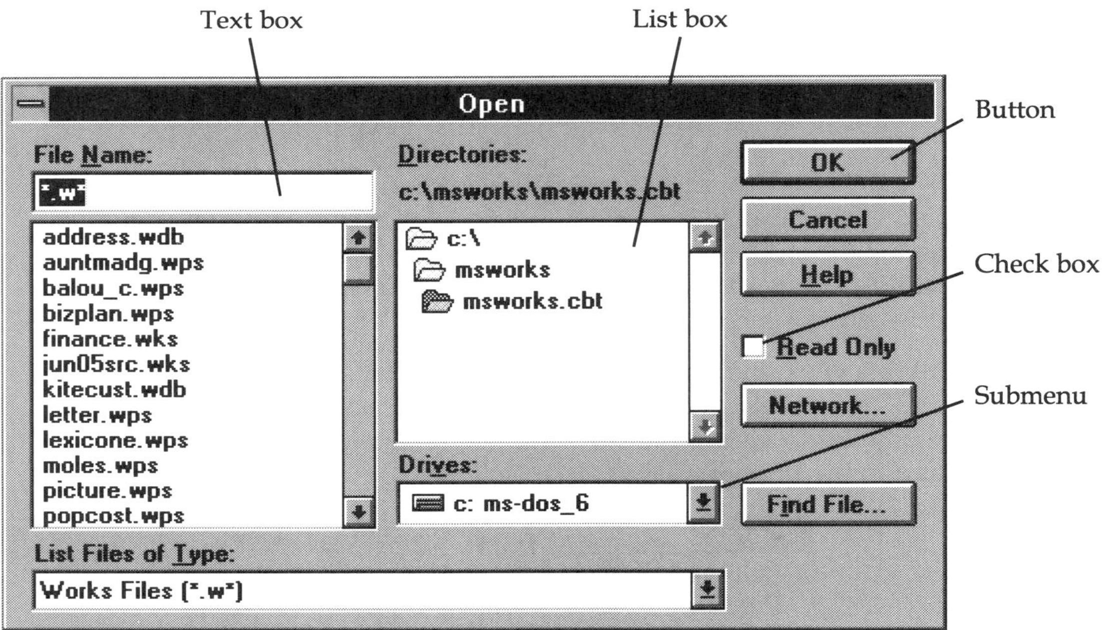

Figure Intro-4. *This dialog box contains examples of most of the major media found in dialog boxes in Works.*

The By Example approach

Microsoft Works for Windows By Example follows the unique *By Example* learning approach.

Graphic screen images

Because Windows programs rely heavily on graphics-based interaction with the user, *Microsoft Works for Windows By Example* includes more than 1,000 screen images taken directly from Works itself.

At each step in the learning process, figures will show you the appearance of the Works screen or dialog box being discussed.

Figure Intro-5 shows the Works editing screen as it appears when the program is first started.

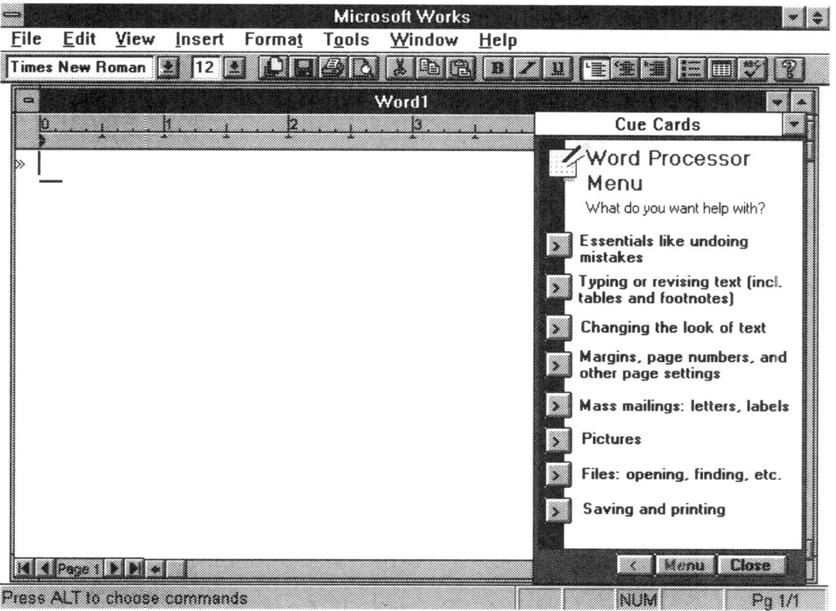

Figure Intro-5. *The Works editing screen which appears when the program is first started.*

Interactive examples

The best way to master any computer program, particularly a program such as Works which is very interactive, is to use it. The chapters in this book are designed in the form of interactive examples.

While you can read each chapter individually for reference, it will greatly enhance your learning process to follow through each chapter on your own computer. Each chapter will take you, step by step, through various Works features and commands. By following the steps yourself, you will learn much more quickly. As you follow the examples in each chapter, you can compare the screen images in the book with the appearance of your own screen.

Exercises

To reinforce the information in each chapter, and to provide additional hands-on training, most chapters include an exercise. While it is not essential to the learning process to complete every exercise, they can be helpful in strengthening your grasp on the material. The exercises can also give you an idea of how well you have mastered the subject matter.

Each exercise begins with a concise list of steps that incorporate the concepts and commands covered in the preceding chapter. If you feel comfortable enough with the material, you may want to complete the steps as outlined at the start of the exercise.

Following the initial list of steps, each of the steps is restated, one at a time, along with a detailed account of the commands and selections required to carry out each step. As with the examples in the chapters, each step is accompanied by a complete series of screen images showing the progression from the beginning to the end of the exercise.

To ensure that all readers can derive maximum benefit from the exercises, many are based on the sample files included with Works. You can copy these files to your hard disk when you install Works. Before using these files to complete the exercises, make a second copy of them to a different subdirectory to protect them from accidental modification.

Assumptions and default settings

The screen images and descriptions in this book try to follow, as closely as possible, the way the program will appear on your computer. However, as no two computer systems are organized in exactly the same way, differences between users are inevitable.

Thus, your screen may not always look the same as every screen image in this book and files may not always be in the same subdirectories.

The screen images displayed in this book provide a gray shading, three-dimensional effect, and are all displayed as they would appear on a VGA monitor.

The toolbar

Most of the images of the Works editing screen in this book include the Toolbar along the top of the document window. In Works, the toolbar display is optional. It has been included in this book because it is a useful addition to the screen which enhances the power of the program. We recommend that you use the toolbar when using Works.

If the toolbar does not appear on your editing screen, you can activate it by selecting the *Toolbar* command from the **View** menu, as seen in Figure Intro-6.

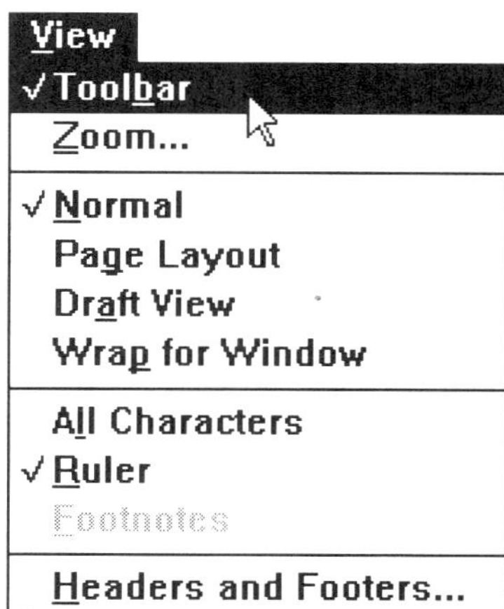

Figure Intro-6. *The Toolbar command in the* ***View*** *menu activates (or deactivates) the toolbar display in the editing screen.*

Subdirectories

When you install Works, you can decide which files are placed in which subdirectories. This decision will depend, in part, on your personal preference. It will also depend on the disk resources available on your computer and on the subdirectories that already exist on your disk before Works is installed.

In this book, a number of the most likely subdirectory structures have been represented throughout different chapters. Though your own system will not match all of our examples, it is likely that it will match with some of them.

Cue cards

When you start Works after installation, the program displays cue cards. These are notes that give you help on your screen while you use Works. You may want to switch off the cue cards because they obscure about one-third of your document window. To do this, choose the *Cue Cards* command from the **Help** menu as shown in Figure Intro-7. Works removes the check mark from this command when you switch off cue cards. You can choose this command again if you do want to see cue cards at any time.

In this book we show what your screen looks like with cue cards switched off.

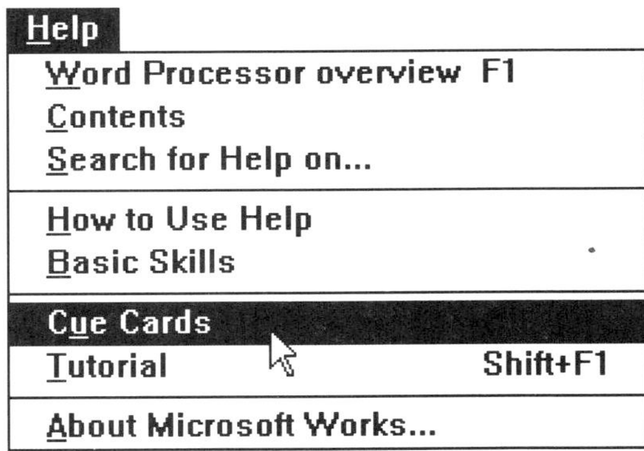

Figure Intro-7. *The Cue Cards command in the **Help** menu deactivates (or activates) the cue cards display in the editing screen.*

The Word Processor Screen

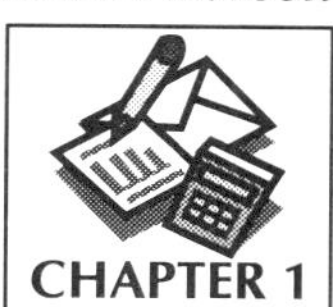

In this chapter you will learn how to start up the word processor from the Microsoft Works *Startup* dialog box. Once a document has been loaded, you will be shown the various components of the screen. It is important to become familiar with these as they give you access to the many features of the Works word processor.

Starting the word processor

The word processor can be accessed in two ways, either by creating a new file or opening an existing file. By clicking on the *Word Processor* button in the *Startup* dialog box, Works will create a new file with which you can work. To open a file which has already been created, select the *Open an Existing Document* button or click on one of your *Recently used files* in the *Startup* dialog box.

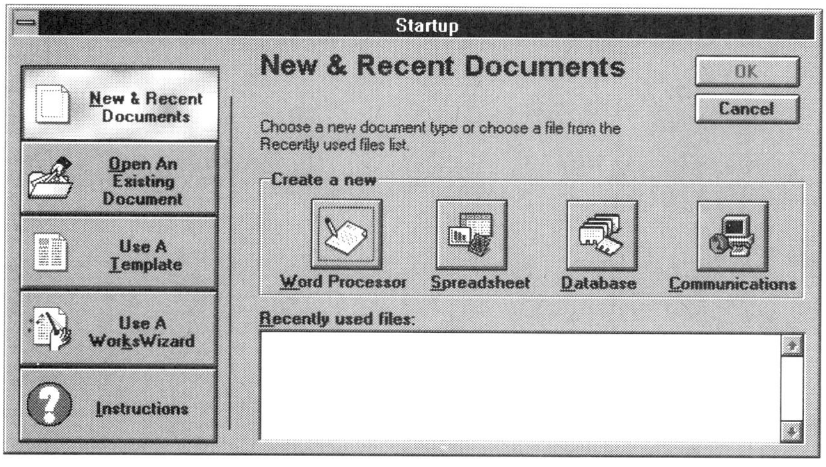

Figure 1-1. The Works Startup dialog box.

However, there are times when the *Startup* dialog box does not appear. This happens particularly when you have been using another part of Works, such as the database. If this does happen, you will need to access a new file or open an existing one through the **File** menu. The option you will choose will either be *Create New File*, or *Open Existing File*, depending on your needs.

Most of the work you do in the word processor takes place in the editing screen. To make the most of this program, you must be able to identify, and use, the various tools and components of this screen.

The editing screen is made up of many elements, which combine to give you access to the different word processor functions and commands. In the next chapter **Creating Documents**, you will be looking at the different parts of the editing screen shown below in Figure 1-2. The following chapters of this book will cover, in more detail, each of the elements introduced to you here.

Parts of the word processor screen

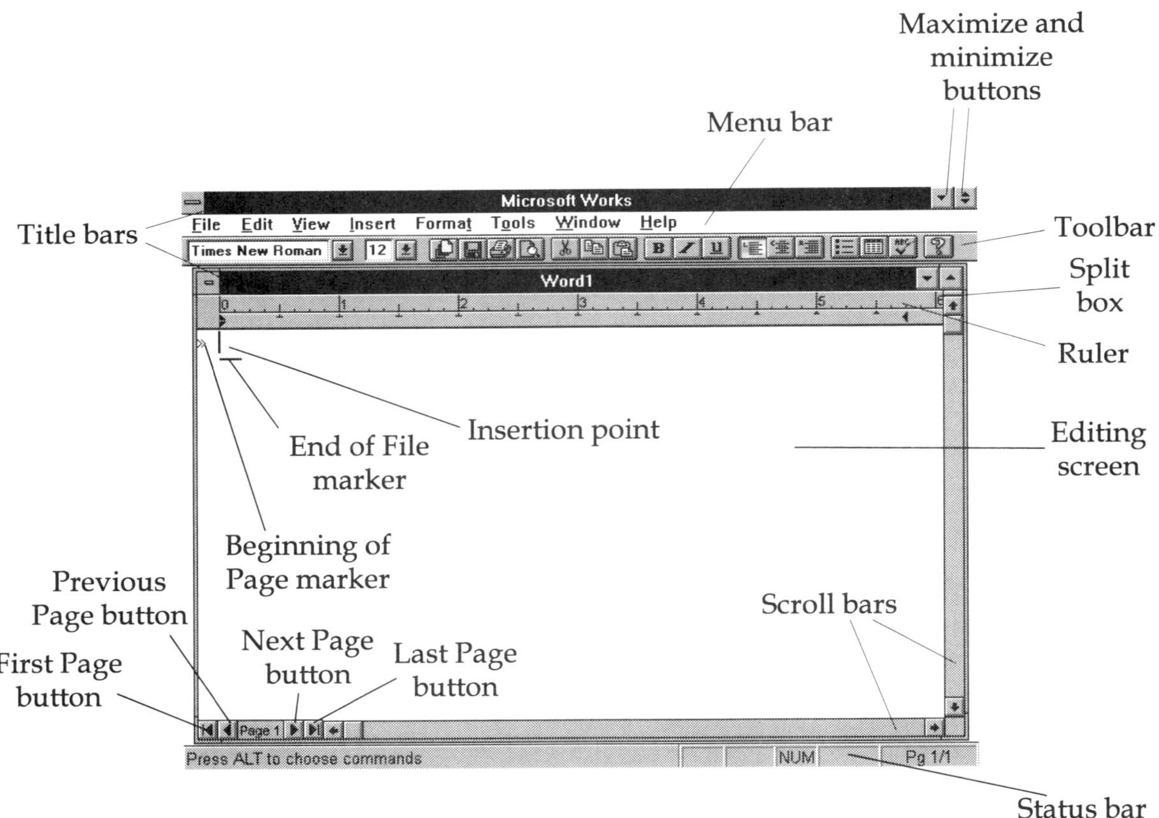

Figure 1-2. *Works word processing screen.*

TITLE BAR

When you open a new file you will see two title bars (Figure 1-2). One is at the top of the application window and tells you that you are using Works. The other, at the top of the document window, tells you the name of the document. If it is a new file, Word1 is displayed and remains until the file is saved. This is a generic label used to identify and number documents that have not yet been given a unique name (Figure 1-3).

Figure 1-3. *Document window title bar showing that the file has not been saved.*

When you save a file for the first time, you give it a name and assign it to a specific disk drive and subdirectory. The file name will be displayed in the title bar, replacing the generic Word title (Figure 1-4).

When you open or retrieve a file, the title bar will change to reflect the name of that file.

Figure 1-4. *Document window title bar showing that the file has been saved.*

It is not essential, however, to have two title bars on the screen at the same time. To consolidate the screen into one window, the document window needs to be maximized, a standard Windows feature. When the maximize button, shown in Figure 1-2, is clicked, the screen will display just one title bar. The name of the application as well as the name of the file will be on this consolidated title bar (Figure 1-5). Most examples in this book will display the application window maximized.

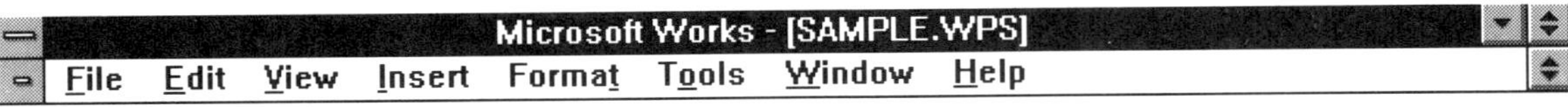

Figure 1-5. The maximized title bar, combining the application and document windows.

MENU BAR

At the top of your screen, below the title bar, are displayed the words **File, Edit, View, Insert, Format, Tools, Window,** and **Help**. These are the titles of the command menus that make up the Works menu bar.

File Edit View Insert Format Tools Window Help

Figure 1-6. The Works menu bar.

To select an option from the menu using the mouse, move the pointer onto **File,** for example, and click. The various commands associated with the **File** menu will then appear on the screen as shown in Figure 1-7. Alternatively, you may use the keyboard—hold down the Alt key and press the underlined letter in the option you wish to access—in this case the F key. Once the menu is open, just press the letter which is underlined to select the option you require. See the **Command Menus and Dialog Boxes** section in the **Introduction** for more information on selecting menu commands with the mouse or keyboard.

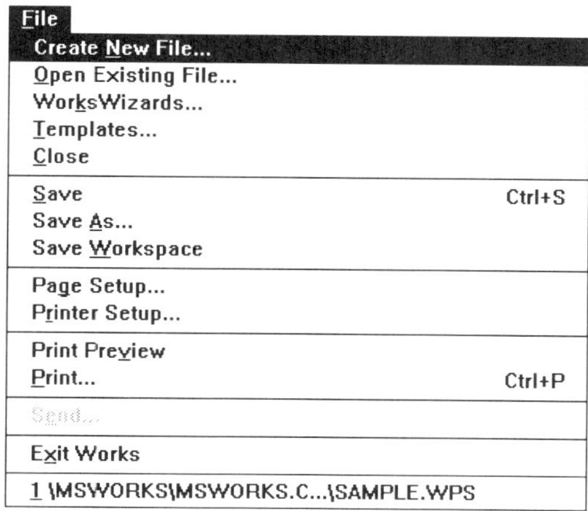

Figure 1-7. *The Works* ***File*** *menu.*

Toolbar

The toolbar is intended to save time and effort by enabling quick access to the most frequently used commands in Works. Using the toolbar, you can change the appearance of highlighted text, align paragraphs, or save your document for example. The toolbar also gives you access to the printing commands within Works.

Figure 1-8. *The Works toolbar.*

When you hold the mouse pointer over a toolbar button, Works displays its function below the pointer. Clicking the mouse pointer on one of the buttons activates the corresponding menu command. When a command is activated, the button on the toolbar appears depressed. To deactivate the command, just click on it again.

The toolbar can be turned on or off from the *Toolbar* command in the **View** menu.

The next diagram illustrates each toolbar button and its function:

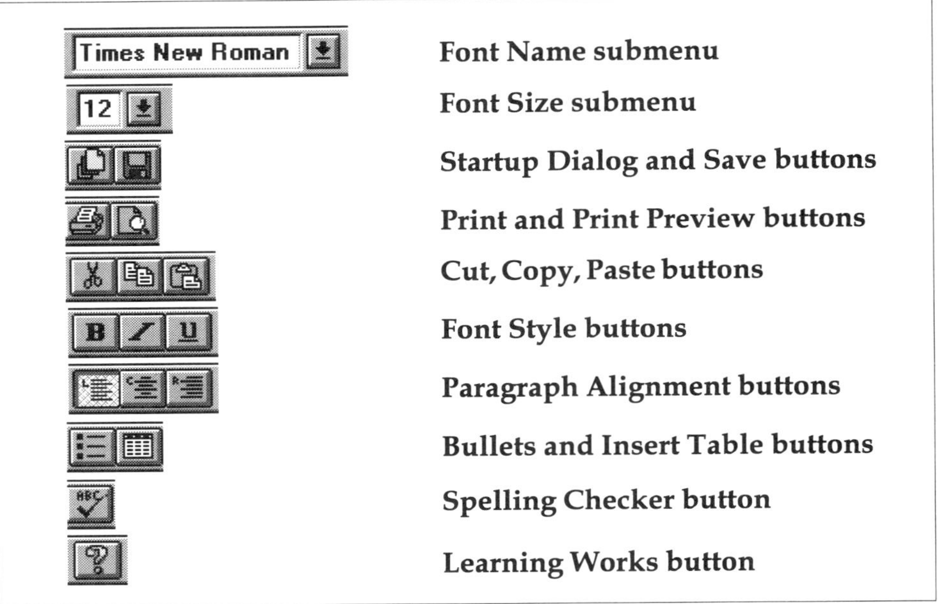

Figure 1-9. *The Works toolbar buttons.*

RULER

The ruler, if selected, appears at the top of the document screen. The ruler's measurements can be displayed in inches, centimeters, picas, points, and millimeters.

The ruler will vary according to the settings you have given to a particular document. These settings appear along the bottom of the ruler and include margins, tab marks, and indents.

The margin indicators show the exact positions of the left and right margins of the document. The right margin is marked by the triangle on the right and the left margin, by the bottom small triangle on the left. The left margin indicators are also used to indent text on your page. The default margins for Works are 1.25 inches for both left and right. On the screen, the left margin is always denoted as 0 on the ruler (see Figure 1-10).

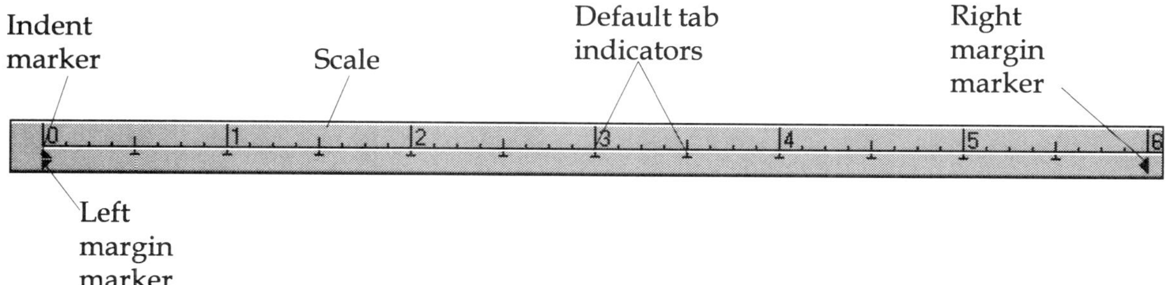

Figure 1-10. *The Works ruler.*

In taking a closer look at the ruler, you will notice that below the measuring scale are small upside-down Ts. These are the default tab indicators and are used to show what tabs have been set for the document. You can change these tabs to suit your own needs and we will discuss this later in the book.

The ruler can be turned on or off from the *Ruler* command in the **View** menu (Figure 1-11). A check mark against this command indicates when you have selected it.

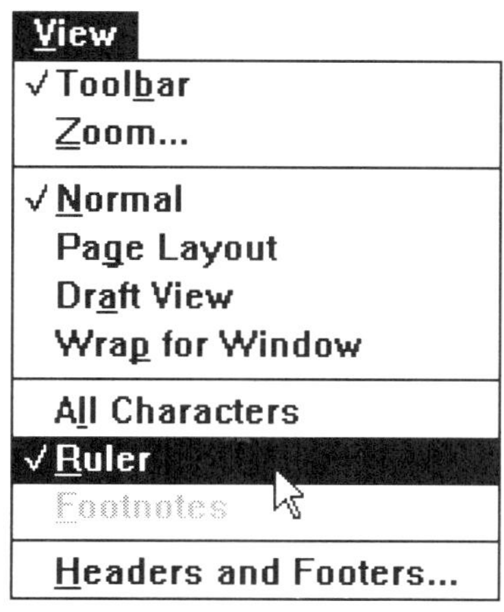

Figure 1-11. *The Ruler command in the **View** menu.*

SCROLL BARS

The scroll bars are situated along the bottom and right-hand sides of the screen (Figure 1-2) and allow you to shift your view to any part of the document. Scroll bars are a standard Windows feature.

STATUS BAR

The status bar appears at the bottom of the screen below the horizontal scroll bar. It is used to display a series of instructions and messages.

These messages include a description of an active menu option; whether CAPS or NUM Lock is on; your position in the document and information specific to the word processing tool. The status bar in Figure 1-12 shows the cursor is on page 1 of a 6 page document, as an example.

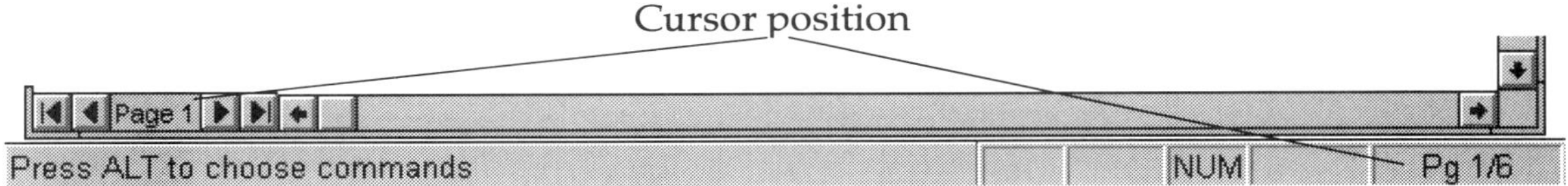

Figure 1-12. *The Works status bar showing that the cursor is on page 1 of a 6-page document.*

The status bar can be turned on or off through *Options* in the **Tools** menu. The *Show status bar* option in the *Options* dialog box in Figure 1-13 is checked, therefore the status bar will show on the screen.

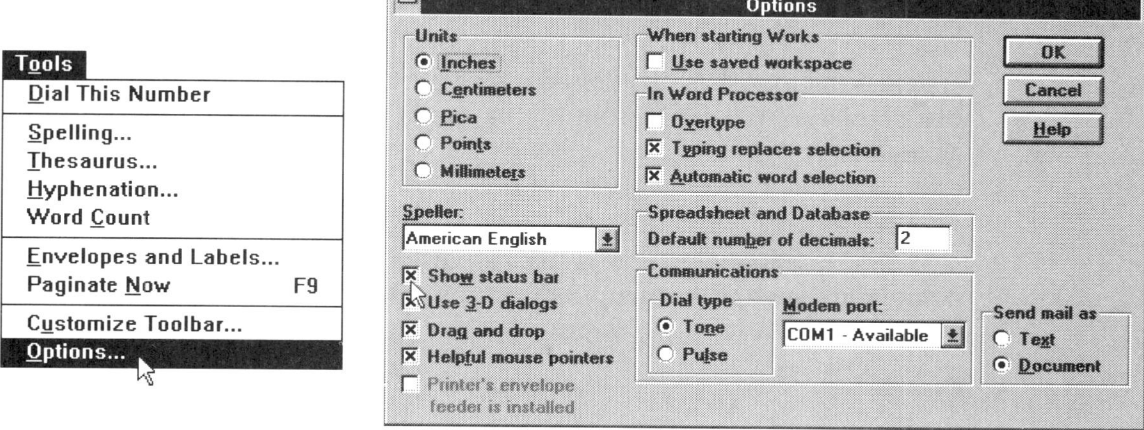

Figure 1-13. *The Show status bar check box in the Options dialog box, obtained from choosing Options from the* ***Tools*** *menu, turns the status bar on or off.*

Editing screen

When you open a new document, the editing screen will be blank except for the insertion point, beginning-of-page and end-of-file markers. These are highlighted in Figure 1-2.

These markers are always displayed in the word processor. The end-of-file marker moves down the screen as you insert more text into your document. It is impossible to move the insertion point below this mark.

Insertion point (text cursor)

The insertion point appears on the screen as a blinking vertical line, showing you exactly where the next character will be entered in the document.

You can move the insertion point around by using either the mouse or the cursor movement keys. Each of these methods will be discussed in **Chapter 2, Creating Documents**.

MOUSE POINTER

When the mouse is positioned over a part of the screen where text can be placed, the position of the mouse is marked by an "I-beam" shaped icon: .

When the mouse pointer is over a part of the screen for selecting commands, such as the menus or the ruler, it takes the form of a hollow arrow: .

Display options

Works enables you to change how the editing screen appears without changing the actual content of the document. These options, which are outlined below, are particularly useful when creating and editing large or complex documents.

VIEW ALL CHARACTERS

The *All Characters* command is in the **View** menu shown in Figure 1-14. It enables you to view not only the text and its attributes, but also the special characters which are placed into the document as you type. These are placed there as instruction codes. This feature is frequently used when editing a document.

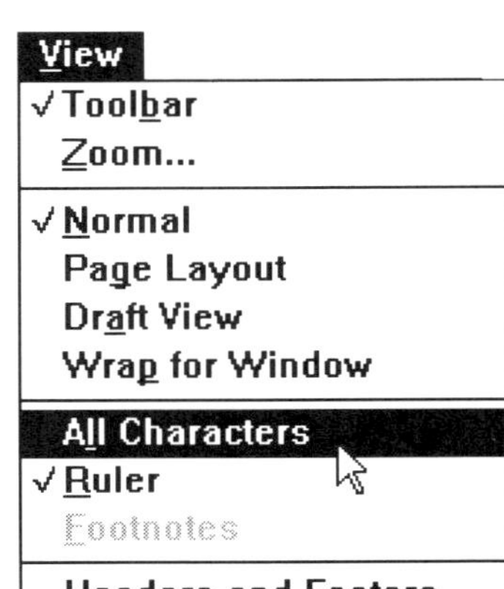

Figure 1-14. *The All Characters command in the **View** menu.*

Some of the more common special characters are the paragraph mark, the tab mark, the end-of-line mark, and the space mark, all shown in Figure 1-15. When the document is printed, these special characters are replaced with what they are representing. For instance, if you have put in a tab, the arrow is not printed.

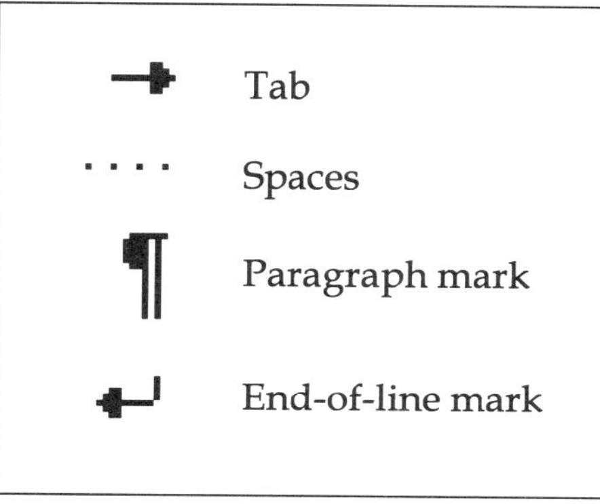

Figure 1-15. *Some special Works characters.*

Wrap for Window

The *Wrap for Window* option in the **View** menu (see Figure 1-14) ensures that all text on the page can be seen on the screen without having to alter the right margin. When *Wrap for Window* is active, Works does not use the right margin as a guide for word wrap, but instead wraps the words onto the next line at the edge of the window. When the document is printed, however, a new line is determined by the right margin.

Normal, Page Layout, and Draft View

Works lets you choose any one of the *Normal, Page Layout,* and *Draft View* options from the **View** menu (Figure 1-14).

Page Layout lets you view your document including margins, objects, pictures, columns, headers, footers, and footnotes as they will appear when you print your document. Using this option decreases the speed at which you can scroll through your document but may save you from printing an incorrectly formatted document.

When you select *Page Layout* Works disables the *Wrap For Window* option so that you see your document as it appears on paper. *Page Layout* is similar to *Print Preview* but also allows you to edit your document (see **Chapter 7, Printing Word Processed Documents** for information on *Print Preview*).

When *Draft View* is selected from the **View** menu (see Figure 1-14), the screen will display the text in one font only. *Draft View* increases the speed at which you can scroll through a document.

Draft View is used particularly with long and complex documents which contain a variety of fonts, font sizes, attributes, and styles. It does not alter the document but will not display the different fonts, graphics, borders, or charts on the screen.

Select the *Normal* option to compromise between the speed of your screen display and the accuracy of what you see compared with the printed page. This is the default option.

Zoom

You can choose *Zoom* from the **View** menu if you want to increase or decrease the scale of your view of the document on screen. Select the magnification you want from the *Zoom* dialog box and click on *OK*. You can open this dialog box again and select *100* from the *Magnification (%)* options if you want to set the magnification of your view back to its normal setting (see Figure 1-16).

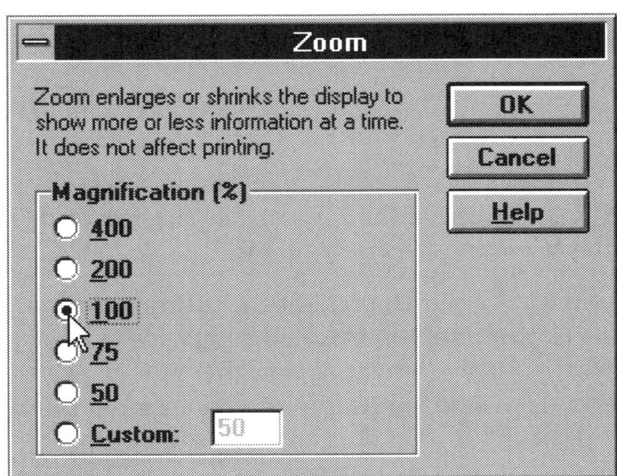

***Figure 1-16.** Select 100 from the Zoom dialog box to set magnification to normal.*

SPLITTING THE EDITING SCREEN

When working with a long document, it is sometimes necessary to compare two parts of the document which are not close to each other. In order to do this you need to split the screen. The word processor in Works enables you to split the screen horizontally (Figure 1-17) into two areas called *panes*.

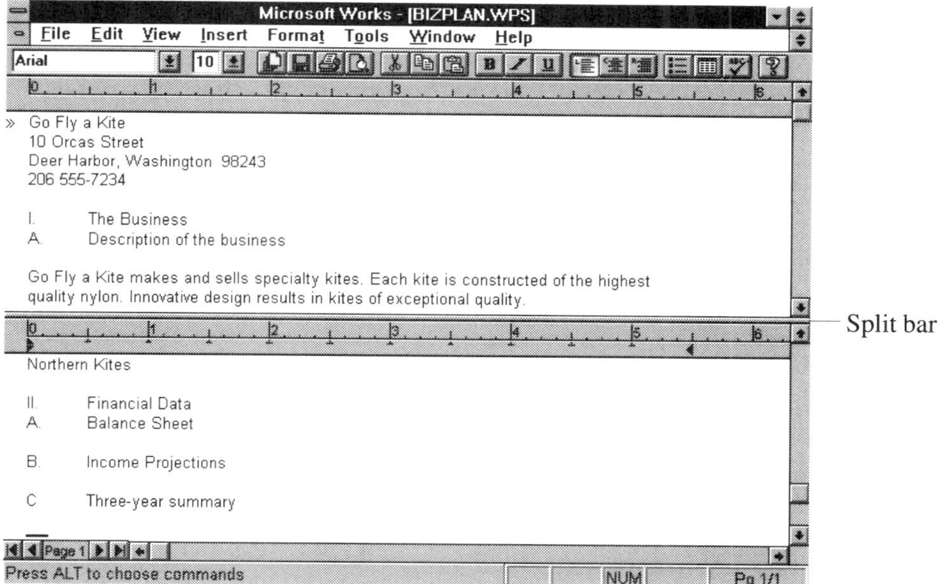

Figure 1-17. *The Works word processing screen split horizontally.*

There are two ways of splitting the screen. The first is to click and drag the split box (refer to Figure 1-2) to the location where you require the split to be. The second way is to choose *Split* from the **Window** menu as in Figure 1-18, then drag the split bar that appears on the screen, to the location where the screen is to be split, and click the mouse button once.

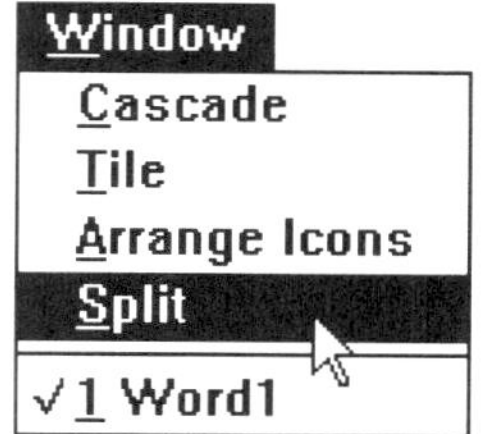

Figure 1-18. *Use Split from the* ***Window*** *menu to split the screen.*

You can move between panes by clicking the mouse pointer on the pane in which you want to be, or by pressing F6. To unsplit the window, double-click on the split bar. Alternatively, select *Split* in the **Window** menu, and drag the split onto the ruler. When you click the left mouse on the ruler, the split disappears.

Closing a file

A file can be closed in Works by choosing *Close* from the **File** menu. Although it is not essential that a file is closed before another is opened, it is wise to do so if you no longer need to use it. Many files open at the same time can slow processing time down.

If a file has not been saved before it is closed, Works will warn you that the file has not been saved. Choose *Yes* if you need to save the changes you have made and *No* if they can be discarded. *Cancel* will cancel the *Close* command completely.

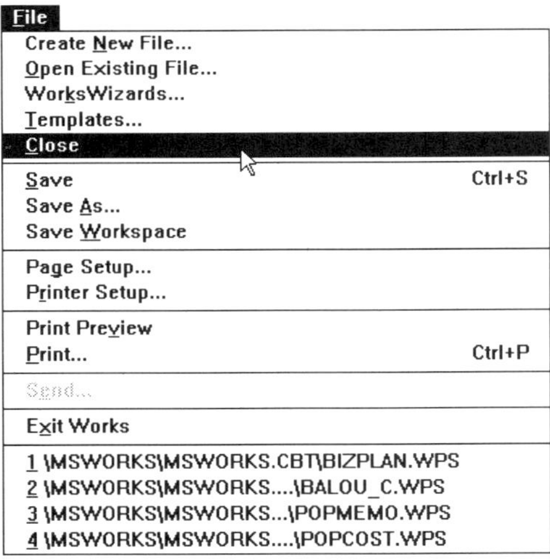

***Figure 1-19.** To close a file in Works, choose Close from the **File** menu.*

Creating Documents

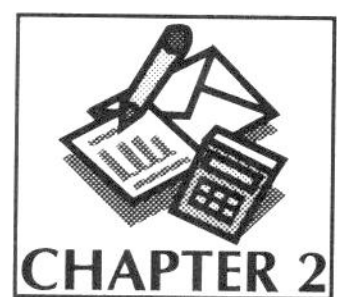

This chapter discusses entering text into the Works word processor. Throughout the chapter we will be referring to the sample file ***auntmadg.wps***, which is located in the ***msworks.cbt*** subdirectory.

Typing text

When you start the Works word processor, the program places a blank page on the screen. The insertion point is automatically placed at the top left-hand side of the page. Entering a new document is like typing on a clean piece of paper.

To enter text into a document, simply start typing and the text is inserted to the left of the flashing insertion point. In this chapter, however, you will be using the sample file mentioned above.

To open this file, select *Open an Existing Document* from the *Startup* dialog box (Figure 1-1 in Chapter 1), click on ***auntmadg.wps*** from the *Open* dialog box that appears (Figure 2-1), and click on *OK*. You may need to change directories to find this file.

When you open a sample file you may receive the message "Cannot change: file is read-only." This means that you can save changes to this file under a new file name or to a new directory only. Click on *OK* to clear this message.

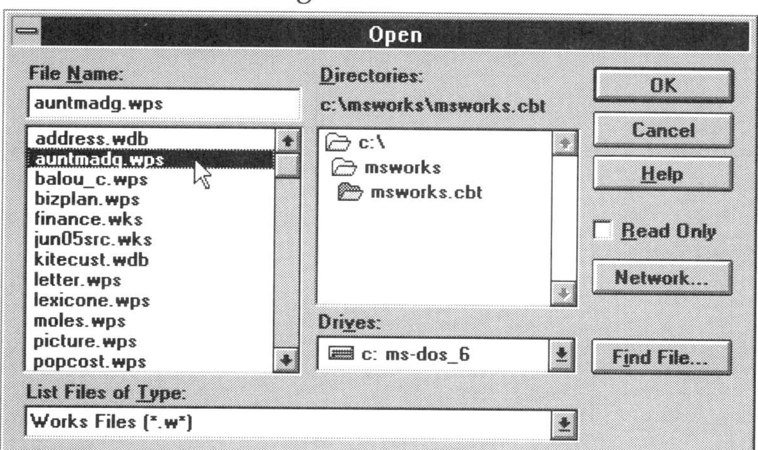

Figure 2-1. *The Open dialog box appears when you select Open an Existing Document from the Startup dialog box or Open Existing File from the* ***File*** *menu.* ***auntmadg.wps*** *is highlighted.*

If the *Startup* dialog box does not appear, close all files and double-click on the screen. The *Startup* dialog box then appears.

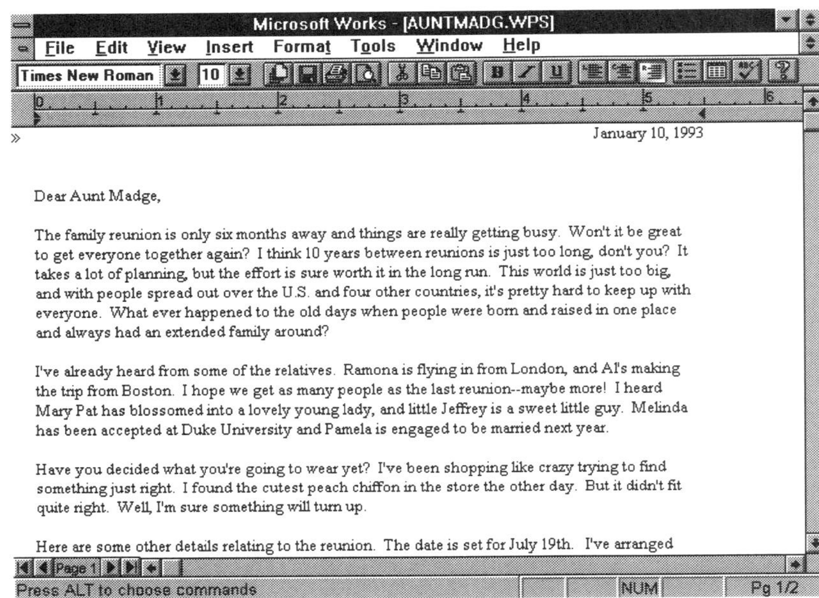

Figure 2-2. *The Works word processor screen with **auntmadg.wps** loaded.*

Insert mode

By default, Works operates in *Insert* mode. When you type in Insert mode, text to the right of the insertion point is pushed along the line to make room for what you're typing. Existing text, therefore, is not replaced by the new text. Works lets you move the insertion point anywhere in your document. We will discuss this later in the chapter.

Overtype mode

The alternative to Insert mode is *Overtype* mode. When Overtype mode is active (Figure 2-3), characters typed into a document replace, or overtype, text which is already to the right of the insertion point. Work's doesn't push existing text over to make room for new text.

Press ALT to choose commands. NUM OVR Pg 1/2

Figure 2-3. *The letters OVR appear on the right-hand side of the status bar to show that Overtype mode is active.*

You activate Overtype mode either by pressing the Insert key or selecting *Overtype* from the *Options* dialog box through the **Tools** menu. Works indicates that Overtype mode is on by displaying "OVR" on the right-hand side of the status bar as seen in Figure 2-3. Pressing the Insert key again, or deselecting *Overtype* from the *Options* dialog box returns Works to Insert mode and removes "OVR" from the status bar.

Moving the insertion point

It is important to be able to move the insertion point around when you type in a document as, in most cases, you can't see the entire document on the screen at one time. Works gives you three methods of moving the insertion point—the navigation keys, the mouse, and the *Go To* command.

Navigation keys

You can move the insertion point around the screen with the navigation keys on the keyboard. The navigation keys are the arrow

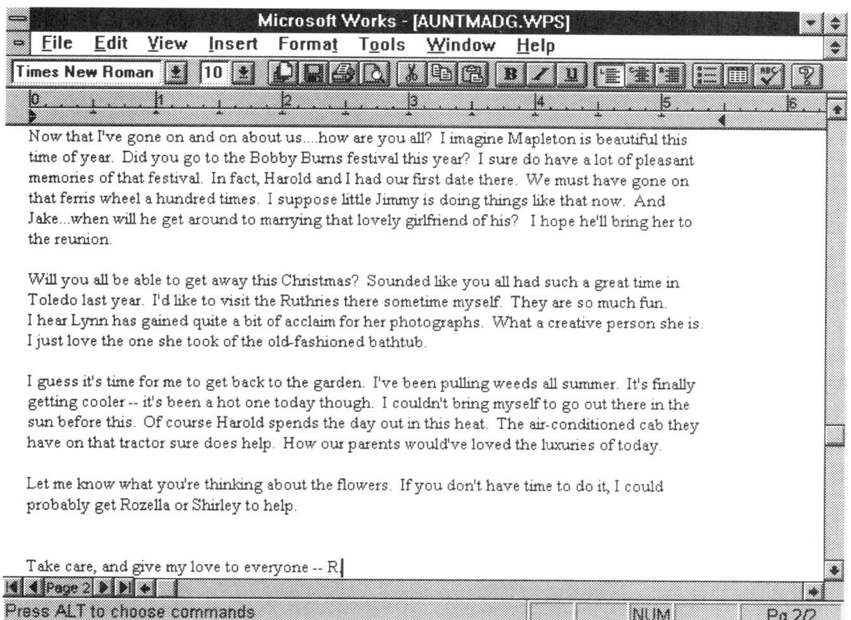

Figure 2-4. You can move the insertion point with the navigation keys.

keys, Home, End, Page Up, and Page Down keys. Pressing any of these keys moves the insertion point to a particular part of the document according to where your insertion point currently is and which key you press.

The left- and right-facing arrow keys move the insertion point one character in the appropriate directions. The up and down arrow keys move the insertion point either up or down a single line at a time.

To move to the beginning of a line quickly, you simply press the Home key (Figure 2-5). Likewise, to move to the end of a line, press End. Page Up and Page Down move up and down one window at a time.

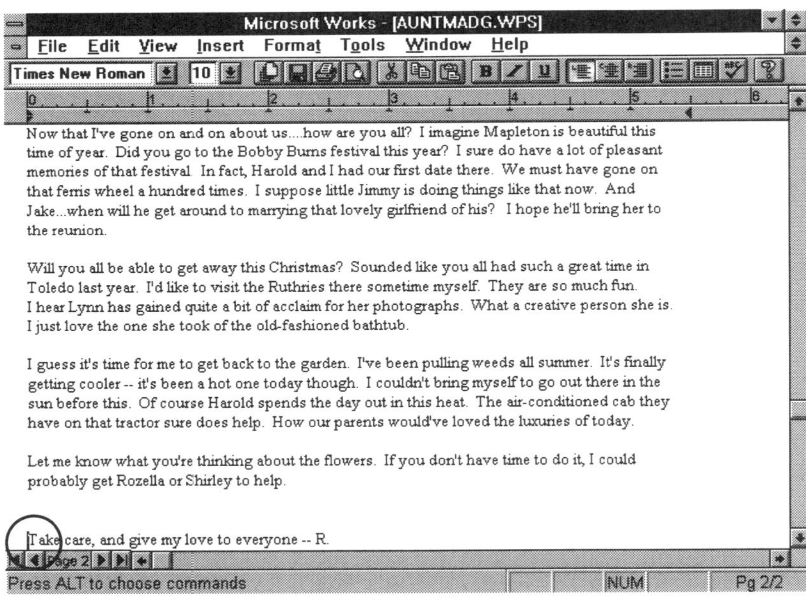

Figure 2-5. The insertion point is sitting at the beginning of the line after pressing Home.

Works has an extended set of movements which gives you greater flexibility in moving the insertion point around the document. You get these extra movements by using the Ctrl key in conjunction with the navigation keys.

To move the insertion point one word at a time, hold down the Ctrl key and tap either the left or right arrow key as appropriate. All the different keystrokes and their functions appear in the table on the following page.

Test these movements out in the ***auntmadg.wps*** sample file—the more you use them the easier they are to remember!

Movement keys

The following table summarizes the various key movements for the insertion point available in Works.

Key	**Cursor Movement**	**Key**	**Cursor Movement**
Left arrow	Left one character	Right arrow	Right one character
Up arrow	Up one line	Down arrow	Down one line
Ctrl-left arrow	Left one word	Ctrl-right arrow	Right one word
Ctrl-up arrow	Up one paragraph	Ctrl-down arrow	Down one paragraph
Home	Beginning of line	End	End of line
Ctrl-Home	Beginning of document	Ctrl-End	End of document
Page Up	Up one screen	Page Down	Down one screen
Ctrl-Page Up	Start of screen	Ctrl-Page Down	End of screen

Moving with the mouse

You can also move the insertion point using the mouse. The position of the mouse is indicated by the "I-beam" (see Figure 2-6) and is called the mouse pointer. This "I-beam" represents the mouse position only and should not be confused with the insertion point, where text will be inserted.

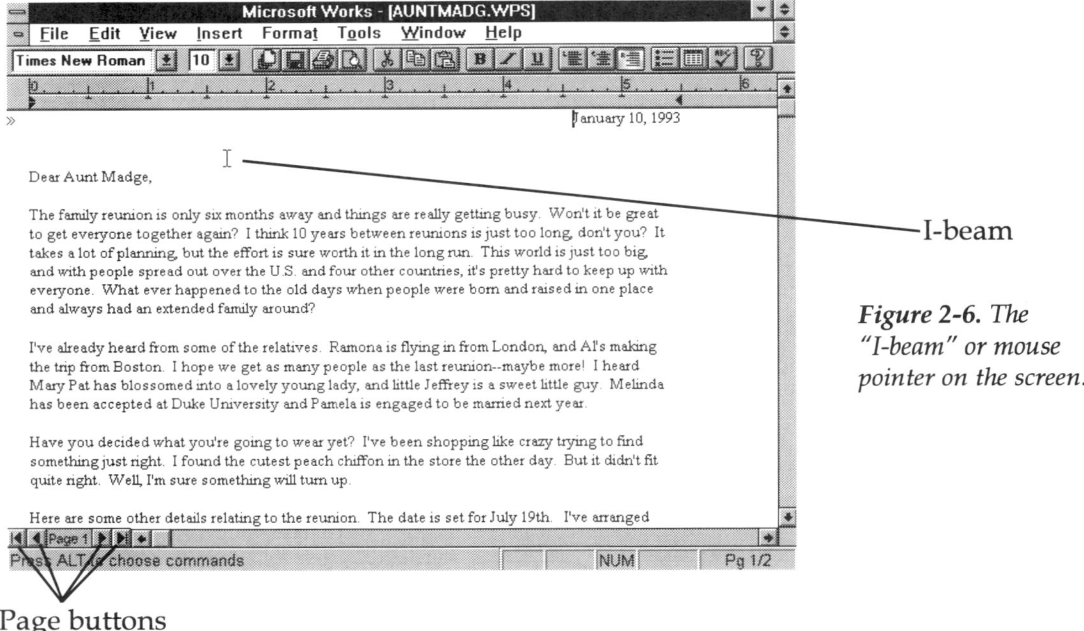

***Figure 2-6.** The "I-beam" or mouse pointer on the screen.*

To select a new insertion point using the mouse, place the I-beam in the document where you want the insertion point and click the left mouse button. Works adds the insertion point wherever the I-beam was when you clicked the mouse button.

You can also move among the pages of your document by clicking on one of the page buttons just above the status bar.

In the sample file, ***auntmadg.wps***, use the mouse to move the insertion point to the beginning of the second paragraph and then back to the beginning of the document.

Moving with the Go To command

You use the *Go To* command in Works to move you to a specific place in your document. It can move the insertion point to the top of a page you want or to a *bookmark*. You use *Go To* by either pressing F5 or selecting *Go To* in the **Edit** menu as in Figure 2-7.

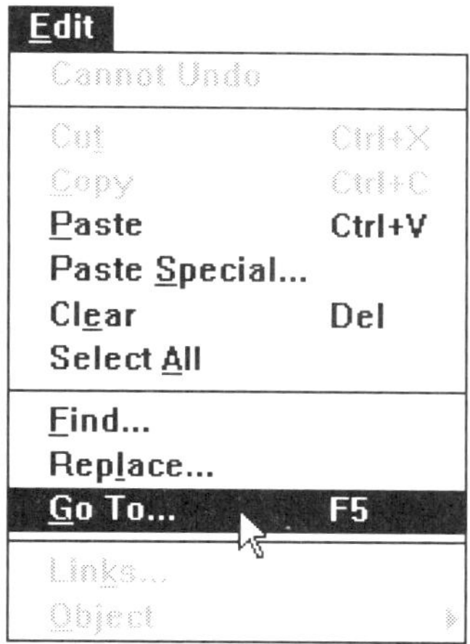

Figure 2-7. *Choose Go To from the* ***Edit*** *menu.*

To move to a particular page, press F5 and the *Go To* dialog box appears (see Figure 2-8). When you type in the page number you want and click *OK*, your insertion point will be placed on the top of that page.

To move to the top of page 2 in ***auntmadg.wps***, press F5 then type "2", and click on *OK*. Your insertion point is now at the top of page 2.

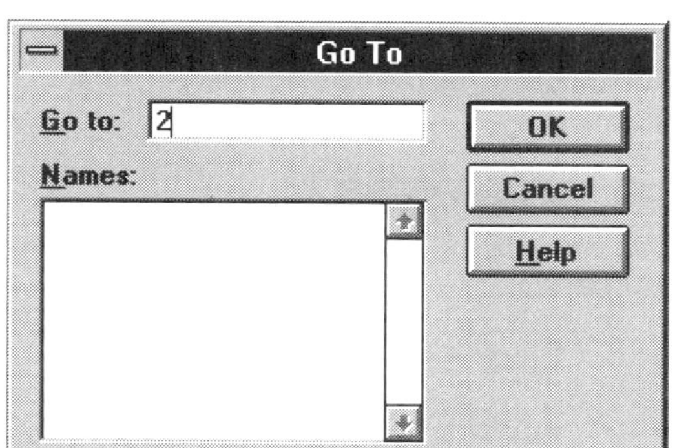

Figure 2-8. *The Go To dialog box.*

The *Go To* command can also take you a to bookmark that you have placed in your document. Bookmarks mark important parts of your document so you can move there quickly.

To create a bookmark in the sample file, you first move the insertion point to where you want the bookmark. In this exercise, mark the reference to the outfit the author will be wearing—"the cutest peach chiffon"—in paragraph 3, as shown in Figure 2-9. Now choose *Bookmark Name* from the **Insert** menu (Figure 2-10).

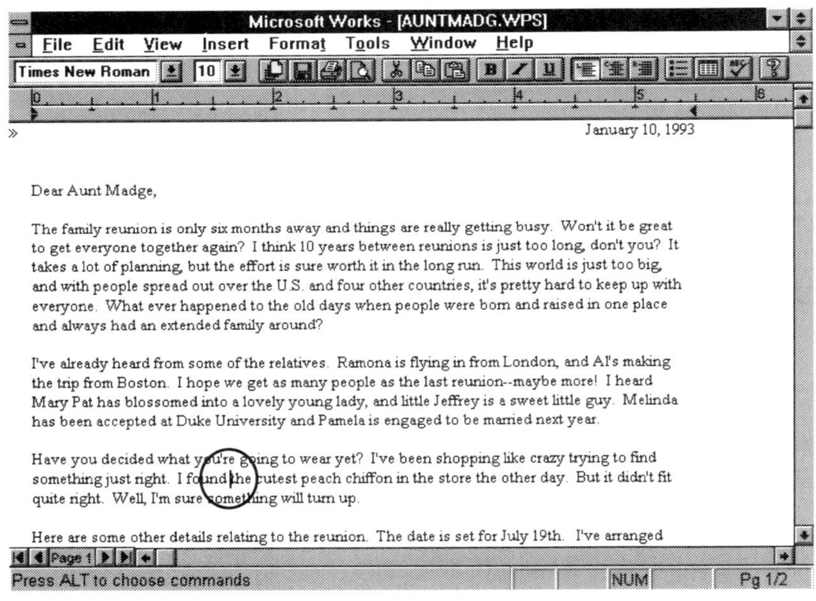

***Figure 2-9.** Move the insertion point in front of "the cutest peach chiffon."*

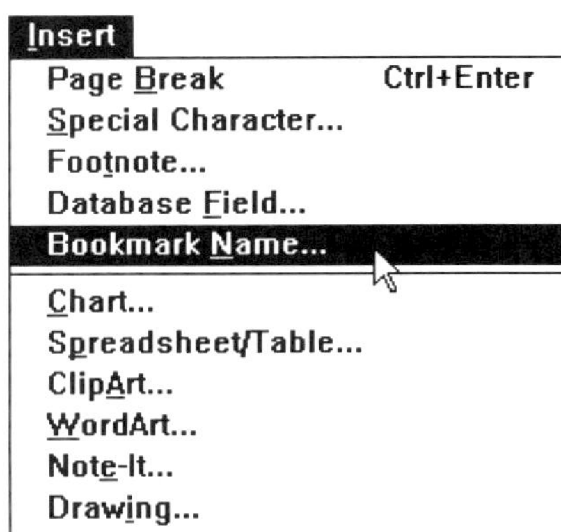

***Figure 2-10.** Select Bookmark Name from the **Insert** menu to create a bookmark.*

The *Bookmark Name* dialog box appears on the screen (see Figure 2-11).

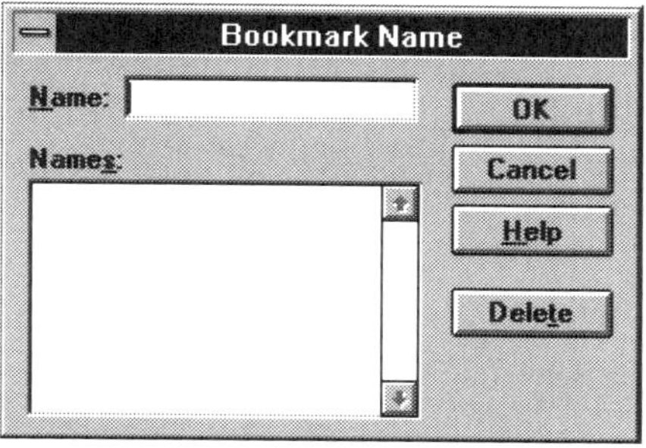

Figure 2-11. *The Bookmark Name dialog box.*

To create the bookmark, type in "outfit" as the bookmark name and click on *OK* (see Figure 2-12).

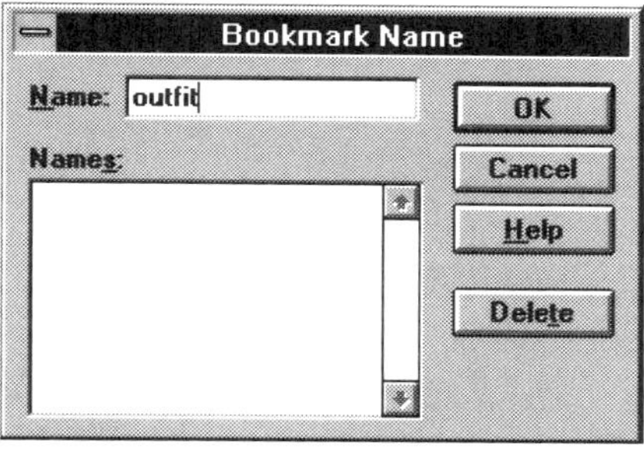

Figure 2-12. *Type in the name of the bookmark.*

"Outfit" will now be available in the *Names* list box in the *Go To* dialog box (Figure 2-13), which appears when you choose *Go To* from the **Edit** menu. Move to the top of the document now and use the *Go To* command to move down to "the cutest peach chiffon."

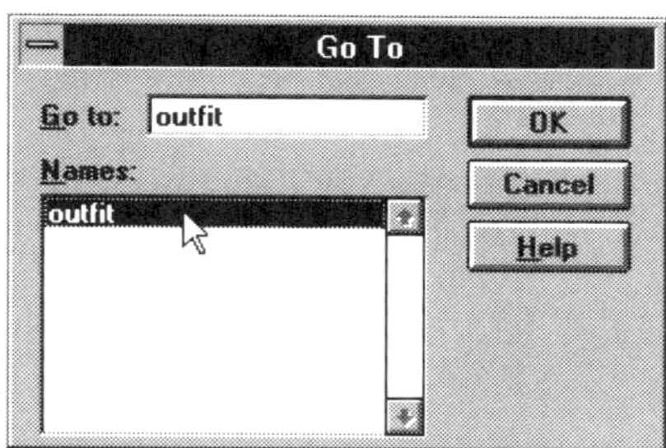

Figure 2-13. *The bookmark name you created appears in the Names text box in the Go To dialog box.*

Using the editing keys

Some of the keys on the keyboard have specialized editing functions. In particular, the Backspace and Delete keys each have special properties that are invaluable in typing and editing documents.

The Backspace key

Using the Backspace key deletes the character to the left of the insertion point.

With ***auntmadg.wps*** on the screen, use the Backspace key to remove some text. Move the insertion point after the "x" in "six" in the first line and delete the word from the document using the Backspace key. Now replace it with "ten". Your document now looks like the one in Figure 2-14.

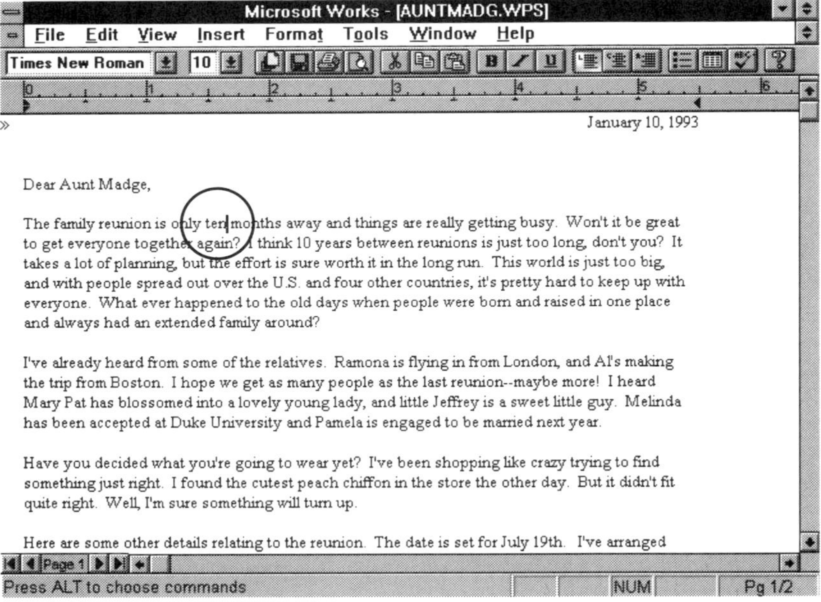

Figure 2-14. *Use the Backspace key to replace "six" with "ten."*

The Delete key

The Delete key removes the character to the right of the insertion point.

Use the Delete key to change "ten" back to "six" in the sample document (Figure 2-15).

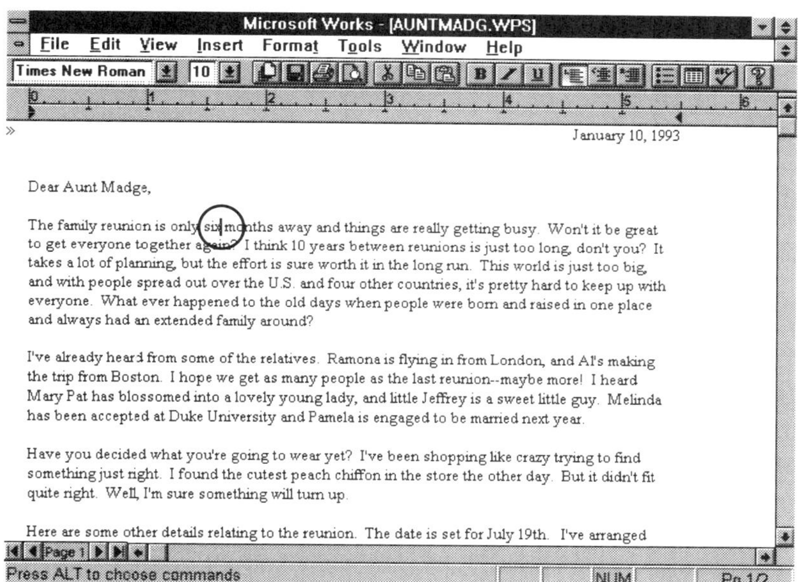

***Figure 2-15.** Use the Delete key to replace "ten" with "six."*

The Undo command

The *Undo* command, which is in the **Edit** menu, is a safety feature that you can use to correct accidental changes to a document. Selecting the *Undo* command reverses the effects of the most recently completed function or command. Though a powerful tool, this command reverses only the last step you have taken.

For example, delete the word "Madge" (second line) in your letter. Now select *Undo* from the **Edit** menu (Figure 2-16). The word "Madge" will be inserted back into the document. The shortcut for activating the *Undo* command is Ctrl-Z.

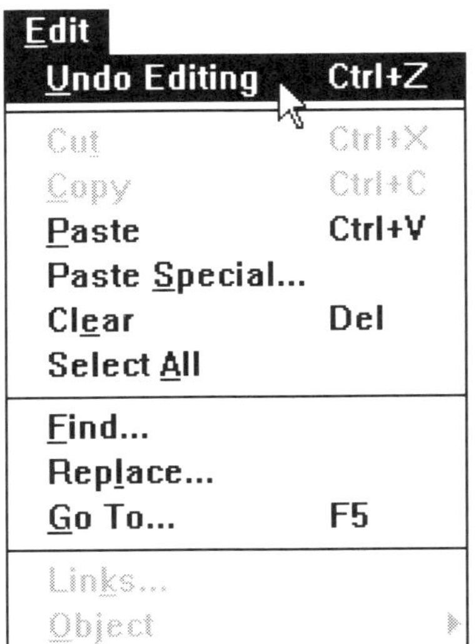

Figure 2-16. *The Undo command in the* ***Edit*** *menu.*

Try using the *Undo* command in a few other places in the sample document. Always remember: only the most recently completed action will be undone.

Saving files

When you create or edit your document, it is important that you save your work to disk at regular intervals. Before a document is saved, documents you create and make changes to in Works are stored temporarily only in your computer's memory.

To keep a document, and also to protect it against accidental loss of data, you have to create a disk file of the document. You create disk files using the *Save* or *Save As* commands in the **File** menu (Figure 2-17). You can activate either one of these commands any time you are working on the document, without losing your place in the document.

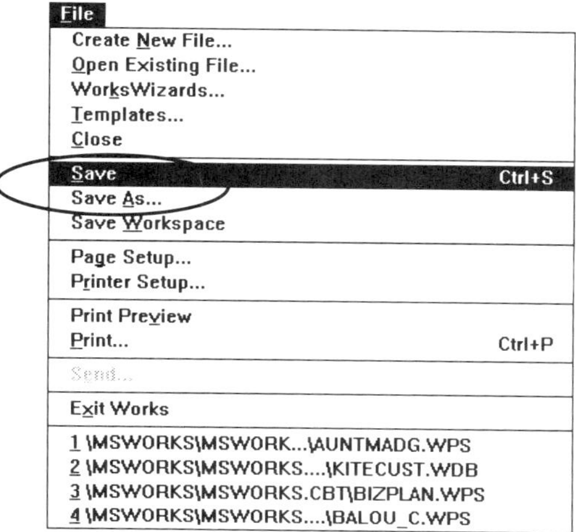

Figure 2-17. *The Save and Save As commands in the **File** menu.*

The Save As command

The main function of the *Save As* command is to give a name to a document that you have not previously saved. If the file is not already saved, the title bar of Works simply says *Word* and a number, for instance *Word1,* shown in Figure 2-18. The *Save As* command lets you create and name a file for the document you're currently editing.

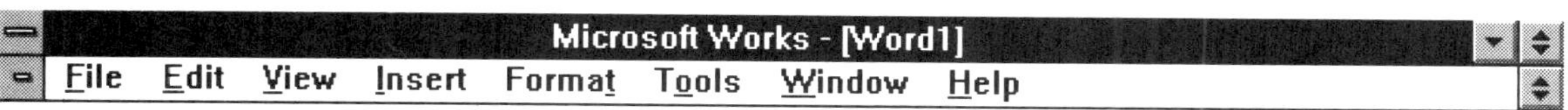

Figure 2-18. *The unsaved document title bar.*

Simply enter the name you want for your file in the *File Name* text box of Figure 2-19. Clicking on *OK* saves your file with this new name.

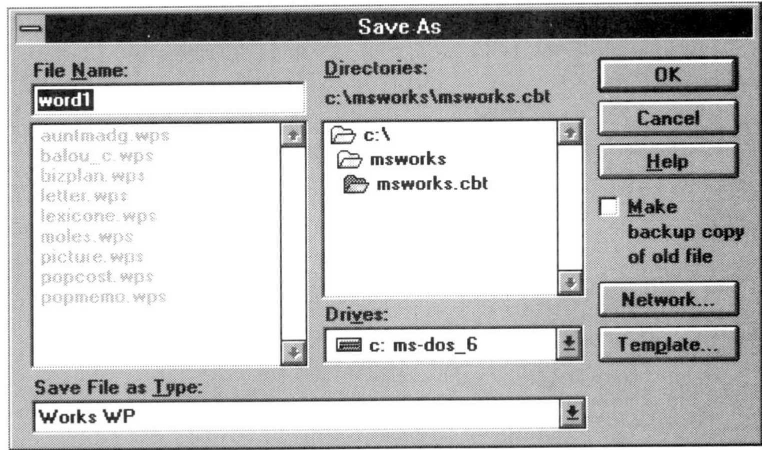

Figure 2-19. *The Save As dialog box.*

You can also use the *Save As* dialog box to change the name of a file which already exists. The original file still remains on disk, giving you a second copy of the document.

Change the name of the sample file to ***reunion.wps*** by selecting *Save As* from the **File** menu. The current name of the file, ***auntmadg.wps***, will be highlighted in the *File Name* text box. As it is highlighted, the new name will replace the current one as soon as you type the first letter. Type in *reunion* at this point, Works gives it the extension "***.wps***" automatically (Figure 2-20).

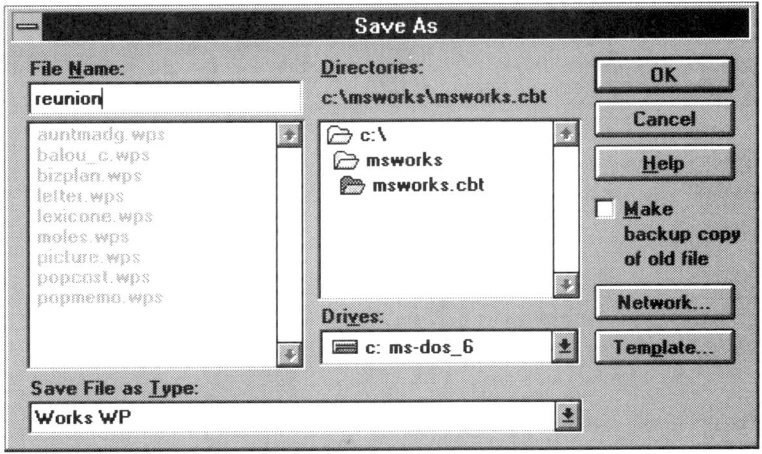

Figure 2-20. *Type the name "reunion" into the File Name text box of the Save As dialog box.*

Click on *OK*. As shown in Figure 2-21, the title bar now displays the new file name ***reunion.wps***.

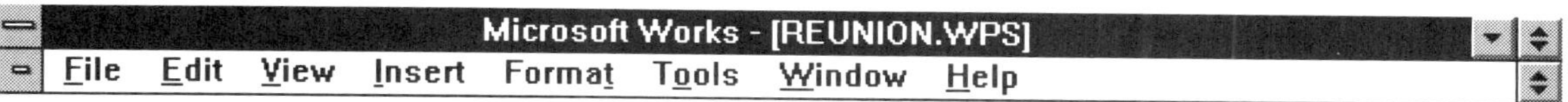

Figure 2-21. *The new file name appears in the title bar.*

The Save command

You use the *Save* command when you have already named the file through the *Save As* command. The *Save* command replaces the existing file on the disk with an up-to-date record of the document.

The *Save* command uses the name you previously gave the file. Once the file is saved, the file name appears on the title bar (Figure 2-22). A shortcut to using the *Save* command is to hold down the Ctrl key and press the S key (Ctrl-S).

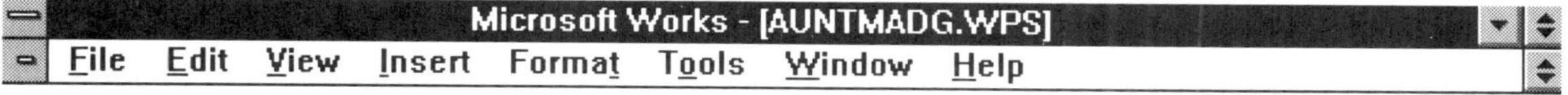

Figure 2-22. *The sample document's name "**auntmadg.wps**" appears on the title bar on the top of the Works word processor screen.*

Editing Documents

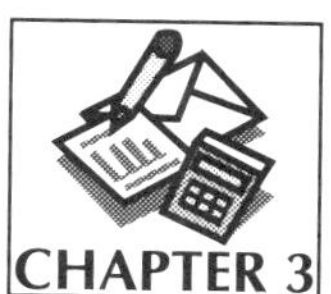

At any time during the creation of your document, text can be altered to suit your own requirements. Such alterations include deleting, copying, and moving text as well as changing text attributes such as bold or underlining.

Works can also change the format of a paragraph. Formatting includes changing the line spacing from single to double spacing; adjusting the alignment from centered to left or right; and adding space to the bottom or top of the paragraph.

In this chapter you will be asked to change the format of the sample document, ***auntmadg.wps***, which is the sample file used in **Chapter 2, Creating Documents**. To open this file, follow the instructions below.

Opening files

The *Open Existing File* command (Figure 3-1) in the **File** menu is used to load an existing file into an editing screen. The file you open must have been saved previously.

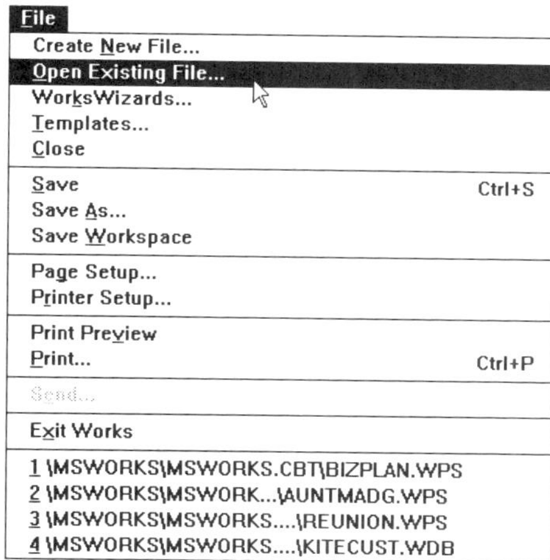

Figure 3-1. *An existing file is opened through the Open Existing File command in the **File** menu.*

To open the file ***auntmadg.wps***, start Works by double-clicking on the Microsoft Works icon in Windows, then choose the *Open an Existing Document* button from the *Startup* dialog box. The *Open* dialog box will appear with the words "Opens existing Works file" remaining in the status bar while the dialog box is on the screen.

The *Open* dialog box in Figure 3-2 is very similar to any other Windows dialog box but contains some special features which will be discussed later in the book.

The *Directories* list box on the right lets you change into the subdirectory from which you wish to open the file. Works displays a series of folders to enable you to change into the required subdirectory. To change into another subdirectory, double-click on the appropriate icon to select the subdirectory which contains the sample file, in this case, ***msworks.cbt***.

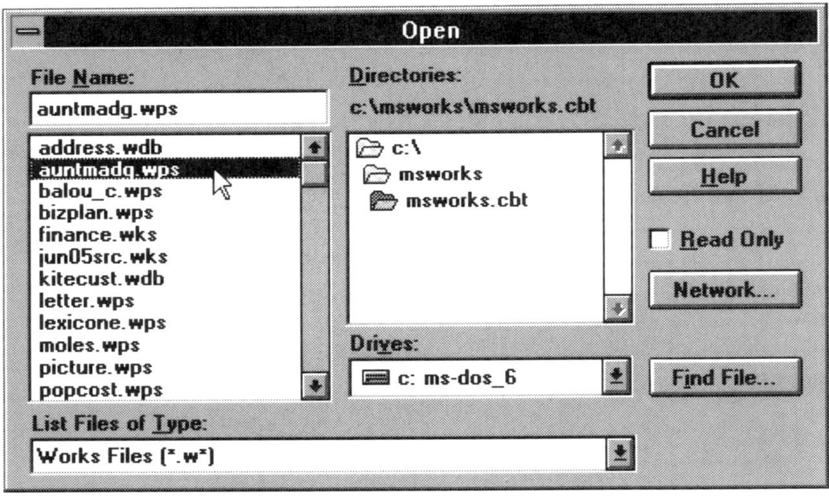

***Figure 3-2.** The Open dialog box is accessed either from the Startup dialog box or from the **File** menu. Click on **auntmadg.wps** and then OK to open the file.*

To change disk drives, for instance, from the hard disk drive to a floppy disk drive, choose the *Drives* submenu. A list of the drives in your system will appear. Clicking on the drive you wish to access will then give you a list of all the files in that drive in the *Files* list box. If you click on a floppy disk drive, and no disk is actually inserted in that drive, an error message will appear.

The *Files* list box appears on the left of the dialog box and contains a list of files from the selected directory. It is not always possible to see all of the files within the subdirectory and, for this reason, Works has provided scroll bars to enable you to move through the list.

By default, the *File Name* text box contains the wild-card combination **.w**, which allows all the files with an extension starting with "w" to be listed. To be more specific, Works enables you to choose from the *List Files of Type* submenu (bottom left of Figure 3-2).

Find the ***auntmadg.wps*** file in the *Files* list box and select it by clicking on it once. Open the file by clicking on *OK*. As with other Windows file selection dialog boxes, you can simply double-click on the file you wish to load into the editing screen.

Menu shortcuts for opening files

In the **File** menu, Works keeps track of the last four files which have been opened most recently. You can click on any of the files listed to open that file without having to access the *Open* dialog box (Figure 3-3).

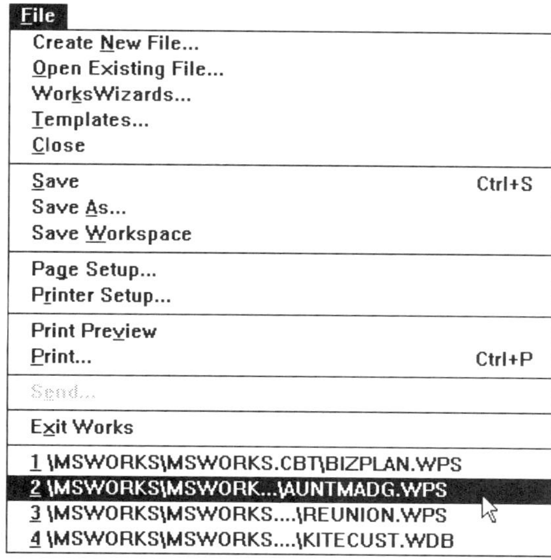

Figure 3-3. *A list of the last four files opened in the* ***File*** *menu. To open one of these files, just click on the name of the file you want to open.*

Highlighting text

Once a document has been typed, it will probably need to be altered in a number of ways. You may decide to change the attributes of the characters to bold or italics, or change the order of the document by cutting and pasting. Before any formatting tasks can be performed, the text you want to format needs to be selected or highlighted. Highlighted text appears reversed—white on black instead of black on white—on the screen—as shown in Figure 3-4.

There are a number of ways of selecting text in Works—*swiping* with the mouse or the cursor keys, clicking with the mouse, or through the **Edit** menu. Each of these will be discussed in this section.

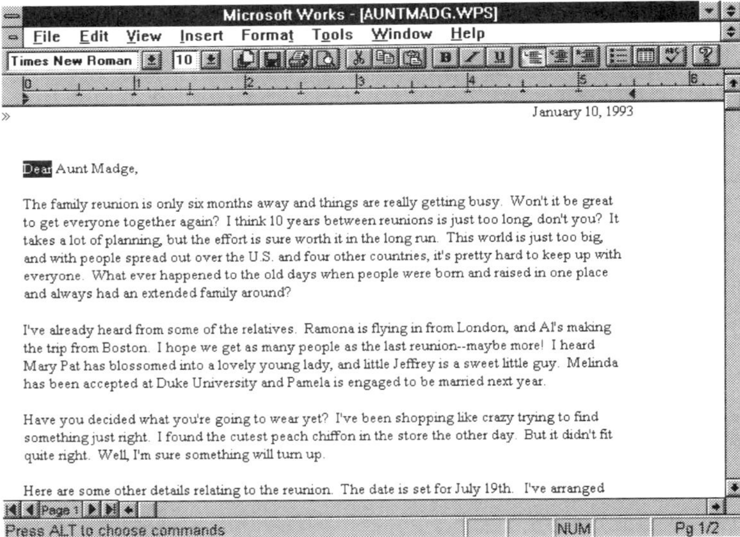

***Figure 3-4.** The word "Dear" has been highlighted.*

Swiping with the mouse or cursor keys

One of the easiest, and most efficient ways, of selecting text is the *swiping* method. There are several ways in which you can swipe text in Works. By completing the following examples, you will see the two most useful techniques. Other methods are listed in Appendix A.

To use the *dragging* method of swiping text, place the insertion point in front of the word "Dear." Click and hold the mouse button and, without releasing, move the pointer to the end of this word. Release the mouse button. The word "Dear" now appears reversed, as seen in Figure 3-4, indicating that it has been selected.

To cancel highlighting, click the left mouse button or press any of the arrow keys.

The *shift-click* method of swiping is useful for selecting larger blocks of text with the mouse. Add the insertion point at the beginning of the word "The" in the first paragraph. Without clicking, position the I-beam at the end of the second paragraph. Hold down the Shift key and click the left mouse button while the I-beam remains at the end of the second paragraph. All the text between the two insertion points — the first two paragraphs of the letter — will be selected as in Figure 3-5.

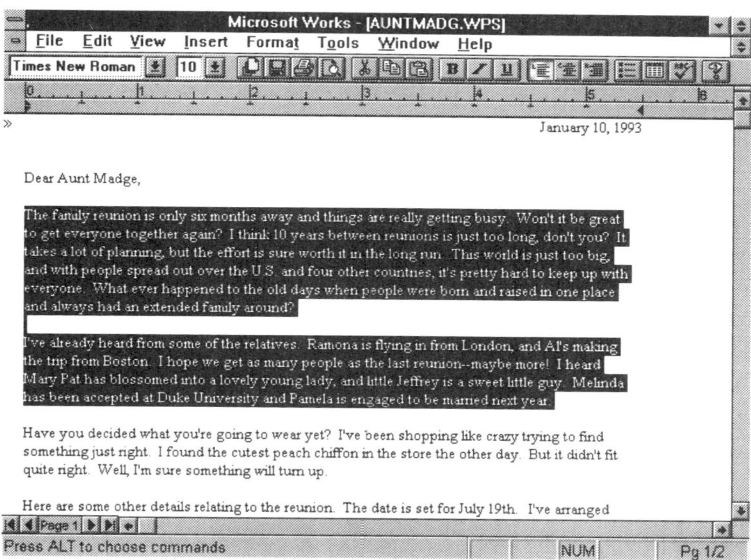

***Figure 3-5.** The first two paragraphs of the sample document are selected using the "shift-click" method to highlight text.*

Extended Highlight mode

Text can also be selected by extending the cursor. This method is used for highlighting large blocks of text with the keyboard. Extended Highlight is activated by pressing the F8 key. The status bar will indicate that you are in Extended Highlight mode by displaying EXT.

Move the insertion point to the word "reunion" in the first paragraph and turn Extended Highlight on by pressing the F8 key. To highlight the word "reunion," press F8 again. To cancel the selection, Extended Highlight must first be deactivated by pressing the Esc key. Notice that EXT is no longer on the status bar. For a complete list of the F8 cursor extensions available in Works, refer to Appendix A.

Select All

If you want to highlight your entire document in order to format it uniformly, you can choose the *Select All* command from the **Edit** menu (Figure 3-6).

An alternative to this, using the mouse, is covered in the next section.

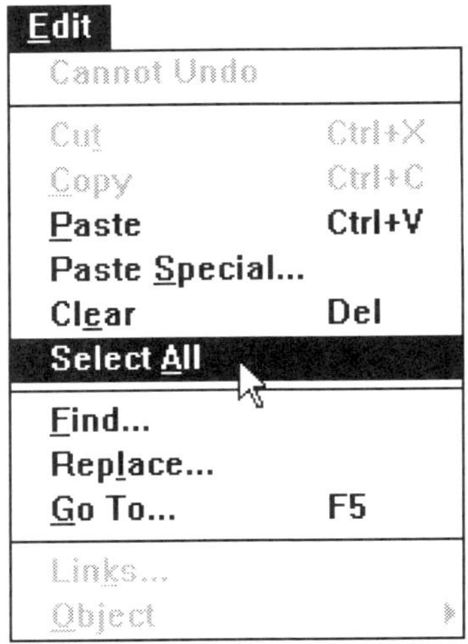

Figure 3-6. *The Select All command is used to highlight the entire document.*

Clicking with the mouse

Clicking with the mouse can be a quick and easy alternative to the methods outlined above. By clicking the mouse button a certain number of times and in certain places on the screen, you can select specific quantities of text.

Double-clicking the mouse will highlight the word under the I-beam. Double-click the mouse over the word "barbecue" in the fourth paragraph and the whole word becomes highlighted.

To highlight more than one word in Works, it is easiest to move the pointer into the left margin of the document window where it becomes the arrow pointer. This can be used to highlight larger blocks of text, such as lines and paragraphs, by clicking the mouse using various combinations.

To highlight a line of text in your document, move the pointer into the left-hand margin and click the mouse pointer next to the second line down in the first paragraph. The entire line will be highlighted (Figure 3-7). Several lines can be highlighted by moving into the left margin, and clicking and dragging the mouse pointer up or down.

Double-clicking the pointer in the left margin beside a paragraph will highlight the whole paragraph. Try using this method to highlight the fourth paragraph in the sample document.

The entire document can be highlighted by holding down the Ctrl key and clicking once in the left margin.

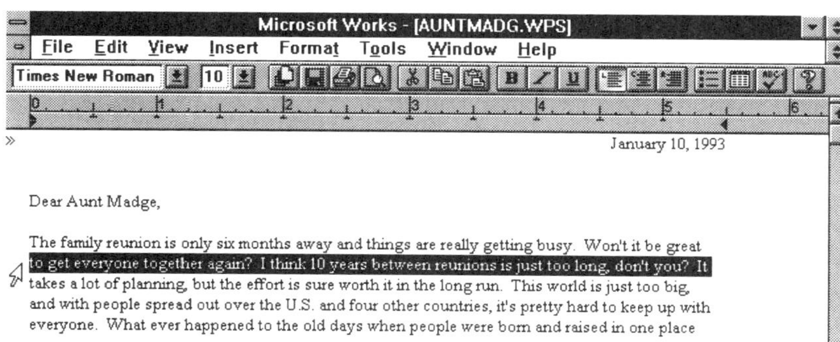

***Figure 3-7.** The margin pointer used to highlight text.*

Typing replaces selection option

The *Typing replaces selection* option is used to replace highlighted text with the new text being typed. It avoids having to delete unwanted text between highlighting it and typing in the new text.

Typing replaces selection is turned on or off in the *Options* dialog box, selected from the **Tools** menu (see Figure 3-8).

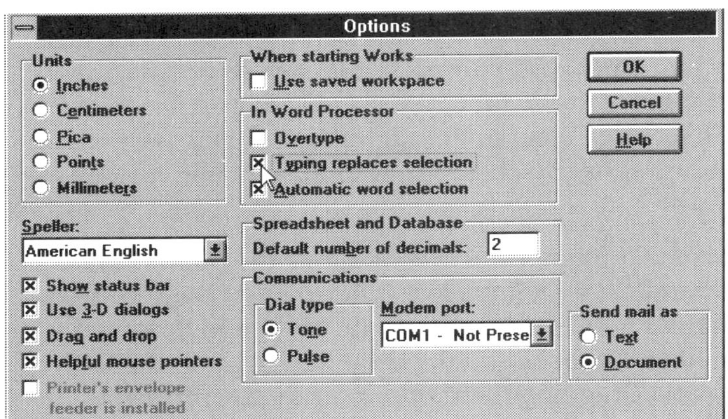

Figure 3-8. *The Typing replaces selection option.*

Formatting paragraphs

Works enables you to change characteristics such as alignment, line spacing, and the amount of space under or above a paragraph. When part of a paragraph is formatted, the whole paragraph will be affected. The end of a paragraph in Works is defined by a paragraph mark which is inserted by pressing Enter. A paragraph can be one word or a number of lines, which are wrapped automatically by Works.

You should place the insertion point in the paragraph you want to format before formatting that paragraph. Alternatively, you can highlight one or more paragraphs using any of the methods discussed above. This way, you can format more than one paragraph at a time so that they are the same.

To change the format of a paragraph as it is being typed, select the option required and then type the text. The paragraph being typed will reflect the choice made.

All of the paragraph formatting options are available through the *Paragraph* dialog box which you open from the **Format** menu. Many of these options have keyboard shortcuts which you can find tabulated in Appendix A.

The shortcut for bringing the *Paragraph* dialog box onto the screen is to double-click on one of the markers referred to in Figure 3-9.

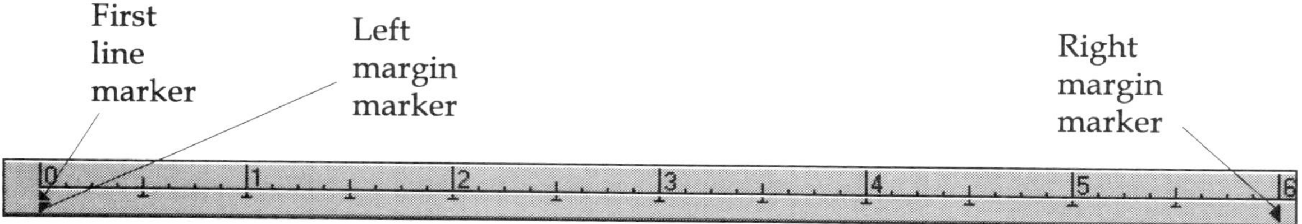

Figure 3-9. *The markers in the Works ruler.*

Quick Formats

When you first open the *Paragraph* dialog box, Works presents options for you to apply *Quick Formats* (Figure 3-10).

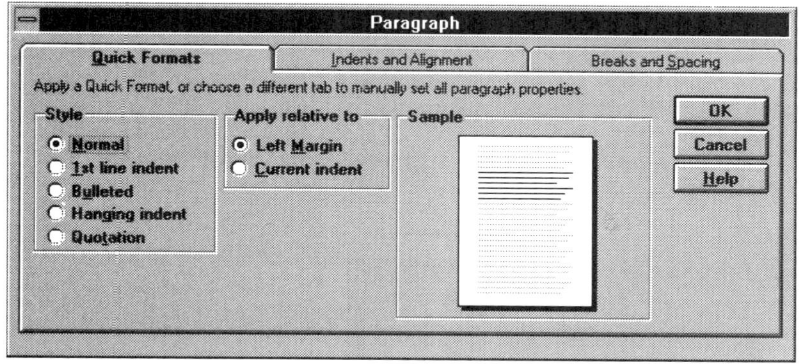

Figure 3-10. *Works displays the Quick Format options when you choose Paragraph from the* ***Format*** *menu.*

You can control the overall *Style* of the paragraph you selected and decide whether to indent this paragraph from the *Left Margin* or the *Current indent*. of your text. Figure 3-11 shows an example of each *Style*.

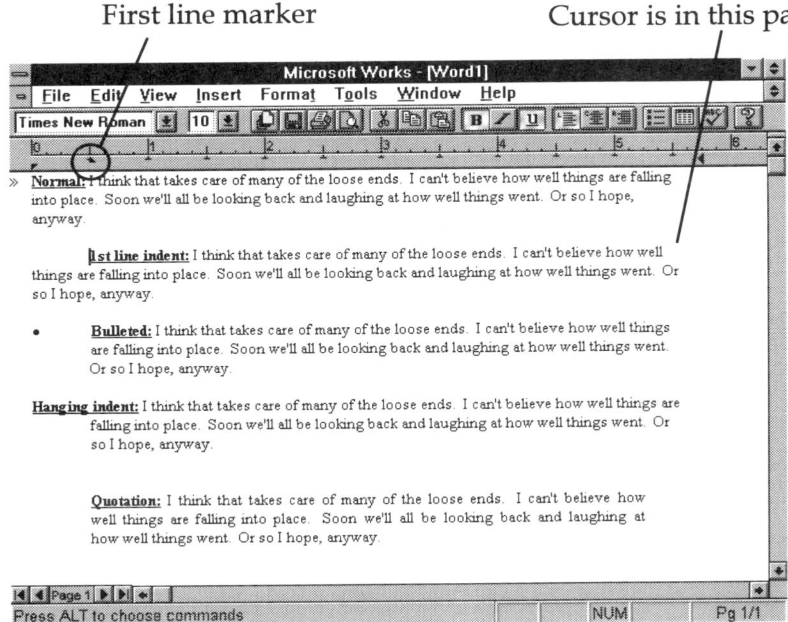

Figure 3-11. *The five types of paragraph style available in Works.*

Indents

The *Paragraph* dialog box is one of a number of dialog boxes which Works displays with "tabs." These tabs are like the tabs that you often find on the edge of paper dividers in a lever arch file. You click on the tab corresponding to the set of options you want to access from this dialog box and Works brings those options to the front.

To access the *Indents and Alignment* options from the *Paragraph* dialog box click on the central tab as shown in Figure 3-12.

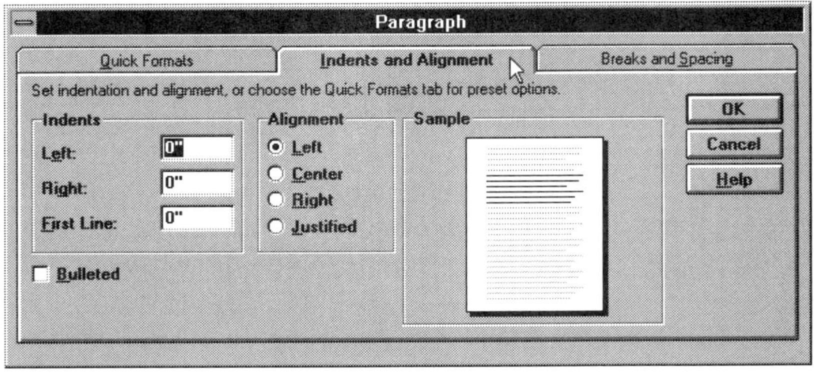

Figure 3-12. *Click on the central tab to display the Indents and Alignment options.*

Indents can be set either through the *Paragraph* dialog box, or by clicking and dragging the indent and margin markers on the ruler (Figure 3-9). Setting indents through the *Paragraph* dialog box ensures more precise measurements, as you can type in the exact position of the indent. Indents and margin changes you set in this dialog box will be reflected on the ruler.

The most common indent used is to indent the first line of a paragraph. Figure 3-11 displays the result of such an indent—notice the first line marker has moved on the ruler.

To achieve this through the Paragraph dialog box, you must place the text cursor in the paragraph to be altered first, for example the paragraph beginning "The family reunion is" in the file ***auntmadg.wps***. Open the *Paragraph* dialog box by double-clicking on a margin marker on the ruler, or select *Paragraph* from the **Format** menu.

Click on *Indents and Alignment* if that tab is not on top, type "1" in the *First Line* text box and click on *OK*. The paragraph and the ruler are indented and look like Figure 3-13. To do this on the ruler, click on the first line marker and drag it to the 1 inch position.

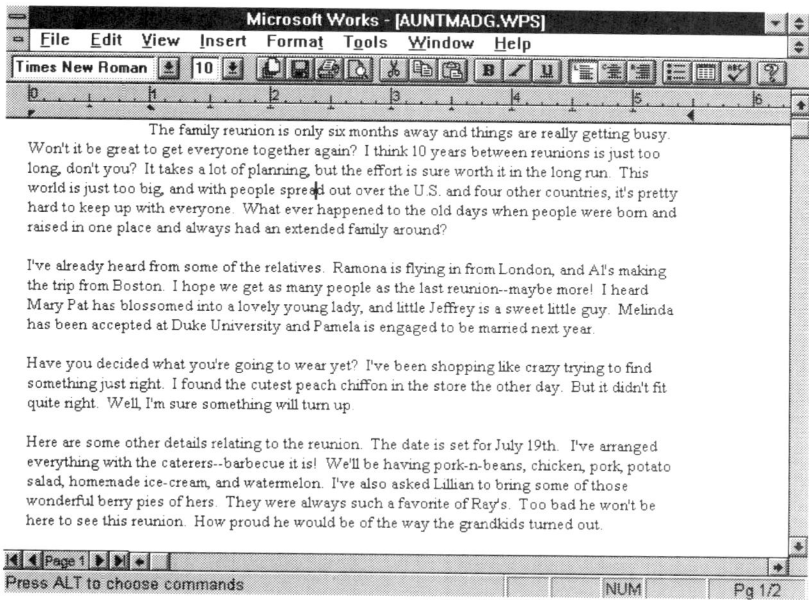

The family reunion is only six months away and things are really getting busy. Won't it be great to get everyone together again? I think 10 years between reunions is just too long, don't you? It takes a lot of planning, but the effort is sure worth it in the long run. This world is just too big, and with people spread out over the U.S. and four other countries, it's pretty hard to keep up with everyone. What ever happened to the old days when people were born and raised in one place and always had an extended family around?

I've already heard from some of the relatives. Ramona is flying in from London, and Al's making the trip from Boston. I hope we get as many people as the last reunion--maybe more! I heard Mary Pat has blossomed into a lovely young lady, and little Jeffrey is a sweet little guy. Melinda has been accepted at Duke University and Pamela is engaged to be married next year.

Have you decided what you're going to wear yet? I've been shopping like crazy trying to find something just right. I found the cutest peach chiffon in the store the other day. But it didn't fit quite right. Well, I'm sure something will turn up.

Here are some other details relating to the reunion. The date is set for July 19th. I've arranged everything with the caterers--barbecue it is! We'll be having pork-n-beans, chicken, pork, potato salad, homemade ice-cream, and watermelon. I've also asked Lillian to bring some of those wonderful berry pies of hers. They were always such a favorite of Ray's. Too bad he won't be here to see this reunion. How proud he would be of the way the grandkids turned out.

Figure 3-13. *The first line of the first paragraph has been indented 1 inch. The first line marker on the ruler confirms this.*

To set a hanging indent through the *Paragraph* dialog box (refer back to Figure 3-11), you need to adjust the settings in both the *Left* and *First Line* text boxes. When a hanging indent is set, the first line actually begins before the left margin, which means the *First Line* has a negative number as its position.

To format the paragraph beginning "I've already heard..." with a hanging indent, move the insertion point into that paragraph and open the *Paragraph* dialog box. The hanging indent in Figure 3-14 was created with the settings as shown in Figure 3-15. Use these to format your paragraph with a hanging indent and, when you click on *OK*, the sample file will look like Figure 3-14.

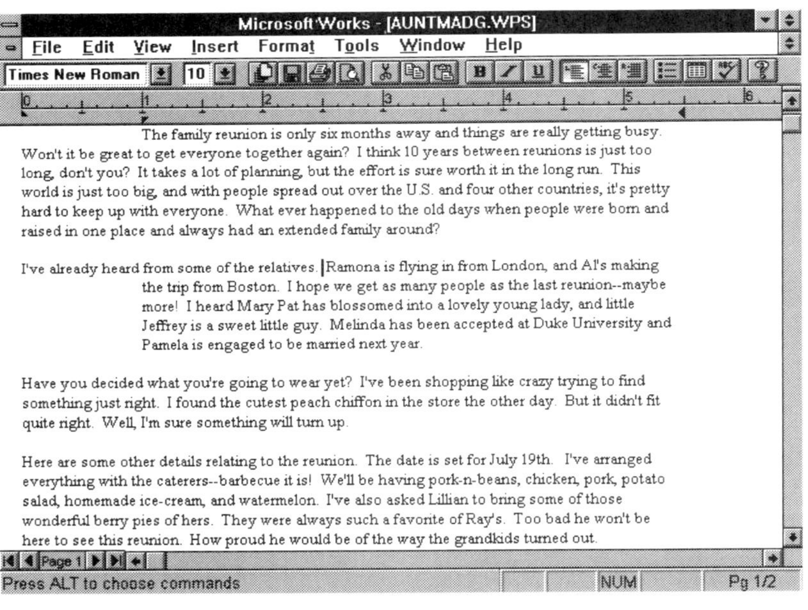

***Figure 3-14.** The second paragraph in the sample file has been formatted with a hanging indent.*

To create a hanging indent using the ruler, hold down the Shift key and drag the left margin marker to the required position and release. The first line marker will remain in the original position and can then be adjusted by dragging it back or forward along the ruler.

Indents in a paragraph can be cancelled in the *Paragraph* dialog box by typing 0 (zero) in the text box of the indent to be canceled. Using the ruler to cancel, drag the indent markers back to their original position at zero. When removing a hanging indent, however, hold down the Shift key to return the left margin marker to the first line marker.

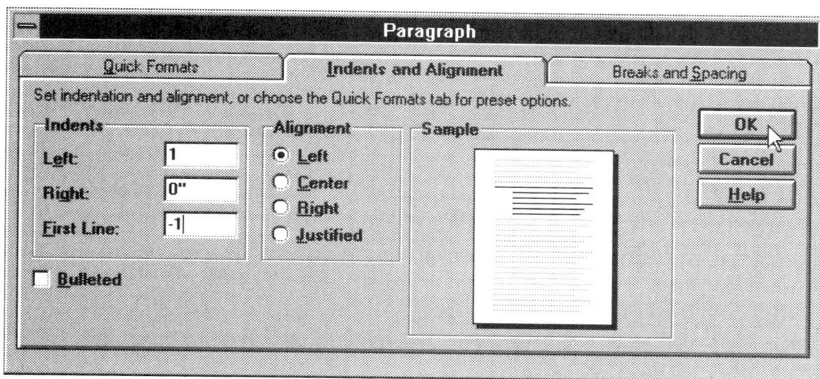

Figure 3-15. *To set a hanging indent as shown in Figure 3-14, we set the Left indent at 1 inch and the First Line indent at -1 inch.*

Alignment

Alignment is the positioning of text across the page. Changing alignment can bring attention to a paragraph, which is useful for headings and other important pieces of text. There are four types of alignment available in Works — *Left, Right, Center,* and *Justified* — which are shown in Figure 3-16.

By default, the alignment in Works is *Left*, which positions the text on the page with an even left margin and an unaligned or ragged right margin. The captions for the figures in this book have been left justified.

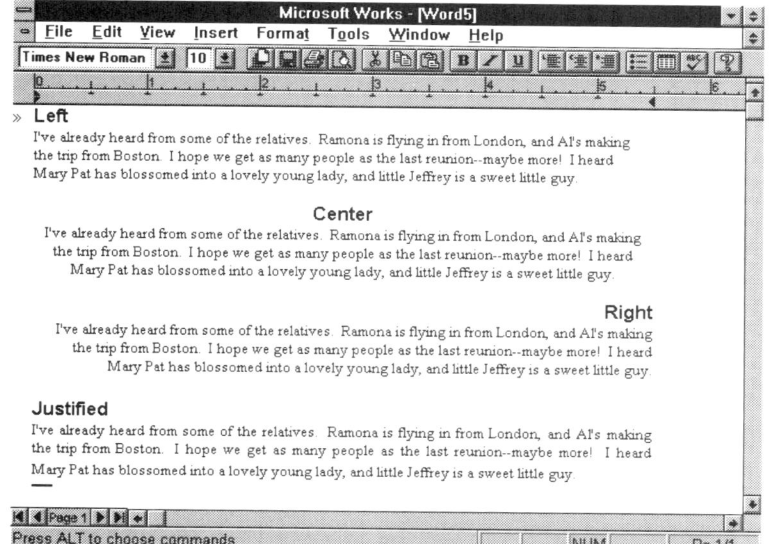

Figure 3-16. *You can align paragraphs in four different ways.*

Text formatted with the *Center* option will be centered between the left and right margins.

Choosing *Right* aligns the text to the right margin, leaving a ragged left margin.

The *Justified* option will align the text evenly between the left and right margins, like most of the paragraphs in this book. You can access all of the alignment options except *Justified* from the toolbar.

Try changing the alignment of the first paragraph in the sample document from *Left* to *Center* alignment. To do this, click the insertion point anywhere in the first paragraph, then click on the *Center* alignment button on the toolbar. Your document will now look like the example in Figure 3-17.

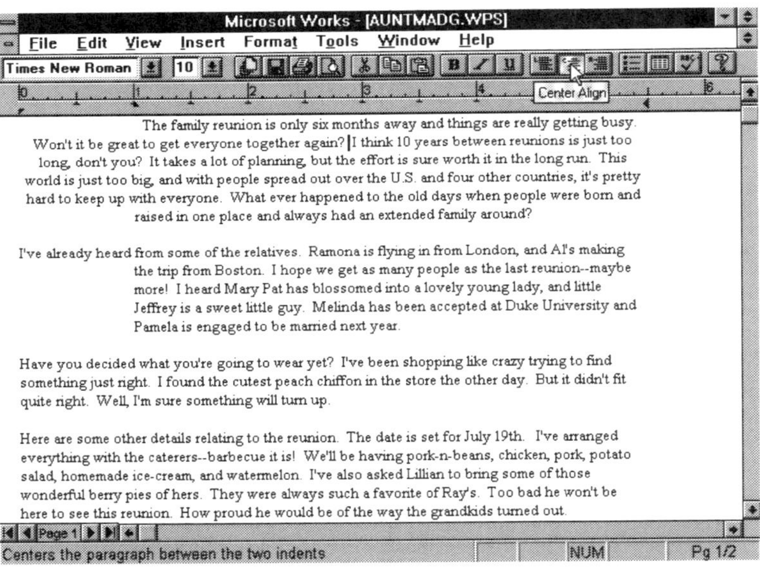

Figure 3-17. *Click on the Center button to center the current paragraph between the indents shown on the ruler.*

Breaks

In some cases it is essential that a paragraph or a series of paragraphs should not be split by a page break. Selecting the *Breaks and Spacing* tab in the *Paragraph* dialog box enables you to control this.

To ensure that Works will not break a paragraph with a page break, choose the *Don't break paragraph* check box. Instead of allowing a page break in the middle of a paragraph Works will force the paragraph to start over the page. By choosing the *Keep paragraph with next* check box, Works will not insert a page break between the text selected and the next paragraph.

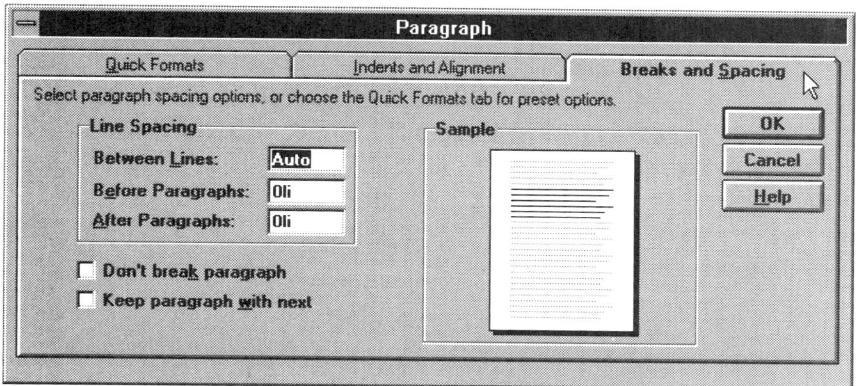

Figure 3-18. *Click on the Breaks and Spacing tab to access these options.*

Spacing

You can adjust line spacing within a document to add to the readability of the text. Line spacing can be changed through the *Breaks and Spacing* tab in the *Paragraph* dialog box. You can set line spacing using whole numbers or decimals (e.g. 0.75, 1.5, etc.) depending on your requirements.

To change the line spacing in the third paragraph to double, first click in that paragraph. Open the *Paragraph* dialog box, click on the *Breaks and Spacing* tab if it is not on top and type in "2" in the *Between Lines* text box, as in Figure 3-19.

The shortcut for applying double spacing is to press Ctrl-2. A complete list of the shortcuts for paragraph formats is found in Appendix A.

Line Spacing
Between Lines: 2
Before Paragraphs: 0li
After Paragraphs: 0li

Figure 3-19. *Change the line spacing in the third paragraph to double spacing.*

Works gives you the option of leaving some blank space at the top or bottom of a paragraph. This option is available in the *Paragraph* dialog box under *Line Spacing* (Figure 3-20). The *Before Paragraphs* and *After Paragraphs* options are measured in lines by default, but you are able to use points, inches, or centimeters by typing in a suffix—"in" for inches, "cm" for centimeters, and "pt" for points.

It is also possible to use these other suffixes in the *Between Lines* text box.

To leave a half-inch space below "Dear Aunt Madge," position the insertion point in that paragraph and select *Paragraph* from the **Format** menu. Click on the *Breaks and Spacing* tab if it is not on top and double-click on *After Paragraphs* text box. As the paragraph has no additional space after it at this stage, the text box currently displays "0li". Type in "0.5in" and click on *OK* (see Figure 3-20).

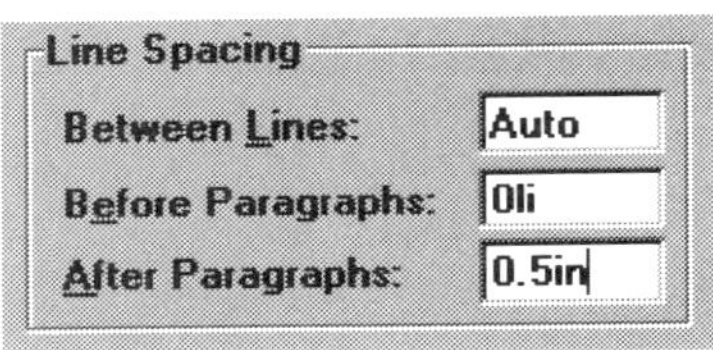

***Figure 3-20.** Type in "0.5in" to replace the current setting in the After Paragraphs text box.*

The first paragraph of the body of the letter moves down the screen to allow for the space below "Dear Aunt Madge," as you can see in Figure 3-21.

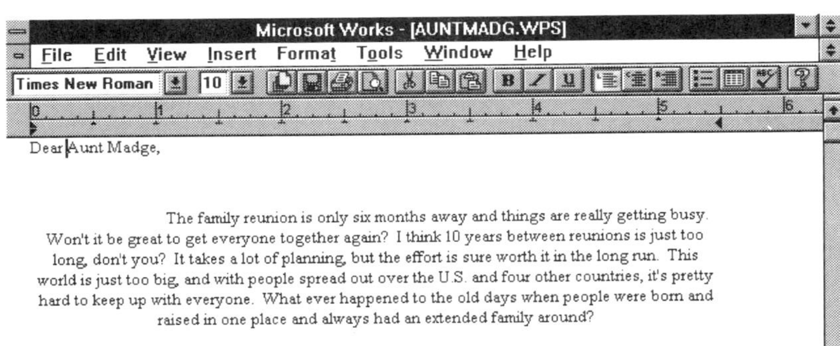

***Figure 3-21.** Works leaves a gap after "Dear Aunt Madge" when you click on OK.*

Formatting text

In a document, text needs to be formatted to enhance the document's appearance and readability. Types of formats include changing the font, font size, and attributes of text. The format of text can be changed in two ways, either by highlighting existing text and applying the format required, or presetting the format by turning it on before the text is typed.

Font submenu in the toolbar

A font is a style which is applied to a set of characters, incorporating both text and numbers. Thousands of fonts are available but each of these relies on your printer being able to produce them. Some of the more common fonts include Times Roman, Helvetica, and Courier.

A list of fonts available in Works is in the *Font* submenu on the toolbar, which can be accessed by clicking on the down arrow to the right of the submenu. The list will vary according to the printer attached to your computer.

Figure 3-22. *The Font submenu located on the toolbar.*

Changing the font using the toolbar is very easy. If the text has already been typed, highlight the text to be changed using the techniques previously mentioned, access the *Font* submenu by clicking on the down arrow, and select a different font.

Try this out by changing the date on the first line in ***auntmadg.wps*** to a font of your choice. Remember to highlight the date first and then choose the font from the *Font* submenu.

To preset a font before text has been inserted into a document, select the appropriate font from the *Font* submenu and start typing. The characters will be displayed in the font you have chosen.

Size submenu in the toolbar

The size of characters is determined in Works by its *Point* size. One point is 1/72 of an inch. Standard text for reading is usually 10 or 12 point and headings are much larger, perhaps 14 or even 24 point. Font sizes are also printer dependent.

The size of text can be formatted in the same way as a font can be changed—either by highlighting existing text or presetting new text. The *Font Size* submenu is on the toolbar next to the *Font* submenu (see Figure 3-23).

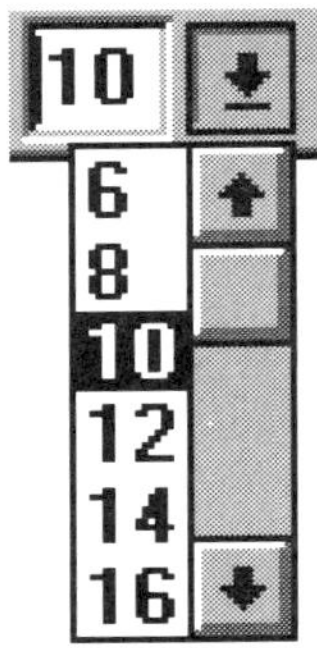

Figure 3-23. *The Font size submenu on the toolbar shows the sizes which are available to you.*

Using the *Font Size* menu, add a heading to the letter in the sample file. Move to the end of the line containing "Dear Aunt Madge" and press Enter to insert a new line. Click on the *Center* button on the toolbar and then choose a larger point size, "16" for example, and type "Family Reunion." You document will now look like the one in Figure 3-24.

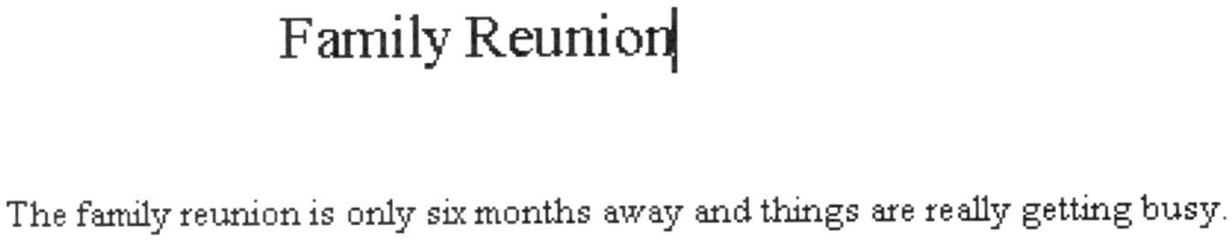

Family Reunion

The family reunion is only six months away and things are really getting busy.

Figure 3-24. *The heading "Family Reunion" was preset to a 16 point font size before it was typed.*

Style buttons on the toolbar

The style of text is often changed to bring attention to it. Bold, underline and italics are used in documents for this purpose. One, or more than one, of these styles can be applied to text.

Styles are applied either by highlighting existing text or presetting new text and using the style buttons on the toolbar (Figure 3-25). For shortcuts to changing the style of text please refer to Appendix A.

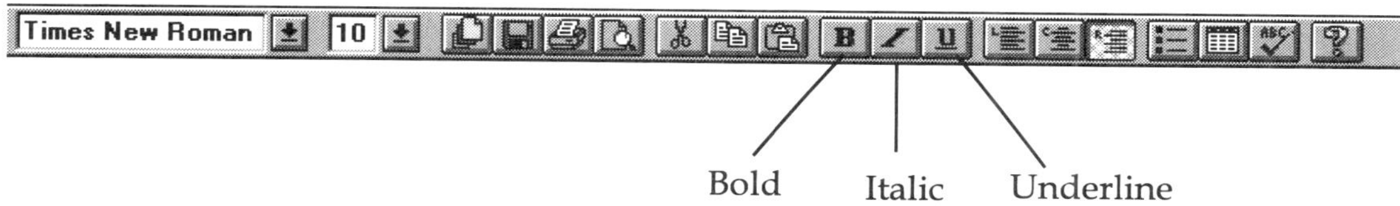

Figure 3-25. *The style buttons on the toolbar – B for bold, I for italics, and U for underline.*

To make the heading you just inserted in ***auntmadg.wps*** even more prominent, change the style to bold. As the text is already part of the document, highlight "Family Reunion" and click the *Bold* style button on the toolbar.

The Font and Style command in the Format menu

The *Font and Style* dialog box, activated through the *Font and Style* command in the **Format** menu, contains all the text formats outlined above as well as *Position* and *Color.*

Position refers to the placement of text on a line. *Normal* will place text on the line, *Superscript* will place text above the line and *Subscript* will place text below the line. An example of *Superscript* in use is 15°, where the degrees symbol is a lowercase smaller point size "o" in a superscript position.

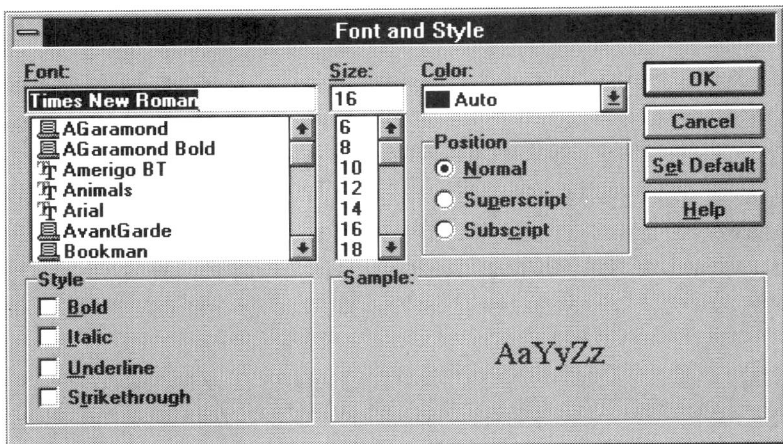

Figure 3-26. *The Font and Style dialog box.*

You can change the color of your text by choosing from the *Color* drop-down list box.

The formats outlined above can be changed using this dialog box either by highlighting or presetting text, and then choosing the font, size, or style required.

Setting tabs

Tabs are positions on a page, usually measured from the left margin. Pressing the Tab key will immediately move the insertion point to the next tab position. Tabs are set for a paragraph or a selection of paragraphs and are used to align text into columns in a table or list.

Works displays a tab as an arrow when *Show All Characters* in the **Options** menu is active (see **Chapter 1, The Word Processor Screen**). For this section, turn *Show All Characters* on.

The tab markers are below the ruler's measurement scale. Works sets default tabs at every half inch and these are indicated by upsidedown Ts. You can change default tabs or set custom tabs. Setting a custom tab will remove any default tabs to the left of the custom tab. A custom tab is displayed on the ruler as an arrow representing the type of tab which has been set (Figure 3-27).

For this section of the chapter, you will need a new document, so go to the **File** menu and select *Create New File*. From the *Startup* dialog box, click on the *Word Processor* button.

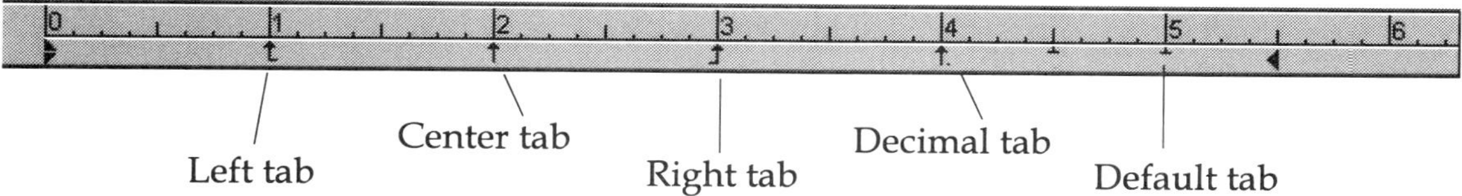

Figure 3-27. *Custom tabs are displayed by an arrow. The style of arrow indicates the type of tab. Default tabs are marked by upside down "T"s.*

Types of tabs

There are four types of tabs, represented by a different style of arrow. These types are: *Left Align, Right Align, Center,* and *Decimal Align* (see Figure 3-27).

Left Align tabs align the left edge of the text at the tab position. *Right Align* tabs align the right edge of the text at the tab position. *Center Align* tabs center text around the tab position.

Decimal Align tabs are used to align columns of figures by their decimal place. The decimal point will automatically be placed on the tab position.

A *Leader* tab can be used in conjunction with any tab type. The leader tab fills the space between the insertion point with a series of characters. Works has four types of leader characters: dots (.....), dashes (-----), double dashes (====), and underlining (___).

Using the ruler

Left Align tabs can be set by clicking the mouse pointer on the bottom half of the ruler where a tab is required. An arrow will be displayed at the new tab position. Any default tabs to the left of this mark will be deleted. Put in a *Left Align* tab at the 1 inch mark by clicking on the ruler at 1 inch. Press the Tab key and type in "Staff No."

To move a tab on the ruler, click and drag the arrow to the new tab mark. Do this for the tab mark at the 1 inch mark, moving it back to 0.5 inches. You will notice that "Staff No." moves back to the new position (see Figure 3-28).

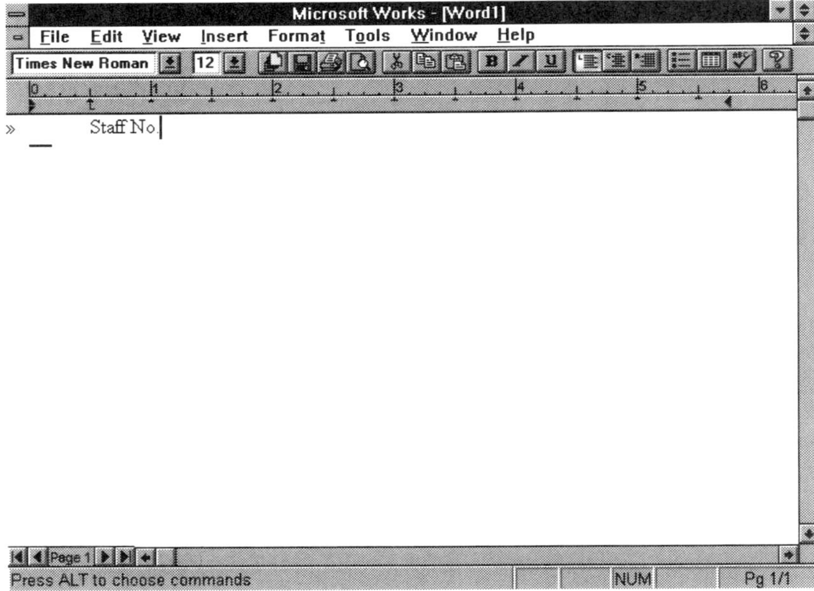

Figure 3-28. *The document has a 0.5 inch left tab, where "Staff No." is located.*

Using the Tabs command in the Format menu

Tabs can also be set through the *Tabs* command in the **Format** menu. It is essential to use the *Tabs* dialog box to change the type of tab and put in a leader character.

A quick way to open the *Tabs* dialog box is to double-click on the measuring scale of the ruler. You will notice the 0.5 inch tab which was inserted using the ruler is recorded in the *Position* list box as in Figure 3-29.

To insert a tab using the *Tabs* dialog box, you type in the tab position in the *Position* text box. Clicking on *Insert* will place it in the *Position* list box, and keep the *Tabs* dialog box on the screen.

To add a *Center* tab at 2 inches using the *Tabs* dialog box, first type in the position—2 inches in our case—then click on the *Center* check box and click on *Insert*. Follow the same procedure to add a *Right Align* tab at 3.5 inches.

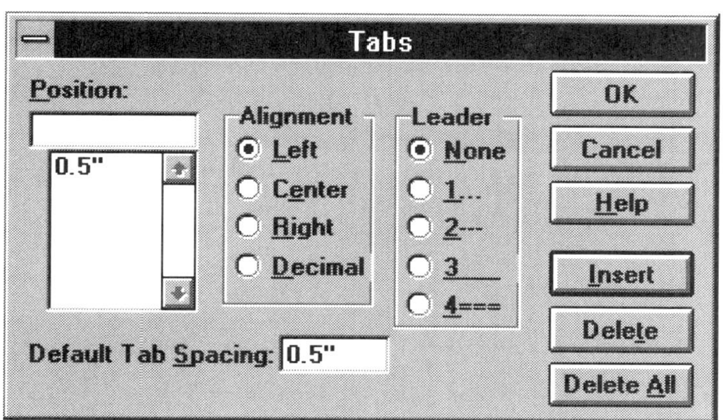

Figure 3-29. *The Tabs dialog box has recorded the 0.5 inch tab from Figure 3-27 in the Position dialog box.*

A *Leader* tab is inserted in much the same way, only before choosing *Insert*, you must click on the check box of the style of leader you require. We need a *Decimal* "dot" leader tab at the 5.5 inches mark, so type "5.5" in the *Position* text box and choose *Decimal* from the *Alignment* list box. To put in the leader, click on "1..." in the *Leader* box and then click on *Insert*.

Your *Tabs* dialog box should now look like the dialog box of Figure 3-30.

Now that all the tabs are in position, click on *OK* in Figure 3-30 to return to the document. Type in the information as shown in Figure 3-31 using the Tab key to align the columns.

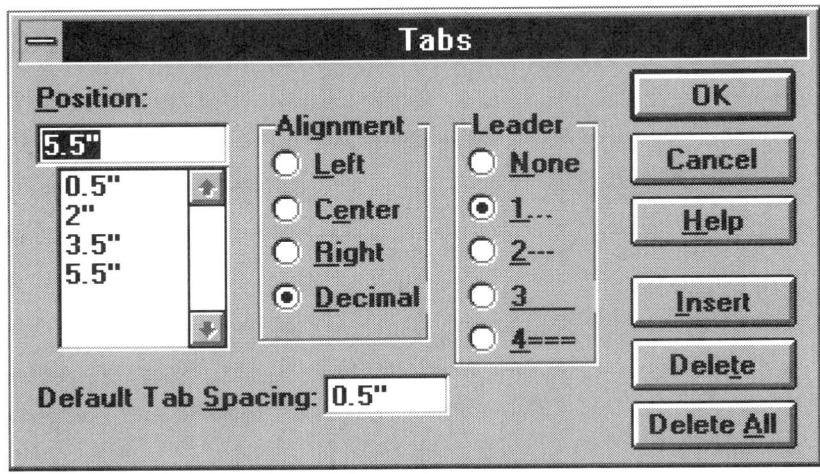

Figure 3-30. *The Tabs dialog box displaying the four tabs you have just inserted.*

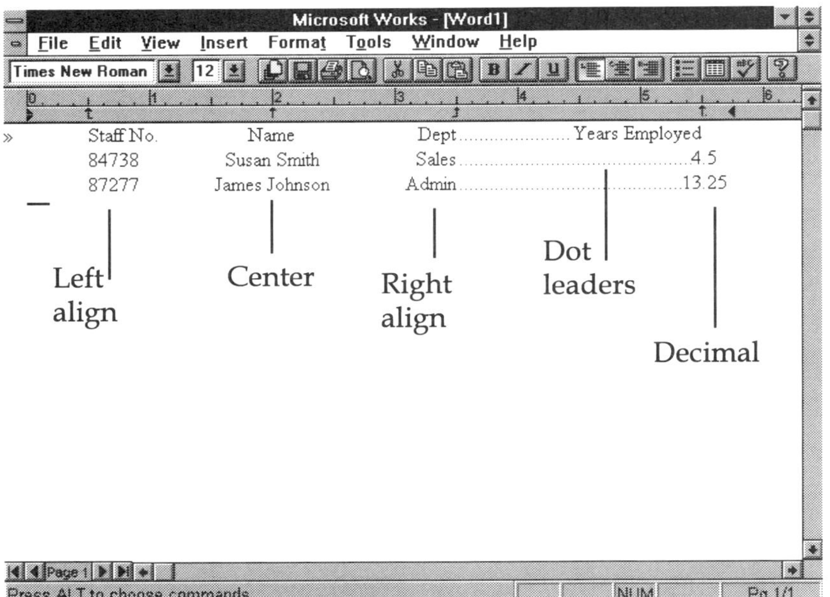

Figure 3-31. *Type in this information using the Tab key to move between columns.*

Note the different types of tabs and their respective formats.

Changing a tab

To change a tab through the *Tabs* dialog box, it must first be selected in the *Position* list box. When a tab is selected, it will appear in the *Position* text-box as well as the list box. Once selected, the position, alignment, and leader can be altered or the entire tab mark can be removed completely using the *Delete* button.

You will notice that the tab mark for the column heading "Years Employed" appears to be out of alignment because of the *Decimal* tab used. To change this heading, click the insertion point in the top paragraph and choose the *Tabs* option from the **Format** menu or double-click on the ruler.

Click on "5.5" in the *Position* list box, then choose *Center* from the *Alignment* list box, now click on *OK*. The heading does not require the leader. To remove the leader click on the *None* check box before clicking on *OK*. The heading "Years Employed" is now centered over that column in Figure 3-32.

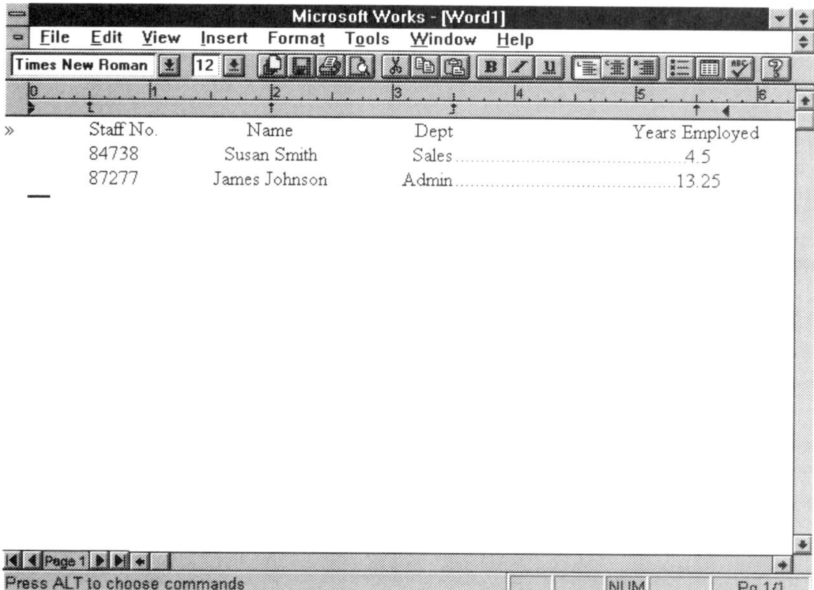

Figure 3-32. *The layout of the page looks much better with "Years Employed" using a Center tab.*

Cut, Copy and Paste commands

Three commands in the **Edit** menu, shown in Figure 3-33, allow you to use the Windows Clipboard as an editing tool in Works. You can also access these commands using buttons on the toolbar, as you can see in Figure 3-33.

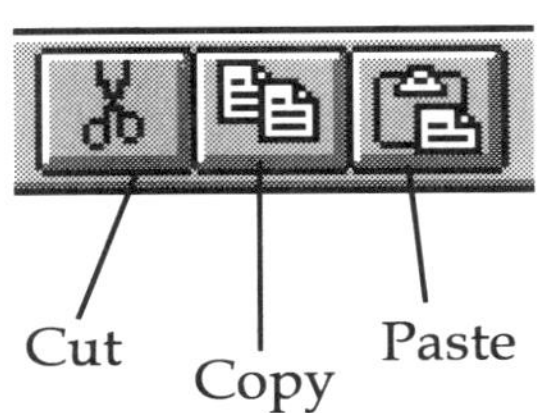

Edit	
Undo Editing	Ctrl+Z
Cut	Ctrl+X
Copy	Ctrl+C
Paste	Ctrl+V
Paste Special...	
Clear	Del
Select All	
Find...	
Replace...	
Go To...	F5
Links...	
Object	

Figure 3-33. The Cut, Copy, and Paste commands use the Windows Clipboard.

Cutting and copying text or graphics will store that information temporarily in the Windows Clipboard. It will remain in the Clipboard until something else is either cut or copied. The contents of the Clipboard can then be inserted or pasted into another position in the document or into another document altogether.

The Cut command

The *Cut* command in the **Edit** menu enables you to remove text from your document. It also allows you to bring it back in another position, if required. This is very different to simply deleting the text, as deleted text cannot be reinserted.

To cut text from a document, highlight the information to be cut and choose *Cut* from the **Edit** menu, as in Figure 3-34. There is no limit to the amount of information which can be cut.

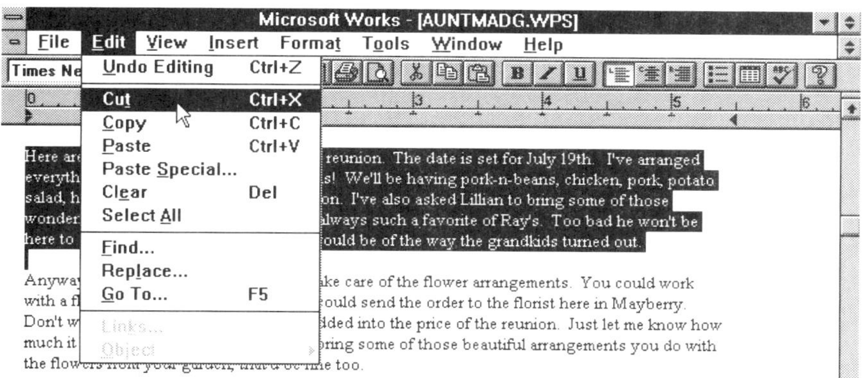

Figure 3-34. Choose Cut to remove the paragraph you highlighted.

The Copy command

The *Copy* command in Works works in a similar fashion to the *Cut* command, except that it doesn't remove the selection from the document. A copy is placed on the Clipboard and can be reinserted anywhere in the document.

To copy information, highlight the text or objects to be copied and choose *Copy* from the **Edit** menu.

The Paste command

Choosing *Paste* from the **Edit** menu after a selection has been cut or copied will insert the contents of the Clipboard into the document at the insertion point. It is important, therefore, to move the insertion point to the correct position before pasting. As the Clipboard contents are not removed as they are pasted, you can paste the same information into several places just by repasting.

Try using the *Cut* and *Paste* commands to rearrange the order of the paragraphs in ***auntmadg.wps***. To move the fourth paragraph after the fifth, highlight the fourth paragraph, including the blank line below. Now choose *Cut* from the **Edit** menu, as shown in Figure 3-33, to remove the paragraph you selected.

It is important at this stage to move the insertion point to where the paragraph is to be inserted — at the beginning of the sixth paragraph. When the insertion point is positioned correctly choose *Paste* from the **Edit** menu to complete the reordering.

Advanced Document Editing

This chapter discusses the advanced formatting techniques which can be applied to a document in Works. Throughout this chapter we use the sample file, ***letter.wps***, to demonstrate the use of these advanced formatting techniques. The sample file is in the ***msworks.cbt*** subdirectory.

Page Setup and Margins

Page setup and margin settings affect how a document will appear on a page when it is printed. Margins are the white area around the edge of a page within which the text and graphics appear. In Works, the default top and bottom margins are 1 inch (2.5 cm) and the left and right margins are 1.25 inches (3.2 cm). However you can alter these as you wish, by changing the settings in the *Page Setup* dialog box (Figure 4-1), which you open from the **File** menu.

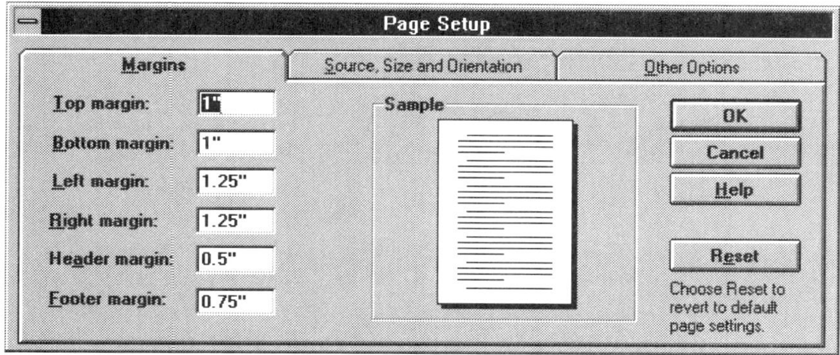

Figure 4-1. *The Page Setup dialog box.*

As well as defining a global margin setting, which affects the whole document, specific paragraphs, tables or graphics can have margins individually set. This is often used to bring attention to a particular piece of text, for instance a quote from a book.

To do this, the block to be changed needs to be highlighted or the insertion point placed in the paragraph if you wish to change only one paragraph. Then move the right or left margin indicators (Figure 4-2) on the ruler to the new position. The left margin indicator begins at zero, which allows for the default left margin width.

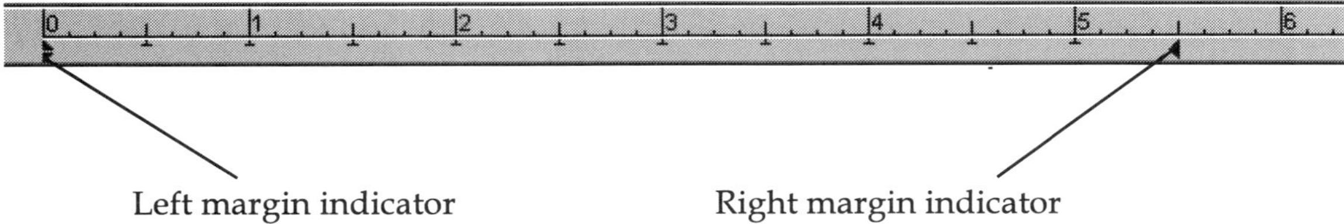

Figure 4-2. *The left and right margin indicators on the ruler.*

Try changing the margin settings in the paragraph beginning "The family reunion" in the sample file ***letter.wps***. Move the insertion point into that paragraph to begin with. Now drag the left margin indicator, with the mouse, to the 1 inch (2.5 cm) position, and the right margin indicator to the 5 inches (12.5 cm) position, on the ruler. Your document should now look like the one in Figure 4-3.

The left margin indicator is now at 1 inch (2.5 cm), which means the text starts 2.25 inches (5.7 cm) from the left side of the page (original 1.25 inch margin plus extra 1 inch margin).

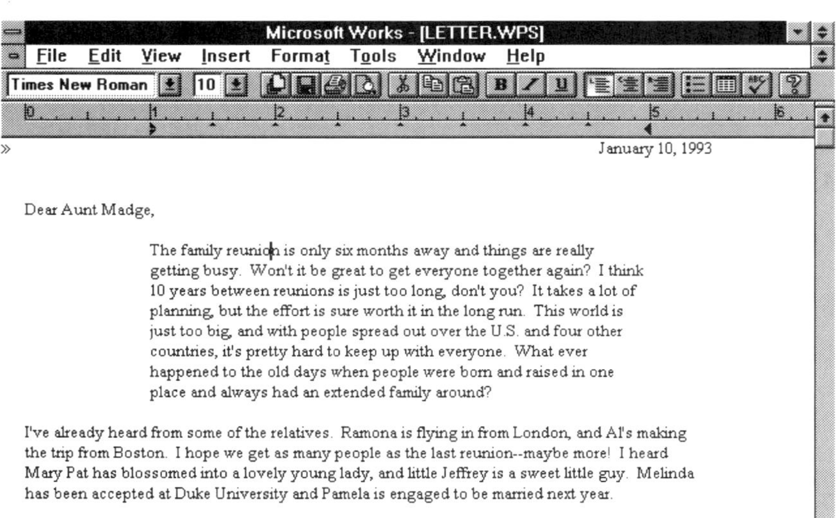

Figure 4-3. *The left margin changes to 2.25 inches – the left margin indicator is at the 1 inch marker on the ruler. The right margin changes to 2.25 inches, therefore the right margin indicator sits at the 5 inches mark – 2.25 inches in from the right edge of the page.*

The absolute right margin is computed as follows:

Width of paper (8.5 inches, 21.4 cm) less the sum of new left margin (2.25 inches, 5.7 cm) plus difference between margin markers (4 inches, 10 cm). This brings the right margin to 2.25 inches (5.7 cm), and is made up from the original 1.25 inch (3.2 cm) default margin plus the additional 1 inch (2.5 cm) margin in moving the right margin indicator to the 5 inch (12.5 cm) position. You can also change the paper size used in you document. To change the paper size, you access the *Page Setup* command in the **File** menu and click on the *Source, Size and Orientation* tab as shown in Figure 4-4.

You can choose a predefined page size from the *Paper Size* submenu or specify a custom size by changing the page dimensions in the *Width* and *Height* text boxes.

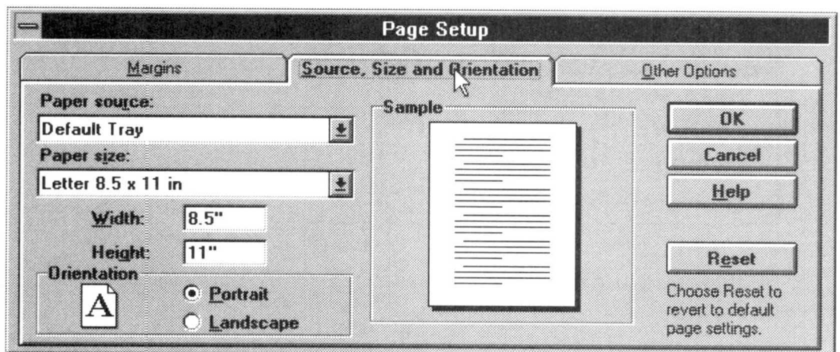

Figure 4-4. *Click on the Source, Size and Orientation tab to access these options.*

Inserting page breaks

Works automatically creates new pages as needed to hold text and graphics. Automatic page breaks are marked by Works with two small arrows in the left margin where the automatic page break has been inserted. The two small arrows are the new page markers and are displayed in Figure 4-5.

» Harold and I are planning our vacation in California

Figure 4-5. *Automatic page breaks are marked in the left margin.*

There are cases, however, when you may need to force the creation of a new page, independent of whether or not the current page has been filled.

Before creating such a page break, move the insertion point to the start of the third paragraph in the sample file as in Figure 4-6. This is where you are going to force a new page break to occur—at the left of the insertion point.

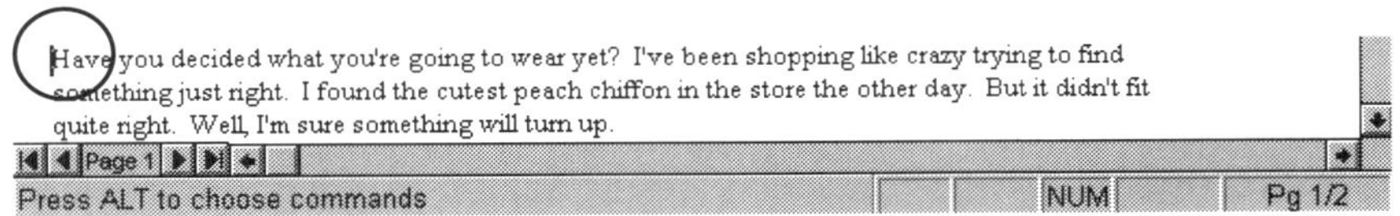

Figure 4-6. Put the insertion point at the beginning of the third paragraph.

To add a page break at the insertion point, select *Page Break* from the **Insert** menu (Figure 4-7). Alternatively, press Ctrl-Enter to insert a page break when the insertion point is positioned correctly.

Figure 4-7. The Page Break command.

A forced page break is indicated in a document by a single broken line across the page. In addition, the new page indicator (two small arrows) will be inserted to the left of the first word on the new page. Figure 4-8 displays both of these. (Note that the automatic page break includes the arrows but not the broken line.)

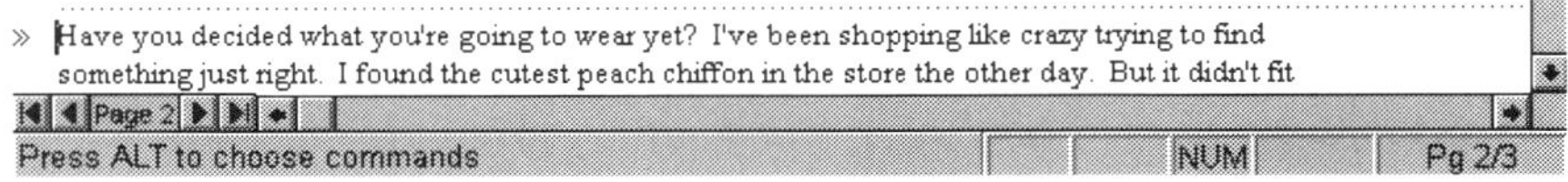

Figure 4-8. Works updates the page number when you insert a page break.

To remove a page break, move the insertion point to the beginning of the new page (Figure 4-8) and press Backspace. Leave the page break in this document as it is used in the **Headers and Footers** section.

The Paginate Now command

The *Paginate Now* command in the **Tools** menu, Figure 4-9, is used by Works to update the page break information within a document. The total number of pages on the status bar, as well as the page indicators on the screen, are updated. By selecting *Paginate Now*, you are certain that Works is displaying the most recent pagination information.

Try using that command to update any changes you have made to the number of pages in your document.

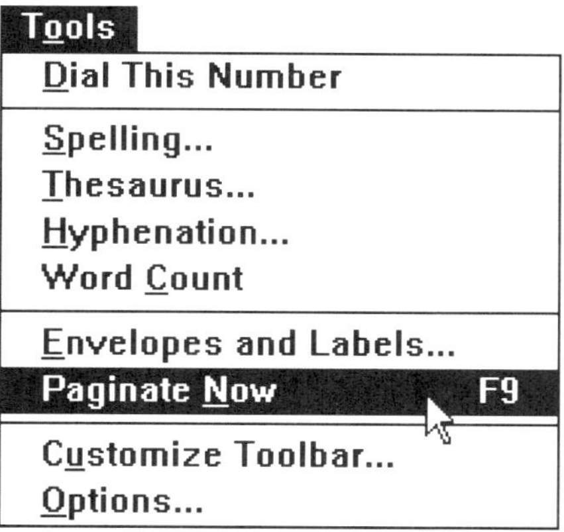

*Figure 4-9. The Paginate Now command in the **Tools** menu.*

Headers and footers

Headers and footers are the text that is repeated across the top (header) and bottom (footer) of pages in a document (see Figure 4-10). In this book, for example, there is a header on all left-hand pages which reads ***Microsoft Works By Example***. On the right-hand pages, the header changes with each chapter — in this chapter, it reads ***Chapter 4 — Advanced Document Editing***. The footer in this book consists of the current page number.

Header

Footer

Figure 4-10. *A header is the information repeated at the top of all, or most pages, in a document, and a footer is repeated at the bottom.*

Special codes can be typed into a header or footer to tell Works to print the page number, the date or time. The header and footer will center text by default, and these codes can be used to alter the alignment of the text. Some of the codes are shown in the table below.

Code	Result	Code	Result
&l	Left align characters after code	&f	Insert filename
&r	Right align characters after code	&d	Insert date
&c	Center characters after code	&n	Insert date in long format
&p	Insert page number	&t	Insert time

In Works, there are two types of headers and footers—single line and paragraph. Lines are used for short, concise headers and footers. The paragraph style enables you to use more than one line for the header, and automatically sets the footer as a page number appearing in the center of the page.

To put in a single line header and footer in the sample document, choose *Headers and Footers* from the **View** menu as in Figure 4-11.

The *Headers and Footers* dialog box appears, into which you type the header and footer information. Type in the contents of the text boxes in Figure 4-11. Also ensure that the *Use header and footer paragraphs* box is not checked. Click on *OK* when finished.

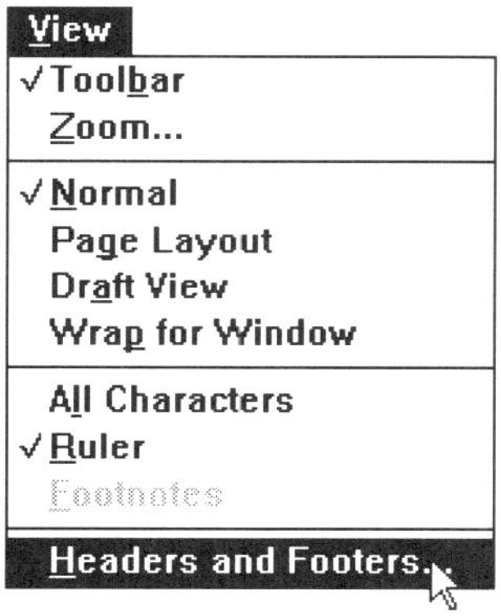

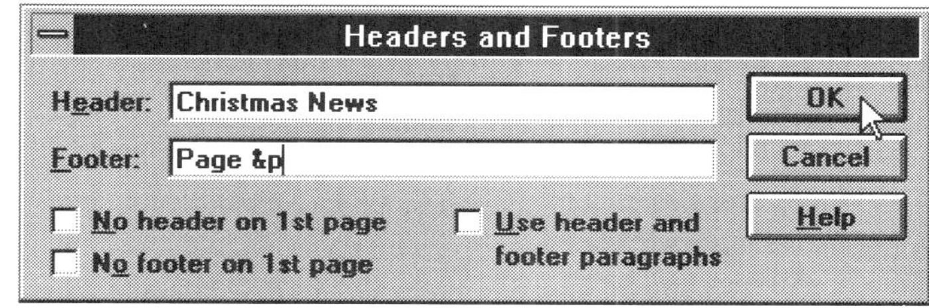

Figure 4-11. *Choose Headers and Footers from the* ***View*** *menu and enter the information shown here.*

To view the document as it will appear when it is printed — showing the headers and footers — choose *Print Preview* from the **File** menu (refer to **Chapter 7, Printing Word Processed Documents**, for more details on printing).

To access the paragraph header and footer option, the *Use header and footer paragraphs* option must be checked in the *Headers and Footers* dialog box as in Figure 4-12. Choosing this option will automatically override any one line headers and footers which have been placed into the document. The header and footer set previously are grayed out in Figure 4-12.

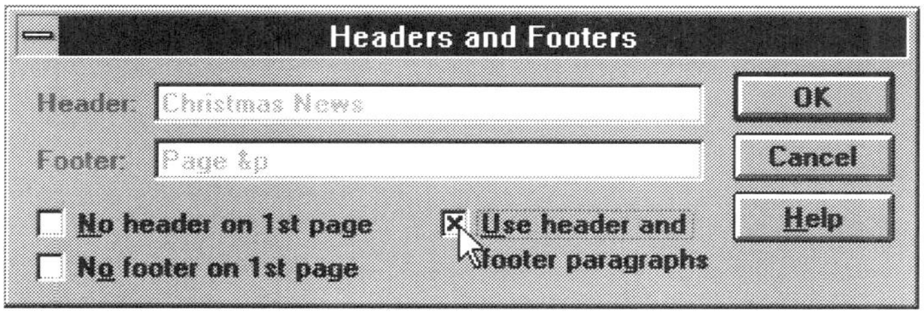

Figure 4-12. *Click on Use header and footer paragraphs.*

Click on *OK* and you return to the document. At the top of the first page, Works has inserted an "H" and an "F." You insert the paragraph header next to the "H," so move the insertion point to this point and type in the following text (Figure 4-13):

I will write with more exciting news of our reunion next month. Watch this space for developments!

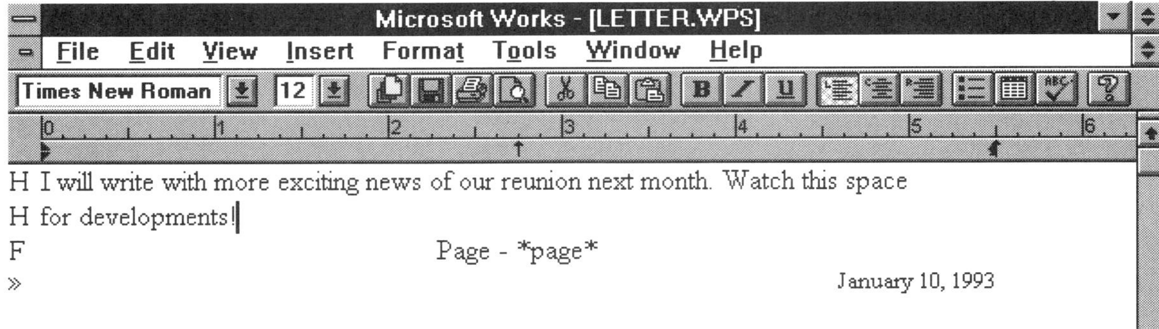

Figure 4-13. *Enter the text as shown for the header paragraph.*

The footer is automatically inserted in the paragraph style of footer and will print the page number at the bottom of the page. The footer can be changed to suit your needs, but leave it in this example. To view the headers and footers, choose *Page Layout* from the **View** menu.

It is possible to suppress the header and footer on the first page. This is done by selecting the *No header on 1st page* or *No footer on 1st page* options in the *Headers and Footers* dialog box (Figure 4-14). This option is very useful for title pages, where a header and footer is not always necessary.

Headers and Footers

Header: Christmas News

Footer: Page &p

No header on 1st page

No footer on 1st page

Use header and footer paragraphs

OK

Cancel

Help

Figure 4-14. *The No header on 1st page and No footer on 1st page options.*

Footnotes

Footnotes are commonly used to cite quotations and add extra information into a document without cluttering the body text.

A footnote is referenced by a predefined character, such as an asterisk, or an automatic numbering system which is the default in Works. The reference mark is placed in the document and the information in the footnote appears at the end of the document. Once a footnote has been placed in a document, the text and the format can be changed or deleted.

To insert a footnote, move the insertion point to where the reference point is to go, at the end of the first sentence in the body of the letter "...really getting busy." Choose the *Footnote* command in the **Insert** menu as in Figure 4-15, which opens the Footnote dialog box as shown.

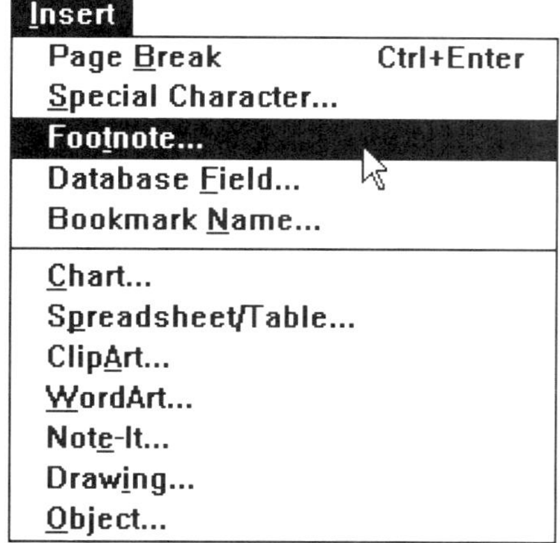

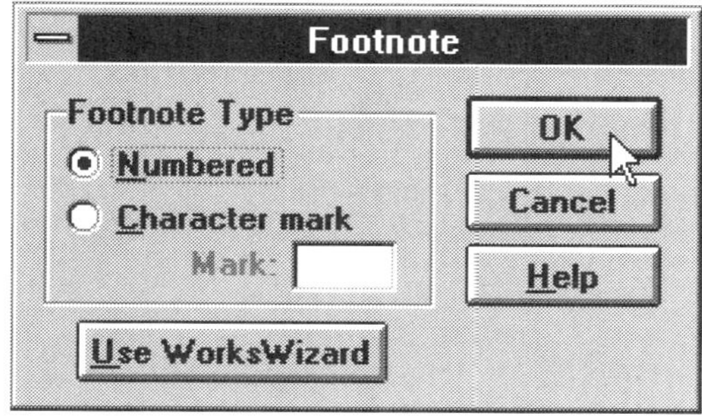

Figure 4-15. *Position the insertion point at the end of the first sentence and choose Footnote from the* ***Insert*** *menu.*

The *Footnote* dialog box gives you the choice of inserting sequentially numbered footnotes, using a character as a reference mark, or using a WorksWizard. See **Chapter 26, Using WorksWizards and AutoStart Templates** for information on this final option. For this example use the default setting, which is the numbered footnote, so click on *OK* or press Enter. Once this has been done, you return to the document where the screen has been split, and you can insert the text for your footnote. Press the space bar to move away from the reference number, and type in:

Never a dull moment around here!

The footnote pane remains on the screen until it is removed by double-clicking on the split bar, which is shown in Figure 4-16, or by choosing *Footnotes* from the **View** menu.

Only the reference mark of the footnote is visible in *Normal* view when the footnote pane is cleared. To view the document as it appears when it is printed, choose *Print Preview* from the **File** menu (refer to **Chapter 7, Printing Word Processed Documents** for more details on printing).

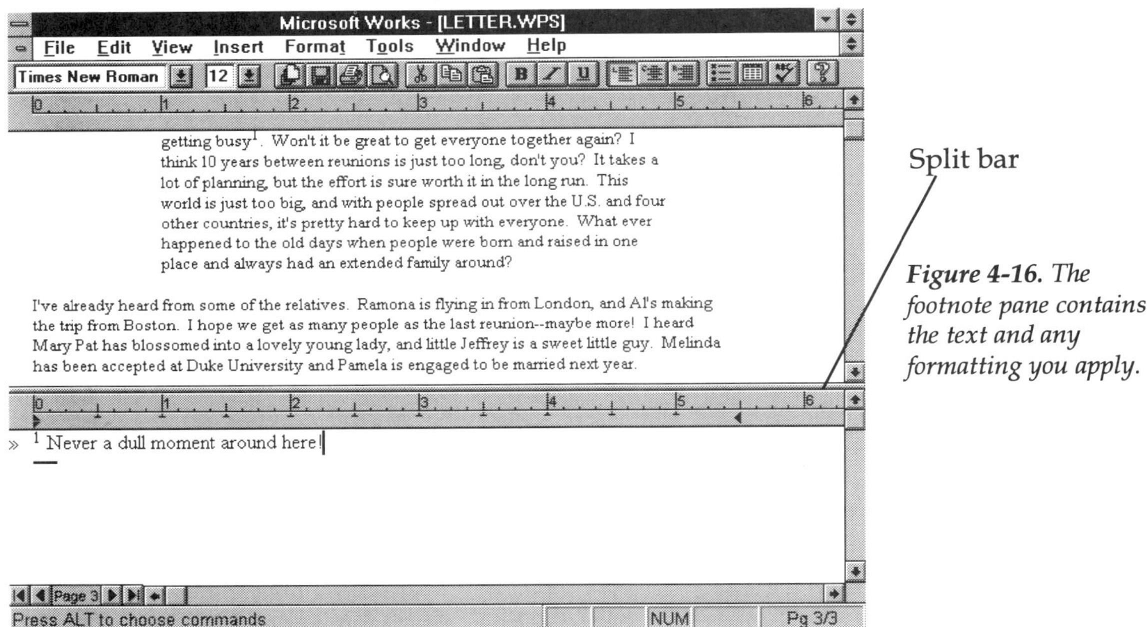

***Figure 4-16.** The footnote pane contains the text and any formatting you apply.*

Inserting special characters

Inserting special characters into a document changes the way a document looks and prints. A special character may simply move text to a tab mark or end a line, or it may be more complex, such as printing the current time on the page.

Chapter 1, The Word Processor Screen, discussed how to display these characters with the *All Characters* command in the **View** menu. This section outlines how to insert some special characters into your document.

Special characters are inserted through the *Special Character* command in the **Insert** menu (Figure 4-17). The right-hand side of the *Special Character* dialog box displays a brief description of the special character currently selected.

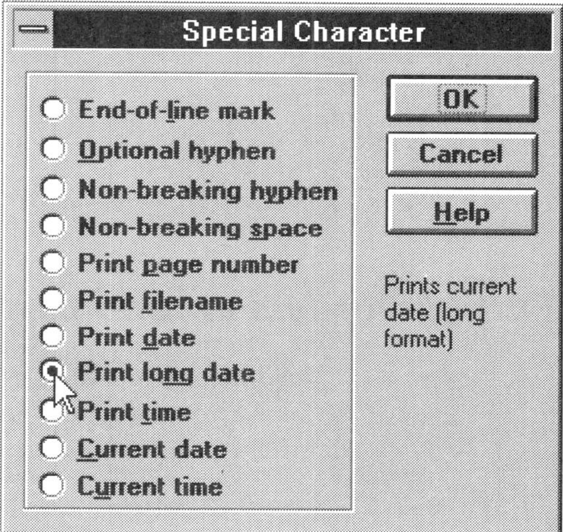

Figure 4-17. *Choose Special Character from the* ***Insert*** *menu to open this dialog box.*

From the *Special Character* dialog box, you can select the special character you require. It is inserted at the insertion point. To remove that character, move the insertion point immediately before the character and press Delete. The character no longer appears on the screen.

As an example, replace the date with the "*longdate*" special character at the top of ***letter.wps***. The first step is to delete the existing date. Now choose *Special Character* from the **Insert** menu and select *Print long date,* as shown in Figure 4-18.

The top of your document with the "*longdate*" special character will now look like Figure 4-18. To see the new character on your screen, choose *Print Preview* from the **File** menu.

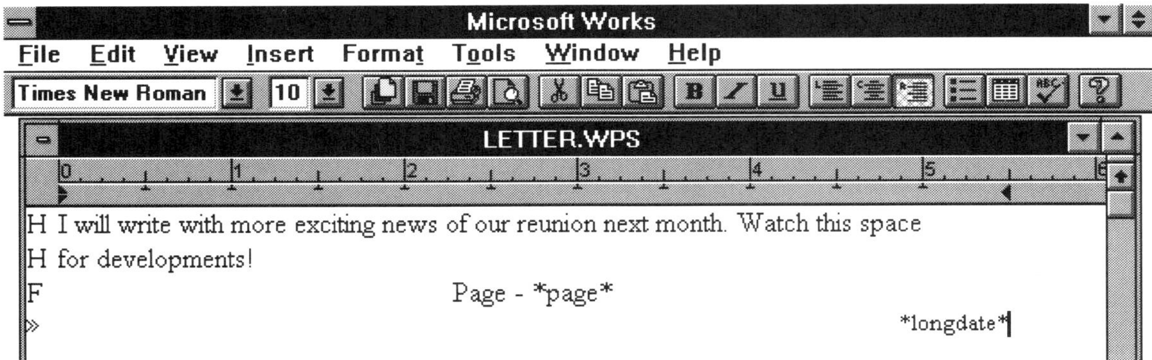

***Figure 4-18.** The "*longdate*" special character in **letter.wps**.*

Putting borders around paragraphs

Borders are used to emphasize paragraphs and to enhance the general appearance of the document. A border can be placed around just one paragraph, a series of paragraphs, or a whole page.

To set a border, select the paragraph or paragraphs which need borders and choose *Border* from the **Format** menu. One paragraph can be chosen just by clicking in it. Figure 4-19 displays the *Border* dialog box in which you can select various positions and styles of borders.

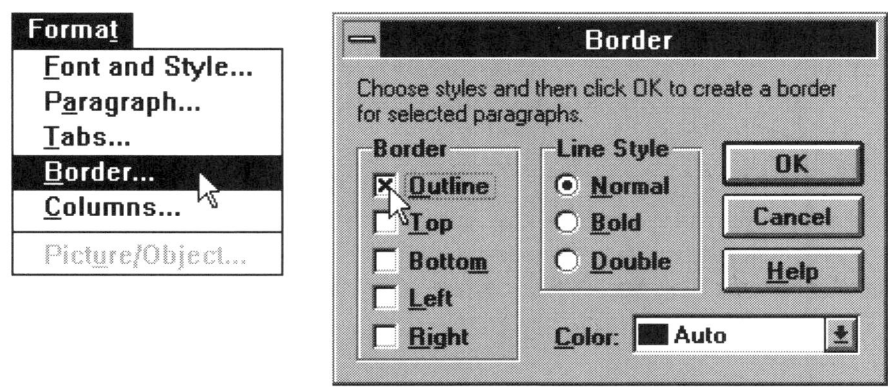

***Figure 4-19.** Choose Border from the **Format** menu to open this dialog box.*

Test the *Border* command by placing a border around the paragraph beginning "Have you decided what..." as shown in Figure 4-20. Click on the paragraph and choose *Border* from the **Format** menu. You can now use this dialog box to select a border.

There are four places in which a paragraph can have a border—*Top*, *Bottom*, *Left*, and *Right*. *Outline* combines all of these to give you a closed border around the entire selection.

Three styles of borders are available to you in Works—*Normal* (a single line), *Bold*, and *Double*. You can also choose a color for your border.

In this example choose the *Outline* option, style, and color of your choice. Your document should now look like Figure 4-20, but perhaps with a different style.

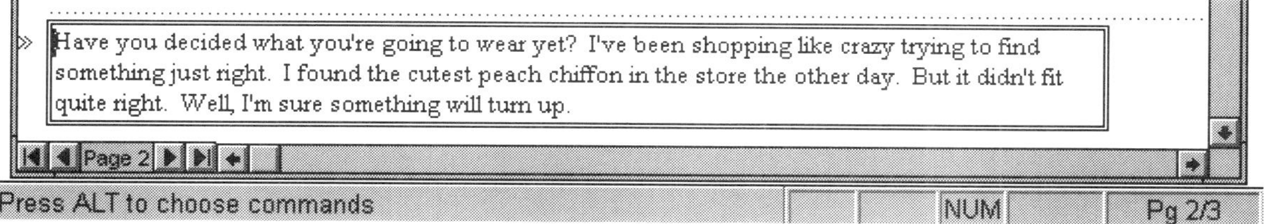

Figure 4-20. *Your document should now look similar to this.*

Find and Replace

Find and *Replace* are useful features of Works which enable you to edit your document quickly and efficiently. Both of these are located in the **Edit** menu as seen in Figure 4-21.

It is always a good idea to move to the beginning of a document before using the *Find* command, so do this now in the sample file ***letter.wps***.

The Find command

When activated, the *Find* command searches through a document for the first occurrence of a specific string of text or numbers and even special characters. It is used often to move the insertion point to a particular part of the document—a heading, for example—quickly.

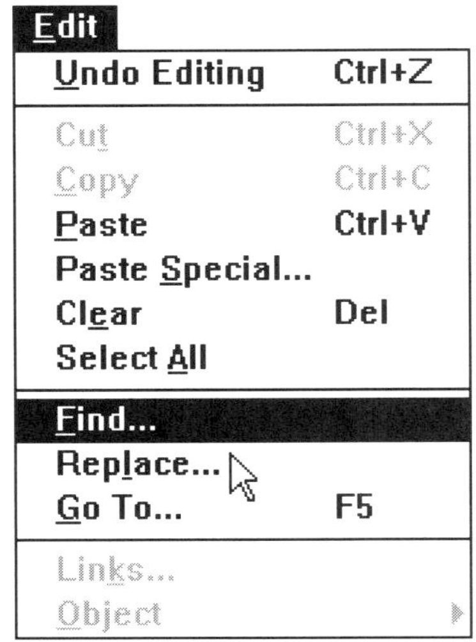

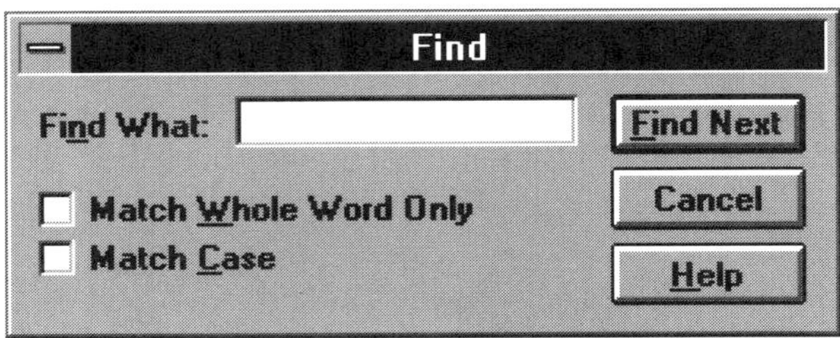

Figure 4-21. *The Find and Replace commands in the* ***Edit*** *menu.*

The *Find* dialog box specifies which occurrences of a word you wish Works to find, using the options. These options are:

Match Whole Word Only will find the word as a whole only. For instance, with this option selected if you were to search through a document for "the," Works would only find "the" as a whole word and not part of another word, such as "other."

Match Case is mainly used to find names, as it enables you to specify the case of the text string Works is to find. For example, typing in "Grant" and checking *Match Case* ensures Works will not find "grant."

Move to the top of the document and use the *Find* command in the **Edit** menu to find the reference made to "flying." Type the word you are looking for into the *Find What* text box as in Figure 4-22 to specify what you want Works to find. Click on *Find Next* and notice that "flying" is highlighted in the document.

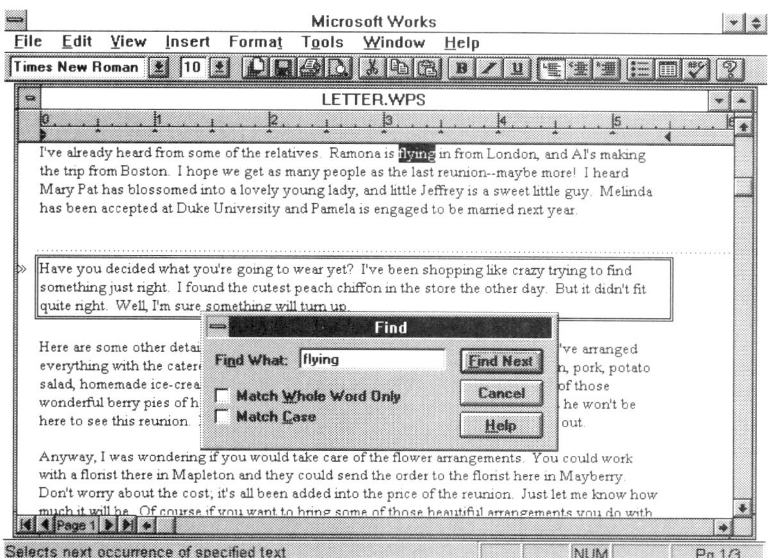

Figure 4-22. Works highlights "flying" when you click on the Find Next button.

The Replace command

The *Replace* command works in a similar fashion to the *Find* command, but takes it one step further by replacing the text you ask Works to find with what you define in the *Replace* text box. In Figure 4-23, we want Works to replace "flowers" with "tulips." Use the *Replace* command in the ***Edit*** menu to do this—move to the beginning of the document first.

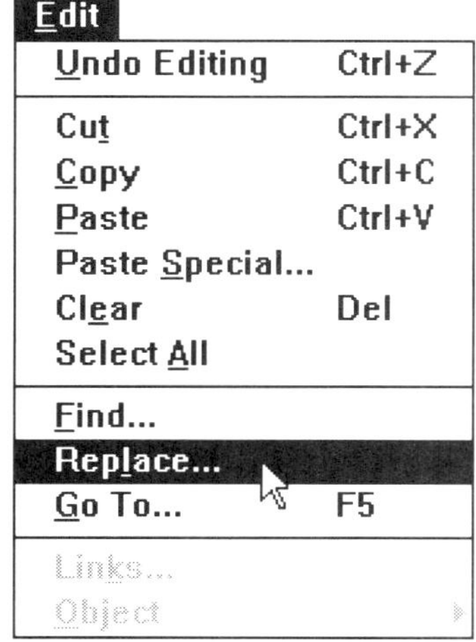

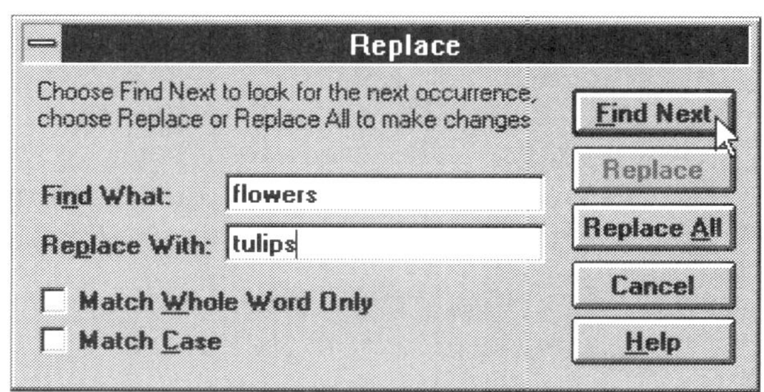

***Figure 4-23.** Move to the top of your document and replace "flowers" with "tulips."*

Clicking on *Find Next* activates the *Replace* command and highlights the first occurrence as in Figure 4-24. Click on *Replace* if you want to change this particular occurrence or click on *Find Next* to move on.

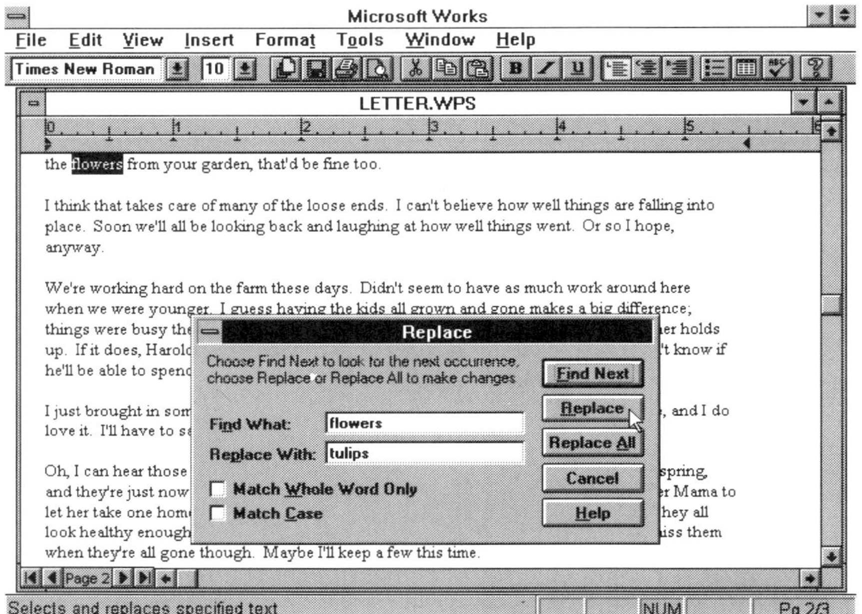

***Figure 4-24.** Click on Replace if you want to replace this occurrence.*

Choosing *Replace All* in Figure 4-24 replaces all occurrences that match the specifications you made in the *Replace* dialog box.

Using columns

In Works you can format your document into "newspaper columns." Like in a newspaper, you start reading text formatted in this way at the top of the left-hand column. When you reach the bottom of one column, you continue reading from the top of the next.

Let's start with a fresh copy of your sample file with which to work. Choose *Close* from the **File** menu and click on the *No* button to abandon the edits you made up to this point. Now choose *\MSWORKS\MSWORKS.CBT\LETTER.WPS* from the **File** menu to open the file afresh.

To format your entire document in columns choose *Columns* from the **Format** menu as in Figure 4-25. Type the *Number of columns* you want to place across the page. You can alter the size of the *Space between columns* and select or deselect the *Line Between* option to further customize the appearance of your document. The *Sample* section shows you a sample page formatted in the way you choose.

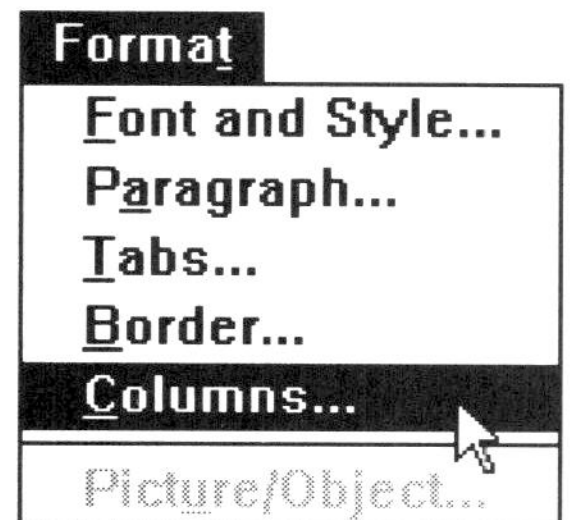

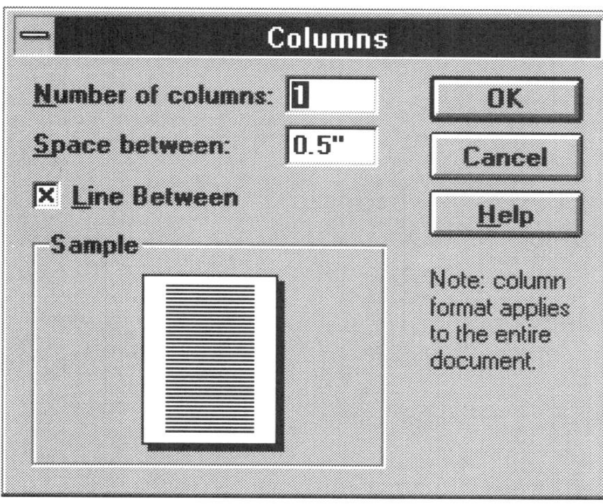

Figure 4-25. Choose Columns from the ***Format*** *dialog box.*

As an example, type 2 in the *Number of columns* text box and click on *OK*. Works asks whether you want to switch to *Page Layout* view to see your columns on screen. Click on *Yes* as shown in Figure 4-26.

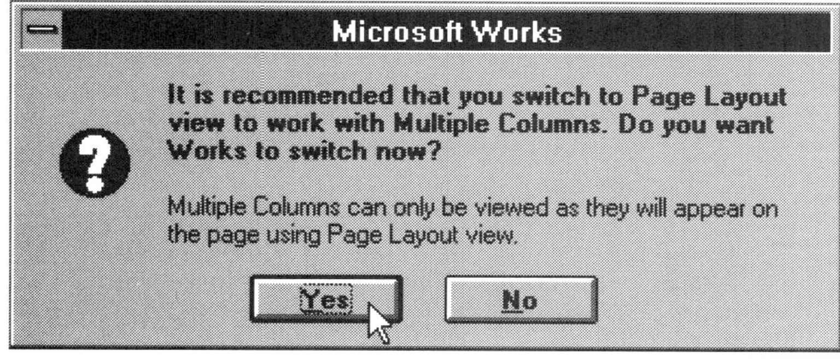

Figure 4-26. Click on Yes to see your 2 columns on the screen.

Figure 4-27 shows you how ***letter.wps*** now looks in *Page Layout* view. Choose *Normal* from the **View** menu when you want to end *Page Layout* view.

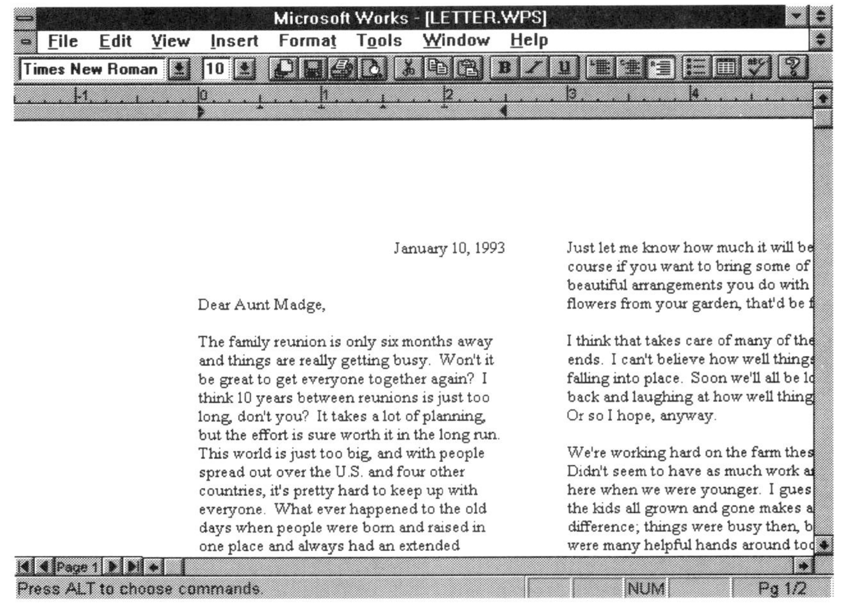

Figure 4-27. Works displays your document in Page Layout view.

Alternatively, you can choose *Print Preview* from the **File** menu if you want to see the line between your columns (see **Chapter 7, Printing Word Processed Documents** for details of using Print Preview).

Inserting ClipArt

Works allows you to add sample pictures to your documents for increased visual appeal. This sample art is available through the ClipArt Gallery which comes with Works. Once you add some ClipArt, you can move, resize, copy or delete the pictures that you added to your document.

Works inserts your chosen ClipArt at your current insertion point in your document. Move the insertion point in front of the phrase "This world is just too big" halfway through the first paragraph of ***letter.wps***. Figure 4-28 shows the insertion point location in *Normal* view while the document is still divided into columns. To start the ClipArt Gallery choose *ClipArt* from the **Insert** menu as shown in Figure 4-28.

The family reunion is only six months away and things are really getting busy. Won't it be great to get everyone together again? I think 10 years between reunions is just too long, don't you? It takes a lot of planning, but the effort is sure worth it in the long run. This world is just too big, and with people spread out over the U.S. and four other countries, it's pretty hard to keep up with everyone. What ever happened to the old days when people were born and raised in one place and always had an extended family around?

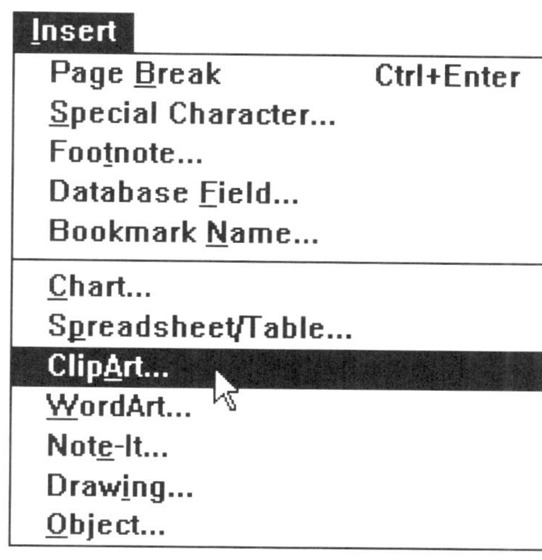

Figure 4-28. *Place the insertion point as shown and then choose ClipArt from the **Insert** menu.*

If there is no art in the ClipArt Gallery yet, Works asks whether you want to add art now as shown in Figure 4-29. Click on *Yes* to add art to the gallery.

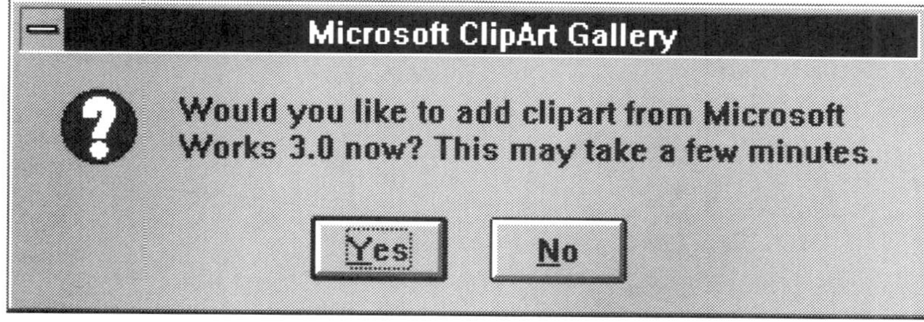

Figure 4-29. *Click on Yes or press Enter to add art to the Gallery.*

Works now opens the dialog box shown in Figure 4-30. You can choose an image by scrolling through those shown in this dialog box. You can also select from the *Choose a category to view below* list box if you want to look among only certain images. By default, Works makes *All Categories* of art available.

Click on the image of the globe at the end of the second line of art among *All Categories* as shown in Figure 4-30 and then click on *OK*.

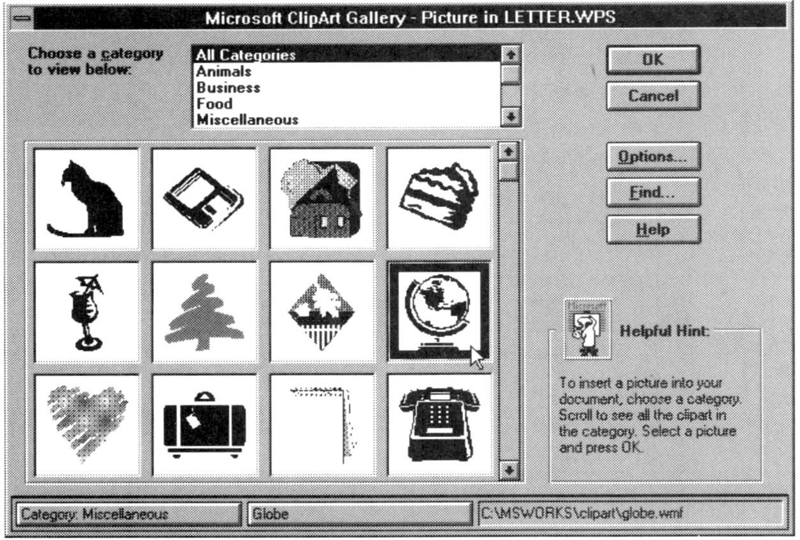

Figure 4-30. *Choose the Globe ClipArt and click on OK.*

Works returns you to your document with the ClipArt you chose inserted to the right of your insertion point. Click on the image of the globe to select the art as shown in Figure 4-31.

Figure 4-31. *Click on the ClipArt to select it.*

With the ClipArt selected in your document you can now adjust the size of the image to suit your needs. Move your mouse pointer onto the top-left corner of the ClipArt so that Works displays the word "RESIZE" beneath the pointer. Click the mouse button and drag the mouse down and to the right until the image outline is roughly the size shown in Figure 4-32.

but the effort is sure worth it in the long run.
RESIZE
This world is
just too big, and with people spread out over

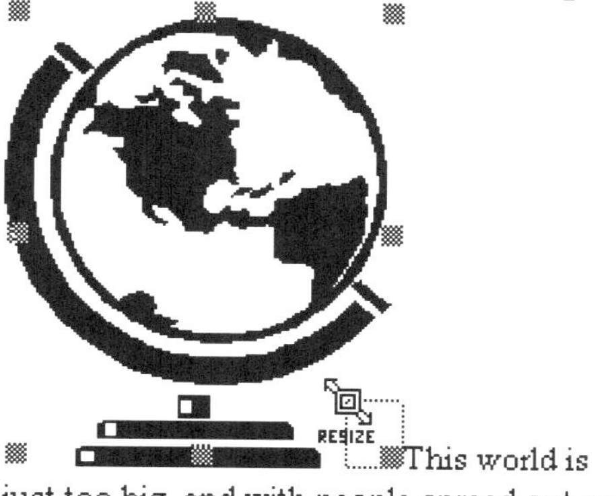

Figure 4-32. *Drag the corner of the art until the outline appears as shown.*

When you click outside of the image, this part of your document should look like Figure 4-33. You can increase or further decrease the size the image by dragging one of its corner handles as you just did. If you want to move the ClipArt, click on the image and drag it to a new position in your document.

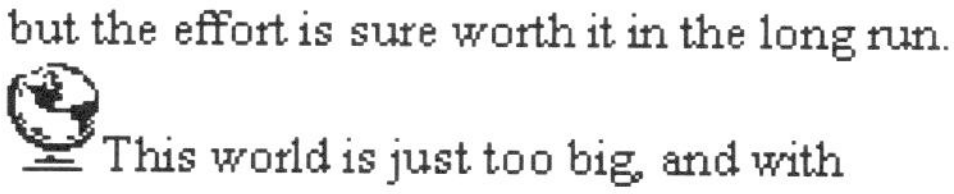

but the effort is sure worth it in the long run.
This world is just too big, and with

Figure 4-33. *Click outside of the art to complete the change in size.*

Inserting WordArt

You can insert text captions into your documents using the WordArt feature of Works. WordArt allows you to apply professional effects such as curvature, shading, and rotation to the text within the caption.

As with ClipArt, Works lets you move, resize, copy, and delete your WordArt as a single object. In addition, you can use special WordArt commands to apply different effects to the contents of your caption.

Click on the line below the date at the top of your document as shown in Figure 4-34, ready to insert some WordArt. To start using WordArt choose *WordArt* from the **Insert** menu.

» January 10, 1993

Dear Aunt Madge,

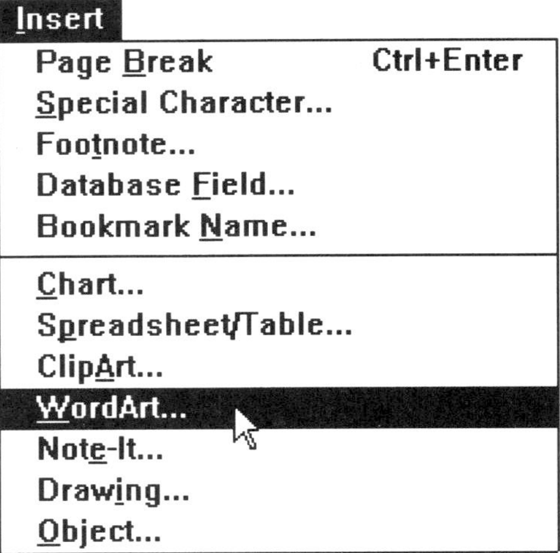

Figure 4-34. *Click on the line below the date and choose WordArt from the **Insert** menu.*

Your screen should now look similar to Figure 4-35. Works changes the menus and toolbar to provide commands specific to the WordArt feature. While the toolbar shown in Figure 4-35 remains on your screen, any commands or formats that you choose will apply to your WordArt only.

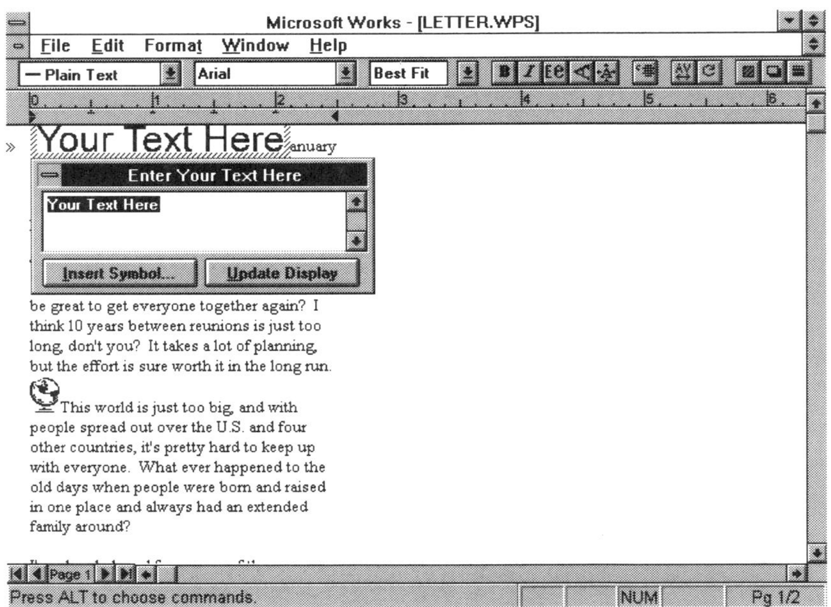

Figure 4-35. *Works displays the WordArt menus and toolbar.*

When you choose the *WordArt* command from the **Insert** menu of the word processor tool, Works selects a default caption which reads "Your Text Here." Press the Delete key on your keyboard to remove this text and type the caption "Not long now!" in its place. Click on the Update Display button to see your new text as it will appear in your document, as shown in Figure 4-36.

Figure 4-36. *Press Delete, type "Not long now!" and click on Update Display.*

The following paragraphs describe the effects which you can apply to your WordArt. You can choose each of these effects from the WordArt toolbar.

The *Text Shape* submenu lets you apply a different overall shape to the text in your WordArt. Choose the *Deflate (Top)* shape shown in Figure 4-37 to alter the shape of the words in your caption.

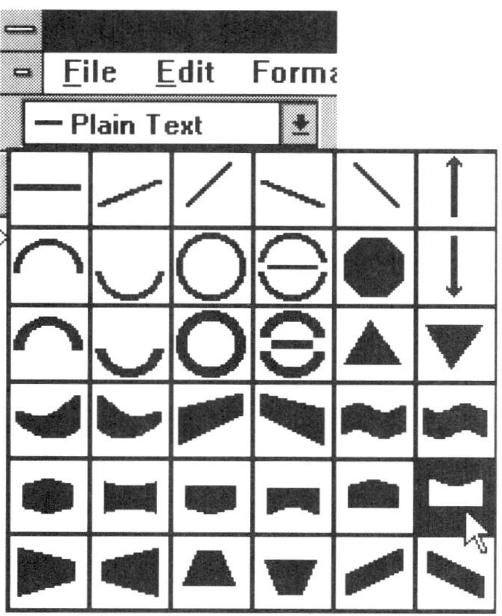

Figure 4-37. *Choose this shape from the Text Shape submenu.*

The *Font Name* and *Font Size* submenus on the WordArt toolbar are similar to those in the word processor, but in addition the *Font Size* submenu provides the *Best Fit* option. *Best Fit* causes Works to choose the largest font size that fits inside the frame around your WordArt (Figure 4-38).

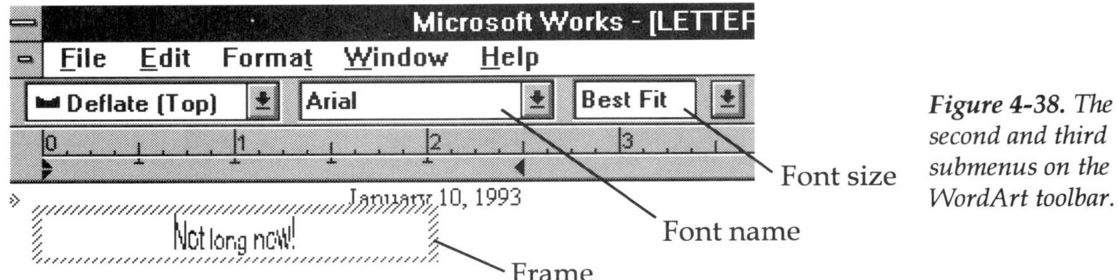

Figure 4-38. The second and third submenus on the WordArt toolbar.

The *Bold* and *Italic* buttons on the WordArt toolbar apply bold and italic formatting respectively. The *Equal Letters* button shown in Figure 4-39 causes uppercase and lowercase letters to occupy the same height. You can use the *Orientate* button to rotate all of the individual characters in your WordArt, and the *Stretch To Frame* button to cause your caption to fully occupy its frame.

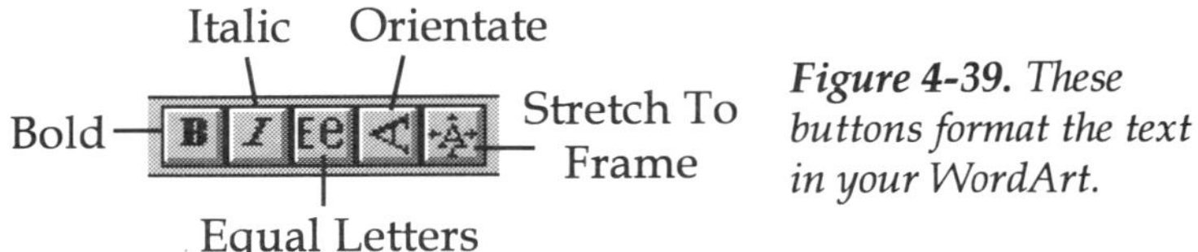

Figure 4-39. These buttons format the text in your WordArt.

Choosing the *Centering and Alignment* button (Figure 4-40) gives you options controlling the horizontal alignment of your WordArt. The *Kerning and Spacing* button lets you control the spacing between the characters in your WordArt. The last button shown in Figure 4-40, the *Rotate and Slide* button, allows you to rotate and skew the entire text within your WordArt caption.

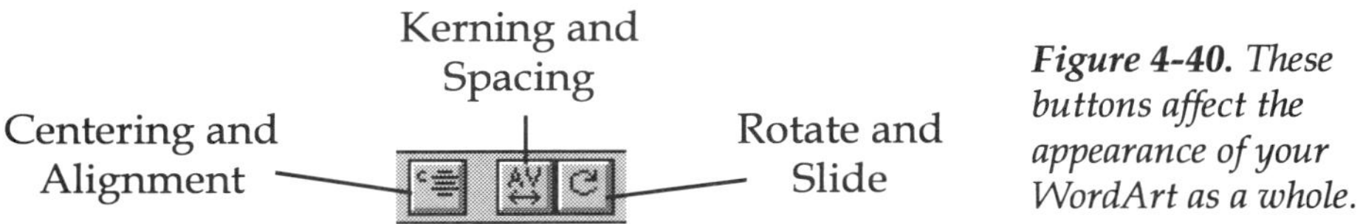

Figure 4-40. These buttons affect the appearance of your WordArt as a whole.

Finally, Works provides the WordArt buttons shown in Figure 4-41. You can use the *Shading*, *Shadow*, and *Border* buttons to apply colors, patterns, and related effects to your WordArt.

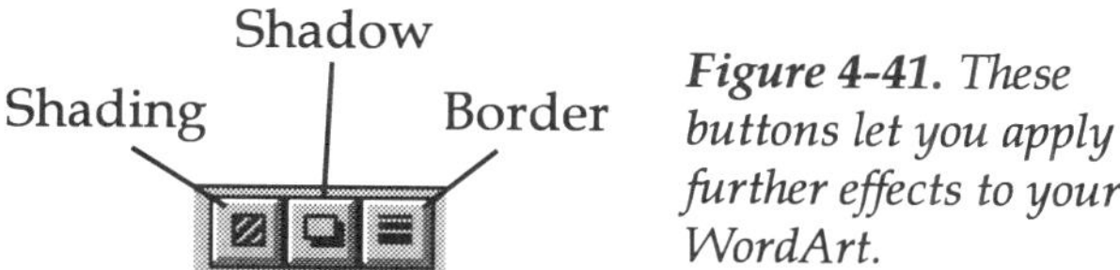

Figure 4-41. *These buttons let you apply further effects to your WordArt.*

To finish using WordArt, click on your document outside of the WordArt caption (Figure 4-42). Works reinstates the normal word processor menu and toolbar. You can double-click on your WordArt to display the WordArt toolbar and menu again if wish to alter your WordArt.

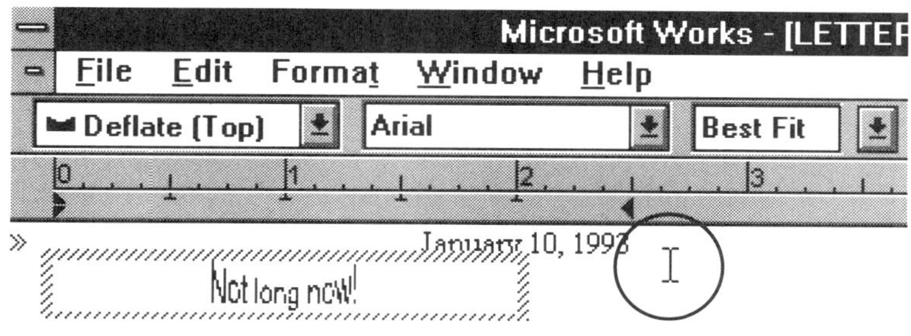

Figure 4-42. *Click on your document outside of the WordArt frame to exit WordArt.*

The Spell Checker and Thesaurus

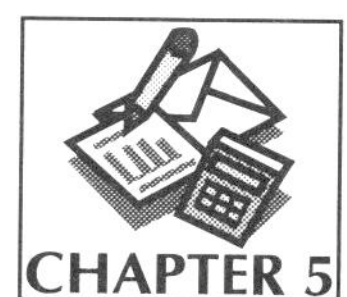

In this chapter we look at the spell checking and thesaurus features of Works. The Works spell checker searches through your text for incorrectly spelled words. On finding a word it thinks is incorrect, it can offer alternative spellings. The thesaurus in Works is designed for the same purpose as a thesaurus in book form—as a list of synonyms. As with the spell checker, Works offers alternative words and you can insert your choice into the document through the thesaurus.

Checking spelling

Works uses a dictionary containing more than 110 000 words as the basis of the *Spelling* function. The spell checker searches through the document from the insertion point, or through selected text, for words which are incorrectly spelled, use the wrong capitalization or hyphenation, or are repeated.

To invoke the spell checker, you can choose *Spelling* from the **Tools** menu (Figure 5-1) and it will begin to move through the document, searching for words which are not in its dictionary. Alternatively, click on the *Spelling Checker* button.

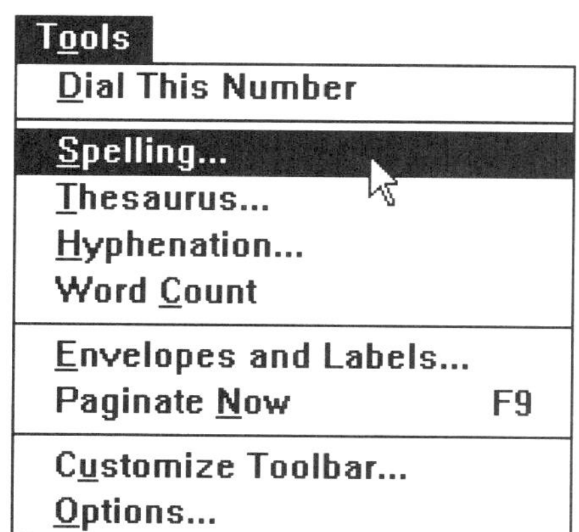

Figure 5-1.** Choosing Spelling from the* ***Tools *menu or choosing this button from the toolbar will activate the spell checker.*

When the spell checker finds a word which it cannot match with its dictionary, the *Spelling* dialog box appears on the screen telling you it can't find that word in its dictionary (Figure 5-2).

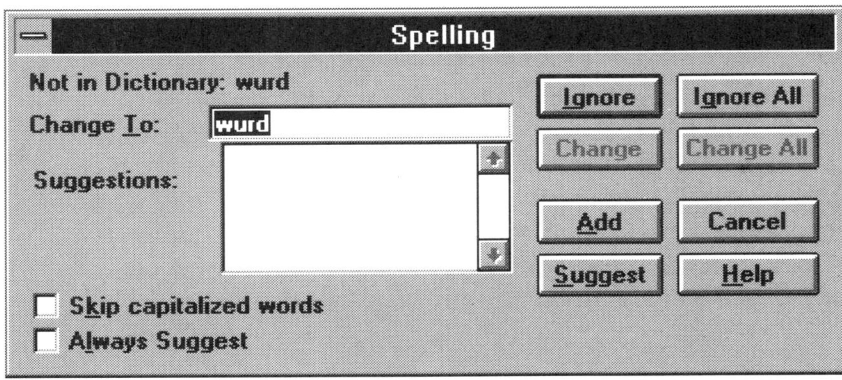

Figure 5-2. *The Works for Windows Spelling dialog box.*

An explanation of the options in the *Spelling* dialog box follows:

Change To-—lets you type in the correct spelling of the word in the text box.

Ignore—leaves the highlighted word unchanged.

Ignore All—ignores every occurrence of the highlighted word.

Change—changes the highlighted word to what appears in the *Change To* text box.

Change All—changes every occurrence of the highlighted word to what appears in the *Change To* text box.

Add—adds the word to the user dictionary.

Suggest—places words which are similar to the spelling of the highlighted word in the *Suggestions* list box.

Skip capitalized words—ignores words with capital letters such as names.

Always Suggest—inserts alternative spellings of the found word in the *Change To* box without your having to press *Suggest*.

To test this feature of Works, type in the following text—mistakes and all!

> There are other ways of acheiving contrast than coloor. You may try changing the font to Palatino, use italics for a key word, or use a slightly larger point size. Contrast should make the text talk. It should make the person reding the the message accent certain words.

Move to the beginning of the document and start up the spell checker by clicking on the *Spelling Checker* button in the toolbar (Figure 5-1).

The dialog box in Figure 5-3 will then open. The first incorrect word it finds is "acheiving." To change the spelling of this word, first click on *Suggest*. The list of alternative spellings appears in the *Suggestions* list box. The correct spelling, "achieving" is in that list box, so click on it and then click on *Change*.

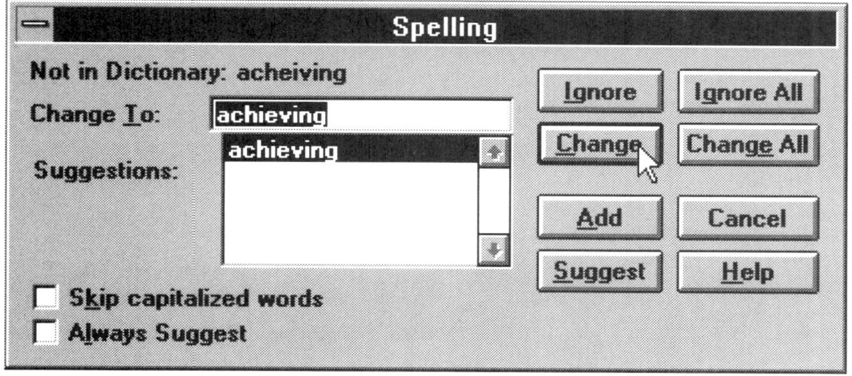

Figure 5-3. This dialog box appears when Works for Windows finds the first incorrectly spelled word — "acheiving." Click on Suggest for the list of suggestions to appear.

The next word it finds is "coloor." Do the same to this word by repeating what you did for "achieving."

Works now moves through the document and finds "Palatino" which is the name of a font. It is appropriate to add it to the dictionary so choose *Add*.

The next word the spell checker cannot find in the dictionary is "reding" and, unfortunately, when you ask for suggestions the correct word does not appear in the list box. To correct this spelling error, you must change the word manually in the *Change To* text box and then click on *Change*, as in Figure 5-4.

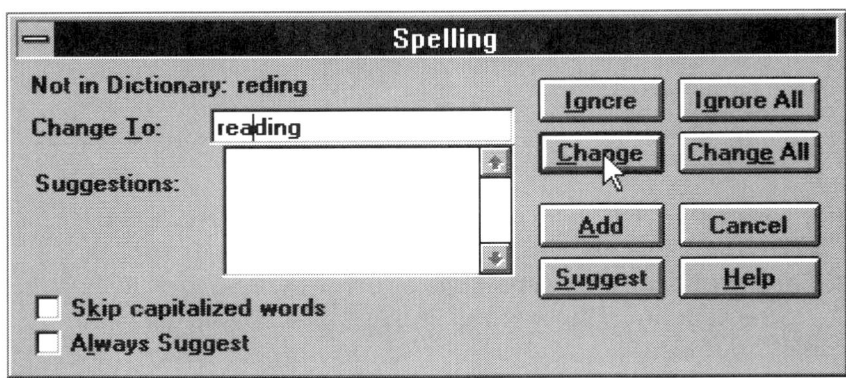

Figure 5-4. *Change "reding" to "reading" in the Change To text box, then click on Change.*

The final alteration to be made is to remove the duplicate "the." To remove it, click on *Change*.

When the spell check is complete, Works displays the dialog box in Figure 5-5. Click on *OK* to return to the document.

Figure 5-5. *The dialog box informs you that there are no more errors in your document, according to the Works dictionary.*

The thesaurus

The thesaurus in Works contains synonyms for 190,000 words. Using the thesaurus is an excellent way of adding variety to text to make it more interesting. To start the thesaurus you can choose *Thesaurus* from the **Tools** menu (Figure 5-6).

For Works to search through the thesaurus for synonyms of a word, you must highlight the word first. Highlight the word "certain" in the last line, as an example, and choose *Thesaurus* from the **Tools** menu. Works will open the dialog box of Figure 5-6.

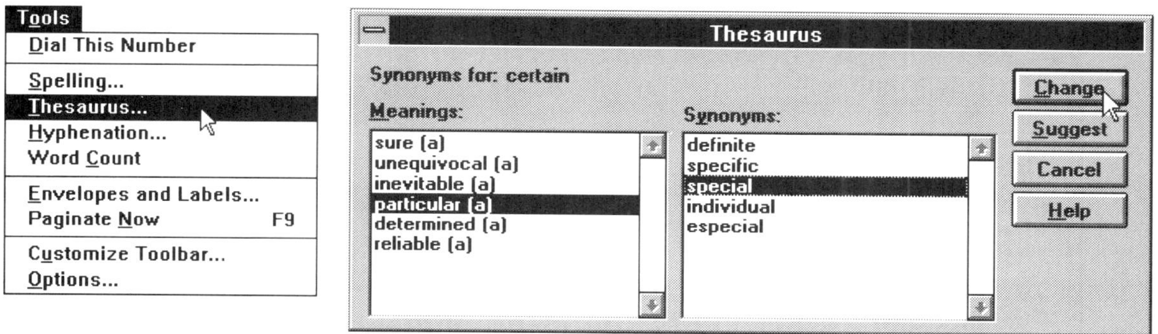

Figure 5-6. *Choose Thesaurus from the* ***Tools*** *menu.*

Works suggests possible meanings of the word that you want for a synonym in the *Meanings* list box; it has found a total of six for the word "certain." The most suitable word for the context of this document is "particular," so click on this to see the synonyms. Figure 5-6 shows the list and, for this exercise, choose "special" from the *Synonyms* text box. To insert the new word into the document, click on *Change*.

The *Suggest* button lets you extend the search for synonyms. This facility is used when the list shown is not adequate. To see the extended list, click on one of the synonyms and then on *Suggest*.

Word count

Often you need to know the exact number of words in a document. Works counts the number of words using the *Word Count* command in the **Options** menu (Figure 5-7).

Works can count the number of words in either a selection of text or the entire document. Using the file created in this chapter, select *Word Count* from the **Options** menu. Make certain that no word is highlighted. All of the words, including footnotes, headers, and footers, are counted. A dialog box, similar to the one in Figure 5-7 will tell you how many words are in the document.

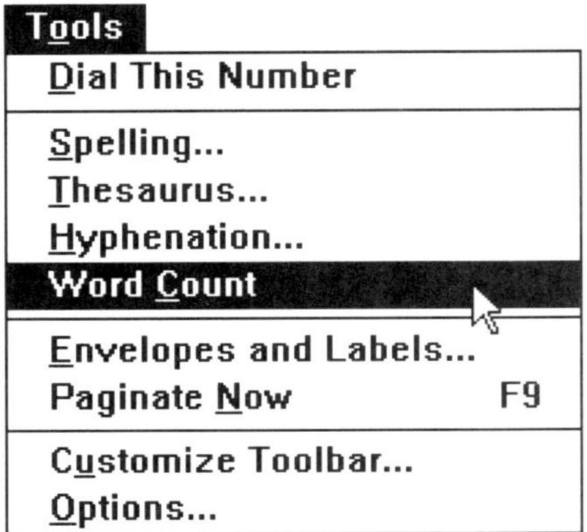

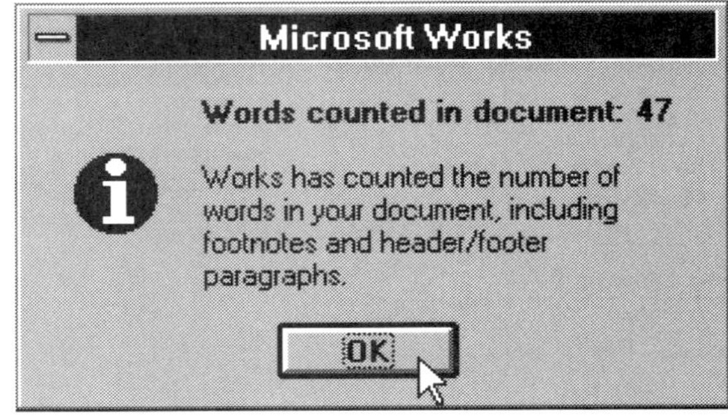

Figure 5-7. *Choose the Word Count command in the* ***Tools*** *menu to find out the number of words in your document.*

The Drawing Program (MS Draw)

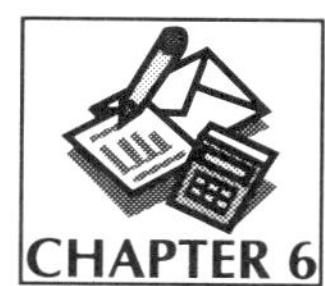

MS Draw is a standard part of Works and is added during the installation process. It can be used to create pictures, diagrams, or logos—depending on what you need—you are only limited by your imagination.

Starting MS Draw

You load MS Draw through the word processing part of Works. To start MS Draw, choose *Drawing* from the **Insert** menu as shown in Figure 6-1.

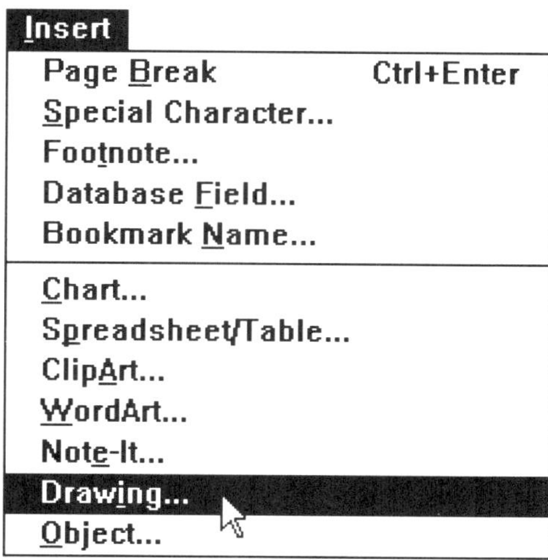

Figure 6-1. *Start MS Draw from the* ***Insert*** *menu.*

The drawing screen

When MS Draw is first loaded, the drawing screen appears and contains the features highlighted in Figure 6-2.

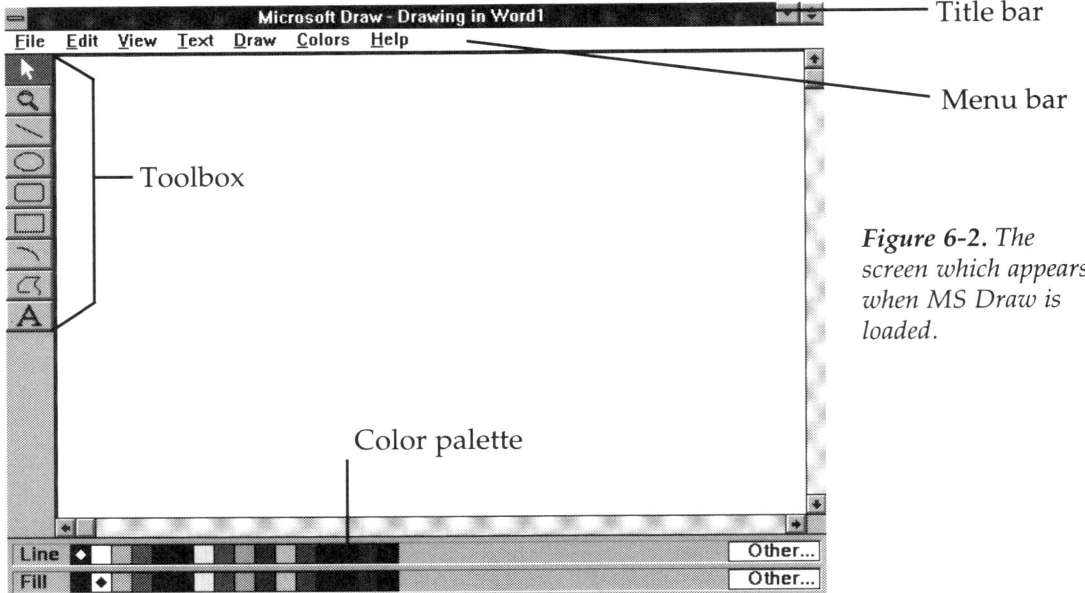

Figure 6-2. The screen which appears when MS Draw is loaded.

THE MENU

You can use the menus and commands in the same way as in the word processor. The menu structure, however, is different, containing **File, Edit, View, Text, Draw, Colors,** and **Help** menus. We discuss these in this chapter.

THE TOOLBOX

The toolbox on the left-hand side of the screen contains the nine tools you can use in MS Draw for different effects. You can select a tool by clicking on the tool you want in the toolbox. When the pointer returns to the drawing area, it represents the tool selected by a specific icon. The pointer in Figure 6-3 is for the tool which draws straight lines.

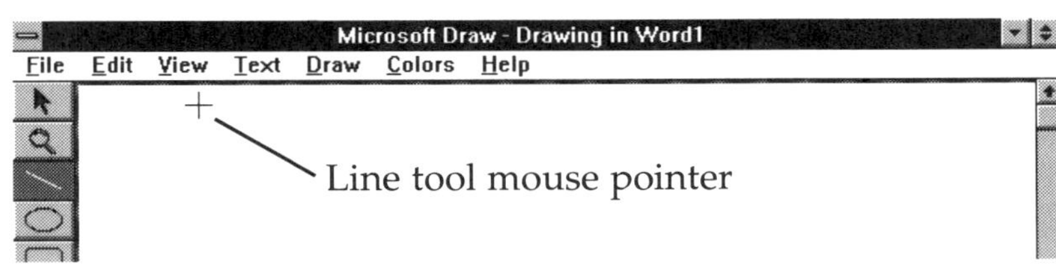

Figure 6-3. The pointer on the drawing screen represents the Line tool.

We explain the nine drawing tools shown in Figure 6-4, below.

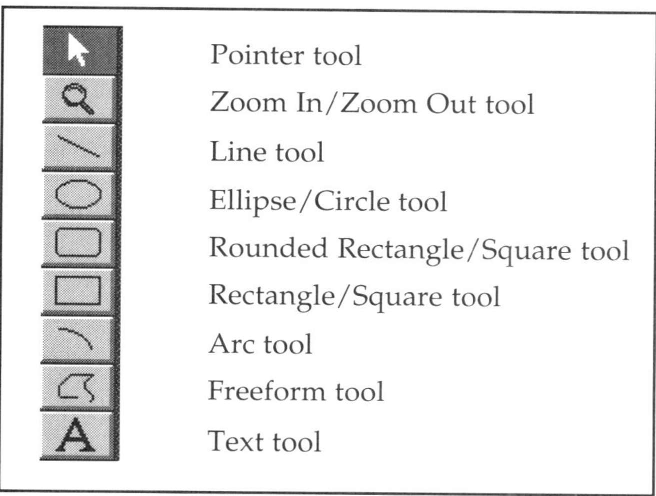

Figure 6-4. *The nine tools available in Draw.*

You use the *Pointer* to select objects. Once selected, the object can be moved, the color changed, or it can be deleted.

When you choose the *Zoom In/Zoom Out* tool you can change the size of the graphic on screen from 25 percent to 800 percent. Clicking the left mouse button zooms in and holding down the Shift key and clicking the left mouse button zooms out. The position of the magnifying glass is important as this will be what is in the center of the screen when "zoomed." An alternative to using this tool is to use the **View** menu as shown in Figure 6-5.

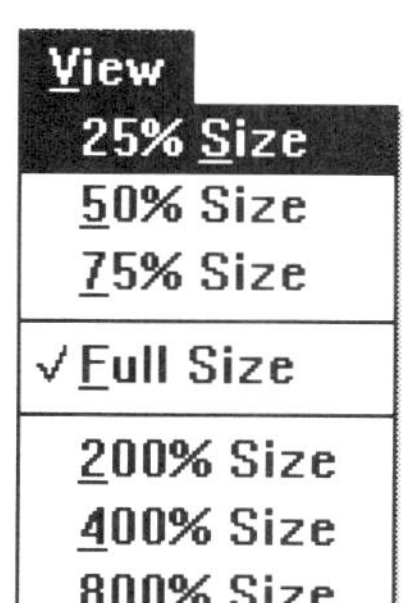

Figure 6-5. *The **View** menu lets you see your drawing at various sizes.*

You select shapes by clicking on the appropriate tool in the toolbox. The tools are outlined in Figure 6-4 and described in more detail below.

To draw a line, select the *Line* tool, then click and drag until you have a line the length you want. Lines are restricted to angles of 45 degrees, if you hold down the Shift key while you draw the line.

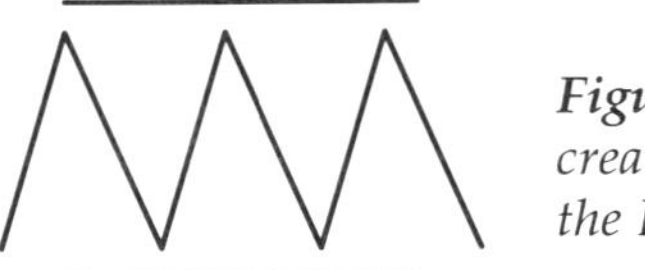

Figure 6-6. *You create lines with the Line tool.*

To draw an ellipse, select the *Ellipse/Circle* tool and click and drag over the drawing screen. If you hold down the Shift key when doing this, you get a circle (see Figure 6-7). If you want to draw the ellipse from the center rather than the edge, hold down the Ctrl key.

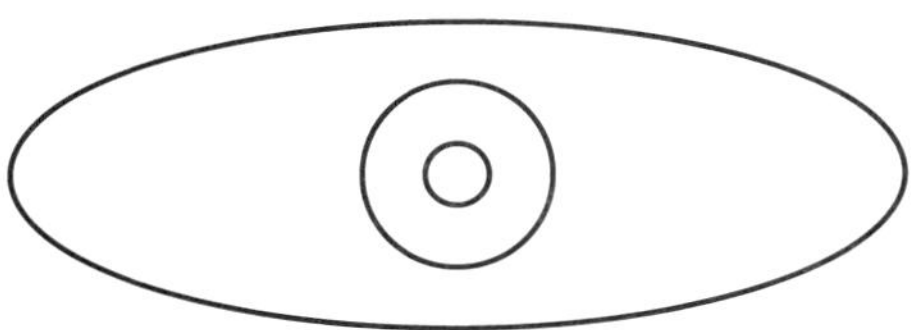

Figure 6-7. *You draw ellipses and circles using the Ellipse/Circle tool.*

The *Rounded Rectangle/Square* tool lets you draw a rectangle with rounded corners. Click and drag the pointer across the screen to do this. The tool draws a square with rounded corners when you hold down the Shift key (see Figure 6-8). If you want to draw from the center, hold down the Ctrl key.

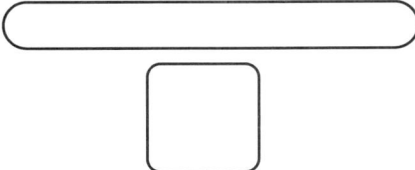

Figure 6-8. *You draw rectangles and squares with rounded corners with the Rounded Rectangle/Square tool.*

The *Rectangle/Square* tool lets you draw rectangles and squares, except the corners are not round. Holding down the Shift key as you draw constrains the object to a square. Holding down the Ctrl key when using this tool draws the shape from the center of the object (see Figure 6-9).

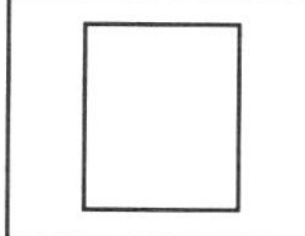

Figure 6-9. *If you need to draw a rectangle or a square, use the Rectangle/Square tool.*

The *Arc* tool draws filled and unfilled arcs. An unfilled arc appears very differently to a filled arc as can be seen in Figure 6-10.

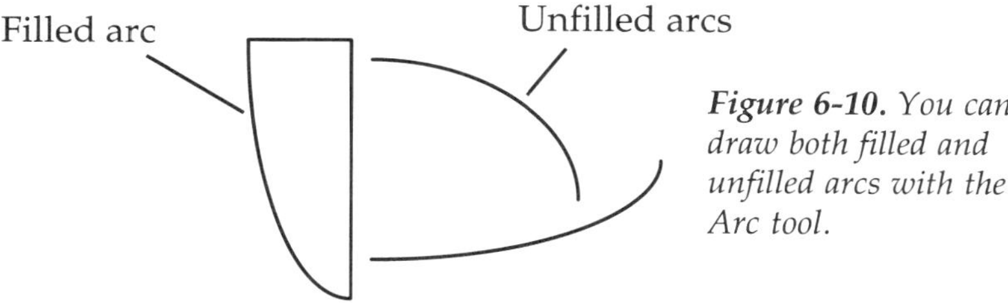

Figure 6-10. *You can draw both filled and unfilled arcs with the Arc tool.*

To draw interesting shapes of your own, use the *Freeform* tool. Figure 6-11 shows some of the shapes you can produce with this tool. Clicking the mouse adds a straight section and dragging it gives a freehand line. Works always tries to create a filled shape when you use this tool. To leave ends open, as in Figure 6-11, click outside the drawing screen to complete the drawing.

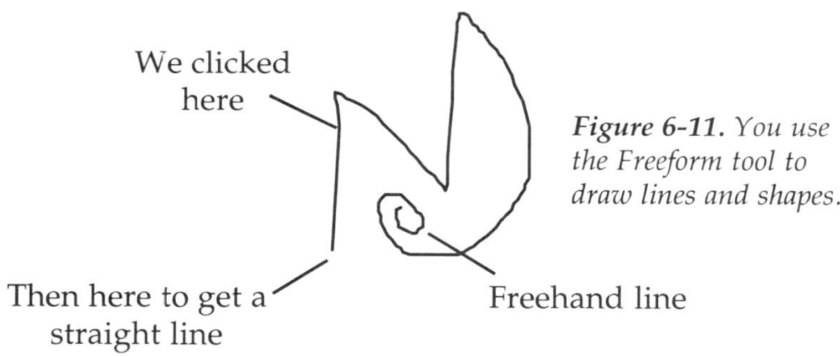

Figure 6-11. *You use the Freeform tool to draw lines and shapes.*

The last tool in the toolbox is the *Text* tool which lets you input text into your creation as in Figure 6-12.

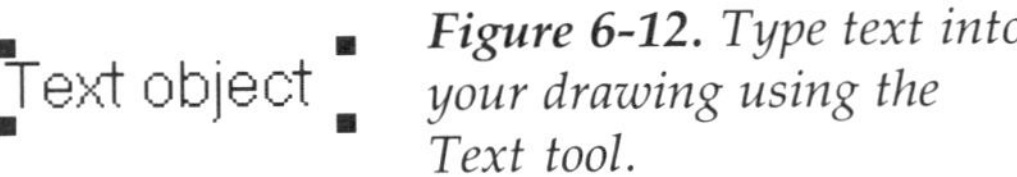

Figure 6-12. *Type text into your drawing using the Text tool.*

Test these tools by using each of them to draw a picture.

The color palette

The color palette is displayed in Figure 6-2. There are two parts to the color palette: *Line* and *Fill*. Line affects such things as the color of lines, borders and text, and Fill affects the color inside an object or shape.

Black is the default line color in MS Draw and white is the default fill color. These colors are indicated by a diamond on the color palette. When you select a different color for a specific object, the color will be marked by a check mark.

You can turn the color palette on and off through the *Show Palette* option in the **Colors** menu (see Figure 6-13). A check mark next to this command indicates that the color palette is turned on.

Figure 6-13. *To turn the color palette off, select the Show Palette command in the* ***Colors*** *menu. Select again to turn the palette on.*

Working with MS Draw

A wide variety of shapes can be drawn on screen by selecting one of the many tools from the toolbox. A circle has been drawn in Figure 6-14.

Selecting objects

You select a shape by clicking on it with the pointer tool. A selected shape is highlighted in MS Draw when it has square handles at the corners. The circle in Figure 6-14 is selected. Once you have selected an object, you can change it.

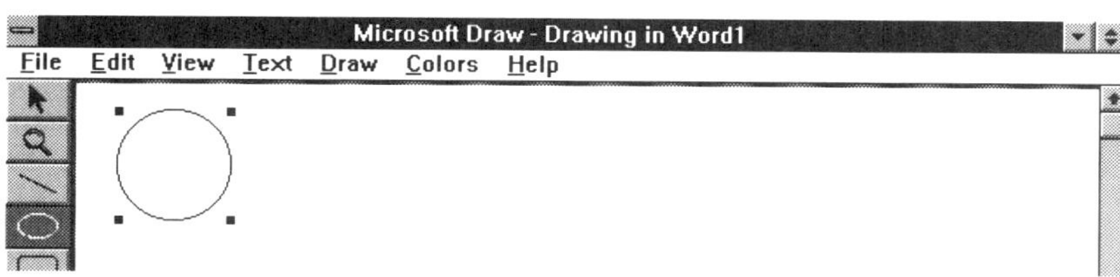

Figure 6-14. *The handles confirm that the circle is selected.*

Selecting colors

You can add color to a selected object by choosing from the range of colors in the palette. As an example, draw a circle on your screen by choosing the *Ellipse/Circle* tool and clicking and dragging across the drawing area. The object you drew most recently remains selected until you click the pointer again (Figure 6-15).

Change the line color to red. The color palette will show that you have selected red by adding a check mark to the red box. The circle remains selected, which allows you to further change that object.

Choose blue as the fill color. Draw adds a check mark on the blue box in the color palette (Figure 6-15).

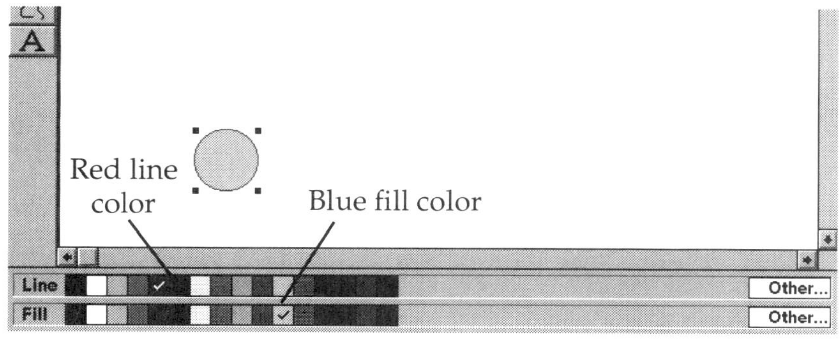

Figure 6-15. *The selected circle has a red border— "Line" and a blue interior—"Fill."*

SELECTING FILL PATTERNS

As well as changing the fill color, you can also alter the style of fill. As shown in Figure 6-16, there are seven patterns you can choose from the *Pattern* submenu in the **Draw** menu. Use this to change the fill to a different pattern of your choice.

The default fill pattern paper is a plain style which will give the object a solid interior. Occasionally, you don't need a fill (making the object transparent), and you do this by deselecting *Filled* in the **Draw** menu.

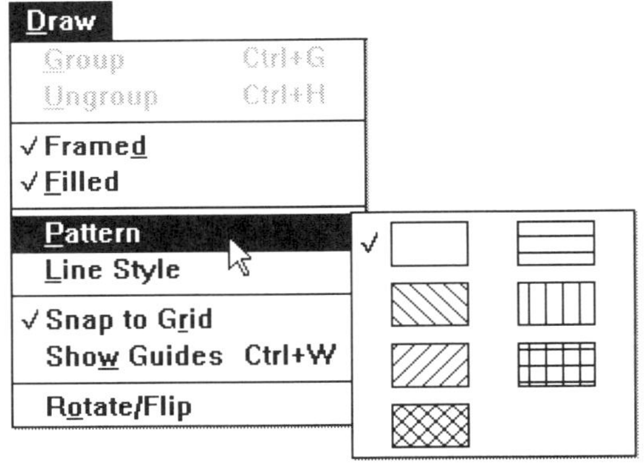

Figure 6-16. *The fill patterns available in MS Draw.*

SELECTING OUTLINE STYLES

You change the style of line in much the same way as the fill pattern. Selecting *Line Style* from the **Draw** menu, as in Figure 6-17, opens a range of styles such as dotted or dashed, and line widths. You can set widths to anything you need through the *Other* command. Experiment with the line styles by changing the border of the rectangle.

Turn lines off by deselecting the *Framed* option in the **Draw** menu. Any new object you draw will have the default line style of 1 point.

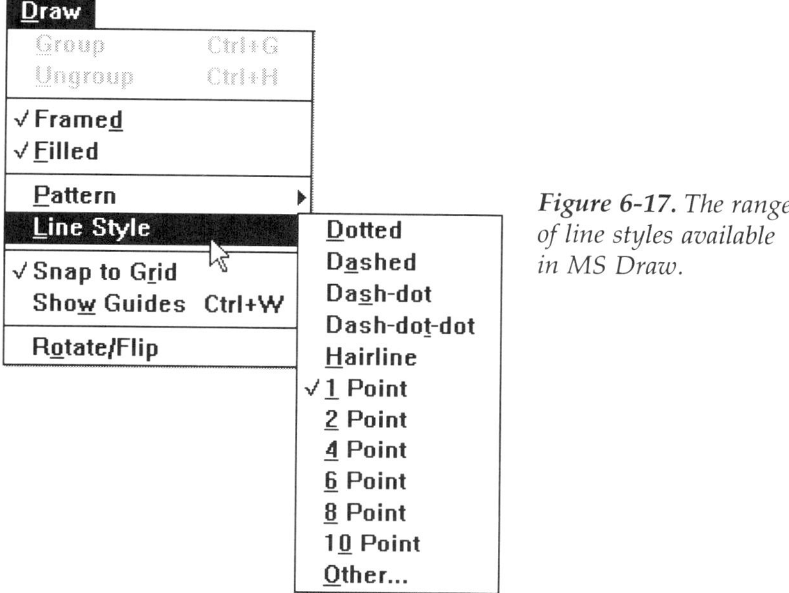

Figure 6-17. The range of line styles available in MS Draw.

Including text in a drawing

You can add text into a drawing with the text tool. For this example, select the text tool, click anywhere on the screen and type in "Look'n'Good Design Co." and press Enter.

Your text is now a complete object which has handles and can be moved around the drawing screen. You can't change individual characters, but you can format the text through the **Text** menu (Figure 6-18).

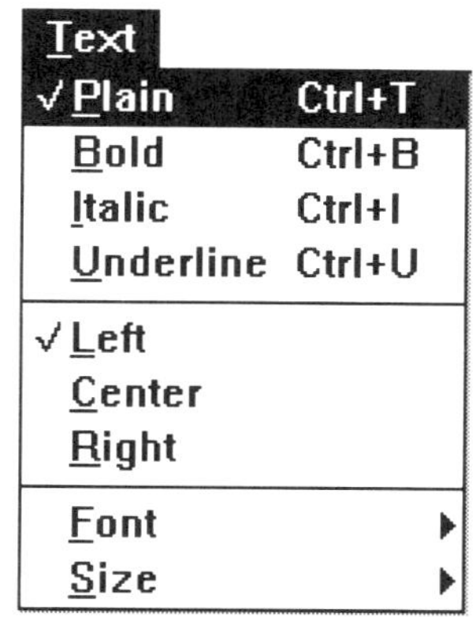

*Figure 6-18. The **Text** menu in MS Draw.*

SELECTING THE TEXT FONT

You change fonts through the *Font* command in the **Text** menu. The number of fonts available depends on how many you have installed. If the text is not selected, click on it with the pointer tool. Move up to the **Font** menu and choose a different font. We have selected *AvantGarde* in Figure 6-19.

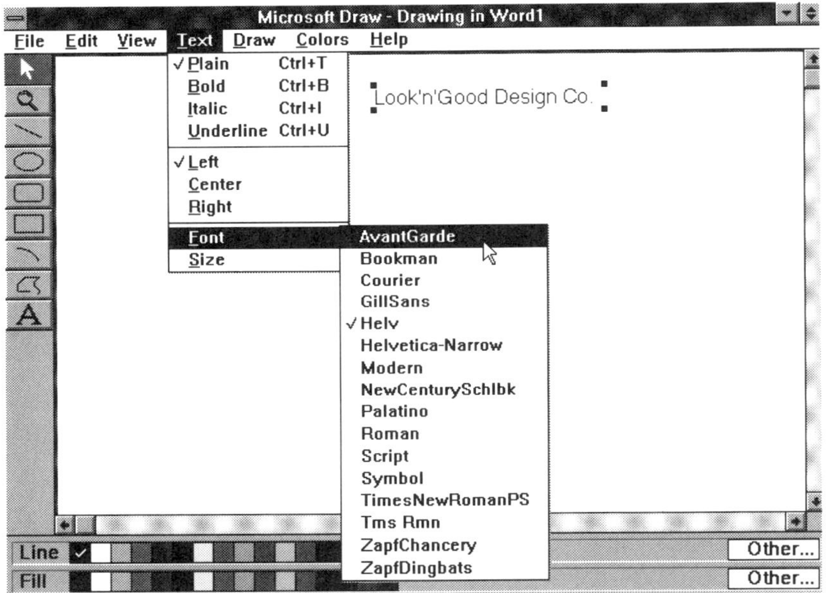

Figure 6-19. Select the font AvantGarde after you have selected the text object.

SELECTING THE TEXT SIZE

A list of text sizes appears when you select the *Size* command from the **Text** menu, as in Figure 6-20. Change the font size to 18 point by clicking on 18 in the submenu.

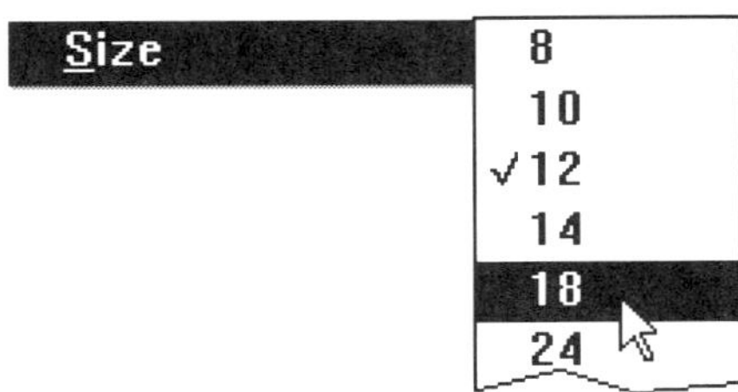

*Figure 6-20. The Size submenu in the **Text** menu.*

Selecting text style

The font styles available in MS Draw are *Plain, Bold, Italic,* and *Underline*. You change the style of font by selecting a text object and clicking the mouse on one of these styles in the **Text** menu.

Use this menu to change the font style to *Bold*.

Selecting text color

You change the color of text with the color palette. When text is selected, only the line colors are available. Black, being the default text color, has a diamond on it. To change the color to pink, for example, click on the pink box. A check mark will appear on the pink box whenever you select that text object.

Selecting text alignment

Left, Right, and *Center* are the alignments available in the drawing package. Alignment follows the same principle as in the word processor. To change alignment of "Look'n'Good Design Co." to center, choose *Center* from the **Text** menu.

The color palette

The color palette, shown in Figure 6-2, allows you to change the color of objects. The palette is set with 16 colors originally. You can add colors and save or delete whole palettes of colors you have chosen. You do all of this through the **Colors** menu (Figure 6-21).

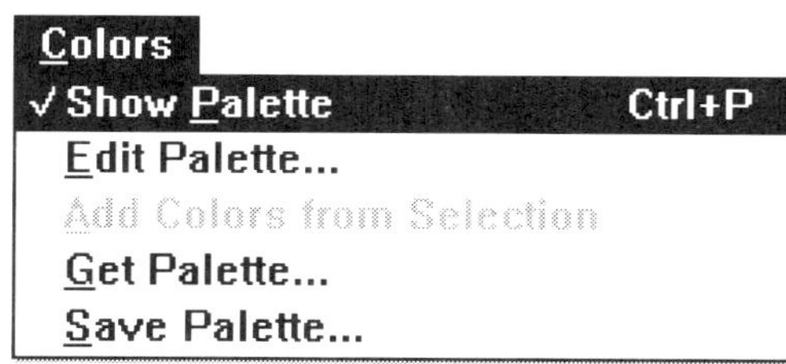

Figure 6-21. The **Colors** *menu.*

Adding colors

You add colors to the palette through the *Edit Palette* dialog box, which is illustrated in Figure 6-22.

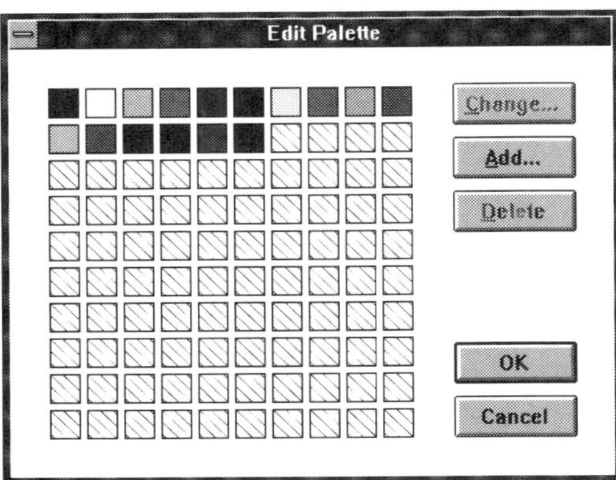

Figure 6-22. *The Edit Palette dialog box.*

To use this feature to add a new bright green color to the palette, select *Edit Palette* from the **Colors** menu to open the *Edit Palette* dialog box. Click on *Add* to open the *Add Color* dialog box (Figure 6-23). To change colors, drag the color refiner and luminosity cursors, which change the values in the appropriate text boxes. Alternatively, type in the values you want. In here, the left-hand side of the *Color Solid* box displays the color being created and the right displays the closest solid color.

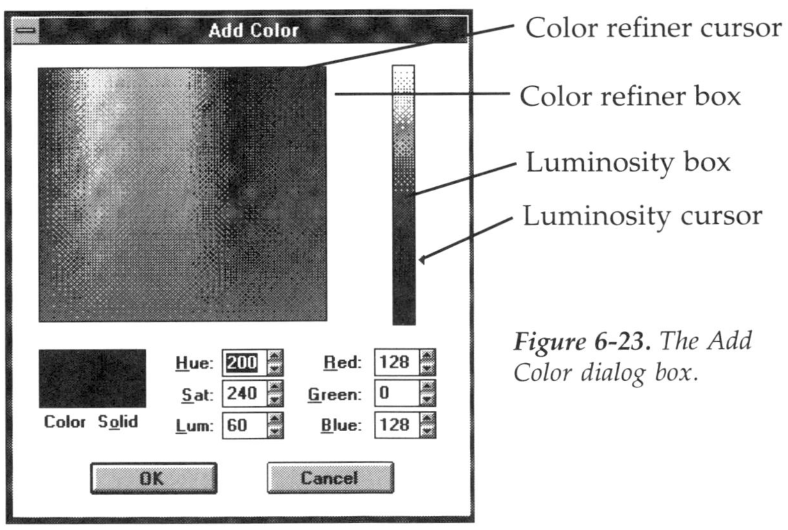

Figure 6-23. *The Add Color dialog box.*

Drag the color refiner cursor to the green area of the color refiner box. The brightness of a color is set in the luminosity box. Move this up to make the green lighter. To add the new color to the palette, click on *OK* in the *Add Color* dialog box and *OK* in the *Edit Palette* dialog box.

Deleting colors

To delete a color, first open the *Edit Palette* dialog box through the **Colors** menu. You can select any color on the current palette at this point. To select the bright green we just "mixed," click on it with the mouse. A dark border shows it as being selected, as in Figure 6-24.

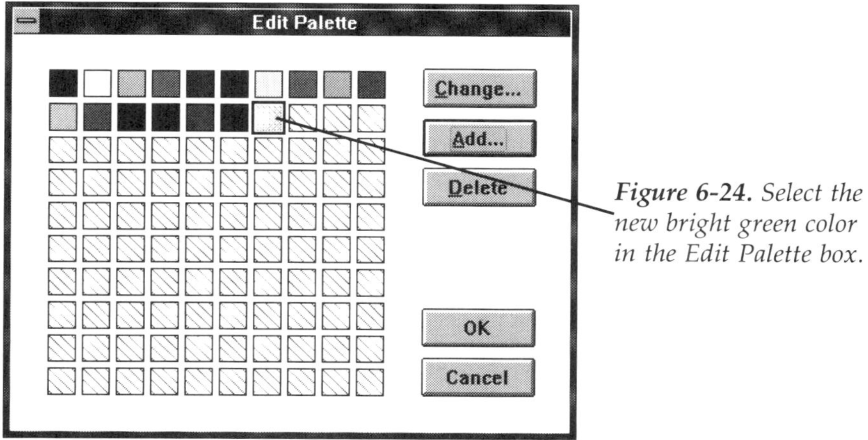

Figure 6-24. *Select the new bright green color in the Edit Palette box.*

The next step is to click on *Delete* and then *OK*. Back at the drawing screen, the color isn't on the color palette.

Saving palettes

You can save a palette of colors that you use regularly for a particular purpose, such as a logo.

To save a palette, choose *Save Palette* from the **Colors** menu. This command brings up the *Save Palette* dialog box which appears in Figure 6-25. The insertion point flashes in the *Save Palette As* text box, waiting for you to type in the new palette name. Type in "Rainbow"—Works adds the extension ***.pal*** automatically—and click on *OK*. Works will save the palette in the ***msdraw*** subdirectory.

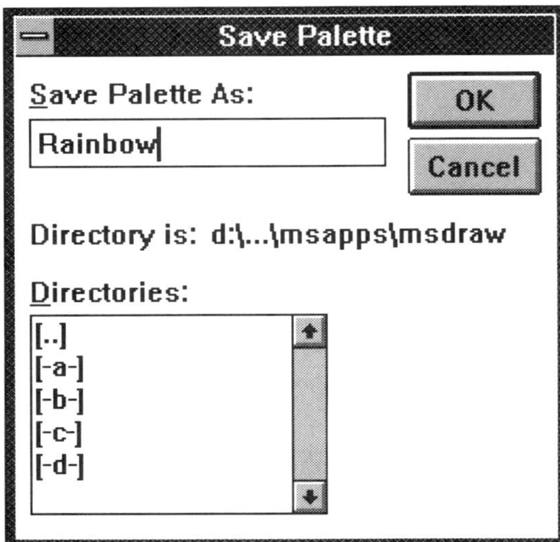

Figure 6-25. The Save Palette dialog box with the new name—Rainbow—in the Save Palette As text box.

Retrieving palettes

You can open a palette you have saved through the *Get Palette* command in the **Colors** menu. To choose another palette, click on ***47colors.pal***, for example, as shown in Figure 6-26. The new palette will then be displayed on screen in place of the 16-color default palette.

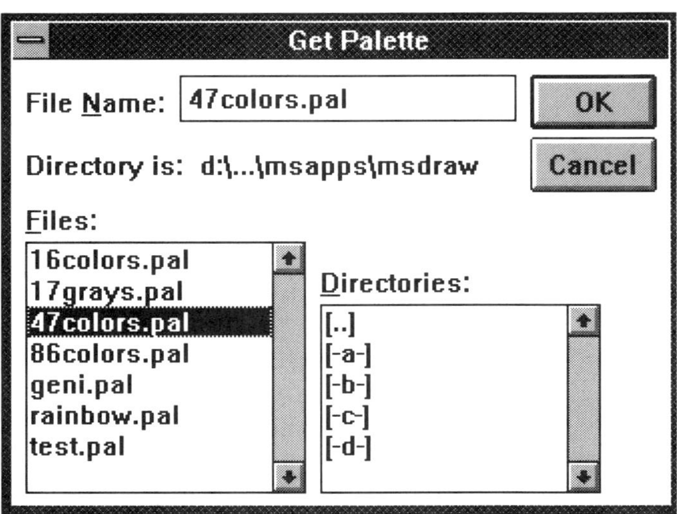

*Figure 6-26. Click on **47colors.pal** in the Get Palette dialog box.*

Editing drawn objects

You must select an object before you can edit it. You select an object by clicking on it with the pointer tool.

MOVING AN OBJECT

You move an object to another position on the drawing area by dragging. For example, create a rectangle and move the text object—"Look'n'Good Design Co." that you created earlier in this chapter—inside the rectangle. Click on the text object and, while it is selected, drag it inside the rectangle.

MS Draw leaves the object in its original position while you press the mouse button. The new location is shown by a broken dotted line, the exact dimensions of the object. Figure 6-27 shows this feature. When you release the mouse button, the object appears at the new position.

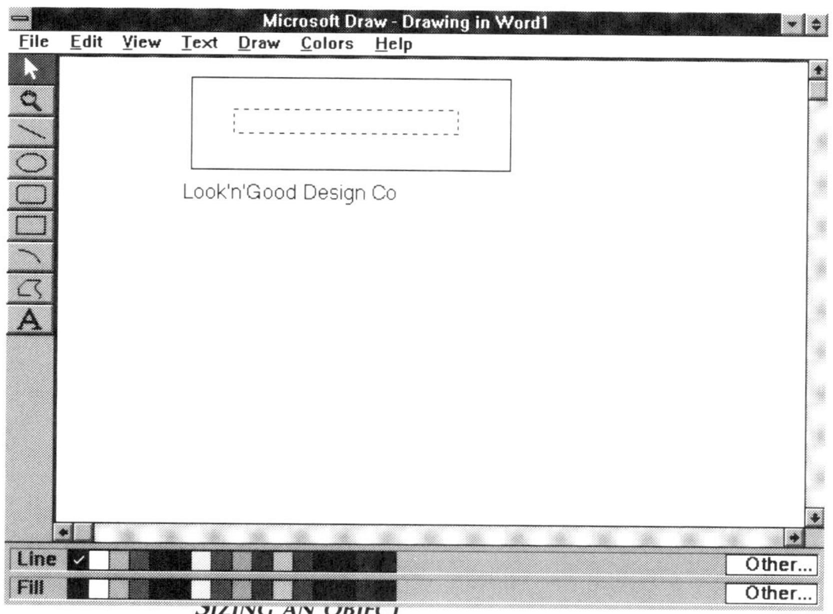

Figure 6-27. The broken dotted line represents the object being moved.

SIZING AN OBJECT

You can resize an object already on the screen to individual specifications with the handles. Click on the handles of the rectangle to adjust the size to fit more comfortably around the text. In this way, you can change the size of any object you draw in MS Draw—except for text.

LAYERING OBJECTS

Works layers objects on the page in the order you draw them. For instance, if you drew a square and you add a circle on top of it, the circle would be on top of the drawing.

You adjust the layers in a drawing for special effects in graphics. To change the layer of an object, you need to use the *Bring to Front* and *Send to Back* commands in the **Edit** menu. Figure 6-28 shows these commands.

To test these commands, select the text object on your screen, then the *Send to Back* command in the **Edit** menu. The text is no longer

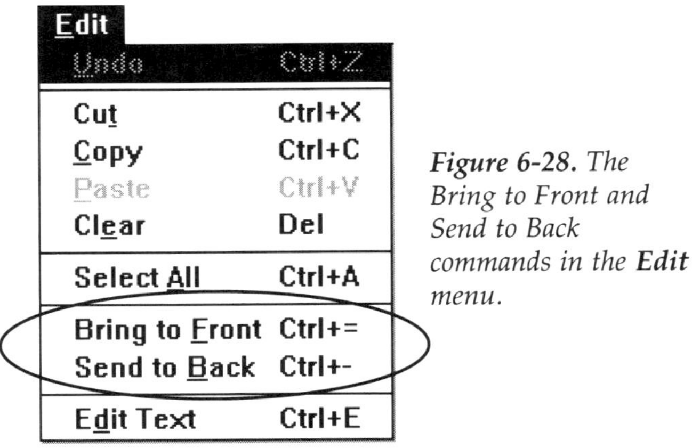

***Figure 6-28.** The Bring to Front and Send to Back commands in the **Edit** menu.*

visible because it is hidden by the rectangle. The text will appear on the screen again when you select the rectangle and send that to the back in the same way.

Grouping objects

You can group a number of objects used to make up one picture into one object, such as the text and the rectangle in Figure 6-29. Try this for the picture you are creating.

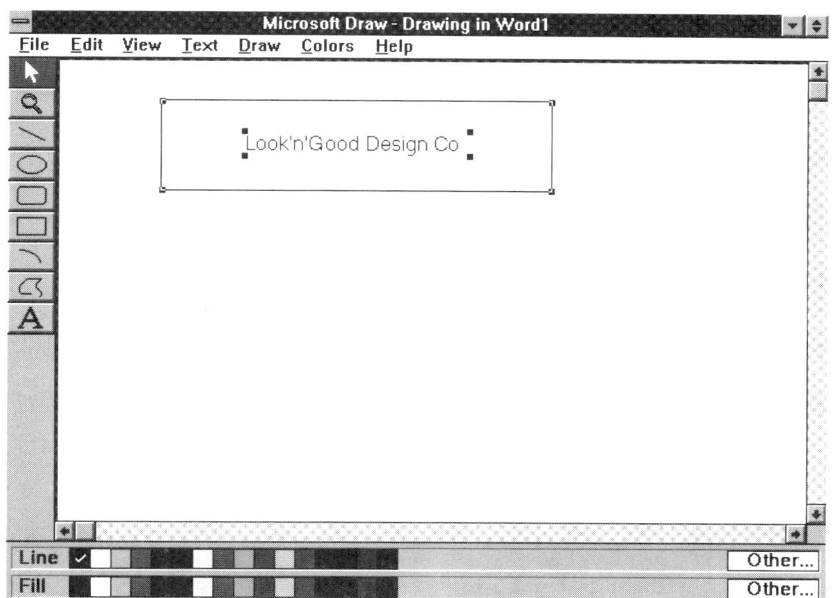

Figure 6-29. The two objects which make up this picture can be grouped to make one object.

The objects to be grouped need to be selected at the same time. (If you hold down the Shift key you can select multiple objects.) Once you have selected all the objects you want, choose *Group* from the **Draw** menu (Figure 6-30). The two objects now share one set of handles.

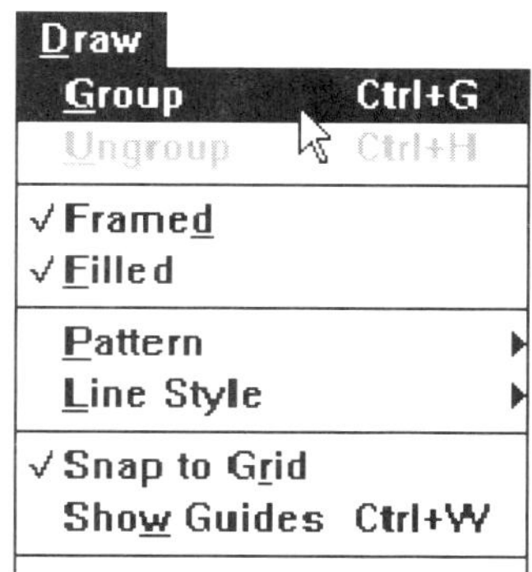

*Figure 6-30. To combine different objects, choose Group from the **Draw** menu.*

Reversing the group is done by selecting *Ungroup* from the **Draw** menu. Try this now.

Importing graphics

In MS Draw you are provided with a number of graphics files. These are stored under the ***clipart*** subdirectory (in the ***msworks*** directory) and have an extension of *.wmf*.

You import clip art with the *Import Picture* command in the **File** menu. The *Import Picture* dialog box will show, by default, the ***clipart*** subdirectory and the graphics files available.

Bring the file you want by clicking on the name of the file—***present.wmf*** for example—and then on *OK*. The graphic appears on the screen and you can move or resize it to what you need. Adjust the objects to look like Figure 6-31.

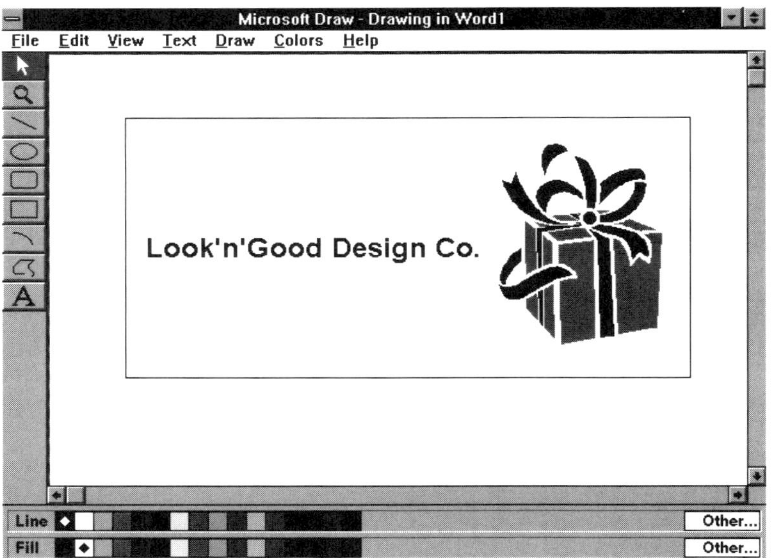

Figure 6-31. *Import* ***present.wmf*** *into your drawing.*

Using the word processor

The drawing is now complete and you are ready to place it into the word processor document. The *Exit and Return to Word1* command in the **File** menu lets you do this (Figure 6-32).

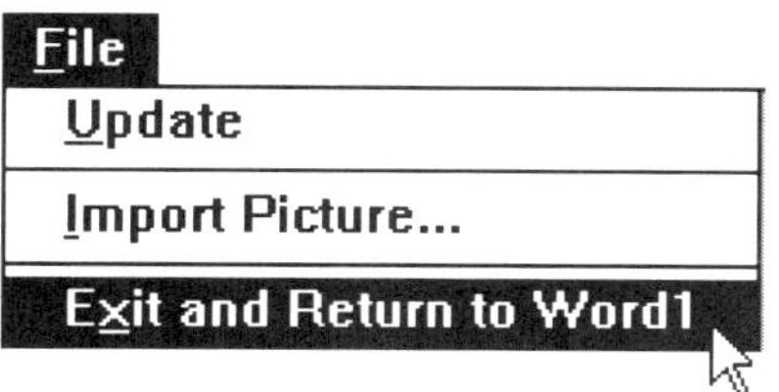

Figure 6-32. Exit and Return to Word1 command in the **File** menu.

After you choose this command, Works asks you whether you want to update ***Word1*** (or the name of the file) in the dialog box shown in Figure 6-33. Click on *Yes* to place the drawing into the word processing document.

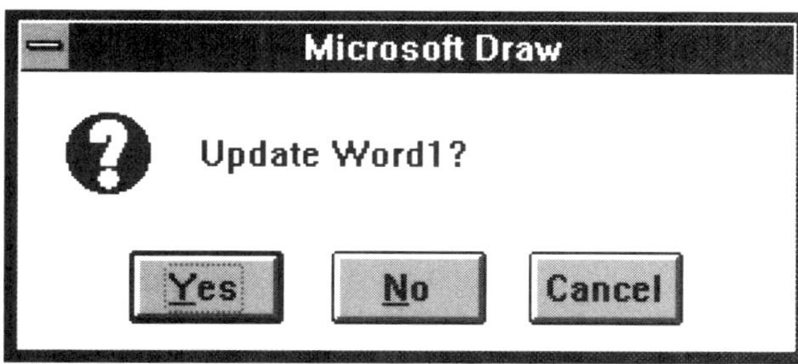

Figure 6-33. To place the drawing into the document, click on Yes.

The graphic is placed into the word processor as a piece of text. You can cut, copy, and paste it as well as align and delete it.

Implementing change

It is not unusual to need to change a graphic that you have placed into a document. To do this, you need to open MS Draw again with the desired graphic loaded. You do this with the *Microsoft Drawing Object* command in the **Edit** menu of the word processor, which is shown in Figure 6-34. This command, however, is only available when a graphic from MS Draw is highlighted in the word processor.

Choosing this command activates a submenu. Choose *Edit* from the submenu as shown. This opens the drawing program again, where you can edit the drawing using the techniques outlined in this chapter.

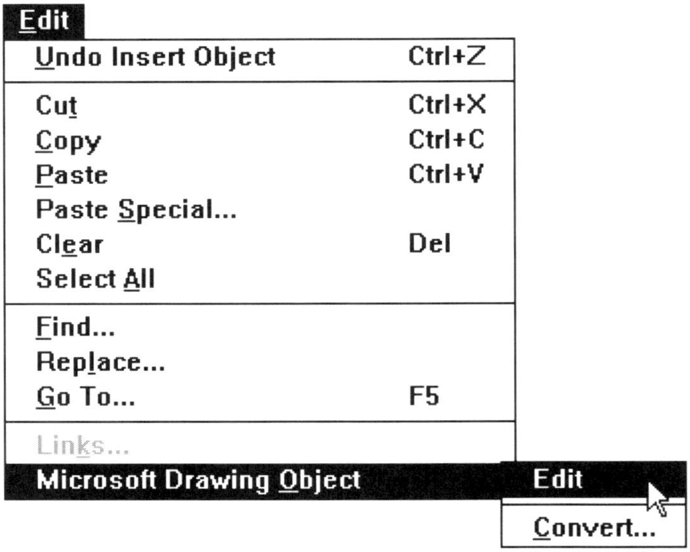

Edit
Undo Insert Object Ctrl+Z
Cut Ctrl+X
Copy Ctrl+C
Paste Ctrl+V
Paste Special...
Clear Del
Select All
Find...
Replace...
Go To... F5
Links...
Microsoft Drawing Object
Edit
Convert...

Figure 6-34. *The Microsoft Drawing Object command in the* ***Edit*** *menu of the word processor.*

Printing Word Processed Documents

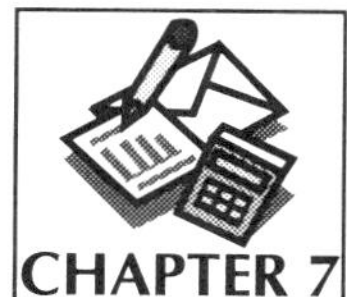

Printing in Works is quite simple. There are, however, many options available to assist you in using the printer most efficiently. We discuss these in this chapter using the sample file ***auntmadg.wps*** (located in the ***msworks.cbt*** subdirectory). Please load this file now.

Selecting a printer

Before you can print to your printer for the first time, you must tell Works which printer you are using. You select printers with the *Printer Setup* command in the **File** menu. In most cases, the printer is set up when you install Works on your system. Figure 7-1 shows this command and the associated dialog box.

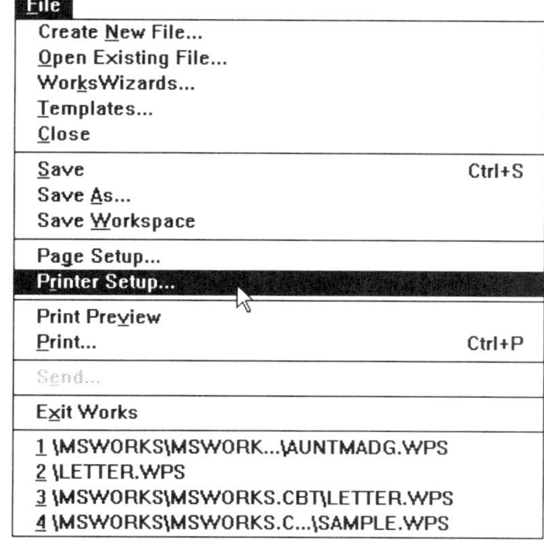

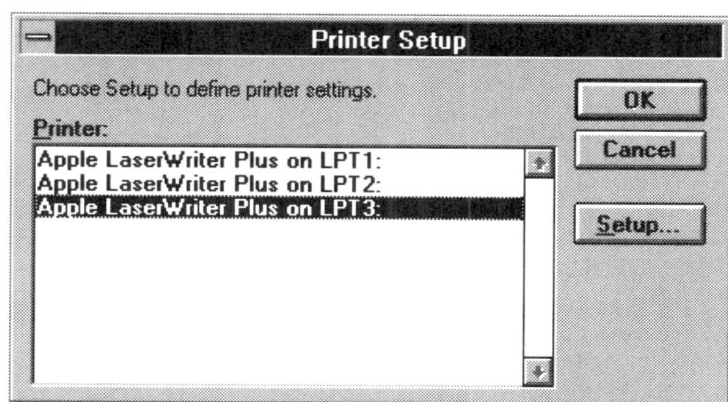

Figure 7-1. *The Printer Setup command in the* ***File*** *menu opens the Printer Setup dialog box.*

Print Preview

A time-efficient and environmentally friendly method of printing is to use the *Print Preview* option before sending the document to the printer. *Print Preview* shows the general page layout—including page breaks, headers and footers—on the screen.

Activate *Print Preview* by selecting *Print Preview* from the **File** menu or by clicking on the *Print Preview* button on the toolbar (Figure 7-2).

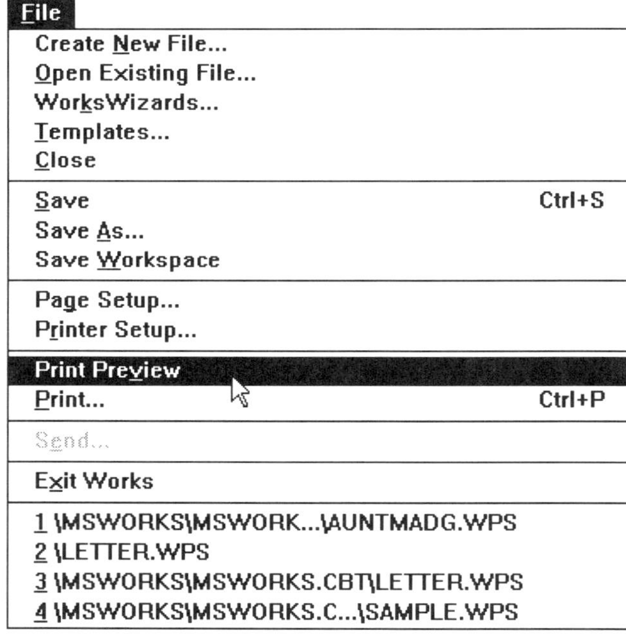

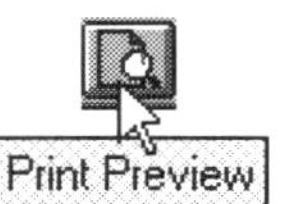

***Figure 7-2.** The Print Preview command in the **File** menu and the Print Preview button on the toolbar both activate the Print Preview facility.*

Viewing different pages

Regardless of where the insertion point is at the time you start *Print Preview*, Works always shows the first page of the document. The *Previous* and *Next* buttons move you through the document as in Figure 7-3.

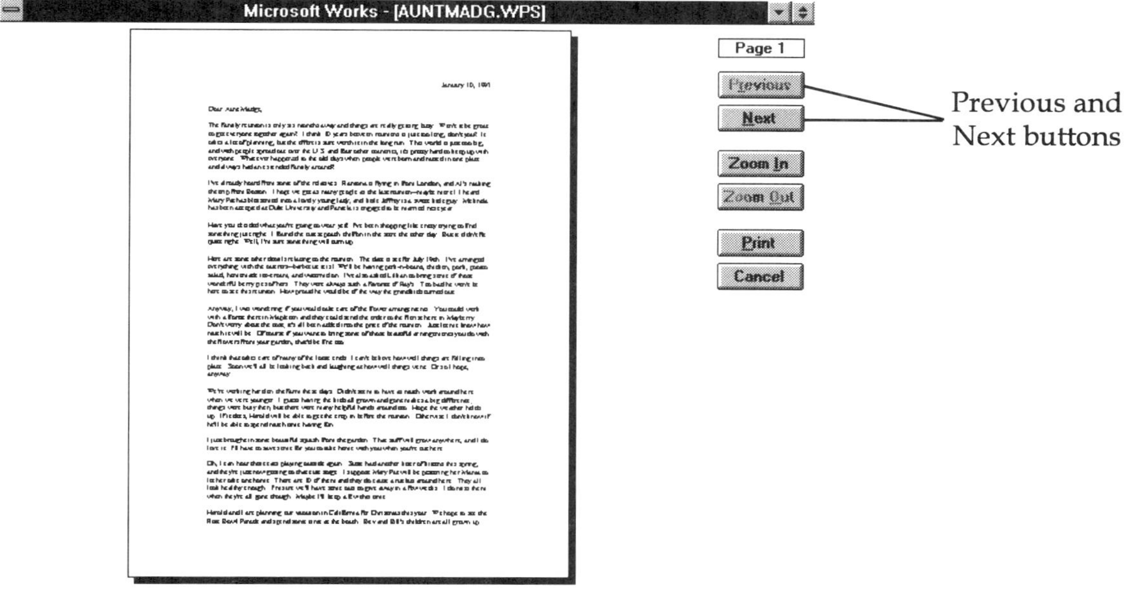

Figure 7-3. *The Print Preview screen. Use the Previous and Next buttons to display different pages of* ***auntmadg.wps****.*

The *Next* button shows the next page of the document and *Previous* shows the page before. If a document is currently showing the final page, the *Next* button will be grayed out. Likewise, when you are viewing the first page, *Previous* is grayed out. Use these buttons to view the two pages of ***auntmadg.wps***.

Zooming in and out

There are three views of the page which you can select in *Print Preview*. *Standard view* shows the entire page on the screen at once. *Half-zoom view* (click the *Zoom In* button) displays the page half the size of the document window and *full-zoom view* (click *Zoom In* again) displays the page the same size as in the document window. Scroll bars appear automatically in half- and full-zoom views.

The *Zoom In* and *Zoom Out* buttons change views according to what view of the page you have. For instance, if full-zoom is active and you click *Zoom Out*, half-zoom displays (see Figure 7-4).

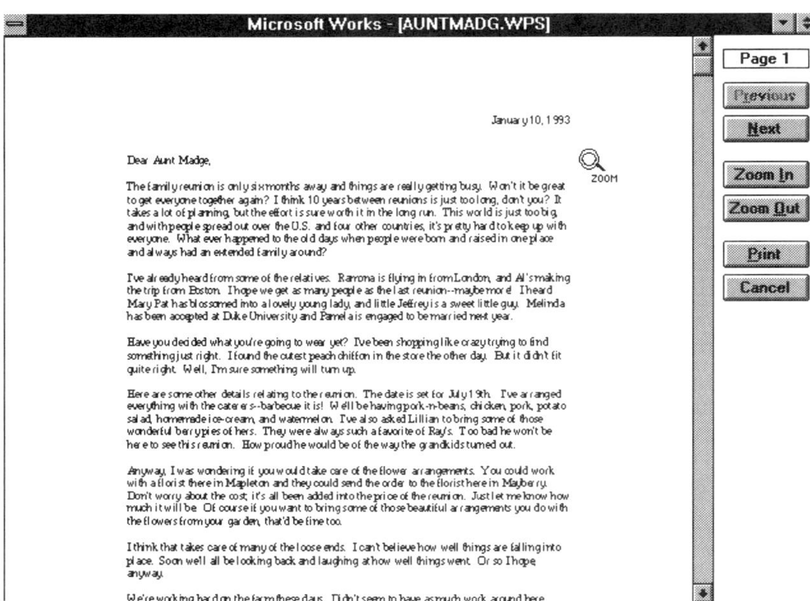

Figure 7-4. *Half-zoom view where a scroll bar appears automatically.*

When you move the mouse pointer onto the page it becomes a magnifying glass. Clicking the left mouse button also changes views, placing whatever is at the cursor position in the middle of the screen.

Use these methods to zoom in and out of the sample document.

Print Preview shortcuts

To ...	Mouse	Keyboard
Move to the next page	Click on Next	Page Down
Move to the previous page	Click on Previous	Page Up
Zoom In	Click on Zoom In or on the page	Alt-I
Zoom Out	Click on Zoom Out or on the page	Alt-O
Print	Click on Print	Alt-P
Return to document window	Click on Cancel	Esc

Printing the document

To print a document using default settings, click on the *Print* button on the *Print Preview* screen or the toolbar. To print your document using custom settings select *Print* from the **File** menu. In this case, the *Print* dialog box appears, which is displayed in Figure 7-5. Click on *OK* when you want to print using the settings you see in this dialog box.

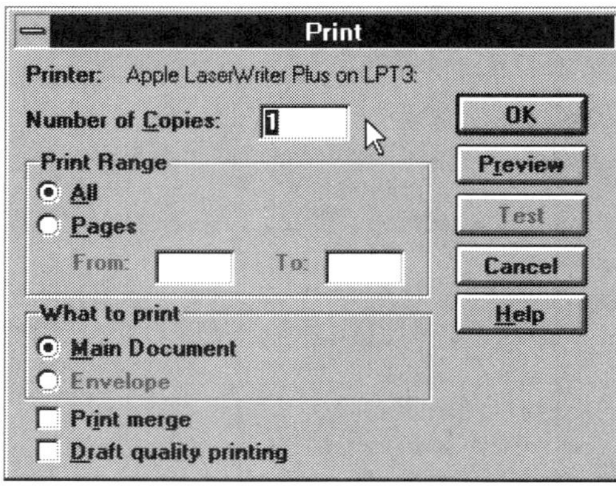

Figure 7-5. *The Print dialog box.*

The *Envelope* and *Print merge* options let you handle database information in your document. See **Chapter 25, Including Databases in a Word Processor Document** for information on this capability.

Number of copies

Works prints the number of copies in the *Number of Copies* text box. One copy of a document is printed by default. Change this by typing the number of copies you want in the *Number of Copies* text box. In Figure 7-6, we have changed the number of copies to be printed to 2.

Number of Copies: 2

Figure 7-6. *This tells Works to print 2 copies.*

Printing page ranges

If you don't change the *Print* dialog box, Works prints every page in the document. To specify a range of pages to be printed, select the *Pages* option. *To* and *From* let you specify the page or page range you want to print.

Use this option to print only page two. Click on the *Pages* option and type 2 into both the *From* and *To* text boxes. Figure 7-7 shows this.

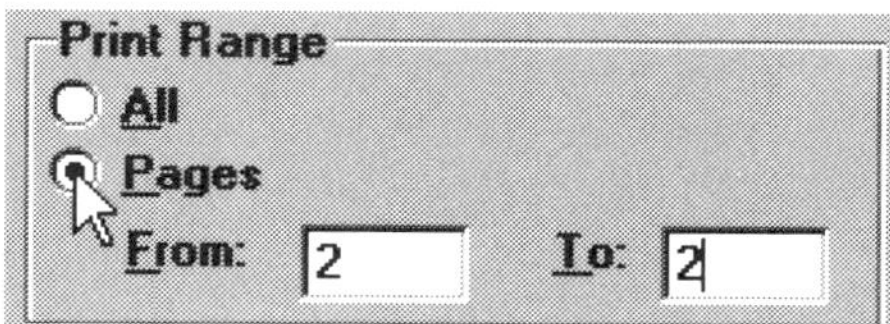

Figure 7-7. *Works will print only page 2 of the document.*

Draft printouts

Works prints in draft mode when you check *Draft quality printing* (Figure 7-8). Printing in draft mode is useful when you need a quick printout. You save time because different fonts, font styles, colors, and graphics are not printed.

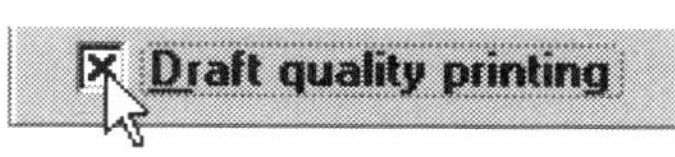

Figure 7-8. *Draft quality printing is checked in the Print dialog box.*

For practice, you may like to review the features covered in this chapter using a different file. Practise until you are fully satisfied with your progress.

The Spreadsheet Screen

In this chapter you are shown how to start up the spreadsheet tool in Works. The spreadsheet screen is similar to the word processing screen; however, there are some fundamental differences which are covered in this chapter.

Starting the spreadsheet

A new spreadsheet file is loaded into the computer's memory by clicking on *Spreadsheet* in the *Startup* dialog box (Figure 8-1).

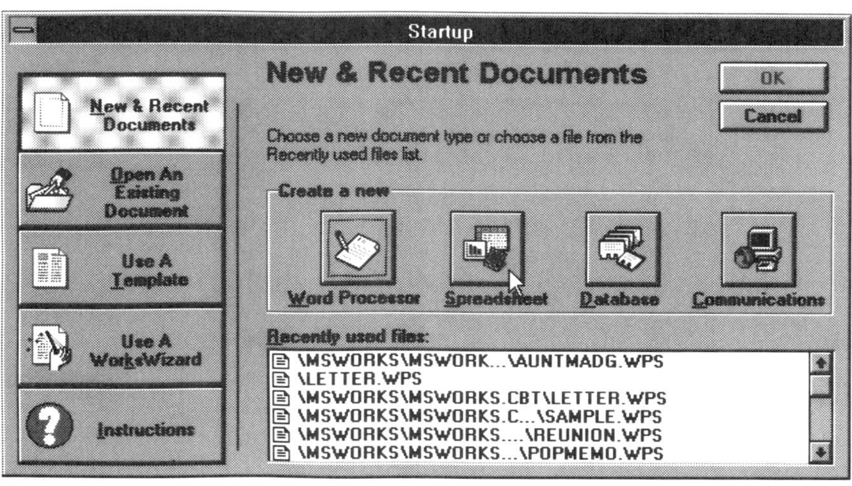

Figure 8-1. *Click on Spreadsheet in the Startup dialog box.*

Another way to start the spreadsheet is to select *Create New File* in the **File** menu (Figure 8-2), which displays the *Startup* dialog box also. Clicking on *Spreadsheet* opens a new spreadsheet file (Figure 8-3).

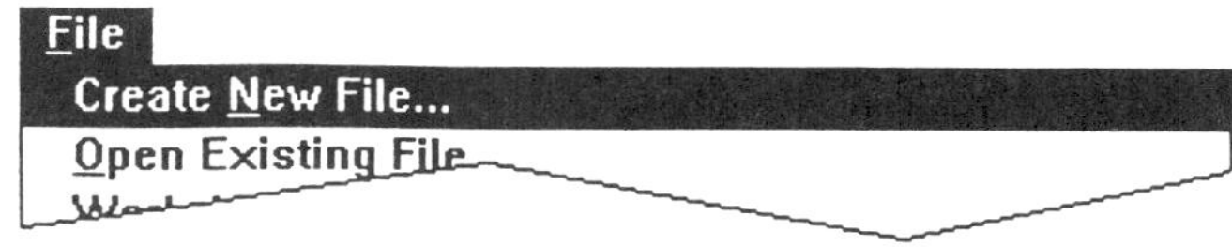

Figure 8-2. *Create New File in the* ***File*** *menu.*

Parts of the spreadsheet screen

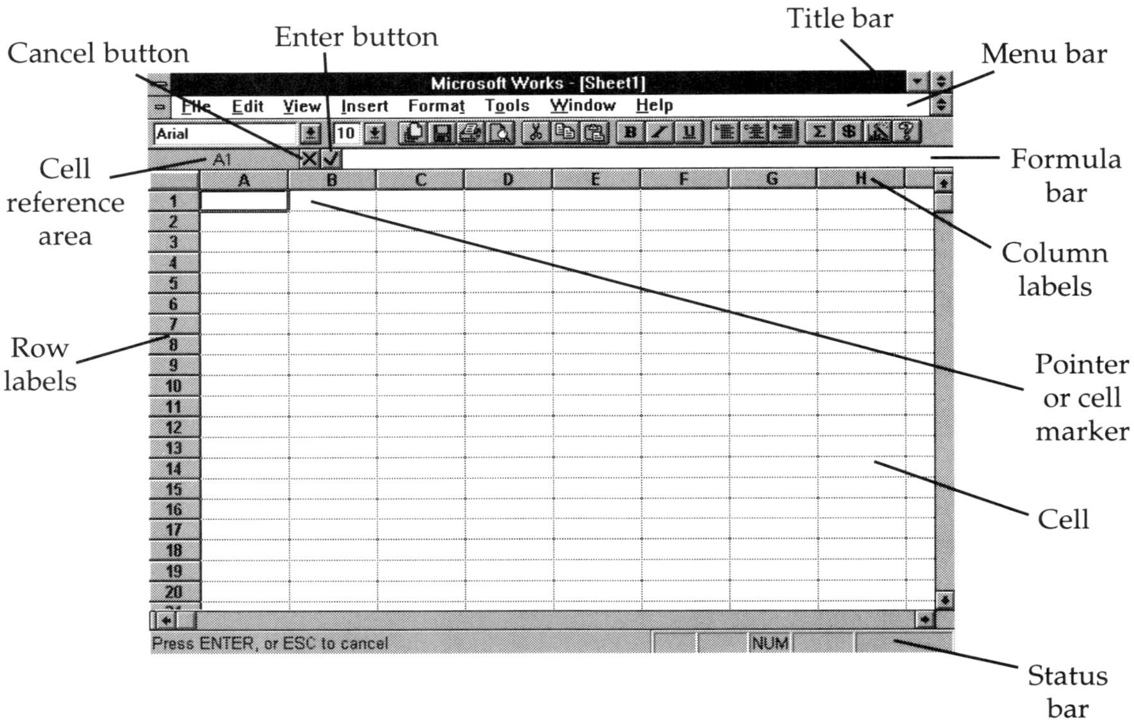

Figure 8-3. *The Works spreadsheet screen.*

The title bar

The title bar in the spreadsheet tool in Works is exactly the same as in the word processor. The screen is not maximized when it is opened for the first time. Click on the maximize button to maximize the windows. For more information about the Title Bar, refer to **Chapter 1, The Word Processor Screen**.

The menu bar

The menu bar, just below the title bar, contains the menu structure of the spreadsheet tool. Although choosing a menu in the spreadsheet is exactly the same as in the other tools, some menus are quite different. The menus are: **File, Edit, View, Insert, Format, Tools, Window,** and **Help** (Figure 8-4).

File Edit View Insert Format T

Figure 8-4. *The menu bar in the spreadsheet tool.*

The toolbar

The toolbar contains a number of submenus and buttons which enable you to do a number of tasks, such as format your spreadsheet quickly. The need to go into a full menu is eliminated as the buttons and submenus are shortcuts for some menu options.

The toolbar in the spreadsheet is similar to that in other tools in Works, but does contain some buttons specifically designed for the spreadsheet. The buttons are displayed in Figure 8-5.

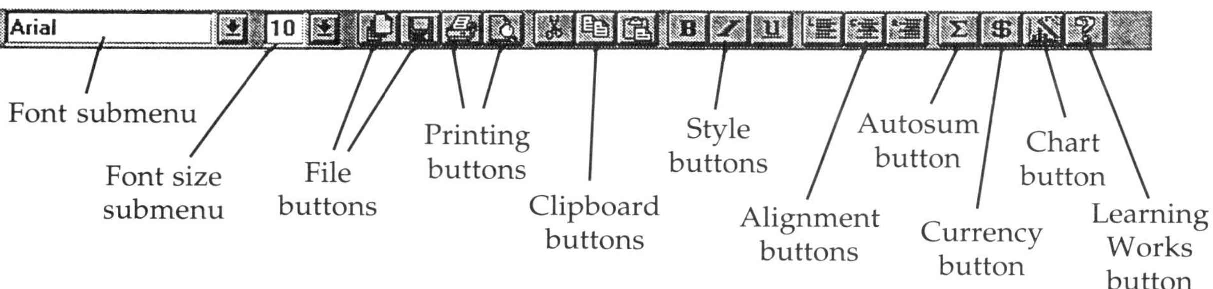

Figure 8-5. *The tools on the spreadsheet toolbar.*

The reference bar

The reference bar is positioned just below the toolbar. It contains a number of important features including the cell reference area, *Cancel* button, *Enter* button and the formula bar. Figure 8-6 highlights these features.

Cancel button

Enter button

A1

Cell reference area

Formula bar

Figure 8-6. *The reference bar.*

The cell reference area displays the cell reference address of the current pointer position. If the pointer is in cell A1, for instance, then "A1" is displayed in the cell reference area. If more than one cell is highlighted, Works displays the first and last cells in the block. For example if the cells A1 through A5 are highlighted, "A1:A5" appears in the cell reference area.

The Cancel and Enter buttons are for the mouse. Clicking on the Cancel button has the same effect as pressing Escape on the keyboard (cancelling your current cell entry). Clicking on Enter does the same as when Enter is pressed on the keyboard (confirming your current cell entry). In Figure 8-7, the Enter button is used.

Figure 8-7. *Clicking on Enter is the same as pressing Enter on the keyboard.*

The formula bar displays what is typed into a cell. The insertion point flashes in the formula bar as the information is being typed, which Figure 8-8 displays. The insertion point remains in the formula bar until you press Enter or click on the Enter button.

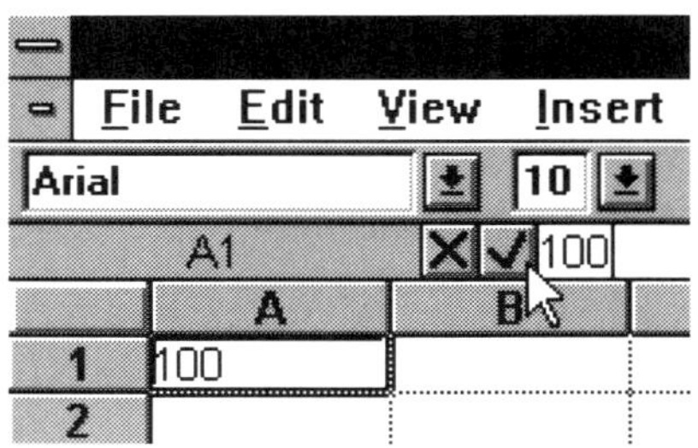

Figure 8-8. *"100" has been typed into cell A1. The insertion point is still in the formula bar as Enter has not yet been pressed.*

Rows

A row, going across the spreadsheet, is labeled by numbers. There are 16,384 rows in the Works spreadsheet.

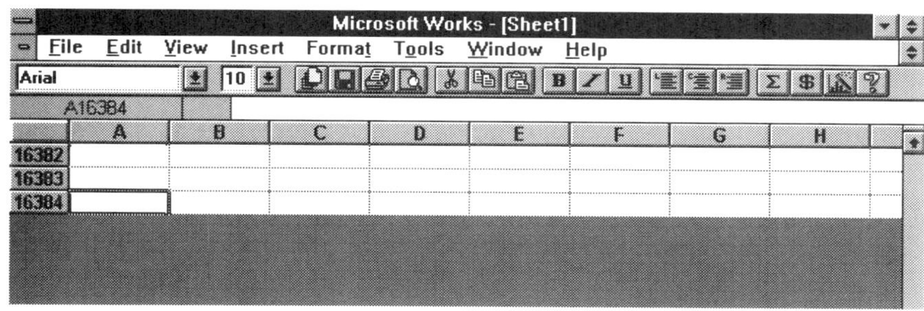

Figure 8-9. *The last row in the spreadsheet is 16,384.*

Columns

A column, going down the spreadsheet, uses letters as its labels. There are a maximum of 256 columns. Columns after "Z" use double letters as labels. "AA," for example, follows column Z. The next column is AB. The column following AZ is BA, then BB, etc. Columns in Works are labeled to IV.

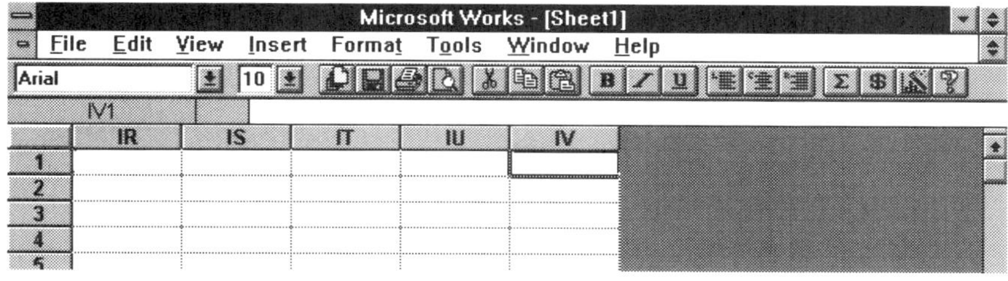

Figure 8-10. *The last column in the spreadsheet is column IV.*

Cells

Cells are the rectangular shapes on the spreadsheet into which numbers and text are typed. These individual pieces of information in cells make up a spreadsheet. There are 4,194,304 cells in the Works spreadsheet.

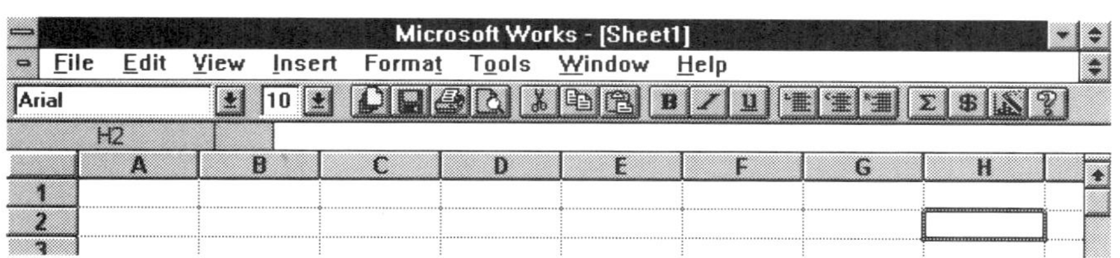

Figure 8-11. *Cell H2 is marked by the cell pointer.*

The cell address—the name of the cell—is determined by the intersection of the row and the column where the cell lies. The cell in Figure 8-11 is called H2, as it intersects row 2 and column H. The current cell, H2 in Figure 8-11, is marked on the spreadsheet by the cell pointer—a dark outline of the cell.

The scroll bars

The scroll bars appear along the bottom and right-hand sides of the screen indicating your relative position in the spreadsheet. They are a standard Windows feature.

The mouse pointer

The mouse pointer indicates the location of the mouse on the screen. The shape of the mouse pointer changes in different places on the screen. For example, the pointer becomes a cross when placed over the cells; an arrow when near a menu; and an I-bar when in a text box or the formula bar (Figure 8-12).

Figure 8-12. *The mouse cursor becomes an I-beam when it is in the formula bar.*

The status bar

The status bar is under the horizontal scroll bar at the bottom of the screen. It displays a series of comments and indicators to inform you of the status of the spreadsheet. It is important to keep watching the status bar for warnings and other indicators which can help solve problems which may be occurring in the spreadsheet. "EDIT" is one of those warnings which is displayed in Figure 8-13.

The status bar can be turned on and off in Works. The procedure to follow is outlined in Figure 1-13, **Chapter 1, The Word Processor Screen**.

Figure 8-13. *"EDIT" is an indicator on the status bar informing you that you can edit the current cell.*

Display options

The screen display can be altered to suit your requirements, some of which are discussed below. For this section, open the file ***popsales.wks*** from the ***msworks.cbt*** subdirectory. This file is used to test the display options in the Works spreadsheet.

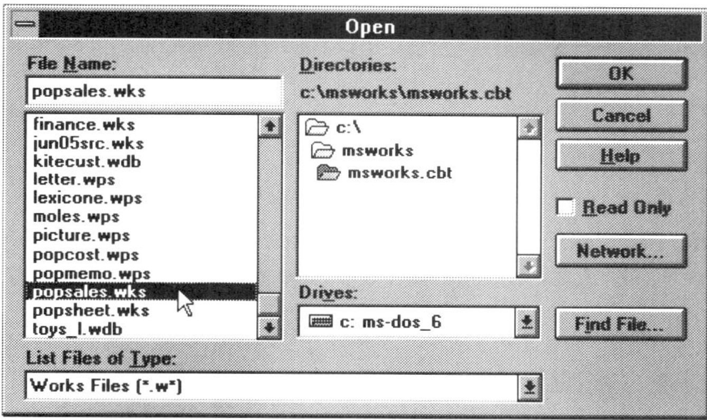

Figure 8-14. *Open the file **popsales.wks** from the **msworks.cbt** subdirectory.*

Show gridlines

Gridlines are the horizontal lines on the screen which mark cells. They clearly show the layout of the spreadsheet and are on by default.

It is not always helpful, however, to display gridlines. When placing borders around cells, sometimes the gridline can be confused for the border. In such a case, the gridlines need to be removed from the screen—through the *Show Gridlines* command in the **View** menu. The command is illustrated in Figure 8-15.

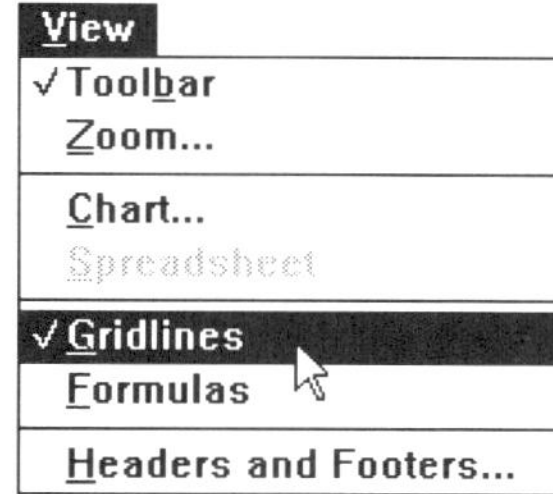

Figure 8-15. *Gridlines are currently on as indicated by the check mark next to the Gridlines command.*

Turn the gridlines off on your screen by deselecting *Gridlines* in the **View** menu. Figure 8-16 shows the screen with no gridlines.

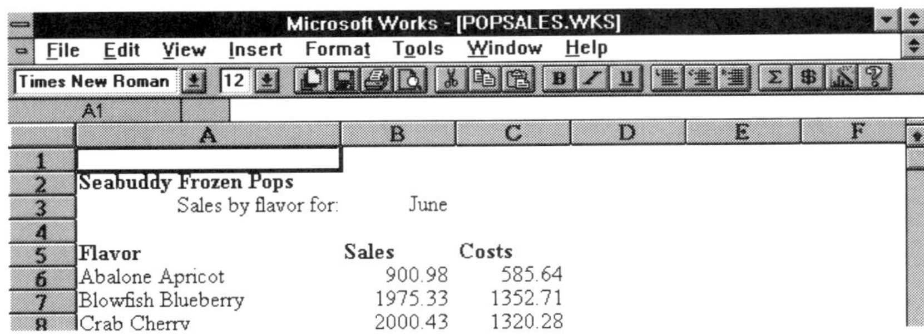

Figure 8-16. *The gridlines have been turned off in the sample file.*

To turn them back on, select *Gridlines* from the **View** menu again, and the screen returns to its original display mode (Figure 8-17).

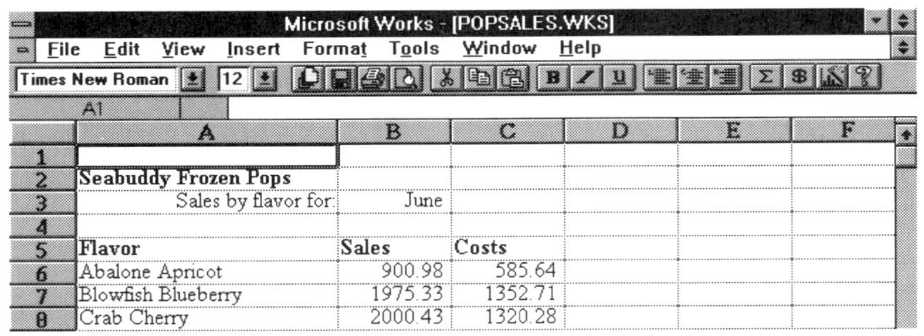

Figure 8-17. *The gridlines are displayed again in your file.*

Freezing titles

When creating a large spreadsheet, it is often important that the titles or headings in a column or row are visible in areas of the spreadsheet other than where they were inserted originally.

Freezing titles depends on the position of the pointer. The pointer must be under the row and to the right of the column to be frozen. Columns and rows can be frozen simultaneously by finding the intersecting point. To freeze column A in the sample file, move the pointer into cell B1 by clicking the mouse on that cell, see Figure 8-18.

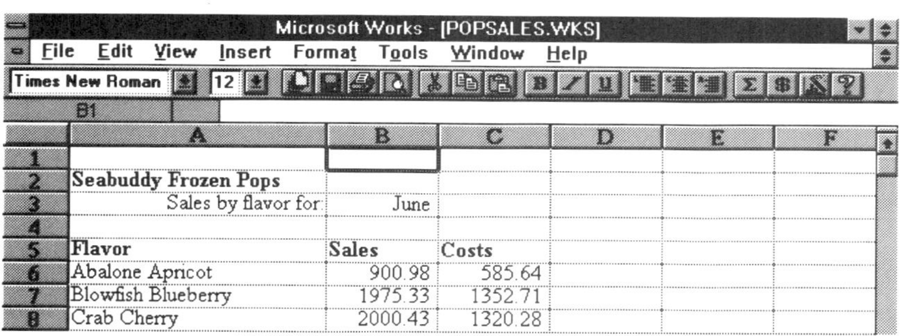

Figure 8-18. *Click the mouse in cell B1 to highlight that cell. The titles in column A are frozen when Freeze Titles is selected.*

To freeze titles in column A, select *Freeze Titles* from the **Format** menu. This command is illustrated in Figure 8-19.

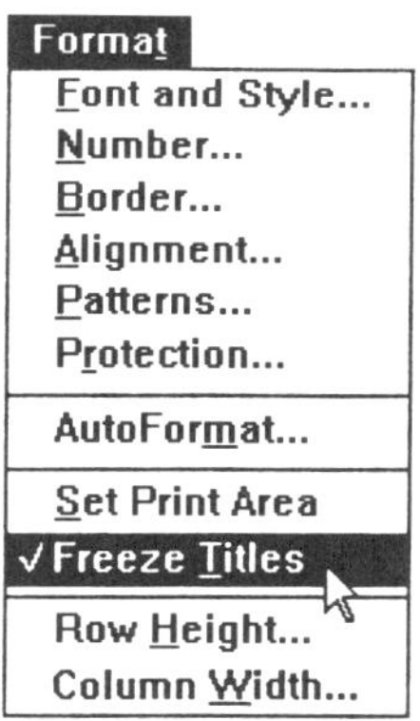

Figure 8-19. *The Freeze Titles command in the* ***Format*** *menu.*

Check to see that the titles have been frozen by scrolling across the spreadsheet using the horizontal scroll bar. The screen looks like Figure 8-20.

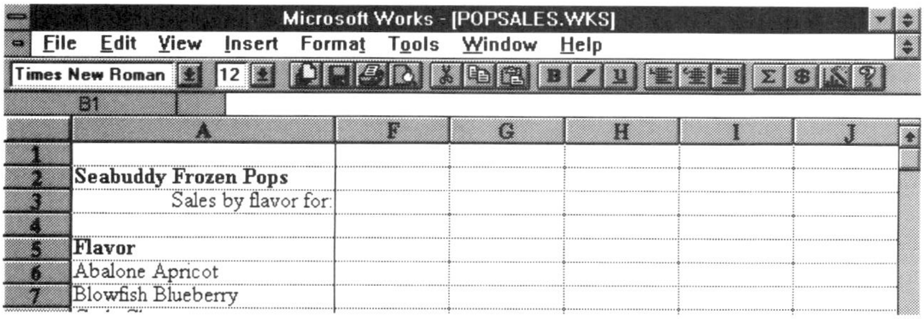

Figure 8-20. *The titles you froze still appear when you scroll right.*

Turning frozen titles off is simply a matter of deselecting *Freeze Titles* from the **Format** menu. Scrolling across the spreadsheet now does not show the titles in column A as it did previously.

Splitting the spreadsheet screen

The screen can be split in a number of ways. This is very useful for comparing different parts of the spreadsheet which could not otherwise be brought together.

The screen is split horizontally (Figure 8-21) by dragging the split box to the positions where the split is to go. Double-clicking on the split bar unsplits the screen. By choosing *Split* from the **Window** menu, you can split the screen into a maximum of four panes (side-by-side and upper and lower). For further details on splitting and unsplitting the screen refer to **Chapter 1, The Word Processor Screen**.

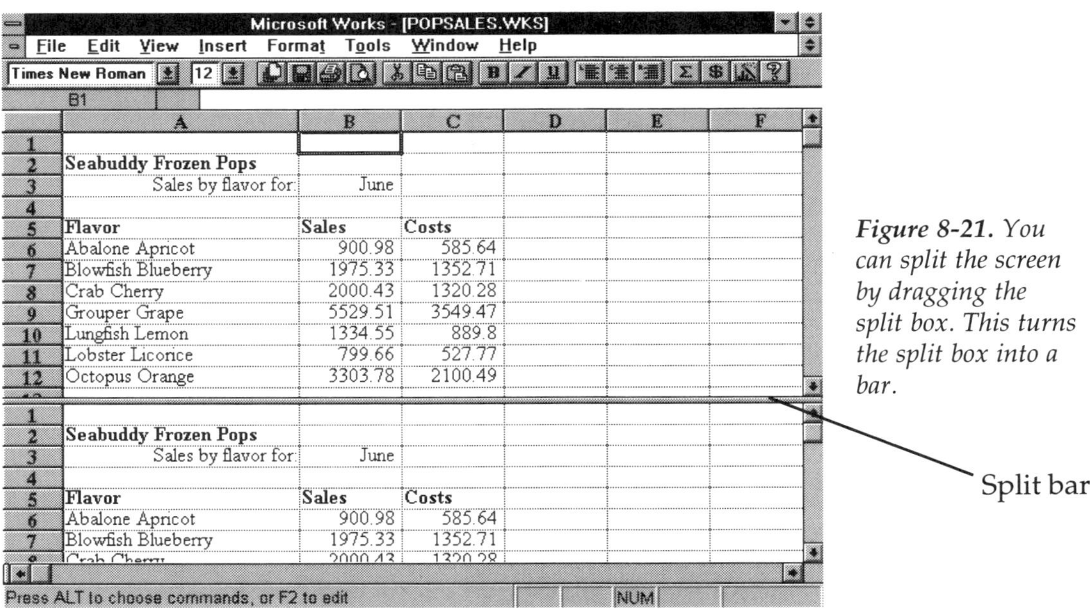

Figure 8-21. *You can split the screen by dragging the split box. This turns the split box into a bar.*

Closing the spreadsheet

To close a spreadsheet in Works, the **File** menu needs to be accessed. From this menu, select *Close* (Figure 8-22) and the file closes automatically. If the file has not been saved, however, Works warns you of this.

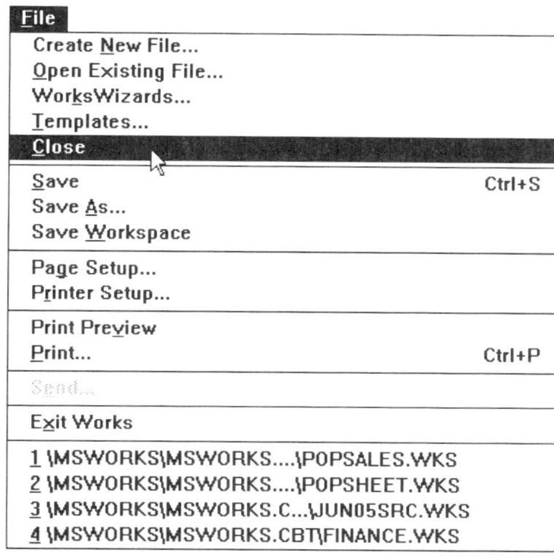

Figure 8-22. *The Close command in the* ***File*** *menu.*

Entering Spreadsheet Data

Entering data (text, numbers, and formulas) is the basis for using a spreadsheet. Text is useful for column and row headings, and spreadsheet titles.

Moving to a cell

The address or name of a cell, as mentioned in the previous chapter, is determined by the intersection of the column and row where it is. Figure 9-1 illustrates this naming procedure.

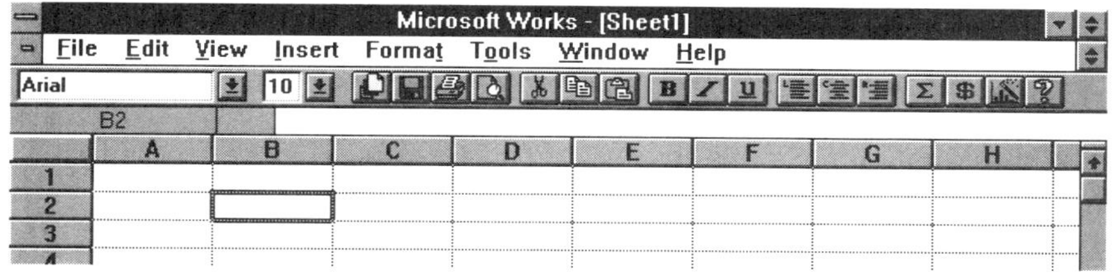

Figure 9-1. The cell is called B2 as it intersects row 2 and column B.

Using the correct name of a cell is essential to using the spreadsheet. Cell names are used in many of the commands outlined in this book as well as in formulas, discussed in this chapter.

Spend a few minutes studying the spreadsheet, determining the cell address of a particular cell, and checking the address in the cell reference area at the top of the screen.

Changing the active cell

The active cell is the cell which has the dark line around its edge. The dark line is referred to as the pointer or the highlight (Figure 9-2).

Figure 9-2. The active cell marked by the cell pointer or highlight.

The active cell is changed by using the cursor keys, clicking the mouse on the cell required, or using the *Go To* command. Each of these is detailed below.

THE CURSOR KEYS

Pressing the arrow keys moves the pointer one cell left, right, up, or down, depending on the arrow key pressed. Using these keys is a quick way of moving around the part of the spreadsheet you can see on the screen.

A spreadsheet, however, often extends beyond the screen boundary and Works has built-in shortcuts for rapid movement through the entire spreadsheet.

For example, to move to the end of the row that the pointer is in, press End, and to move to the beginning of that row, press Home. These and other cursor movements are listed in the table below.

To Move	Keyboard	To Move	Keyboard
Left one cell	Left arrow or Shift Tab	Up one row	Up arrow
Right one cell	Right arrow or Tab	Down one row	Down arrow
To beginning of row	Home	To beginning of spreadsheet	Ctrl-Home
To end of row	End	To end of spreadsheet	Ctrl-End
Up one screen	Page up	Left one screen	Ctrl-Page Up
Down one screen	Page Down	Right one screen	Control-Page Down

The mouse

To move to a specific cell using the mouse, click the mouse cursor—the cross—over the cell. The cell where the mouse is clicked is immediately made active. Figure 9-3 illustrates this process.

Often the cell required is not on the screen. To view another part of the spreadsheet, the scroll bars must be used. Scroll the spreadsheet so the cell Z20 appears on the screen and make Z20 active by clicking on it (Figure 9-3).

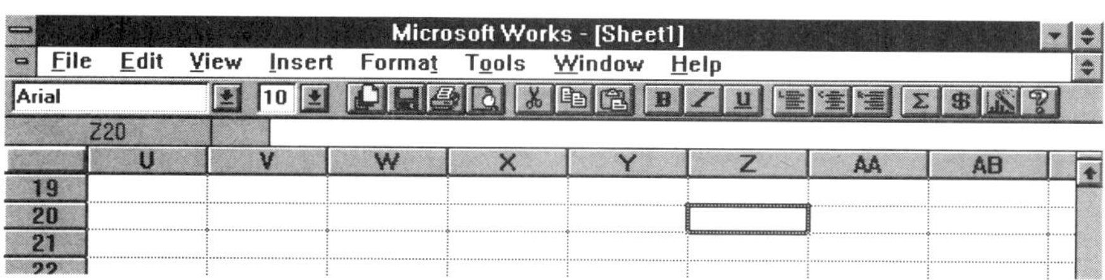

Figure 9-3. *Z20 is made active by scrolling to it and clicking in this cell with the mouse.*

The Go To command

The *Go To* command enables you to quickly position the pointer at a specific cell or range of cells (see **Chapter 10, Editing Spreadsheets**, for more information on ranges).

The *Go To* command is activated by pressing F5 or through the **Edit** menu shown in Figure 9-4.

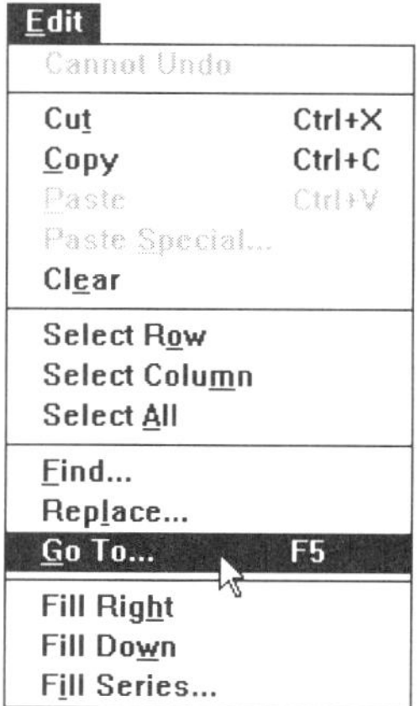

Figure 9-4. *The Go To command.*

Try using this command to position the pointer in cell W50. Press F5 to open the *Go To* dialog box and type in "w50" in the *Go to* text box. This is shown in Figure 9-5. Click on *OK* and you will now return to the screen with cell W50 selected.

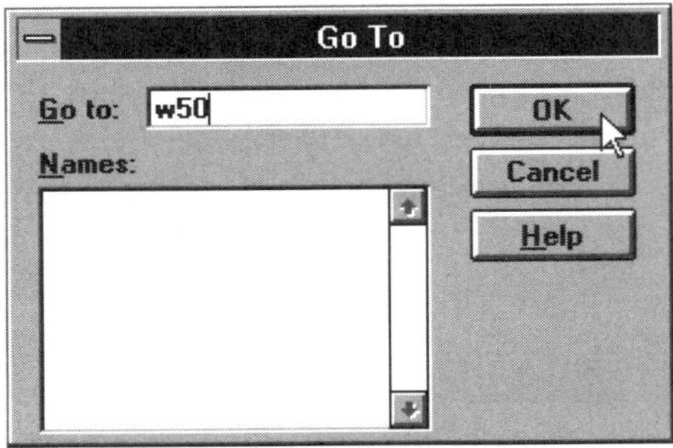

Figure 9-5. *Type in the cell address to go to—w50—in the Go to text box.*

Entering information

Information is entered using the Enter key. It is also entered using the up or down arrow key. The arrow keys are especially useful when entering a list of information.

There are three valid entries which can be inserted into a cell. These are text, values, and formulas.

Text

Text is simply a word or a series of words used for headings and labels which give a spreadsheet added meaning. The moment you start typing text into a cell, the insertion point appears in the formula bar. The text is inserted into the active cell and the formula bar simultaneously. Insert the text "Toy Shop" into cell A1 as in Figure 9-6.

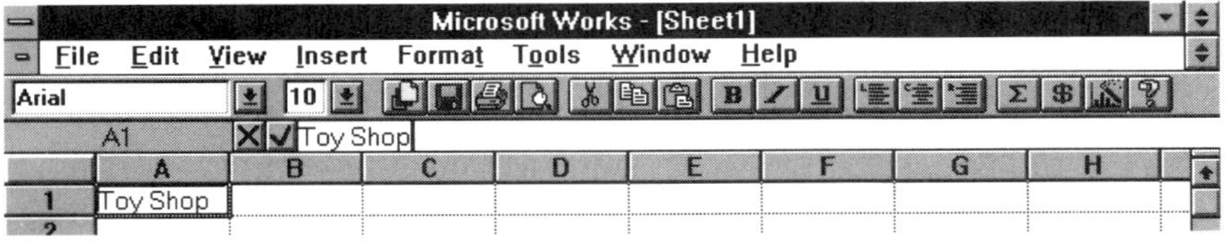

Figure 9-6. *The insertion point is in the formula bar as "Toy Shop" is put into cell A1.*

When Enter is pressed or the *Enter* button clicked on with the mouse, the text becomes part of the cell "officially." It is given a double quote text prefix (") automatically, which appears in the formula bar only. The prefix is used to differentiate between the different types of entries in Works.

Put the following text into the cell specified:

B1 Quantity
C1 Cost
D1 Total Cost
A2 Skates
A3 Roller Boards
A4 Total

Your spreadsheet should look like Figure 9-7 when complete.

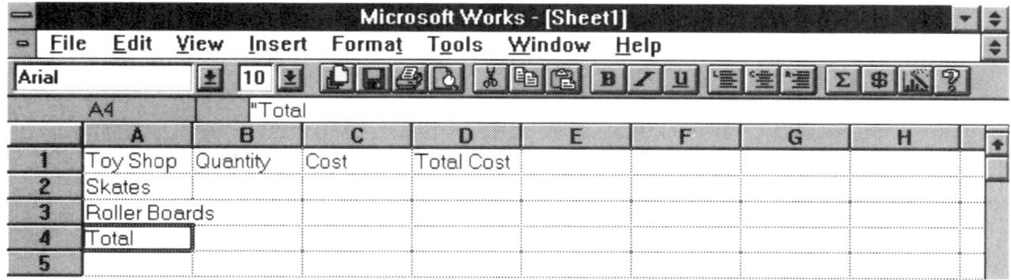

Figure 9-7. *Insert this text into your spreadsheet.*

Values

Values are the numbers which are used in the spreadsheet. These have an actual value of the number represented and are used in calculations.

The value required is typed in using the numeric keypad or the numbers above the letters on the keyboard. The value "100" is entered into cell B2 in Figure 9-8 and appears in both the formula bar and the cell. To confirm this entry, you need to press the Enter key, click on the *Enter* button, or use the arrow keys.

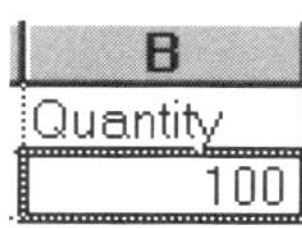

Figure 9-8. *Give B2 the value of 100.*

Continue using the spreadsheet you started above and key in these values; the completed spreadsheet looks like Figure 9-9.

B2	100
B3	175
C2	60
C3	80

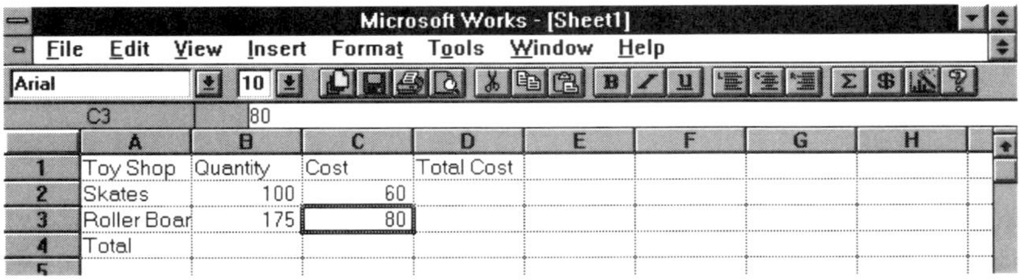

Microsoft Works - [Sheet1]

File Edit View Insert Format Tools Window Help

C3 80

	A	B	C	D	E	F	G	H
1	Toy Shop	Quantity	Cost	Total Cost				
2	Skates	100	60					
3	Roller Boar	175	80					
4	Total							

Figure 9-9. *The spreadsheet looks like this when the values are keyed in.*

Keying in the value in cell B3 has *cut off*—truncated—the "ds" from "Roller Boards" in cell A3. This happens because "Roller Boards" is too long for cell A3. When B3 was empty, it used that cell for the extra characters. Text is truncated when it does not fit into the cell.

Values are not truncated, but change the format of the number to scientific notation. To overcome such problems, the column needs to be widened, which is looked at in **Chapter 10, Editing Spreadsheets**.

Formulas

Formulas are used to calculate equations. The equation appears in the formula bar and the answer, by default, appears in the cell.

It is essential to put in a formula prefix when inserting a formula into a spreadsheet. The formula prefix is an equals sign (=) and tells Works to calculate the equation that follows.

The golden rule for using formulas, however, is to be in the cell in which the result is to go *before* beginning the formula with an equals sign.

A basic formula uses at least one of the four mathematical operators: addition (+), subtraction (-), division (/), and multiplication (*). Brackets () can be used to group parts of the formula together to ensure the order required is adhered to.

In cell B4, a simple formula to add the values above could be "=100+175" (refer back to Figure 9-9). This would put the answer of 275 in cell B4 and appears to be perfect. However, if the number of Skates increases to 200 and you put this in cell B3, the answer of 275 would be incorrect. Figure 9-10 illustrates this problem.

To avoid such things occurring, use cell addresses in the formulas rather than values.

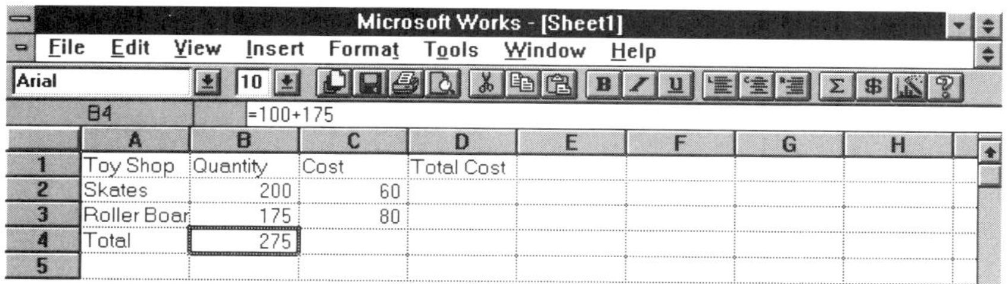

Figure 9-10. *Using values in formulas can lead to errors in a spreadsheet if other values are changed.*

Using cell addresses in formulas

The cell address is inserted into a formula in one of three ways: by typing it in, pointing to it, or moving to it with the cursor keys. This section looks at each of these methods using the "Toy Shop" text and values entered above.

The first cell requiring a formula is B4, to add the two cells above it. Move to that cell by clicking on it with the mouse. To tell Works that the information being keyed in is a formula, the formula prefix (=) needs to be inserted. The formula can now be typed, using the addition operator (+). Complete the formula by typing "B2+B3". As you type, the formula appears in the formula bar as well as in the cell, shown in Figure 9-11.

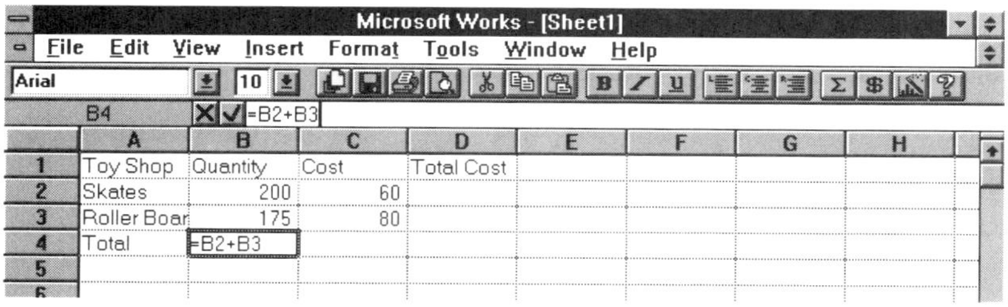

Figure 9-11. *"=B2+B3" appears in the formula bar and the cell B4, as it is typed.*

The answer does not appear in the cell until Enter is pressed. Do this now and your screen will look like Figure 9-12.

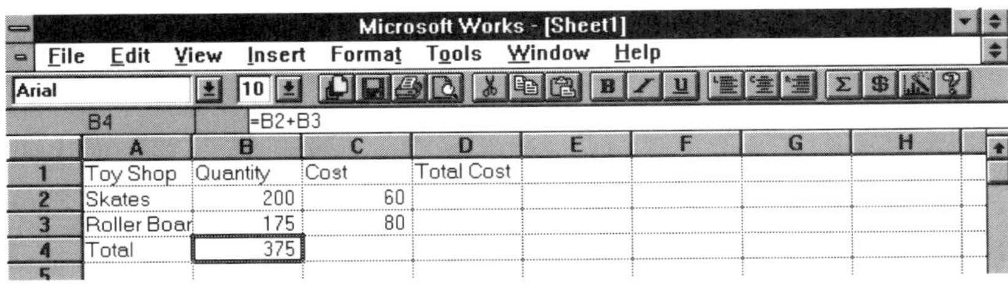

Figure 9-12. *The answer of "375" is in cell B4 while the formula still appears in the formula bar.*

Typing in a formula, however, is not as accurate as using the *pointing* method. *Pointing* is moving to the appropriate cell when creating the formula, using either the keyboard or the mouse.

Move to cell C4, and type in a formula which adds the two cells above (=C2+C3). The formula prefix is initially entered into the cell when using the pointing method as it ensures that the answer appears in the correct cell—type in "=".

Now click on C2. Figure 9-13 displays how your screen should look.

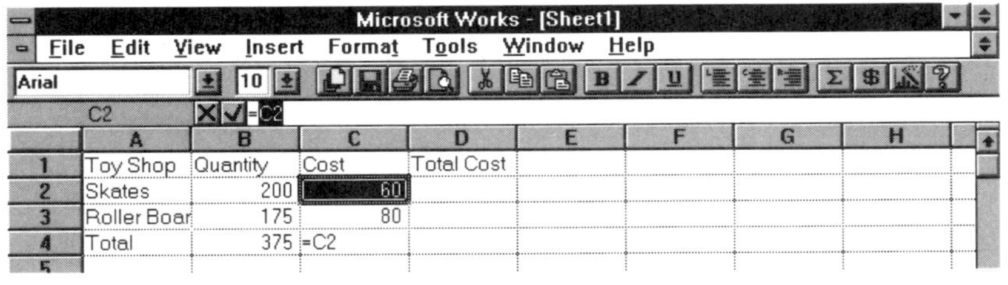

Figure 9-13. *"=C2" appears in the formula bar.*

When the operator (+) is keyed in, it appears in the formula bar and the pointer moves back to the original cell automatically (Figure 9-14).

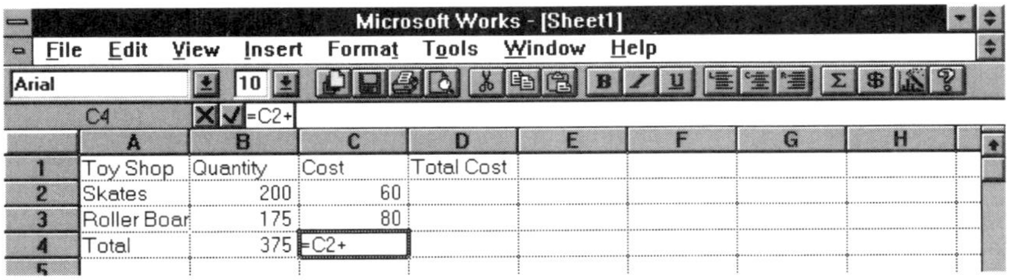

Figure 9-14. *The formula bar displays "=C2+" and the pointer moves back to C4.*

The formula is completed by pointing to C3; Figure 9-15 shows the result to this point. The answer "140" appears in the cell, as shown in Figure 9-16, when the *Enter* button is clicked or the Enter key is pressed.

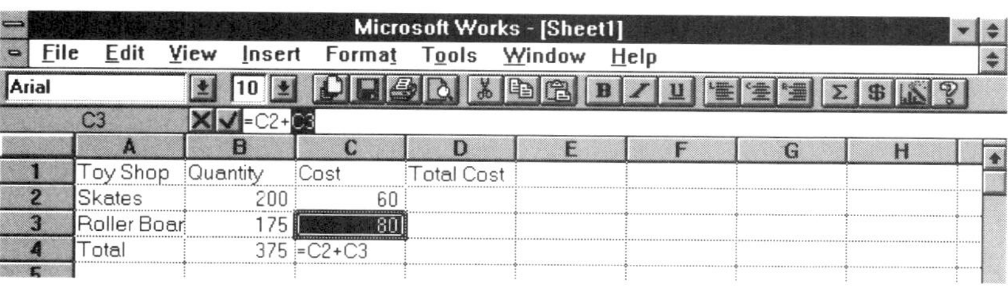

Figure 9-15. The formula is completed by clicking on cell C3.

Creating a formula pointing with the keyboard is very similar to using the mouse, except the arrow keys are used. To test this method, put the formula "=B2*C2" in cell D2 to calculate the total cost.

Move into cell D2 and enter the formula prefix. Now move into cell B2 with the cursor keys and look at the formula bar—"=B2" is showing. Press the * key and the pointer moves back to cell D2. To finish the formula, press the left arrow to move to cell C2 and press Enter. The answer "12000" is in D2 as shown in Figure 9-16.

Put the formula "=B3*C3" into D3 using any of the methods outlined above. Figure 9-16 now displays the spreadsheet, with an additional formula (B3*C3) in cell D3.

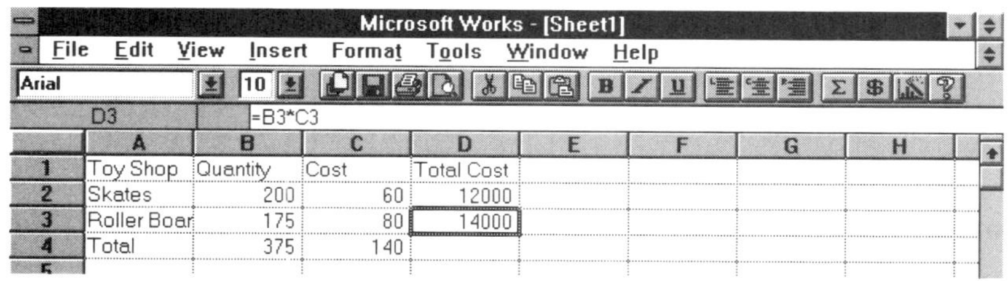

Figure 9-16. The spreadsheet now has four formulas.

The Formulas command in the View menu

The default display in Works is to show the formulas in the formula bar only. It is necessary at times to see the formulas in the spreadsheet, especially when the structure of the spreadsheet, rather than the figures, is important. To show formulas in this way, choose *Formulas* in the **View** menu (Figure 9-17).

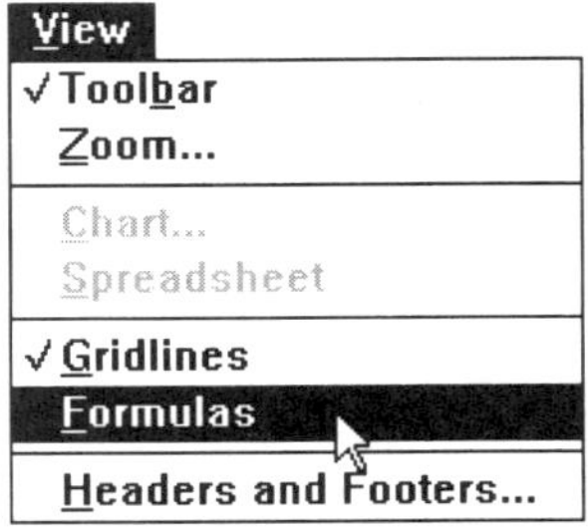

Figure 9-17. *The Formulas command in the* ***View*** *menu.*

The columns are automatically widened to fit the formulas, displaying the screen as shown in Figure 9-18. To turn *Formulas* off, select it again from the **View** menu.

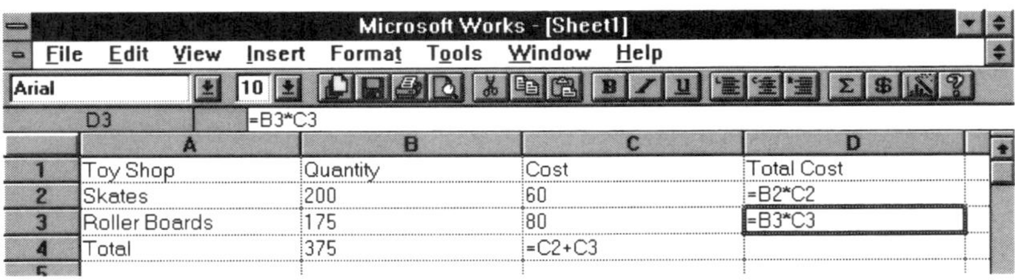

Figure 9-18. *The screen as it appears when Formulas is activated in the* ***View*** *menu.*

Manual calculation

By default, Works calculates a spreadsheet automatically, immediately after an entry is made. For example, move into cell B2 and change that value to 300 by typing over it and pressing Enter. The new total in B4 is 475, and 18,000 in D2.

Recalculating after each entry is time consuming when using a complex spreadsheet with many formulas. *Manual Calculation* is activated to alleviate the problem of slow processing. Manual calculation is turned on through the *Manual Calculation* command in the **Tools** menu (Figure 9-19). Turn *Manual Calculation* on.

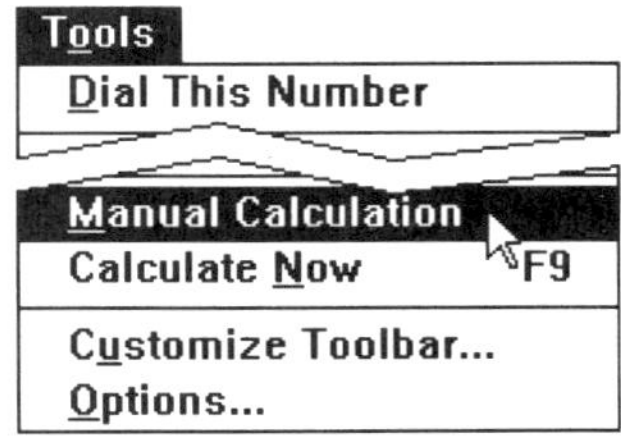

Figure 9-19. *The Manual Calculation command in the* ***Tools*** *menu.*

When values are changed in the spreadsheet, with *Manual Calculation* active, formulas are not automatically updated. Change the value in B3 to 300 to test this—the totals in B4 and D3 remain constant.

THE CALCULATE NOW COMMAND

The *Calculate Now* command calculates the formulas in the spreadsheet when *Manual Calculation* is on. *Calculate Now* is in the **Tools** menu (Figure 9-20). F9 is the shortcut to the *Calculate Now* command. It is essential that you recalculate the spreadsheet before printing, to avoid inaccurate results appearing on paper.

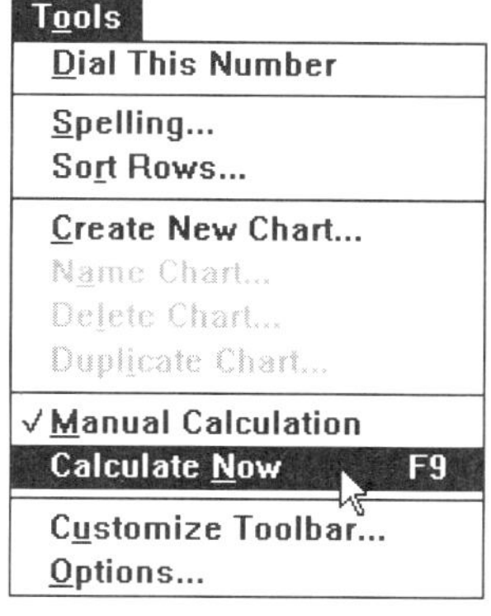

Figure 9-20. *Calculate Now in the* ***Tools*** *menu.*

Choose this command and notice the totals in B4 and D3 change to 600 and 24,000 respectively. The results are shown in Figure 9-21.

Microsoft Works - [Sheet1]

File Edit View Insert Format Tools Window Help

B3 300

	A	B	C	D	E	F	G	H
1	Toy Shop	Quantity	Cost	Total Cost				
2	Skates	300	60	18000				
3	Roller Boar	300	80	24000				
4	Total	600	140					
5								

Figure 9-21. *When Manual Calculation is active, totals are calculated by selecting Calculate Now from the* ***Tools*** *menu.*

Be sure to turn *Manual Calculation* off now by selecting it from the **View** menu.

Functions

Functions are preprogrammed equations which are a standard feature of Works. There are 76 functions of frequently used equations designed to save time and increase efficiency.

Some of these functions include SUM, which adds a group of cells, ROUND, which rounds values, and AVG, which calculates the average value of a group of cells. A complete list of functions used in Works can be found in Appendix A of the Works manual.

For this example, enter the numbers 10, 12, 14, 16, 18, 20 in cells A10 to A15. In cell B10 enter 20 and in C10 enter 30. You may like to drag the scroll box down the vertical scroll bar so that the column labels are nearer to your data. See Figure 9-22 for the screen layout.

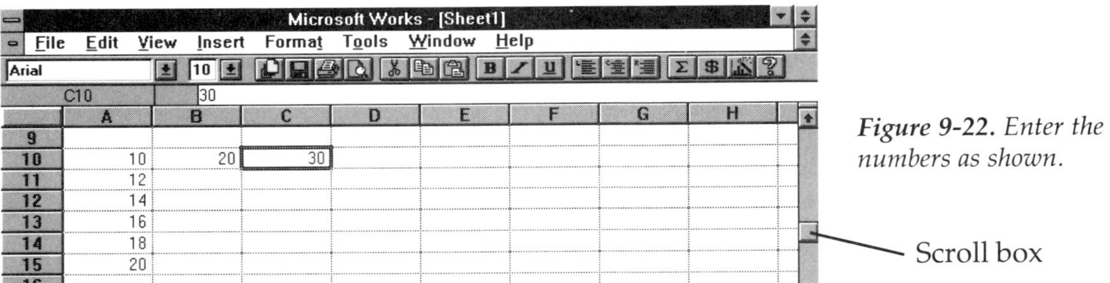

Figure 9-22. Enter the numbers as shown.

The Autosum button

The *Autosum* button is a shortcut to the SUM function, which is used to add a column or row of numbers. When the *Autosum* button is activated, Works looks for cells above it first, then it looks to the left. A cell range reference is then displayed in the formula bar for you to check. Pressing Enter accepts the formula and inserts it into the cell.

If no cells to be summed can be found, Works displays =SUM(). You can type in your choice of cell reference to sum between the parentheses.

To quickly add the numbers in cells A10 through A15, the first step is to move to the cell where the answer is to be—A16. Click in this cell now. Clicking on the *Autosum* button places the SUM function in the cell in the formula bar and the cell, with the cell range inserted.

Figure 9-23 displays the screen after you click on the *Autosum* button.

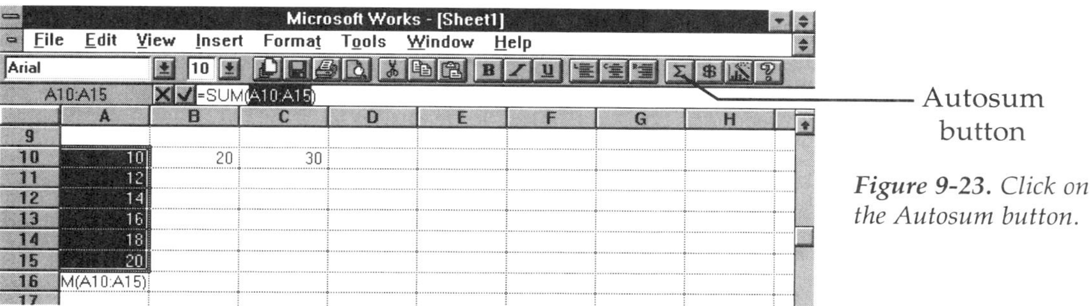

Figure 9-23. Click on the Autosum button.

To complete the formula, press Enter and the total—90—appears in A16. This, as you can see, is a very fast way of adding a group of cells together.

Entering functions

Not all functions are as easy to insert as the SUM function using the *Autosum* button; however, the basic syntax of a function remains constant.

As with any formula, the pointer must be located in the cell where the result of the function is to appear. The basic syntax of a function is as follows:

=FUNCTION NAME(range of cells)

The function name can be typed in either upper or lowercase.

The function used in this example is AVG, which is to calculate the average of the numbers in cells A10, B10, and C10, and is to insert the result in cell D10. To put this function in, click in cell D10, and type "=AVG(" (Figure 9-24).

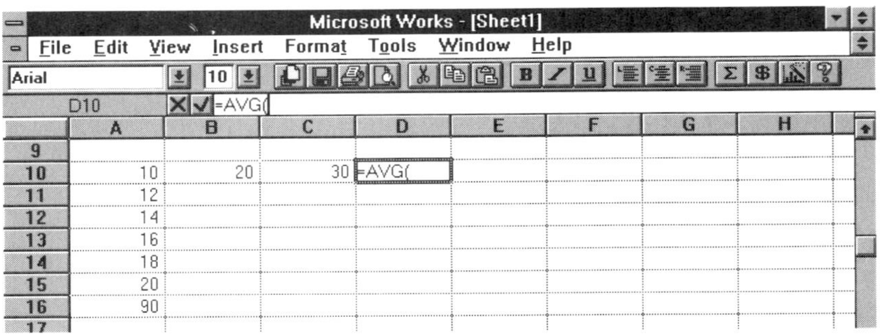

Figure 9-24. *The AVG function is started in cell D10 to determine the average of 10, 20, and 30.*

Cell references can be inserted in two ways: pointing with the mouse or highlighting with the keyboard.

To highlight the cells using the mouse, click on A10 and drag over to C10. Using the keyboard, press the left arrow until it is on cell A10. The pointer now needs to be anchored, so it can be extended over to C10. Press the colon (:) to anchor the pointer and move the pointer over to C10.

Use either of these methods to insert the cell range into the AVG function as in Figure 9-25.

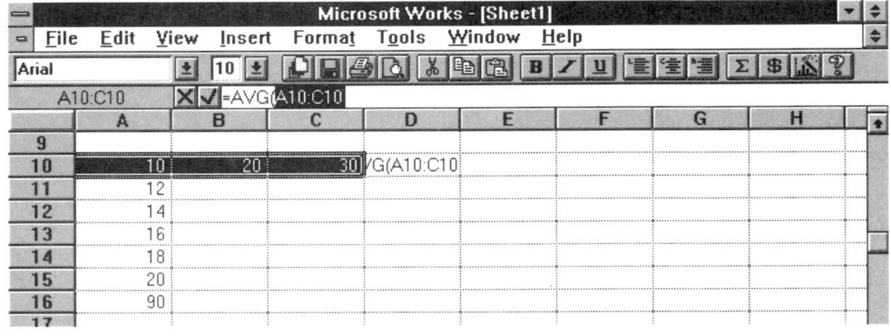

Figure 9-25. *The cell range is inserted into the function with the mouse or the cursor keys.*

The right parenthesis needs to be typed in to complete the function. Do this now and press Enter so the result—20—appears in D10.

The Protection command

Protecting data is an essential part of creating a complex spreadsheet. Any unprotected cell can easily be deleted or edited accidentally, which may cause you to lose valuable data.

When you first open a file in Works, all of the cells are "locked." The cells in the spreadsheet, however, do not use the "locked" feature until you "protect" the locked cells. To protect all locked cells from change, choose *Protection* from the **Format** menu and select *Protect Data* as Figure 9-26 shows.

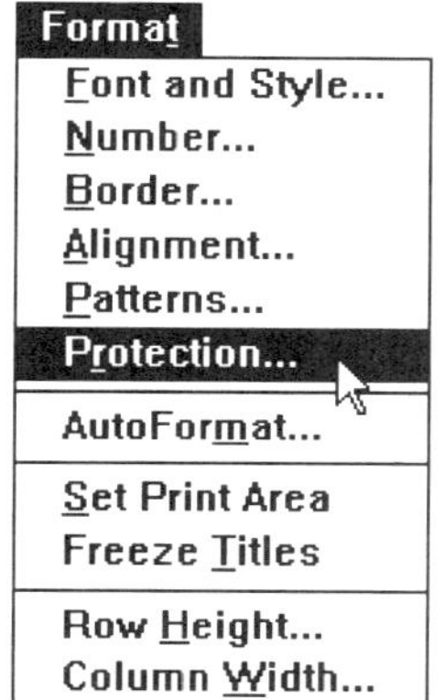

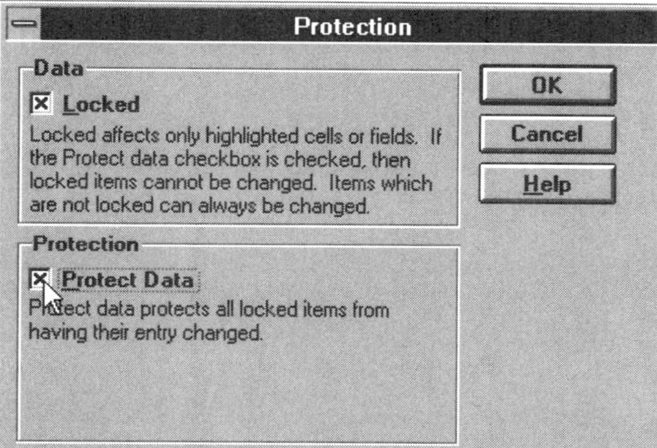

Figure 9-26. *Choose Protection from the **Format** menu and select Protect Data.*

No locked cell in the spreadsheet can be changed while this command is active. Try changing the figure in B4 to 300 to see that the spreadsheet is protected. When you try to change the entry, a dialog box appears explaining that the cell contents cannot be changed, which is illustrated in Figure 9-27.

Figure 9-27. *Works warns you with a dialog box that a protected cell cannot be changed.*

It is not always beneficial to lock every cell in the spreadsheet, as some values may need to be changed. You can unlock selected cells through the *Protection* command in the **Format** menu.

Move to cell B2 as this is the cell to be unlocked and open the *Protection* dialog box. The *Locked* check box is checked as this is the default. To deselect it, click on the check box until it is blank and then click on *OK* (Figure 9-28).

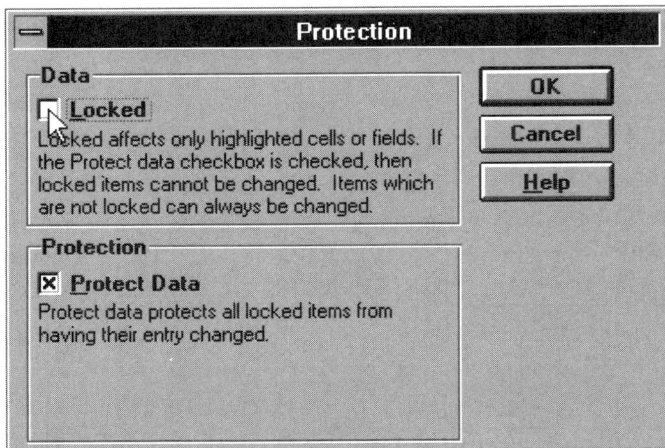

Figure 9-28. *Deselect Locked in the Protection dialog box to enable changes to your cell selection.*

To test that this has unlocked B2, change the value in the cell to 500. You can change the contents of this cell only if it has been unlocked.

Most of the menu commands in Works are unavailable if you are in a locked cell while *Protect Data* is on. Turn *Protect Data* off by deselecting it in the *Protection* dialog box through the **Format** menu.

Saving files

The spreadsheet needs to be saved as a disk file if it is to be used again. For extra details about saving files, refer to **Chapter 2, Creating Documents**, in this book. For an outline on saving a spreadsheet, refer to the sections below.

The Save command

The *Save* command in the **File** menu (Figure 9-29), saves a previously saved file again. The new version of the file overwrites the one already on disk. The shortcut for saving a file is Ctrl-S.

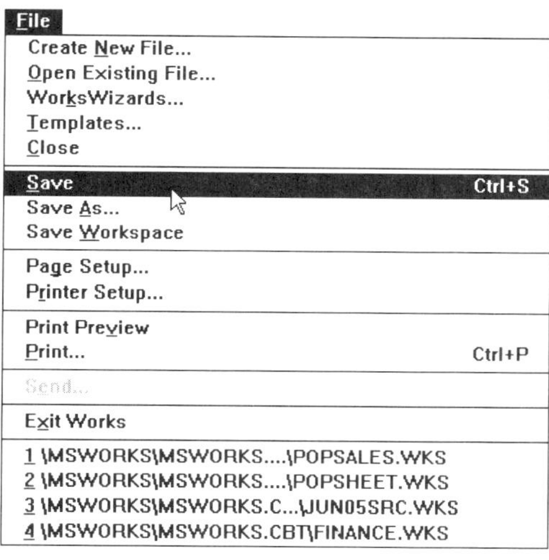

*Figure 9-29. The Save command in the **File** menu.*

The Save As command

The *Save As* command creates a new disk file for the document on the screen. When saved initially, the *Save As* dialog box appears as in Figure 9-30.

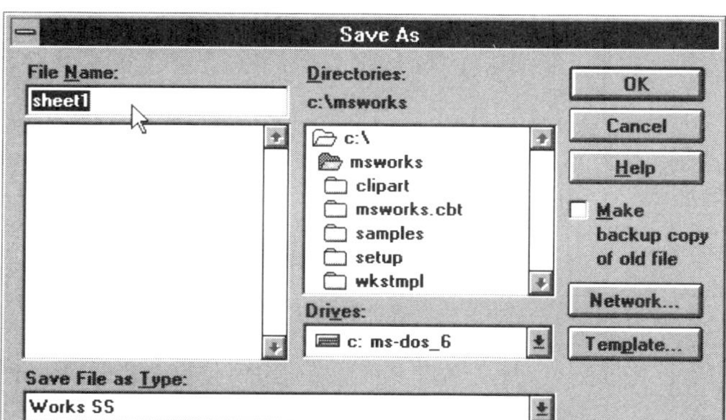

Figure 9-30. The Save As dialog box.

The name of the file is keyed into the *File Name* text box. It is not necessary to add the extension as this is added automatically when the file is saved. The file extension in the spreadsheet is ***.wks***.

Works knows that this is a spreadsheet file because of the *Save File as Type* text box in the *Save As* dialog box. The type of file, by default, in the spreadsheet tool is *Works SS* which can be seen in Figure 9-30.

Editing Spreadsheets

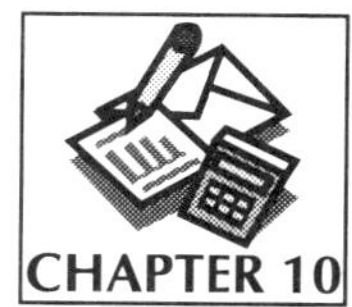

The basic data in a spreadsheet can be formatted in a number of ways to enhance its appearance and readability. Some of these formats are discussed in this chapter.

Throughout this chapter, we will be using the sample file ***popsales.wks*** to which we will apply the formats in the examples. Open this file, which is in the ***msworks.cbt*** subdirectory (Figure 10-1).

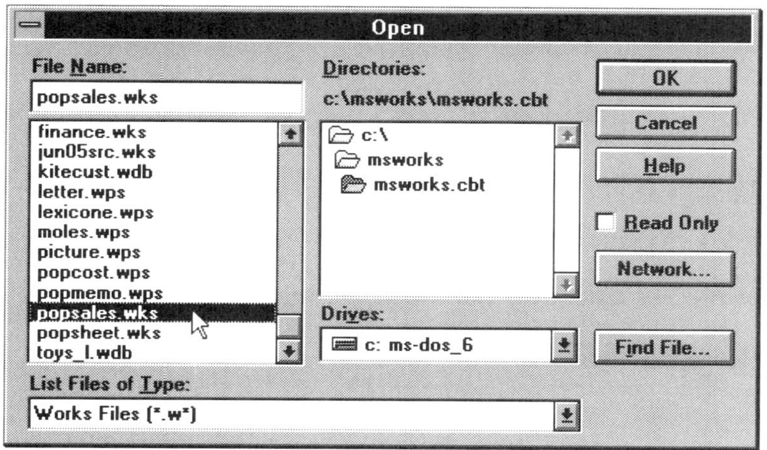

Figure 10-1. *Open the sample file* ***popsales.wks****.*

Selecting cells

To apply most of the formats outlined in this chapter, it is necessary to highlight the cells which are to be affected. There are a number of methods of highlighting text: using the cursor keys, using the mouse or through the **Edit** menu.

Using the cursor keys

To select a cell with the cursor keys, you simply move to the required cell. The pointer outlines that cell and it is then active, selected or highlighted. As Figure 10-2 depicts, cell A3 is selected, as the pointer outlines the cell, and the cell address is in the cell reference area.

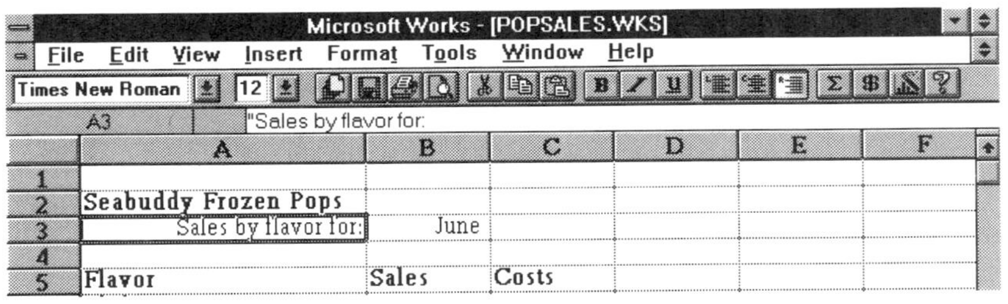

Figure 10-2. Cell A3 is selected by moving to it with the arrow keys.

A row in the spreadsheet is selected with the cursor keys by moving to the appropriate row and pressing Ctrl-F8. A column is selected in a similar way, except Shift-F8 is pressed. When a row or a column is selected in this way, the entire row or column is selected—to column IV or row 16,384, which Figure 10-3 shows.

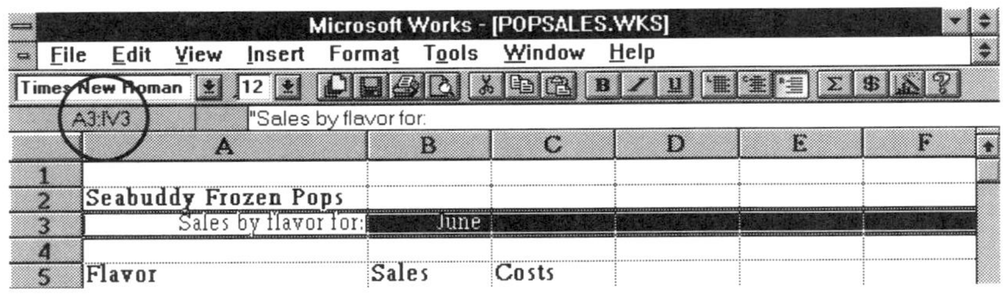

Figure 10-3. Row 3 is selected by pressing Ctrl-F8.

The pointer can be extended to highlight a group or block of cells. F8 is the extension key and when active, EXT appears in the status bar (Figure 10-4). Extending the cursor enables you to move around the screen with the arrow keys, highlighting all of the cells from the original cursor position. In Figure 10-4, the cells B6 to B12 are selected using the F8 key. This is done by moving to B6, pressing F8, and then moving the cursor using the arrow keys to B12. Press the Esc key if you want to make a new selection.

To highlight the entire spreadsheet using the keyboard, press Ctrl-Shift-F8. Test each of these selection methods by selecting combinations of cells in ***popsales.wks***.

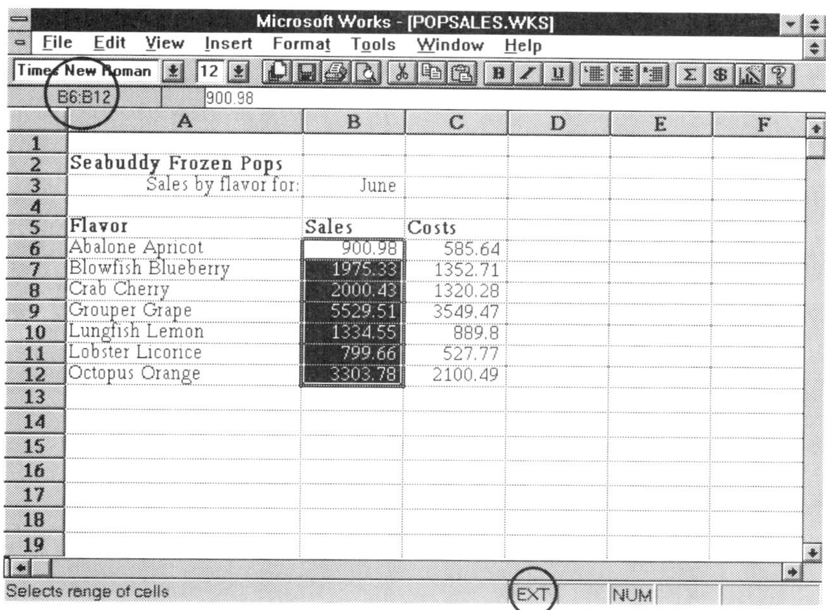

Figure 10-4. *B6 to B12 are selected by extending the cursor with the F8 key. EXT appears in the status bar and B6:B12 is in the cell reference area.*

Using the mouse

Selecting cells with the mouse requires clicking on specific parts of the screen. For example, to select a cell, click on the cell required with the mouse. A row of cells is selected by clicking on the number of the row in the frame around the spreadsheet (Figure 10-5).

In the same way, a column is selected by clicking on the letter of the column on the frame in the spreadsheet.

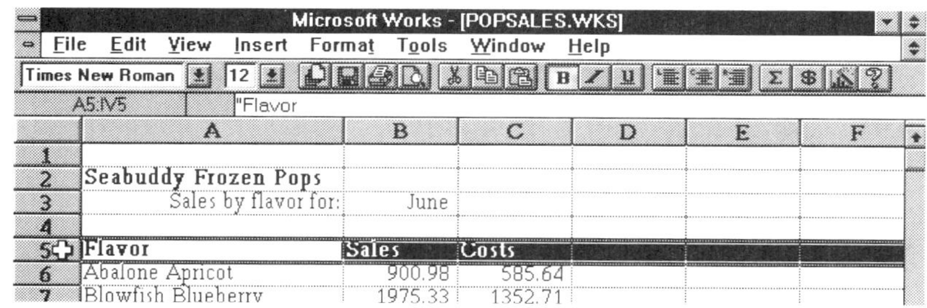

Figure 10-5. *Row 5 is highlighted by clicking on "5" in the frame.*

Cells B5 through C12 are highlighted in Figure 10-6. This is achieved, using the mouse, by first clicking on the upper left cell—B5—and dragging down to the lower right cell—C12.

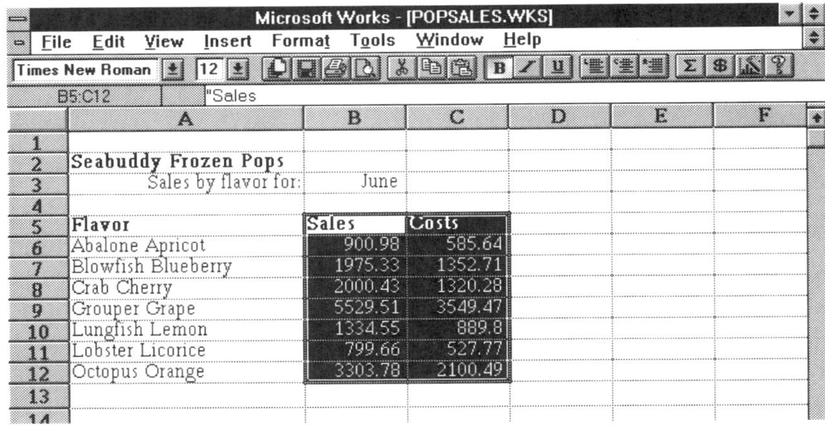

Figure 10-6. *Cells B5 through C12 are highlighted using the mouse.*

Selecting the entire spreadsheet using the mouse requires a click on the button at the top left corner of the spreadsheet frame, see Figure 10-7. Try using these methods of selecting cells in the sample file.

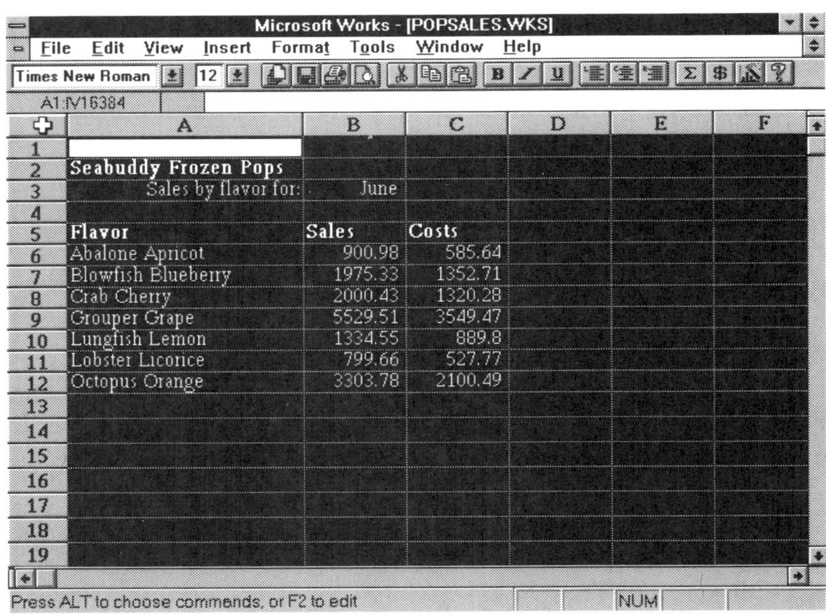

Figure 10-7. *The entire spreadsheet is selected by clicking on the button in the top left corner of the frame. (Note position of mouse cursor.)*

The following table summarizes the mouse and keyboard methods of selecting cells.

To Highlight	Mouse	Keyboard
A cell	Click on the cell	Press arrow key to cell
A row	Click on the row number	Ctrl-F8
A column	Click on column letter	Shift-F8
A block of cells	Drag pointer over cells	F8 to extend then use arrow keys to move to cells
The entire spreadsheet	Click on button in the top left corner of frame	Ctrl-Shift-F8

Using the Edit menu

Cells can be selected through the **Edit** menu in Figure 10-8.

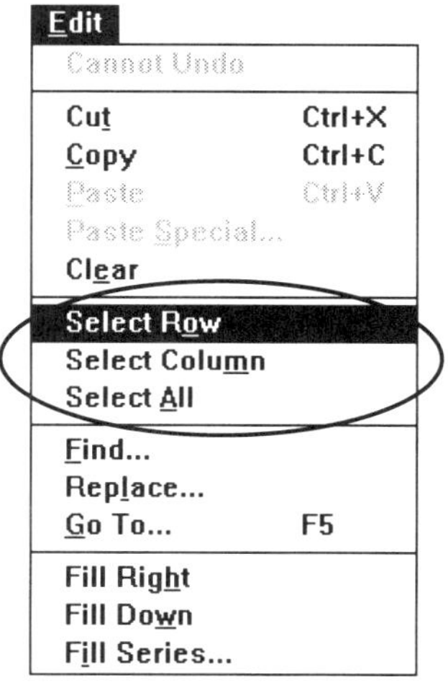

Figure 10-8. *The commands for selecting cells in the* ***Edit*** *menu.*

The row in which the pointer is located is selected when you click on *Select Row* in the **Edit** menu. Likewise, the column in which the pointer is situated is selected by choosing *Select Column*. Column D in ***popsales.wks*** is selected in Figure 10-9.

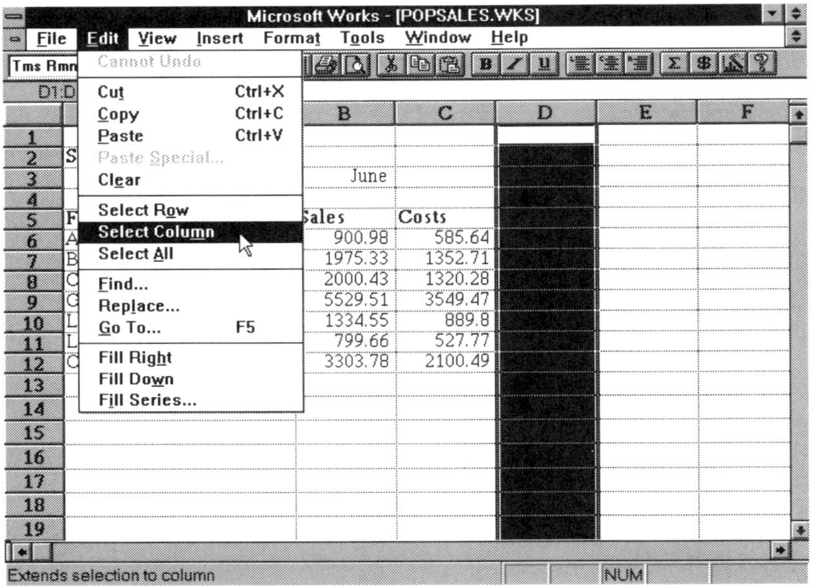

Figure 10-9. *Column D is selected through the* ***Edit*** *menu.*

Choosing *Select All* from the **Edit** menu (Figure 10-10) highlights every cell in the spreadsheet. Use the **Edit** menu to highlight some cells in the sample file.

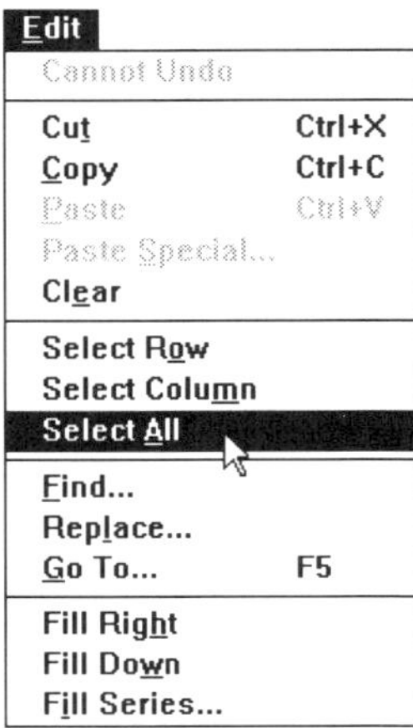

Figure 10-10. *Choosing Select All in the* ***Edit*** *menu highlights the 4,194,304 cells in the spreadsheet.*

Naming ranges of cells

A range of cells which is frequently referred to is often given a name. A range name is used with the *Go To* feature, in a formula or function, or in a chart. Range names are much easier to recall than cell references as they use words, such as "Income" or "Profit". There is no limit to the number of range names a spreadsheet can have.

Using this feature, give the cells B6 through B12 the range name "Sales". To do this, highlight the cell range using any of the selection methods outlined above. Choose *Range Name* from the **Insert** menu (Figure 10-11).

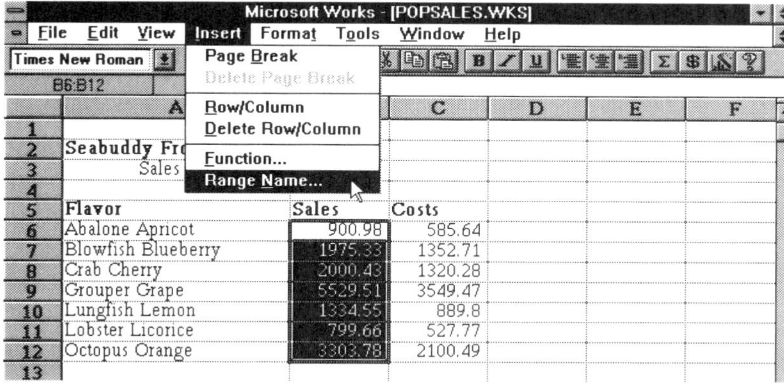

Figure 10-11. *The Range Name command in the **Insert** menu.*

The *Range Name* dialog box appears on the screen as in Figure 10-12. The text in cell B5—"Sales"—is suggested for the name of the range as it is in the cell immediately above the range of cells being named. This can be changed by typing in the new name in the *Name* text box. In this example, however, keep this name and click on *OK* to create the *Range Name*.

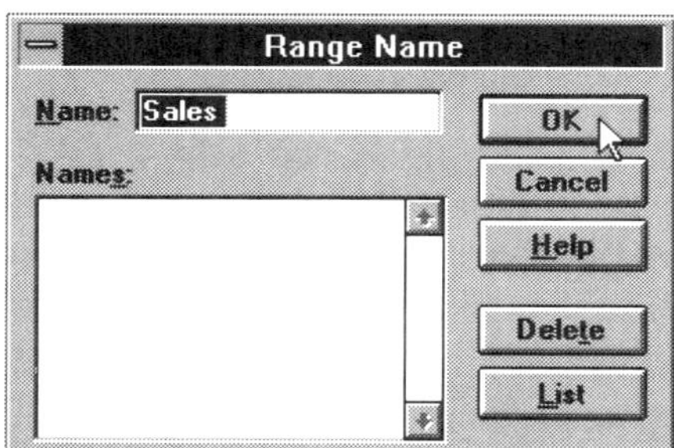

Figure 10-12. *The Range Name dialog box.*

The range name now becomes part of the spreadsheet. It appears in the *Names* list box in the *Range Name* dialog box displaying the name of the range as well as the cells it represents (Figure 10-13).

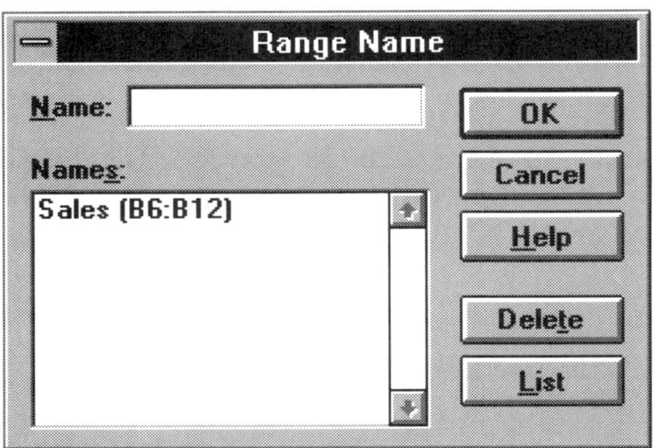

Figure 10-13. *The Range Name dialog box with the recently created range name – Sales.*

To quickly highlight a range which has been given a name, use the *Go To* key which is F5. This displays the *Go To* dialog box on the screen with the list of range names in the *Names* list box. Double-clicking on the range name to be highlighted (Figure 10-14), highlights the cells in the spreadsheet.

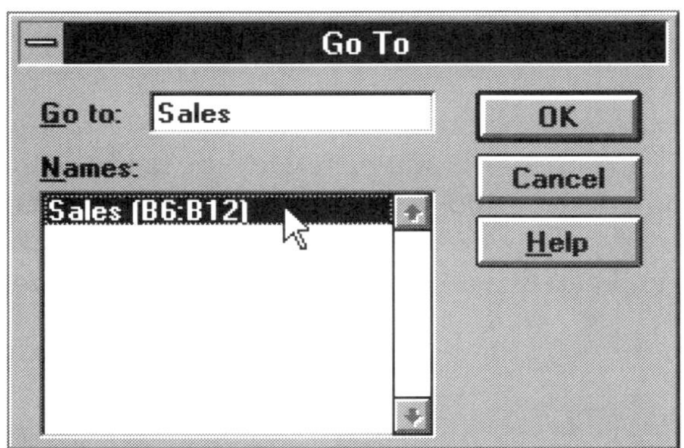

Figure 10-14. *Double-click on Sales or click once on Sales, and then on OK, to highlight the range of cells.*

Range names are used also in formulas and functions. For example, to add the sales figures putting the result in cell B13, move to B13, and click on the *Autosum* button. The function appears in the formula bar using the range name rather than the cell references, which Figure 10-15 illustrates. Press Enter to input the function into cell B13.

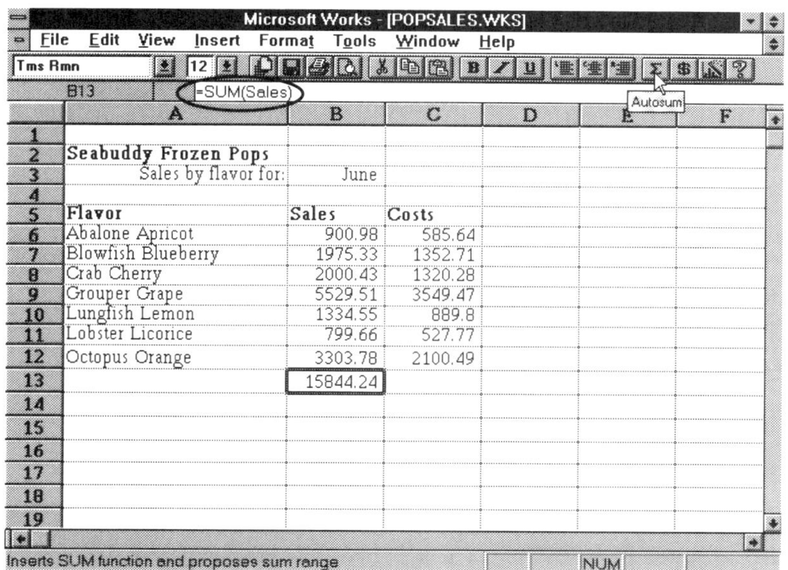

Figure 10-15. The SUM function uses the range name as the cell reference.

Changing cell contents and appearance

Cell entries can be edited, deleted and/or new values entered. Cells may be formatted with different numeric styles and also have text attributes changed. Column widths can also be altered in a number of ways.

Cell content editing

One method of changing or editing cell entries is to retype the text, value or formula and press Enter. This replaces the old entry with the new.

This is not the most time efficient way of editing, however, as often only one or two characters need changing. To change just a few characters, you need to access the cell contents in the formula bar. The text cursor is reinserted into the formula bar using the mouse or the F2 key. While in "Edit Mode," EDIT appears on the status bar.

EDITING WITH F2

For this example, you can change "June" in cell B3 to "July;" click in B3 now to do this. As only the last two characters in "June" need changing, use the F2 key to edit the cell, rather than retyping the cell completely. Press F2 now and the text cursor jumps to the formula bar (Figure 10-16).

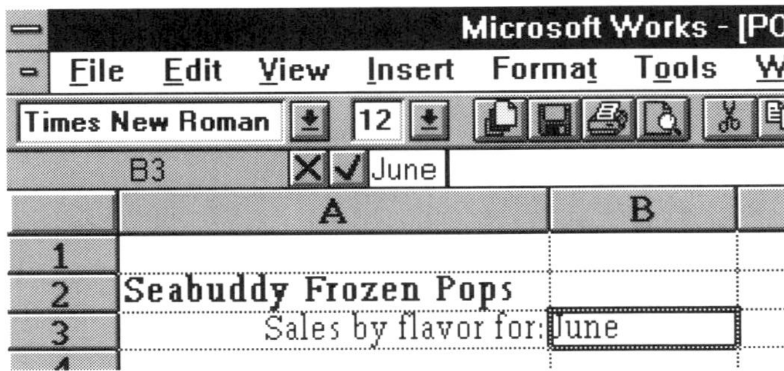

Figure 10-16. *The text cursor is in the formula bar as F2 has been pressed.*

Once in the formula bar, the cursor can be moved using the arrow keys or Home — to move to the beginning of the entry, or End — to move to the end. The Backspace and Del keys are used to remove characters from the formula bar.

The Del key removes a character to the right of the text cursor and the Backspace key removes characters to the left.

The text cursor is currently sitting at the end of the word. Press Backspace until only "Ju" remains, as in Figure 10-17. You can now key in "ly" to complete the word "July."

Figure 10-17. *Remove the end of the entry using the Backspace key.*

Editing the cell using the keyboard is completed using the Enter key. If you wanted to return to the original cell entry—June—the Esc key would bring it back into the formula bar (but only before you press Enter). Press Enter to insert "July" into B3.

Editing with the mouse

The mouse cursor becomes an I-beam when positioned over the formula bar. Clicking the I-beam at this position inserts the text cursor in the formula bar, allowing you to edit the cell. Do this now to edit B3 again.

The text cursor is moved by clicking it in another position on the formula bar when using the mouse. Text is removed by using the Backspace key or by swiping it with the mouse and typing in the new text. Try using this method to change "July" back to "June." Highlight "ly" as in Figure 10-18 and key in "ne."

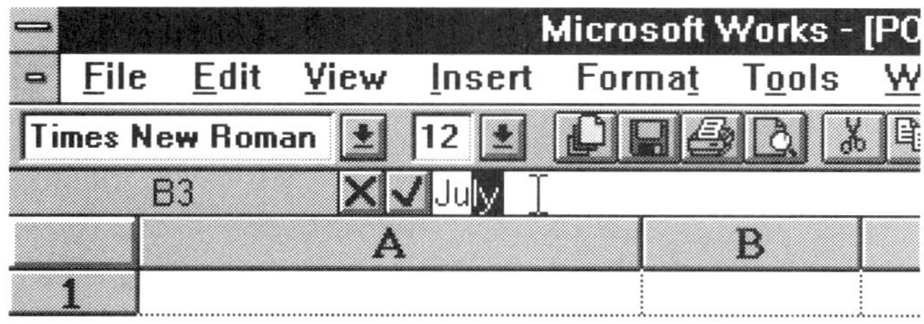

Figure 10-18. *The I-beam over the formula bar.*

The *Enter* button (check mark) next to the formula bar can be used to input the data into the spreadsheet. Click on this now (Figure 10-19). To cancel this entry and return to "July," you would click on the *Cancel* button (cross) instead of the *Enter* button.

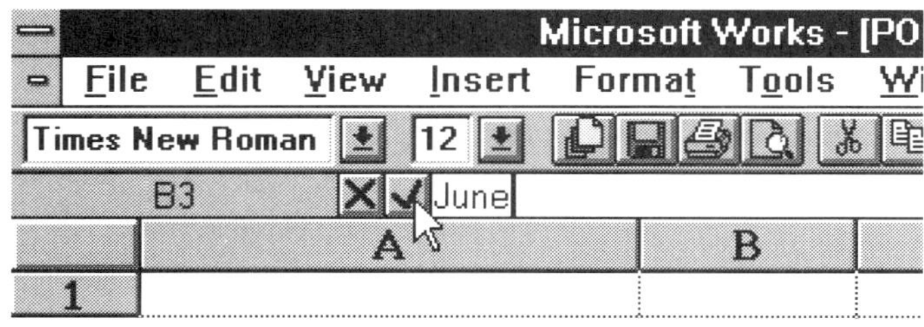

Figure 10-19. *Click on the Enter button to insert June into cell B3.*

Deleting a cell

You can delete your current cell selection, whether a single cell or a range of cells, by pressing the Del key. Alternatively, you can choose *Clear* from the **Edit** menu.

Formatting selected cells

Cells may be formatted with different numeric types. This is useful depending upon the type and size of numbers being used.

Numeric formats

There are twelve formats which can be applied to values in Works. Each of these is available through the **Format** menu as in Figure 10-20, and are described on the following pages.

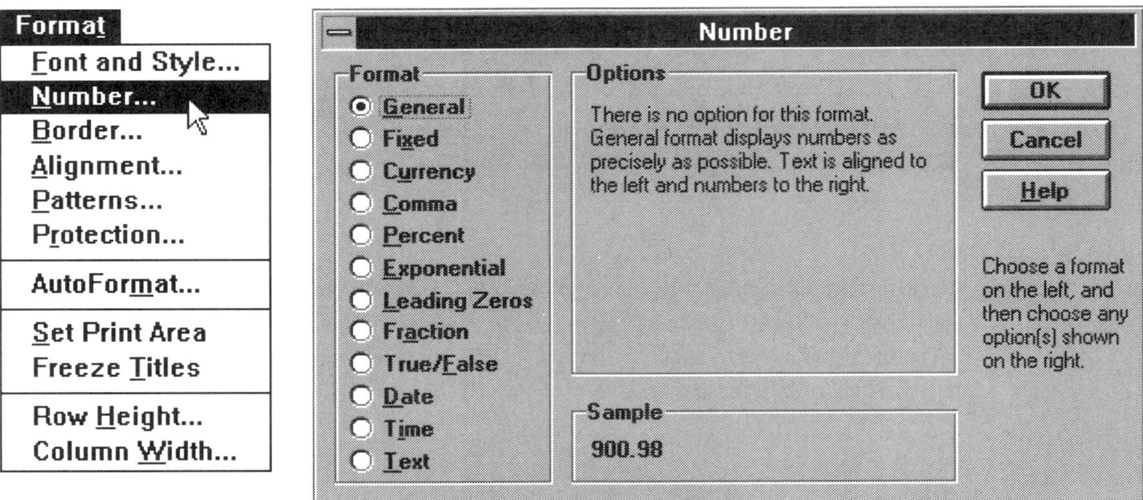

*Figure 10-20. The Number formats available through the **Format** menu.*

General format (Figure 10-21) is the default format which each value is initially given as it is entered. The value is not rounded, but uses the number of decimal places originally inserted. Negative numbers use a minus sign (-) prefix and numbers which are too long use exponential or scientific notation.

Figure 10-21. *General format.*

A *Fixed* format (Figure 10-22) is allocated a specific number of decimal places and rounds any digits past this point.

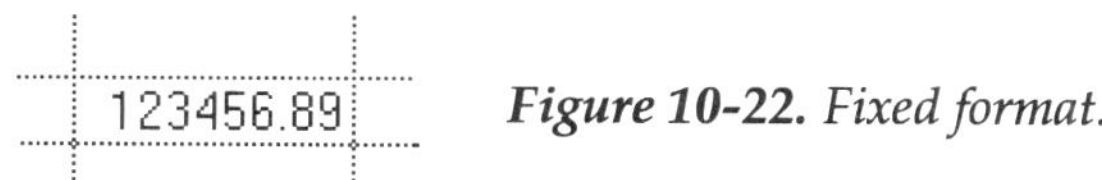

Figure 10-22. *Fixed format.*

Currency format (Figure 10-23) adds a dollar sign prefix to the number. A comma is used to separate thousands, and the desired number of decimal places can be specified. You can also apply this format by clicking on the Toolbar button shown here.

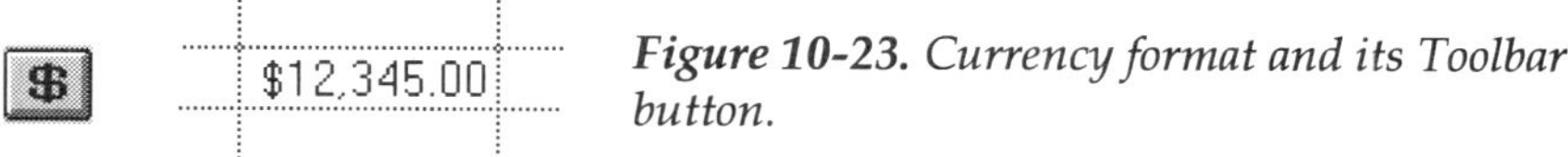

Figure 10-23. *Currency format and its Toolbar button.*

Comma format (Figure 10-24) is identical to *Currency* format, but does not add a dollar sign prefix to the number. A comma is used to separate thousands.

Figure 10-24. *Comma format.*

The *Percent* format (Figure 10-25) adds a percent sign to the end of a number. The desired number of decimal places can be specified using this format.

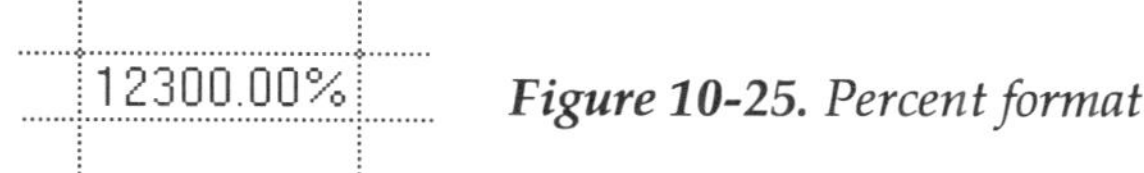

Figure 10-25. *Percent format.*

Using the *Exponential* format (Figure 10-26) converts the value to exponential or scientific notation. This is used particularly when dealing with very large or very small numbers.

Figure 10-26. *Exponential format.*

The *Leading Zeros* format (Figure 10-27) enables you to specify a specific length of digits which your value must have. Zeros are added before any unfilled digits.

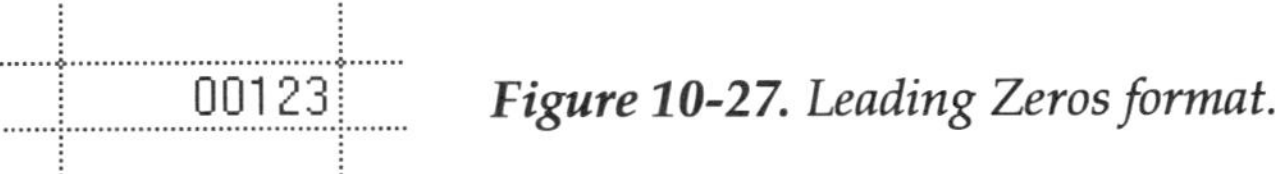

Figure 10-27. *Leading Zeros format.*

The *Fraction* format lets you display a number with a fractional part rather than with a decimal point.

Figure 10-28. *Fraction format.*

True/False (Figure 10-29) is a logical format which displays non-zero numbers as "TRUE" and zero numbers as "FALSE."

Figure 10-29. *True/False format.*

The *Date* and *Time* formats (Figure 10-30) allow you to format dates and times into various styles, such as "month, year" or "hour:minute".

Figure 10-30. *Date and Time formats.*

Text format is useful for treating entries consisting of digits, such as product codes or postal codes, as if they were non-numeric.

In the sample file, ***popsales.wks***, click on cell B13, which contains the total you inserted previously. As this is an important figure, make it stand out by applying a currency format to it. Currency is the numeric format available on the toolbar, so click on the *Currency* button as in Figure 10-31.

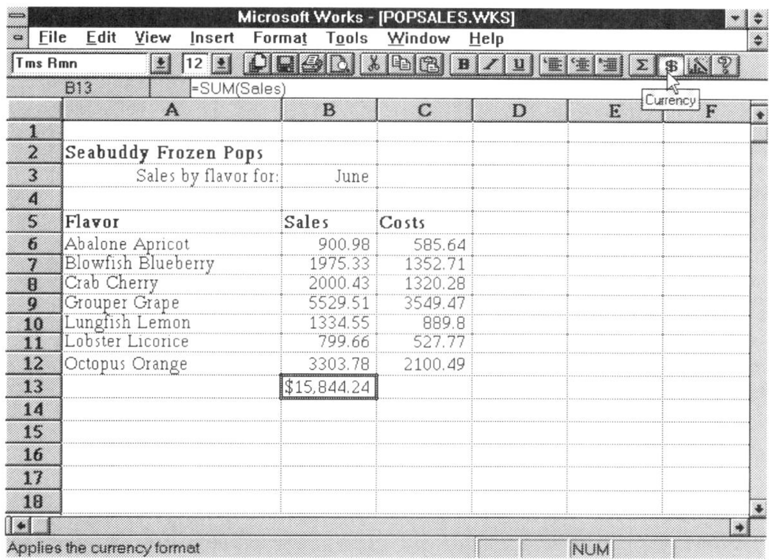

Figure 10-31. *The format of cell B13 is changed by clicking on the Currency button in the Toolbar.*

To change cells C6 to C12 to a *Fixed* format with no decimal places, they must be highlighted. Highlight these cells using one of the highlighting techniques outlined in this chapter. *Fixed* format can be applied through the **Format** menu only. Select *Number* from the **Format** menu and then choose *Fixed* (Figure 10-32).

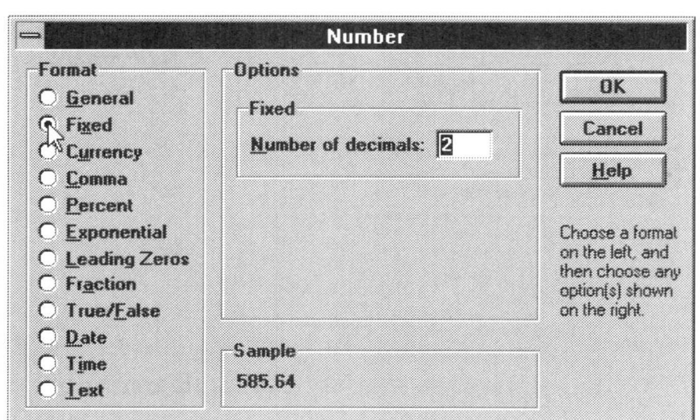

Figure 10-32. *Choose the Fixed number format.*

The number of decimals is currently two which is the default. Type "0" into the *Number of decimals* text box and press Enter to change the format of this block.

Cell B3 was changed to a date format when the spreadsheet was created originally. Click on this cell and choose *Number* from the **Format** menu. The *Date* option has been selected for that cell. The *Number* dialog box displays as in Figure 10-33.

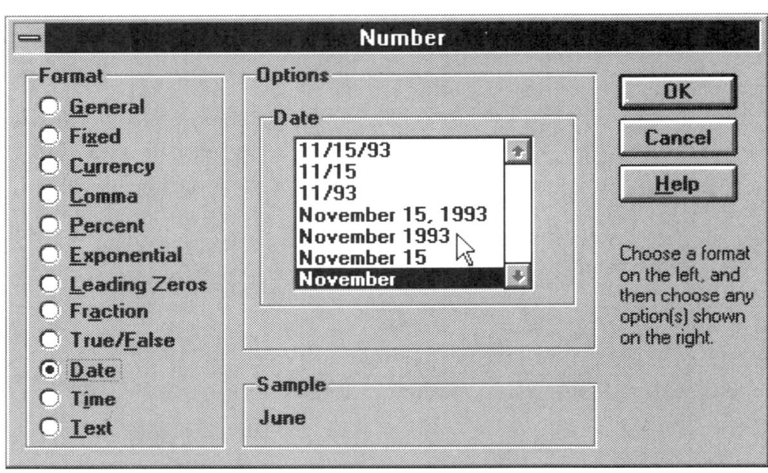

Figure 10-33. *The Date option.*

Click on *November 1993* and then on *OK*. The screen displays cell B3 as in Figure 10-34.

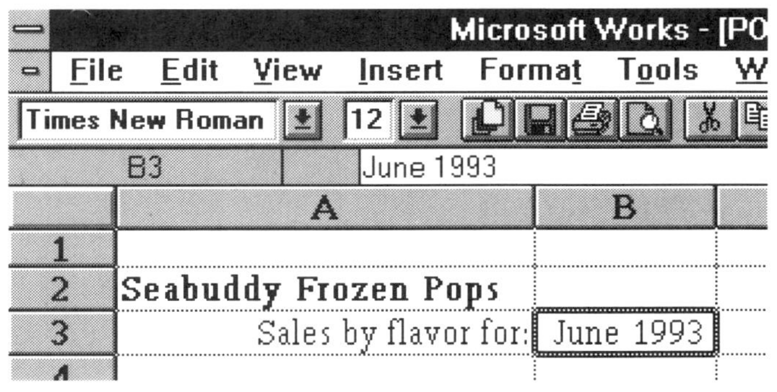

Figure 10-34. *The Date format is changed to Month, year.*

Changing text attributes

It is possible to change the font, size, style and alignment of text in a spreadsheet.

Selecting text fonts

You can change the font through the *Font* command in the **Format** menu or the *Font* submenu on the toolbar (Figure 10-35).

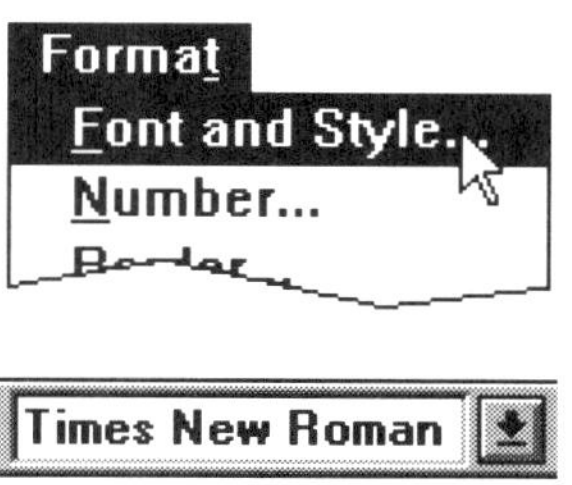

Figure 10-35. *The Font and Style command in the* ***Format*** *menu or the Font submenu on the toolbar can be used to change font type.*

Change the font of cell B3 to Helvetica by selecting that cell and then choosing *Helvetica* from the *Font* submenu on the toolbar.

Selecting font sizes

In this example, change the font size of cell B3 to Helvetica 8 point through the *Font and Style* command in the **Format** menu. Selecting the *Font and Style* command displays the *Font and Style* dialog box on the screen as shown in Figure 10-36. Click on 8 and then on *OK* to change the font size.

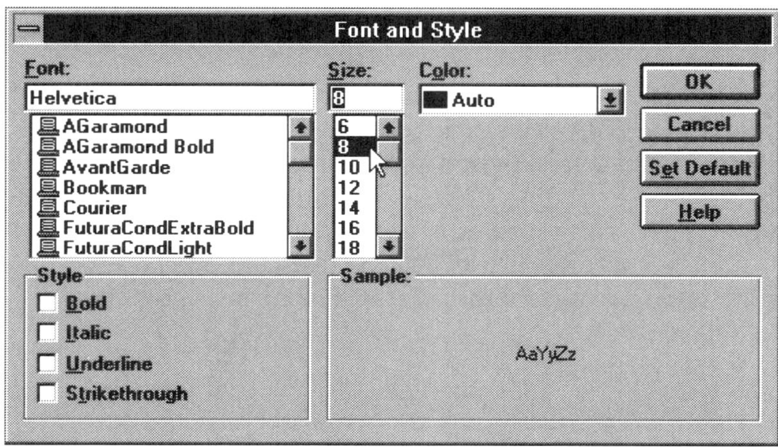

Figure 10-36. *Click on 8 in the Size drop-down list in the Font and Style dialog box.*

SELECTING TEXT STYLES

Styles can be applied to cells of your choice. Cell A2, for example, is bold. Move to this cell. The *Bold* button on the toolbar is depressed. A style can be added to a cell through the *Font and Style* command in the **Format** menu or using the tools on the toolbar.

Choose this command to bring the *Font and Style* dialog box onto the screen. Currently, as A2 is bold, the *Bold* check box is selected. To add another style, such as italic, click on the *Italic* check box and click on *OK*. Figure 10-37 displays this.

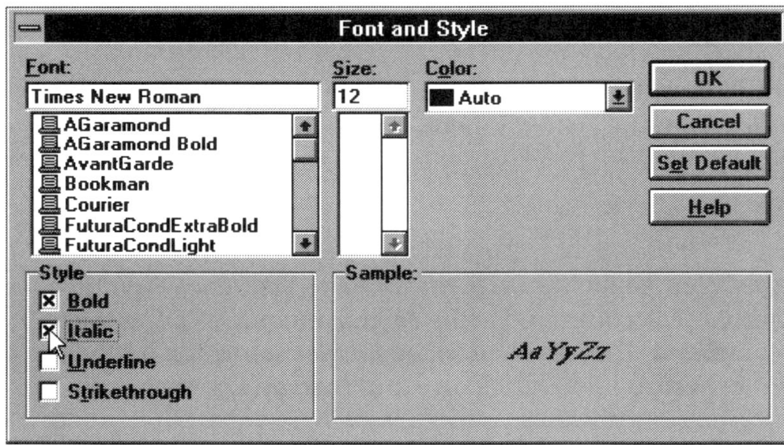

Figure 10-37. *Click on Italic in the Font and Style dialog box.*

SELECTING ALIGNMENT

There are six types of horizontal alignment a cell entry can have: *General*, *Left*, *Right*, *Center*, *Fill*, or *Center across selection*. By default, text which is inserted into a cell is left aligned and value and formula cells are aligned to the right — this is known as *General* alignment. Use *Fill* to occupy one or more cells with repeated characters. This is useful for creating effects such as lines of asterisks (*). You can use *Center across selection* to center an entry across several cells rather than just across the cell it occupies.

Horizontal alignment is changed either by clicking on the *Alignment* buttons on the toolbar, or through the *Alignment* dialog box (Figure 10-38). Change the alignment of cell A3 to *Center* using the *Alignment* dialog box as shown in Figure 10-38.

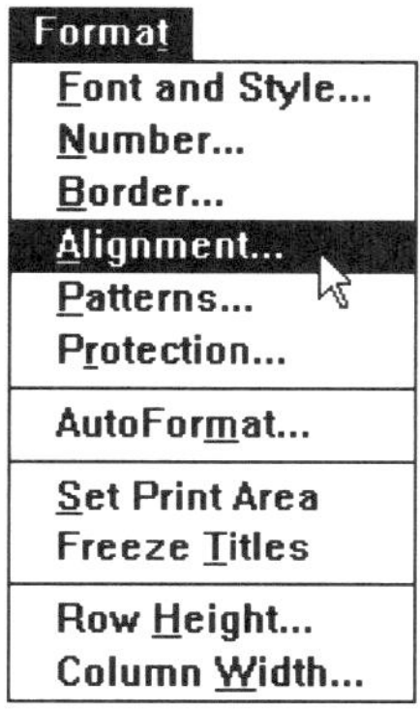

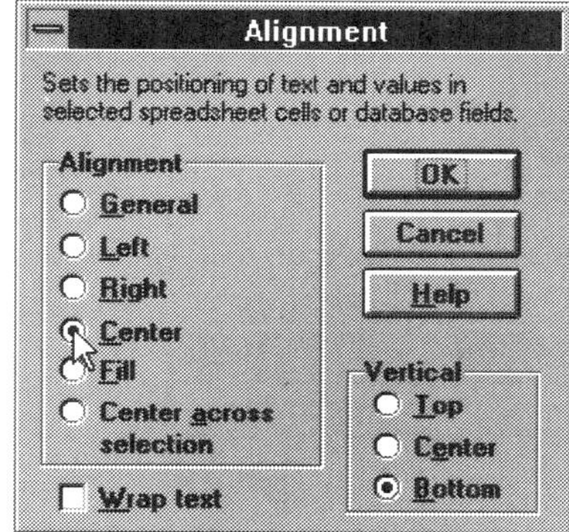

Figure 10-38. *Change cell A3 to Center alignment using this dialog box.*

You can choose a *Vertical* alignment for your cell selection where the row height exceeds the height of your cell entries. Finally, the *Wrap text* check box lets you have text entries automatically increase the height of their row and wrap within their cells rather than overlap neighboring cells (Figure 10-39).

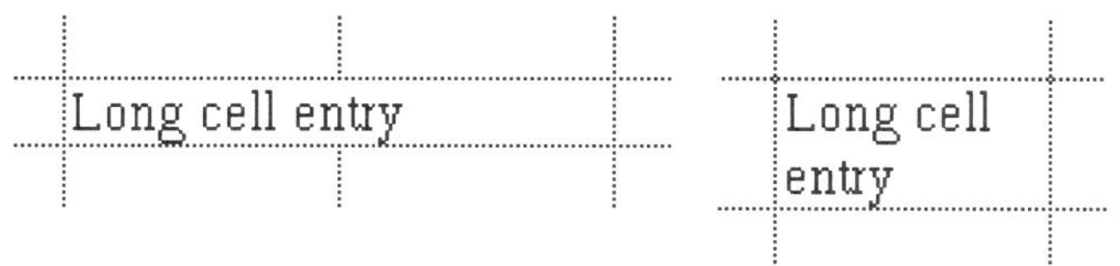

Figure 10-39. *A long text entry and the same entry formatted using the Wrap text check box.*

Changing column width or row height

You can change the width of columns and height of rows to suit your needs. The default column width in Works is 10 characters.

Using commands

The width of selected columns can be changed through the *Column Width* command in the **Format** menu. You can change the height of selected rows also, using the *Row Height* command (Figure 10-40).

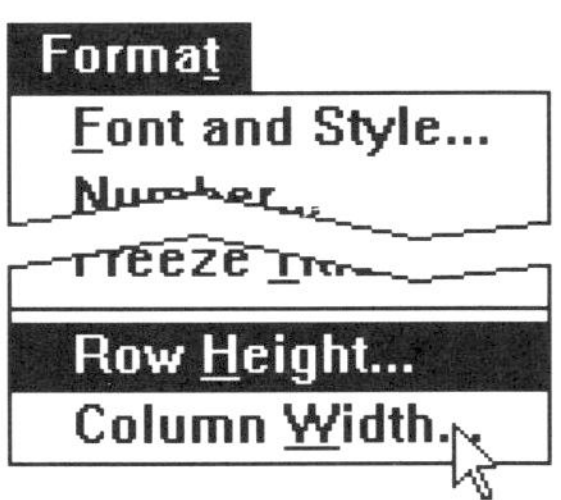

Figure 10-40. *The Row Height and Column Width commands in the* ***Format*** *menu.*

Select the rows or columns whose height or width you want to change before choosing the related command. To change the width of column A in ***popsales.wks*** click in column A and select *Column Width* from the **Format** menu. The *Column Width* dialog box appears on the screen as Figure 10-41 displays.

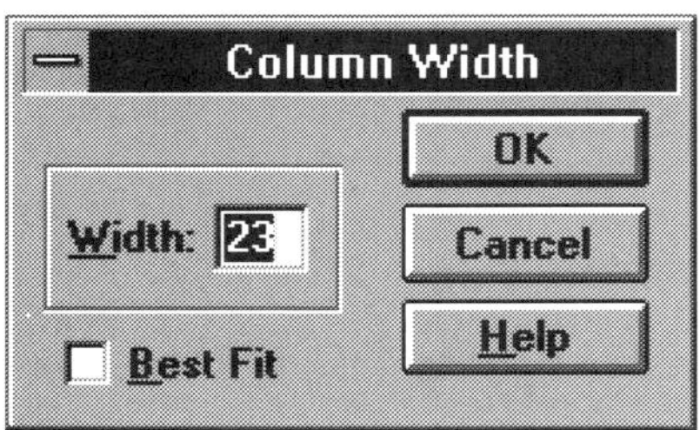

Figure 10-41. *The Column Width dialog box showing that the width of column A in* ***popsales.wks*** *is 23.*

The *Column Width* dialog box informs you of the current width of the selected column through the *Width* text box. Column A in this spreadsheet had previously been set to 23. Type in 30 and click on *OK* to make the column 30 characters wide. The spreadsheet now looks like Figure 10-42.

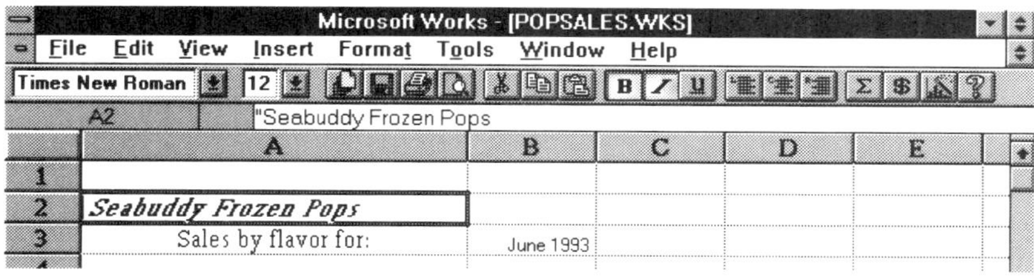

Figure 10-42. *Column A is now 30 characters wide.*

To change the width of each row you selected to fit its widest entry click on the *Best Fit* check box in the *Column Width* dialog box. You can apply this option to row heights also, through the *Row Height* dialog box.

Using the mouse

Individual column widths or row heights can be changed using the mouse. The mouse pointer alters when it is moved near the column or row separators on the frame (Figure 10-43).

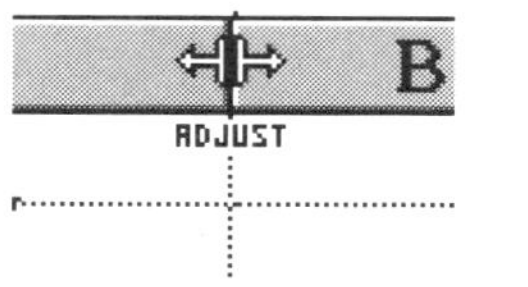

Figure 10-43. *The mouse pointer changes to adjust column widths or row heights.*

Dragging this pointer along the frame changes the width of the column to the left of the pointer or the height of the row above the pointer.

You can double-click on a column label in the frame to change the width of that column to fit its widest entry. Similarly, you can double-click on a row label to make the height of that row fit its tallest entry.

Inserting columns and rows

The layout of a spreadsheet often changes as it is created, requiring rows and columns to be inserted for new information. Select the column label to the right of where you want to insert a new column or the row label below where you want to insert a new row. You can insert multiple rows or columns by highlighting the number of columns or rows you want to insert.

Inserting a column or row is done through the *Row/Column* command in the **Insert** menu (Figure 10-44).

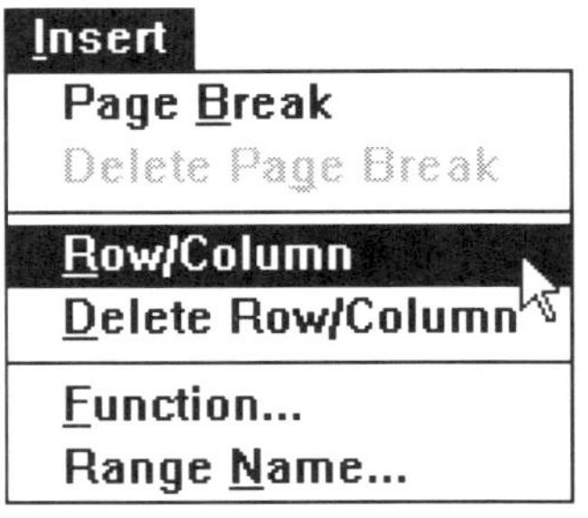

***Figure 10-44.** The Row/Column command in the **Insert** menu.*

Select row 3 by clicking on *3* in the worksheet frame and choose the *Row/Column* command in the **Insert** menu, to insert a new row above it. Figure 10-45 shows the result.

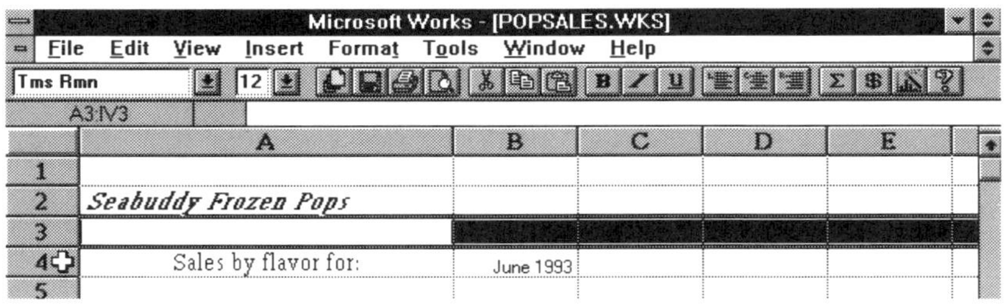

***Figure 10-45.** The newly-inserted row 3.*

Deleting columns and rows

Columns and rows are deleted using the *Delete Row/Column* command in the **Insert** menu. The position of the pointer determines which part of the spreadsheet is deleted. A number of columns or rows are deleted by highlighting the appropriate rows or columns before selecting the *Delete Row/Column* command.

Caution should be taken when deleting, as the entire column or row is deleted. No warning is given if cells contain data in the row or column being deleted.

Delete row 3 which you just inserted. You can do this by ensuring that the row is highlighted and selecting the *Delete Row/Column* command from the **Insert** menu (Figure 10-46).

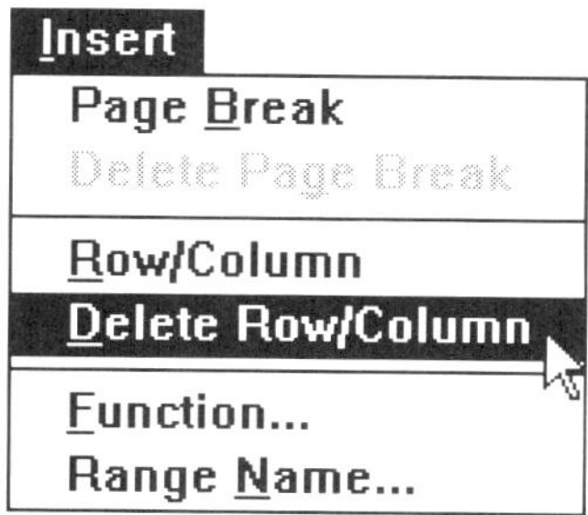

Figure 10-46. *Choose Delete Row/ Column to delete the selected row.*

Moving, Copying, and Addressing Cells

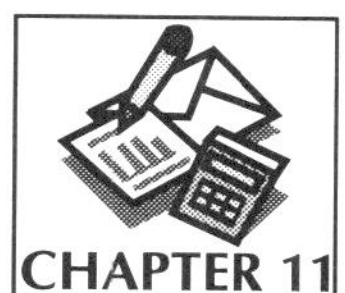

This chapter looks at various features within Works which enable you to use information which has already been inserted into cells. Cells are moved and copied to rearrange the layout and expand the spreadsheet without unnecessary typing. Cell addressing in formulas gives you added flexibility. The *Fill* commands eliminate the need to input a series of data.

The sample file ***popsales.wks*** (Figure 11-1) in the ***msworks.cbt*** directory is referred to in the examples within this chapter. Close any open copy of this file without saving changes and open a fresh copy to work on.

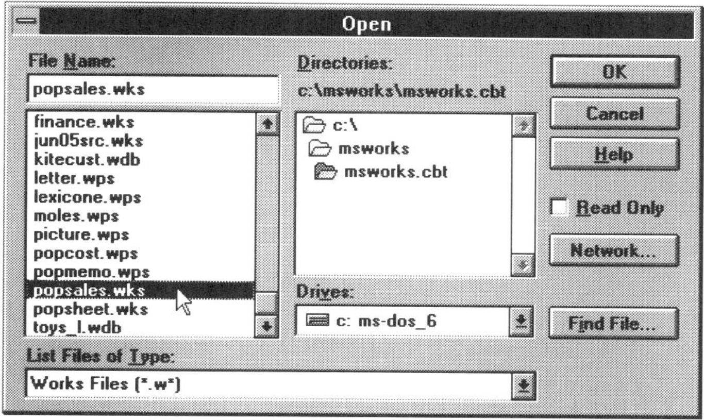

Figure 11-1. *Open the sample file* ***popsales.wks****.*

Moving cell contents

The contents of selected cells can be moved to another part of the spreadsheet by dragging the edge of your selection elsewhere. Text, values, and formulas are all moved in the same way. By moving cell contents, the layout of your spreadsheet is altered without the need to retype existing data.

In the sample file the heading "Seabuddy Frozen Pops" is in cell A2. As an example, we will move the contents of this cell into cell A1.

Click on cell A2 and move the mouse pointer onto the edge of the cell so that the pointer displays the word "DRAG" as shown in Figure 11-2.

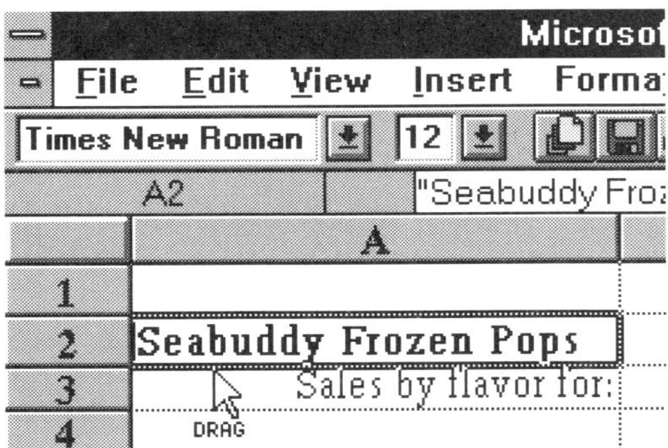

Figure 11-2. Click on cell A2 and move the mouse pointer onto the edge of the cell.

Hold down the mouse button and move the tip of the mouse pointer into cell A1. When you release the mouse button, Works moves the data you selected into cell A1 (Figure 11-3).

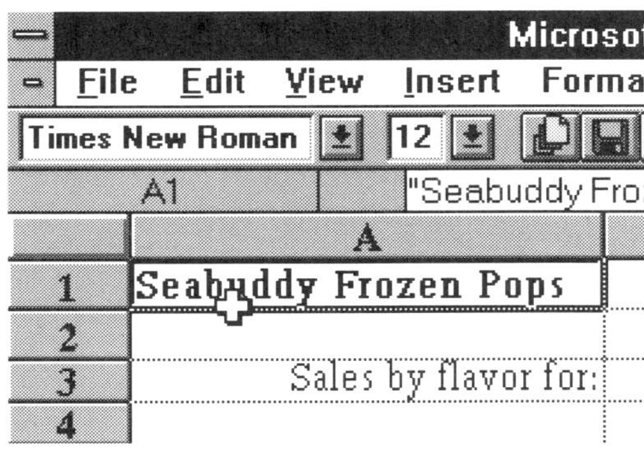

Figure 11-3. Drag the mouse pointer into cell A1 and release the mouse button.

Moving a value can be as simple as moving text in a spreadsheet. However, problems may arise if you move a value from a cell at one end of a range. To demonstrate this click on cell C13 and then on the *Autosum* button in the toolbar (Figure 11-4). Works creates the formula =SUM(C6:C12) shown in the formula bar. Press Enter to accept the formula.

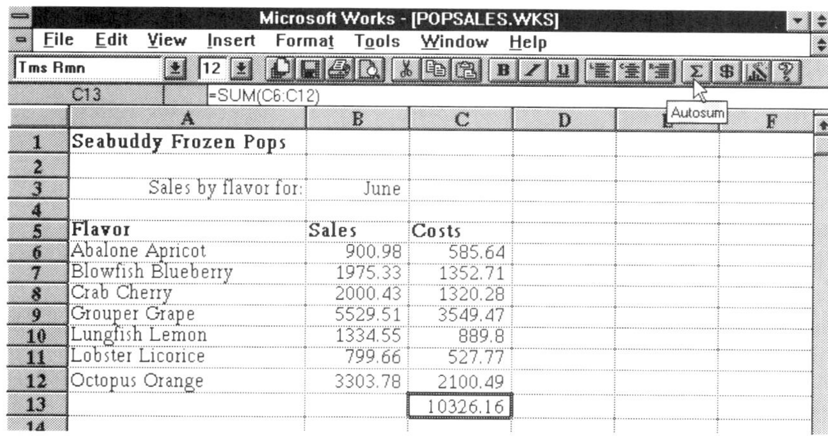

***Figure 11-4.** Click on cell C13, then click on the Autosum button and press Enter.*

Now move the contents of cell C6. This cell begins the range C6:C12 in your formula. Drag the contents of C6 to C15 and click on cell C13 to see the effect on your formula (Figure 11-5). The range in your formula now includes the cell in which you stored the formula itself. This is because you moved one of the ends or "anchor points" of the range so that the formula now lies in a cell within the range. The previous result of the formula is added into the SUM every time Works recalculates the spreadsheet.

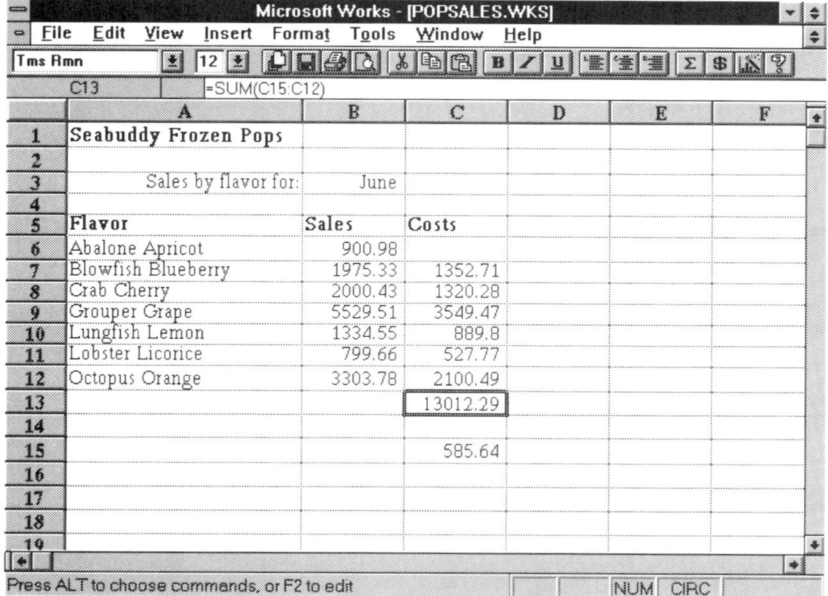

***Figure 11-5.** Including your formula within the range referred to in the formula causes CIRC to appear in the status bar.*

The value you moved remains the same, but there is now a fundamental error in the spreadsheet. The total in cell C13 has increased and continues to increase with each spreadsheet recalculation (press F9). The status bar warns of this error—called a circular reference—with the CIRC indicator shown in Figure 11-5.

The problems arising from a circular reference are evident. It is important to be careful when moving values and even more important to stop and find the circular reference immediately. To remove the circular reference, move the contents of cell C15 back to C6.

A formula is also moved in Works in the same way as text and values. The formula does not change in relation to its new position in the spreadsheet, but remains the same as it was in its original cell address (Figure 11-6).

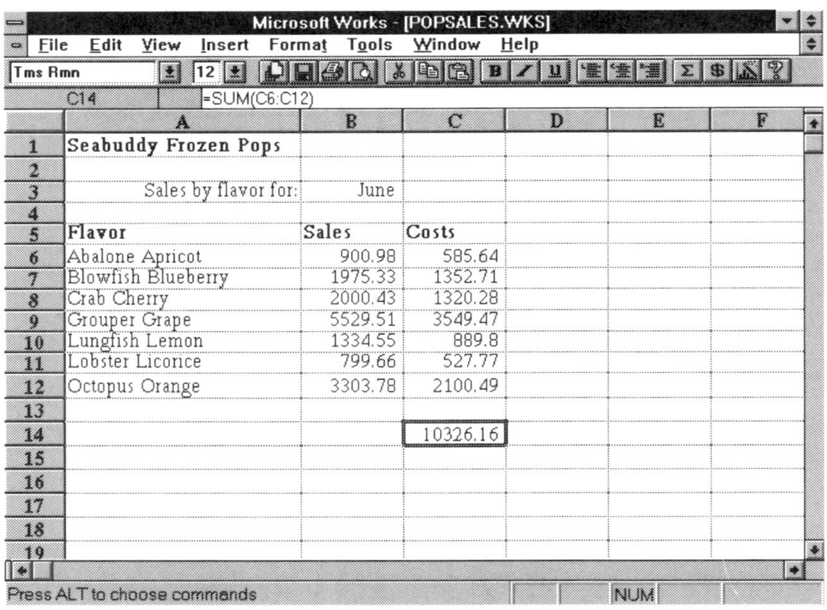

Figure 11-6. C13 is moved to C15, but the formula remains the same.

Copying cell contents

Cell contents are copied with the *Copy* command in the **Edit** menu or using the *Copy* button illustrated in Figure 11-7.

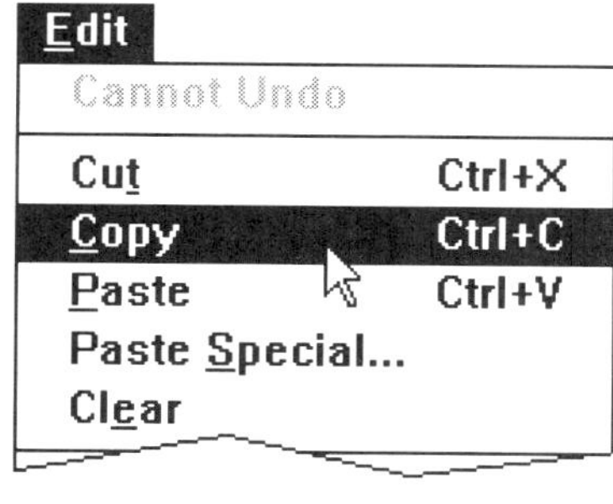

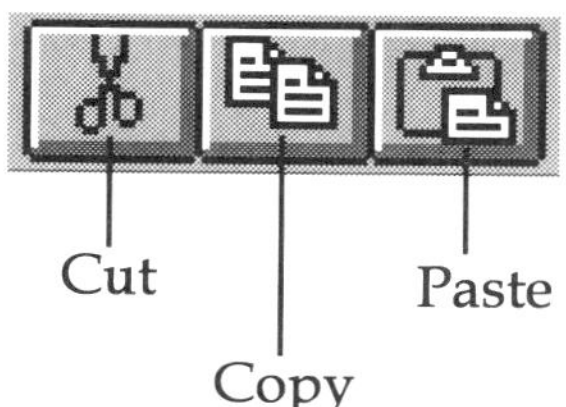

Figure 11-7. *The Copy command and related toolbar buttons.*

Text, values, and formulas are reinserted into the spreadsheet through the *Paste* command. Copy the formula in cell C14 into B14. The first step is to move into C14 and select *Copy* from the **Edit** menu. The contents of C14 remain on the screen, but are copied onto the clipboard.

Now move to the new location—B14—and choose *Paste* from the **Edit** menu. Figure 11-8 shows that the formula now appears in both B14 and C14 as it has been copied.

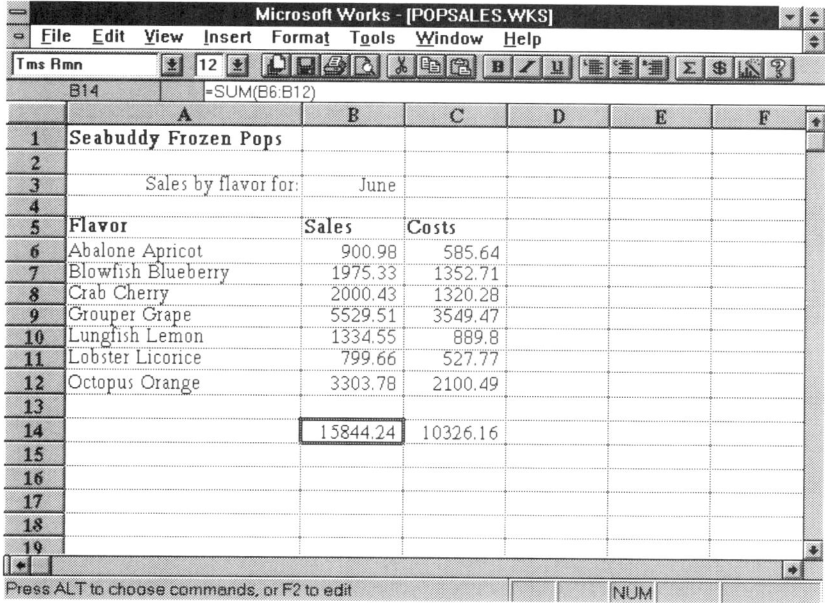

	A	B	C	D	E	F
1	Seabuddy Frozen Pops					
2						
3	Sales by flavor for:	June				
4						
5	Flavor	Sales	Costs			
6	Abalone Apricot	900.98	585.64			
7	Blowfish Blueberry	1975.33	1352.71			
8	Crab Cherry	2000.43	1320.28			
9	Grouper Grape	5529.51	3549.47			
10	Lungfish Lemon	1334.55	889.8			
11	Lobster Licorice	799.66	527.77			
12	Octopus Orange	3303.78	2100.49			
13						
14		15844.24	10326.16			
15						
16						
17						
18						
19						

Figure 11-8. *Paste the copied formula into cell B14.*

You copy text or values in Works in exactly the same way. Copying does not affect formulas in the same way as moving a value can.

Copying formulas in a spreadsheet can be a very powerful and time efficient tool. The formula need be inserted once only and then copied into the appropriate cells. The reason for this is that Works copies cells relatively, which is discussed in detail in the next section.

Works enables you to paste an object a number of times as the contents of the clipboard remain until something new is cut or copied.

The following table outlines the shortcuts for cutting, copying, and pasting.

Cut	Copy	Paste
Ctrl-X	Ctrl-C	Ctrl-V
Shift-Del	Ctrl-Ins	Shift-Ins

Cell addressing in formulas

There are two types of cell references in a formula: relative and absolute. The type of reference used depends on the requirements of your spreadsheet.

Relative addressing

A relative cell address is most commonly used in the Works spreadsheet. It is also the default. A relative cell address is concerned with the position of the cell in relation to the location of the formula.

As an example, insert the formula "=B6-C6" into cell D6. Figure 11-9 shows the result.

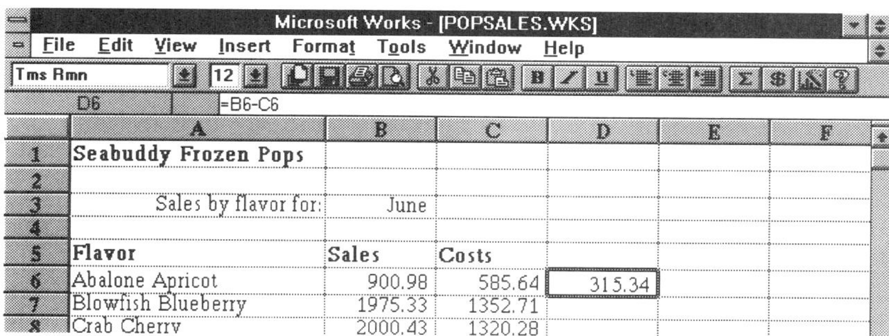

Figure 11-9. Insert this formula into cell D6.

This formula essentially says "find the difference in value between the two cells on the left." If this was copied to any other cell in the spreadsheet it would always "find the difference in value between the two cells on the left," as it is relative. To test this, copy the formula in D6 to D7 so the screen looks like Figure 11-10.

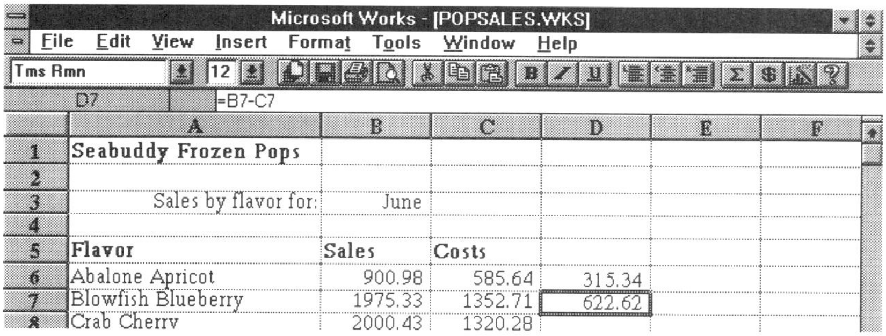

Figure 11-10. Copy and paste your formula into cell D7.

As you can see in Figure 11-10, the function in D7 still "finds the difference in value between the two cells on the left," displaying a different result, but the same relative formula. Copy the formula into cells D8 through D12. These formulas also find the difference in value between the two cells to the left of where the formula is placed. Type the text "Profit" into cell D5 and click on the *Bold* toolbar button to complete column D.

Absolute addressing

A relative address in a formula is not always appropriate—an absolute reference may be required. An absolute cell address refers back to the same cell, regardless of its position and the position of the formula on the spreadsheet. A cell address is made absolute when it is referred to by formulas in a number of other cells. The commission rate for a group of sales managers, for example, could be used as an absolute cell reference.

An absolute cell address is indicated by a dollar sign ($) in front of the row or column label or both. A cell address "A1" indicates that both the column and the row are absolute—always referring back to the same cell.

The other combinations available are "$A1" in which the row may change but the column is constant and "A$1" means that the column is relative and the row is absolute. "A1" refers to a relative cell reference where both the row and column are relative. Figure 11-11 displays these options.

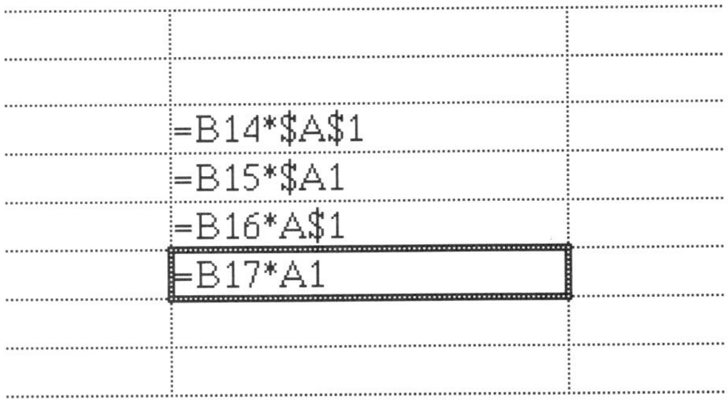

=B14*A1
=B15*$A1
=B16*A$1
=B17*A1

***Figure 11-11.** The four cell address options in a formula.*

The dollar sign is inserted by keying it in as the formula is being created, or by using the F4 key. F4 is a toggle switch which offers each of the options, outlined above, in turn.

In the sample file, we will use an absolute cell reference to project a profit increase of 2%. Type in the heading "Projection:" in E4 and 102% in E5 (Figure 11-12).

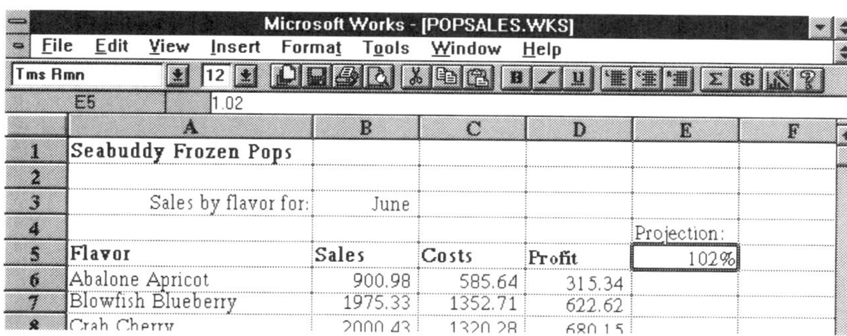

Figure 11-12. *Type "Projection:" in cell E4 and "102%" in cell E5.*

The formula — D6*E5 — is now ready to be inserted into E6. Move into cell E6, key in the formula prefix "=", and click on D6. Type a multiplication sign (*) and click on E5 to continue the formula. While in this position, the cell reference needs to be made absolute by pressing the F4 key, as in Figure 11-13.

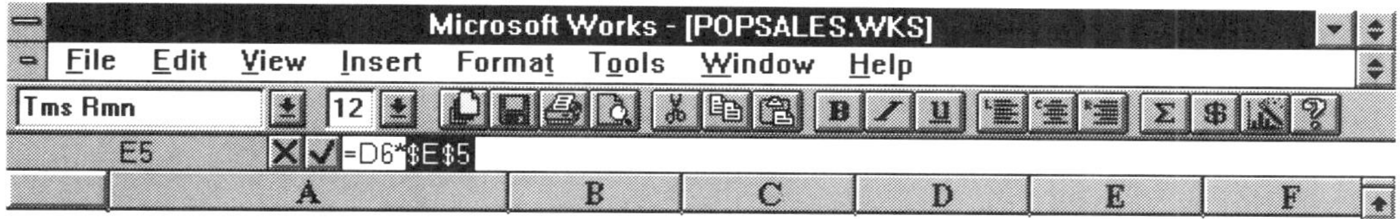

Figure 11-13. *Your reference to cell E5 is made absolute using the F4 key.*

Press Enter and the formula is inserted, calculating a total of 321.6468. Copy this into cell E7 and the formula changes to "D7*E5", where the absolute cell remains constant, as shown in Figure 11-14.

Microsoft Works - [POPSALES.WKS]

File Edit View Insert Format Tools Window Help

Tms Rmn 12

E7 =D7*E5

	A	B	C	D	E	F
1	Seabuddy Frozen Pops					
2						
3	Sales by flavor for:	June				
4					Projection:	
5	Flavor	Sales	Costs	Profit	102%	
6	Abalone Apricot	900.98	585.64	315.34	321.6468	
7	Blowfish Blueberry	1975.33	1352.71	622.62	635.0724	

Figure 11-14. *Copy your formula to cell E7.*

In this case, absolute cell addressing eliminates the need to change formulas to adjust the percentage of projected profit. For example, change the 102% to 105% and all of the figures recalculate accordingly.

Sorting rows

Sorting rows enables a spreadsheet to be organized in alphabetical or numerical order. Entire rows are sorted, not just individual cells. Works allows you to sort according to the contents of up to three columns at once.

For example, imagine that a staff list contains last names in column A, first names in column B and the middle initial in column C. To sort the list logically, the last name is sorted into alphabetical order first. Column B, which contains the first names is sorted next, followed by the middle initial.

To sort data, *Sort Rows* is selected from the **Tools** menu (Figure 11-15).

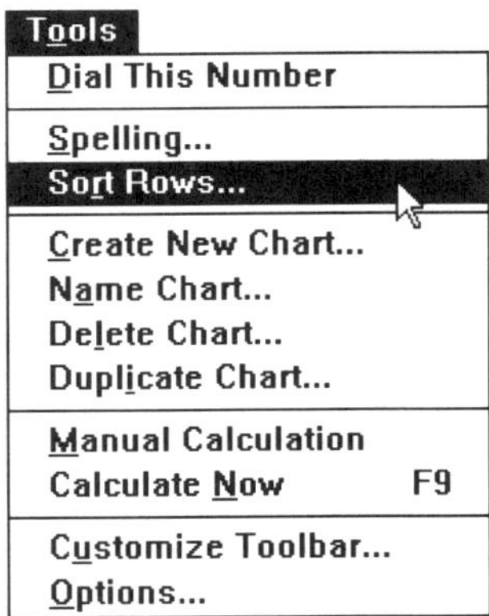

Figure 11-15. *Sort Rows in the* ***Tools*** *menu.*

Sort the flavor data in the sample file into ascending order of profitability. Highlight the rows to be sorted, in this case rows 6 to 12, and choose *Sort Rows* from the **Tools** menu.

As only one column is being used to determine the order, fill in only the *1st Column* area. Type "D" in the *1st Column* text box since this is the column which contains profitability. As we want to arrange rows in increasing or ascending order, select *Ascend A*. Figure 11-16 shows how the *Sort Rows* dialog box should be set. Press Enter to begin the *Sort* process.

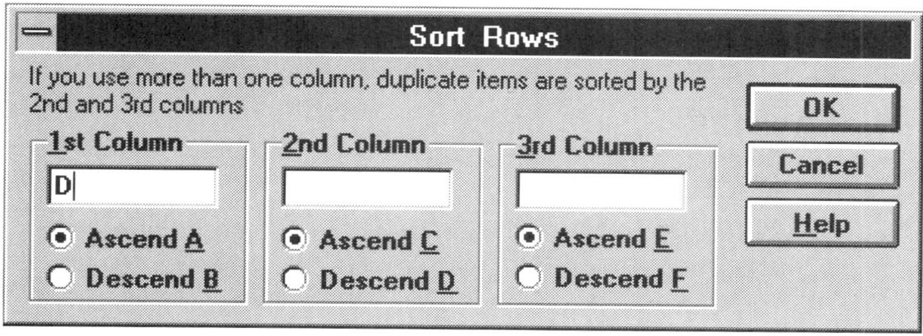

Figure 11-16. *The Sort Rows dialog box set up to sort the flavors into order of profitability.*

Once sorted, the spreadsheet looks like Figure 11-17.

Microsoft Works - [POPSALES.WKS]

File Edit View Insert Format Tools Window Help

Times New Roman 12

A6:M12 "Lobster Licorice

	A	B	C	D	E	F
1	Seabuddy Frozen Pops					
2						
3	Sales by flavor for:	June				
4					Projection:	
5	Flavor	Sales	Costs	Profit	105%	
6	Lobster Licorice	799.66	527.77	271.89	285.4845	
7	Abalone Apricot	900.98	585.64	315.34	331.107	
8	Lungfish Lemon	1334.55	889.8	444.75	466.9875	
9	Blowfish Blueberry	1975.33	1352.71	622.62	653.751	
10	Crab Cherry	2000.43	1320.28	680.15	714.1575	
11	Octopus Orange	3303.78	2100.49	1203.29	1263.4545	
12	Grouper Grape	5529.51	3549.47	1980.04	2079.042	
13						

Figure 11-17. *Your sample file is now sorted.*

Filling selected cells

The *Fill* commands are used in Works to copy data to many cells simultaneously. Using the *Fill Down* and *Fill Right* commands, the same cell entry is copied down a column or across a row. A series of values or dates are inserted using the *Fill Series* command. Cells are filled using one of the *Fill* commands in the **Edit** menu (Figure 11-18).

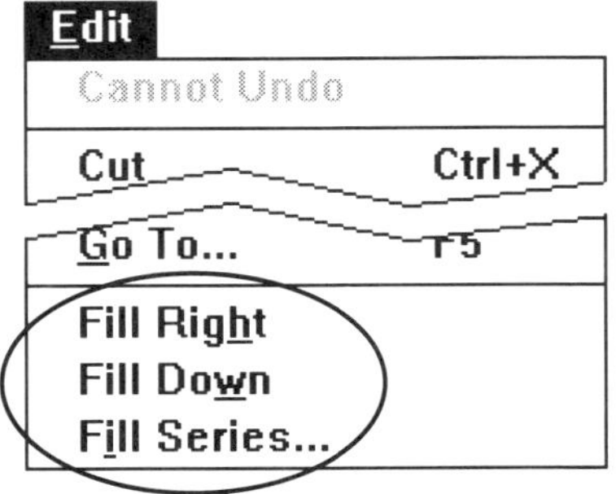

Figure 11-18. *The Fill commands in the* ***Edit*** *menu.*

Fill Down and Fill Right

The *Fill Down* command fills adjacent cells down a column with identical information. Type the entry you want to reproduce and highlight all the cells you want to fill, starting with that cell (Figure 11-19).

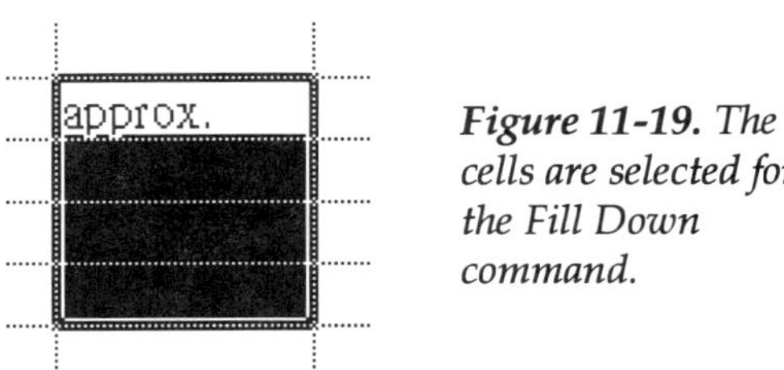

Figure 11-19. *The cells are selected for the Fill Down command.*

To fill the cells, select *Fill Down* from the **Edit** menu and the spreadsheet displays the values in the highlighted block, as shown in Figure 11-20.

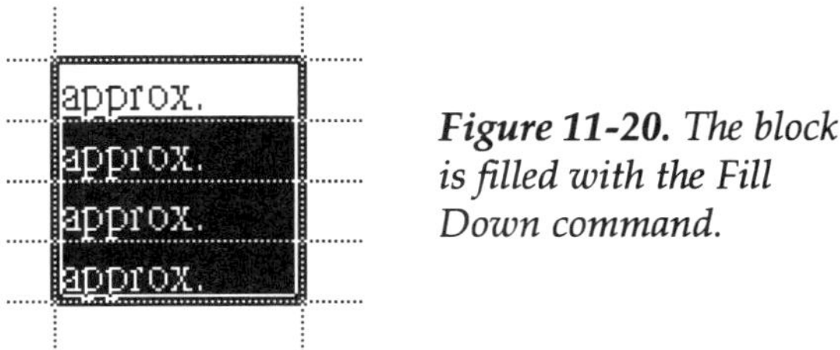

Figure 11-20. *The block is filled with the Fill Down command.*

The *Fill Right* command is used in exactly the same way as *Fill Down*, except cells are highlighted and filled to the right of the first cell.

Fill Series

The *Fill Series* command fills a block of highlighted cells with a series of values or dates according to specific data inserted in the *Fill Series* dialog box. The first value in the series must be entered for the *Fill Series* dialog box to appear.

In the sample file give each flavor a number in a new column inserted before column A. First insert the column as Figure 11-21 illustrates. For more information on inserting columns, refer to **Chapter 10, Editing Spreadsheets**.

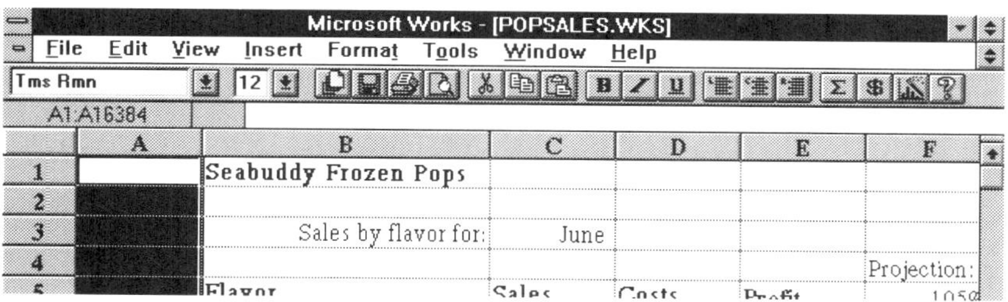

Figure 11-21. *A new column is inserted.*

The numbering of the flavors begins in cell A6, so the number "1" needs to be entered into this cell. The cells which are to be filled (A6 through A12) are highlighted (Figure 11-22).

Microsoft Works - [POPSALES.WKS]

File Edit View Insert Format Tools Window Help

Tms Rmn 12

A6:A12 1

	A	B	C	D	E	F
1		Seabuddy Frozen Pops				
2						
3		Sales by flavor for:	June			
4						Projection:
5		Flavor	Sales	Costs	Profit	1059
6	1	Lobster Licorice	799.66	527.77	271.89	285.4845
7		Abalone Apricot	900.98	585.64	315.34	331.107
8		Lungfish Lemon	1334.55	889.8	444.75	466.9875
9		Blowfish Blueberry	1975.33	1352.71	622.62	653.751
10		Crab Cherry	2000.43	1320.28	680.15	714.1575
11		Octopus Orange	3303.78	2100.49	1203.29	1263.4545
12		Grouper Grape	5529.51	3549.47	1980.04	2079.042
13						
14			15844.24	10326.16		

Figure 11-22. *The first number – 1 – is entered and the cells are highlighted.*

Select *Fill Series* from the **Edit** menu to display the *Fill Series* dialog box shown in Figure 11-23.

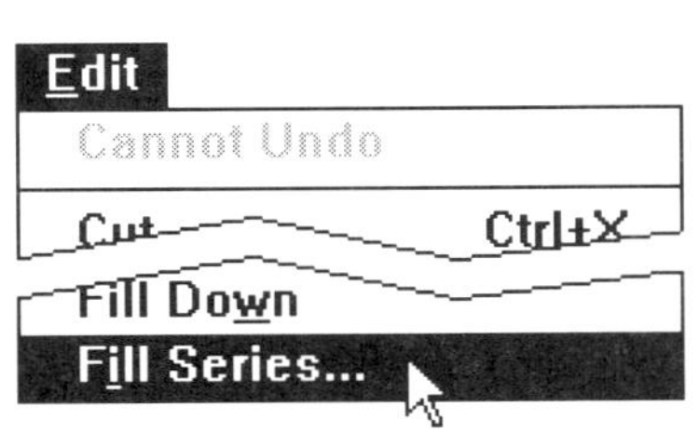

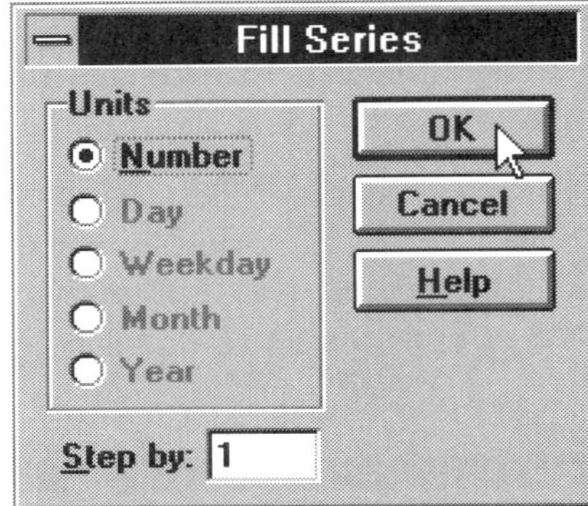

Figure 11-23. *The Fill Series dialog box.*

The options available in the *Units* section depend on the type of series being created. If the first entry is a number, only *Number* is available in the *Units* section. If the first value in your series is a date, the unit may be a *Day* (7 day week), a *Weekday* (5 day week), a *Month* or a *Year*.

The units increment by the amount specified in the *Step By* text box. The default value is 1, which is what is required in this case, but any amount can be entered. A negative number decreases the series.

As "1" is a number, Works selects *Number* automatically in this example. Ensure that the *Fill Series* dialog box is identical to Figure 11-23 and click on *OK* to number the cells automatically.

Works inserts the numbers in a series increasing by 1 each time until all highlighted cells are filled. The completed spreadsheet is shown in Figure 11-24.

5		Flavor	Sales	Costs	Profit
6	1	Lobster Licorice	799.66	527.77	271.89
7	2	Abalone Apricot	900.98	585.64	315.34
8	3	Lungfish Lemon	1334.55	889.8	444.75
9	4	Blowfish Blueberry	1975.33	1352.71	622.62
10	5	Crab Cherry	2000.43	1320.28	680.15
11	6	Octopus Orange	3303.78	2100.49	1203.29
12	7	Grouper Grape	5529.51	3549.47	1980.04
13					

Figure 11-24. *Your data should now look like this.*

Formatting and Printing Spreadsheets

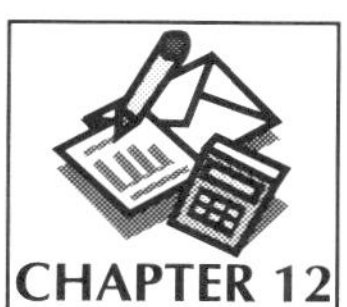

CHAPTER 12

In this chapter, the file ***popsheet.wks*** is used as a sample file. It is located in the ***msworks.cbt*** subdirectory. Please load this file now.

Headers and footers

Headers and footers are standard pieces of text which appear at the top (header) and bottom (footer) of a printed page. Information in a header or footer often includes the page number and other information relevant to the spreadsheet, such as the name of the spreadsheet and the date it was printed.

Headers and footers are inserted into a spreadsheet created in Works through the *Headers and Footers* command in the **View** menu (Figure 12-1).

View

√ Toolbar
Zoom...

Chart...
Spreadsheet

√ Gridlines
Formulas

Headers and Footers...

Figure 12-1. *The Headers and Footers command in the* ***View*** *menu.*

The alignment of headers and footers is set to the center by default. This can be altered using a code. Alignment codes and special codes (such as page numbering) are identical to those used by the word processing tool in Works. For further details of headers and footers refer to **Chapter 4, Advanced Document Editing**.

The header required for this spreadsheet is one which inserts the heading "Pop Sales" in the center of the page, and the date on the right. The text which creates this header is "Pop Sales&r&d".

The footer need display the page number only on the left side of the page and therefore reads "&l&p". The *Headers and Footers* dialog box, in Figure 12-2, appears with this information. Enter this information for the sample file.

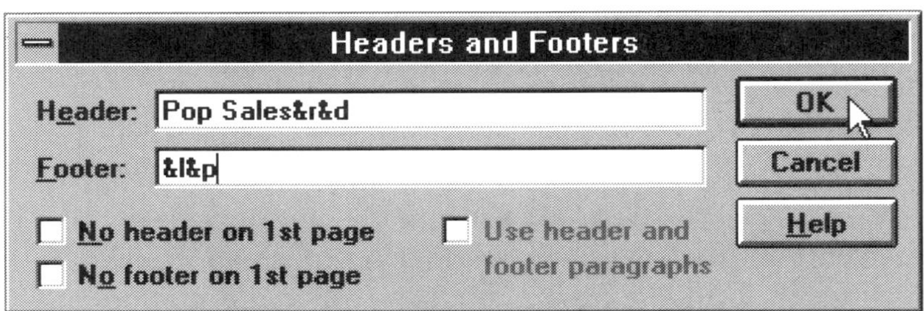

***Figure 12-2.** The Headers and Footers dialog box information with the correct codes inserted.*

Inserting a page break

In many cases a spreadsheet is too large to fit on one piece of paper. When it prints, it breaks the spreadsheet into pages according to the paper size and orientation. These "soft" page breaks do not always display your spreadsheet in the best way. Because of this, "hard" page breaks—put in manually—are inserted in appropriate places.

A hard page break is indicated by a dotted line and can be used to break a spreadsheet by columns or rows. The row or column is highlighted by clicking on the label where the page break is to go. For example, the sample file is to have a page break above row 8, which is highlighted in Figure 12-3.

***Figure 12-3.** Row 8 is highlighted to insert a page break.*

The page break appears when you choose *Page Break* from the **Insert** menu (Figure 12-4).

A page break, as mentioned above, is indicated by a dotted line above the row or to the left of the column which is highlighted. In Figure 12-4, the dotted line is displayed above row 8. When printed, row 8 is the first row on page 2.

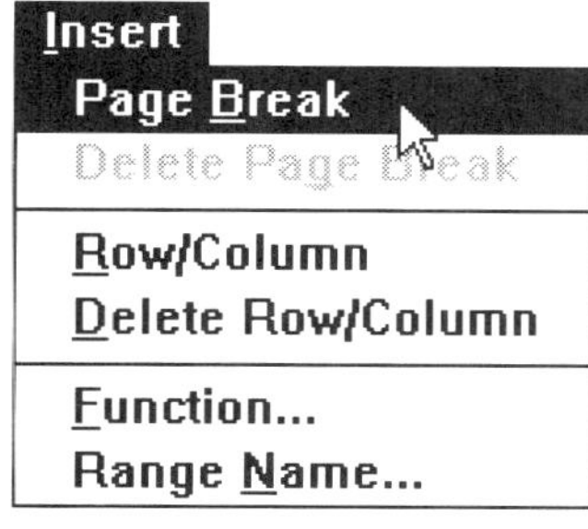

7	Perch	$0.06	$255.61	4575
8	Grouper	$0.06	$530.33	9000
9	Lungfish	$0.06	$231.53	4028

Figure 12-4. *The dotted line marking a page break appears above row 8.*

A page break is deleted by moving into the row below or the column to the right of the page break. The *Delete Page Break* command in the **Insert** menu is active only when the cell pointer is in the correct position (Figure 12-5). You do not need to highlight the whole row or column.

7	Perch	$0.06	$255.61	4575
8	Grouper	$0.06	$530.33	9000
9	Lungfish	$0.06	$231.53	4028

Figure 12-5. *Place the cell pointer immediately below or to the right of a page break before deleting the page break.*

Printing a spreadsheet

Printing is an important part of creating a spreadsheet. There are a number of options within Works that enable you to specify how the spreadsheet is printed.

Print Preview

Print Preview is a feature which is used to view the spreadsheet before it is printed on paper. Headers, footers and the actual page breaks (not just the dotted lines) can be seen only when printed or in *Print Preview*.

Print Preview is activated using the *Print Preview* button on the toolbar (Figure 12-6) or through the *Print Preview* command in the **File** menu (Figure 12-7).

***Figure 12-6.** The Print Preview button.*

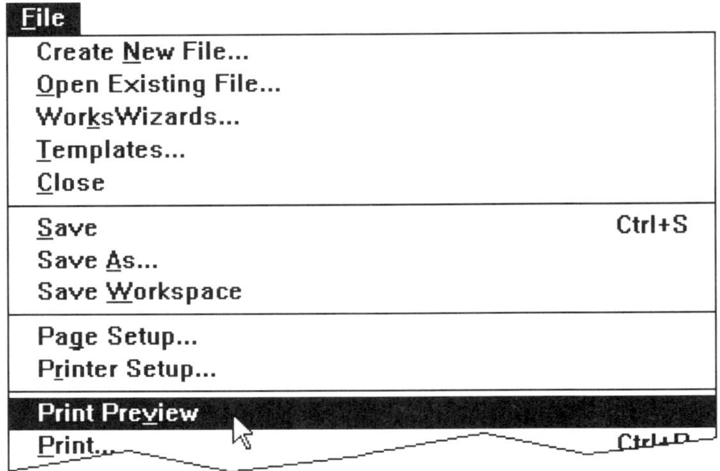

***Figure 12-7.** The Print Preview command in the **File** menu.*

Details of the *Print Preview* feature, such as changing views, are outlined in **Chapter 7, Printing Word Processed Documents**. For this file, however, click on the *Print Preview* button to display the screen shown in Figure 12-8.

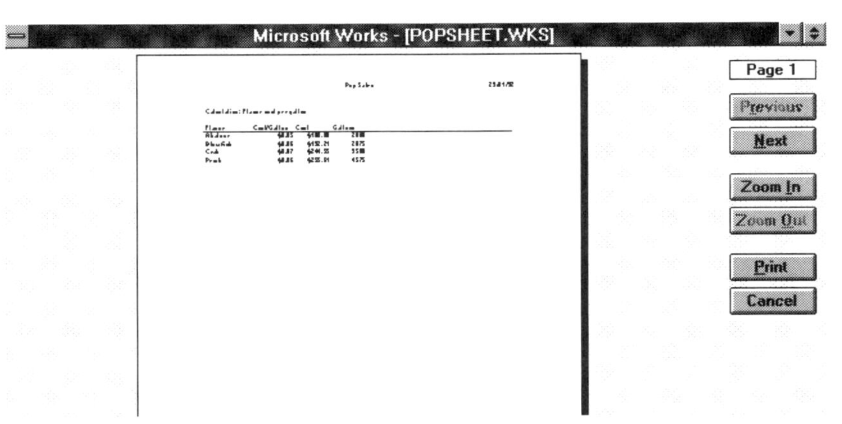

***Figure 12-8.** The Print Preview screen showing the top of the first page of **popsheet.wks**. This view assumes that the page break of Figure 12-4 is still inserted.*

The header and footer appear on the top and bottom of the page. The *Next* button is active, telling you that there is more than one page in this spreadsheet. Click on *Next* and page 2 appears on the screen. The headers and footers remain, as in Figure 12-9.

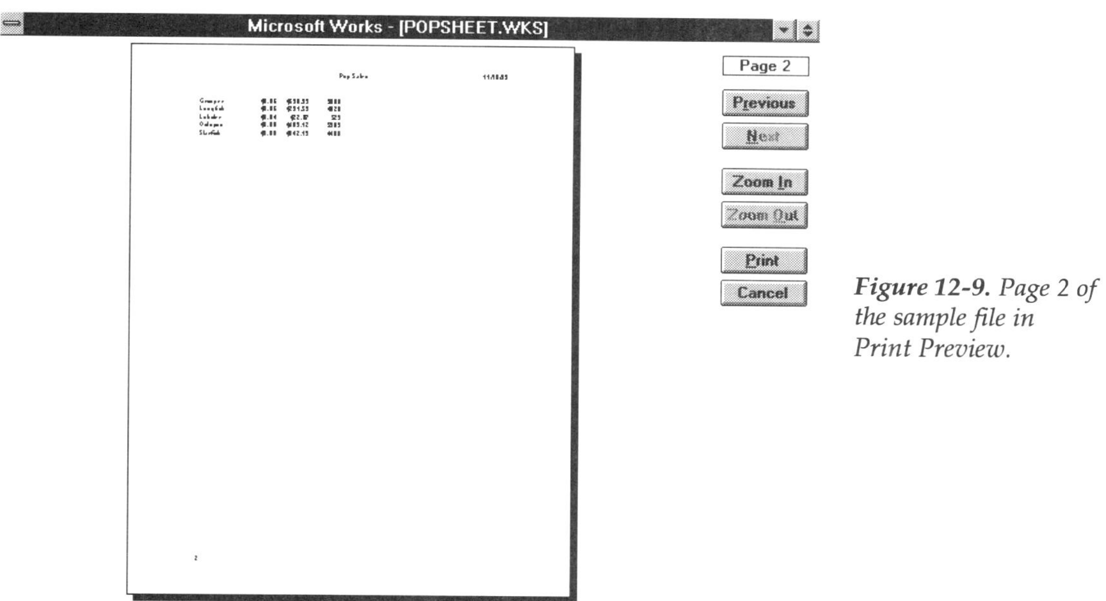

Figure 12-9. *Page 2 of the sample file in Print Preview.*

Setting the print area

The print area set automatically in Works includes every cell entry in the spreadsheet. To specify a portion only of the spreadsheet, a new print area is defined. Cells included in the print area are highlighted using any of the selection techniques covered in this book.

Do this now in the sample file as displayed in Figure 12-10.

3	Flavor	Cost/Gallon	Cost	Gallons
4	Abalone	$0.05	$100.00	2000
5	Blowfish	$0.06	$132.21	2075
6	Crab	$0.07	$244.55	3500
7	Perch	$0.06	$255.61	4575

Figure 12-10. *Highlight the cells to be printed.*

The print area is set by selecting *Set Print Area* from the **Format** menu (Figure 12-11).

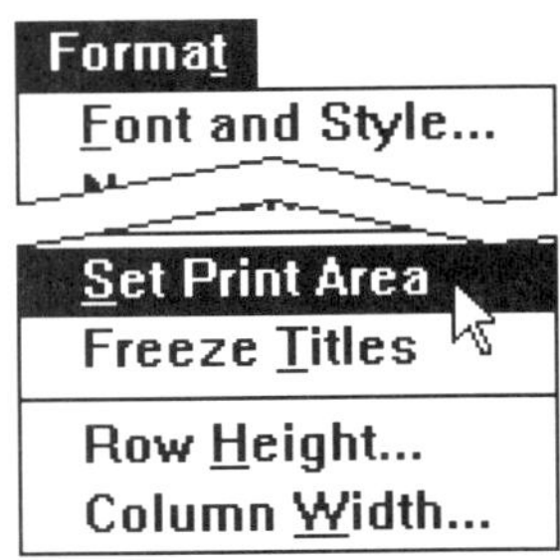

***Figure 12-11.** The Set Print Area command in the **Format** menu.*

The print area is reset by selecting the entire spreadsheet and then choosing *Set Print Area* from the **Format** menu.

Page Setup command

The *Page Setup* command in the **File** menu (Figure 12-12) is very similar to the same command in the word processor. Changing the paper size and margins follows the same process (**Chapter 4, Advanced Document Editing**). Figure 12-13 illustrates the *Other Options* tab of the *Page Setup* dialog box.

Printing the grid lines and row and column headings makes the spreadsheet easier to read on paper. They are printed by checking the *Print gridlines* and *Print row and column headers* options shown in the *Page Setup* dialog box in Figure 12-13.

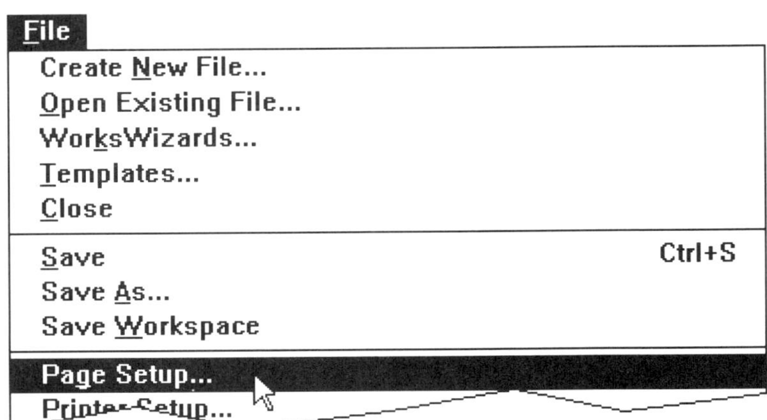

***Figure 12-12.** The Page Setup command in the **File** menu.*

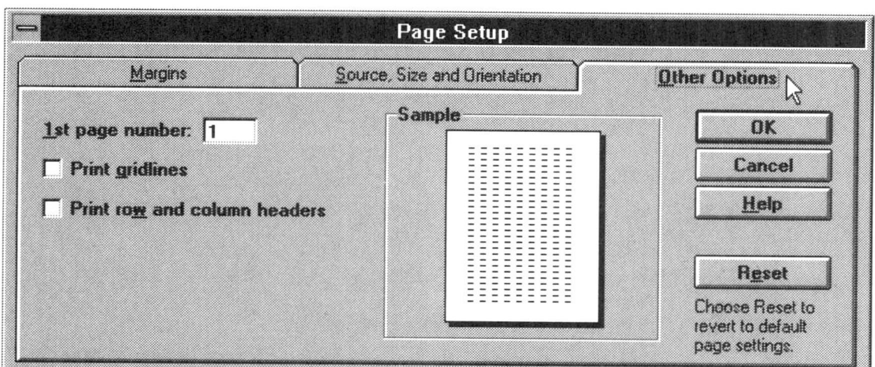

Figure 12-13. *The Print gridlines and Print row and column headers options.*

Printing

The spreadsheet is printed by selecting *Print* from the **File** menu as Figure 12-14 illustrates. Alternatively, click on the *Print* button on the *Print Preview* screen, or the *Print* button in the toolbar.

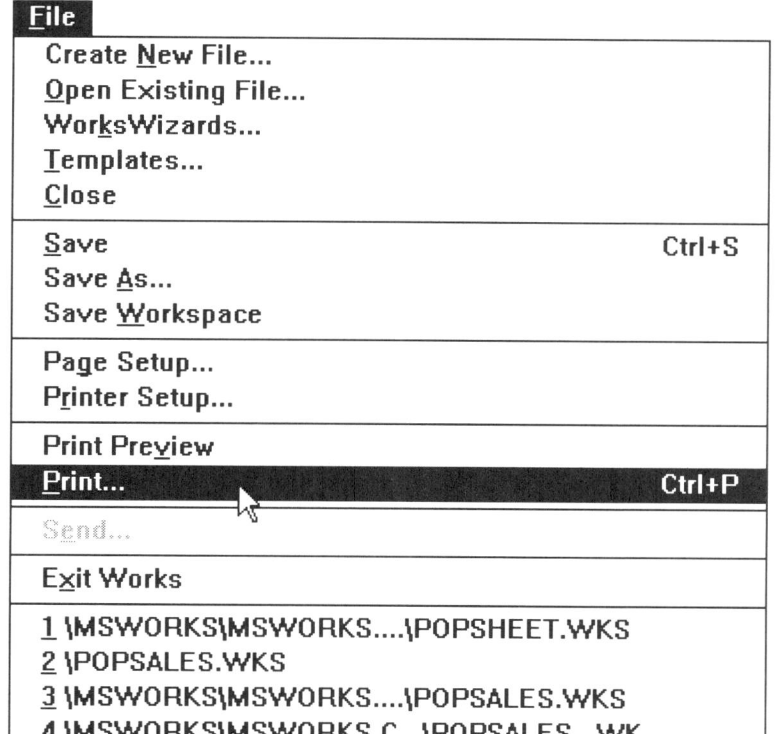

Figure 12-14. *The Print command in the* ***File*** *menu.*

The *Print* button on the toolbar prints a copy of your spreadsheet without displaying the *Print* dialog box. All of the other methods, as well as the shortcut Ctrl-P, display the dialog box shown in Figure 12-15.

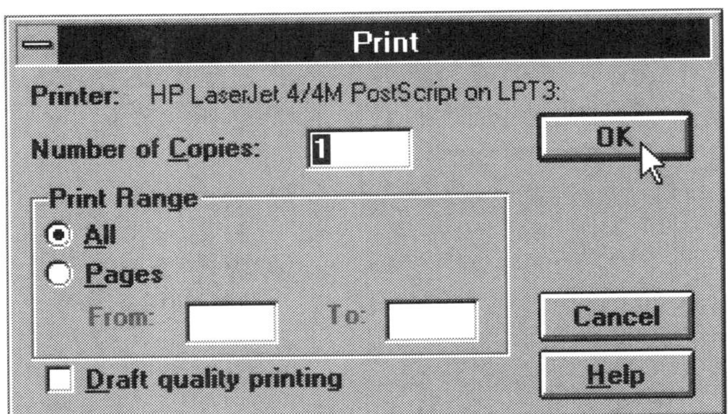

Figure 12-15. *The Print dialog box.*

The *Print* dialog box contains a number of options to specify the type of printout required, the pages to be printed, and the number of copies. Further information about each of these options can be found in **Chapter 4, Advanced Document Editing**.

Print the sample file by clicking on *OK* in the *Print* dialog box.

As an exercise, you may like to go through the steps covered in this chapter again using a different sample spreadsheet file.

Creating Charts

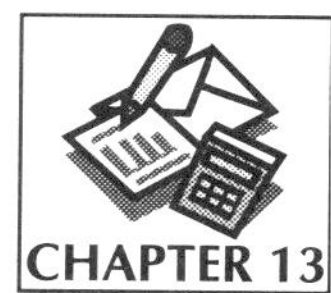

In this chapter, you are shown how to create a chart in Works. A chart enables you to interpret the data visually. Charts created in Works use the information already placed in the spreadsheet.

A chart is created in the sample file ***popsales.wks***. The chapter then looks at some of the options available for formatting, printing, and using multiple charts. Open ***popsales.wks*** from the ***msworks.cbt*** subdirectory to follow the examples in the chapter.

Activating the chart facility

The chart facility is activated only when a block of cells is highlighted. The cell contents are used by Works as the data to create the chart. A new chart is created automatically when the chart facility is opened. To create a new chart, highlight the cells A5:C12 as Figure 13-1 displays.

4			
5	Flavor	Sales	Costs
6	Abalone Apricot	900.98	585.64
7	Blowfish Blueberry	1975.33	1352.71
8	Crab Cherry	2000.43	1320.28
9	Grouper Grape	5529.51	3549.47
10	Lungfish Lemon	1334.55	889.8
11	Lobster Licorice	799.66	527.77
12	Octopus Orange	3303.78	2100.49
13			

Figure 13-1. *The cells A5:C12 are highlighted.*

You can activate the chart facility through the *Create New Chart* command in the **Tools** menu or by using the *Chart* button on the toolbar. Figure 13-2 displays both of these.

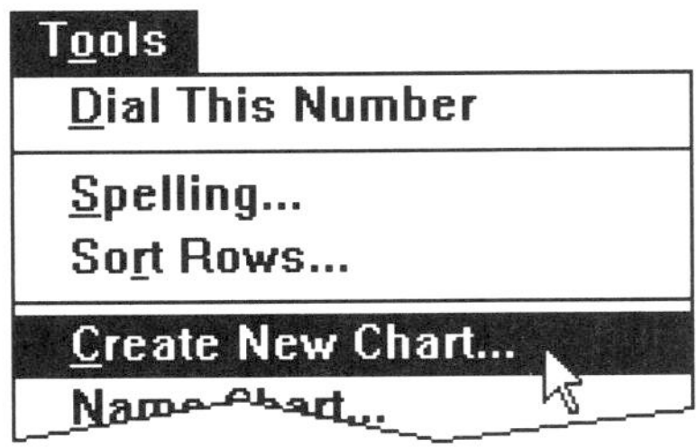

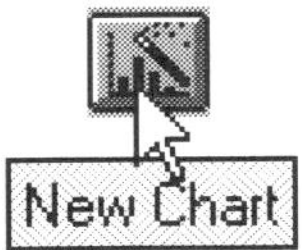

Figure 13-2. *Alternatives for activating the chart facility within Works.*

The dialog box which appears on the screen is illustrated in Figure 13-3. Click on *OK* to create a chart using the current settings.

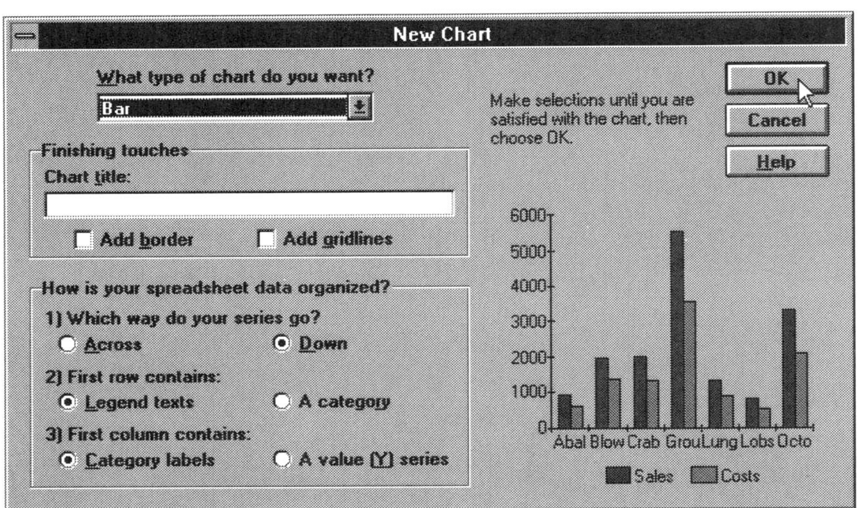

Figure 13-3. *The New Chart dialog box.*

The menu bar in the charting facility differs from the menu bar in the spreadsheet tool. The chart menu bar consists of the following options: **File, Edit, View, Gallery, Format, Tools, Window, Help.** Some of these menu titles, such as the **Edit** menu, use the same menu title as the spreadsheet tool, but contain different commands. These menus are used in this chapter. The menu bar is displayed in Figure 13-4.

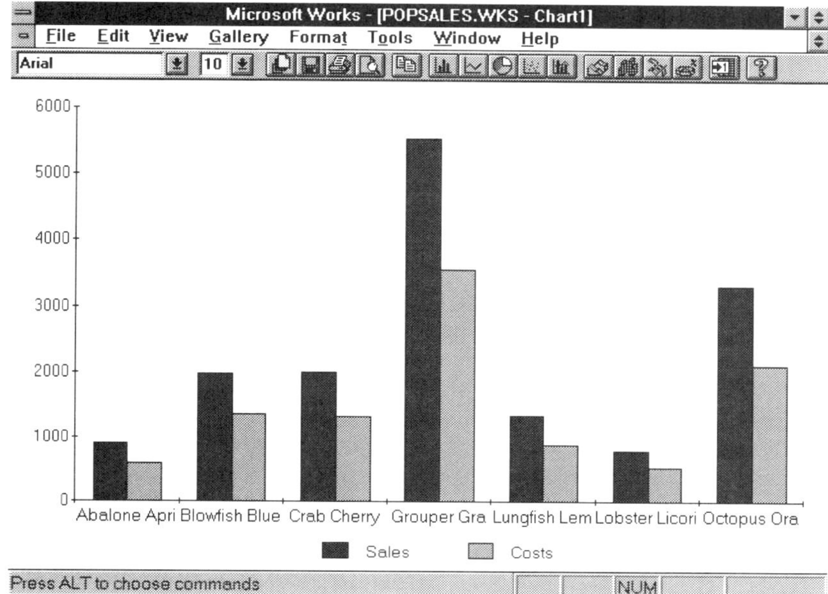

Figure 13-4. Your chart should look like this.

The **Window** menu is used to move between the chart and the spreadsheet. The **Window** menu lists all of the open "windows," placing a check mark to the left of the active window. In Figure 13-5, the active window is *POPSALES.WKS - Chart 1*. To move to the spreadsheet, click on *POPSALES.WKS* in the **Window** menu. Return to the chart when done.

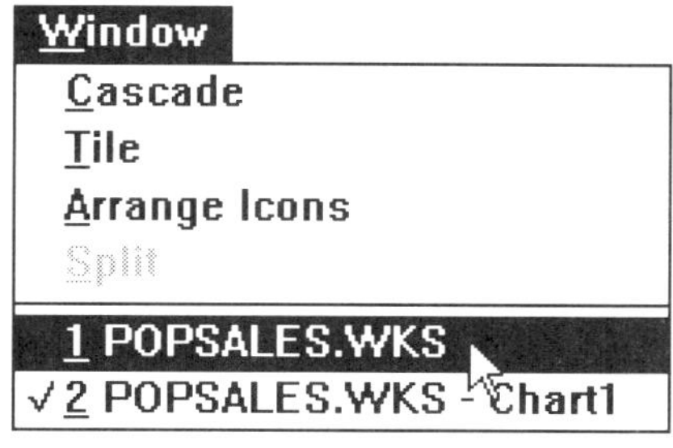

*Figure 13-5. The **Window** menu uses a check mark to indicate that the chart is active.*

Defining charts

The parts of a chart are highlighted in the following diagram. Each of these is discussed in this section.

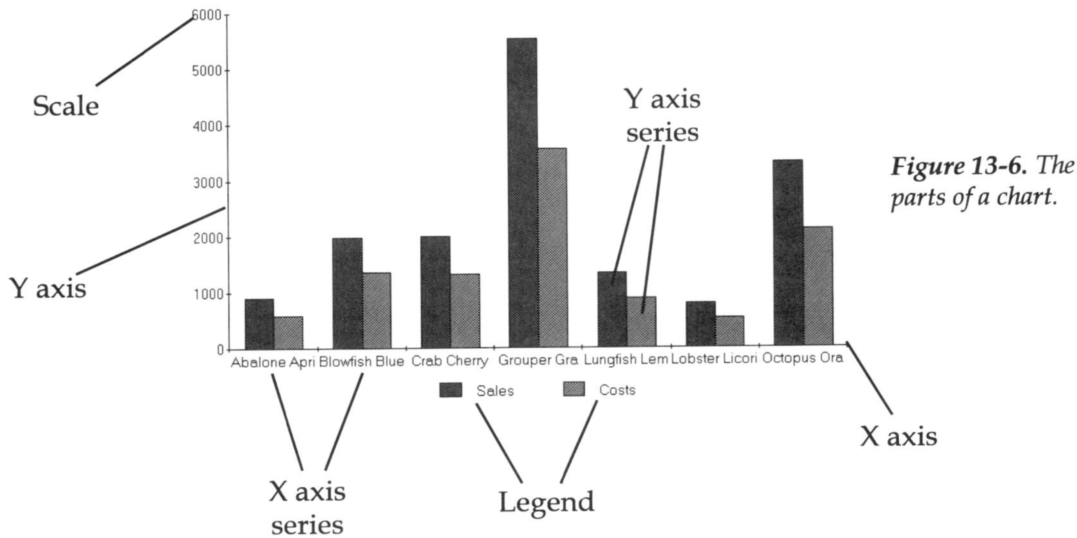

***Figure 13-6.** The parts of a chart.*

Identifying the X and Y series

The information displayed in a chart is determined by the cells highlighted in the spreadsheet. When cells are highlighted, Works breaks these cells down into *series* which give the chart a logical appearance. There are two kinds of series: X and Y.

The X series are placed on the X axis, which is the horizontal axis. In the chart (Figure 13-6) the X series consist of the names of the flavors. Looking back to the spreadsheet, these words are in cells A6:A12. The X series, therefore is A6:A12 (Figure 13-7).

5	Flavor	Sales
6	Abalone Apricot	900.98
7	Blowfish Blueberry	1975.33
8	Crab Cherry	2000.43
9	Grouper Grape	5529.51
10	Lungfish Lemon	1334.55
11	Lobster Licorice	799.66
12	Octopus Orange	3303.78
13		

***Figure 13-7.** The X axis series is cells A6:A12.*

The Y series relate to the Y axis, which is the vertical axis on the chart. The Y axis is automatically given a scale, which is used to determine the size of each Y series. The chart in Figure 13-6 uses a scale of the numbers 0 to 6000, incrementing by 1000.

A chart can have up to six Y series. The chart above uses two. The first data series is "Sales" and displays the sales generated for each flavor—the X series. These figures are in cells B6:B12 in the spreadsheet (Figure 13-8.

5	Flavor	Sales
6	Abalone Apricot	900.98
7	Blowfish Blueberry	1975.33
8	Crab Cherry	2000.43
9	Grouper Grape	5529.51
10	Lungfish Lemon	1334.55
11	Lobster Licorice	799.66
12	Octopus Orange	3303.78

***Figure 13-8.** The first Y series uses the values in cells B6:B12.*

The other Y series in the chart displayed in Figure 13-6 is "Costs" (cells C6:C12).

The series are set in a chart when it is created. Series can be altered, deleted, and new Y series inserted, through the *Series* command in the **Edit** menu when the chart is on the screen (Figure 13-9).

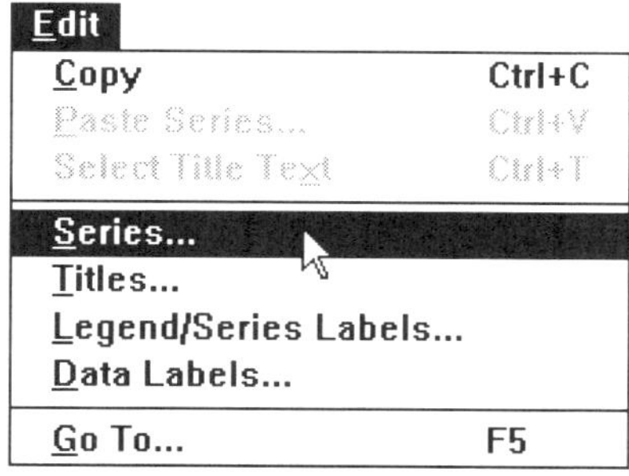

***Figure 13-9.** The Series command in the **Edit** menu.*

The *Series* dialog box (Figure 13-10) indicates the series being used in the current graph. Changing the cell addresses in any of the series text boxes alters the series in the chart. Cells can be copied directly from the spreadsheet and placed in the text box by clicking on the *Paste* button.

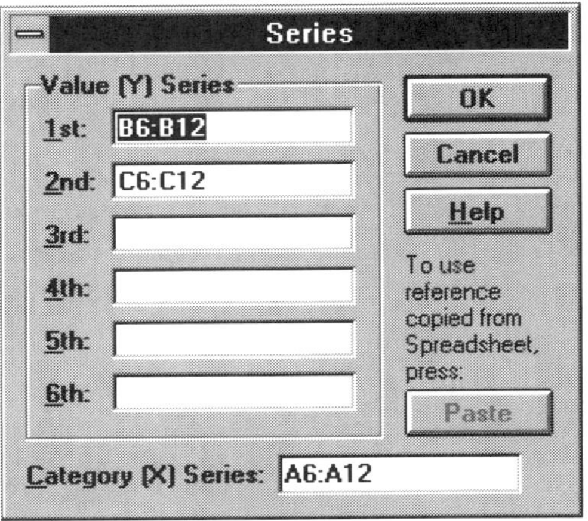

Figure 13-10. *The Series dialog box shows the two Y series and the X series in the chart.*

The Go To command

The *Go To* command is in the **Edit** menu as shown in Figure 13-11. The shortcut keystroke is F5.

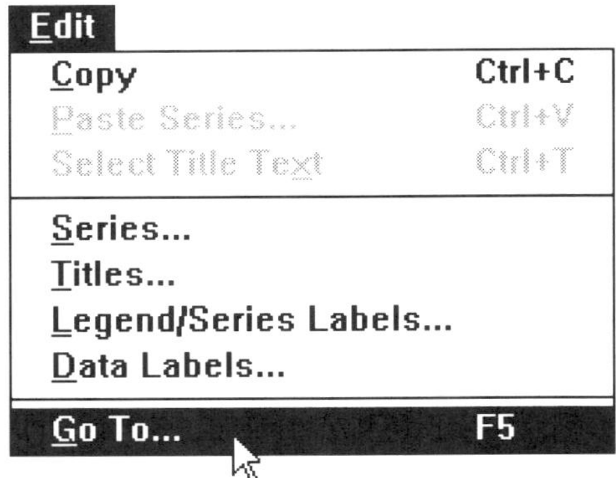

Figure 13-11. *The Go To command.*

The *Go To* command in the charting facility is used to highlight the series in the spreadsheet that you select in the *Go To* dialog box. Use this feature to select the second series. Click on the *2nd* check box and then on *OK* (Figure 13-12).

Move back to the chart using the **Window** menu.

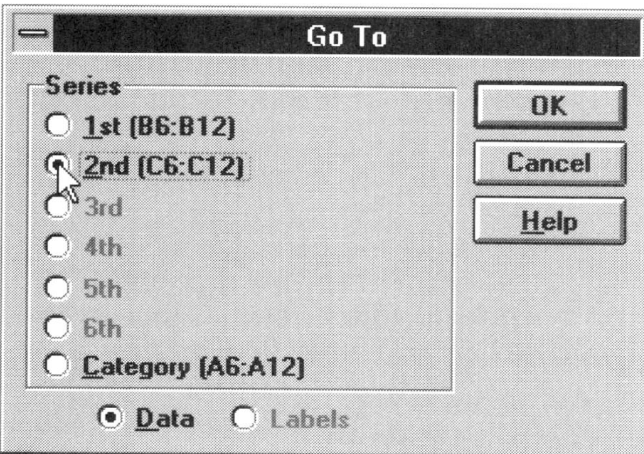

Figure 13-12. Click on the second series in the Go To dialog box to highlight related cells in the spreadsheet.

Selecting chart types

There are twelve types of charts which can be applied in Works. These are all shown in the **Gallery** menu in Figure 13-13. The type of the current chart is marked with a check mark. Each type is outlined in this section.

Changing the type of the current chart can either be done through the **Gallery** menu or the *Type* buttons on the toolbar (Figure 13-13).

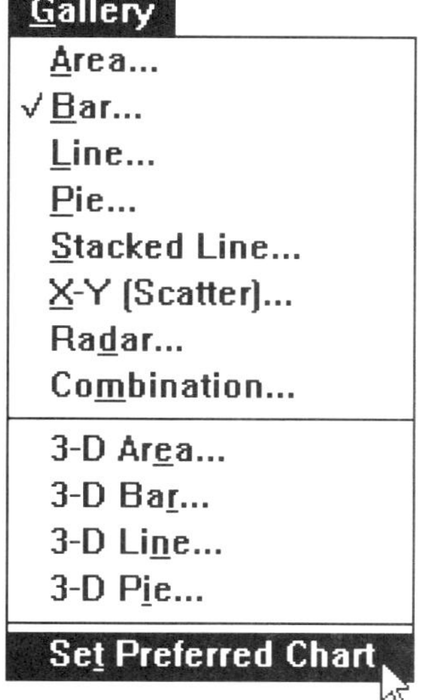

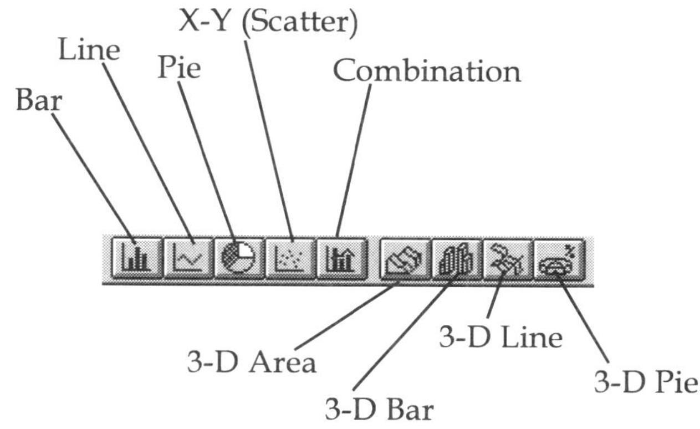

*Figure 13-13. The **Gallery** menu and the Type buttons.*

The default type is a bar chart. You can change the type of chart that Works uses as the default type. To change the default chart type to the currently selected type, choose *Set Preferred Chart* from the **Gallery** menu (Figure 13-13).

Area chart

Choose an area chart to represent your data as an area enclosed by a line. The five types of area chart are shown in Figure 13-14.

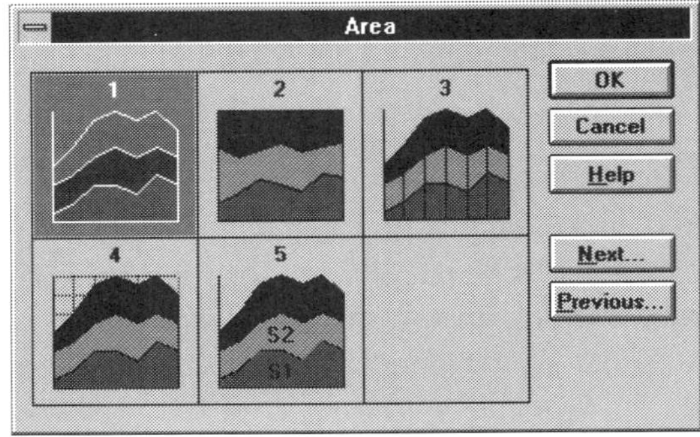

Figure 13-14. *The area charts.*

Bar chart

A bar chart uses bars to display the information, comparing it with the scale on the vertical axis. There are six styles of bar charts which are displayed in Figure 13-15.

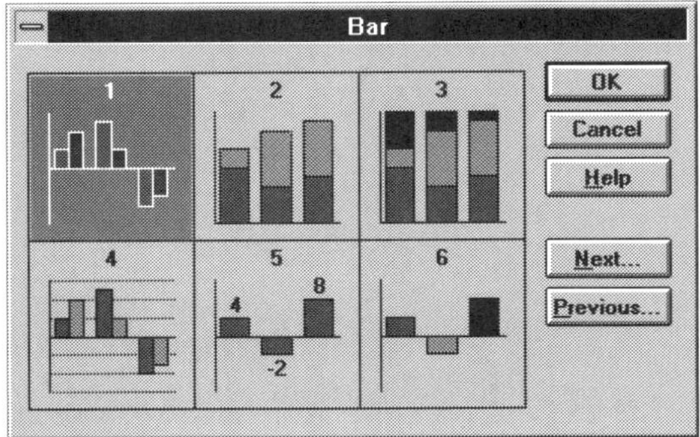

Figure 13-15. *The bar charts.*

Line charts

A line chart uses a line to display the values in the Y series. Line charts are commonly used to indicate trends in the data. Figure 13-16 shows the six line charts in Works.

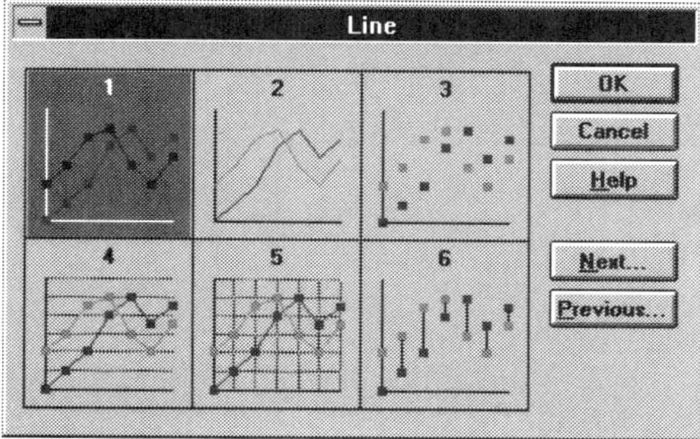

Figure 13-16. *The line charts.*

Pie charts

A pie chart is used to represent one Y series on its own. The pie displays information as segments of a circle. Each represents a percentage of a whole Y series. There are six types of pie charts (Figure 13-17).

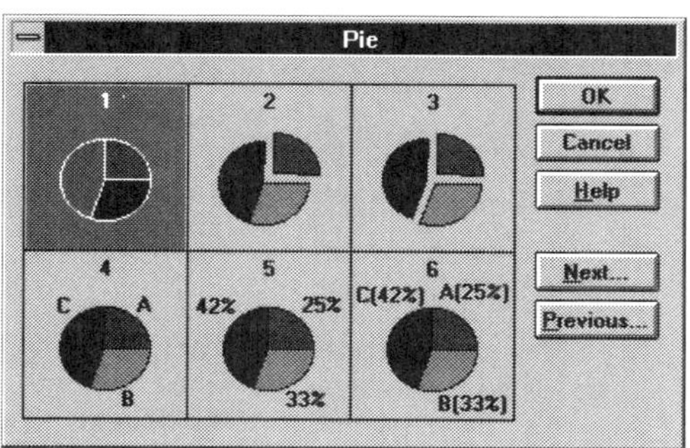

Figure 13-17. *The pie charts.*

Stacked line charts

A stacked line chart compares the different Y series using a number of lines stacked into a chart. Each series is represented by a line. Four line charts are available and displayed in Figure 13-18.

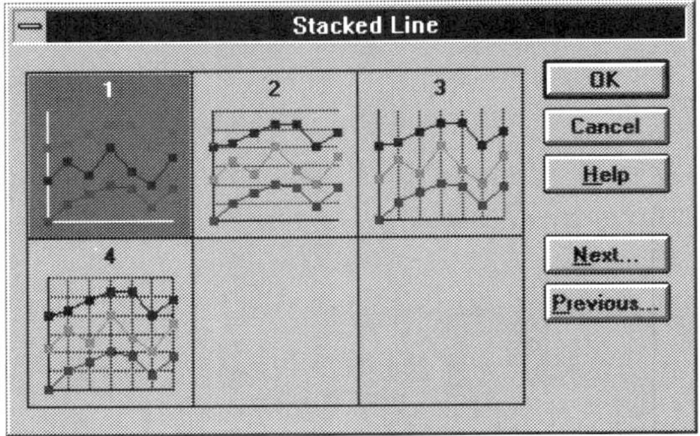

Figure 13-18. *The stacked line charts.*

X-Y (scatter) charts

An X-Y (scatter) chart represents two Y series on a chart using position markers to represent their values. The data is easily compared as the chart uses different markers for each series. You can choose from one of the six types of X-Y (scatter) charts in Figure 13-19.

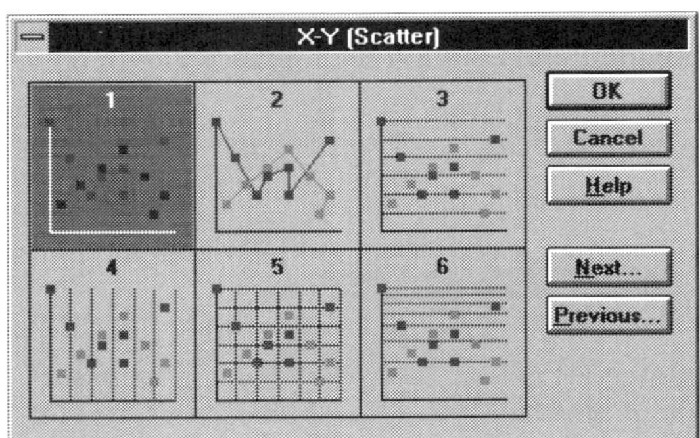

Figure 13-19. *The X-Y (scatter) charts.*

Radar charts

A radar chart plots each Y series as points around a center, rather like the image on a radar screen. There are six varieties of radar charts from which you can choose (Figure 13-20).

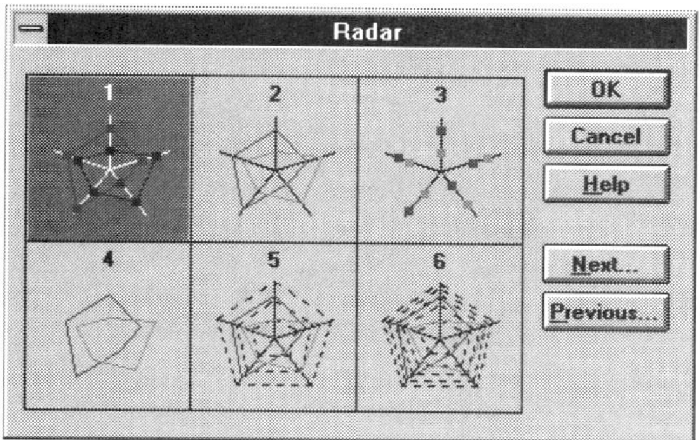

Figure 13-20. The radar charts.

Combination charts

As the name suggests, a combination chart combines two types of charts into one. It is used to compare data in which one piece of the data needs to stand out from the other. There are four types of combination charts in Works (Figure 13-21).

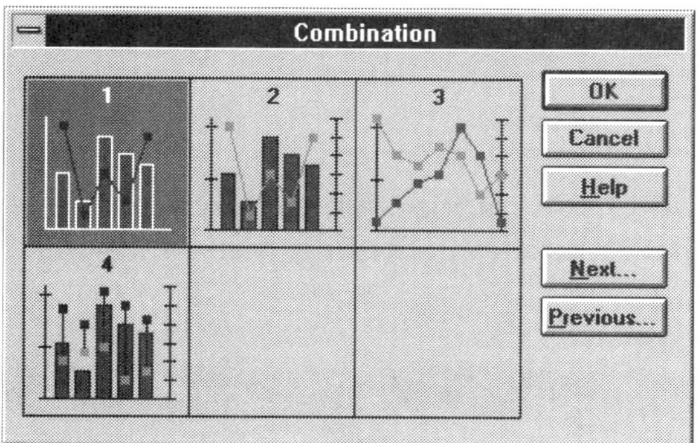

Figure 13-21. The combination charts.

3-D charts

The 3-D charts are like their two-dimensional counterparts, but you can sometimes find them more appropriate because they appeal to our sense of perspective. Works gives you a choice of six 3-D area charts, six 3-D bar charts, four 3-D line charts, and six 3-D pie charts. For example, Figure 13-22 shows the varieties of 3-D bar chart available to you.

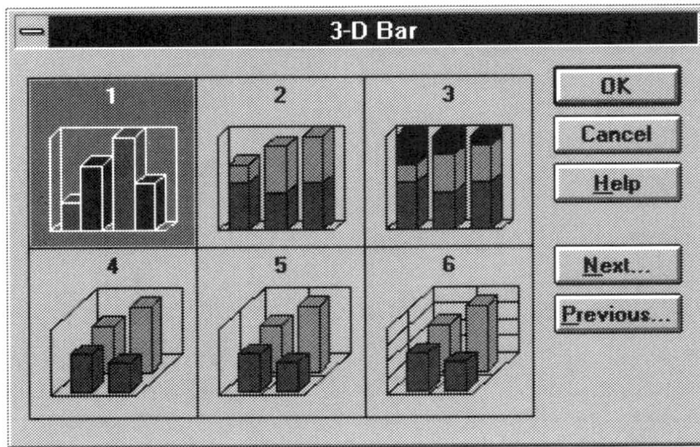

Figure 13-22. The 3-D bar charts.

Formatting charts

The basic bar chart which appears initially can be modified in a number of ways. For example, titles and borders can be added, and the legend can be removed. Fonts can be changed as well as the patterns and colors of the bars and lines. Changing the format of a spreadsheet is covered in this section.

Adding titles

Titles are used to add information to the chart. Titles are inserted through the *Titles* command in the **Edit** menu shown in Figure 13-23.

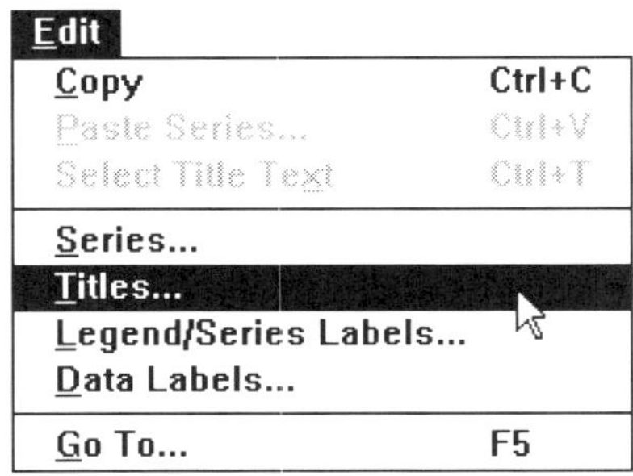

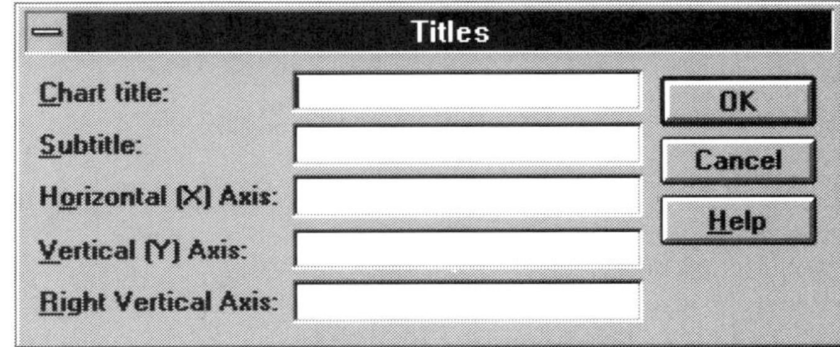

Figure 13-23. The Titles command in the ***Edit*** *menu brings up the Titles dialog box.*

A chart can have up to five titles, depending on the type of chart selected. These are the *Chart title, Subtitle, Horizontal (X) Axis, Vertical (Y) Axis*, and *Right Vertical Axis*. The *Titles* dialog box displays these.

The first four types of titles can be placed in the sample file. Open the *Titles* dialog box through the **Edit** menu. The text in charts can be typed directly into the corresponding text box or referred back to a cell address in the spreadsheet which contains the information for the title.

The first title to insert is the *Chart title* which appears at the top of the chart. This title is "Seabuddy Frozen Pops" and is the contents of cell A2. As the title is part of the spreadsheet, the cell address—"A2"—can be typed in. The *Chart title* text box has been filled in this way in Figure 13-24.

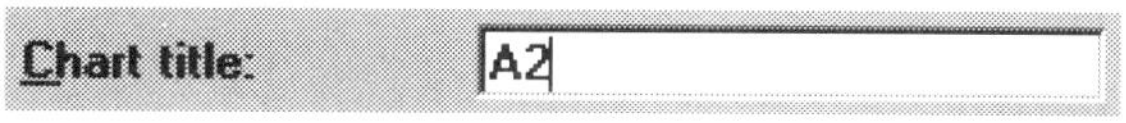

Chart title: A2

***Figure 13-24.** The Chart title text box is using the cell address A2 for the title.*

Click on *OK* to view the title as it appears on the chart (Figure 13-25).

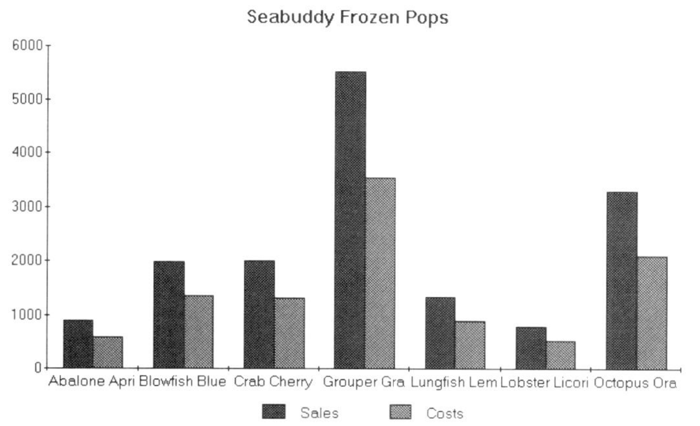

***Figure 13-25.** The chart title is "Seabuddy Frozen Pops."*

The *Subtitle* is the next one to insert. The *Subtitle* is located underneath the *Chart title* in a smaller font size which is not bold. The *Subtitle* is typed into the text box in the *Titles* dialog box as Figure 13-26 displays. Fill in the text box as shown.

Subtitle: Sales versus Costs

***Figure 13-26.** Type "Sales versus Costs" into the Subtitle text box.*

Type in the following axis titles before clicking on *OK*:

Horizontal (X) Axis: Flavors

Vertical (Y) Axis: $$$$

The chart looks like Figure 13-27 when all titles are inserted.

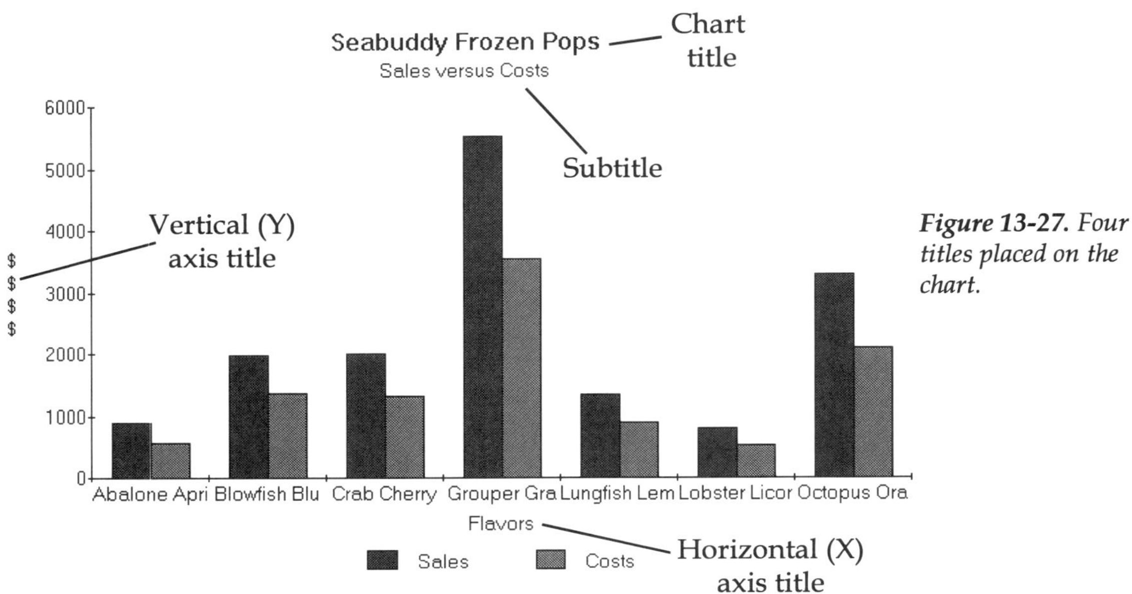

***Figure 13-27.** Four titles placed on the chart.*

Changing fonts

Fonts are a style of type designated to a piece of text. Fonts available depend on the printer selected. The charting facility enables you to change the font, font size, and style of text in your chart.

The font of the chart title shown in Figure 13-28, for example, is now 48 point Script.

Seabuddy Frozen Pops

Sales versus Costs

***Figure 13-28.** The chart title is changed to 48 point Script.*

To achieve this, select the title by clicking on it in your chart or by pressing Ctrl-T. Then choose the *Font and Style* command in the **Format** menu (Figure 13-29) to display the *Font and Style for Title* dialog box.

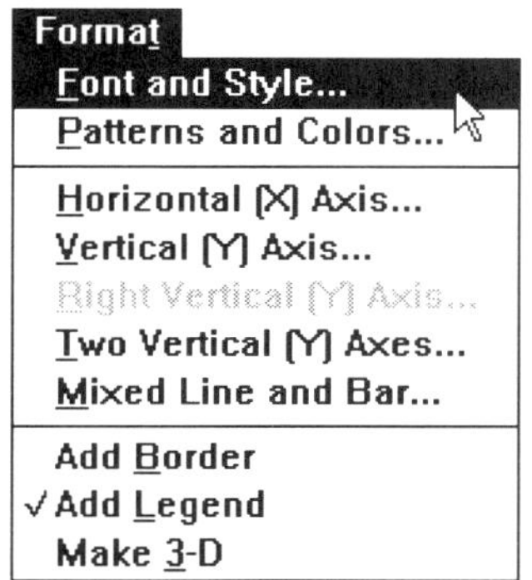

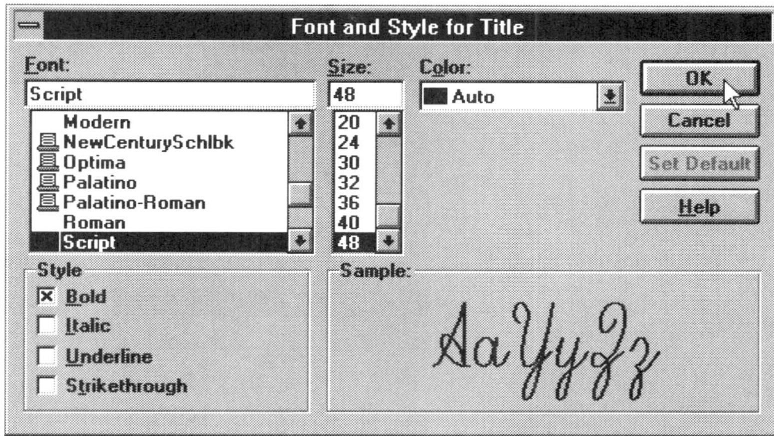

Figure 13-29. *When you select the chart title, the Font and Style command opens the Font and Style for Title dialog box.*

The options in this dialog box allow you to change the font, its size, style and color. The *Font* selected is *Script*, and the *Size* is 48 point. (If this font is not available on your system, choose another.) This is a fairly large font which is good for an important title. The *Bold* check box is selected by default. The dialog box in Figure 13-29 creates the chart title in Figure 13-28.

If you do not first select the title of your chart, the other titles are changed simultaneously with the *Font and Style* command in the **Format** menu. You have the same options in the dialog box opened by this command whether you select the chart title first or not. Click outside the chart title or press Ctrl-T to deselect the title. Now use the *Font and Style* command to change the point size for the rest of your chart to 8 points, making the X axis series more readable.

Legends

A legend appears by default on your charts. To remove the legend, deselect the *Add Legend* command in the **Format** menu.

To redisplay the legend, select *Add Legend* again from the **Format** menu, as in Figure 13-30. Works indicates with a check mark on the menu that you have enabled the legend.

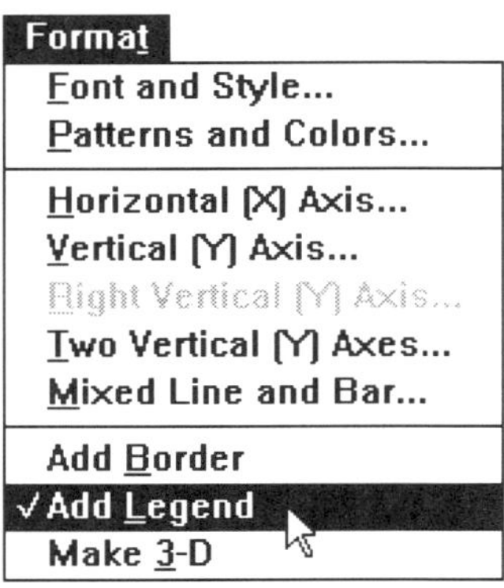

***Figure 13-30.** Turn the legend back on.*

The text which appears in the legend is automatically determined when the chart is created. To change this, select *Legend/Series Labels* from the **Edit** menu. The *Legend/Series Labels* dialog box appears with the cell references containing "Sales" and "Costs" (Figure 13-31). New text or another cell address can be typed in to change the legend text. Alternatively, you can assign a legend which refers to your series simply as "Series 1" and "Series 2" by selecting *Auto series labels*. In the case of an area chart, Works also gives you the choice of *Use as legend* or *Use as area labels* to determine whether your legend appears separately.

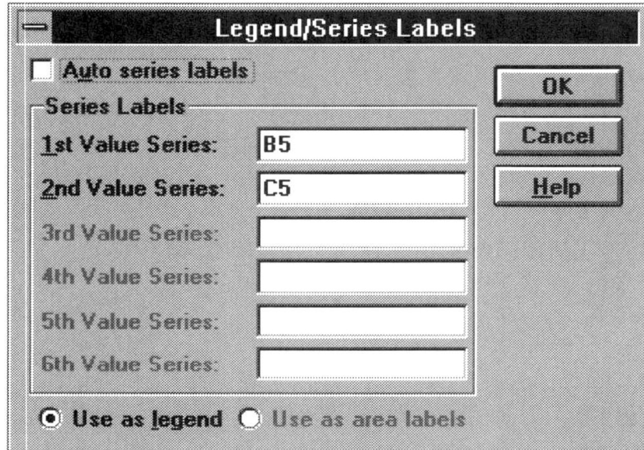

***Figure 13-31.** The Legend dialog box referring to the cells which contain the legend text.*

Data labels

Data labels are used in charts to add more information to one or more Y series. In a bar chart, for instance, a data label showing the exact value represented, is added to the Sales bars in Figure 13-32.

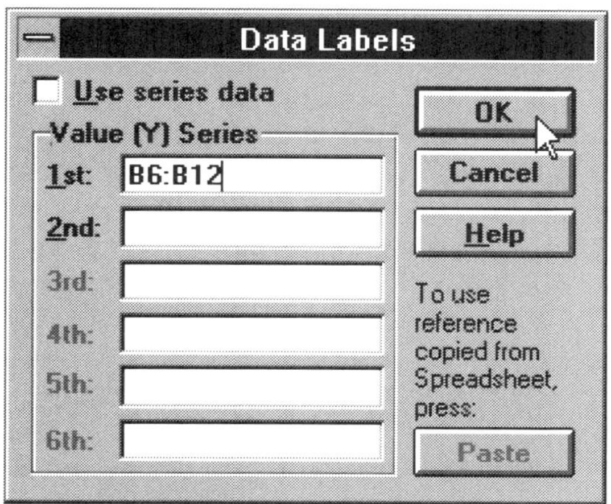

Figure 13-32. The Sales bars show their exact values with a data label.

This is achieved by selecting *Data Labels* from the **Edit** menu to display the *Data Labels* dialog box. "SEASON" is the third Y series, and therefore the cell address of this series — D4:D8 — is inserted in the *3rd* text box. Try adding *Data Labels* to your spreadsheet.

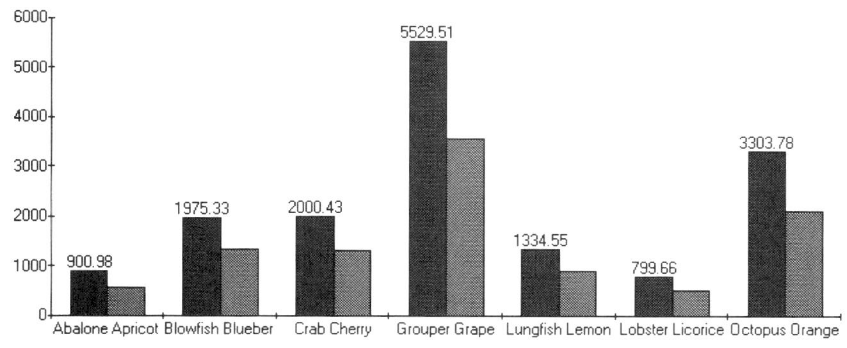

Figure 13-33. The 1st series is given a data label using the cell address of the series.

Borders

The *Add Border* command in the **Format** menu puts a border around your entire chart. Choose this command as in Figure 13-34.

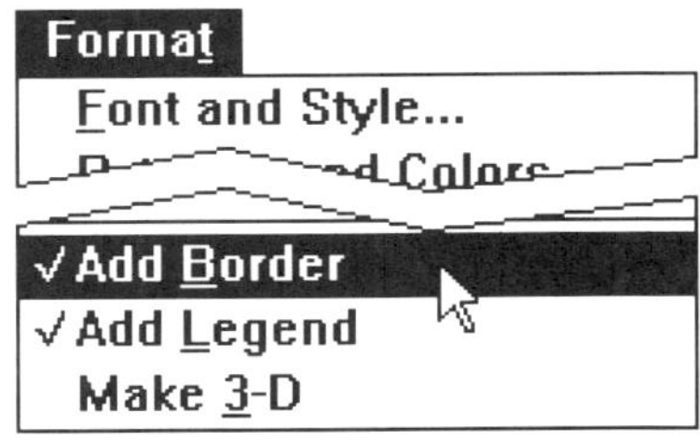

Figure 13-34. *The Add Border command in the **Format** menu.*

Gridlines

Gridlines are added to a chart to assist in comparing parts of the chart with a point on the scale. Vertical, horizontal, or a combination of gridlines are placed through the **Format** menu. To display horizontal gridlines, select *Horizontal (X) Axis* from the **Format** menu and click on the *Show Gridlines* check box (Figure 13-35). Click on *OK* to exit.

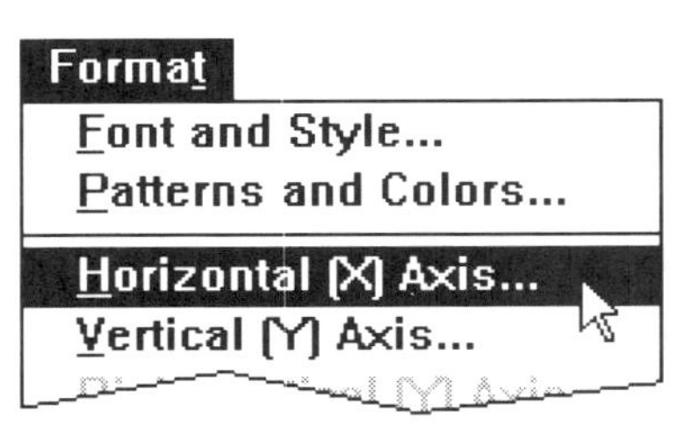

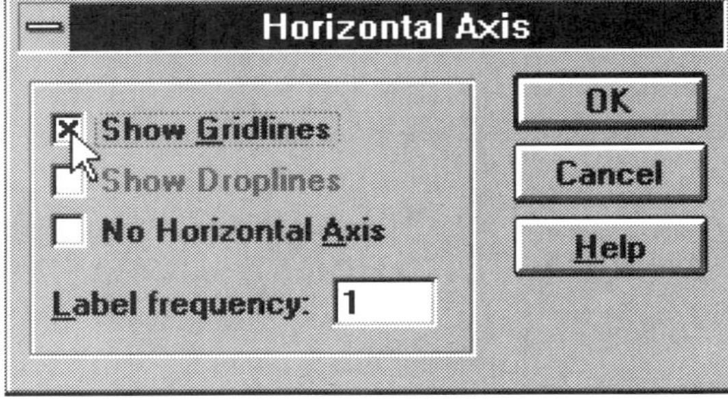

Figure 13-35. *Choose Show Gridlines in the Horizontal Axis dialog box.*

Vertical gridlines are displayed by choosing *Vertical (Y) Axis* in the **Format** menu and checking *Show Gridlines* in the dialog box as shown in Figure 13-36.

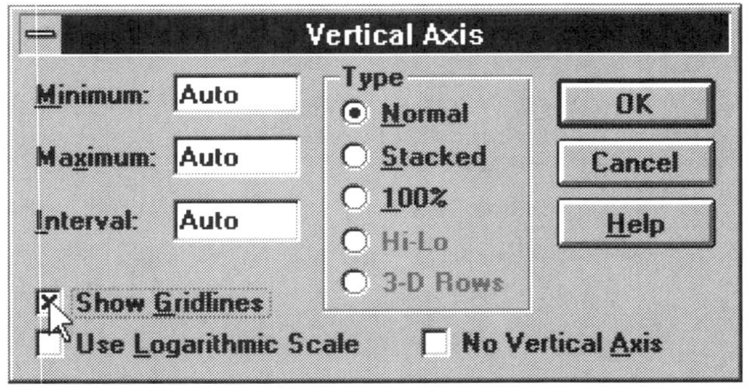

Figure 13-36. *Check Show Gridlines in the Vertical Axis dialog box.*

The chart now displays both sets of gridlines, as in Figure 13-37.

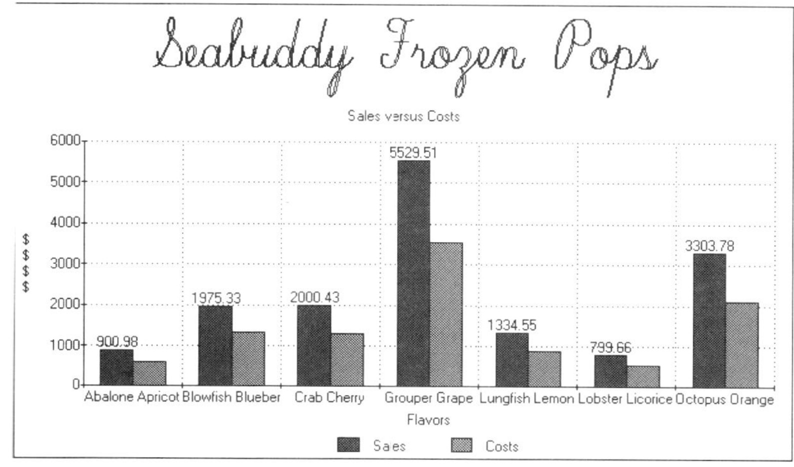

Figure 13-37. The chart with gridlines and a border displayed.

Selecting patterns and colors

Patterns and colors of bars, lines, and markers, as well as segments of a pie chart, can be changed from the default colors specified. Works indicates the default color and pattern schemes with "Auto" in the submenus in the *Patterns and Colors* dialog box.

Patterns and colors are printer dependent, particularly the colors. If your printer cannot print color, Works automatically changes it to black and white before printing.

The colors in the chart created previously in this chapter use the default colors provided. Select the *Patterns and Colors* command in the **Format** menu to change these (Figure 13-38).

Figure 13-38. The Patterns and Colors command.

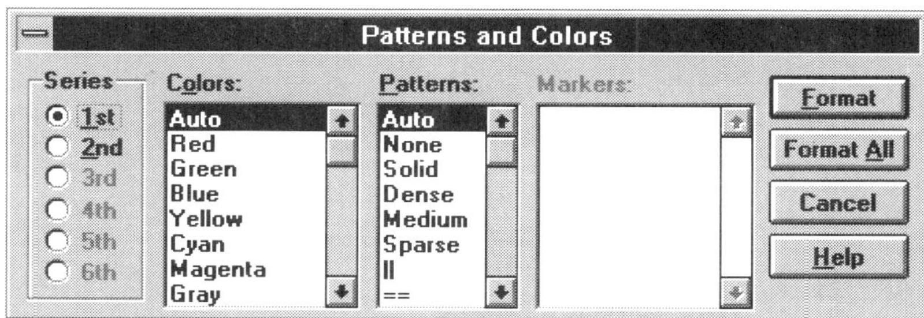

In the *Series* list, you choose the series to be altered. With a pie chart, *Slices* is available, referring to the segments of a pie.

Explode Slice (Figure 13-39) is available only when a pie chart is active. Selecting this check box separates the current slice from the rest of the pie to make it stand out.

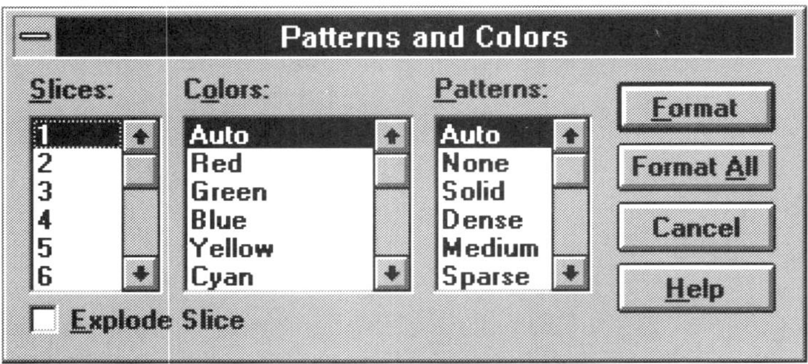

Figure 13-39. *The Patterns and Colors dialog box used for Pie charts.*

Colors displays a list of colors which can be applied to a series.

Patterns enables you to change the fill pattern of a series and the style of line. This is especially important when printing in black and white.

Markers (Figure 13-40) affect the points on a line chart. The shape of these is altered in this list box.

The *Format* button on the right of the dialog box sets the format selected for the particular series or slice and keeps the dialog box open.

Format All sets the same format to all of the series in the chart. This is used especially to reset the patterns and colors back to *Auto*.

Use the *Colors and Patterns* dialog box to change all the series patterns to *Medium* by clicking on *Medium* in the *Patterns* list box as in Figure 13-40 and then on *Format All*. The *Cancel* button changes to *Close* at this point. To close the dialog box, click on *Close*.

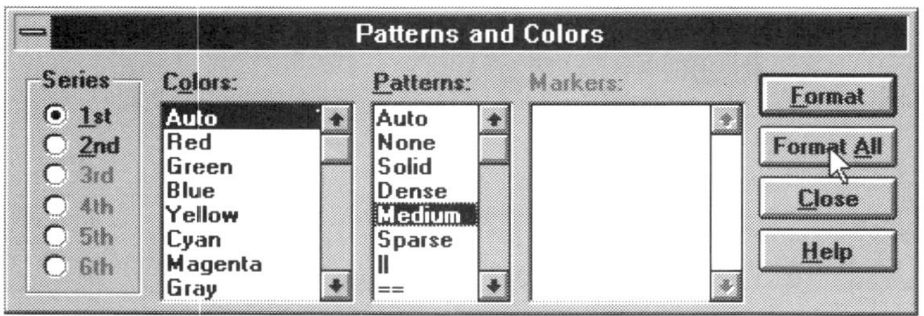

Figure 13-40. *Click on Medium and then on Format All.*

Mixing bar and line charts

You can mix line and bar charts to distinguish clearly between two types of data represented on a chart. The *Mixed Line and Bar* command to do this is in the **Format** menu (Figure 13-41).

In the *Mixed Line and Bar* dialog box, the style of each Y series is decided. As the chart is currently a bar chart, the *Bar* options are active for each of the series. In this example, change the *1st Value(Y) Series* option to *Line* as in Figure 13-41.

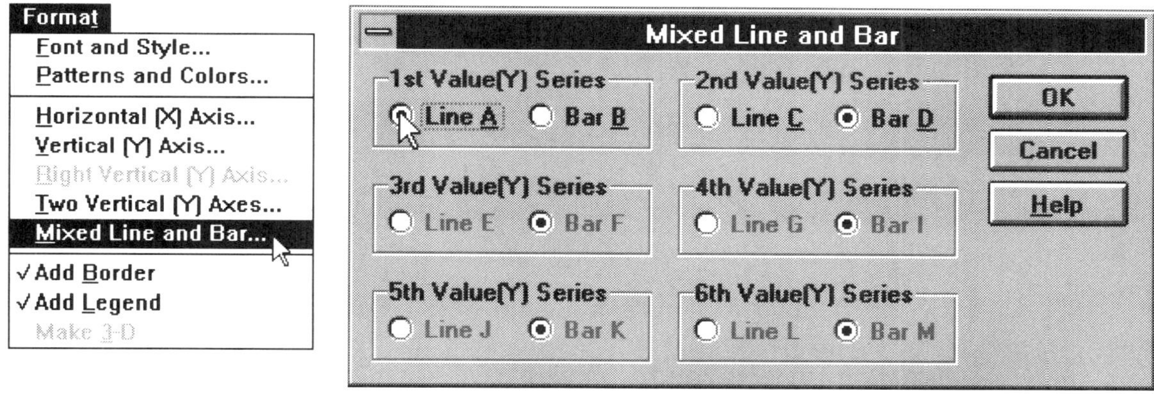

Figure 13-41. *Choose Mixed Line and Bar from the* ***Format*** *menu and click on Line A.*

The chart you see is illustrated in Figure 13-42.

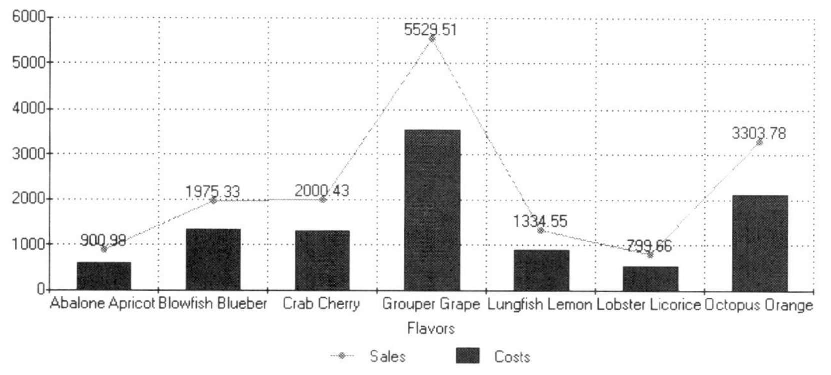

Figure 13-42. *The first series is represented by a line.*

Vertical axis

The scale on a vertical axis is changed to add meaning and impact to your chart. There are a number of options available in the *Vertical Axis* dialog box in Figure 13-43 which is activated through the *Vertical (Y) Axis* command in the **Format** menu.

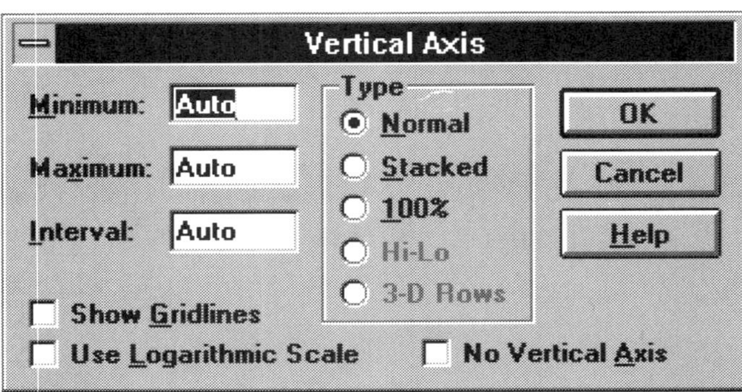

Figure 13-43. The Vertical Axis dialog box.

Works uses an automatic scale which is determined by the Y series values. The automatic scale is indicated by "*Auto*" in the *Minimum, Maximum,* and *Interval* text boxes. To set a specific scale, values are typed into the text boxes to specify the minimum value in the scale, the maximum value, and the increment by which it increases.

The type of scale used can be changed in the *Type* section. A stacked scale, for example, is used in Figure 13-44 by clicking on *Stacked* in the *Vertical Axis* dialog box. We have used the *Mixed Line and Bar* command to change the chart to a conventional bar chart for the purposes of this figure.

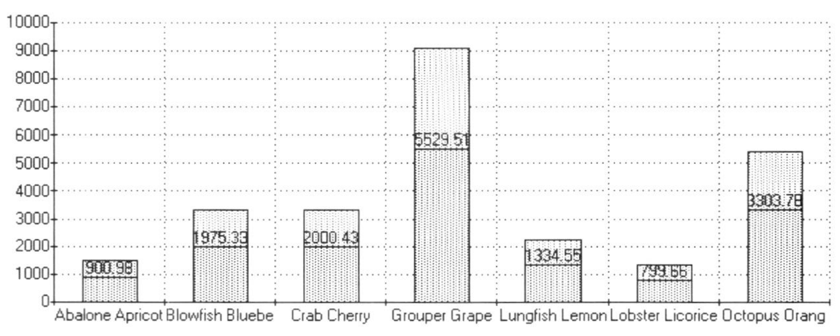

Figure 13-44. We have chosen the Stacked option here.

A right axis can be added to highlight a particular series on the chart. It is especially relevant to the chart in Figure 13-42 where the first series is displayed by a line. A right Y axis could be placed on the chart relating specifically to sales.

The command *Two Vertical (Y) Axes* in the **Format** menu is used for this purpose. Select this now to display the *Two Vertical Axes* dialog box. An option for a left and right axis is allocated for each series — each of these indicating a *Left* axis is current. To insert a right axis which uses the scale related to the first series, click on *Right B* in the *1st Value Series* section (Figure 13-45).

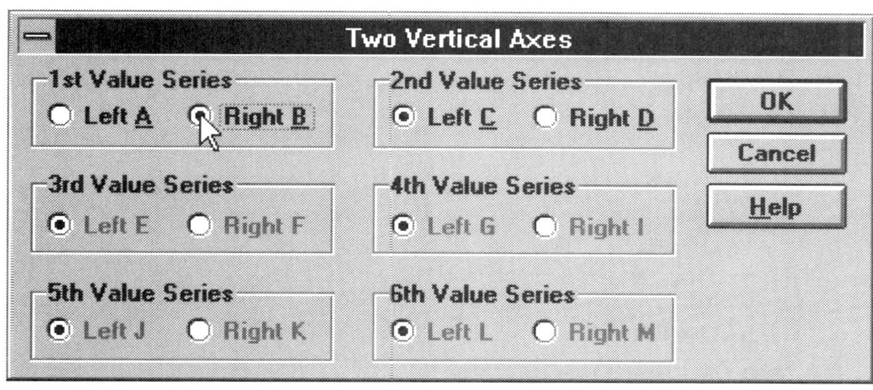

Figure 13-45. Click on Right B for the first series to display a right axis for that value series.

To make the chart even clearer, the right axis is labeled through the *Titles* command outlined earlier in this chapter (Figure 13-23). The chart in Figure 13-46 has been given a right axis title. Also, in the *Vertical Axis* dialog box (Figure 13-43), the *Type* section has been changed back to *Normal.*

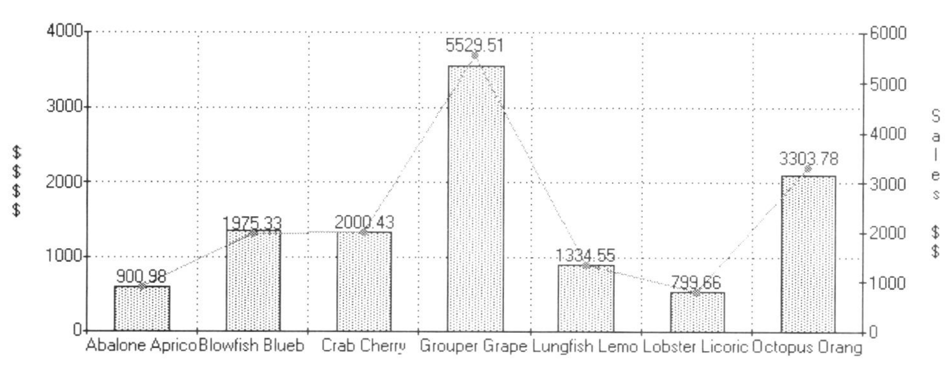

Figure 13-46. The right axis is inserted and given the title Sales $$.

Previewing and printing charts

Charts displayed on the screen are not always represented as they appear on paper. For example, if a non-color laser printer is active, color is not seen when printed – only on the screen.

The Display as Printed command

Works allows you to view the chart as it will print and also provides *Print Preview* facilities.

Works enables you to view the chart as it is printed though the *Display as Printed* command in the **View** menu (Figure 13-47). If your printer is a black and white unit, Works now displays in shades of gray, instead of color.

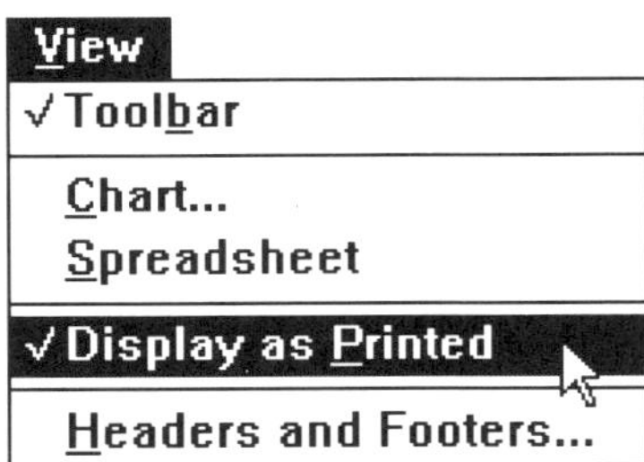

Figure 13-47. *The Display as Printed command.*

The Print Preview command

Print Preview is selected through the *Print Preview* command in the **File** menu or by clicking on the *Print Preview* button on the toolbar.

Print Preview in the charting facility of Works is used in exactly the same way as in the other tools. For more information about *Print Preview*, refer to **Chapter 7, Printing Word Processed Documents**.

The chart is displayed on the page size selected (Figure 13-48).

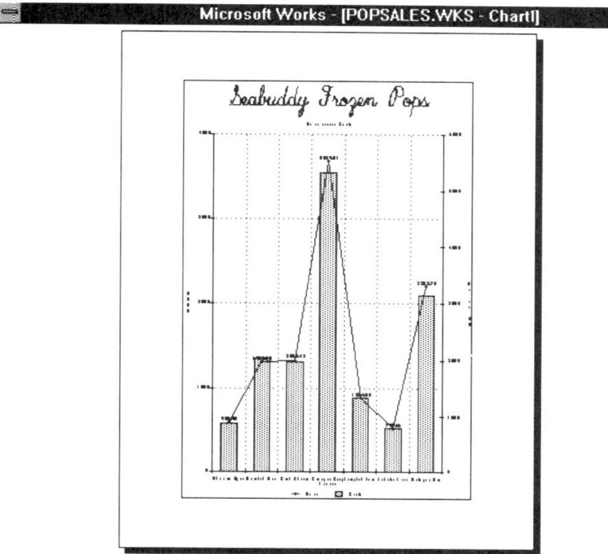

Figure 13-48. The chart in Print Preview.

The Print command

The *Print* command is activated through the **File** menu, by clicking on the *Print* button on the toolbar, or by using the *Print* button in the *Print Preview* screen.

When you choose *Print* from the **File** menu, the *Print* dialog box (Figure 13-49) appears, which gives you the option to print more than one copy of the chart.

Print your chart now using any of these methods.

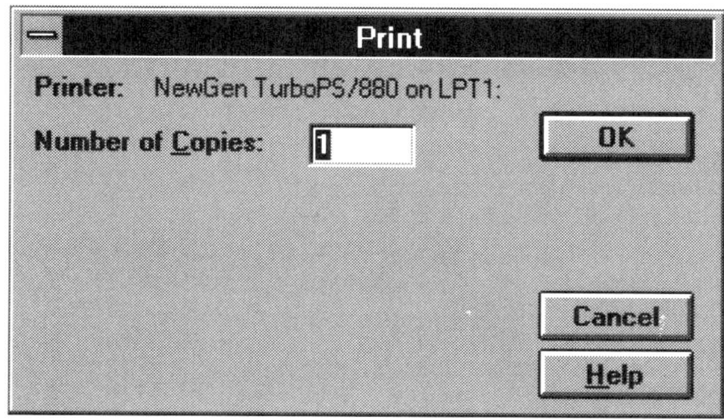

Figure 13-49. The Print dialog box.

Changing the page orientation

Charts are often wider than they are long. The orientation of the page can be adjusted so the chart can fit more comfortably on the page. Landscape and portrait are the two types of page orientation available. A portrait page is longer than it is wide – as the pages in this book are. In landscape orientation, the page is wider than it is long.

A chart in Works is printed in portrait by default. To change to landscape, the *Page Setup* and *Printer Setup* dialog boxes need to be changed.

The *Page Setup* dialog box is activated through the *Page Setup* command in the **File** menu. In Figure 13-50 we have chosen the *Source, Size and Orientation* tab and then selected *Landscape* in the *Orientation* section. This swaps the dimensions in the *Width* and *Height* boxes.

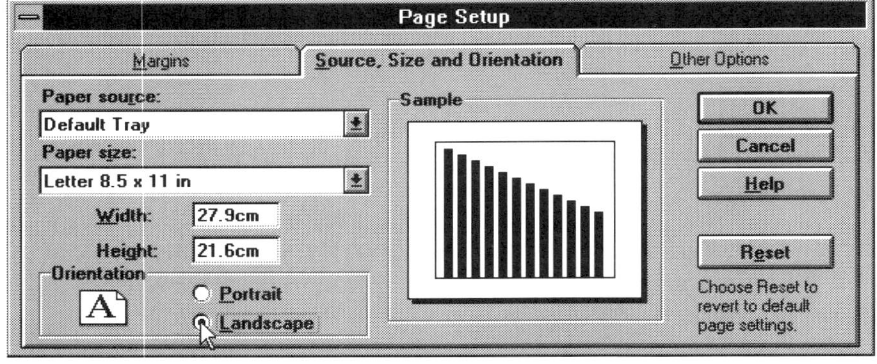

Figure 13-50. *Click on the Source, Size and Orientation tab and then select Landscape.*

Now change the orientation for your printer through the *Printer Setup* dialog box. Choose the *Printer Setup* command in the **File** menu. Click on the *Setup* button to open the dialog box for your printer and choose *Landscape* in the *Orientation* section as in Figure 13-51.

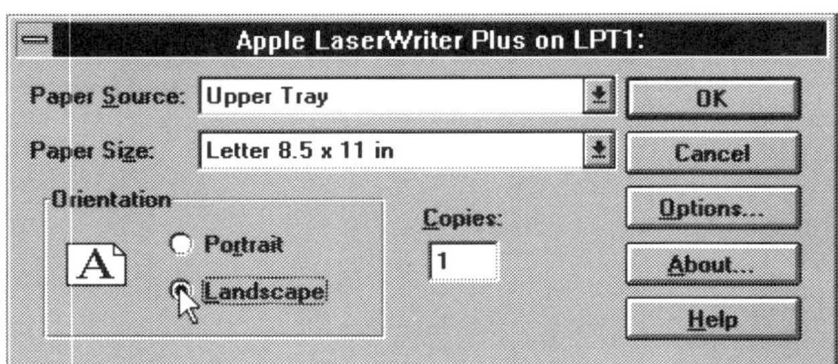

Figure 13-51. *The orientation is changed from Portrait to Landscape through the Printer Setup command.*

Handling multiple charts

There is often a need in a spreadsheet to create more than one chart in which to display the data. Multiple charts may show different parts of the spreadsheets or represent the same data in a different way.

Works enables you to create a number of charts for the same spreadsheet. Each chart is named "Chart" followed by a number, for example "Chart1." This name can be changed to a more meaningful description. The chart can be deleted or duplicated. These features are outlined in this section.

Creating a new chart

Once the cells are selected, a new chart is created using the *Create New Chart* command in the **Tools** menu in the spreadsheet or the charting facility. It is the same procedure as you used to create the original chart at the beginning of this chapter.

Try this now. Move back into the spreadsheet through the **Window** menu (Figure 13-52).

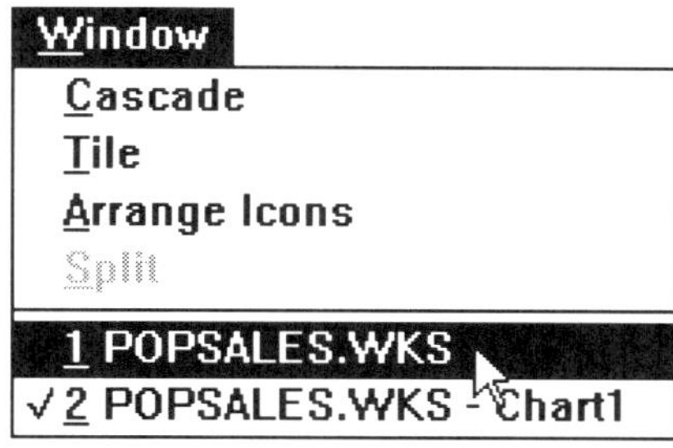

Figure 13-52. *Select POPSALES.WKS from the **Window** menu.*

The cells to select are A5:B12 which are used to create a pie chart as the second chart for this spreadsheet. To create the chart, choose *Create New Chart* from the **Tools** menu and click on *OK*. The new chart appears on the screen as a bar, which is the default. Change it to a pie by clicking on the pie button and select the fourth option in the *Pie* dialog box. Double-click on the option, or click on *OK*. *Chart2* appears on the screen as in Figure 13-53.

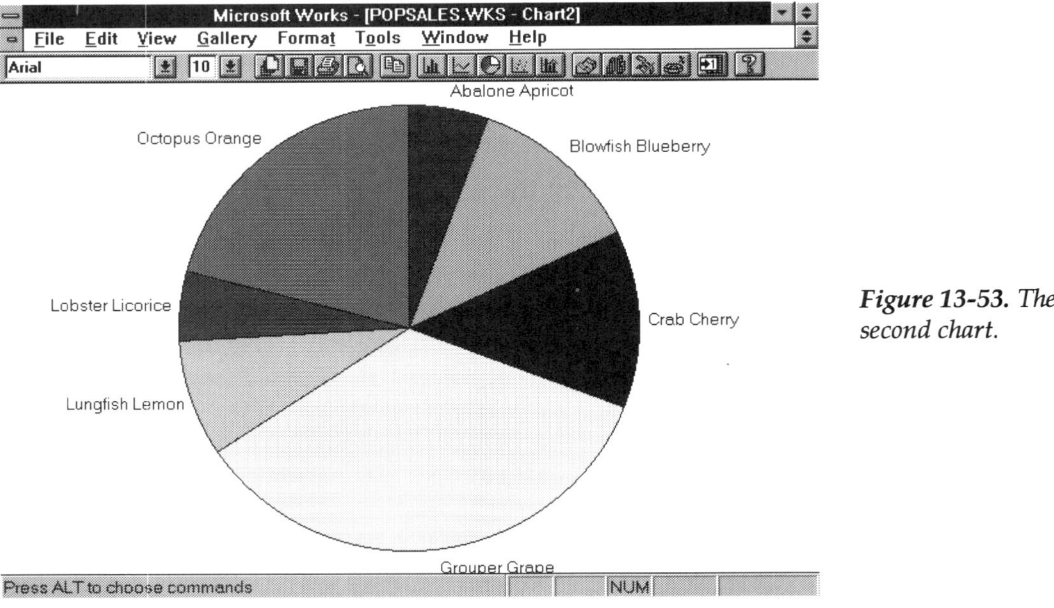

Figure 13-53. The second chart.

Naming, deleting, and duplicating a chart

A chart is named to give it a more meaningful name which makes it easier to identify. The *Name Chart* command in the **Tools** menu (Figure 13-54) displays the *Name Chart* dialog box.

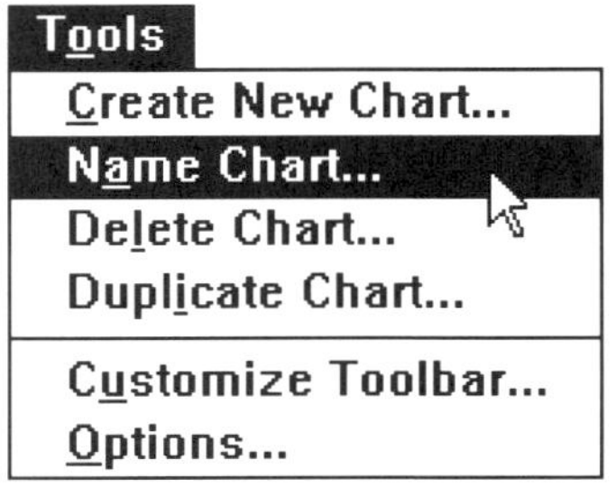

Figure 13-54. The Name Chart command.

The chart you just created displays the sales figures. A logical name for the chart, therefore, is "Sales." The chart being named—Chart2—is selected from the *Charts* list box and the name is typed into the *Name* text box as in Figure 13-55.

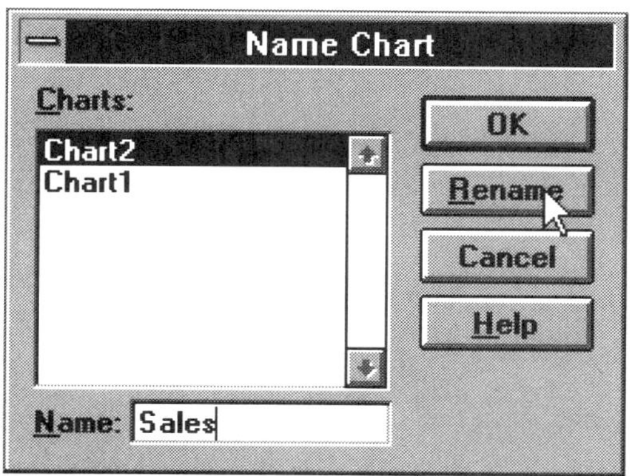

Figure 13-55. *The chart is named "Sales."*

To set the name, click on the *Rename* button and, when done, click on *OK*. The chart is renamed "Sales."

A chart is deleted using the *Delete Chart* command in the **Tools** menu. The chart to be deleted is selected in the *Delete Charts* dialog box and *Delete* is clicked (Figure 13-56). Clicking on *OK* then removes the chart from the system.

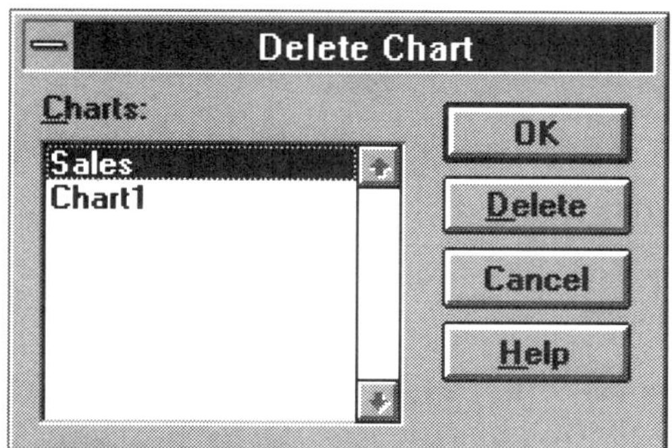

Figure 13-56. *The Delete Chart dialog box.*

An exact copy of a chart is created when the *Duplicate Chart* command is selected in the **Tools** menu.

Duplicate "Chart1" by selecting it in the *Charts* list box in the *Duplicate Chart* dialog box (Figure 13-57). Click on *Duplicate* to create a copy of the chart, called Chart2; then click on *OK*.

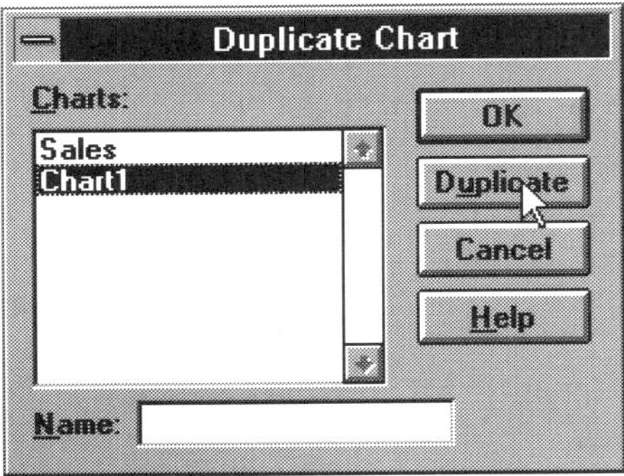

Figure 13-57. *The Duplicate Chart dialog box.*

Switching between charts

The sample file now contains three charts. To move between these charts, you can select the chart you wish to view from the *Charts* dialog box. You open this dialog box by choosing *Chart* from the **View** menu (Figure 13-58).

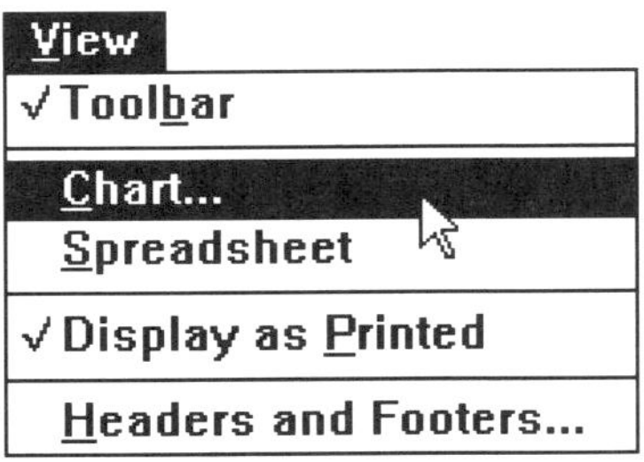

Figure 13-58. *Choose Chart from the* ***View*** *menu.*

Move to Chart1 by double-clicking on *Chart1* in the *Charts* dialog box as Figure 13-59 shows. Once you view a new chart in this way, you can also switch to it from the **Window** menu as you did earlier.

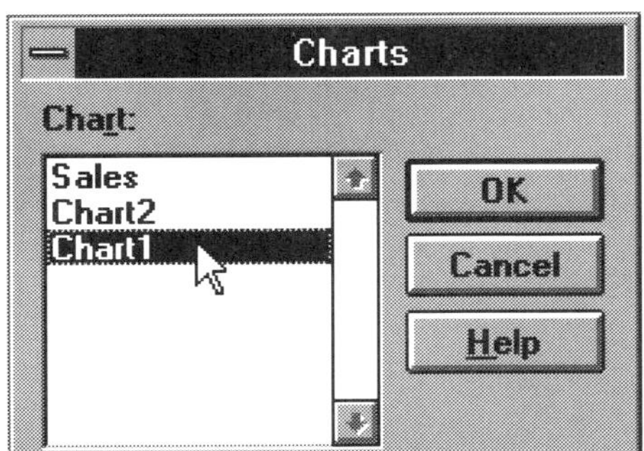

Figure 13-59. *The Charts dialog box.*

The Database Screen

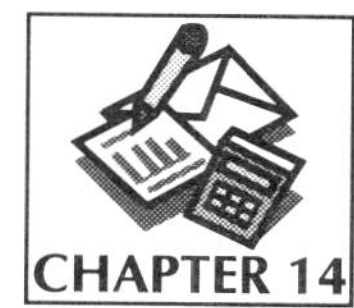

In this chapter you are shown how to start up the database tool in Works. The screen, although similar to the word processor and the spreadsheet, contains a number of different elements unique to the database. These are outlined in this chapter.

Database structure

A database is a collection of information stored in a logical order. People have been using databases for years, and now use computers to build bigger and more accessible databases.

A database consists of records which are broken into fields. A staff list is an example of a database—which could be created electronically—using the basic structure of records and fields.

A simple staff list usually contains the last and first names of a person, the department in which they work, and the telephone extension for each member of staff. The company keeps this information for each person employed.

Those four pieces of information make up one *record* in the database. The record is divided into *fields*—last name, first name, department, and telephone extension. Figure 14-1 shows one record in the "Staff" database created in Works. *Crocker* is a field entry in the *Last name* field.

```
 Last name: Crocker
First name: Jim
Department: Sales
       Ext:                345
```

Figure 14-1. *The Staff database.*

A database can contain up to 32,000 records. A record in Works can have up to 256 fields. Each field can contain up to 256 characters. The structure of a database is discussed in more detail in the next chapter, **Creating a Database.**

Starting the database

A new database file is loaded by clicking on the *Database* button in the *Startup* dialog box (Figure 14-2).

The new file is called "Data" and a number, for instance, "Data1" until you save it and give it a relevant name.

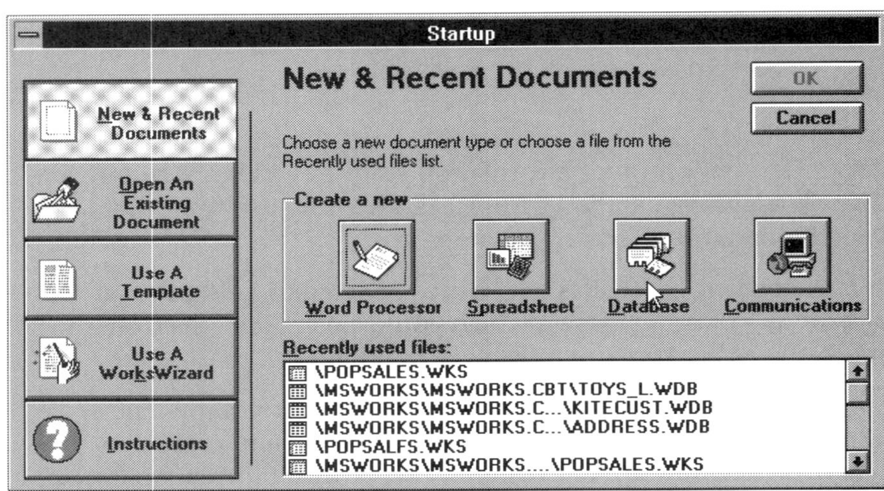

Figure 14-2. *The Database button.*

To open a file already created, you can click on the *Open an Existing Document* button in the *Startup* dialog box, or select *Open Existing File* from the **File** menu.

The *Open* dialog box appears on the screen. All files in this directory are listed in the *Recently used files* list box. To view the database file only—with the extension of *.wdb*—select *Works DB(*.wdb)* in the *List Files of Type* submenu (Figure 14-3).

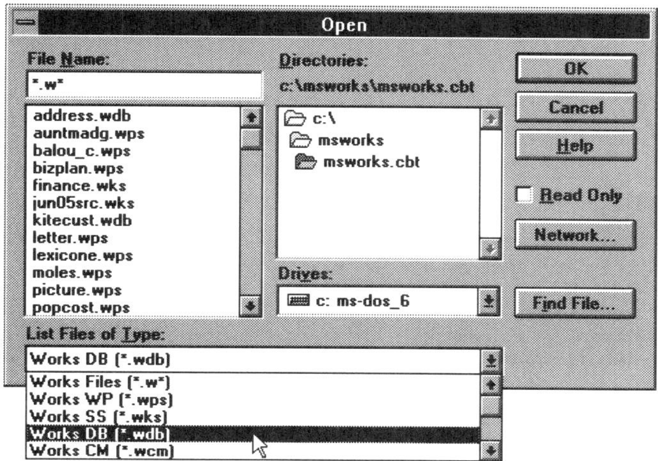

Figure 14-3. You can choose to list database files only with the List Files of Type option.

Common database screen components

Data can be viewed in a variety of ways. In this section, the parts of the screen common to all views are outlined initially (Figure 14-4).

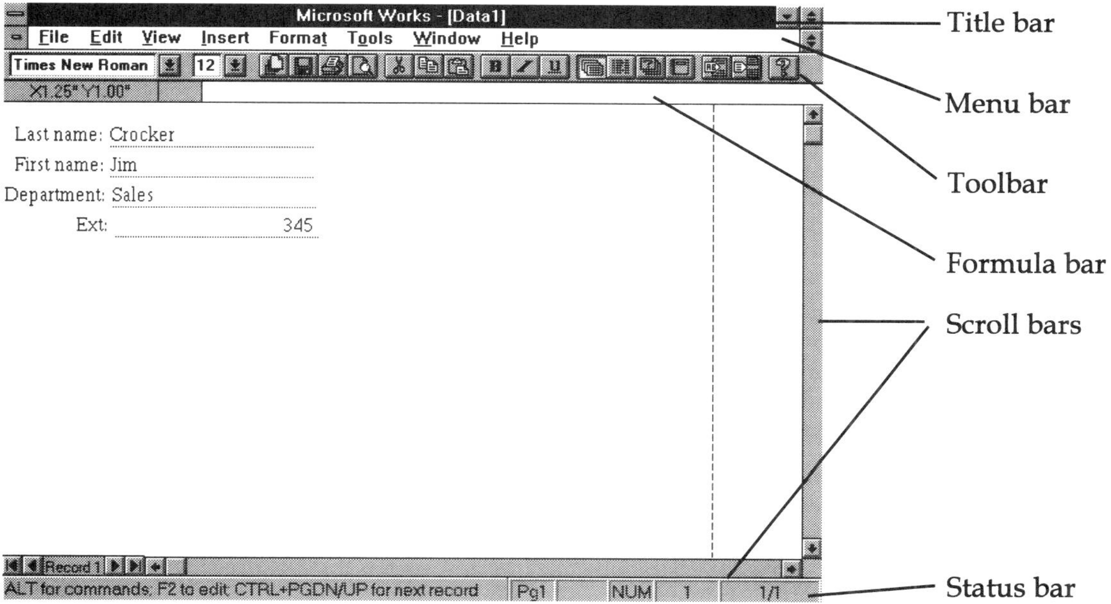

***Figure 14-4.** The parts of the database screen common to all views.*

The title bar

The title bar is a standard Windows feature. The application title bar contains the name of the application—Microsoft Works. The document title bar contains the name of the file. When the document window is maximized, both the application and database file names appear on the title bar (Figure 14-5). More information about the title bar is in **Chapter 1, The Word Processor Screen**.

Figure 14-5. *The application title bar.*

The menu bar

The menu bar is directly under the title bar in the Works database. It contains menu options specific to the database. The options are: **File, Edit, View, Insert, Format, Tools, Window**, and **Help** which are displayed in Figure 14-6.

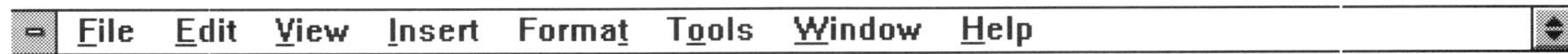

Figure 14-6. *The menu bar.*

The toolbar

The toolbar (Figure 14-7) contains a number of submenus and buttons which are shortcuts to some of the commands in the menus. More information about the buttons you have seen so far is found in **Chapter 1, The Word Processor Screen**.

The *View* buttons are unique to the database and are outlined in more detail in a later section. Also, you can use the *Insert* buttons as shortcuts when you add fields or records to your database.

Figure 14-7. *The database toolbar.*

The formula bar

The formula bar displays the field entry of the current field.

The scroll bars

Scroll bars are a Windows feature which enables you to move around the database screen by clicking the arrows or dragging the box in the scroll bar to a different position.

While in *Form* view, which is discussed in the next section, Works provides buttons to move you through the records. Figure 14-8 highlights these buttons which are on the horizontal scroll bar.

First record
Record 1
Last record
Previous record
Next record

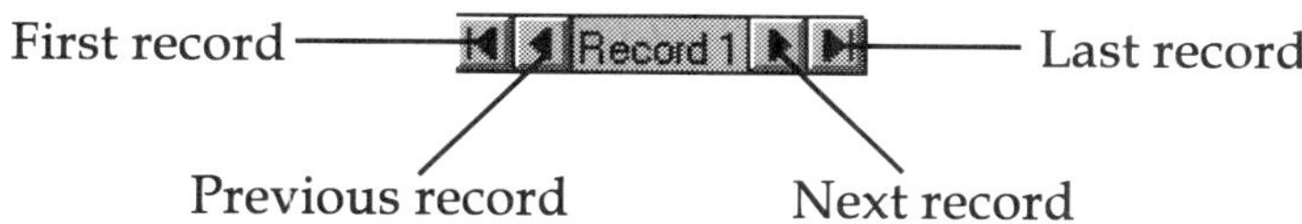

Figure 14-8. *The scroll bar buttons which enable you to move to particular records in Form view.*

The status bar

The left side of the status bar is used to display messages (Figure 14-9). The message displayed could be concerning the menu command chosen or shortcut hints. The status bar also tells you the page number and the record number where the insertion point is.

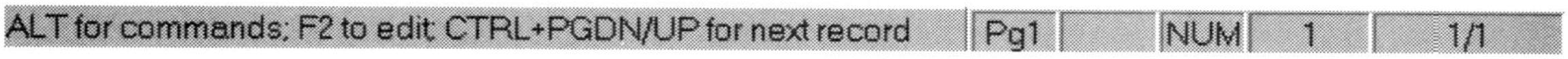

ALT for commands; F2 to edit; CTRL+PGDN/UP for next record
Pg1
NUM
1
1/1

Figure 14-9. *The status bar.*

Database views

As indicated above, data can be viewed on the screen in a number of ways in Works. The view selected displays the data in a particular way, specific to what you need to see at the time.

There are four views: *Form*, *List*, *Query*, and *Report Definition*. *Form* and *List* views are discussed in this section. *Query* and *Report Definition* views are covered in later chapters.

Form view

Any new file created is displayed in *Form* view by default. This view enables you to work with one record in the database at one time. It is a similar concept to using index cards or a printed form. In Figure 14-10, the staff database is displayed in *Form* view.

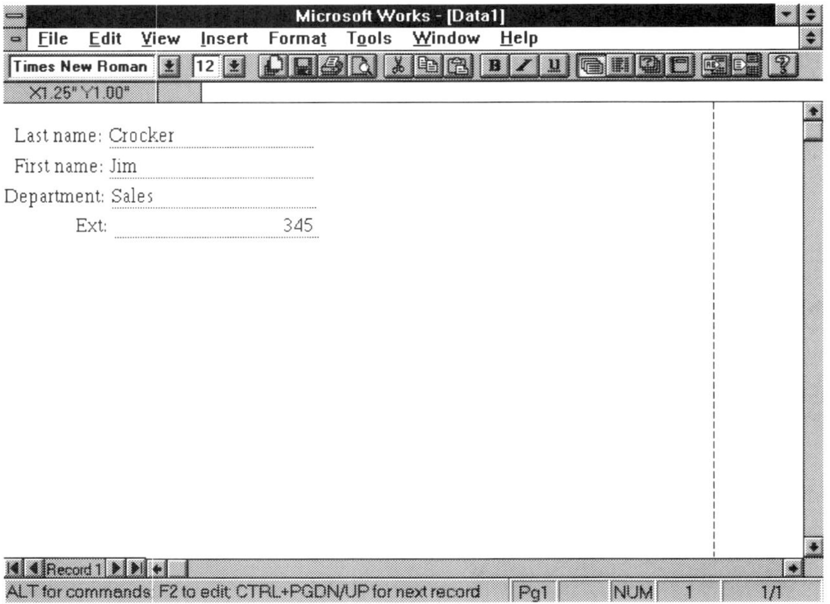

***Figure 14-10.** The staff database in Form view.*

List view

To work with multiple records in the database simultaneously, *List* view is selected. *List* view displays the records in a grid, similar to the spreadsheet layout. Each cell in *List* view contains a field or field entry. Figure 14-11 displays the staff database in *List* view.

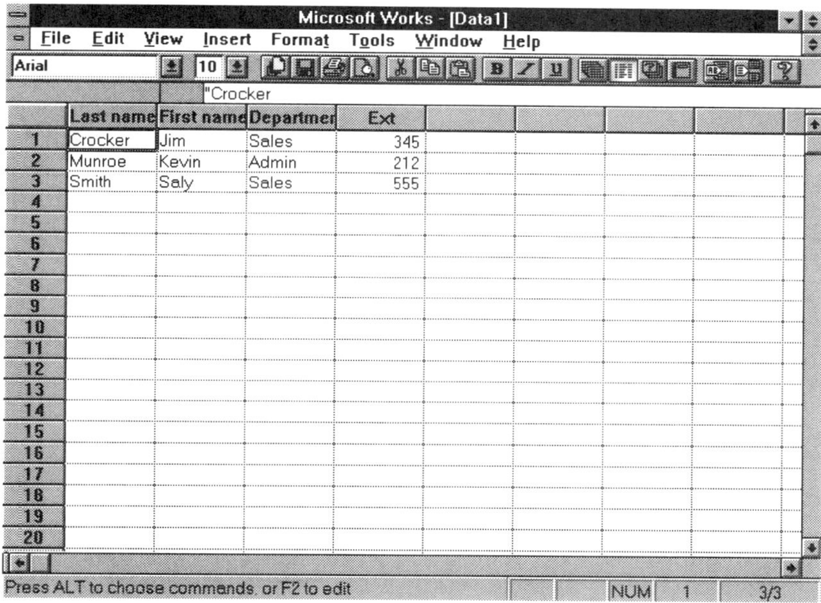

***Figure 14-11.** The staff database in List view.*

Changing views

Swapping between *List* view and *Form* view can be done using the *View* buttons on the toolbar, the **View** menu, or the F9 button.

The *View* buttons are displayed in Figure 14-12.

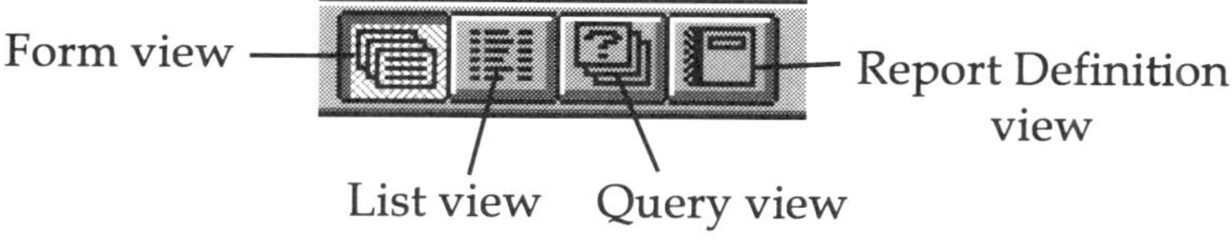

***Figure 14-12.** The View buttons on the toolbar.*

The **View** menu (Figure 14-13) is another way to change views. Select the view required from the menu and the screen adjusts accordingly.

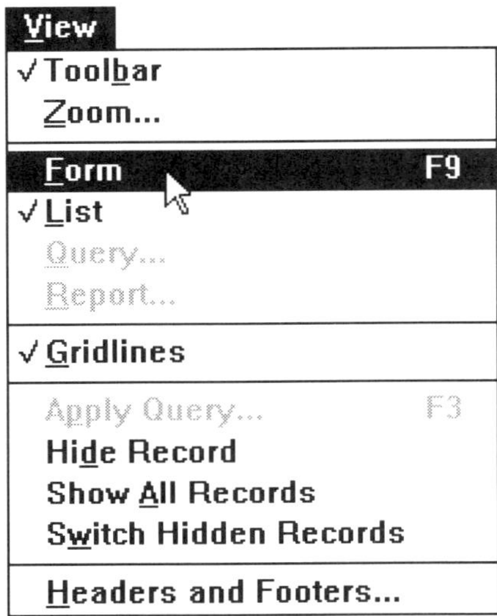

***Figure 14-13.** The **View** menu.*

The F9 key is used in the database as a toggle switch between *List* view and *Form* view. If *List* view is displayed and F9 is pressed, the screen displays the database in *Form* view. The opposite occurs when *Form* view is active.

Closing the database

When you have completed work on your database, you can close it in the same as any other document in Works. As before, choose the *Close* command in the **File** menu.

Creating a Database

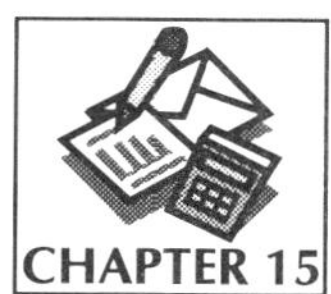

The first step in creating a database is deciding what is to go into the database. Looking at what it will be used for often gives you a few clues.

Creation

The database created in this chapter is of names and addresses used by the "Save the Hippo" group, which needs a database to keep track of the people who donate money to their cause and how much they donate each time.

To create a database from scratch, click on the *Database* button in the *Startup* dialog box as in Figure 15-1.

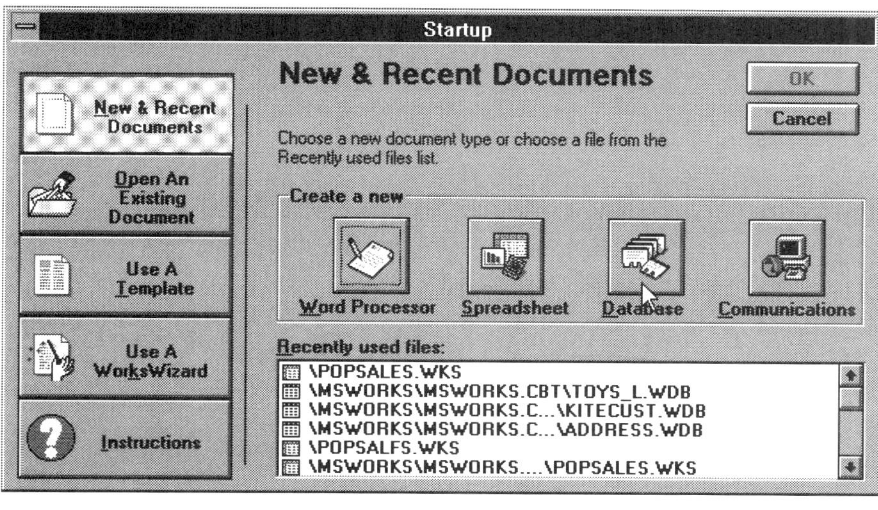

Figure 15-1. *A new database is created by clicking on the Database button in the Startup dialog box.*

The screen display is blank when opened for the first time. The screen is being viewed in *Form* view, by default (Figure 15-2). It has been maximized by clicking on the maximize button and the insertion point appears in the left-hand corner.

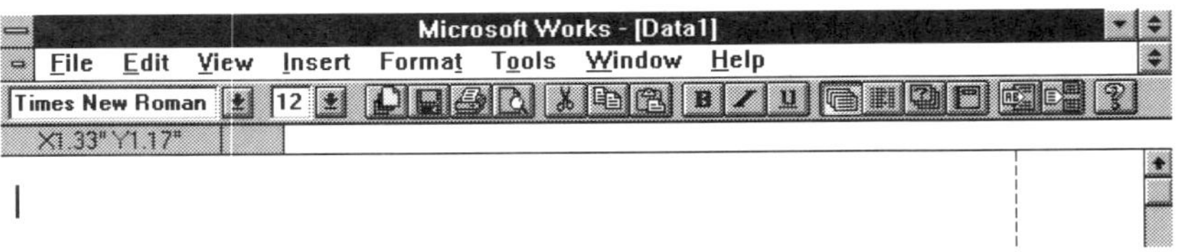

Figure 15-2. The top of the blank Form view screen with the insertion point.

At this point, it is important to consider what fields are required in the database you are developing. Time spent in these early stages pays off in the long term, leading to a more flexible and workable database.

Smaller, more precise fields, which break down the contents of a record, are a much better system to adopt than using large fields which contain a lot of information. This allows for flexibility in sorting and searching, which is covered in **Chapter 17, Viewing the Database**.

The record structure in the database at this stage will contain the following fields: First name, Last name, Address, City, State, Postal Code, and Country.

Adding fields

In Form view

Type in the first field, which is "First name:". It is important to include the colon (:) in the field name. The colon tells Works that what is being typed in is a field and not a label or field entry.

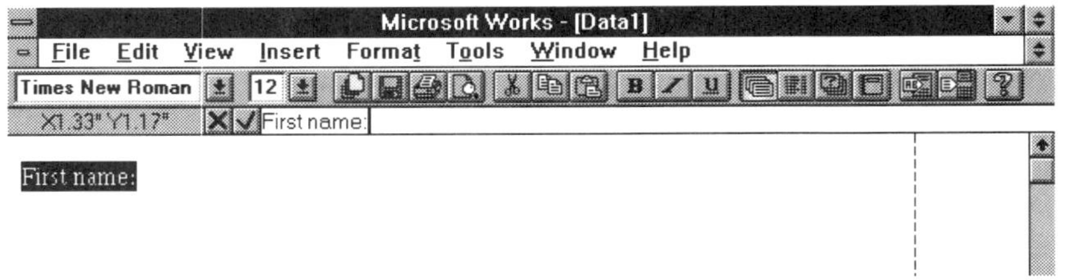

Figure 15-3. Key in "First name:" as the first field.

As you are typing, the field appears highlighted on the screen (where the text cursor is positioned) and also appears in the formula bar, as illustrated in Figure 15-3.

The field is inserted by clicking on the *Enter* button on the formula bar, as shown in Figure 15-4. Another way is simply to press Enter on the keyboard.

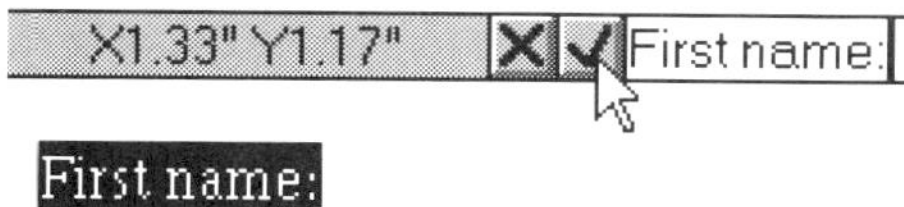

Figure 15-4. *Click on the Enter button.*

When you click on Enter, Works immediately displays the *Field Size* dialog box (Figure 15-5).

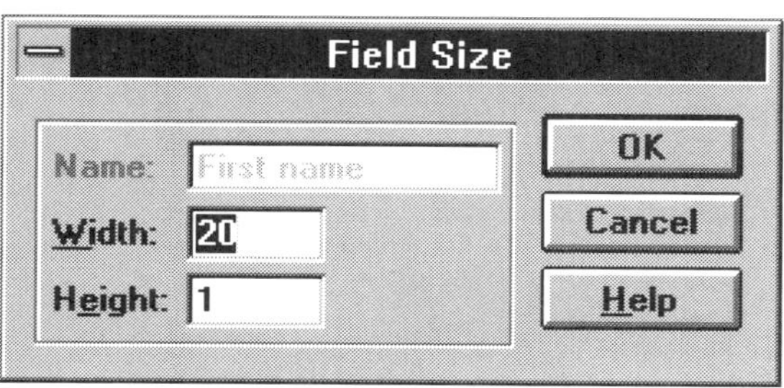

Figure 15-5. *The Field Size dialog box.*

The size of the field dictates how many of the field characters appear on the screen. The default width is 20 characters and this can be changed according to the field being entered. Regardless of the field size set in the *Field Size* dialog box, up to 256 characters can be inserted.

The length of a field is displayed on the screen by a line to the right of the field name (Figure 15-6). A longer line allows you to display more of the field. When creating your database, think about what the field will contain and key in a suitable width, then click on *OK*.

Comments:

Figure 15-6. *The number of lines in this "Comments:" field is set to 5.*

Fields of multiple lines are inserted by adjusting the *Height* measurement in the *Field Size* dialog box. A field of more than one line can be used to keep the information in a field in a compact block rather than a long string across the form.

The number of lines specified in the *Height* text box determines how many lines appear on the screen (Figure 15-6). The length of those lines is still determined by the *Width* figure. Text inserted into that field wraps onto the next line when the end of the line is reached—similar to the word processor.

In your database, 20 characters is probably too long for the "First name:" field. Change the length to 12, as in Figure 15-7, and click on *OK*.

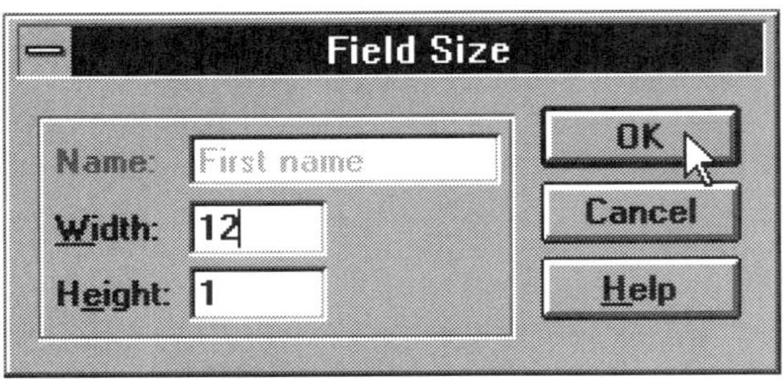

Figure 15-7. *The field size is changed.*

A line 12 characters long is placed next to "First name:" on the screen. Field entries are displayed on this line when inserted into the database. When a field is entered in this way, the insertion point is directly under the first field when you return to the *Form* view screen. Works is ready for you to insert the next field. The new field is placed exactly where the insertion point is in *Form* view. See Figure 15-8.

Figure 15-8. *The insertion point indicates the position of the next field you enter.*

The next field is "Last name:" and, as with all new fields being entered, a colon needs to be keyed in at the end of the field name. Enter the next field by typing "Last name:". Accept 20 characters in length for the field by clicking on *OK* in the *Field Size* dialog box. Your fields now look like Figure 15-9.

First name:

Last name:

***Figure 15-9.** The first and second fields are entered.*

The cursor is currently situated under the "Last name" field. Insert field 3—"Address"—in this position. Remember to type in the colon. When the *Field Size* dialog box appears, change the length of this field to 30 characters. The database displaying the fields inserted at this stage is in Figure 15-10.

First name:

Last name:

Address:

***Figure 15-10.** The database with the first three fields.*

In List view

Fields can be added through *List* view. Change to *List* view now by clicking on the *List* view button on the toolbar (Figure 15-11).

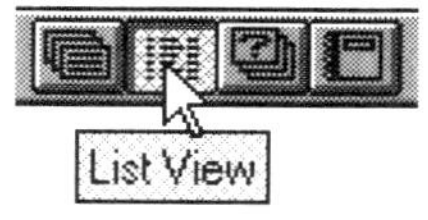

***Figure 15-11.** Change to List view using the toolbar.*

To add a field in *List* view, the insertion point must be in the column which is being used for the new field. As the first three columns are already in use, click in the fourth column for the fourth field (Figure 15-12).

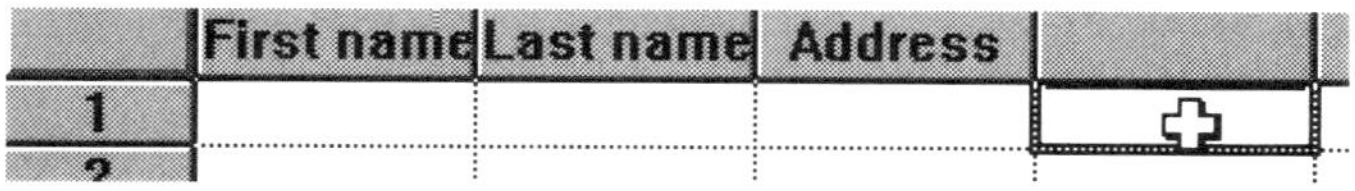

	First name	Last name	Address	
1				

***Figure 15-12.** Click in the fourth column where the "City" field is to go.*

A new field is inserted in List view through the *Field Name* command in the **Edit** menu, as shown in Figure 15-13.

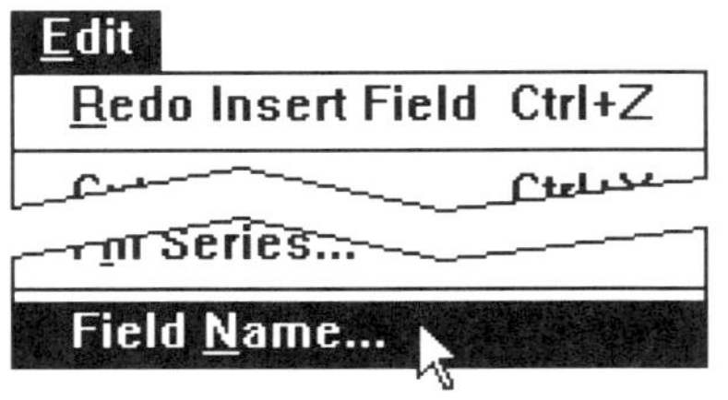

Figure 15-13. *The Field Name command.*

The *Field Name* command in the **Edit** menu brings the *Field Name* dialog box onto the screen. The name of the new field, which is "City," is keyed into the *Field Name* dialog box (Figure 15-14).

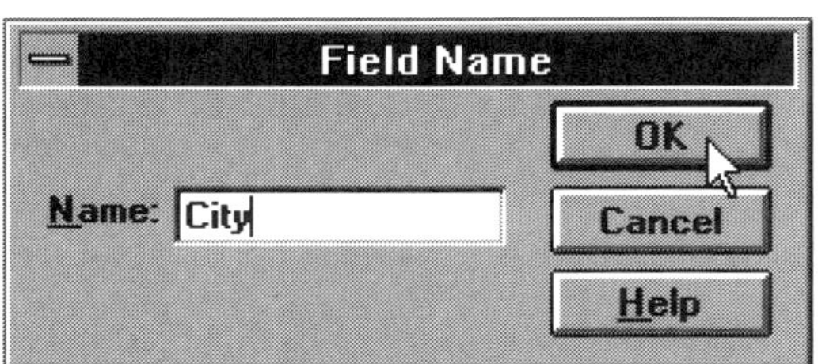

Figure 15-14. *"City" is inserted as the new field.*

Pressing Enter or clicking on *OK* returns you to the *List* view screen. "City" is inserted as the column label in the fourth column. The other fields, entered in *Form* view, are the column labels for the first three columns. Figure 15-15 shows the database in *List* view.

	First name	Last name	Address	City
1				
2				

Figure 15-15. *The database contains four fields which are indicated by column headings in List view.*

The next field to be entered is "State." This can be done in the same way as "City" in *List* view. The first step is to move into the next column. Choose the *Field Name* command in the **Edit** menu, type in "State" and click on *OK*. The dialog box is shown in Figure 15-16.

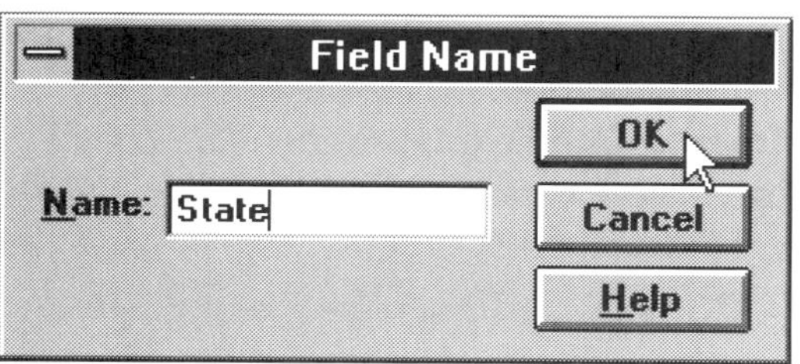

Figure 15-16. *"State" is inserted.*

Enter the last two fields which are Postal Code, and Country. The database with all of the fields entered is shown in Figure 15-17.

	First name	Last name	Address	City	State	Postal Cod	Country
1							

Figure 15-17. *The finished columns.*

Field widths in List view

The columns can be widened and narrowed so all the field names can be read. Adjusting the columns in this way does not affect the width of the field itself, just the column width on the screen. It also does not affect the field width in *Form* view, only columns in *List* view.

The width of a field is changed through the *Field Width* command in the **Format** menu (Figure 15-18).

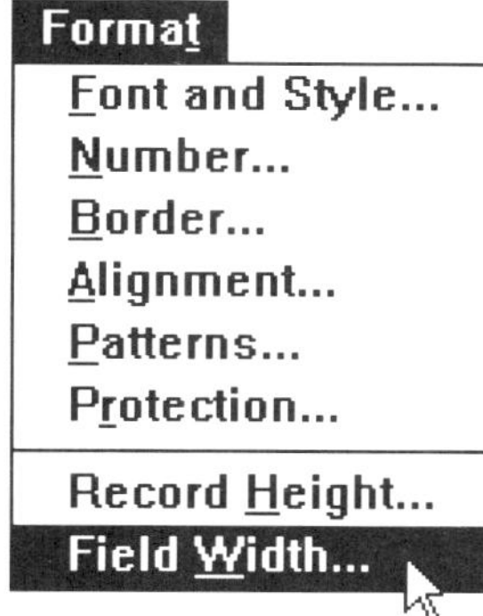

Figure 15-18. *The Field Width command.*

This option displays the *Field Width* dialog box into which the new width is typed. This affects only the width of the columns you have currently selected.

The column which contains the Postal Code field can be widened so the field name is not truncated. Move the pointer into this column and choose *Field Width* from the **Format** menu. The *Field Width* dialog box appears, into which you type "12" as the new width. Figure 15-19 displays this. When done, click on *OK*.

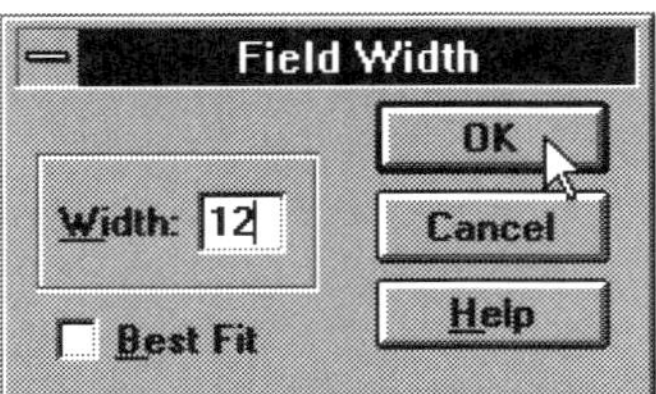

Figure 15-19. *Type 12 in the Width text box and click on OK.*

The *Field Width* dialog box also lets you apply *Best Fit* to the columns you have selected. Works changes the column width to accommodate the widest data item in the column if you select *Best Fit*. However *Best Fit* takes no account of the length of the field name, which is what we are trying to adjust for here.

Instead of changing the width through the **Format** menu, you can use a shortcut. To change the width of the column using the shortcut, position the mouse pointer on the column dividers on the frame. The mouse pointer changes to a double-sided arrow, which is used to move the column dividers to the right or the left.

Move the mouse pointer between the second and third columns. Figure 15-20 shows the new mouse pointer shape which appears when the mouse is moved to the column divider on the frame.

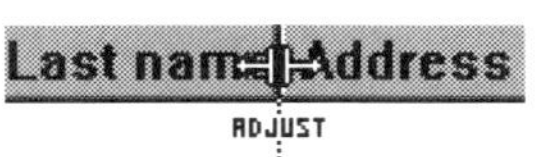

Figure 15-20. *Move the mouse pointer onto the line between Last name and Address in the frame.*

The mouse pointer is dragged to the right to make the column wider and to the left to make it narrower. Make the second column wider by dragging the pointer to the right.

Continue adjusting the field widths for the database using either of the methods outlined above. The database should look similar to Figure 15-21 when complete.

Return now to *Form* view using the *Form view* button on the toolbar.

***Figure 15-21.** Adjust the field widths to new settings.*

Positioning fields in Form view

The fields may be slightly jumbled when you first return to *Form* view. This is easily fixed by dragging the fields to more desirable positions on the screen. Fields are often moved around in *Form* view to unjumble a series of fields after inserting then in *List* view, to make the form more appealing to the eye, or to match a printed form.

To move a field to a more suitable place on the form, click on the field name to select that field. Now the "DRAG" pointer is active, the field can be moved by dragging it to the new position. Try this out by moving City under Country as in Figure 15-22.

***Figure 15-22.** Move City under Country by dragging.*

Use this method to move the State field under City. Your screen should look like Figure 15-23.

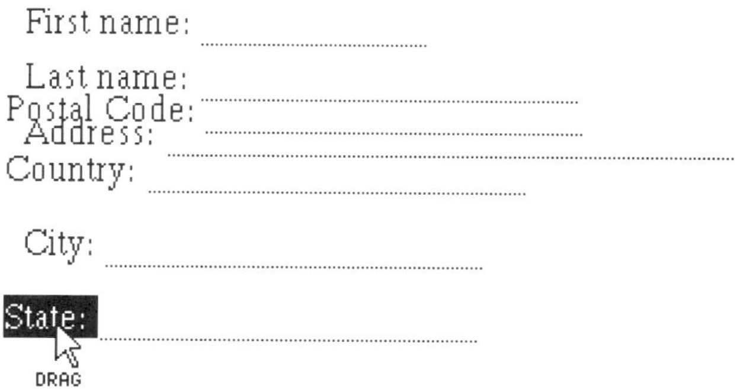

***Figure 15-23.** "State" is now under "City."*

Fields can be moved to an exact location on the screen using the X and Y coordinates which appear in the formula bar (Figure 15-24). X and Y coordinates specify where the pointer is in relation to the edges of the page. The Y coordinate refers to the vertical location and the X coordinate refers to the horizontal location.

Figure 15-24. *The formula bar displays the exact position of the pointer.*

Move all of the fields into a suitable position on the form. An example appears in Figure 15-25. Leave some space at the top of the screen; you will add a title there later.

First name: ....

Last name: ....

Address: ....

City: ....

State: ....

Postal Code: ....

Country: ....

Figure 15-25. *The completed database form.*

Entering data

The basic structure of the database is now in place. The records can be inserted using the fields created. Information stored in a field is called a "field entry." The field entry should be relevant to the field name.

There are three types of entries: text, values, and formulas. Field entries can be inserted in *List* or *Form* view. All types of entries and both methods of inserting field entries are covered in this section.

Entering text

A text entry consists of words and sometimes a combination of numbers and words. It may be a name of a person such as "Peter," or a product such as "Brake pads." It may also be an address such as "57 Hopetown Ave." To type text into a field, you must select the field first. Click on the line next to "First name" to select this field (Figure 15-26).

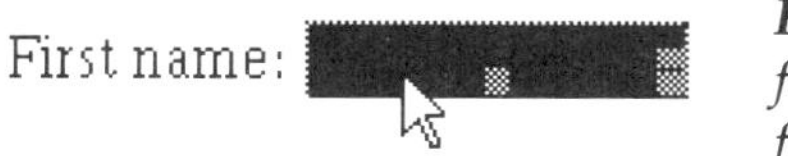

Figure 15-26. *Select the field before typing in the field entry.*

Type in "James" and as you type, the letters appear in the field and in the formula bar. To confirm the entry, press Enter. "James" appears in the field as well as the formula bar.

The field entry is given an inverted commas (") text prefix in the formula bar. This indicates that the entry is left aligned, which is the default. Changing the alignment of fields is outlined in **Chapter 16, Editing a Database**. Enter "Brady" in the Last Name field in the same way. (Click on this field or use the Tab key to move from the First Name field.) Figure 15-27 shows the field entry.

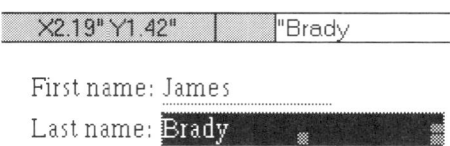

X2.19" Y1.42" "Brady

First name: James

Last name: Brady

Figure 15-27. *"James" and "Brady" are entered into fields 1 and 2 respectively.*

The next field in the database requires an address which, in this case, is made up of a street number and a street. When letters and numbers are combined in this way, the entry is considered text. It therefore is given a text prefix — inverted commas, for example. James Brady lives at 4667 Network Street, so type the address into the Address field. Figure 15-28 shows the entry when Enter is pressed.

First name: James

Last name: Brady

Address: 4667 Network Street

Figure 15-28. *Enter the address "4667 Network Street" into the third field.*

Field entries—text, values, and formulas—can also be made in *List* view. Change to *List* view by clicking on the *List view* button on the toolbar. You may need to adjust the column width of "Address" so that the entire address entry can fit in the cell. If this is not adjusted, the entry will be truncated when something is entered into the adjacent field. This does not affect the contents of the cell entry, but does affect readability.

An entry is made in *List* view where the pointer is located. As the entry needs to be made in the first record of the "City" field, click just under "City." "Wood Hill" is typed in directly, as in Figure 15-29. Adjust the column width if necessary.

	First name	Last name	Address	City	State
1	James	Brady	4667 Network Street	Wood Hill	
2					

Figure 15-29. *"Wood Hill" is the "City" entry.*

Insert the final text entry—CA in "State"—in the same way. The database in Figure 15-30 has all the text entries inserted.

	First name	Last name	Address	City	State
1	James	Brady	4667 Network Street	Wood Hill	CA
2					

Figure 15-30. *The text entries in this record are entered.*

Text can be used as descriptive text in *Form* view. Move back to *Form* view now, using the *Form view* button. Headings and comments can be inserted into relevant places in the form to add more meaning. In this database, you could add a title to the form to describe what the database contains.

A descriptive title is inserted in a similar way to inserting a field name, except that a colon (:) is not keyed in at the end of the text. You can add a heading "Save the Hippo Client List." The insertion point must not be on any field name or entry area, so click on a free area of the screen. Type in the heading and press Enter.

Moving descriptive text is done by dragging, as covered in the **Positioning Fields in Form View** section. Drag the text up to the top of the screen so the form looks like Figure 15-31.

Save the Hippo Client List

First name: James

Last name: Brady

Address: 4667 Network Street

City: Wood Hill

State: CA

Postal Code:

Country:

Figure 15-31. The descriptive title "Save the Hippo Client List."

Entering values

Values are entered in the same way as text. Highlight the "Postal Code" field as this requires a value entry. Type in the entry "93933" and press Enter. A value entry is not given a prefix (Figure 15-32).

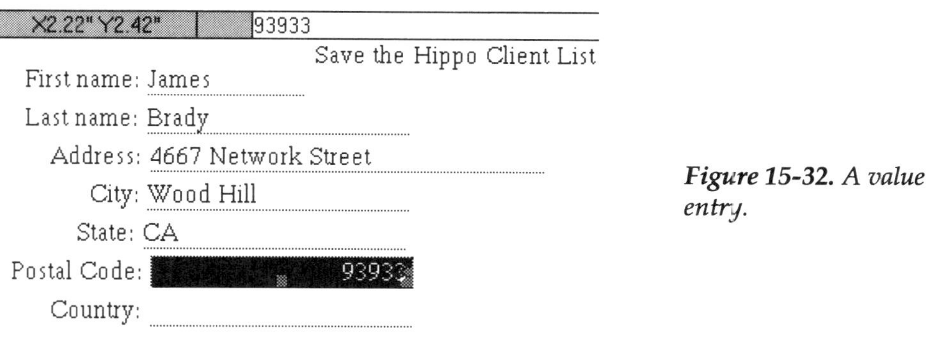

Figure 15-32. A value entry.

Entering formulas

The database requires a number of extra fields and entries to use in the examples for entering formulas. The new field names are: Donation 1:, Donation 2:, Total:, and Average:. Insert these now.

Into the new fields in the first record, enter the following values: Donation 1: - "$45" and Donation 2: - "$100". Rearrange the screen as in Figure 1-33.

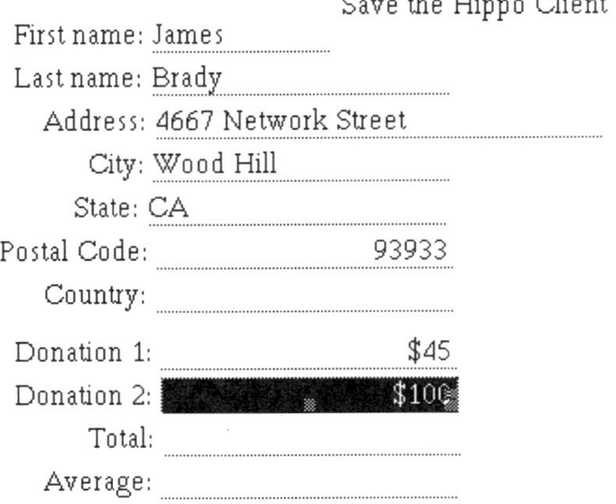

Figure 15-33. The new field names and field entries are added to the database.

Formulas in databases are used in two ways. They are used to calculate the contents of one cell based on entries in other fields. In the Works database, you can also use a formula to enter repetitive entries into fields. These are both covered in this section.

Entering formulas, regardless of the purpose, follows the same procedure. The field where the formula is inserted must be highlighted. It is always given the formula prefix, which is an equals (=) sign and then the formula is simply typed in as normal text.

Once entered, the formula shows the result in the field and the formula in the formula bar. It is possible only to place one formula in a field as the formula is used in the same field of every record.

Formulas can be inserted in either *Form* or *List* view. In this example, *List* view is used. Change to *List* view now.

A formula, as mentioned above, can be used to insert the identical information into the same field in every record of the database. You can use this function to insert "USA" into every Country field that appears in the database. The database at present has one record only, but when more are added, "USA" appears in all of the Country fields.

Move into the Country field area and type in "=" as the prefix. To insert such a field, the text which is to appear is typed in surrounded by inverted commas—""USA"." Type this in now and see Figure 15-34 for the result when Enter is pressed.

=“USA”

	First name	Last name	Address	City	State	Postal Code	Country
1	James	Brady	4667 Network Street	Wood Hill	CA	93933	USA
2							

Figure 15-34. *“USA” will appear in the Country field of every new record.*

If a client from another country is entered into the database, the different country is typed over the top of “USA.”

A formula can be inserted to calculate a figure in a field which is determined by the contents of other cells in the database. In this example, you can find how much James Brady has donated in Total without having to search for a calculator!

Once again, the first step is to move into the field (Total) where the formula is to be entered and key in the formula prefix (Figure 15-35).

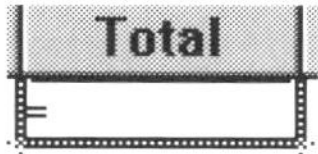

Figure 15-35. *The formula in “Total” is started with “=.”*

The formula required in this field is one which adds the two donation figures and places their total in the Total field. The formula is “=Donation 1+Donation 2” and can be typed in directly, or created by pointing when in *List* view. When you create a formula by pointing, you actually highlight the field required as the formula is being entered. It is the same technique as pointing as discussed in **Chapter 9, Entering Spreadsheet Data**.

The prefix is inserted so, click on the Donation 1 field and press “+.” The pointer automatically jumps back to the Total field. From here, press the left arrow to move into Donation 2 and when you press Enter the total “145” is entered into the Total field, as illustrated in Figure 15-36. Every new record will have that formula in the Total field.

=Donation 1+Donation 2

	City	State	Postal Code	Country	Donation 1	Donation 2	Total
1	Wood Hill	CA	93933	USA	$45	$100	145
2							

Figure 15-36. *The “Total” formula is entered.*

Functions can be used in a database to calculate complex formulas. Functions are preprogrammed equations which are part of Works. You may have used these in the spreadsheet tool. The same functions used in the spreadsheet can be used in the database.

In this example, you insert a function which calculates the average donation in the Average field. The function which performs this function is AVG. Move into this field and type "=AVG(" to start the function, as shown in Figure 15-37.

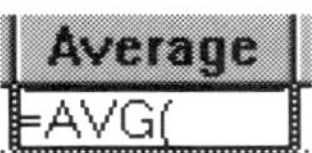

Figure 15-37. *The start of the AVG function in the Average field.*

The list of fields to be averaged is inserted in the brackets. The fields are separated by a comma. In this case the fields are Donation 1 and Donation 2. These can either be typed in or you can create the function by pointing when in *List* view.

To create the function by pointing, click on the Donation 1 field and press the comma. The pointer jumps back to the original field. Click on Donation 2, close the bracket and press Enter to insert the function into Average. The function appears in the formula bar and the result as a field entry in the Average field (Figure 15-38).

=AVG(Donation 1,Donation 2)

	State	Postal Code	Country	Donation 1	Donation 2	Total	Average
1	CA	93933	USA	$45	$100	145	72.5
2							

Figure 15-38. *The AVG function and result in the Average field.*

Adding and deleting records

There is one record only in the database at this stage. A database in Works can contain up to 32,000 records. In this example, you add another two records, making a total of three in the entire database file.

Works informs you of the number of records in the database, and the current record, on the status bar. In Figure 15-39, the left indicator tells you the current record and the right indicator tells you how many displayed records are in the file versus the total number of records. This is particularly useful when querying the database, which is covered in **Chapter 17, Viewing the Database**.

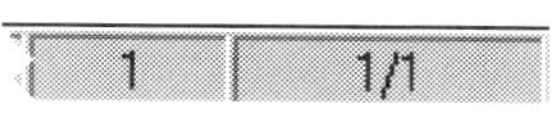

***Figure 15-39.** The record indicators on the status bar.*

Records can be inserted before, after, or between current records. They are added or deleted in both *Form* and *List* view. In this example, the first new record is added in *Form* view. Change to *Form* view now by pressing F9.

To add a record in *Form* view, the *Record* command in the **Insert** menu is selected as in Figure 15-40.

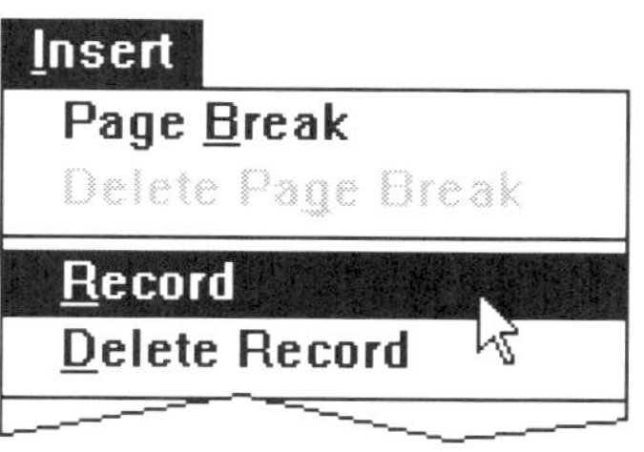

***Figure 15-40.** The Record command in the **Insert** menu.*

The new record is inserted before the current record. For example, if the current record—the one displayed on the screen—is number 3, then the new record will be number 3. The old record 3 is pushed down to fourth place and the subsequent records are renumbered automatically.

To add a record to this database, select the *Insert Record* command from the **Edit** menu. A new record is inserted in the same format as the current record, becoming the first record in the database. The blank "form" appears on the screen as in Figure 15-41. A new record can be inserted at the end of the database in *List* view by pressing Tab.

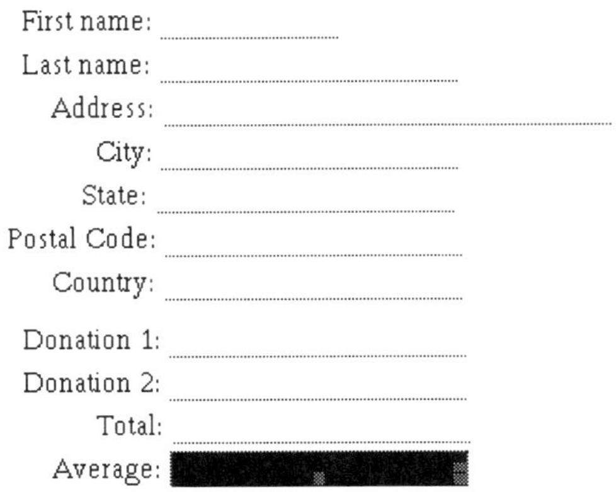

First name:
Last name:
Address:
City:
State:
Postal Code:
Country:
Donation 1:
Donation 2:
Total:
Average:

Figure 15-41. The new record appears as a blank form.

Add the following data to the record as in Figure 15-42:

First name: Penny
Last name: Cassidy
Address: 56 First Avenue
City: Portland
State: OR

Postal Code: 39442

Remember not to put anything in the Country field, as it will automatically be "USA."

Donation 1: 60

Donation 2: 150

The total and the average are calculated automatically because of the formula and function inserted previously.

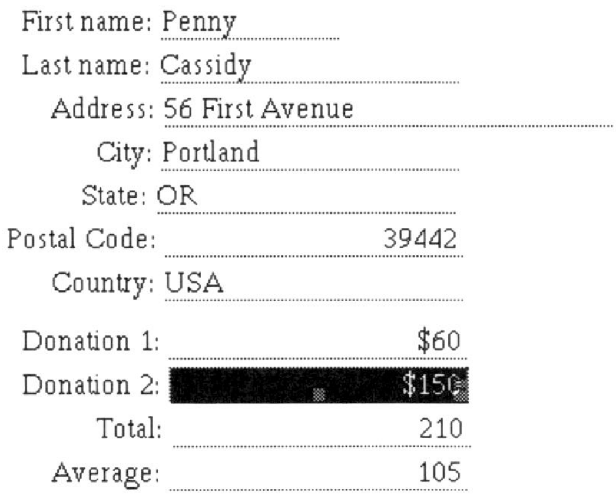

First name: Penny
Last name: Cassidy
Address: 56 First Avenue
City: Portland
State: OR
Postal Code: 39442
Country: USA
Donation 1: $60
Donation 2: $150
Total: 210
Average: 105

Figure 15-42. The new record with the fields complete.

A record is deleted in *Form* view through the *Delete Record* command in the **Insert** menu. Works deletes the current record—without warning! Do not delete any records, as they are required in the next section.

A record can be inserted through *List* view. Change to *List* view now by pressing F9. The *Record/Field* command in the **Insert** menu is used to insert a new record (Figure 15-43).

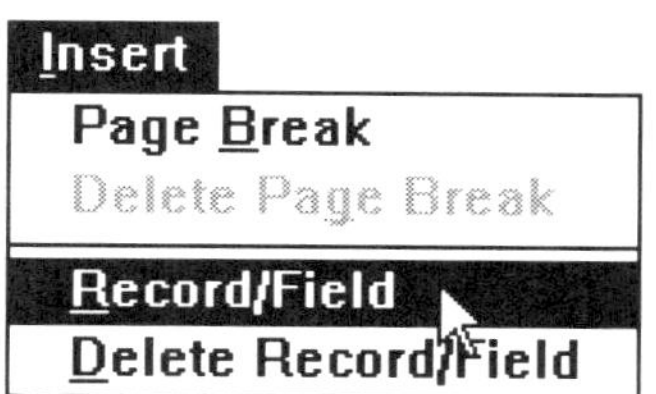

Figure 15-43. *The Insert Record/Field command.*

The record is inserted at the record number where the pointer is situated. Therefore if you want the new record to be record 2, move the cursor to row 2. Do this now (Figure 15-44). The record which is currently record 2 becomes record 3.

	First name	Last name	Address
1	Penny	Cassidy	56 First Avenue
2	James	Brady	4667 Network Street
3			

Figure 15-44. *The new record will be record 2.*

Choose *Record/Field* from the **Insert** menu and the *Insert* dialog box (Figure 15-45) appears on the screen. You are given the choice of inserting a record or a field. Ensure *Record* (the default) is selected and click on *OK*.

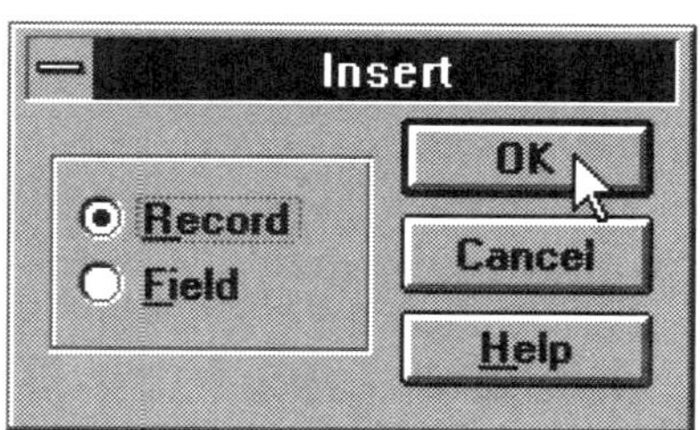

Figure 15-45. *The Insert dialog box.*

A blank record is inserted at row 2. Fill in the information below for the new record. The completed record is in Figure 15-46.

First name: Crystal
Last name: Harper
Address: 78 Scenic Drive
City: Apple Hill
State: IL
Postal Code: 23934
Donation 1: 100
Donation 2: 235

The total and the average are calculated automatically because of the formula and function inserted previously. The Country field is also inserted automatically because of the formula inserted earlier in Figure 15-34.

	First name	Last name	Address	City	State	Postal Code	Country
1	Penny	Cassidy	56 First Avenue	Portland	OR	39442	USA
2	Crystal	Harper	78 Scenic Drive	Apple Hill	IL	23934	USA
3	James	Brady	4667 Network Street	Wood Hill	CA	93933	USA
4							

Figure 15-46. The new record in List view.

Records are deleted in *List* view using the *Delete Record/Field* command in the **Insert** menu as displayed in Figure 15-47.

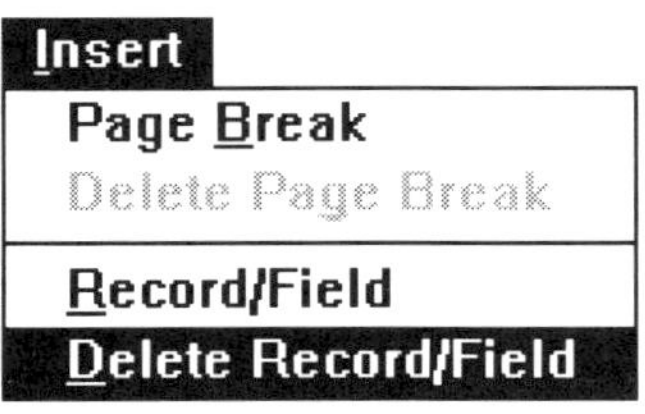

Figure 15-47. The Deleted Record/ Field command.

The current record—where the pointer is located—is the record which is deleted. Multiple records can be deleted by highlighting the rows in which they are located before selecting *Delete Record/Field* from the **Insert** menu. The *Delete* dialog box appears (Figure 15-48), in which you choose *Record* to delete the current or highlighted records. Do not delete any records, as they are required in the next section.

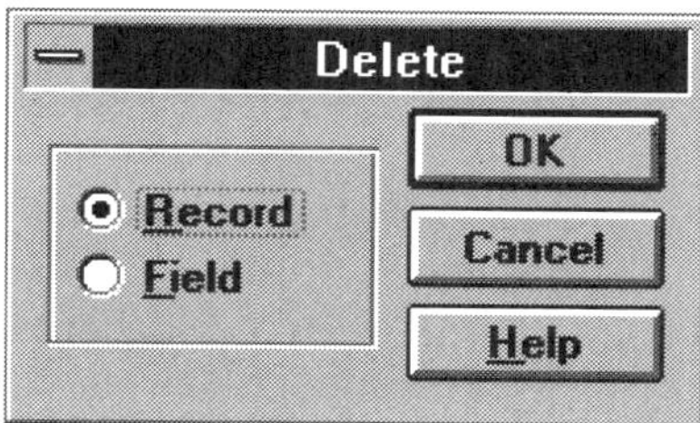

Figure 15-48. The Delete dialog box.

Moving around the database

The database now consists of three records and ten fields. There are a number of shortcuts which enable you to move quickly through the database. These are outlined in the tables below:

Form view	
Move	**Keystroke**
Up or down to next field	Up or down arrow
Next/previous field (unlocked)	Tab/Shift Tab
First/last record	Ctrl-Home/End
Next/previous record	Ctrl-Page Up/Down

List view	
Move	**Keystroke**
First/Last field	Home/End
Next/previous field (unlocked)	Tab/Shift Tab
First/last record	Ctrl-Home/End
Next/previous record	Up or down arrow

Saving a file

The database needs to be saved if you are going to use it in the future. The *Save* command in the **File** menu is shown in Figure 15-49. This command saves the database as a file with a ***.wdb*** extension. Choose this command now.

Figure 15-49. *The Save command.*

Works displays the *Save As* dialog box because you have not yet named your file. The name of the file is typed into the *File Name* text box. It is not necessary to add the extension manually, as Works does this automatically. Type in "hippo" as the name of the file as in Figure 15-47.

Clicking *OK* writes the file to the drive and directory specified. Save the database as ***hippo.wdb*** to a drive and directory of your choice.

Further details on saving can be found in **Chapter 2, Creating Documents**.

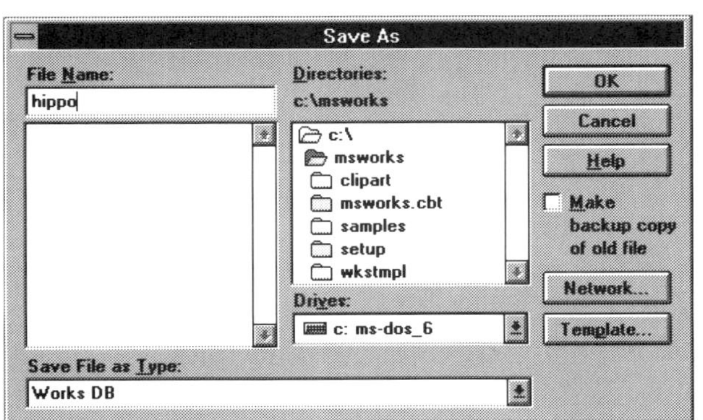

Figure 15-50. *Type in "hippo".*

Editing a Database

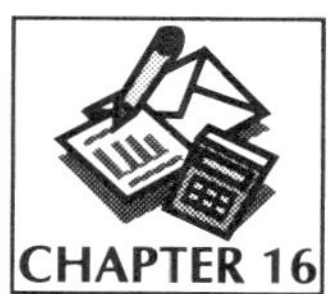

This chapter looks at ways of altering a database after the basic information has been entered. The sample file ***kitecust.wdb*** is referred to throughout the chapter. Open this file now, so you can follow the examples. Figure 16-1 shows that the file is in the ***msworks.cbt*** subdirectory.

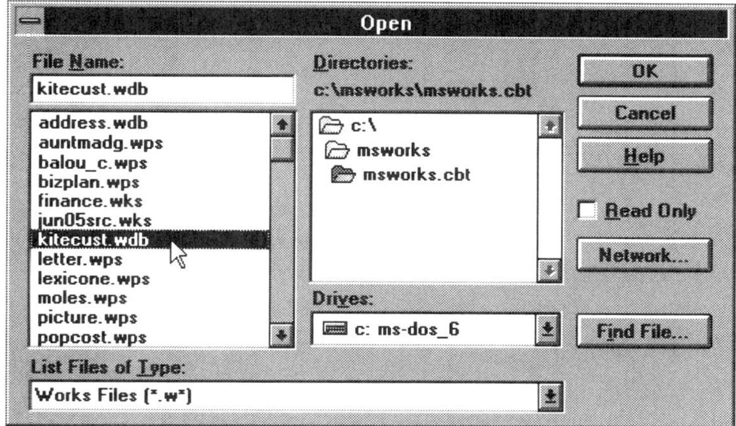

Figure 16-1. *Open the file* ***kitecust.wdb.***

Highlighting

To make any changes to information which is already part of the database, it must be highlighted. Works enables you to highlight a field, a record, a field entry, or multiple entries.

Highlighting techniques differ according to the view selected. These are outlined below. If not in Form view, move to this view now.

Using the mouse in Form view

To highlight a record with the mouse, click on the arrow buttons on the scroll bar until the record required is displayed on the screen. Refer to **Chapter 14, The Database Screen,** for an explanation on each button and its use. A field name, field entry, or label is highlighted by clicking on it (Figure 16-2).

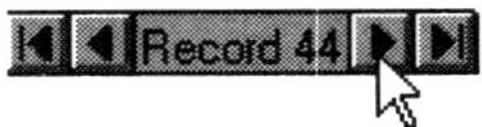

Figure 16-2. A field entry is highlighted.

Using the keyboard in Form view

Pressing Ctrl-Page Down displays the next record in the database. Ctrl-Page Up displays the previous record. The record on the screen in Form view is the current record, which essentially means it is selected. Figure 16-3 shows a current record in **kitecust.wdb.**

Name: Samuel Leather
Street: 45 Duval Road
City: Medina
State/Province: WA
Postal Code: 98033
Telephone: (206) 555-6655

Date of Sale:

Qty:

Unit Price:

Amount of Sale:

Figure 16-3. The current or selected record displayed in Form view.

A field is selected by pressing Tab until the field required is highlighted. Using the arrow keys highlights field names, field entries, and labels.

Try using some of these highlighting techniques to highlight parts of the database in Form view. Now, move to List view.

Using the mouse in List view

A field entry is highlighted by clicking on the appropriate entry in List view. The entry appears with a border around it on the List view screen. The contents of the field entry are shown in the formula bar.

Several field entries are highlighted by clicking in the top left-hand corner of the range being selected and dragging down to the bottom right-hand corner. Figure 16-4 shows several highlighted field entries.

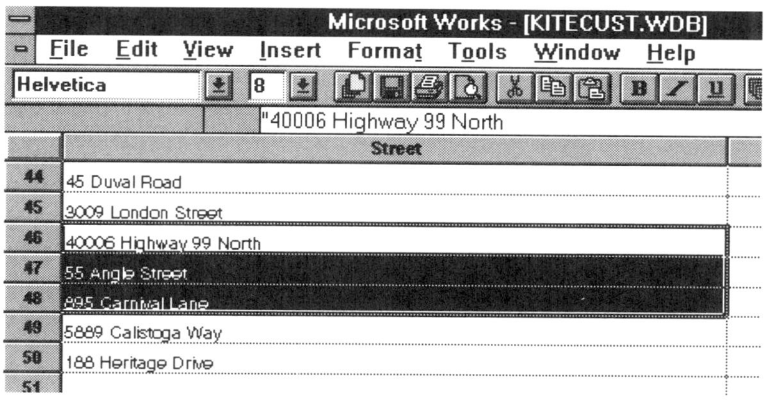

Figure 16-4. *Several field entries are highlighted.*

An entire record is highlighted by clicking on the record number on the frame. All fields are selected by clicking on the field name on the frame. To highlight the entire database, the button in the top left-hand corner of the frame is clicked, irrespective of your position in the database (Figure 16-5).

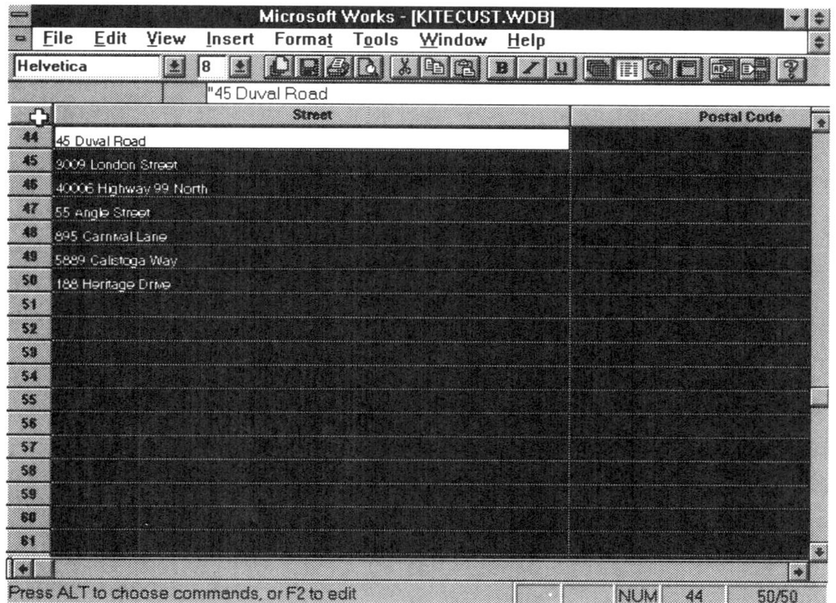

Figure 16-5. *The whole database is highlighted.*

Using the keyboard in List view

A field entry is highlighted by moving onto it with the arrow keys. Several entries are selected when the Shift key is held down and the arrow keys are used to move to the cells which are to be highlighted.

The record in which the pointer is located is highlighted by pressing Ctrl-F8. An entire field is selected by moving into that field and pressing Shift-F8 as shown in Figure 16-6.

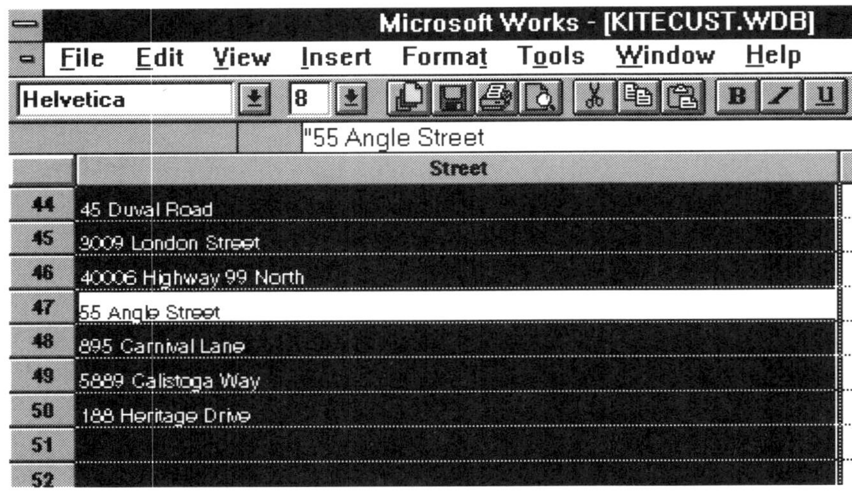

Figure 16-6. *Press Shift-F8 to highlight the entire field.*

Using the keyboard in List view, the whole database is highlighted by pressing Ctrl-Shift-F8.

Using the Edit menu in List view

The **Edit** menu in List view differs from the **Edit** menu in Form view. The **Edit** menu for List view allows you to select an entire record, field or database and is illustrated in Figure 16-7.

Try using some of these highlighting techniques to highlight parts of the database in List view.

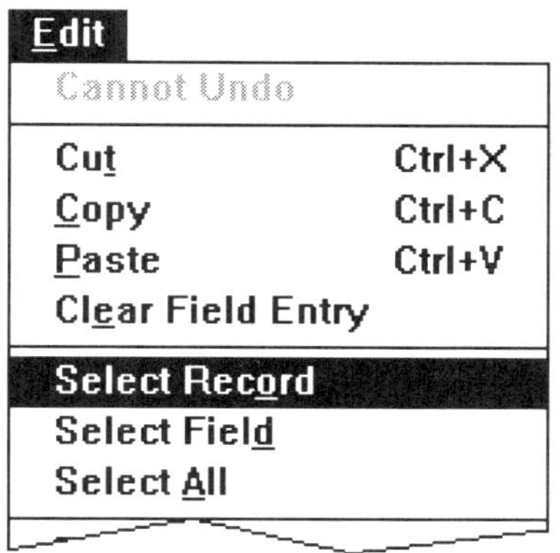

Figure 16-7. The **Edit** *menu in List view.*

Editing records

Often the order of records in a database needs to be changed. Works allows you to move and copy cells using the **Edit** menu. The commands used are *Cut, Copy,* and *Paste*. If a record becomes superfluous, it is deleted through the **Edit** menu as well.

Cutting in Form view

Move to Form view by pressing F9. If a record is to be cut, it must be current. In this example the third record in the sample file is to be cut. Display this record, which is for "Mike Jones," on the screen. The first few fields are shown in Figure 16-8.

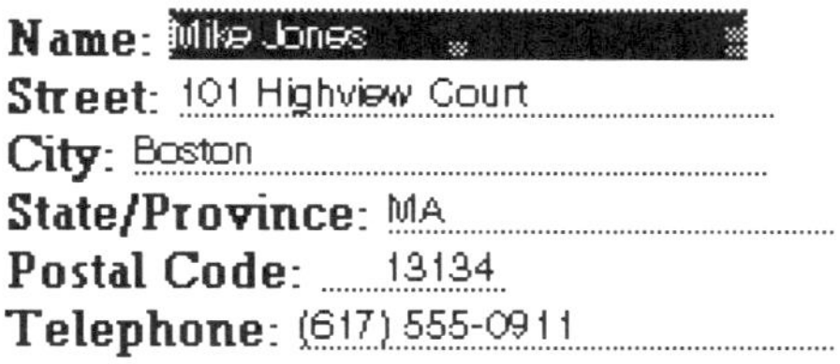

Name: Mike Jones
Street: 101 Highview Court
City: Boston
State/Province: MA
Postal Code: 13134
Telephone: (617) 555-0911

Figure 16-8. The third record is for "Mike Jones."

Select *Cut Record* from the **Edit** menu as in Figure 16-9 and the record is removed from the database. The new third record is for the "Joy Yarrow," which was previously the fourth record.

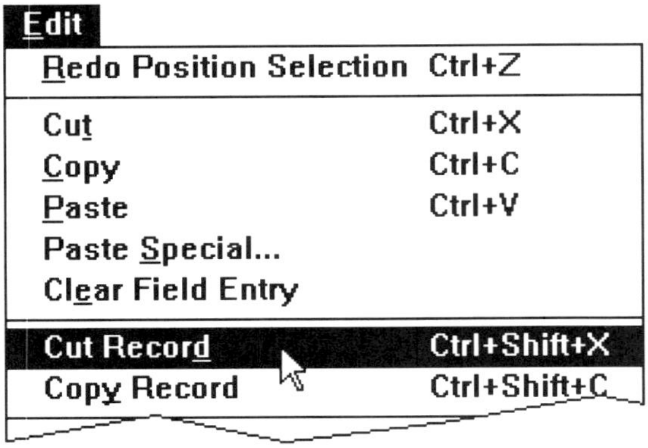

Edit
Redo Position Selection Ctrl+Z
Cut Ctrl+X
Copy Ctrl+C
Paste Ctrl+V
Paste Special...
Clear Field Entry
Cut Record Ctrl+Shift+X
Copy Record Ctrl+Shift+C

Figure 16-9. *The Cut Record command.*

The "Mike Jones" data is currently stored in the Clipboard and can be reinserted into the database through the *Paste Record* command in the **Edit** menu of Figure 16-10.

Edit
Cannot Undo
Cut Ctrl+X
Copy Ctrl+C
Paste Record Ctrl+V
Paste Special...

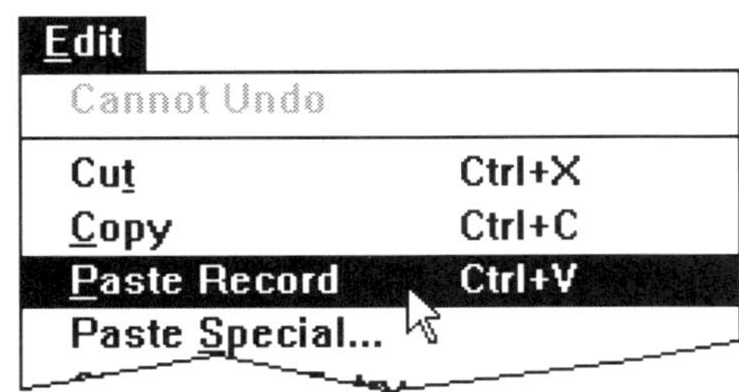

Figure 16-10. *The Paste Record command.*

The record is pasted back into the database before the current record. For instance, choose *Paste Record* now and the "Mike Jones" record becomes number 3 again (Figure 16-11). "Joy Yarrow's" data becomes the fourth record once more.

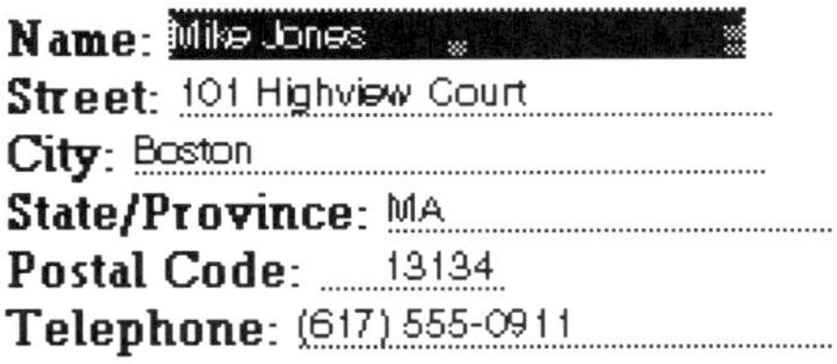

Name: Mike Jones
Street: 101 Highview Court
City: Boston
State/Province: MA
Postal Code: 13134
Telephone: (617) 555-0911

Figure 16-11. *The third record is for "Mike Jones" again.*

Copying in Form view

A record can be copied in Form view, and when pasted back into the database, it replaces the current record.

To copy a record, move to the record which is being copied — in this case, record 5. Choose *Copy Record* from the **Edit** menu (Figure 16-12).

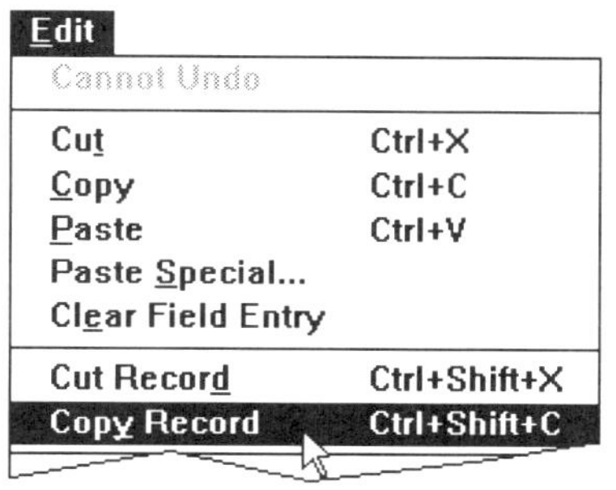

Figure 16-12. *Copy Record in the* ***Edit*** *menu.*

The record remains on the screen when it is copied. Scroll up, using the screen arrows, to the first record, which is where the record is to be pasted. To paste a copy of that record into the database, choose *Paste* from the **Edit** menu.

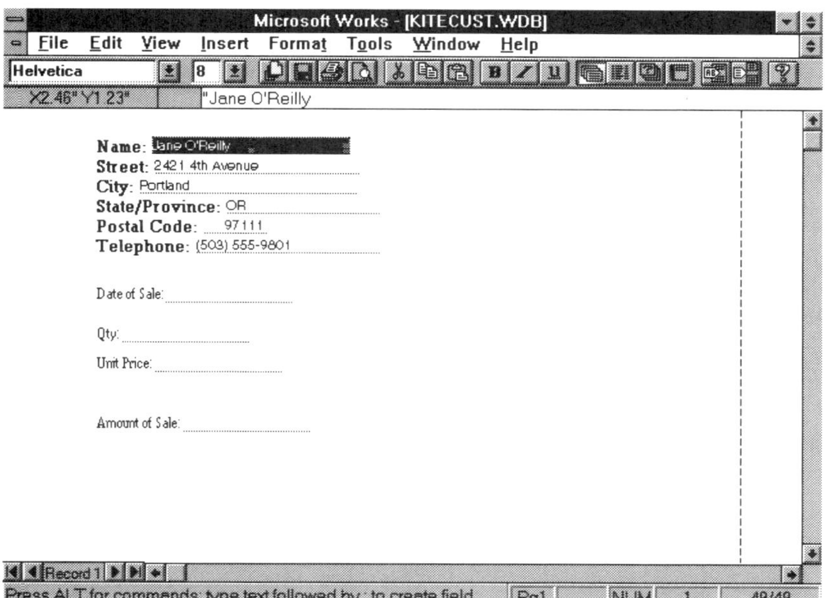

Figure 16-13. *The data is pasted over the first record.*

The information originally in the first record is replaced with what is being pasted (Figure 16-13). To paste—and not lose—data, a new, blank record must be put in (see **Chapter 15, Creating a Database**).

Cutting in List view

Move back to List view by pressing F9. To cut a record in List view, the entire record must be highlighted. Use any of the highlighting techniques outlined above to highlight record 4 (Figure 16-14).

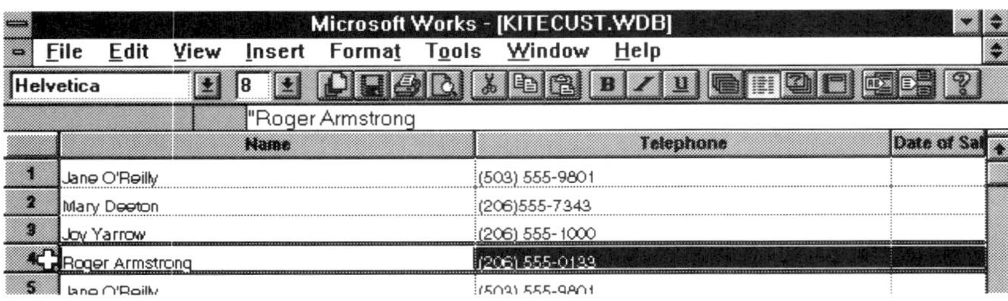

Figure 16-14. *Record 4 is highlighted.*

Choose *Cut* from the **Edit** menu and the record which was previously number 5 is now number 4. The record is placed back into the database by selecting the *Paste* command in the **Edit** menu (Figure 16-15). The record is pasted back as record 4 as the pointer was in that position.

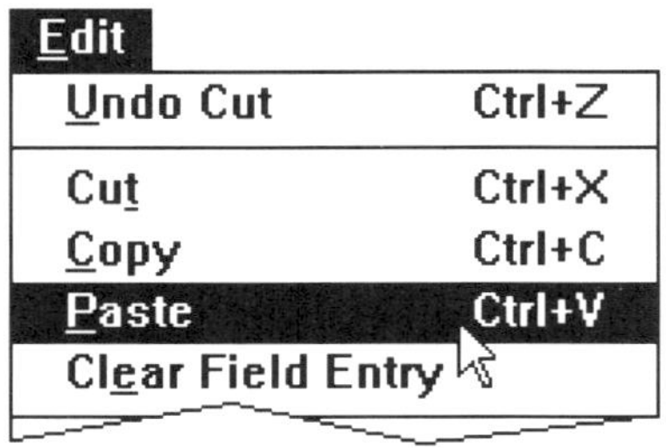

Figure 16-15. *The Paste command in the **Edit** menu.*

Copying in List view

A record is copied by selecting the appropriate record and choosing *Copy* from the **Edit** menu. Select all of record 3 now and choose *Copy*. The original information remains displayed. Move down to record 4 and choose *Paste* from the **Edit** menu. You now have two records for "Joy Yarrow." The data being pasted replaces the data which was in record 4 originally (Figure 16-16).

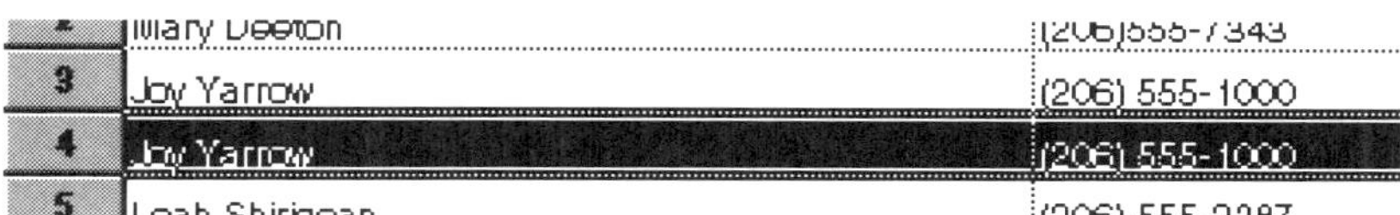

Figure 16-16. *"Jane Yarrow's" record is pasted into record 4.*

Fill commands in List view

There are three *Fill* commands which can be used in the database. These are *Fill Down, Fill Right*, and *Fill Series,* circled in Figure 16-17.

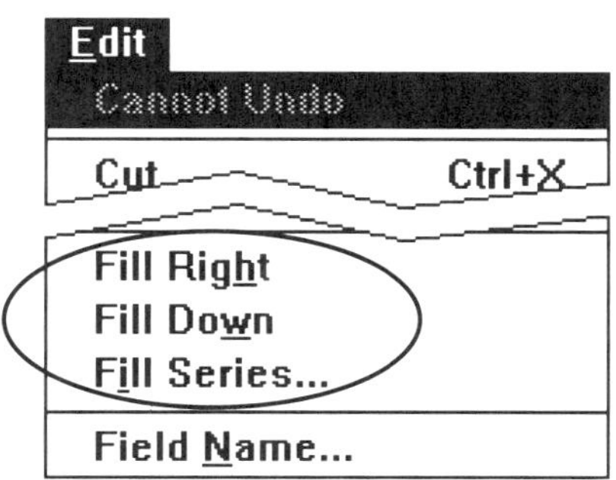

Figure 16-17. *The Fill commands in the **Edit** menu.*

Fill commands are used to insert data into fields quickly. The *Fill Down* and *Fill Right* commands put the same information into highlighted fields. The *Fill Series* command enters a series of numbers or dates which increase by the increment into adjacent records.

Using the *Fill* commands in the database is the same as entering information with the *Fill* commands in the spreadsheet tool of Works. For further details, refer to **Chapter 11, Moving, Copying and Addressing Cells**.

Editing fields

Deleting

A field entry is deleted in either List view or Form view. In List view, a single entry or a block of highlighted fields is deleted using the *Clear Field Entry* command in the **Edit** menu, as shown in Figure 16-18.

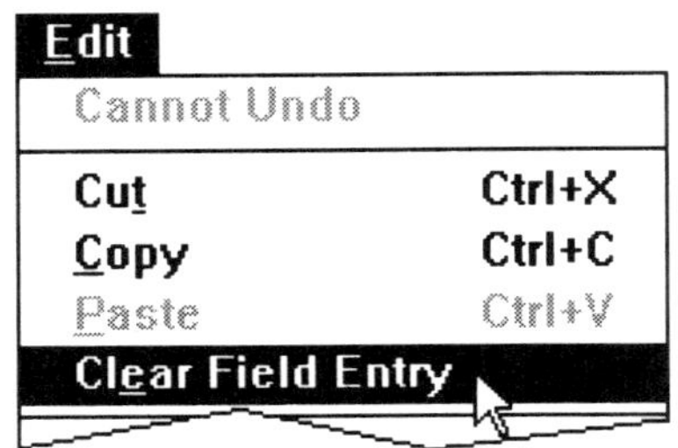

Figure 16-18. *The Clear Field Entry command.*

In both views, however, single field entries are deleted by pressing the Delete key. Delete clears an entry from the formula bar. Pressing Enter while the formula bar is empty, confirms that the field is cleared permanently.

Try using these to delete field entries at random.

Cutting

Field entries can be *Cut* in either Form view or List view. The field entry to be cut needs to be highlighted first and then the *Cut* command is chosen from the **Edit** menu. It is pasted into the database again, by choosing *Paste* from the **Edit** menu.

Copying

The *Copy* command is used to copy a single field entry and the *Paste* command is used to put it back into the database.

Editing field names

Occasionally, a field name which was added when the database was originally created needs to be changed. It may be that the actual field name itself has been changed or that a typing error exists!

Display the database in Form view to begin with. To change a field name in Form view, you simply select the field name to change and it appears in the formula bar. If just a few characters need to be changed, press F2 or click the text cursor in the formula bar to edit. If the entire field name is to be changed, simply start typing while the field name is highlighted.

The field name to be changed in this example is "Telephone." Move into this field now by clicking on it as in Figure 16-19.

***Figure 16-19.** Move into the "Telephone" field.*

You can change just a few of the characters or retype the entire field name. Be sure not to use a field name which is more than 15 characters. It must also end in a colon. In the sample file "Telephone" is being replaced by "Phone." Type in "Phone:" as in Figure 16-20.

X2.00" Y2.07" Phone:

Name: Leah Shirigean
Street: 126 Elm St.
City: Carnation
State/Province: WA
Postal Code: 98644
Phone:

***Figure 16-20.** The new field name "Phone:" is typed into the formula bar.*

When Enter is pressed, "Phone" becomes the name of the field.

Change to List view by pressing F9. In List view, change the name of the fifth field from "Name" to "Full Name." A field name is changed in List view through the *Field Name* command in the **Edit** menu (Figure 16-21).

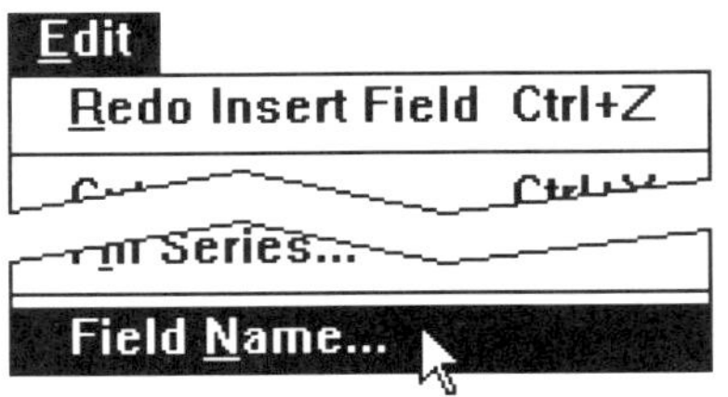

Figure 16-21. *The Field Name command.*

Select the Name field in List view and this command, and the *Field Name* dialog box appears on the screen. You used this command in **Chapter 15, Creating a Database**, to insert new field names, and you can use it now to change field names.

The original field name appears in the dialog box, which is "Name." Click at the beginning of the word, so "Full" can be added (Figure 16-22).

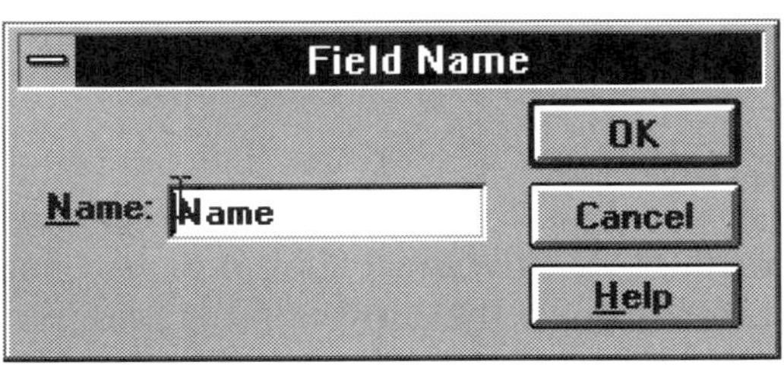

Figure 16-22. *Click in front of "Name" in the Field Name dialog box.*

The name of the field can be edited, rather than retyped. Type in "Full" and a space, then press Enter. The field name on the frame is now "Full Name" and is shown in Figure 16-23.

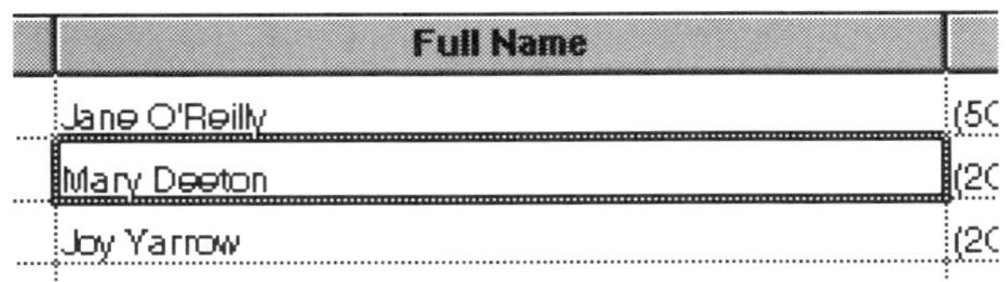

Figure 16-23. *"Full Name" is the new name of the field.*

Adding a field

It is often important that a new field is inserted between two existing fields. In Form view this is easily done by moving the fields around on the screen. This was covered in **Chapter 15, Creating a Database**.

In List view, however, you need to use the *Record/Field* command in the **Insert** menu (Figure 16-24).

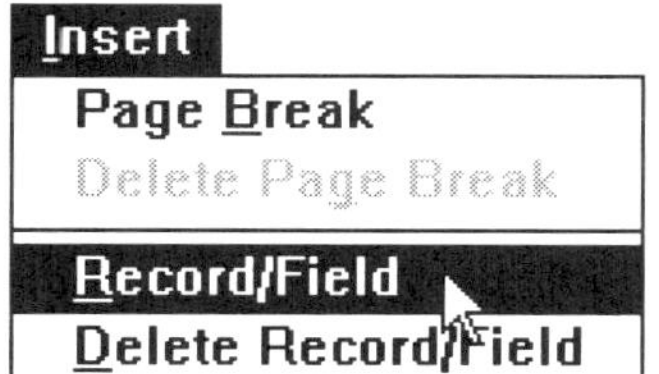

Figure 16-24. *The Record/Field command in the **Insert** menu.*

This command inserts a new column to the left of the pointer. Move into the "Postal Code" field and you can insert a space for a new field to the left of "Postal Code." Choose *Record/Field* and the *Insert* dialog box appears on the screen. In the *Insert* dialog box, you must choose between inserting a field or a record. Click on *Field* in this case, which is in Figure 16-25.

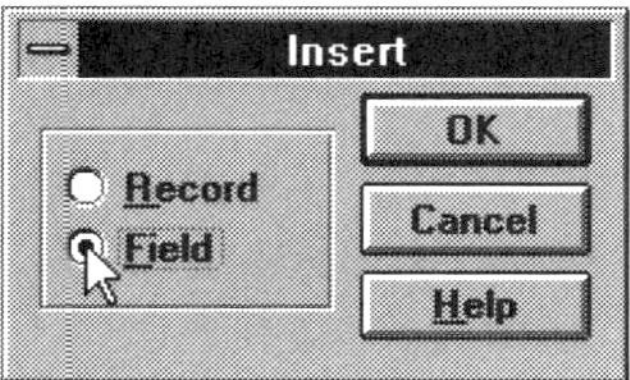

Figure 16-25. *Click on Field in the Insert dialog box.*

Clicking on *OK* returns you to the List view screen, in which the "Postal Code" field is now preceded by a blank column. The field can now be named as any field is in List view.

Deleting a field

A field can be deleted in List view using the *Delete Record/Field* command in the **Insert** menu.

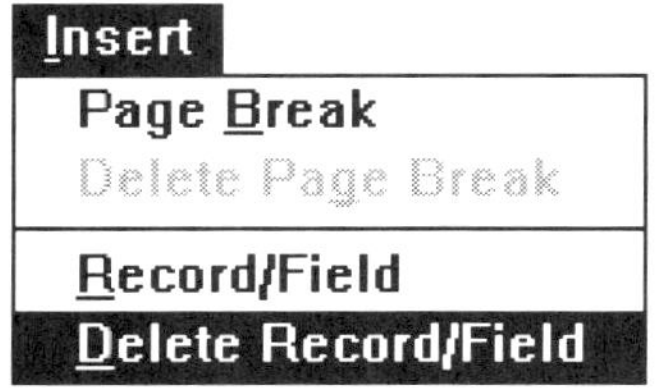

Figure 16-26. *The Delete Record/Field command.*

This operation deletes the currently selected fields. Move into the blank field which was just created and choose *Delete Record/Field* from the **Insert** menu. The *Delete* dialog box appears, in which you specify that a field is to be deleted by clicking on *Field* (Figure 16-27).

When you click on *OK*, the blank field is removed from the screen.

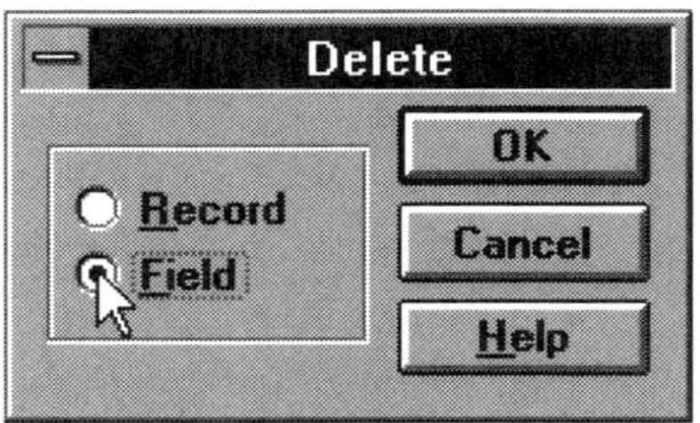

***Figure 16-27.** The Delete dialog box.*

Formatting data

Alignment

There are four main choices of aligning field entries in Works. These are: General, Left, Right, and Center (Figure 16-28).

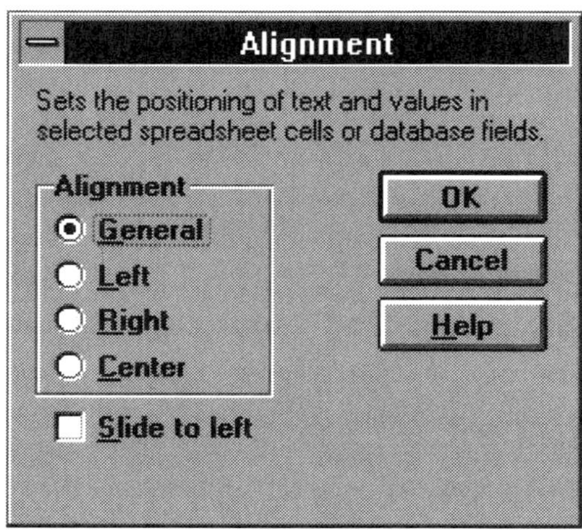

***Figure 16-28.** The Alignment dialog box in Form view.*

General is the default alignment in the database. It places all text to the left of the field entry and all numbers to the right.

Left alignment places all entries at the left of the field entry area. *Right* places entries at the right of the field and *Center* puts the entries in the middle of the field entry area.

You can open the *Alignment* dialog box from the **Format** menu in Form view or List view. The options you have in addition to *General, Left, Right,* and *Center* depend on which view you are using. In Form view, Works also gives you the *Slide to left* option shown in Figure 16-28. Selecting *Slide to left* removes spaces surrounding a field entry when you print your data.

In List view you have three *Vertical* alignment options and a *Wrap text* option (Figure 16-29). As in the Works spreadsheet, the *Vertical* options align selected field entries vertically within their cells.

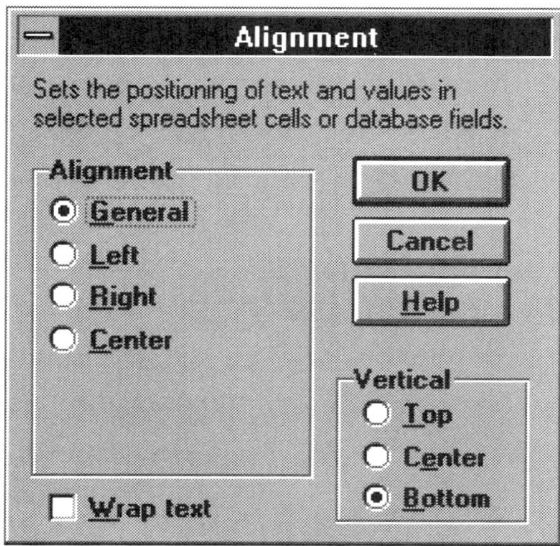

***Figure 16-29.** The Alignment dialog box in List view.*

Wrap text has an effect only when you select text fields. Choosing *Wrap text* causes text fields to automatically increase the height of their record and wrap within their cells rather than overlap neighboring cells. See **Chapter 10, Editing Spreadsheets** for more information on the *Vertical* and *Wrap text* options.

Select the "Full Name" field and change it to *Center* alignment using the *Alignment* command in the **Format** menu. The database in List view now looks like Figure 16-30.

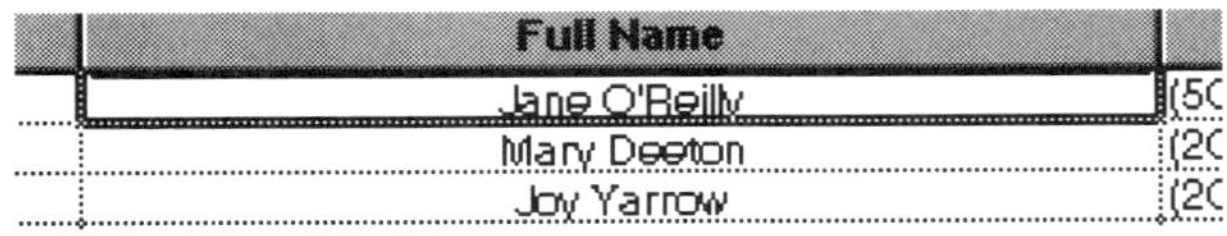

Figure 16-30. *The "Full Name" field is changed to center alignment in List view.*

Text styles

The style of a field can be changed in Works. There are three styles available on the toolbar: bold, italic, and underline.

Figure 16-31. *The Style toolbar buttons.*

The *Font and Style* command in the **Format** menu displays the *Font and Style* dialog box (Figure 16-32). This is the alternative method for changing styles.

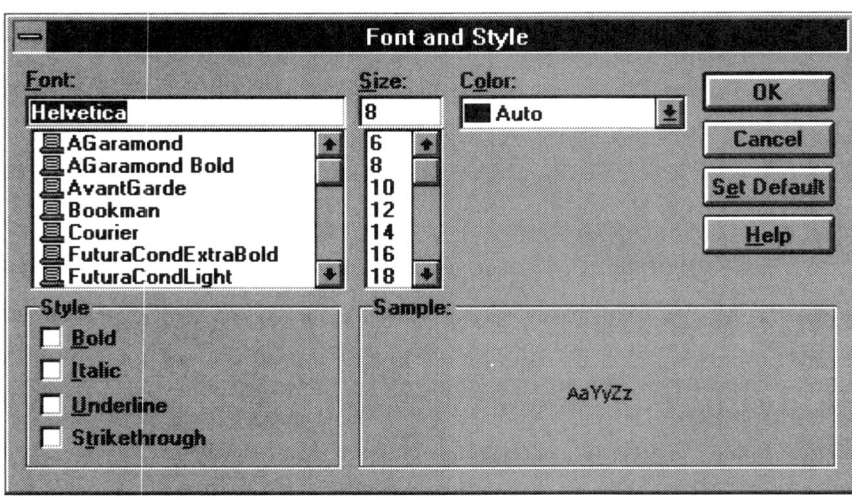

Figure 16-32. *The Font and Style dialog box from the **Format** menu.*

To emphasize the entries in the "Full Name" field, you can change them to bold. The style of a field can be formatted in either Form view or List view. In this example, the style is changed in Form view, so change to Form view by pressing F9.

It is important to select the field which is to be formatted, before adding the new style. Click on the field entry of the "Full Name" field as in Figure 16-33. Changing the field style in any record affects the style in all entries of that field. Because of this, it does not matter in which record the change is made.

Full Name: Jane O'Reilly
Street: 2421 4th Avenue
DRAG
City: Portland
State/Province: OR
Postal Code: 97111
Phone: (503) 555-9801

Figure 16-33. *The field entry in the "Full Name" field is selected.*

To change the style in this case, use the *Bold* button on the toolbar. The field entry immediately changes to bold and, if you scroll through the other records in the database, you will see that all of the "Full Name" data is changed to a bold style (Figure 16-34).

Full Name: **Judi Rapsody**
Street: 75 Harbor Road
City: Oceanside
State/Province: WA
Postal Code: 98008
Phone: (206) 555-6619

Figure 16-34. *The "Full Name" field is now bold.*

Selecting fonts and font sizes

Fonts and font sizes are changed in a database before or after text is entered.

A list of fonts which are available is in the *Font* submenu on the toolbar (Figure 16-35). The fonts in this list depend on the printer you have attached and what soft fonts have been loaded.

Figure 16-35. *The Font submenu.*

The font sizes correspond with the selected font. These also depend on your printer. The *Size* submenu lists the font sizes available to you. Figure 16-36 shows an example of the *Size* submenu.

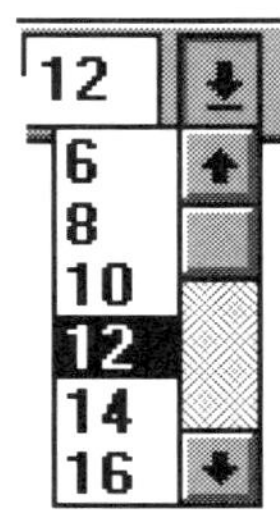

Figure 16-36. *The Size submenu.*

Fonts and sizes affect your selection in the current view only. Changing the font in Form view does not affect List view. For instance, if you change the font to Avant Garde in Form view, the fields, field entries, and labels in your selection in Form view are all changed to Avant Garde. Try this now after selecting the "Full Name" field name, and holding down the Ctrl key and clicking on the corresponding field entry to select it also, as in Figure 16-37.

Full Name: Jane O'Reilly
Street: 2421 4th Avenue
City: Portland
State/Province: OR
Postal Code: 97111
Phone: (503) 555-9801

Figure 16-37. *Select both "Full Name" and its corresponding field entry.*

Choosing *AvantGarde* from the *Font* submenu changes the font as in Figure 16-38. List view fonts, however, will not change.

Full Name: Jane O'Reilly
Street: 2421 4th Avenue
City: Portland
State/Province: OR
Postal Code: 97111
Phone: (503) 555-9801

Figure 16-38. The font is now Avant Garde.

Value formats

Value formats affect the numbers in a field. The value may be a number which has simply been typed in, or a result of a formula. The format of these numbers can be changed in either List view or Form view in exactly the same way. This example shows you how to change a value format in List view. Change to List view by pressing F9.

A number which is keyed into a field is automatically given a General format, which displays the number without thousands separators, dollar signs, or the decimal places required for calculations.

There are 11 other formats, which are listed in the *Number* dialog box (Figure 16-39). Each of these is described in detail in **Chapter 10, Editing Spreadsheets** as they are identical to the value formats in the spreadsheet tool.

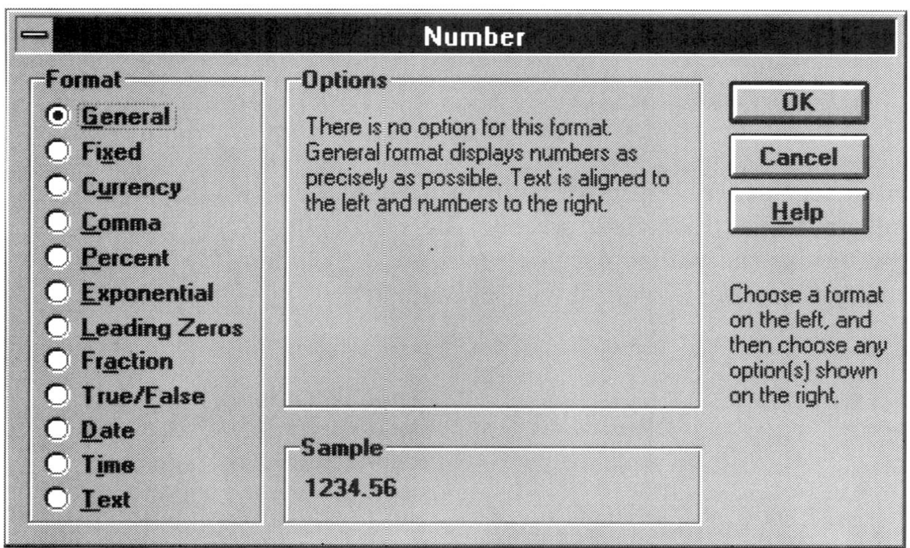

Figure 16-39. The Number dialog box.

As an example, click on the "Qty" field in a record of your choice and type "$100,000". Click on the same field in another record and type "$200,000" as shown in Figure 16-40. Works formats this field with the Currency format with no decimal places because you entered a number of dollars, without cents.

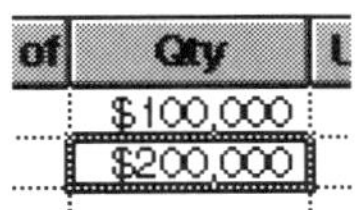

Figure 16-40. *The figures are formatted as Currency with no decimal places.*

You can change figures to any other format through *Number* command in the **Format** menu.

This command can be used to change the format of the numbers in the "Qty" field to something else. Move into the field which is to be changed. In this case, click in "Qty" and choose *Number* from the **Format** menu. Let's increase the number of decimal places displayed for this field. Double-click on the *Number of decimals* text box of the *Currency* section in the *Number* dialog box and type "2". This can be seen in Figure 16-41.

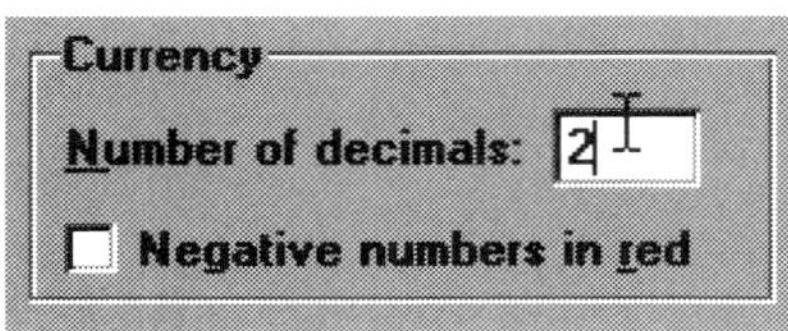

Figure 16-41. *Type "2" in the Currency text box.*

As this field is to change its format to two decimal places, click on *OK* and return to the List view screen. The result, however, may be unexpected, as the values may be replaced with hatch (#) symbols (Figure 16-42), if the field is not wide enough to display all the figures.

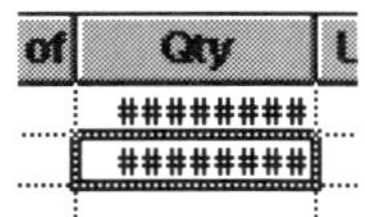

Figure 16-42. *Hatch symbols appear as the field size is not wide enough.*

Works is telling you that the field is too narrow, as the values now have an extra three characters—a decimal point and two places after that decimal point. It is easily fixed by widening the field. Widen the field now and the values appear with the correct format when the field is wide enough. Figure 16-43 shows this.

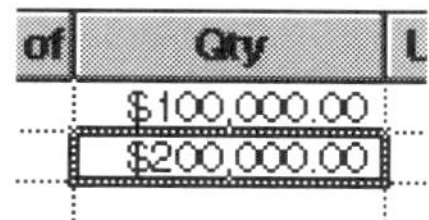

Figure 16-43. *Widen the column to reveal the field entries.*

Protecting the database

Protecting form setup

Setting up the form can take quite some time. It may be set up in a particular way to suit a preprinted form, or for a strong visual effect. Change to Form view to follow the next example.

Moving fields around the form is easy and can quite often be done accidentally. To avoid changing the form unintentionally, the setup of the form can be protected. Choose *Protection* from the **Format** menu (Figure 16-44).

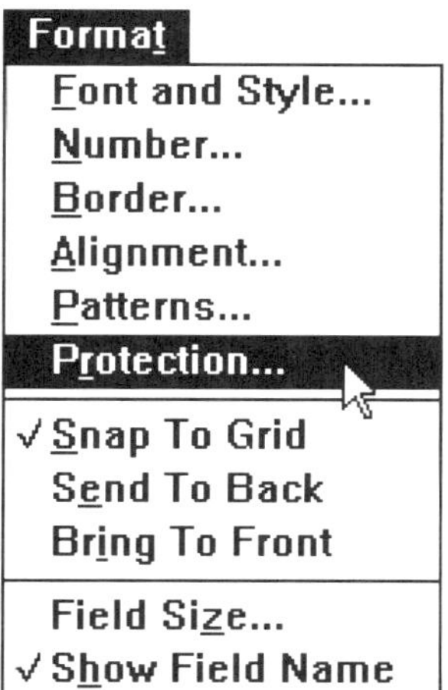

Figure 16-44. *The Protection command in the* ***Format*** *menu.*

When *Protect Form* is selected as in Figure 16-45, the form cannot be altered. Activate this check box and test it by attempting to move the fields around the screen. This option does not appear in the *Protection* dialog box in List view.

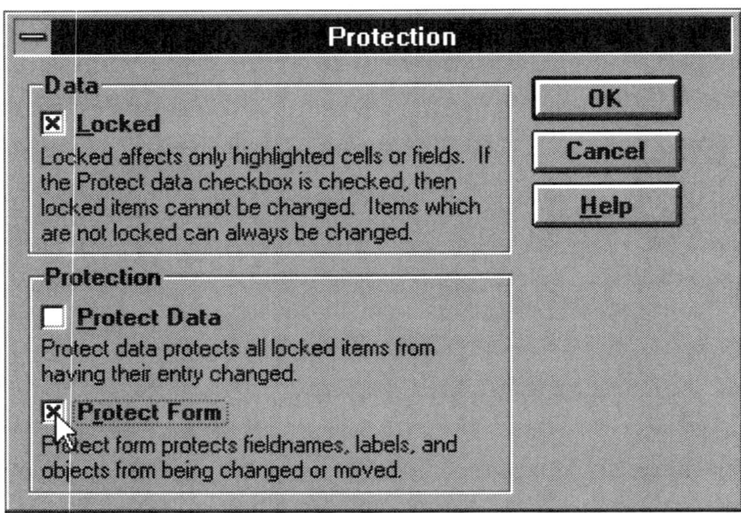

Figure 16-45. *Select Protect Form in the Protection dialog box.*

Protecting data

When you have completed the database, it is often necessary to protect it from accidental changes to field entries and formulas.

All fields are "locked" in Works, as soon as they are inserted into the database. The locking has no effect until you select the *Protect Data* check box in the *Protection* dialog box of Figure 16-45.

When a field is locked, and *Protect Data* is on, the field format and entry cannot be changed. Activate *Protect Data* and try to change a field entry. The dialog box in Figure 16-46 appears, telling you that the field is locked.

Figure 16-46. This dialog box warns you that the field entry cannot be changed as it is locked.

To unlock some fields in the database, and leave others protected, you use the *Locked* check box in the *Protection* dialog box. The *Protect Data* check box in the dialog box must be empty; deselect this now.

The field to be unlocked is the "Postal Code" field. This example shows you the steps in Form view, but the process is identical in List view. Highlight the "Postal Code" field in any record and choose *Protection* from the **Format** menu (Figure 16-44).

The *Protection* dialog box appears, in which you deselect the *Locked* check box. The *Locked* check box is deselected if there is no cross in it, as shown in Figure 16-47.

The final step is to activate *Protect Data* in the *Protection* dialog box again (Figure 16-47). Test that "Postal Code" is unlocked by changing its field entry. Attempt to change the other field entries. The dialog box telling you that the cell is locked appears (Figure 16-46), and the contents remain the same.

Figure 16-47. Clear the Locked check box and select Protect Data to protect all but the currently selected data entries.

Viewing the Database

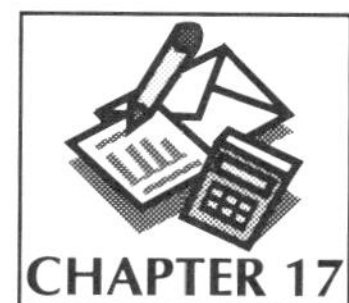
CHAPTER 17

In this chapter you are shown some techniques for displaying specific database information. The sample file used in this chapter is ***toys_l.wdb*** and is in the ***msworks.cbt*** subdirectory.

Hiding and displaying information

In Works, you can choose to hide or display parts of the database, according to the view you are in.

Field perimeters

Field perimeters are borders of fields which are used to separate fields entries in the database.

In List view, the field perimeters are displayed as gridlines. These are turned off by deselecting the *Gridlines* command in the **View** menu (Figure 17-1).

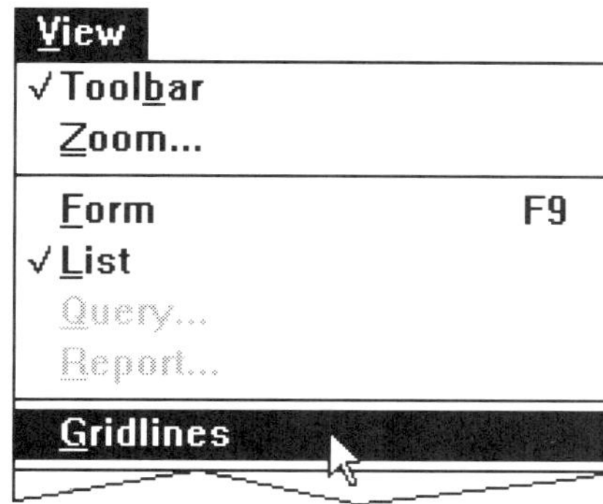

Figure 17-1. *The Gridlines command in the **View** menu.*

When the gridlines are not displayed, the sample file appears as in Figure 17-2.

	Toy	Brand	Supplier	Color	Order
1	Fortran Lea	Computer Fun	Fun Factory	Yellow	7/1/93
2	Rocket Rac	Flying Fun	Fun Factory	Red/Blue	7/14/93
3	Day-Glo Fri	Flying Fun	Fun Factory	Lime/Pink	7/1/93
4	Model Cess	Flying Fun	Fun Factory	Black	7/1/93

Figure 17-2. *The sample file displayed without gridlines.*

In Form view, field lines appear to the right of the field name. If these lines are not to be displayed, the *Field Lines* command in the **View** menu is deselected (Figure 17-3).

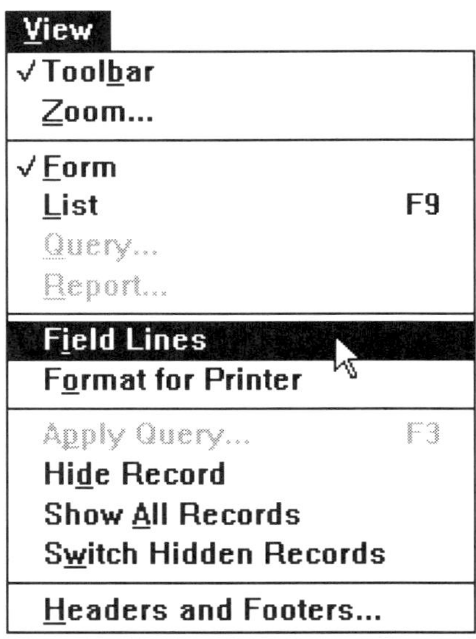

Figure 17-3. *The Field Lines command in Form view.*

Fields

In some cases, it is necessary to hide some fields from view. Change to List view by pressing F9. This may be the wholesale price of an item, for example, which you don't want your retail customers to see.

Fields can only be hidden in List view. This is achieved by changing the width of a column to zero. The *Field Width* command is in the **Format** menu and, when selected, displays the *Field Width* dialog box shown in Figure 17-4. Move into the "Wholesale" field and open this dialog box.

Figure 17-4. *The Field Width dialog box in which the Width is changed to zero.*

When you click on *OK*, you return to the List view screen and "Wholesale" is not shown.

To redisplay the field, the *Go To* command is used. *Go To* is activated by selecting *Go To* from the **Edit** menu, or by pressing F5. This command is used to go to a particular field in the database. The dialog box displays the list of fields.

When redisplaying a hidden field, the hidden field is selected from the *Names* list box as shown in Figure 17-5.

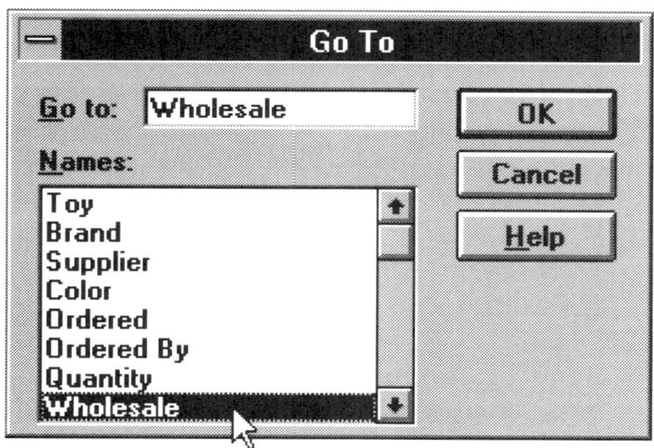

Figure 17-5. *Select "Wholesale" from the Go To dialog box.*

Pressing Enter returns you to the screen where the field is not yet displayed, but is selected. As it is selected, you can simply reenter the width of the field in the *Field Width* dialog box. Try this now by selecting *Field Width* from the **Format** menu and type in "10". Click on *OK* and the screen shows the "Wholesale" field once again.

In Form view, all that can be hidden is the field name itself. When *Show Field Name* in the **Format** menu is selected, the field name appears on the form. Figure 17-6, for example, shows that the *Show Field Name* command is selected, therefore the highlighted field name appears on the form.

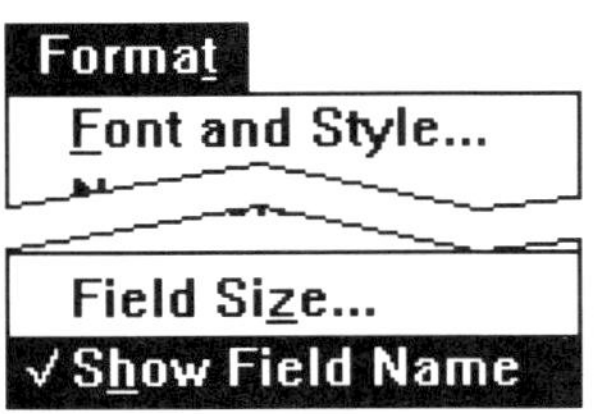

***Figure 17-6.** Show Field Name is selected in the **Format** menu.*

Records

Records can be hidden from view in either List or Form view. To hide a record, the *Hide Record* command is used in the **View** menu. In this example, records are hidden in List view. The process is the same in Form view.

Assuming that the record to be hidden is record 6—the Satellite Launcher—the insertion point needs to be in this record before opening the **View** menu. Move your insertion point there now and select *Hide Record* from the **View** menu, as Figure 17-7 illustrates.

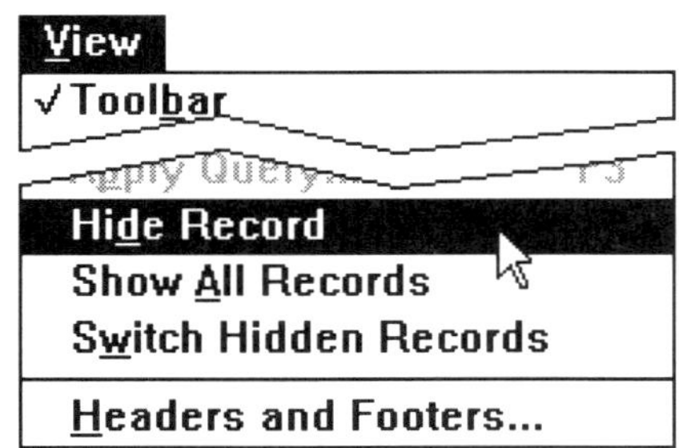

***Figure 17-7.** The Hide Record command in the **View** menu.*

The screen no longer displays record 6. It is obvious that a record is hidden from the frame, as the records are numbered 1, 2, 3, 4, 5, 7.

There are a couple of options in the **View** menu which can be used to redisplay the hidden record or records. *Switch Hidden Records* is a toggle switch which shows you either the hidden records or all other records. Use this command now and record 6 appears on the screen, by itself, as in Figure 17-8. To view the rest of the records again, choose *Switch Hidden Records* from the **View** menu.

Figure 17-8. *The Switch Hidden Records command is used to show only the hidden record in this case.*

To unhide records in the database, the *Show All Records* command is activated from the **View** menu. Select this now, as in Figure 17-9 and the database returns to its original state.

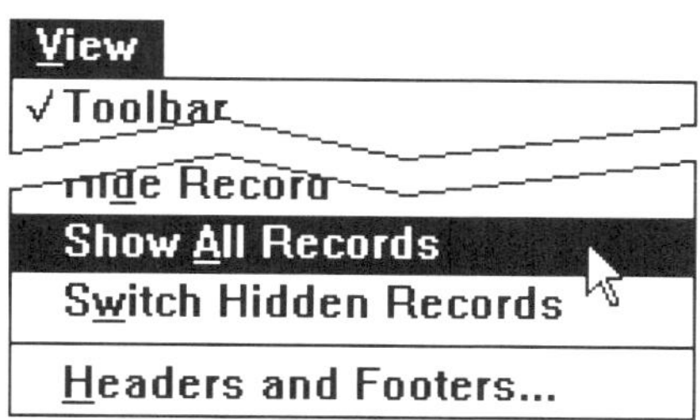

Figure 17-9. *The Show All Records command in the* ***View*** *menu.*

Sorting records

Records can be sorted in alphabetical and numeric order. The sort order can be ascending or descending. It may be important to sort addresses into numeric order based on their postal code, or alphabetical order based on the city.

Works lets you sort on one, two, or three fields. An example of when a three-field sort is used is for a staff list. Staff would first be sorted according to their department, then into alphabetical order of last name, and then perhaps into numeric ascending order of their salary.

In the sample file, a sort will be applied which sorts data using the values in the "Toy" field. Begin the sort by selecting *Sort Records* from the **Tools** menu, which displays the *Sort Records* dialog box. Works uses the first field in your database as a default by which to sort your data. Figure 17-10 shows the dialog box. Click on OK to accept "Toy" as the sort field.

Note that the records are now sorted in alphabetical order of toy name.

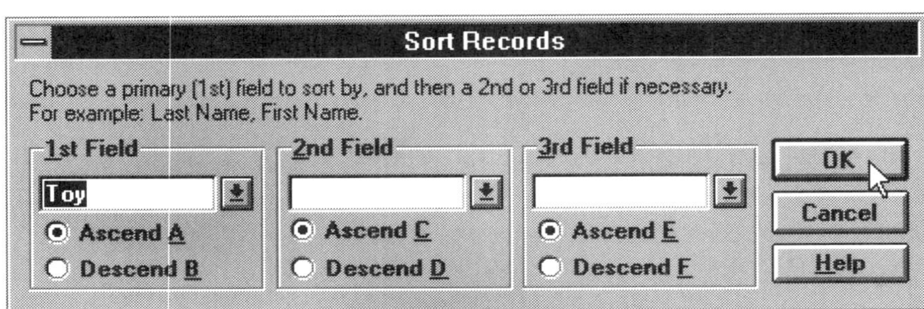

Figure 17-10. *The dialog box to sort the records into order according to toy name.*

Searching

Searching is used to find specific records in the database quickly. For example, you may require a list of New York clients. The *Find* command in the **Edit** menu displays the Find dialog box.

In the *Find What* text box, you specify on what criterion the search is to be based. In ***toys_l.wdb***, you could look for all of the brown toys, according to their "Color" field. Type in "brown" in the *Find What* text box as in Figure 17-11.

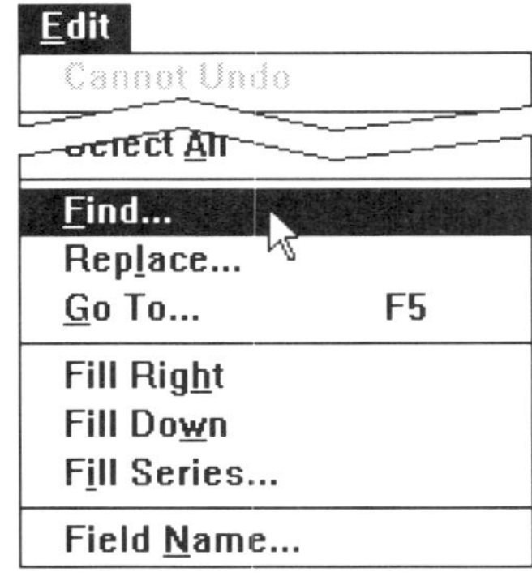

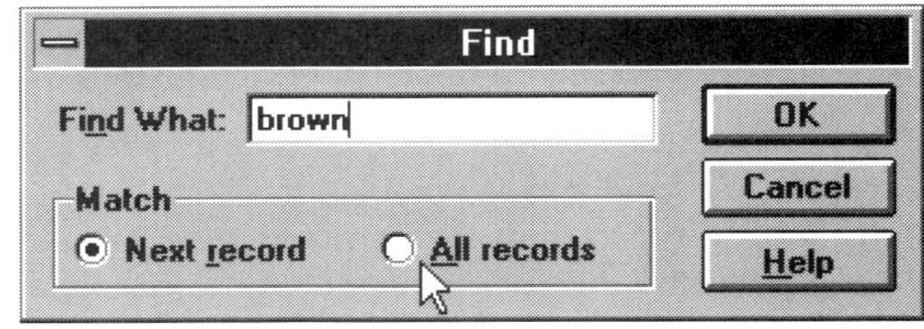

Figure 17-11. *Type "brown" into the Find What text box.*

The type of *Match* is determined next. A search finds the next record in the database which matches the search criteria if *Next Record* is selected. To find the following record you simply repeat the search by pressing F7.

To display a list of all records which match what is selected in the *Find* dialog box, choose *All records.* Do this for this example, and click on *OK*. The screen in Figure 17-12 shows all of the toys which have a brown color.

	Toy	Brand	Supplier	Color	Ordered
4	Dan the Dru	Zap Toys	Toy Barn	Brown	7/5/93
7	Expanding	Rich Folks	GraphInc	Brown	7/5/93
21	Piano Pete	Zap Toys	Toy Barn	Brown	7/5/93
29	Stegosauru	Nature's Kids	Toy Barn	Brown/Olive	7/1/93
31	Thinking Tr	Plastic Pets	Toy Barn	Brown	7/5/93
34	Wooden Tr	Non-Toxic Toys	Toy Barn	Brown	6/25/93
35	Wooden Tu	Non-Toxic Toys	Toy Barn	Brown	6/25/93
36					

Figure 17-12. *The search has been performed and lists all brown toys.*

To display all of the records again, choose *Show All Records* from the **View** menu.

Queries

A query is a more powerful way to display specific records in the database than searching. Works searches through all records, including the hidden ones, and hides any records which do not match the query criteria.

There are a number of types of queries which can be applied to your database. A simple query can find the exact match; for example every client from California. You can ask to find all the clients who owe more than or less than a given amount. A query can be used to match entries in more than one field; for example, clients in California who owe more than $100. A query can also be used to determine the opposite, such as clients who do not owe more than $100.

Defining query parameters

To define a query, click on the *Query View* button on the toolbar or choose *Create New Query* from the **Tools** menu shown in Figure 17-13.

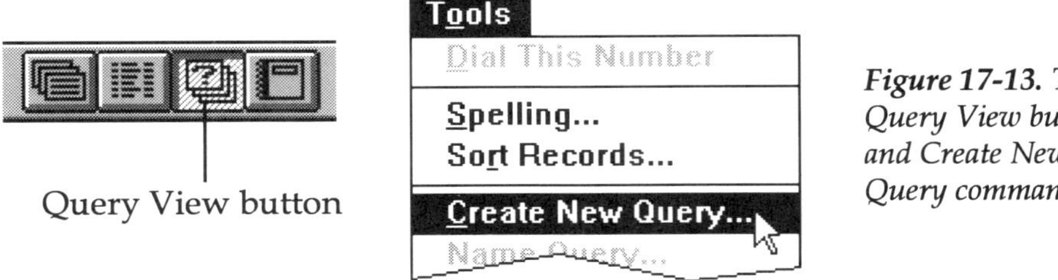

Figure 17-13. *The Query View button and Create New Query command.*

Works opens the *New Query* dialog box for you to define your query. You use this dialog box to create up to three "query sentences" or criteria. Only records that match your criteria will appear when you apply your query.

Suppose you want to find all records for toys whose retail value is over $10. Choose *Retail* from the *Choose a field to compare* submenu as shown in Figure 17-14.

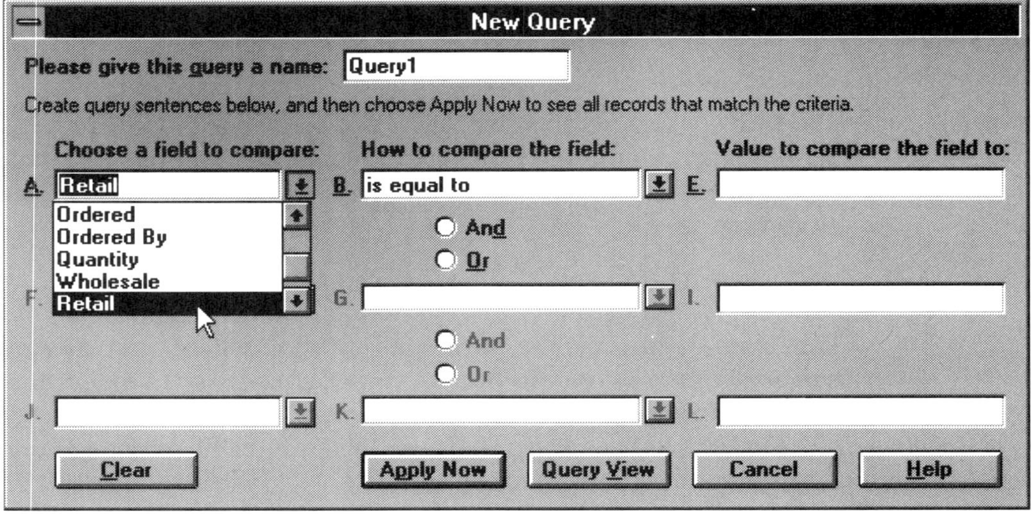

Figure 17-14. *Choose the Retail field in the New Query dialog box as shown.*

Complete your query by choosing *is greater than* from the *How to compare the field* submenu and entering *$10* in the *Value to compare the field to* text box as shown in Figure 17-15.

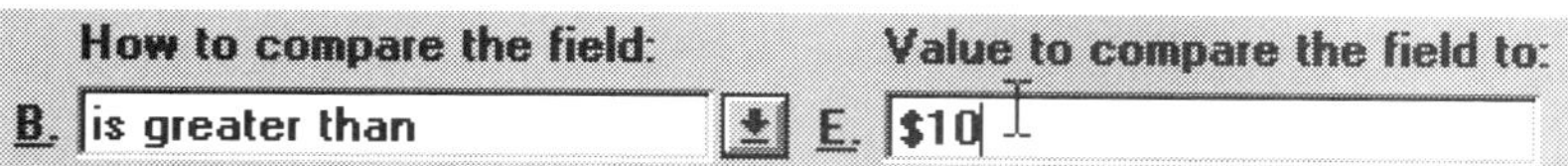

Figure 17-15. *These specifications will find all the toys which sell for more than $10.*

Applying the query

Click on *Apply Now* in the *New Query* dialog box to see the matching records. List view is best for this (Figure 17-16).

	Color	Ordered	Ordered By	Quantity	Wholesal	Retail	S
16	Black	7/1/93	A. Hayes	50	$8.99	$12.14	
20	Magenta	6/23/93	T. Livingston	25	$13.99	$18.89	
26	Silver/Taup	6/24/93	A. Hayes	50	$12.50	$16.88	
28	N/A	7/1/93	T. Livingston	25	$12.50	$16.88	
34	Brown	6/25/93	J.Mathers	25	$8.50	$11.48	
36							

Figure 17-16. *Only the toys over $10 are visible.*

Show All Records

Redisplay all the records by choosing the *Show All Records* command in the **View** menu.

Using wild card characters

There are two wild cards which can be used in a query. These are "*," which substitutes for any number of characters and "?," which substitutes for one character. Using wild cards gives you added flexibility in applying queries.

Change to Query view using the toolbar. Once you have created a query, clicking on the *Query View* button takes you to your most recent query. The Query view screen looks similar to Form view and shows a list of field names which make up the database. On a field entry line, you can see the formula that Works used for your last query (Figure 17-17).

Toy: =Retail>VALUE("$10")
Brand:
Supplier:
Color:
Ordered:
Ordered By:
Quantity:
Stock:
Wholesale:

Figure 17-17. *Query view shows the formula for your most recent query.*

Apply a query now to find all the toys whose names start with "T." Choose *Create New Query* from the **Tools** menu. Rather than having many queries simply named "Query 1," "Query 2," and so on, you can make your queries easier to use by giving them meaningful names. Name this query ""T" toys" using the *Please give this query a name* text box in the *New Query* dialog box. Your query sentence should check whether the "Toy" field is equal to "T*," as shown in Figure 17-18. Press Enter to apply your new query.

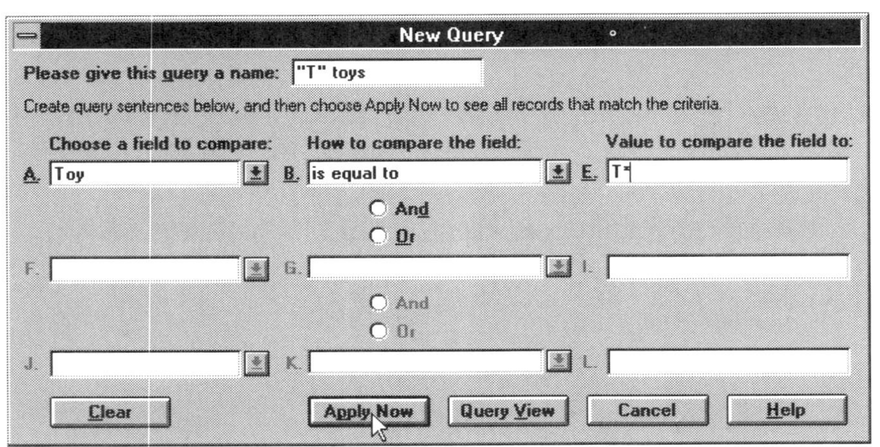

Figure 17-18. *This query is to find all the toys whose names start with "T."*

Return to List view to see the result of your query. The screen should display the two records shown in Figure 17-19.

	Toy	Brand	Supplier	Colc
30	The Enlight	Zen Toys	GraphInc	N/A
31	Thinking Tr	Plastic Pets	Toy Barn	Brown
36				

Figure 17-19. All the toys which start with "T" are on the List view screen.

Manipulating multiple queries

Works provides several commands which become particularly useful when you work with more than one query. To demonstrate some of these commands, return to Query view using the toolbar button.

In Query view the *Query* command in the **View** menu opens the *Queries* dialog box which you use to switch between queries (Figure 17-20). Choose this command now and double-click on *Query1* to switch to your first query.

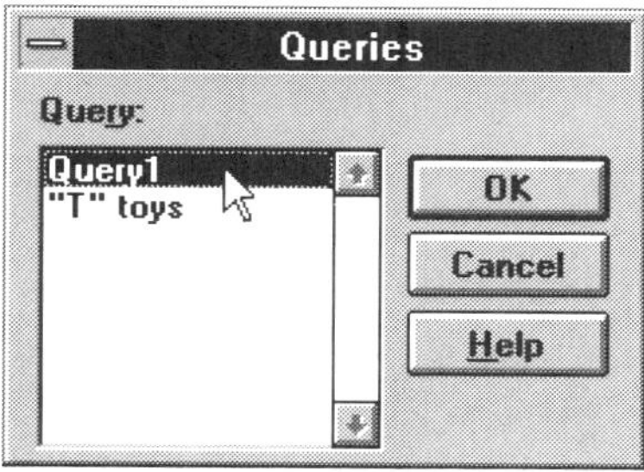

Figure 17-20. Choose Query from the ***View*** *menu and double-click on Query1.*

To delete a query, choose *Delete Query* from the **Tools** menu as shown in Figure 17-21.

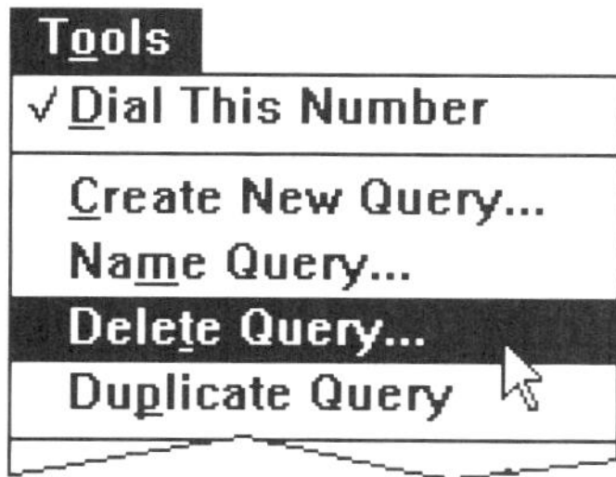

Figure 17-21. The Delete Query command.

Click on the query you want to remove, then click on *Delete* as in Figure 17-22. Click on *OK* to close the dialog box.

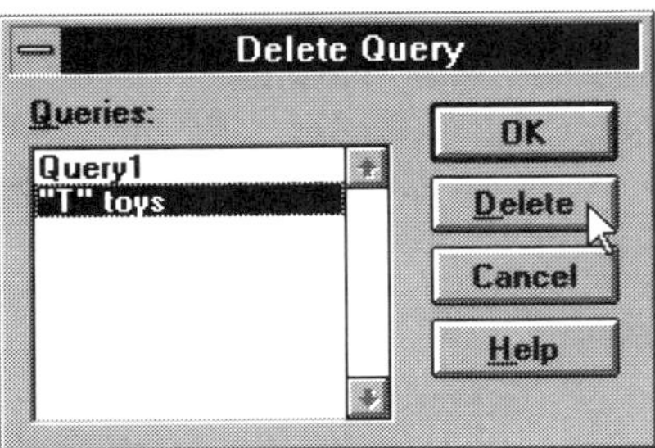

Figure 17-22. *Select the query you want to delete and click on Delete in the Delete Query dialog box.*

Creating Database Reports

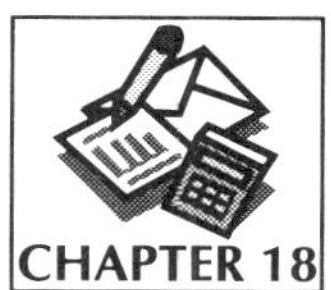

A report in a database allows you to organize information for printing. Often a report consists of a summary of key fields, which are appropriate to the report being printed. A report, therefore, is much more flexible than simply printing the database from List or Form view.

The fields specified as part of the report can be sorted and grouped. The fields can be placed in a certain position on a page. Headings and comments can be added and statistical information can be inserted to add meaning to the report.

This chapter looks at reporting with the Works database. The sample file referred to is ***toys_l.wdb*** which is in the ***msworks.cbt*** subdirectory. Open this file to follow the examples in this chapter as illustrated in Figure 18-1.

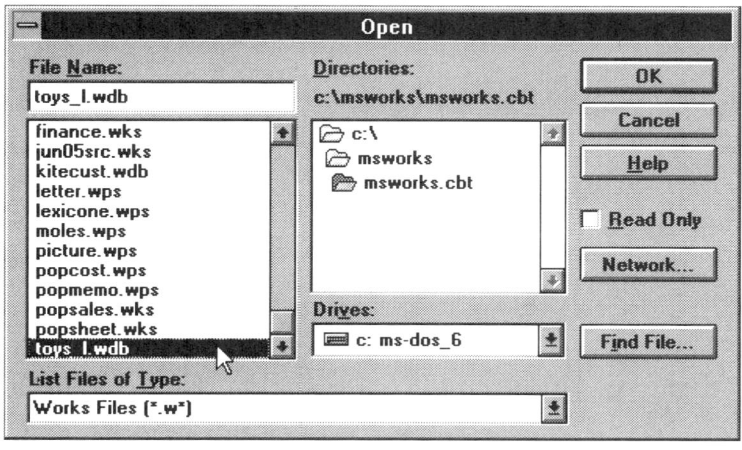

Figure 18-1. *The sample file* ***toys_l.wdb*** *is used as an example in this chapter.*

Creating a new report

A new report is created in the *New Report* dialog box. This is displayed by selecting the *Create New Report* command in the **Tools** menu (Figure 18-2).

Figure 18-2. *Select Create New Report from the* ***Tools*** *menu to display the New Report dialog box.*

The title of the report is entered into the *Report Title* text box in the *New Report* dialog box. The title appears at the top of the first page of the report and gives the reader an indication of the contents of the report.

The report shows the current inventory of Candell Imports. The title should reflect this, so type in "Candell Imports Inventory Report" into the *Report Title* text box as shown in Figure 18-3.

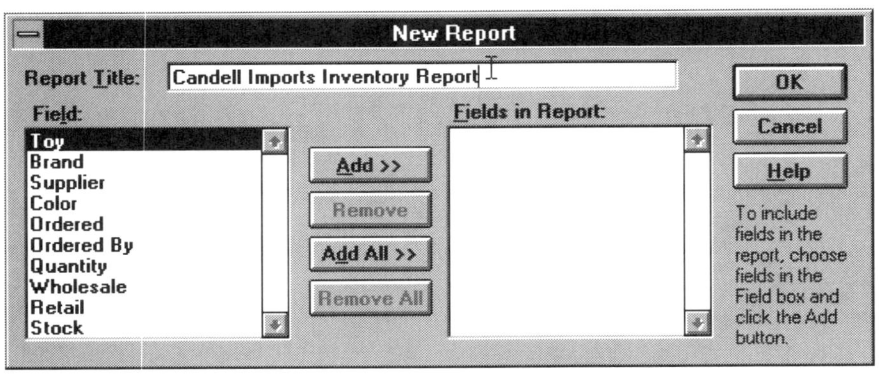

Figure 18-3. *"Candell Imports Inventory Report" is inserted as the title.*

Selecting fields to show in report

As the report need show a summary of the database only, not all fields are added to the report. The fields to go into this report are "Toy," "Brand," "Supplier," "Wholesale," and "Stock."

All the fields in the database are listed in the *Field* list box on the left. They are added to the report by highlighting the field in the list box and clicking on *Add*. Try this for the "Toy" field as Figure 18-4 shows.

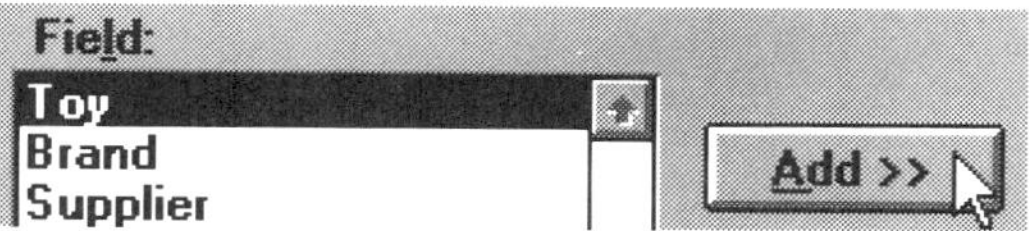

Figure 18-4. *Highlight "Toy" and click on Add in the New Report dialog box.*

The field is added to the *Fields in Report* list box. Add the other four fields listed above. In Figure 18-5, all the fields have been added that will appear in the report. To confirm that the list of fields is correct, click on *OK*.

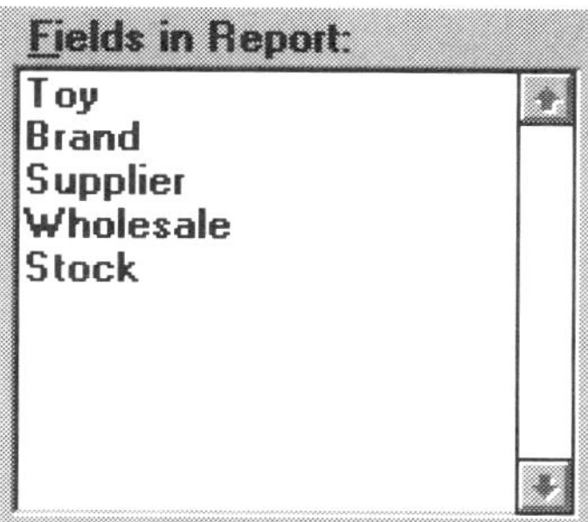

Figure 18-5. *The report contains five fields from the database.*

Selecting statistics to show in report

Works immediately displays the *Report Statistics* dialog box (Figure 18-6).

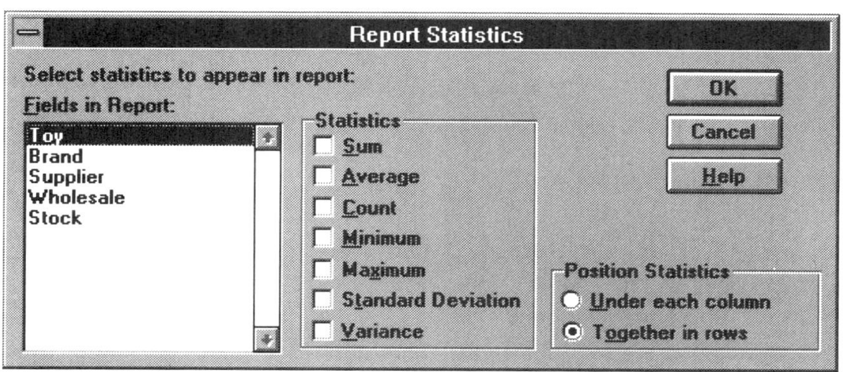

Figure 18-6. *The Report Statistics dialog box.*

Statistics are used in a report to perform calculations on fields in the database. There are seven types of statistics available in the *Report Statistics* dialog box. These are listed below:

Sum—SUM—totals values in a field.

Average—AVG—calculates the average of values in a field.

Count—COUNT—counts the number of entries in a field.

Minimum—MIN—finds the smallest value in a field.

Maximum—MAX—determines the largest value in a field.

Standard Deviation—STD—calculates the standard deviation for a numeric field.

Variance—VAR—calculates the variance for a numeric field.

In this example, for instance, the total figure for the "Stock" field, would be interesting. The type of statistic used to calculate this figure is SUM.

To insert this into the report, the field is selected first and then the type of statistic is selected from the *Statistics* box. For this inventory, click on "Stock" in the *Fields in Report* list box and then choose *SUM* (Figure 18-7).

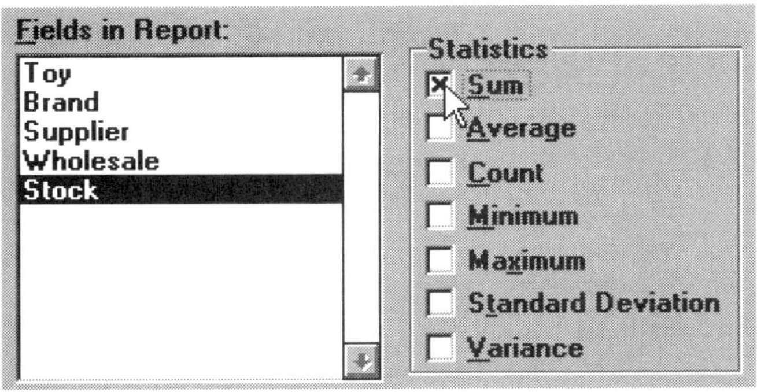

Figure 18-7. *The Statistics to add the total of "Stock" in the report.*

To calculate the number of records in the report, the *COUNT* statistic is used. The most logical field to count is "Toy." Click on "Toy" and then on *COUNT* in the *Statistics* box (Figure 18-8).

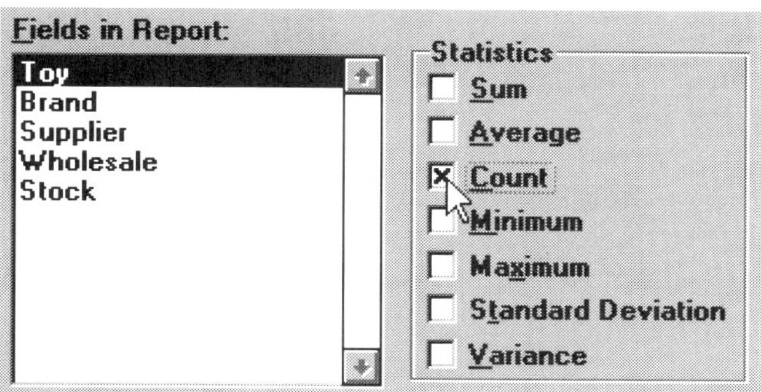

***Figure 18-8.** The COUNT statistic is selected for the "Toy" field.*

The placement of the statistical information in the report is determined in the *Report Statistics* dialog box. There are two choices. *Under each column* places the result of the calculation under the corresponding column. *Together in rows* places the calculations at the end of the report. Works automatically provides a description of the calculation when this option is active.

Leave *Together in rows* checked. Click on *OK* and the report definition is created. A dialog box appears to inform you that the report definition is created (Figure 18-9). Click on *OK* to see the report definition screen.

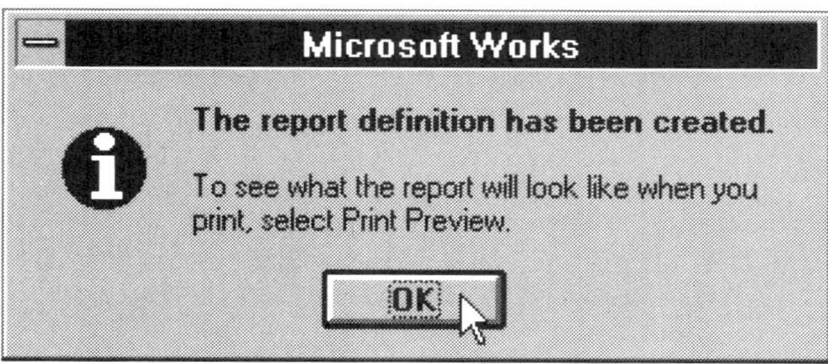

***Figure 18-9.** The dialog box which tells you that the report is defined.*

The report definition screen

The report definition screen displays the report defined in the *New Report* dialog box in columns and rows. When the report definition screen is active, REPORT appears in the status bar. The columns are labeled with letters, but the rows are labeled with parts of the report. Four parts appear in this screen, and are: Title, Headings, Record, and Summary. These are displayed in Figure 18-10.

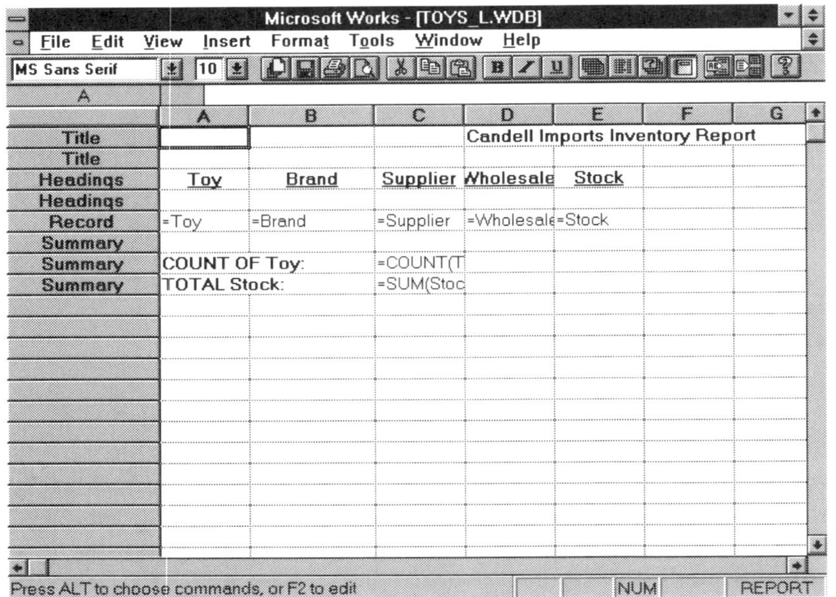

Figure 18-10. *The report definition screen.*

Title rows

The title rows (Figure 18-11) contain the title which was inserted in the *New Report* dialog box (refer back to Figure 18-3). Your title appears in column D and is printed in this position. It is possible to move this to another location, by using the *Cut* and *Paste* commands in the **Edit** menu.

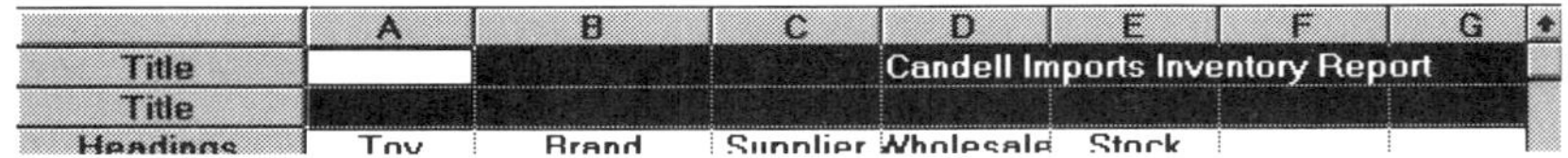

Figure 18-11. *The title rows.*

To separate the title from the rest of the report more clearly, you can insert another row. There are two rows allocated for the title automatically. More rows are inserted using the *Row/Column* command in the **Insert** menu. Select that command after selecting the second title row.

Works asks what type of row is being inserted—Title, Headings, Record, or Summary—in the *Insert Row* dialog box (Figure 18-12).

Click on *Title* and then on *OK*, and a new title row is inserted into the report definition screen.

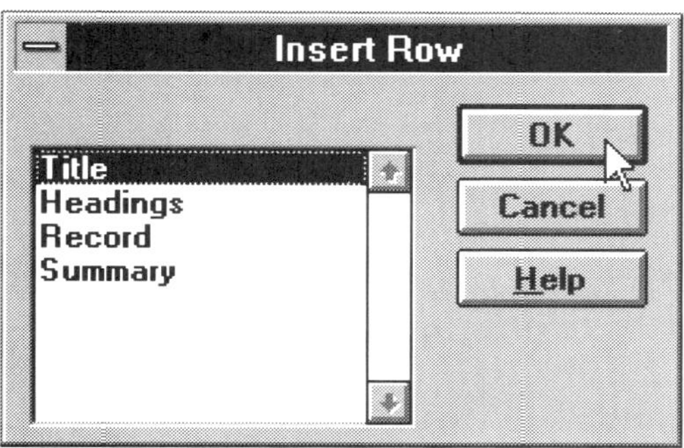

Figure 18-12. *The Insert Row dialog box.*

HEADINGS ROWS

Headings in the heading rows (Figure 18-13) label the fields in the report. By default, the headings are made up of the field names which were entered into the database originally.

Figure 18-13. *The heading rows.*

Headings are underlined automatically, which helps to distinguish them from the records. The text in headings can be changed if necessary. A heading may need to be changed when the field name is not clear enough or is abbreviated.

RECORD ROW

The record row (Figure 18-14) lists the fields specified in the *New Report* dialog box. The field name is prefixed with an equals sign (=). The equals sign tells Works to print all the records in the field specified.

Figure 18-14. The record row.

When the report is printed, data in the summary rows is pushed down, inserting enough rows for all of the records to be printed.

SUMMARY ROWS

The results of calculations are placed in the summary rows in the report definition screen. The calculations are based on the statistics specified in the *Report Statistics* dialog box (refer back to Figure 18-6).

Figure 18-15 displays the two pieces of statistical data entered. We have dragged the column border to the right to widen the column and make these readable. The first statistic counts the total number of records using the "Toy" field. The formula for this is =COUNT(Toy). The second totals the "Stock" field with the formula =SUM(Stock).

Figure 18-15. The summary rows.

Editing reports

A report can be edited easily in Works. The format of numbers and text can be changed, as can column widths. These and other formats are outlined in this section.

Text and value formats

Changing the format of text is the same as changing text formats in other Works tools. Text styles, alignment, colors, fonts, and font sizes are changed through the *Font and Style* command in the **Format** menu. You can change most of these attributes using the buttons on the toolbar.

The row to be formatted is selected before any changes can be made. Select the first title row and click on the italic button on the toolbar (Figure 18-16).

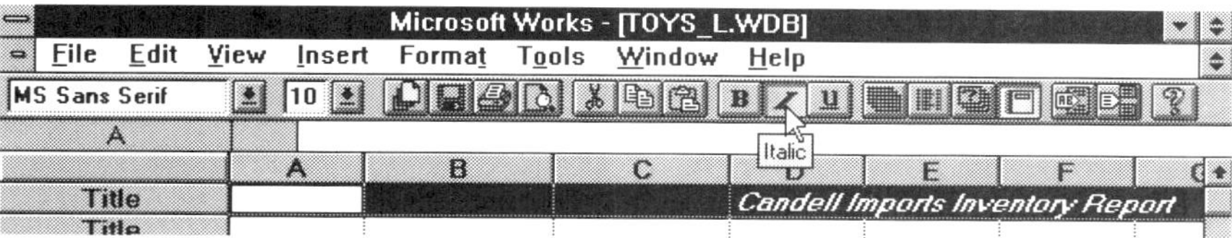

***Figure 18-16.** The title is made italic using the Italic button on the toolbar.*

Value formats can be changed through the *Number* command in the **Format** menu. The *Number* dialog box is shown in Figure 18-17.

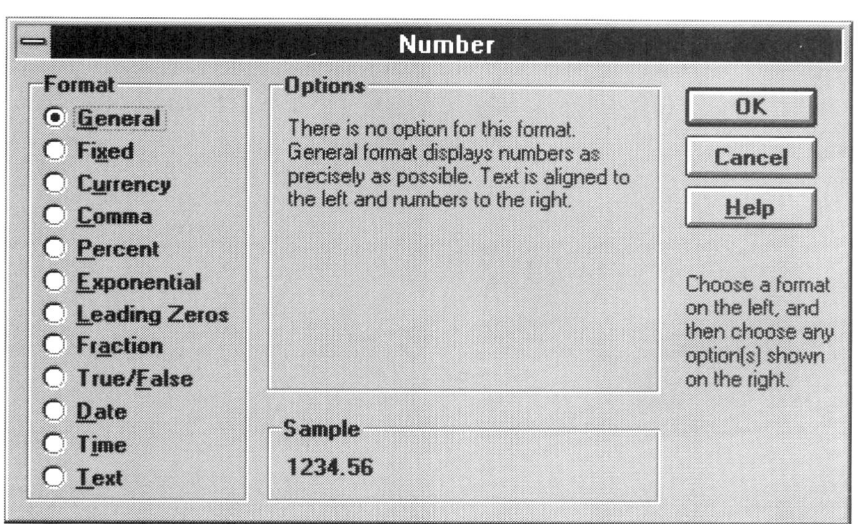

***Figure 18-17.** The Number dialog box displaying the value formats available.*

The part of the report to be formatted needs to be highlighted first. To format an entire field, click on the field name in the record row. To format a total figure calculated by statistics, the cell in which that statistical information is located is highlighted.

In this example, you can change the total of "Stock" to a Comma format without decimal places. Highlight the cell which contains "=SUM(Stock)" is in Figure 18-18.

Figure 18-18. *Select the part of the report to be formatted.*

The *Number* command needs to be selected from the **Format** menu to display the *Number* dialog box. Click on the Comma format. As two decimal places is the default, change the entry in the *Number of decimal places* text box to 0 and click on *OK* to accept the format as shown in Figure 18-19.

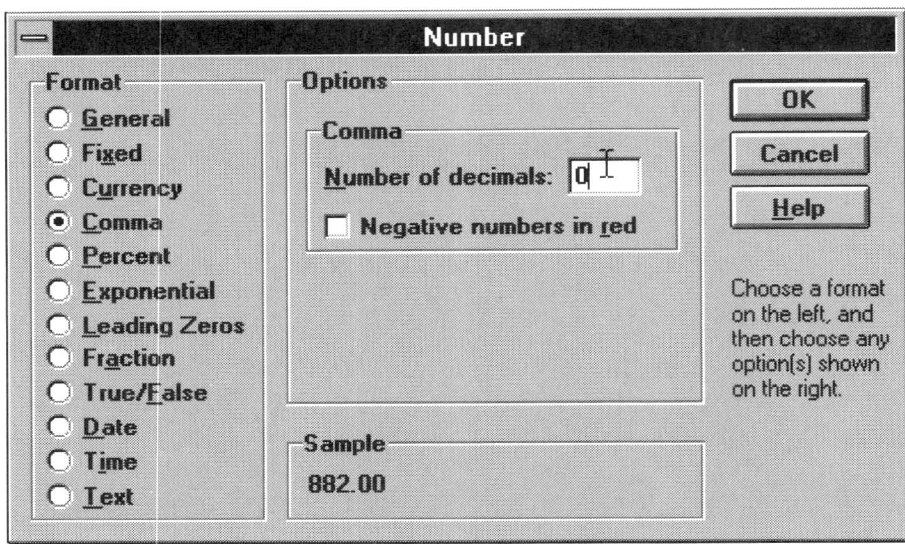

Figure 18-19. *The format is being changed to Comma with no decimal places.*

The report definition screen does not change when a value format is altered. The report needs to be printed or *Print Preview* activated to see the change. These are looked at later in this chapter.

Column widths

Your report definition uses the column widths from List view by default. The width of a column is changed in the report definition screen using the column borders on the frame, or the *Column Width* command in the **Format** menu.

The only columns which need adjusting are the "Toy" and "Wholesale" columns. Use the column border to do this, by moving the pointer up to the frame where column A joins column B, and dragging it across until the column is as wide as shown in Figure 18-20. Widen the "Wholesale" column so you can read the entire field name.

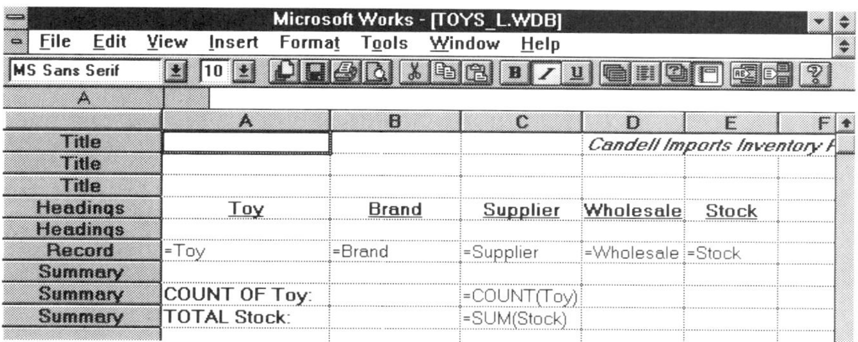

Figure 18-20. *Widen columns A and D using the column border on the frame.*

Inserting and deleting fields

Fields are originally inserted into a report with the *New Report* dialog box (see Figure 18-3). If a report structure changes, however, fields can be inserted directly into the report definition screen.

The pointer must be in the correct position. In this case, you are going to insert the "Retail" field after "Stock," so click in the cell where column F (the next blank column) crosses the record row. You may choose to use the horizontal scroll bar to reach this position.

A record is inserted using the *Field Entry* command in the **Insert** menu (Figure 18-21).

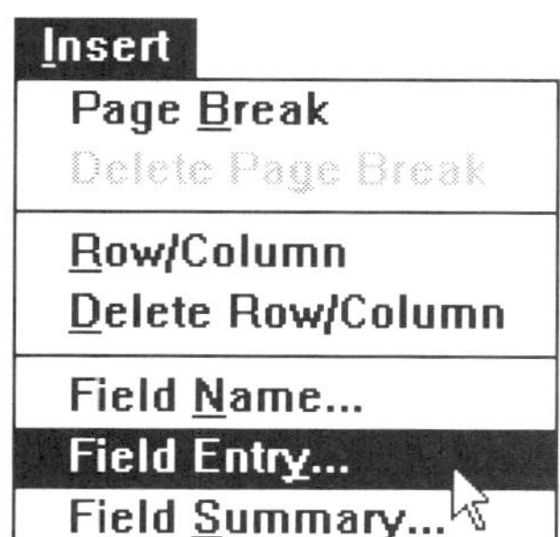

Figure 18-21. *The Field Entry command.*

When this is selected, the *Insert Field Entry* dialog box appears on the screen displaying a list of all fields in the database. Click on "Retail" (use the scroll arrow if necessary) and then *OK* to return to the report definition screen. "=Retail" is entered into the highlighted cell which Figure 18-22 depicts.

Figure 18-22. *"=Retail" is entered into the correct position.*

To insert a heading, the *Field Name* command is used. Click in the cell denoted by the first heading row in column F and select *Field Name* from the **Insert** menu. Works displays the *Insert Field Name* dialog box on the screen which once again lists all the fields in the database. The field name to select is "Retail." Choose this now (Figure 18-23) and click on *OK*.

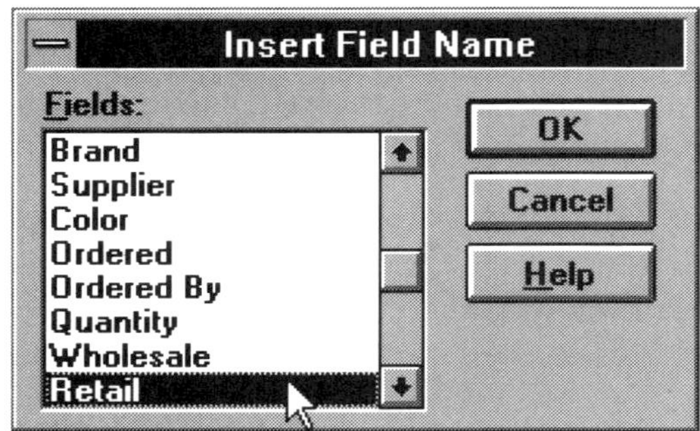

Figure 18-23. *"Retail" is selected from the Insert Field Name dialog box.*

The field name appears in the report definition screen and should be centered with bold and underlining to match the others.

A field is deleted using the *Delete Row/Column* command in the **Insert** menu. Click on the F column label to select the column, and then choose this command. The field and heading you inserted are no longer part of the report.

Be careful when using the *Delete Row/Column* command, as all the data contained in the selected row or column is deleted.

Inserting and deleting statistics

Statistics can be inserted after the basic structure is defined. The command which inserts statistics is *Field Summary* in the **Insert** menu (Figure 18-24).

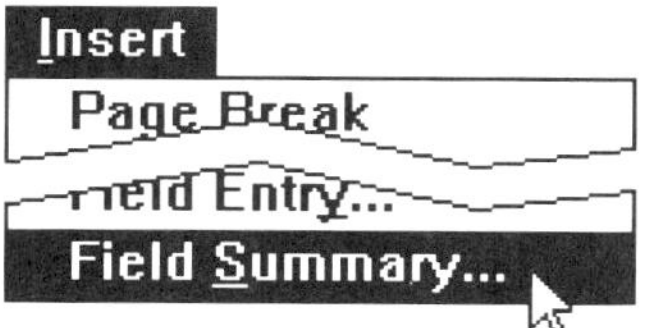

Figure 18-24. *The Field Summary command.*

The field included in statistics does not have to be part of the report. In this report, for example, you could enter a summary which states the maximum "Quantity" field among all orders.

Move into the cell in column C below the other summary statistics. Select the *Field Summary* command from the **Insert** menu to display the *Insert Field Summary* dialog box.

The field required is "Quantity," so click on that in the *Fields* list box. The statistic needed is MAX, so click on this in the *Statistic* section, as in Figure 18-25.

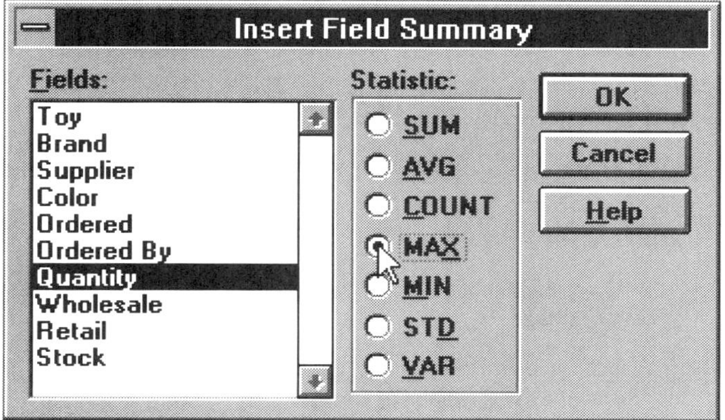

Figure 18-25. *The Insert Field Summary dialog box, with the new statistic entered.*

Click on *OK* and the statistic is inserted into the highlighted cell. Type in the description "MAXIMUM SIZE OF AN ORDER:" into column A of the same row and then Enter. Click on the *Bold* button on the toolbar. Figure 18-26 displays the result.

Figure 18-26. Your entries should look like this.

A summary is deleted through the *Delete Row/Column* command in the **Insert** menu.

Naming reports

Like with queries, a database can have more than one report. Different reports are usually created to highlight different parts of the database. You can list all reports for your database by choosing the *Report* command from the **View** menu as shown in Figure 18-27.

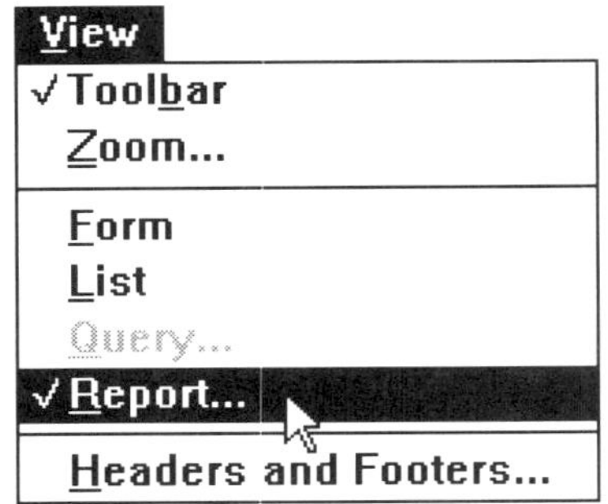

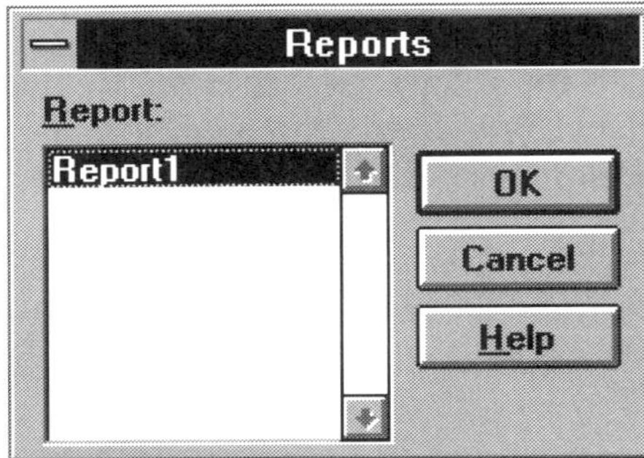

Figure 18-27. All reports in your file are listed in the Reports dialog box.

You can give a name to the report created in this chapter. Naming reports makes it easier to distinguish between different reports.

The *Name Report* command in the **Tools** menu enables you to do this. Choose this command as shown in Figure 18-28.

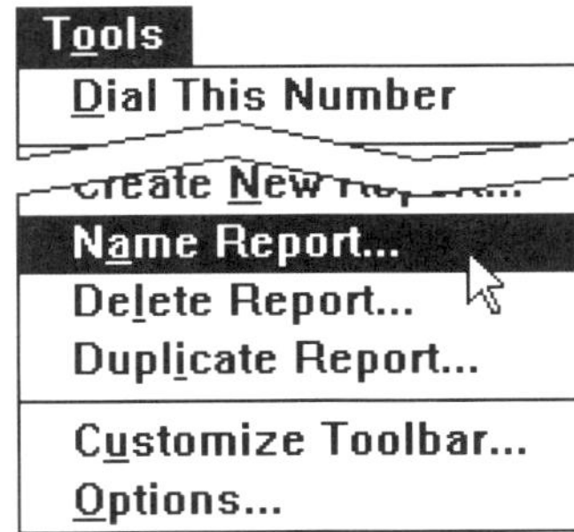

Figure 18-28. The Name Report command.

All reports which are created for the database are listed in the *Reports* list box in the *Name Report* dialog box. If the report has not yet been given a name manually, Works calls it "Report" and a number, for example "Report1." The name of the report developed in this chapter is currently "Report1."

As this report is active, or displayed on the report definition screen, *Report1* is highlighted in the *Reports* list box. Type in "Inventory '93" as the name of the report in the *Name* text box as in Figure 18-29, and click on *Rename*. Click on *OK* in the *Name Report* dialog box to return to the report definition screen.

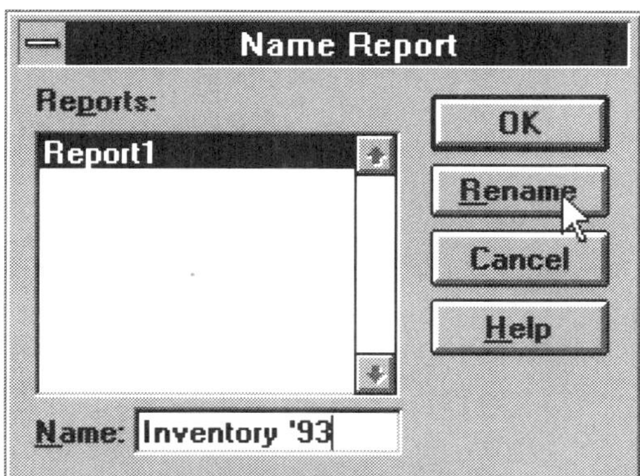

Figure 18-29. *Clicking on Rename will change "Report1" in the Reports list box to "Inventory '93."*

Printing reports

Print Preview

The *Print Preview* command in the **File** menu displays how the report will be printed before it is sent to the printer. The shortcut for activating *Print Preview* is to click on the *Print Preview* button on the toolbar.

The report in *Print Preview* looks like Figure 18-30. Use the *Zoom In* and *Zoom Out* buttons to change views in *Print Preview*. For more information on *Print Preview*, refer to **Chapter 7, Printing Word Processed Documents**.

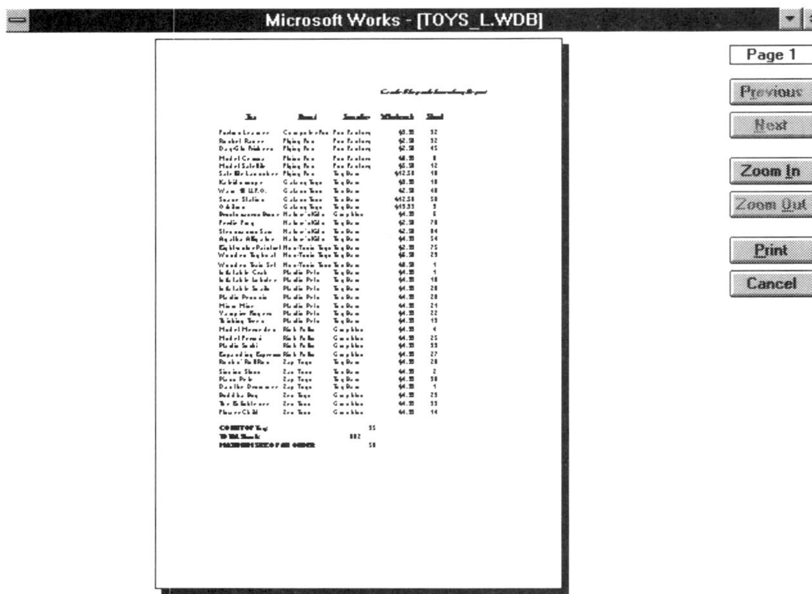

Figure 18-30. *The report in Print Preview.*

Printing

To print directly from *Print Preview*, click on the *Print* button. If you are not in *Print Preview*, select *Print* from the **File** menu. In the *Print* dialog box (Figure 18-31) you can specify how many copies of a document you need to print, which pages need to be printed, and whether it is to be in draft quality or not.

Click on *OK* to print the report.

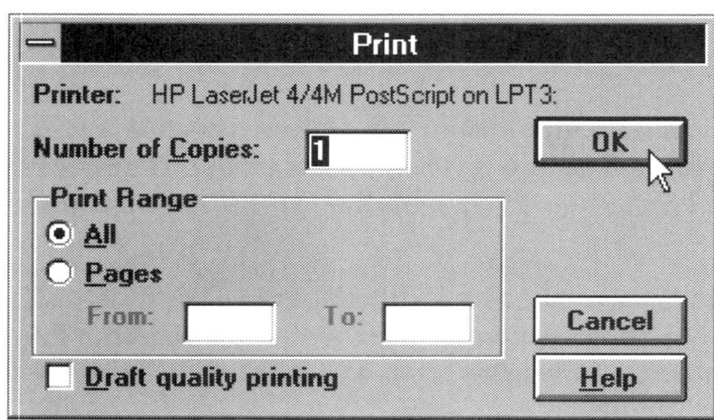

Figure 18-31. *The Print dialog box.*

Printing Databases

The database can be printed from List or Form view, as well as in reports outlined in the previous chapter. This chapter looks at the process of printing from Form and List view.

Printing options

The file ***address.wdb*** in the ***msworks.cbt*** subdirectory is used in this chapter (Figure 19-1).

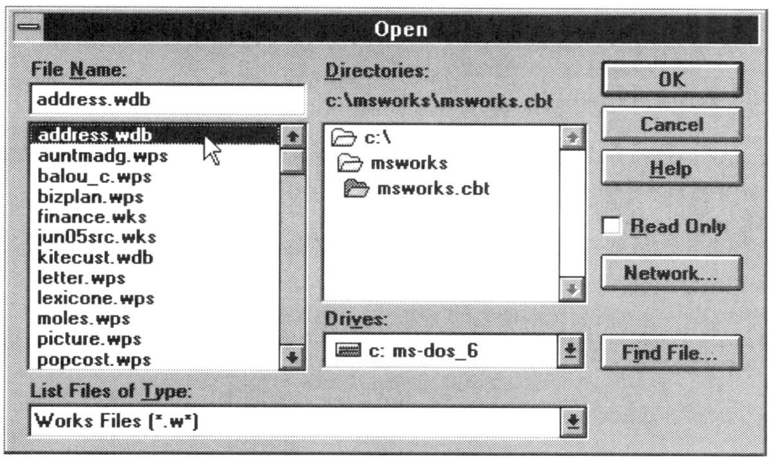

Figure 19-1. *The sample file is opened through the Open dialog box.*

Chapters 7, Printing Word Processed Documents, and **12, Formatting and Printing Spreadsheets**, cover printing in the other tools in Works. Printing is essentially the same in all of the tools in Works. If you need further information about printing, refer to these chapters.

Headers and footers

Headers and footers are inserted into the printed database to show page numbers, and the date or file name for example. A header appears at the top of every page and the footer appears at the bottom. There are many combinations which can be used in headers and footers, some of which are covered in this chapter.

Headers and footers remain the same in List and Form view. To insert a header and footer, use the *Headers and Footers* command in the **View** menu which is illustrated in Figure 19-2.

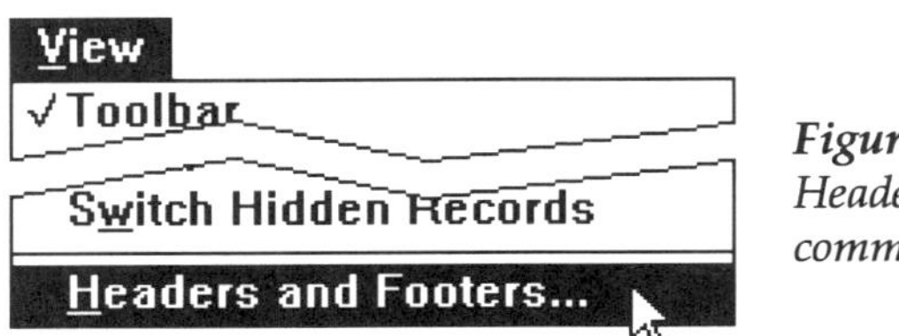

Figure 19-2. *The Headers and Footers command.*

This command displays the *Headers and Footers* dialog box into which the specifications of the headers and footers are inserted. The *Headers and Footers* dialog box is in Figure 19-3.

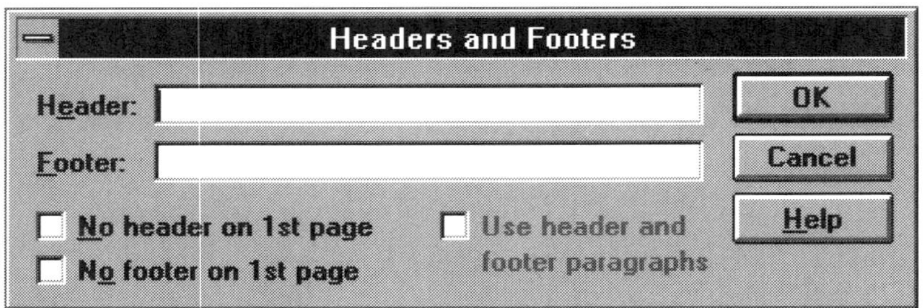

Figure 19-3. *The Headers and Footers dialog box.*

Various codes are typed into the *Header* and *Footer* text boxes which tell Works what to print and how to print the header and footer in a database. These are described in detail in **Chapter 7, Printing Word Processed Documents**.

In this example, insert a header which puts "Address Records" in the center of the page and the filename to the right of the page. The footer simply states the page number in the center of the page.

To create the header, type "&cClimber Records&r&f" into the *Header* text box. This appears in the *Headers and Footers* dialog box as shown in Figure 19-4.

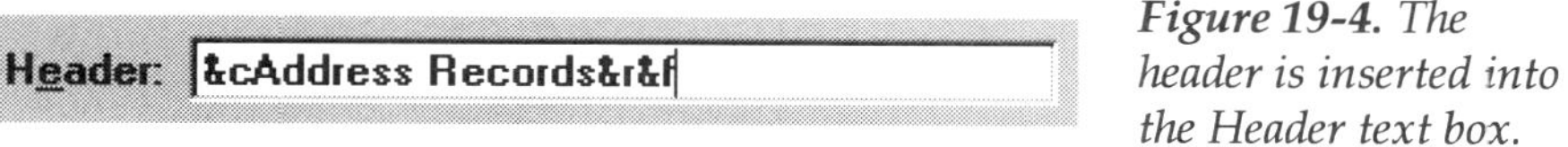

Figure 19-4. *The header is inserted into the Header text box.*

The footer requires the following text in order to place the page number in the center of the page: "&c&p." Type this into the *Footer* text box as in Figure 19-5. (Strictly speaking, the &c code — for centering the text — is not really required as the default location for header and footer text is center.)

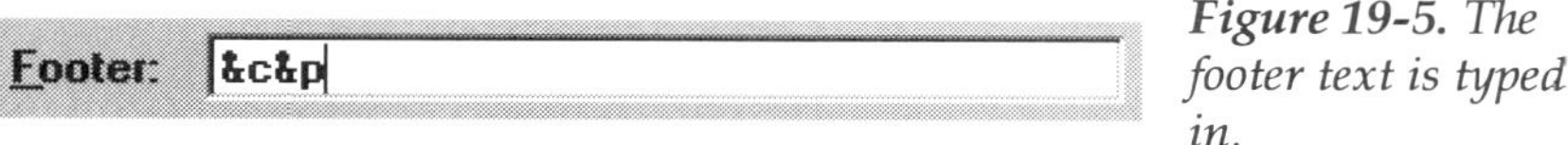

Figure 19-5. *The footer text is typed in.*

Click on *OK* to return to the database. Headers and footers cannot be seen until the database is printed or *Print Preview* is activated. These are covered later in the chapter.

Page breaks

In large databases, it may be necessary to print the database on more than one page. Works inserts an automatic page break when it is essential. Automatic page breaks are not always in appropriate places as far as the look of the printed database is concerned.

Works enables you to have control over page breaks, by letting you set your own. Page breaks are set in both List and Form view but remain independent of each other. Therefore, a page break in Form view does not affect a page break in List view and vice versa.

In Form view, one record only is printed per page. If the record requires more than one page, an automatic page break is inserted when necessary. Manual page breaks can be inserted in Form view and are indicated by a broken line on the screen.

A page break in Form view is inserted either just above the highlighted field or through the middle of it. In this example, insert a page break just above the "City" field in Form view. Highlight "City" as in Figure 19-6.

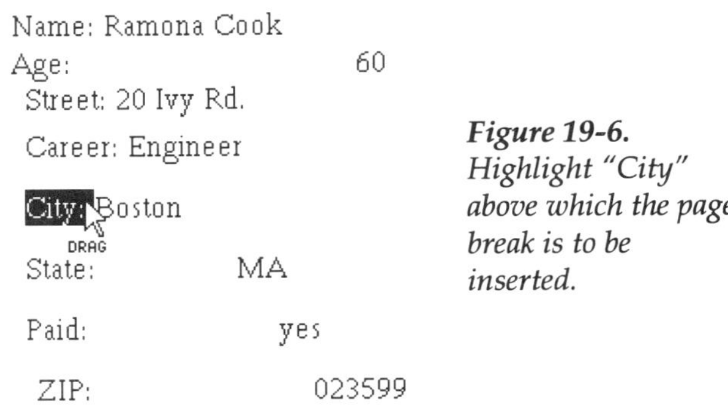

Figure 19-6. *Highlight "City" above which the page break is to be inserted.*

The *Page Break* command in the **Insert** menu is used to set the page break (Figure 19-7).

Figure 19-7. *The Page Break command.*

Choose this command to insert a broken line through or just above "City." The broken line represents the page break. Figure 19-8 shows the page break in place.

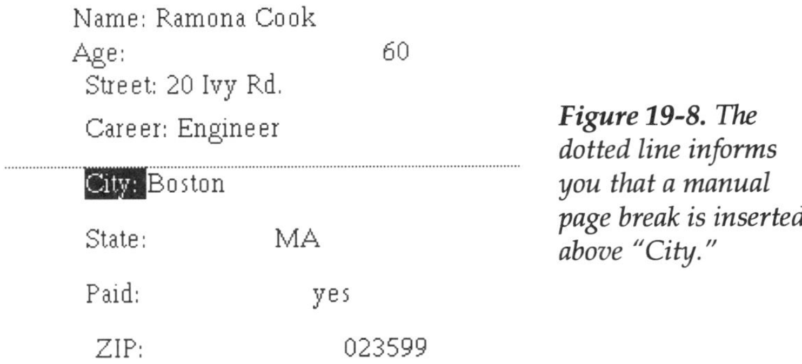

Name: Ramona Cook
Age: 60
Street: 20 Ivy Rd.
Career: Engineer
City: Boston
State: MA
Paid: yes
ZIP: 023599

Figure 19-8. *The dotted line informs you that a manual page break is inserted above "City."*

You can delete your page break after clicking the insertion point on the page break marker. The command used to delete a page break is *Delete Page Break* in the **Insert** menu. If this command is shaded and cannot be selected, it means that the pointer is not in the correct position. Choose this command, as in Figure 19-9, to delete the page break.

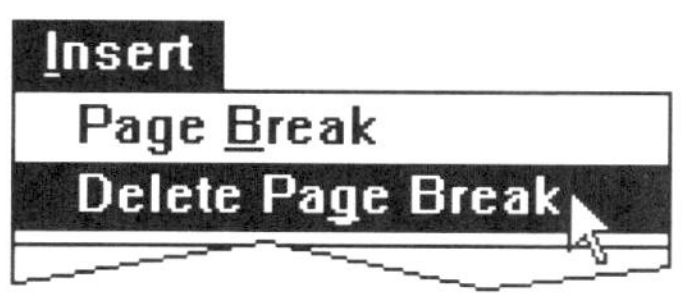

***Figure 19-9.** The Delete Page Break command.*

Page breaks are inserted in a similar way in List view. Change to List view now by pressing F9 and press Ctrl-Home to position the pointer at the beginning of the database.

Page breaks can be inserted in List view either horizontally or vertically. To insert a horizontal page break, the entire record—above which the page break is to go—is to be highlighted (Figure 19-10).

***Figure 19-10.** The horizontal page break will go above row 15 as it is highlighted.*

The *Insert Page Break* command is then selected from the **Edit** menu and a dotted line appears above this row.

Remove the page break by selecting *Delete Page Break* from the **Edit** menu.

To place a vertical page break, the entire field is highlighted. A vertical page break is inserted to the left of the highlighted field. Highlight the "Career" field by clicking on "Career" on the frame as Figure 19-11 shows.

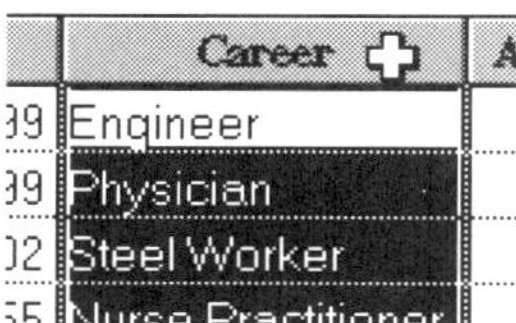

***Figure 19-11.** Highlight the "Career" Field.*

Select the *Page Break* command in the **Insert** menu to set the page break. A broken line appears to the left of the "Career" field which indicates that the data in "Career" will be printed on a new page. Figure 19-12 shows the result.

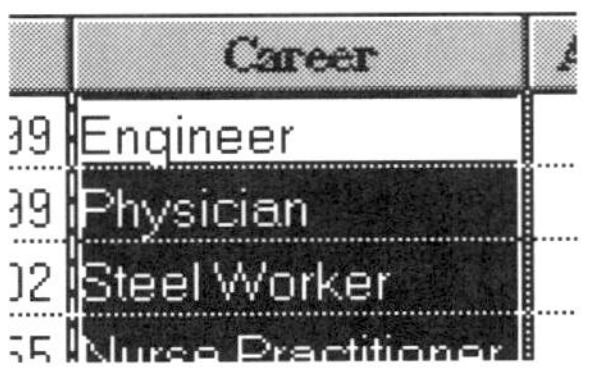

Figure 19-12. *A vertical page break is set at "Career."*

Print Preview

Print Preview is activated in one of two ways. The first of these is to click on the *Print Preview* button on the toolbar (Figure 19-13).

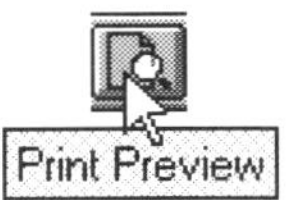

Figure 19-13. *The Print Preview button.*

The second method is to select *Print Preview* from the **File** menu (Figure 19-14).

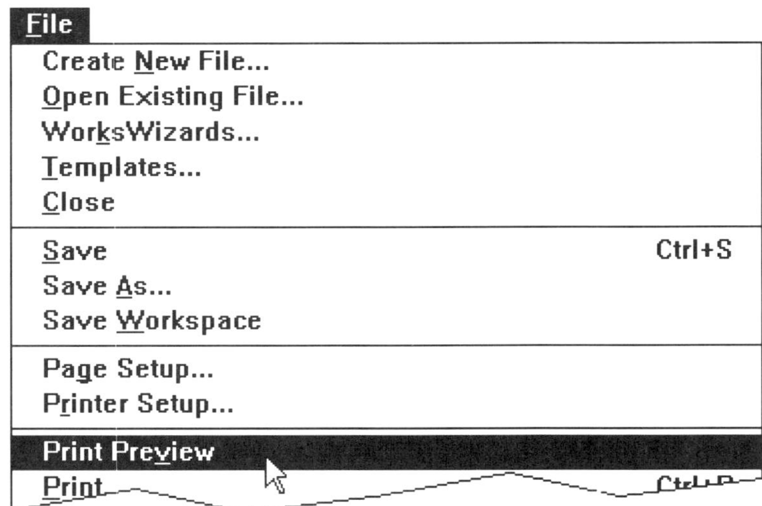

Figure 19-14. *The Print Preview command.*

Print Preview displays the database as it will be printed. The database is printed in List view if it is active at the time *Print Preview* was started. If you were viewing the database in Form view, it will be printed in Form view. In Figure 19-15, *Print Preview* shows the database in List view, as this was the last view selected.

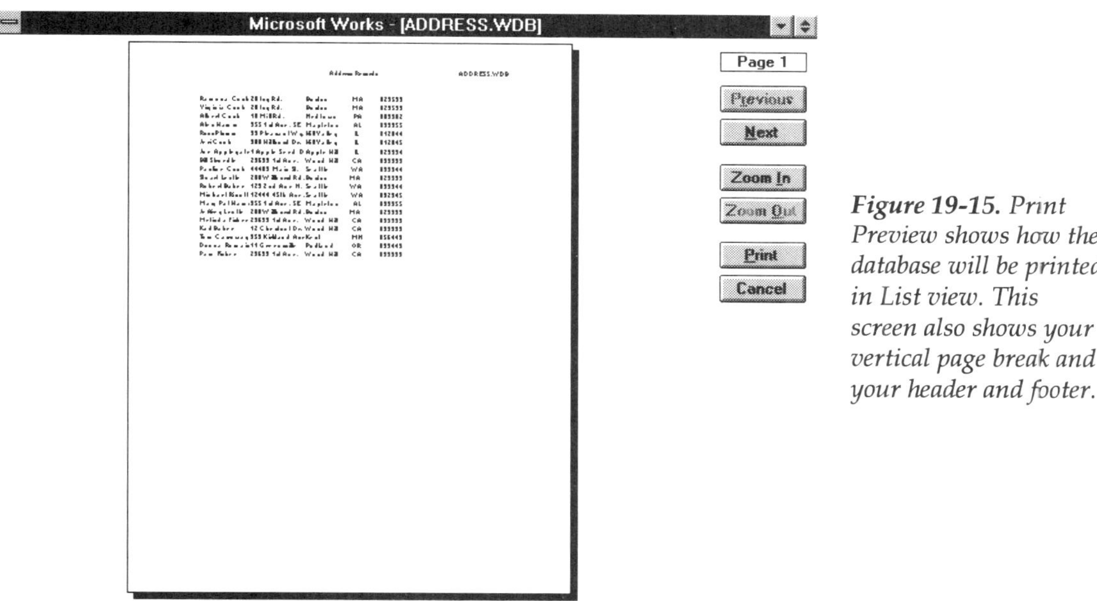

Figure 19-15. *Print Preview shows how the database will be printed in List view. This screen also shows your vertical page break and your header and footer.*

Click on the *Next* button to display the next page to be printed. The data on the second page consists of the fields from "Career" onwards in this case (Figure 19-16).

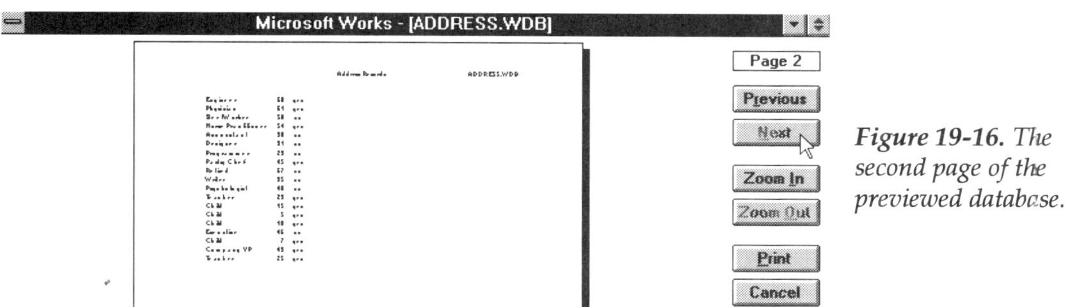

Figure 19-16. *The second page of the previewed database.*

Printing

Works prints the database in the view format which is current on the screen. For example, if List view is active, then the database is printed in List view format and vice versa.

A database can be sorted before it is printed, which means that only records meeting certain criteria are printed. Sorting data is covered in **Chapter 17, Viewing the Database**.

While in *Print Preview*, you can print directly to the printer by clicking on the *Print* button. Figure 19-17 shows this button being used.

Figure 19-17. *The Print button in Print Preview.*

If the database is in List or Form view, the *Print* command in the **File** menu can be used. The *Print* command used in List view displays the *Print* dialog box shown in Figure 19-18.

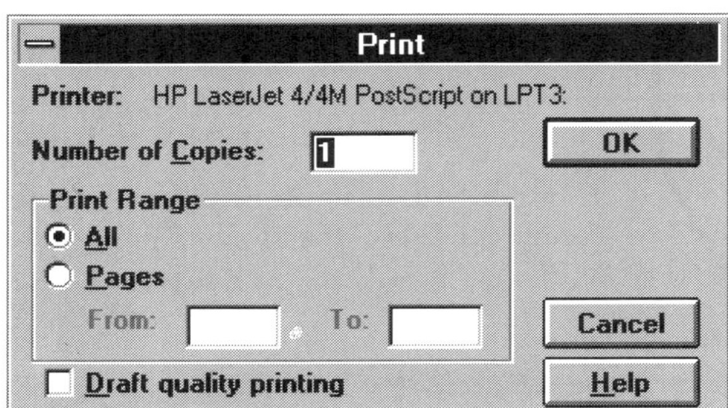

Figure 19-18. *The Print dialog box from List view.*

There are a number of options in the *Print* dialog box which enable you to specify how the printing is to be done. These options are:

Number of Copies in which you choose the number of copies of the database to be printed.

Print Range where the pages to be printed are determined.

Draft quality printing is used to print a database quickly. If the database has been formatted with italic and bold styles, for instance, these are not printed. Grid lines are also not printed. This option is only available when List view is selected.

When you choose the *Print* command from Form view, the *Print* dialog box looks as shown in Figure 19-19.

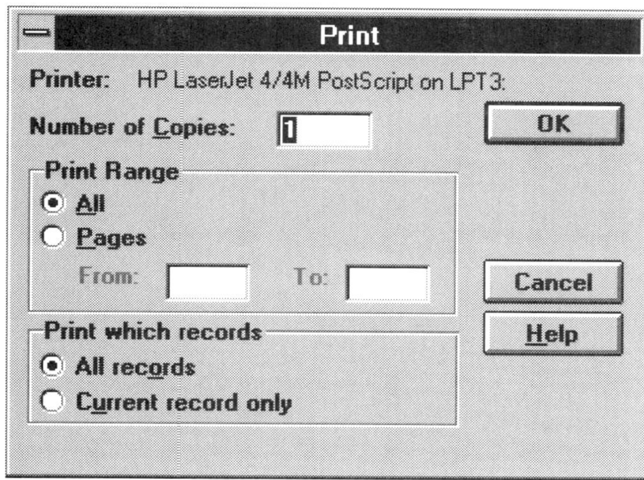

Figure 19-19. *The Print dialog box from Form view.*

In Form view the *Print* dialog box also gives you the *Print which records* options. *All records* is the default but you can choose to print the *Current record only* if you wish.

Try printing your database, experimenting with some of the options listed above. For further practice, you may like to choose a different sample file and work through the features in this chapter using that file.

The Communications Screen

In this chapter you learn how to start up the communications tool in Works. The communications screen, although similar to the word processor, spreadsheet, and database, contains some elements unique to the communications facility. These are discussed in this chapter.

Starting the Communications tool

You start using the communications tool by clicking on the *Communications* button in the *Startup* dialog box (Figure 20-1).

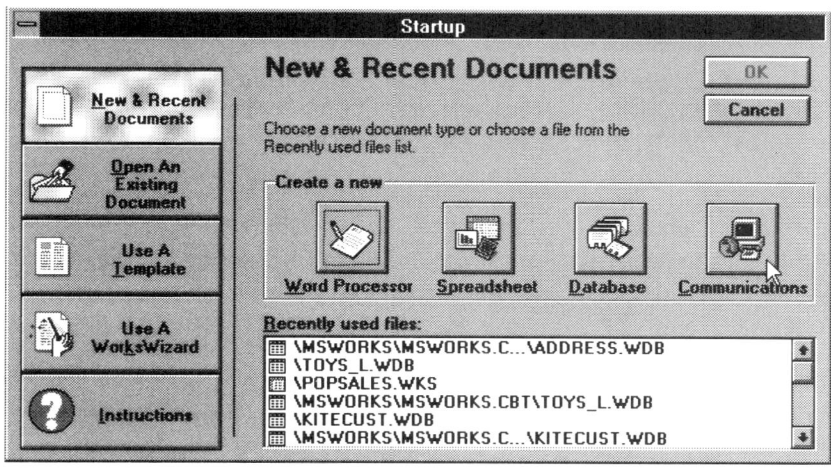

***Figure 20-1.** The Communications button in the Startup dialog box.*

When you start the communications tool for the first time Works opens the *Modem Setup* dialog box. You learn about this and the other communications dialog boxes in the next chapter, **Using Communications**. Click on the *Cancel* button in the *Modem Setup* dialog box to view the rest of the screen. Your screen should now look like Figure 20-2.

Works creates a new file called "Comm" and a number, for example "Comm1," until you save the file and give it a new name.

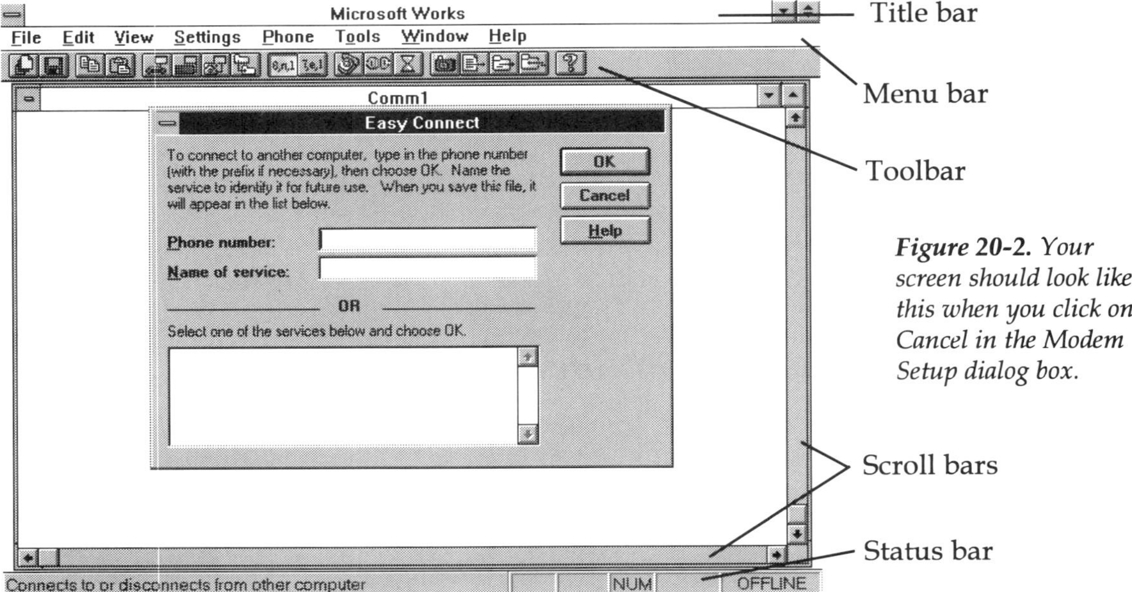

Figure 20-2. *Your screen should look like this when you click on Cancel in the Modem Setup dialog box.*

Works opens the *Easy Connect* dialog box shown in Figure 20-2 when you cancel the *Modem Setup* dialog box. For now, if you want to examine the communications menus, click on *Cancel* in the *Easy Setup* dialog box also.

To open a file you already created, click on the *Open an Existing Document* button in the *Startup* dialog box, or select *Open Existing File* from the **File** menu. This process is very similar to the one you use in the other Works tools.

Parts of the Communications screen

The title bar

As in the other Works tools, when you maximize the document window, both the application and file names appear on the title bar (Figure 20-3). More information about the title bar is in **Chapter 1, The Word Processor Screen**.

Figure 20-3. *The title bar.*

The menu bar

The menu bar is directly under the title bar. It contains menu options specific to the communications tool. The options are: **File, Edit, View, Settings, Phone, Tools, Window**, and **Help** which are displayed in Figure 20-4.

File Edit View Settings Phone Tools Window Help

Figure 20-4. *The communications menu bar.*

The toolbar

The toolbar (Figure 20-5) contains a number of buttons which are shortcuts for some menu commands. We have discussed only a small number of these buttons before — the main communications buttons are explained in the next chapter. For more information on the buttons you have seen so far, see **Chapter 1, The Word Processor Screen**.

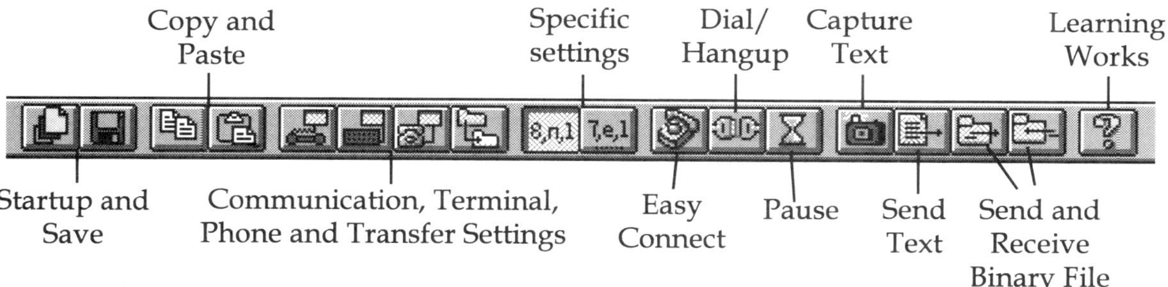

Figure 20-5. *The communications toolbar buttons.*

The scroll bars

You should be quite familiar with the Windows scroll bars at this stage since they appear in all Works tools. Scroll bars enable you to move around the screen by clicking the arrows or dragging the box in the scroll bar to a different position.

The status bar

The left side of the status bar at the bottom of your screen is used to display messages as in the other tools (Figure 20-6). The message displayed could be concerning the menu command chosen or shortcut hints. The status bar also informs you of your connected time during a communications session with a remote computer, and at other times displays OFFLINE, as shown here.

Figure 20-6. *The status bar.*

Closing a file

When you have completed work using your file, you can close it in the same as any other document in Works. As before, choose the *Close* command in the **File** menu.

Using Communications

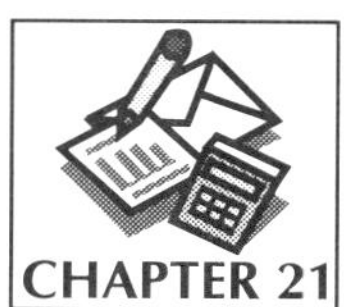

In this chapter you learn how to use the communications tool in Works. Using Works communications tool you can connect to another computer system such as an online bulletin board system (BBS) to exchange information or files. To do this, you need a device called a modem, or a communications cable linking the computers involved. A modem lets your computer send and receive information using a telephone line.

Modem setup

Start using the communications tool by clicking on the *Communications* button in the *Startup* dialog box (Figure 21-1).

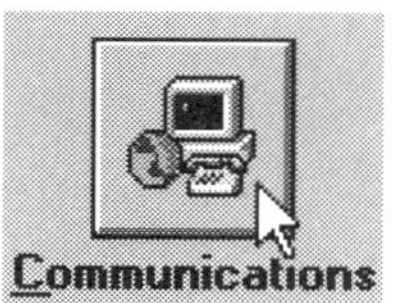

Figure 21-1. *Click on Communications in the Startup dialog box.*

As you saw in **Chapter 20, The Communications Screen**, Works opens the *Modem Setup* dialog box when you use the communications tool for the first time. Click on *Test* to have Works examine each of the communications ports available on your computer and determine which of these to use (Figure 21-2). Click on *OK* to close this dialog box.

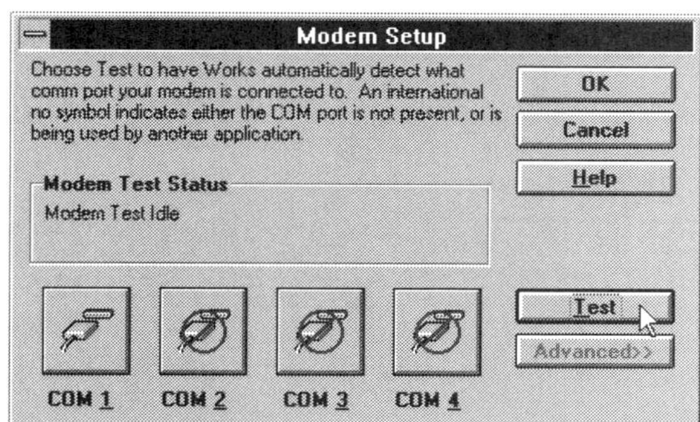

Figure 21-2. *Click on Test in the Modem Setup dialog box.*

You can access the *Modem Setup* dialog box again if you want to change your modem settings by choosing the *Modem* command from the **Settings** menu as shown in Figure 21-3.

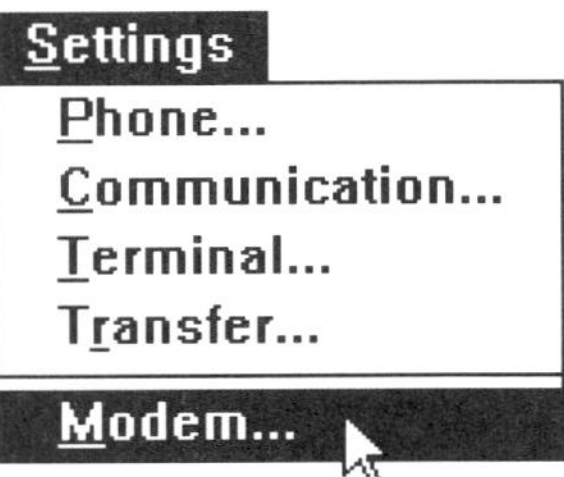

Figure 21-3. *Choose Modem from the* ***Settings*** *menu if you want to open the Modem Setup dialog box again.*

Opening an existing communications file

Works lets you open a file stored on your disk in three different ways. You can choose *Open Existing File* from the **File** menu or choose *Open An Existing Document* from the *Startup* dialog box. You can also click on one of your recently used files in the *Startup* dialog box.

When you open an existing communications file, Works asks whether you want to connect to the service you used previously with this file. Click on *OK* in the *Connect to other computer?* dialog box if you want to connect in the same way as you did when you used this file before (Figure 21-4). Click on *Cancel* if you want access to commands in the communications tool before making your connection.

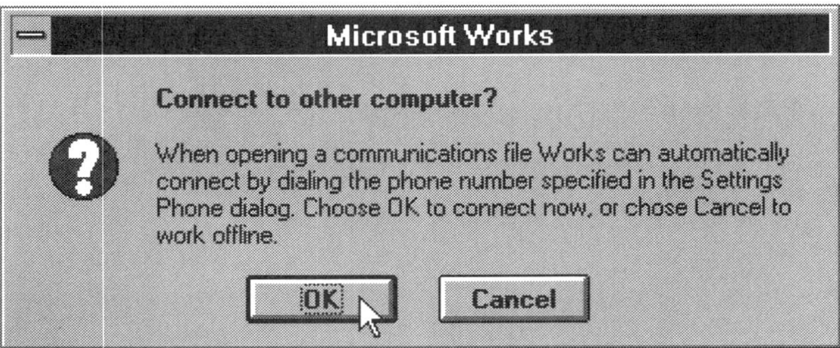

Figure 21-4. *Works opens this dialog box when you open an existing communic-ations file.*

Establishing a connection

Once you let Works know about your modem using the *Modem Setup* dialog box you can establish a connection to another computer system. When you close the *Modem Setup* dialog box for the first time or when you create a new communications file, you see the *Easy Connect* dialog box (Figure 21-5).

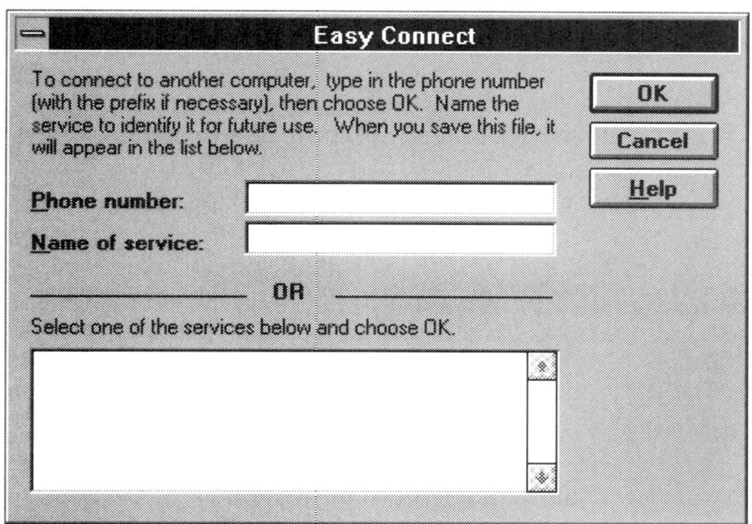

Figure 21-5. *Works uses this dialog box for you to identify a computer system to which to connect.*

Type the telephone number of the modem used by the system to which you want to connect. You enter this telephone number in the *Telephone number* text box as Figure 21-6 shows. If you want to connect to another computer using a cable rather than a modem and the telephone system, simply click on *OK* in the *Easy Connect* dialog box.

You can type a name in the *Name of service* text box to help you identify this telephone number among others to which you may connect using Works. You might type the name of the person or organization to whose system you are connecting.

Phone number: 555 3052
Name of service: Usual bulletin board

Figure 21-6. *Type the number of the remote modem in the Phone number text box. Enter a name in the Name of service text box.*

If you have previously identified a service to which to connect, Works lists it in the list box at the bottom of the *Easy Connect* dialog box as shown in Figure 21-7. You can click on the service to choose it.

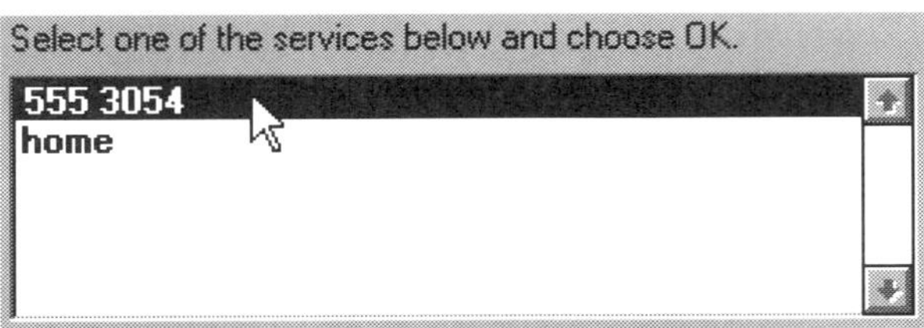

Figure 21-7. *If you have previously identified a service, you can click on the name or number of a service you used before.*

Click on *OK* once you have identified the computer system to which you want to connect. This opens the *Dial Status* dialog box while Works tries to connect to the remote computer system (Figure 21-8).

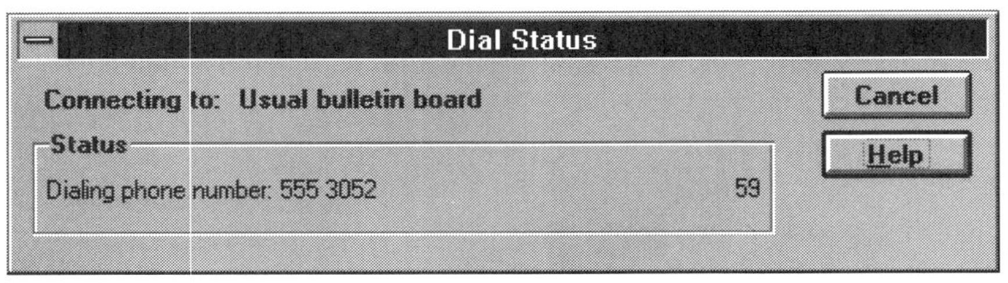

Figure 21-8. *Works displays the Dial Status dialog box.*

When you successfully connect to the remote computer, that system will display some kind of message on your screen. Typically the message you see is some kind of login prompt like the one shown in Figure 21-9.

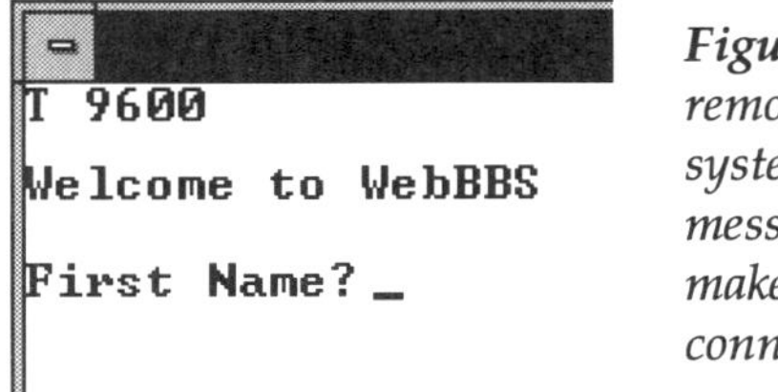

Figure 21-9. *The remote computer system displays a message when Works makes the connection.*

You are now able to follow the procedure for using the remote computer system. How you interact with that system is wholly dependent on the system to which you connect.

As well as in the *Easy Connect* dialog box, Works lists your most recent connections on the **Phone** menu (Figure 21-10). You can choose a service from the **Phone** menu to which you want to connect.

Choose *Dial Again* from the **Phone** menu if you get a "busy" signal when you try to connect.

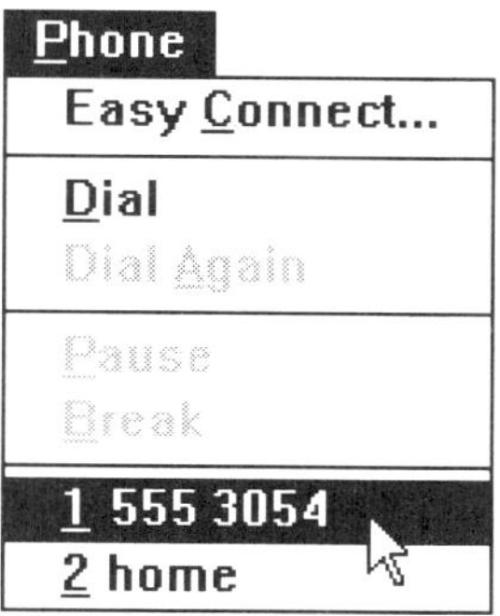

Figure 21-10. *You can choose a previous service from the* ***Phone*** *menu.*

Answering a call

You can also use Works to receive a call from another computer user, rather than making the call. Start the communications tool by clicking on *Communications* in the *Startup* dialog box. Close any communications dialog boxes that Works displays and choose the *Phone* command from the **Settings** menu as in Figure 21-11. Click on *Auto answer* in the *Connect option* group and then on *OK* to receive the call.

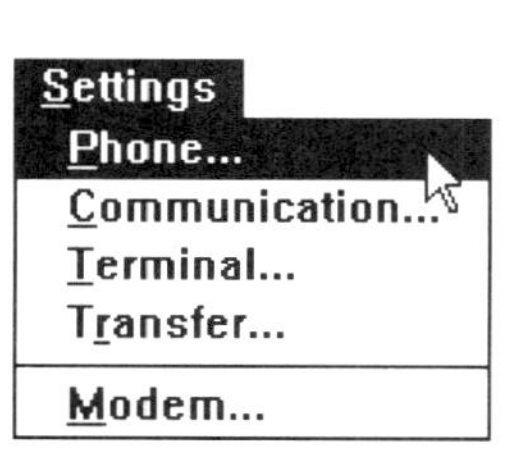

Figure 21-11. *Choose the Phone command from the Settings menu, click on Auto answer and then on OK.*

Saving communications settings

When you save a communications file Works saves the communications settings you used, including the telephone number you specified. Saving the communications file does not save any information that you received from or sent to the remote computer system. The **Saving Information You Receive** section in this chapter tells you how to save the information that you receive during your communications sessions.

As in the other tools in Works, you save your file by choosing *Save* or *Save As* from the **File** menu or by clicking on the *Save* button in the toolbar (Figure 21-12).

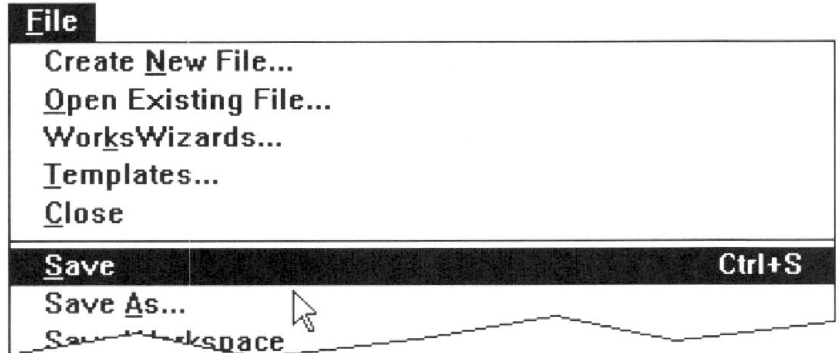

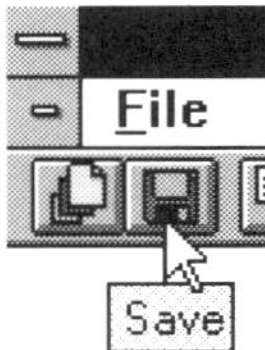

Figure 21-12. *Save your file by choosing Save or Save As from the file menu or by clicking on the Save button.*

Sending a break signal

Sometimes the remote computer system does not respond to your commands once you connect. You can often make the other system respond by choosing *Break* from the **Phone** menu as in Figure 21-13.

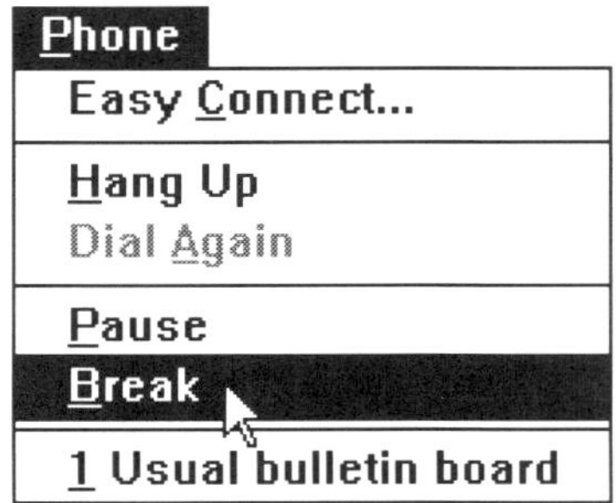

Figure 21-13. *Choose Break from the* ***Phone*** *menu if you need to send a "break" signal.*

Saving information you receive

You can save information that the service to which you connect displays on your screen. You can also receive files sent from the remote computer system.

Selecting information from the screen

Works holds up to 256,000 lines of information that the remote computer system has displayed on your screen in the current session. If the remote system sends more than this number of lines of text, Works discards the oldest text to make room.

Works keeps the text for your current communications session in a temporary document that you can view on your screen in the communications tool. Since Works does not save information sent to you during a session when you save your communications file, this section shows you how to save that information separately.

When information fills your screen, the lines at the top of the document window scroll out of sight. To read information that has scrolled out of sight, choose *Pause* from the **Phone** menu or click on the *Pause* toolbar button as Figure 21-14 shows.

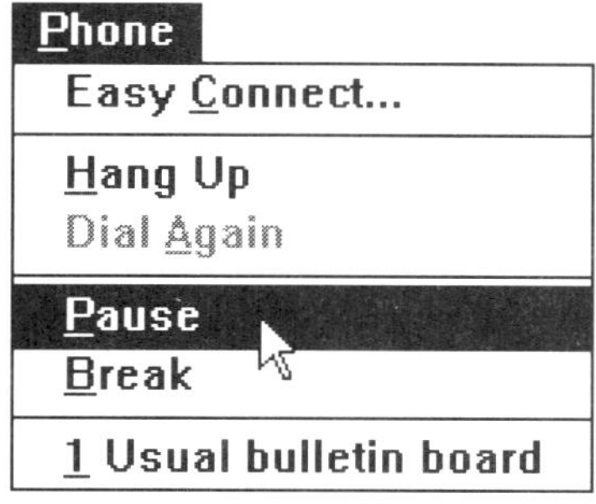

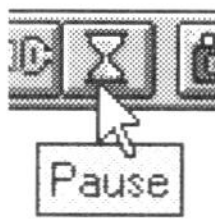

Figure 21-14. *Choose Pause from the* ***Phone*** *menu or click on the Pause button.*

You are now free to scroll through the temporary document using the scroll bars and the cursor movement keys, as you do in the word processor. You can also select text by dragging with the mouse or holding down the Shift key while moving through the document. See **Chapter 2, Creating Documents** and **Chapter 3, Editing Documents** for more information on scrolling and selecting text.

The communications tool also offers several commands for selecting text and copying that text to the Windows Clipboard. You can then switch to another tool such as the word processor or even to a program other than Works and paste that information into a document.

Choose *Copy Text* from the **Edit** menu or click on the *Copy* button to copy your selection to the Clipboard (Figure 21-15).

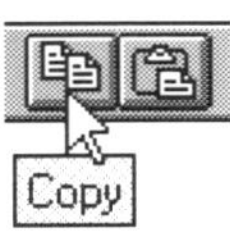

Figure 21-15. *Choose Copy Text from the* ***Edit*** *menu or click on the Copy button to copy your selection to the Clipboard.*

You can select the contents of the entire temporary document by choosing *Select All* from the **Edit** menu shown in Figure 21-16.

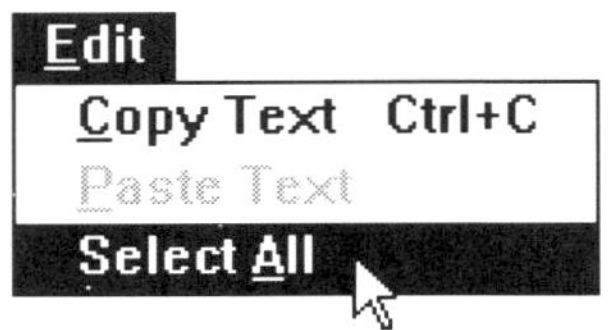

Figure 21-16. *Choose Select All from the* ***Edit*** *menu to select all the information received and held by the communications tool.*

To resume receiving information choose *Pause* again from the **Phone** menu or click on the *Pause* toolbar button (see Figure 21-14).

Automatically capturing text

You can capture text sent by the remote computer system directly into a file, without a limit on the number of lines received. Works saves all text you receive between the time you confirm the *Capture Text* command and the time you choose the *End Capture Text* command.

Choose *Capture Text* from the **Tools** menu or click on the *Capture Text* button to begin text capture. Figure 21-17 shows you these features.

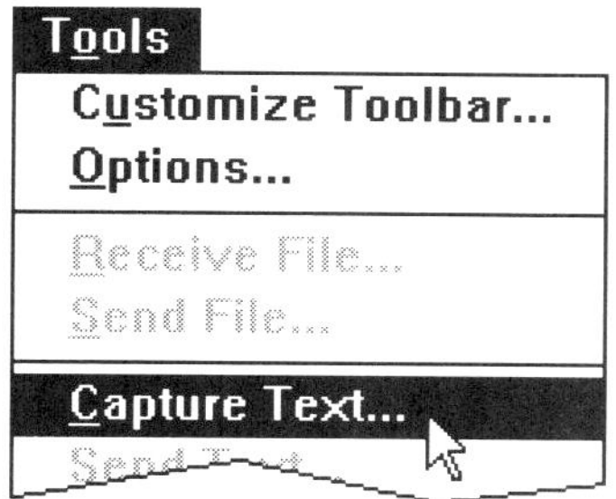

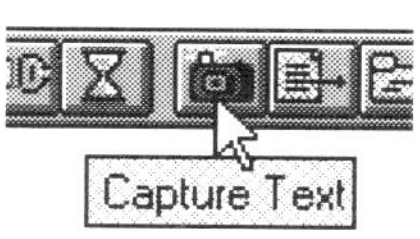

Figure 21-17. Choose Capture Text from the ***Tools*** *menu or click on the Capture Text button to begin text capture.*

Choosing *Capture Text* opens the *Capture Text* dialog box in which you identify the file in which you want to store the information. The default *File Name* is ***capture.txt*** (Figure 21-18). Click on *OK* to enable capture of text to the file you identify.

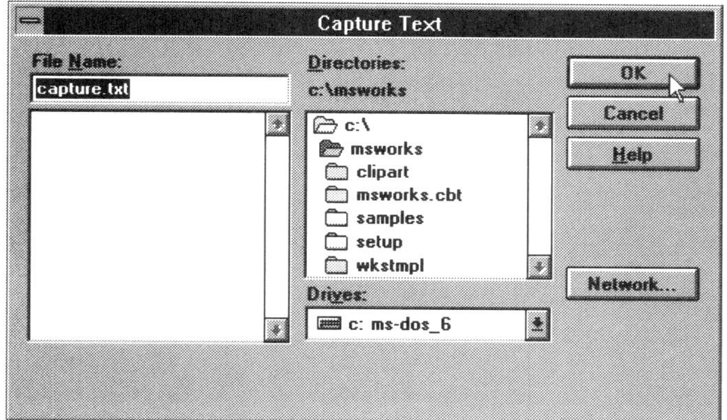

Figure 21-18. Identify the file in which you want to store captured text.

Works warns you with the dialog box shown in Figure 21-19 if the file you nominated already exists. You can choose *Replace* to delete the existing file and replace it with the new text in a file of the same name, *Append* to add new text to the end of the existing file, or *Cancel* to return to the *Capture Text* dialog box to choose a different file name, drive, or directory.

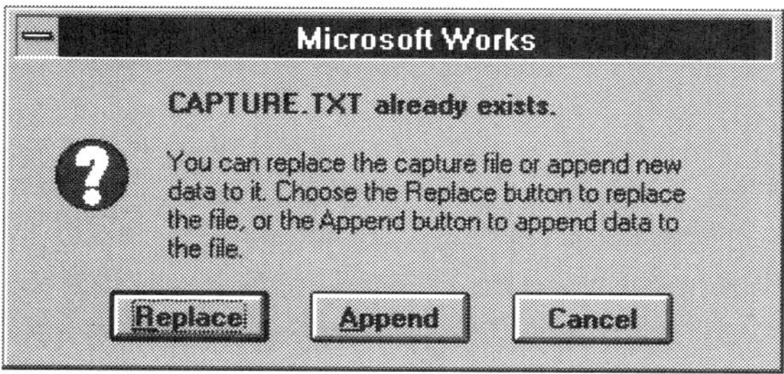

Figure 21-19. Choose to append or to replace an existing file or cancel the operation.

To end text capture choose *End Capture Text* from the **Tools** menu as shown in Figure 21-20 or click on the *Capture Text* button again.

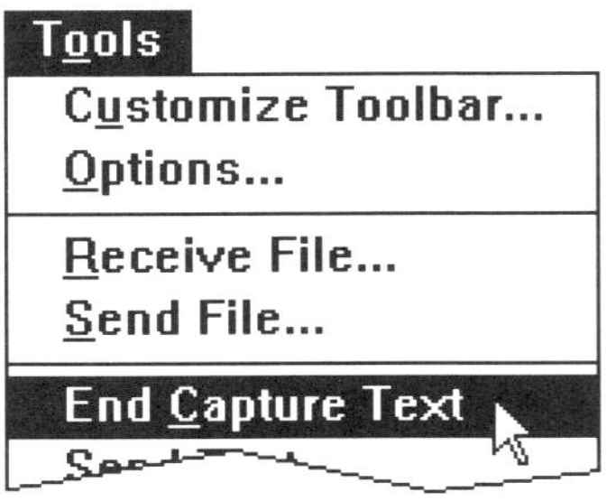

Figure 21-20. *Choose End Capture Text from the **Tools** menu to end text capture.*

Receiving a file

When you receive a file sent from another computer system your own computer must use the same communications settings, known as a protocol. See **Changing Communications Settings** below for information on changing the communications protocol in Works.

When the remote system sends the file, choose *Receive File* from the **Tools** menu or click on the *Receive Binary File* button (Figure 21-21) to open the *Receive File* dialog box shown in Figure 21-22.

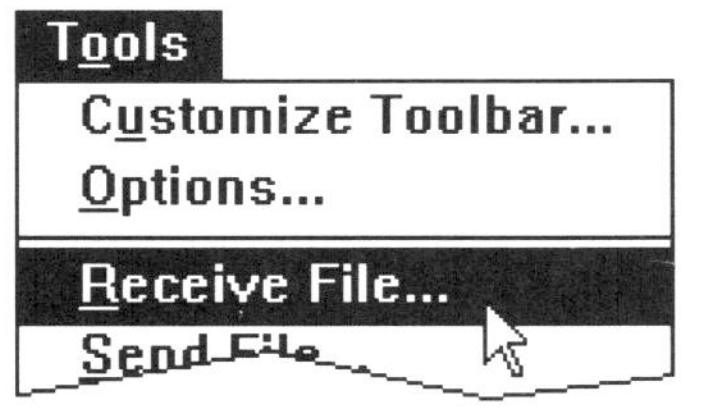

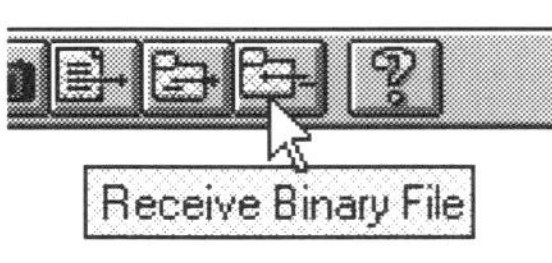

Figure 21-21. *Choose Receive File from the **Tools** menu or click on the Receive Binary File button.*

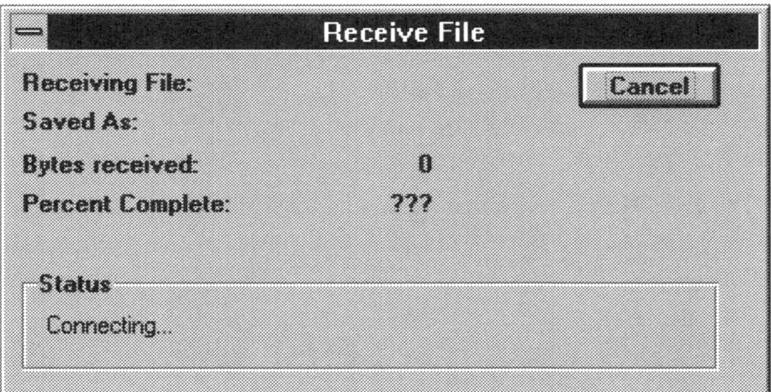

Figure 21-22. *Choosing Receive File opens this dialog box.*

You can give the file a new name if you use the protocol known as *Xmodem.* Otherwise Works uses the original filename for the new copy on your own system.

Sending information

You can send information to a remote computer as well as receive information. This section explains how to send text and files.

Sending Clipboard text

You can send text from the Windows Clipboard as though you had typed the information directly into the communications tool. Because Works sends the text as though you typed it in the communications tool, Works does not send any character or paragraph formatting. See **Sending a File** below for information on sending data other than unformatted text.

You can copy text to the Clipboard from a Works tool or from another program. See **Chapter 3, Editing Documents** for information on copying text to the Clipboard.

Once you connect to the remote computer system choose *Paste Text* from the **Edit** menu or click on the *Paste* button as shown in Figure 21-23.

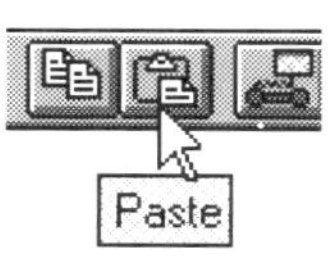

Figure 21-23. *Choose Paste Text from the* ***Edit*** *menu or click on the Paste button to send text from the Clipboard.*

Sending a file

When you send a file to another computer system your own computer must use the same communications settings, known as a protocol. See **Changing Communications Settings** below for information on changing the communications protocol in Works.

Choose *Send File* from the **Tools** menu or click on the *Send Binary File* button as shown in Figure 21-24.

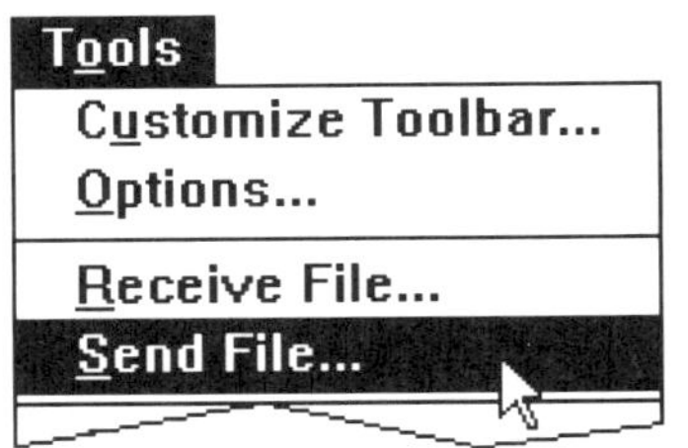

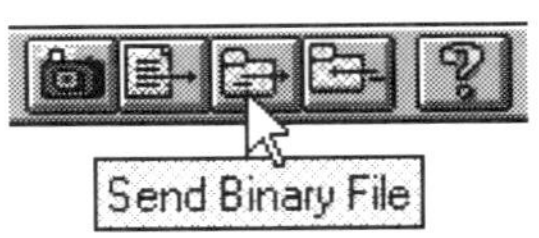

Figure 21-24. *Choose Send File from the **Tools** menu or click on the Send Binary File button.*

Now choose the *Drive, Directory,* and *File Name* of the file you want to send and click on *OK* to send the file (Figure 21-25).

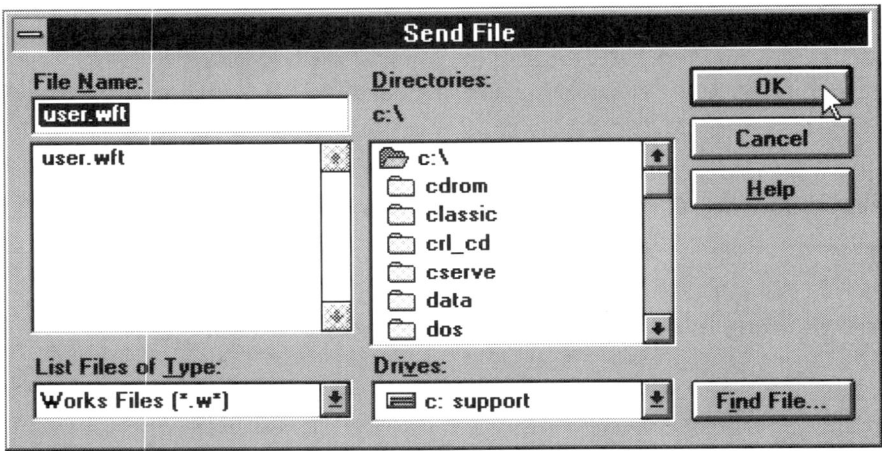

Figure 21-25. *From this dialog box, choose the file you want to send.*

Ending a connection

Be sure to follow the correct sequence for closing your session on the remote computer system. How you do this depends entirely on the system to which you connect.

Once you log out using commands on the remote computer system you can end your connection to it. Choose *Hang Up* from the **Phone** menu or click on the *Dial/Hangup* button as shown in Figure 21-26.

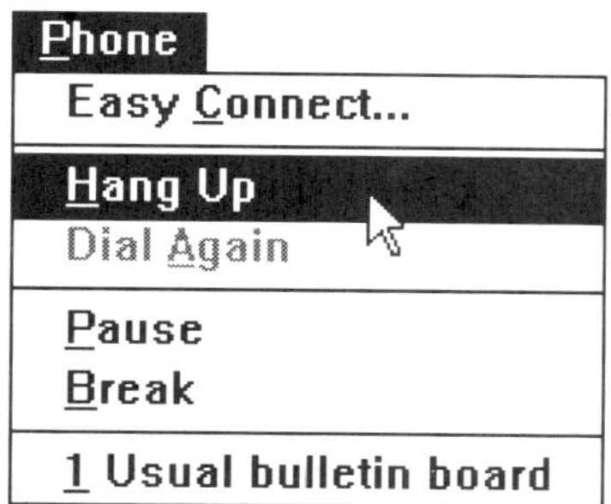

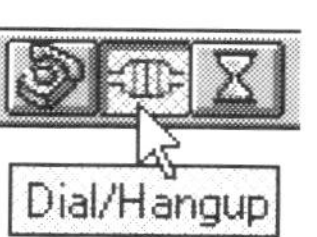

Figure 21-26. *Choose Hang Up from the **Phone** menu or click on the Dial/Hangup button to end your connection.*

Works asks you to confirm that you wish to disconnect as in Figure 21-27. Click on *OK* to hang up.

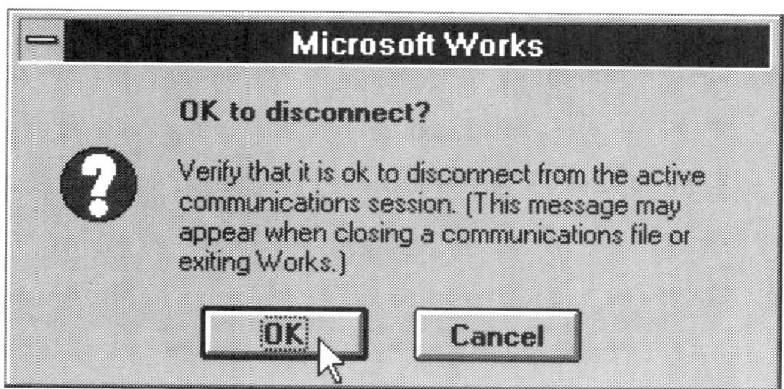

Figure 21-27. *Click on OK to confirm your decision to hang up.*

Changing communications settings

Choose *Phone, Communication, Terminal,* or *Transfer* from the **Settings** menu or click on one of the *Settings* buttons shown in Figure 21-28 if you need to change settings used by the communications tool. The **Modem Setup** section above discusses the *Modem* command.

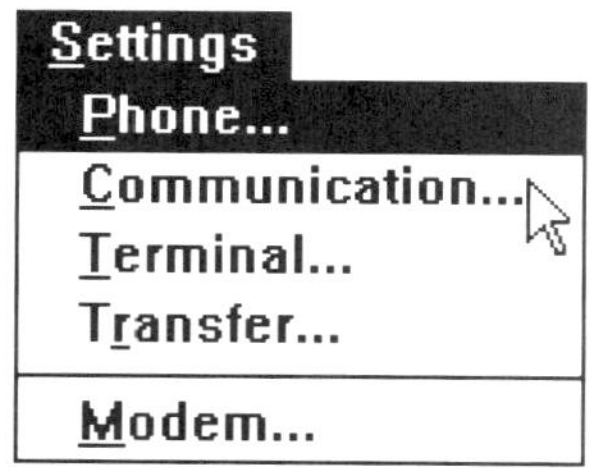

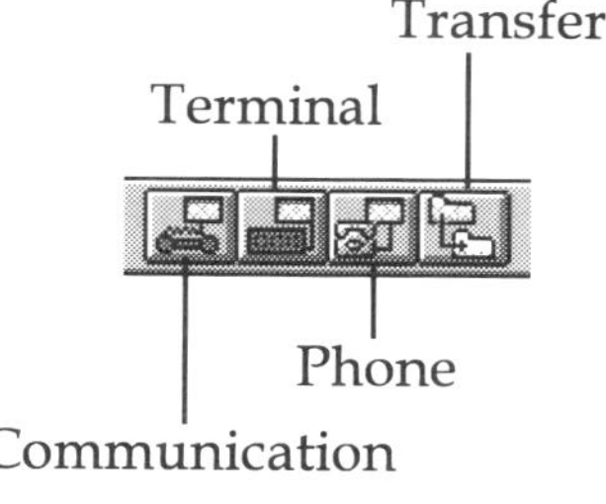

Figure 21-28. *Choose from the **Settings** menu or click on one of the Settings buttons to open the Settings dialog box.*

Works displays a different tab on top of the *Settings* dialog box shown in Figure 21-29 depending on which command you select from the **Settings** menu. For example, this figure shows the result of choosing *Phone* from the **Settings** menu.

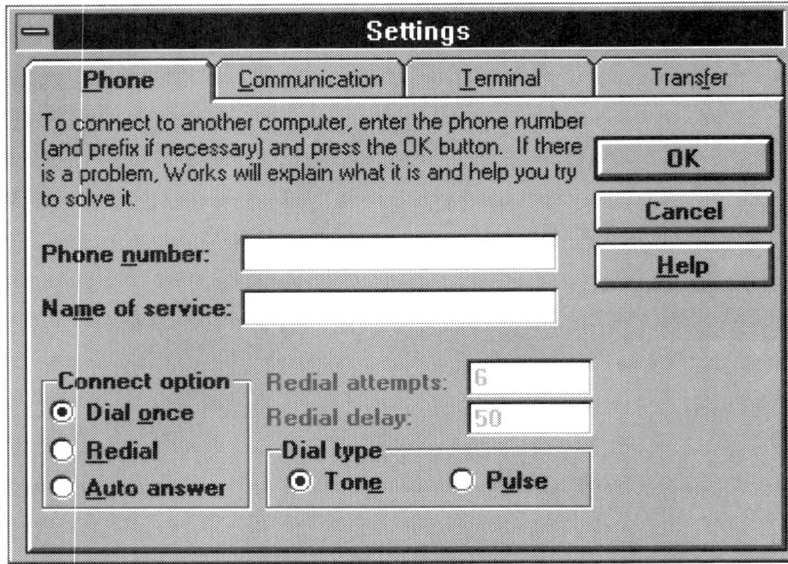

Figure 21-29. *Choose Phone from the* ***Settings*** *menu to open this dialog box.*

Choose the *Transfer* command from the **Settings** menu or click on the *Transfer* tab in this dialog box to change the communications protocol before transferring files between computer systems.

You should take great care if you alter technical settings on any tab in the *Settings* dialog box. Only alter settings to match with those of your communications hardware or those of the remote computer system to which you want to connect.

Closing a communications file

When you have completed work using your communications file, you can close it in the same as any other document in Works. As before, choose the *Close* command in the **File** menu. Remember that Works only ever saves communications data in a communications document. You must separately save any information sent by the other computer system if you want to keep that information. See **Saving Information You Receive** above for details.

Speaking with someone by telephone

If you have a telephone modem attached to your computer you can use it to call someone on the telephone. Once your modem dials the telephone number, pick up the telephone used by your modem and speak to the other person.

You can use this facility only in the Works word processor, spreadsheet, or database. To do so, highlight the telephone number in your document and choose *Dial This Number* from the **Tools** menu (Figure 21-30).

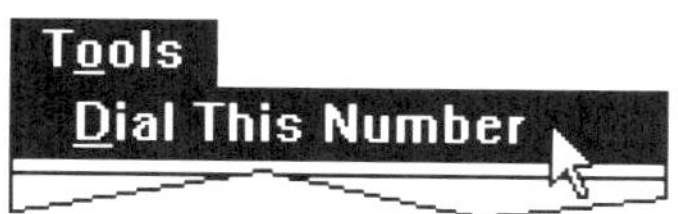

Figure 21-30. *Choose Dial This Number from the* ***Tools*** *menu to dial the number you highlighted.*

Handling Multiple Documents

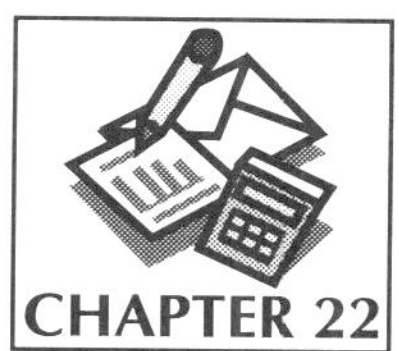

One of the most convenient features of Works is that a number of documents can be open at the same time. This is especially convenient in an integrated product such as Works as the tools (word processor, spreadsheet, and database) which make up the package are designed to work together. Information from the spreadsheet and database are easily integrated into the word processor.

In the following chapters of this book, we look at ways to integrate the tools in Works most efficiently. This chapter looks at the basics of working with multiple documents.

Multiple document windows

A number of document windows (up to eight) can be open at the one time in Works. These can be any type of Works file—word processor, spreadsheet, communications, or database.

Opening windows

Documents which have been saved previously are opened using the *Open Existing File* command in the **File** menu (Figure 22-1). From the Open dialog box, choose the file ***balou_c.wps*** from the ***msworks.cbt*** subdirectory.

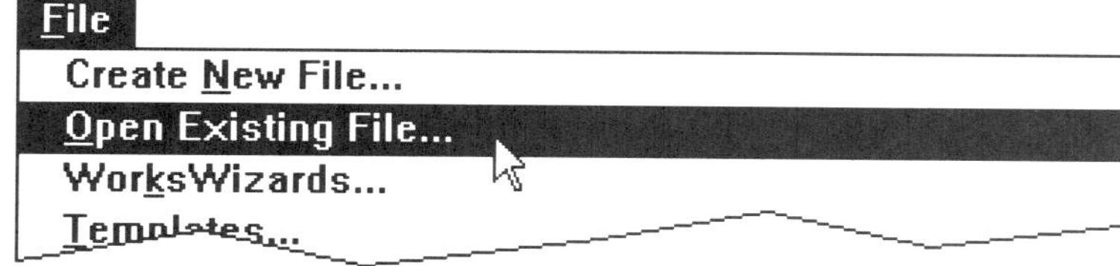

Figure 22-1. *The Open Existing File command in the* ***File*** *menu.*

The file is placed into a document window. The document window is not maximized by default. Maximize it by clicking on the maximize button as Figure 22-2 illustrates.

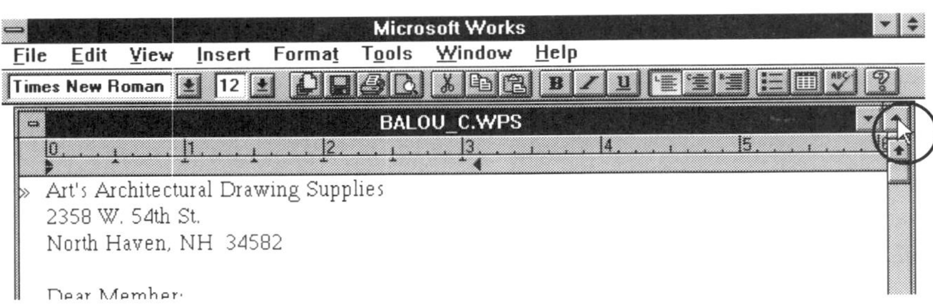

***Figure 22-2.** The file is placed into a document window and maximized with the maximize button.*

Select the *Open Existing File* command again, to open the file ***address.wdb*** also from the ***msworks.cbt*** subdirectory. This second file is placed into its own document window, on top of ***balou_c.wps.*** Maximize this document too as shown in Figure 22-3.

To open a new file, choose *Create New File* from the **File** menu and select the type of file to open in the *Startup* dialog box (Figure 22-4).

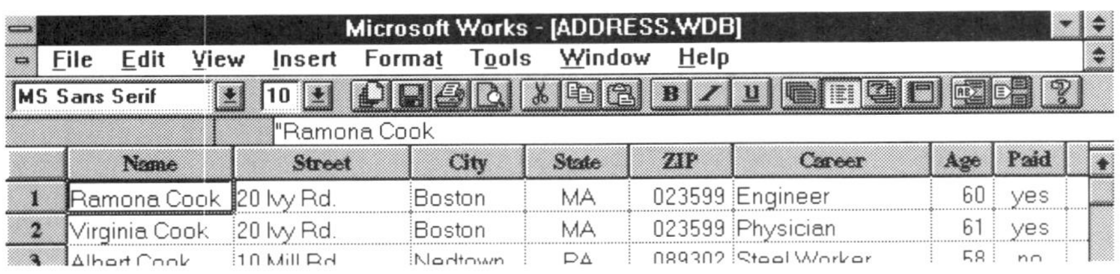

***Figure 22-3.** When you maximize the database file it covers **balou_c.wps**, which was opened first.*

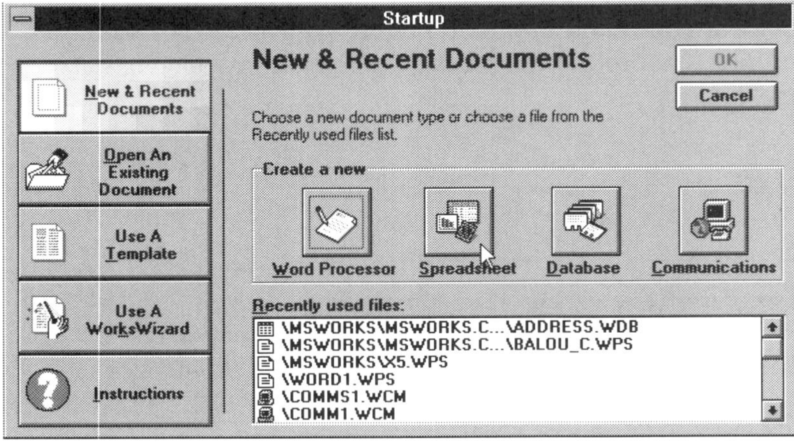

***Figure 22-4.** Choose to create a new spreadsheet using the Startup dialog box.*

Open a new spreadsheet file now. The new file is also placed in a separate document window, at the top of the "pile" of open files. It too is maximized as are the previous two files opened (Figure 22-5).

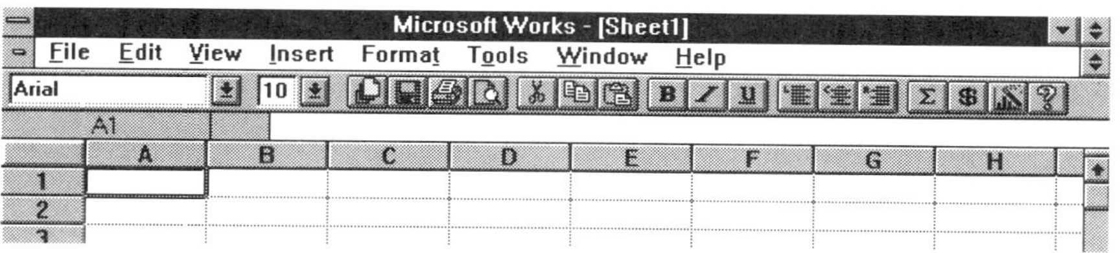

Figure 22-5. *A new spreadsheet file is opened, called* ***Sheet1****.*

There are three files open in Works at this stage. One of these is a word processor file, one was created in the database, and one from the spreadsheet. Only one of these files is visible on the screen at present.

Making open files active

As the documents are opened, they are listed in the **Window** menu and numbered in the order in which they were opened. The first file opened was ***balou_c.wps*** and therefore is number 1 in the **Window** menu. The other two documents are numbered accordingly (Figure 22-6).

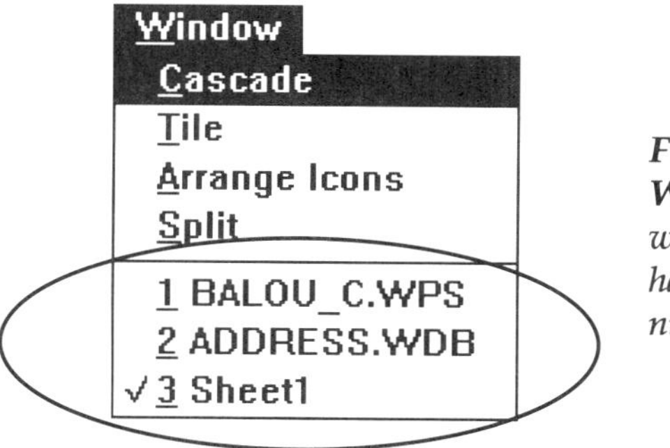

Figure 22-6. *The* ***Window*** *menu in which the files that have been opened are numbered.*

The **Window** menu is used to move between multiple documents which are open in Works. To move to another document, you simply select it from the **Window** menu. The document selected becomes "active."

Open the **Window** menu and select *1BALOU_C.WPS* as illustrated in Figure 22-7.

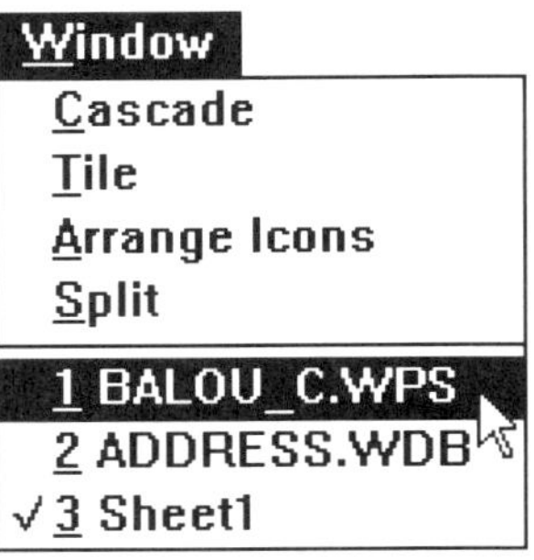

Figure 22-7. *To make* ***balou_c.wps*** *active, select it from the* ***Window*** *menu.*

There are keyboard shortcuts which can be used instead of going to the **Window** menu. Ctrl-F6 displays the previous document window and Ctrl-Shift-F6 shows the next document window.

Experiment with these methods of changing the active document window, using the documents currently open. See that ***balou_c.wps*** is active when you have finished.

Arranging document windows

It is often necessary to see more than one window on the screen at one time. This may be to compare information in two or more documents or simply to remind you which documents are open without having to refer to the **Window** menu.

Although a number of documents can be on the screen at one time, only one of these is active at any time.

The position and size of windows can be altered using the *Cascade* and *Tile* commands in the **Window** menu (Figure 22-8).

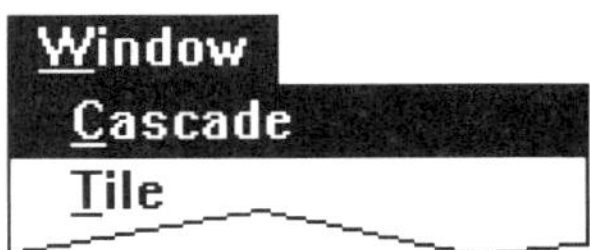

Figure 22-8. *The Cascade and Tile commands in the* ***Window*** *menu.*

The Cascade command

The *Cascade* command is used to view the title bars of all document windows on the screen simultaneously. Select the *Cascade* command from the **Window** menu.

The screen displays all of the document windows stacked in the same order as in the **Window** menu. In this example, ***balou_c.wps*** was active when *Cascade* was selected. It remains the active window—placed at the top of the stack of windows (Figure 22-9).

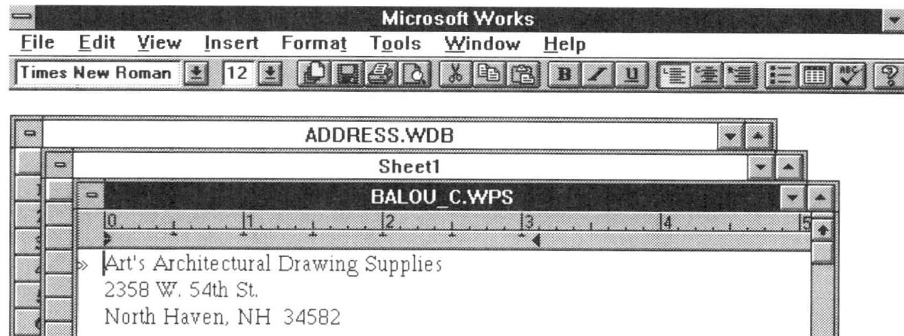

Figure 22-9. *The document windows in Cascade view.*

You can easily change to another window by clicking on the title bar of the window you require. In Figure 22-10, *Sheet1* is selected by clicking on the title bar which says *Sheet1*.

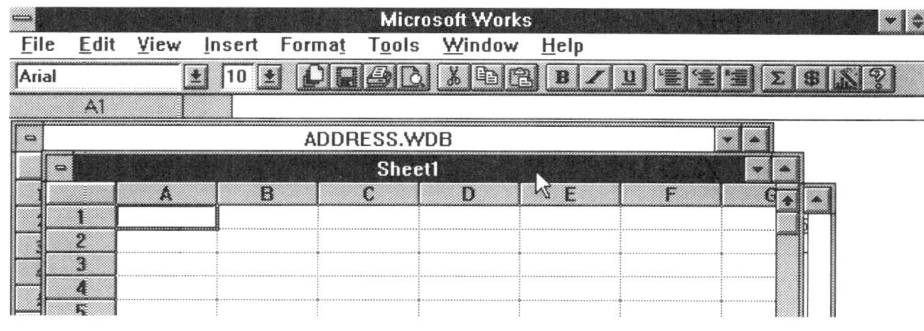

Figure 22-10. *Sheet1 is made active by clicking on its title bar.*

The Tile command

The *Tile* command in the **Window** menu arranges the screen so that all of the windows are visible at the one time. The active window has scroll bars which enable you to move around in that document. Select the *Tile* command to tile the three document windows as shown on the screen in Figure 22-11.

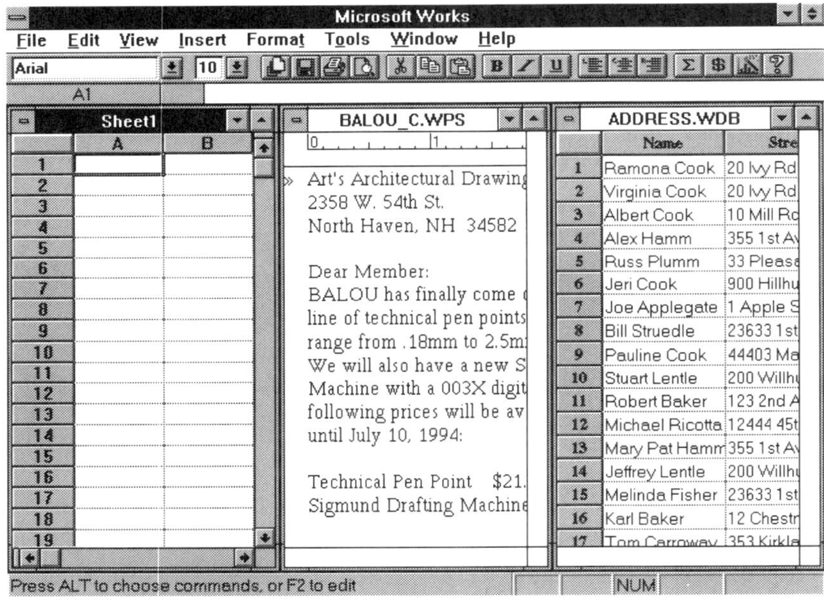

Figure 22-11. The documents are tiled using the Tile command in the ***Window*** *menu. Sheet1 is the active window.*

Using the mouse

A window is moved using the mouse by clicking on the active title bar and dragging it to a new position. Try moving the ***balou_c.wps*** window around the screen in this way, as in Figure 22-12. It is made active by clicking anywhere in the ***balou_c.wps*** document window.

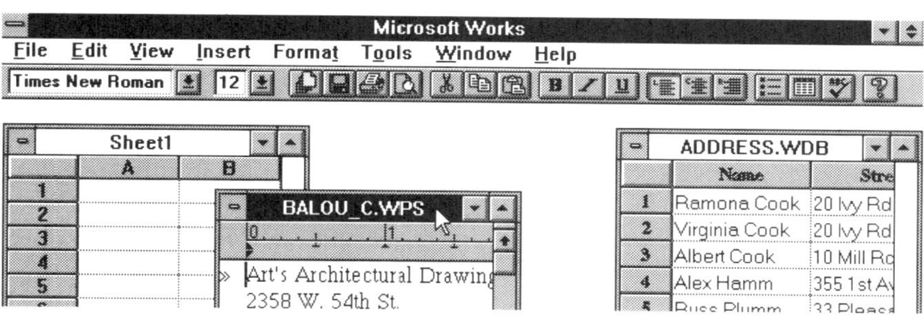

Figure 22-12. Move the word processor document by dragging its title bar.

Windows can be resized by moving the pointer to the border of a window and dragging the border to the size required. The window can be made larger or smaller in this way. Use the window border to resize the ***balou_c.wps*** window (Figure 22-13).

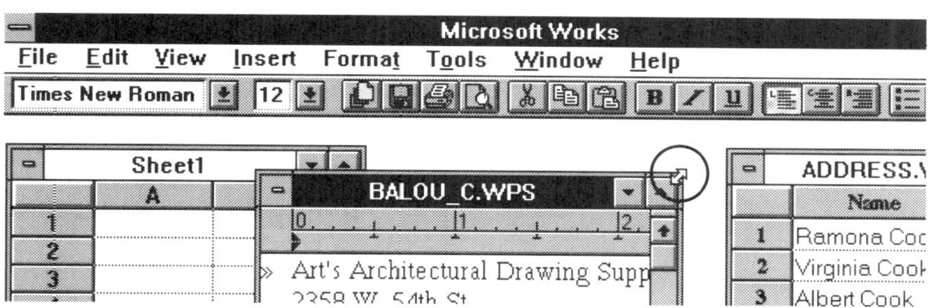

Figure 22-13. Resize the document window using the mouse.

The Save Workspace command

The workspace refers to the part of the screen below the toolbar where windows and icons are displayed. The screen in Figure 22-14 displays three document windows which have been moved and resized in this chapter.

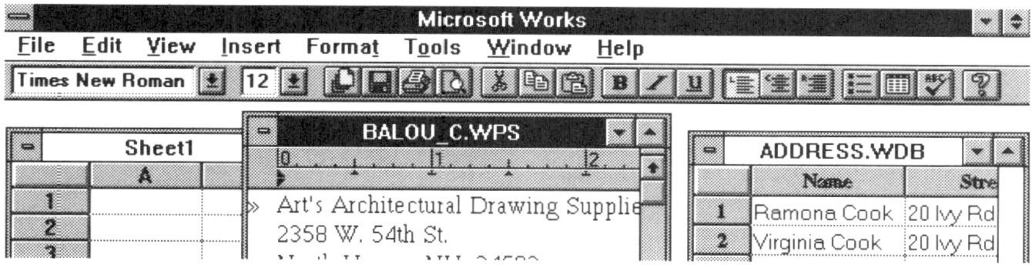

Figure 22-14. The workspace contains three document windows.

Works enables you to save the layout of the screen using the *Save Workspace* command in the **File** menu (Figure 22-15).

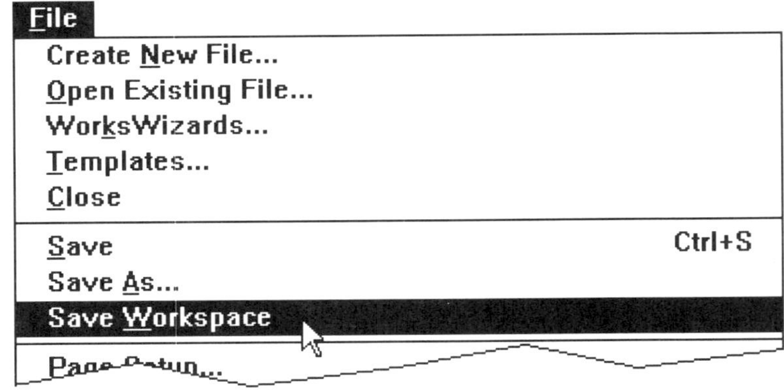

***Figure 22-15.** The Save Workspace command in the **File** menu.*

The layout of the screen includes the arrangement of open files, any files which have been minimized and the size of all document windows. When the workspace is saved, the same screen is available to you next time Works is opened—automatically.

Adjust the screen to look like Figure 22-16. The document window of ***balou_c.wps*** has been minimized using the minimize button. The other two windows are "tiled."

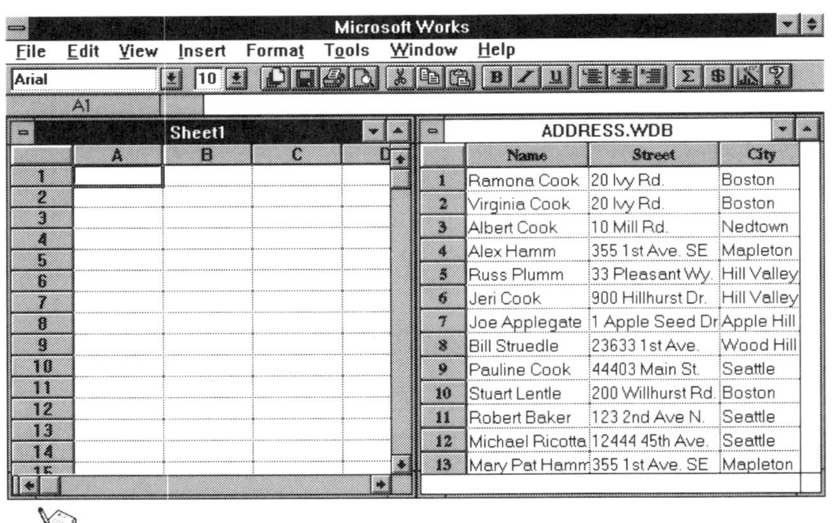

***Figure 22-16.** The screen is ready to be saved, with **balou_c.wps** minimized.*

Choose the *Save Workspace* command from the **File** menu. Works informs you that some of the documents in the workspace have not yet been saved through the dialog box shown in Figure 22-17. The document which needs saving is ***Sheet1***. If this was not saved, it would not be part of the workspace being saved. Click on *Cancel* to cancel the *Save Workspace* command. Activate the ***Sheet1*** document window and save it now as ***test.wks*** using the *Save* command in the **File** menu.

Figure 22-17. *The dialog box warning you that a file has not been saved.*

Choose *Save Workspace* again and Works saves the workspace, indicating this in the status bar as it is being saved. The workspace will be opened next time Works is started from the Windows Program Manager.

To test this, you need to exit from Works altogether, using the *Exit Works* command in the **File** menu (Figure 22-18).

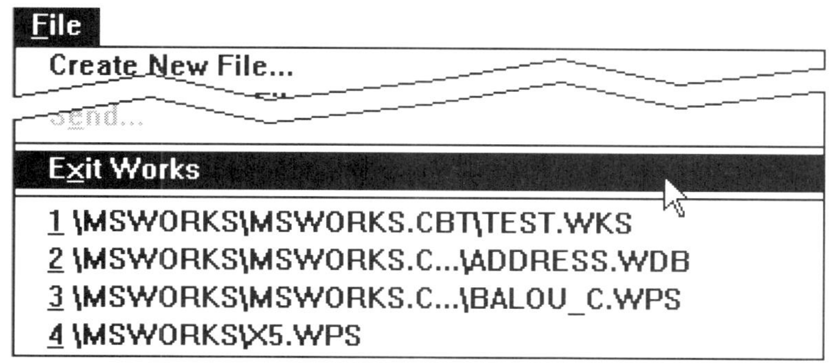

Figure 22-18. *The Exit Works command in the **File** menu.*

When Works is restarted, the workspace saved previously appears on the screen automatically. Restart Works by double-clicking on the Microsoft Works icon in Program Manager as in Figure 22-19. You see a similar screen to that in Figure 22-16, the only difference being the name of your worksheet—***test.wks***.

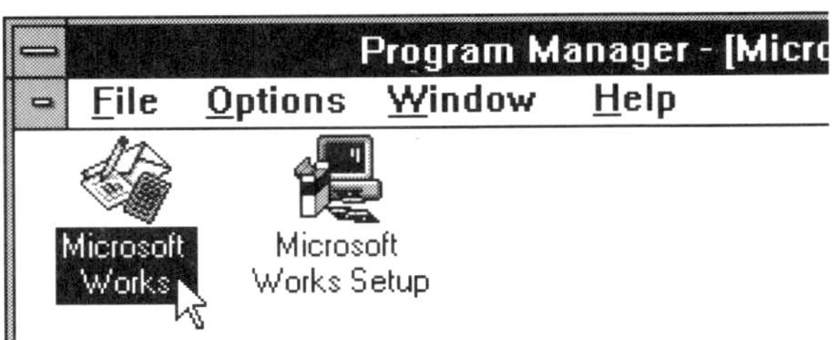

Figure 22-19. *Restart Works from Windows Program Manager. Your screen may look different to this, depending on how you have Windows set up.*

Works recorded the saved workspace as a setting in the *Options* dialog box. This dialog box is displayed by selecting *Options* from the **Tools** menu. *Used saved workspace* in the *When starting Works* section is checked when a workspace is saved.

Deselecting this option cancels the workspace which has been saved. Deselect the *Use saved workspace* check box so Works no longer uses your saved workspace when you next begin using Works (Figure 22-20).

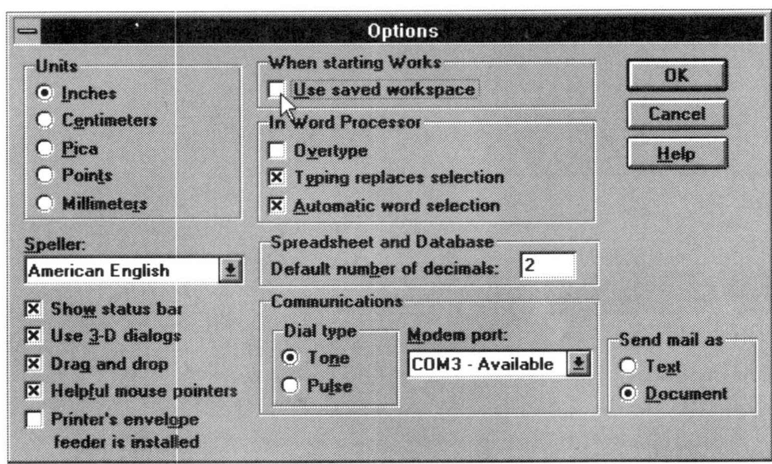

Figure 22-20. *Deselect the Use saved workspace check box in the Options dialog box.*

Including Spreadsheets in a Word Processor Document

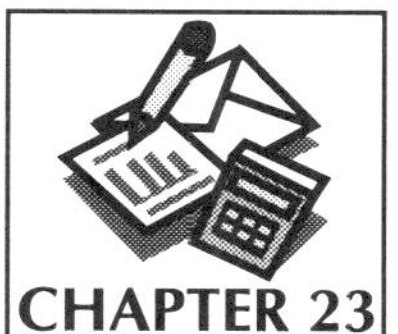

Incorporating data from different tools in Works can save time and lead to greater consistency in your documents. The tools in Works are designed to work together.

Data sharing in Works is powerful. Information copied from one tool to another can be linked. When data is linked, any changes made are automatically updated in all documents into which the data is copied.

Copying and linking

This chapter covers copying data from the spreadsheet tool into the word processor. A simple copy—without linking data—is discussed first. Linking the spreadsheet to the word processor document is covered later in the chapter.

There are two sample files used in this chapter. The spreadsheet file is ***popsales.wks*** and the word processor file is ***popmemo.wps***. They are both in the ***msworks.cbt*** directory. Open these files. Maximize ***popsales.wks*** and when ***popmemo.wps*** is open, it too is maximized as in Figure 23-1.

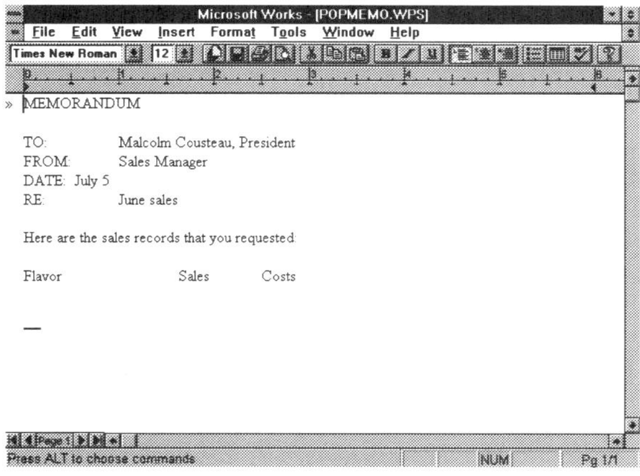

Figure 23-1. *Open* ***popsales.wks*** *and* ***popmemo.wps*** *maximizing the screen.* ***Popsales.wks*** *is hidden behind* ***popmemo.wps***.

It is essential to determine which part of the spreadsheet data is to be used in the word processor document. Studying ***popmemo.wps***, you can see that the information required is the sales records for the drinks of various flavors.

From the spreadsheet, the information on the *Flavor*, *Sales*, and *Costs* columns are to be copied. Figure 23-2 shows the headings in ***popmemo.wps*** under which the spreadsheet data is to be inserted.

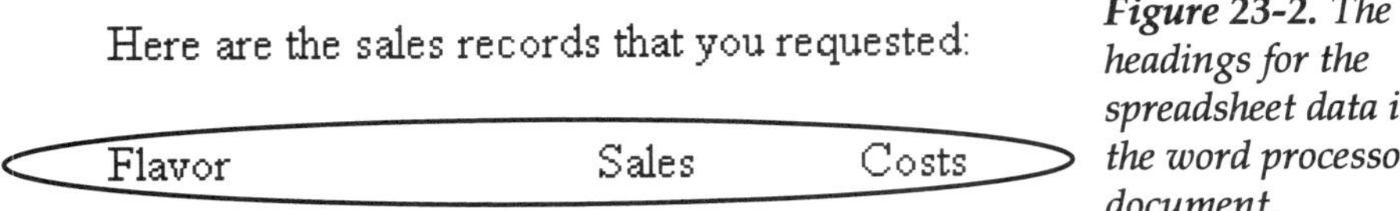

Figure 23-2. *The headings for the spreadsheet data in the word processor document.*

By copying the information from the spreadsheet, you can be assured that the data is identical in both documents. This saves repetitive typing and avoids the possibility of a typing error in one of the sales figures.

Copying data between documents is done in a similar way to copying data to another position in the same document. The process involves highlighting the data to be copied, selecting *Copy* from the **Edit** menu, moving the cursor to where it is to be pasted, and selecting *Paste* from the **Edit** menu.

Selecting data from the spreadsheet

In this example the data to be copied is in the spreadsheet file—***popsales.wks***. Display this file now by clicking on ***popsales.wks*** in the **Window** menu (Figure 23-3).

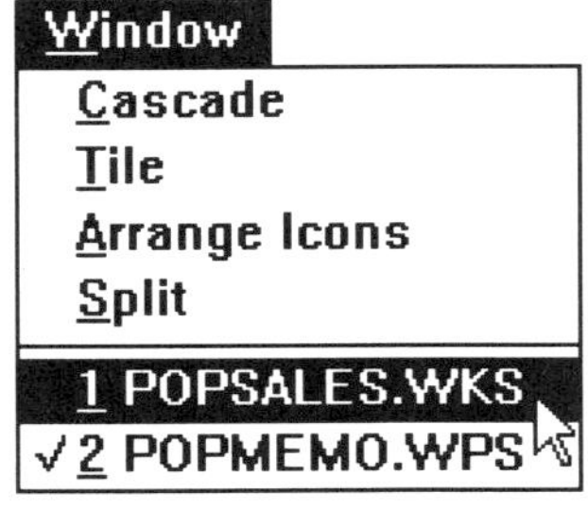

Figure 23-3. *Display* ***popsales.wks*** *using the* ***Window*** *menu.*

The information needed in the word processing document is in cells A6:C12. The labels in cells A5, B5, and C5—*Flavor*, *Sales*, and *Costs*—confirm this. Highlight cells A6:C12 by dragging over them with the mouse as in Figure 23-4.

	Flavor	Sales	Costs
6	Abalone Apricot	900.98	585.64
7	Blowfish Blueberry	1975.33	1352.71
8	Crab Cherry	2000.43	1320.28
9	Grouper Grape	5529.51	3549.47
10	Lungfish Lemon	1334.55	889.8
11	Lobster Licorice	799.66	527.77
12	Octopus Orange	3303.78	2100.49

Figure 23-4. *The cells A6:C12 are highlighted for copying into **popmemo.wps**.*

Copying spreadsheet data into a word processor document

To copy cells—without linking—the *Copy* command in the **Edit** menu is selected. As with all material which is copied, the data is stored on the Clipboard. It is through the Clipboard that information can be copied between documents in Works.

The copied data is inserted into its new position using the *Paste* command in the **Edit** menu. When pasted into the word processor document, the data is inserted in tabular form.

Continuing the example in the sample files, select *Copy* from the **Edit** menu while the cells in the spreadsheet are highlighted. The cells are on the Clipboard and you can now move back to ***popmemo.wps***.

The cells which are copied from a spreadsheet are pasted into the document at the insertion point in the word processor document. The information needs to go under the headings in ***popmemo.wps***. Move the insertion point into this position as in Figure 23-5.

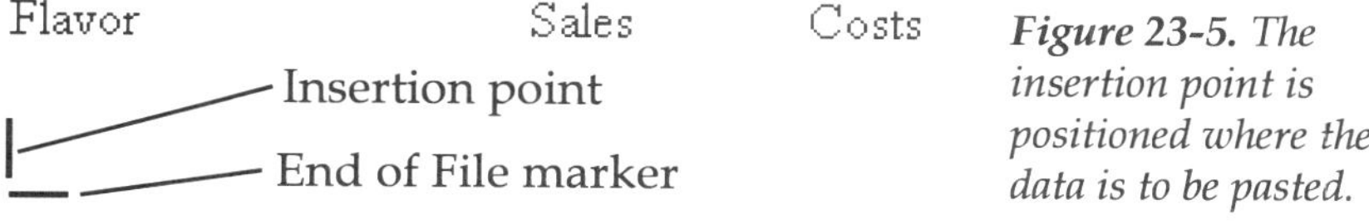

Figure 23-5. *The insertion point is positioned where the data is to be pasted.*

To insert cells A6:C12 into the word processor document, choose *Paste* from the toolbar or the **Edit** menu (Figure 23-6).

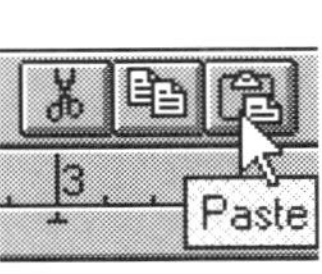

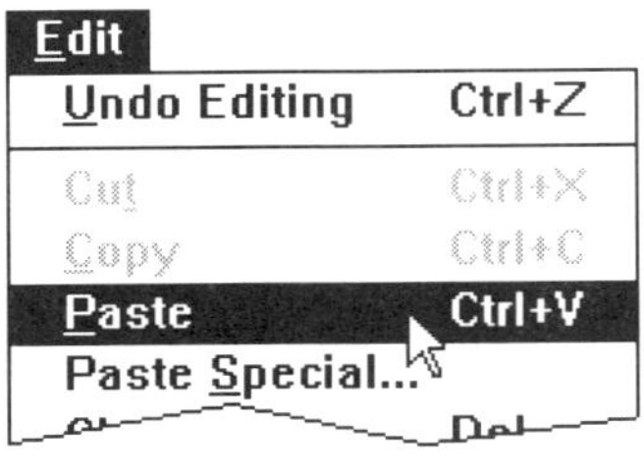

Figure 23-6. *The Paste command.*

The spreadsheet data is now part of ***popmemo.wps.*** The headings do not match the width of the new columns exactly. The tabs of the document need to be changed to allow for the new information. Make these changes if you like, referring back to **Chapter 3, Editing Documents**, if necessary. The reformatted document looks like Figure 23-7 when done.

Here are the sales records that you requested:

Flavor	Sales	Costs
Abalone Apricot	900.98	585.64
Blowfish Blueberry	1975.33	1352.71
Crab Cherry	2000.43	1320.28
Grouper Grape	5529.51	3549.47
Lungfish Lemon	1334.55	889.8
Lobster Licorice	799.66	527.77
Octopus Orange	3303.78	2100.49

Figure 23-7. *The spreadsheet data is pasted into **popmemo.wps** and the tabs are adjusted.*

Linking spreadsheet data to a word processor document

This section requires the same two sample files which were used previously. ***Popsales.wks*** has not been changed in any way but ***popmemo.wps*** has changed quite considerably. The following example requires the original document. To revert to the original document, reopen the file by clicking on ***popmemo.wps*** in the **File** menu (Figure 23-8).

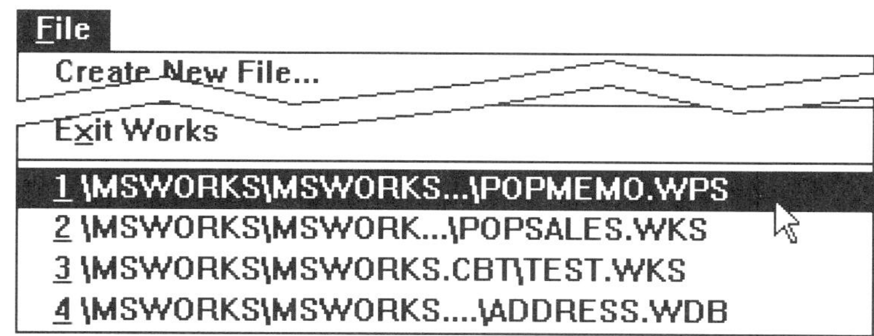

Figure 23-8. *Reopen **popmemo.wps** through the **File** menu.*

Works warns you in a dialog box that any changes you have made will be lost (Figure 23-9). Click on *OK* to continue and the original copy of the file appears on the screen.

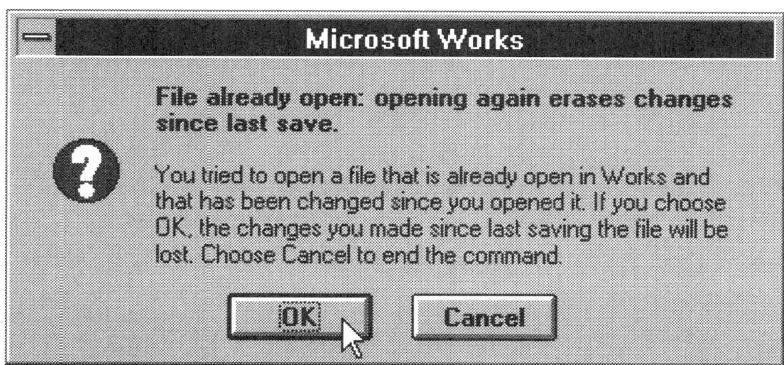

Figure 23-9. *Works warns you that changes will be lost if you proceed.*

Linking data

Linking spreadsheet data is particularly important when the spreadsheet data is dynamic. Linking avoids having to make the same changes to information in a word processor document, which has been copied from a spreadsheet document. Linking ensures greater consistency between documents and less chance of error.

The Paste Special command

To link data, the *Paste Special* command is used in the **Edit** menu (Figure 23-10). The *Paste Special* dialog box appears when this command is selected. In the *Paste Special* dialog box, you specify the details of the link.

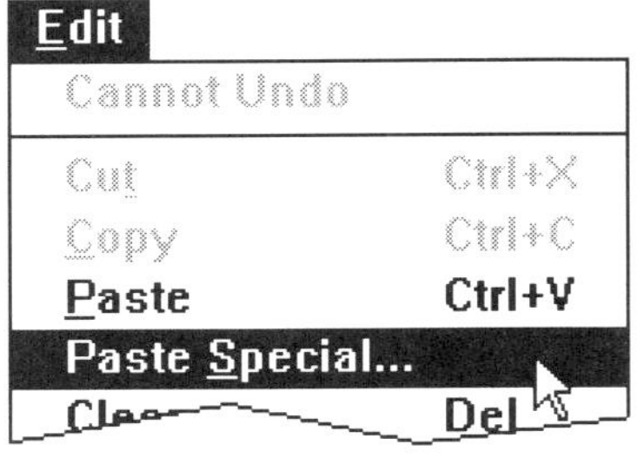

*Figure 23-10. The Paste Special command in the **Edit** menu.*

In this example, you paste the same spreadsheet information into the word processor file used previously. This time, however, the information is linked by using the *Paste Special* command.

As before, the information required in the spreadsheet is highlighted first. Display ***popsales.wks*** and highlight the block A6:C12. It may still be highlighted from the example outlined above. Choose *Copy* from the **Edit** menu and return to ***popmemo.wps*** through the **Window** menu.

The insertion point once again determines the placement of the data being pasted. Move the insertion point to the end of the word processor document, leaving one line between the headings and the spreadsheet data.

The *Paste Special* command in the **Edit** menu is selected to link data (Figure 23-10). Choose this now to display the *Paste Special* dialog box shown in Figure 23-11.

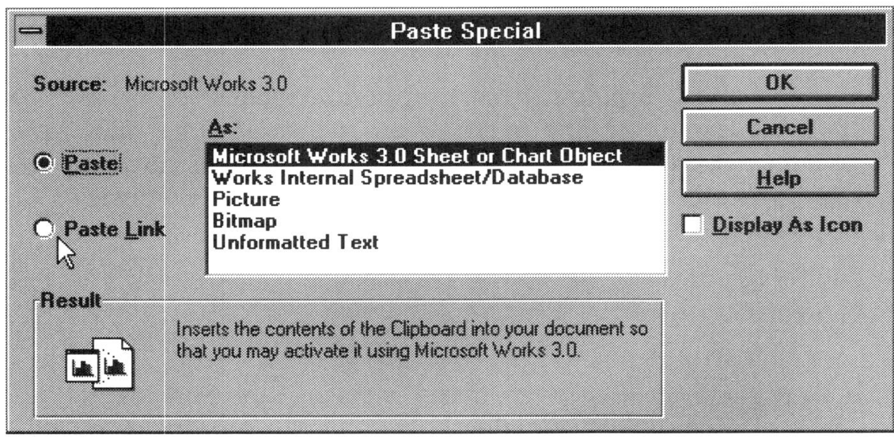

Figure 23-11. The Paste Special dialog box.

It is in this dialog box that the specifications of the link are determined. Works automatically specifies the *Source* by recalling where the information came from before it was copied to the Clipboard. In this case the source is *Microsoft Works 3.0*.

Select *Paste Link* and click on *OK* and the data is inserted into the word processor document (Figure 23-12).

Here are the sales records that you requested:

Flavor Sales Costs

Abalone Apricot	900.98	585.64
Blowfish Blueberry	1975.33	1352.71
Crab Cherry	2000.43	1320.28
Grouper Grape	5529.51	3549.47
Lungfish Lemon	1334.55	889.8
Lobster Licorice	799.66	527.77
Octopus Orange	3303.78	2100.49

Insertion point

Figure 23-12. *The data is pasted into **popmemo.wps** and linked to **popsales.wks**.*

Like when you use *Paste*, the spreadsheet data is inserted into the word processor in a table format with the gridlines visible. The table is actually one object. As it is one object, Works uses only one insertion point for the entire table as is in Figure 23-12.

The table can be highlighted in the word processor. The only thing you can change, however, is alignment. All other formatting changes need to be made in the spreadsheet. Highlight the table by clicking on it with the mouse and change it to center aligned using the *Center* button on the toolbar (Figure 23-13).

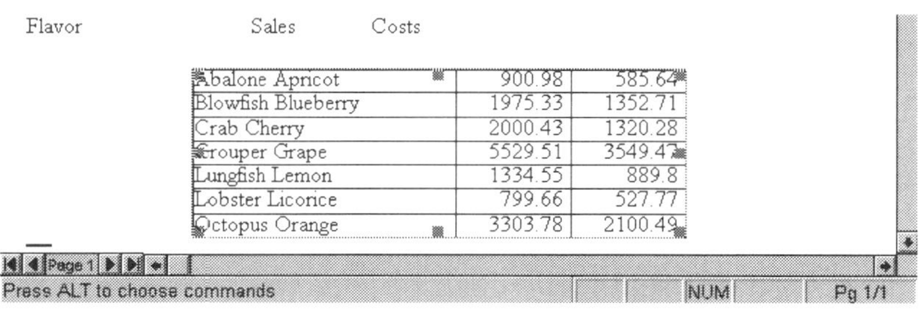
Flavor Sales Costs

Abalone Apricot	900.98	585.64
Blowfish Blueberry	1975.33	1352.71
Crab Cherry	2000.43	1320.28
Grouper Grape	5529.51	3549.47
Lungfish Lemon	1334.55	889.8
Lobster Licorice	799.66	527.77
Octopus Orange	3303.78	2100.49

Figure 23-13. *The Table is center aligned.*

It is impossible to change information in the table from the word processor. You need to return to the spreadsheet to change data. To return to the spreadsheet you can either use the **Window** menu or the shortcut of double-clicking on the table. Double-click on the table and the spreadsheet appears.

UPDATING LINKED DATA

Any change in the spreadsheet will automatically update the word processor when the information is linked.

In this example, click on cell B11 and change the Lobster Licorice sales figure to 1000 as in Figure 23-14. Remember to press Enter.

11	Lobster Licorice	1000	527.77

Figure 23-14. *The Lobster Licorice sales figure is changed to 1000 in the spreadsheet.*

Return to ***popmemo.wps*** through the **Window** menu and you will see that the change made in the spreadsheet file is automatically reflected in the word processor file (Figure 23-15).

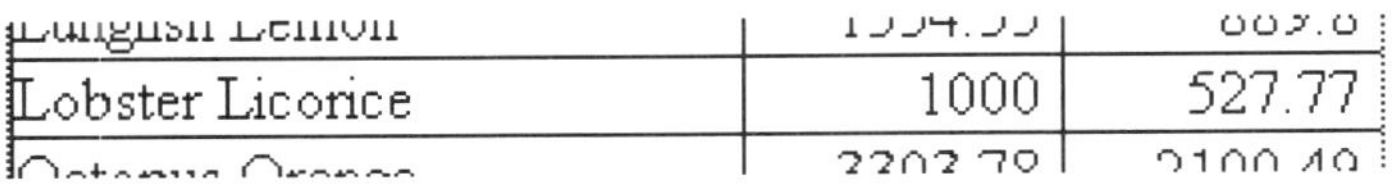

Lobster Licorice	1000	527.77

Figure 23-15. *The Lobster Licorice sales figure is changed to 1000 in the word processor because of the link set with the Paste Special command.*

Including Charts in a Word Processor Document

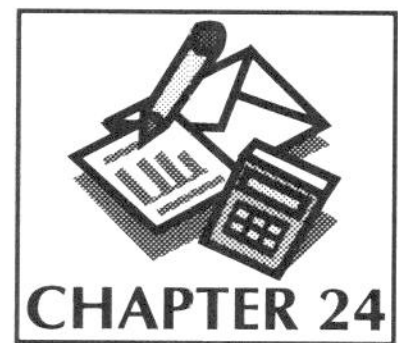

Charts are a visual method of displaying a collection of information and are much more eye catching than raw figures. Many people use charts to display data from a spreadsheet in a word processor document to avoid long lists of numbers.

As with spreadsheet data, charts created in a spreadsheet file can be inserted into a word processed document by copying. To link the chart, the *Paste Special* command is used.

Linking spreadsheet charts

In the previous chapter, the sample files ***popsales.wks*** and ***popmemo.wps*** were used to demonstrate copying information from a spreadsheet into a word processor document. These files are used again in this chapter to link a chart to a word processor document. Open ***popsales.wks*** and ***popmemo.wps*** and ensure ***popsales.wks*** is active (Figure 24-1).

Microsoft Works - [POPSALES.WKS]

File Edit View Insert Format Tools Window Help

Times New Roman 12

A1

	A	B	C
1			
2	**Seabuddy Frozen Pops**		
3	Sales by flavor for:	June	
4			
5	**Flavor**	**Sales**	**Costs**
6	Abalone Apricot	900.98	585.64
7	Blowfish Blueberry	1975.33	1352.71

Figure 24-1. Popsales.wks *is active.*

Selecting a chart

The chart being copied needs to be selected in the spreadsheet file and copied onto the Clipboard before it can be pasted into the word processed document. There can be a number of charts belonging to one spreadsheet and it is important to select the right one. The chart is selected when it appears on the screen—no highlighting is required.

In the sample file ***popsales.wks***, a chart has already been created. The name of the chart is Popsales and it is displayed on the screen by selecting it from the *Charts* dialog box—please do this now. Figure 24-2 shows you how to open this dialog box by choosing *Chart* from the **View** menu. Select *Popsales* in the *Charts* dialog box and click on *OK*.

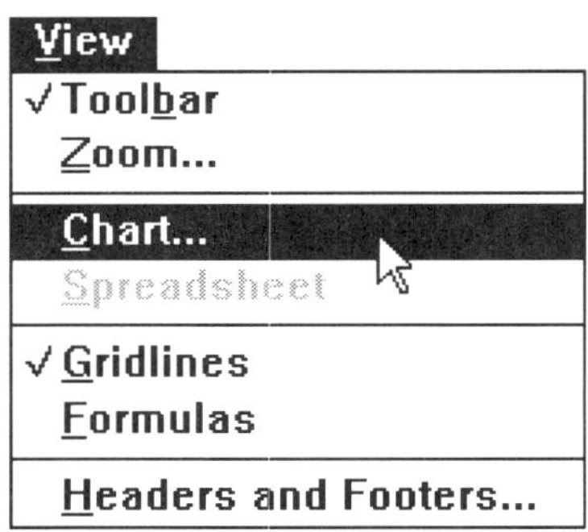

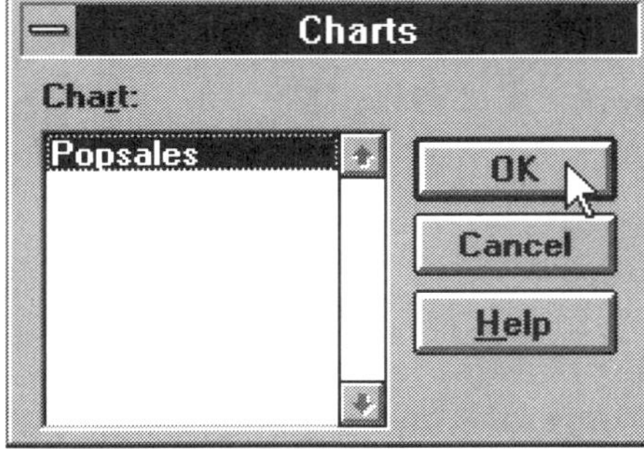

Figure 24-2. *The Popsales chart is selected from the Charts dialog box.*

The chart to be used in the word processed document needs to be copied, using the *Copy* command in the **Edit** menu or the *Copy* toolbar button, while the chart is displayed (Figure 24-3). Select this command to copy the chart onto the Clipboard.

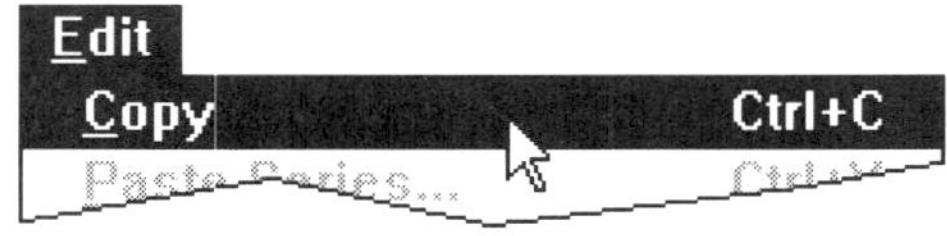

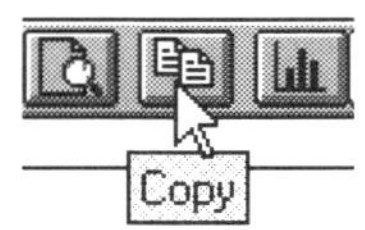

Figure 24-3. *Choosing Copy copies the chart which is displayed on the screen.*

Linking charts to the word processor

As mentioned above, charts can be linked to a word processor document in the same way as basic spreadsheet data is. The chart must be copied first, and then the *Paste Special* command in the **Edit** menu is selected to insert the chart into the word processor (Figure 24-4).

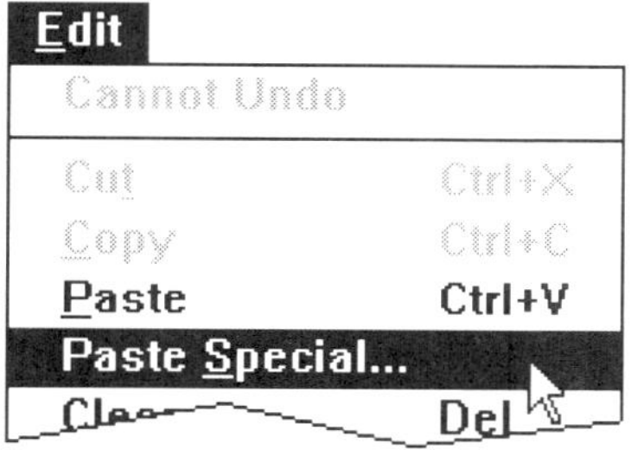

***Figure 24-4.** The Paste Special command in the **Edit** menu of the word processor.*

Return to ***popmemo.wps*** using the **Window** menu. Since the column headings are no longer appropriate, remove the line which reads "Flavor Sales Costs." The document is now ready for the chart. Move the insertion point to the end of the document as shown in Figure 24-5.

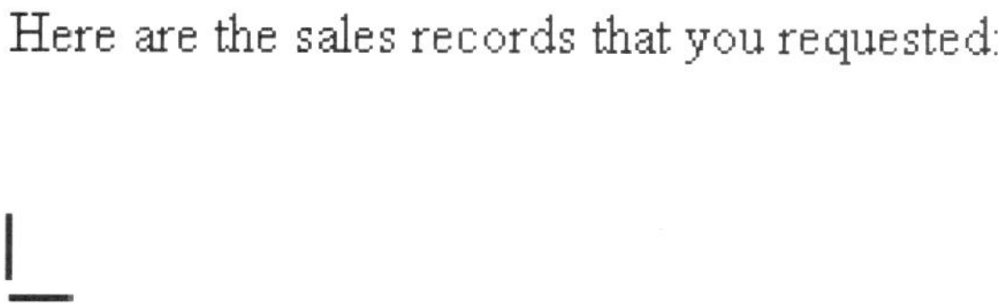

Here are the sales records that you requested:

***Figure 24-5.** The text has been altered and the insertion point is located where the chart will be inserted.*

Using the Paste Special command

The *Paste Special* command pastes information into the word processor from other Works tools. In this case, the information to be inserted is a chart, which has been copied from ***popsales.wks*** and is currently on the Clipboard.

The Paste Special dialog box appears on the screen when *Paste Special* is selected from the **Edit** menu. Select *Paste Special* so the type of data being pasted can be determined.

The chart which was created in the spreadsheet uses the type *Microsoft Works 3.0 Chart Object*, which is already selected when the *Paste Special* dialog box appears. To insert the chart into the word processor document, click on *Paste Link* and then on *OK* (Figure 24-6).

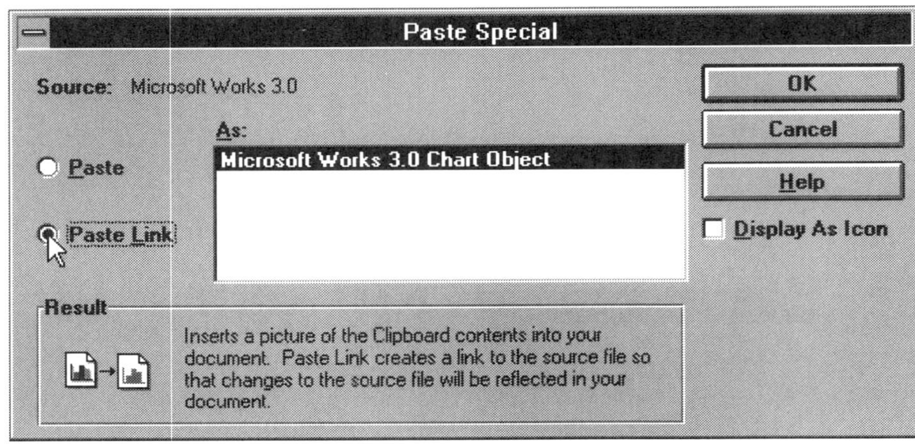

Figure 24-6. *The chart is inserted by selecting Paste Link.*

Figure 24-7 shows the chart inserted into the document. Notice the large insertion point which is to the left of the chart. This informs you that the chart is one object in the word processor document.

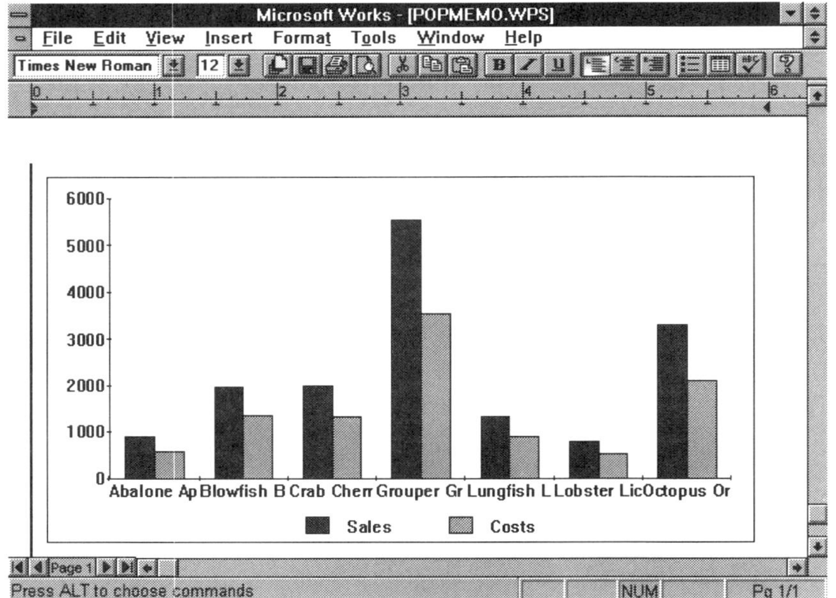

Figure 24-7. *The chart in the word processor document.*

UPDATING LINKED DATA

The alignment of the chart can be altered from within the word processor, but all other changes need to be made back in the charting facility. The charting facility can be accessed through the **Window** menu, or by double-clicking on the chart. Try double-clicking on the chart to return to the charting screen (Figure 24-8).

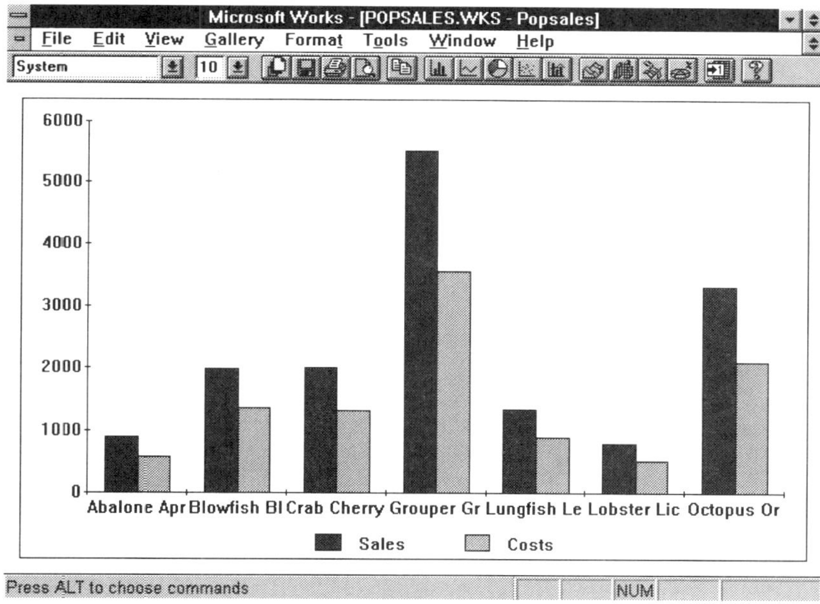

Figure 24-8. *The charting screen.*

The type of graph used will be changed in this example. When the change has been made, you can return to the word processor and check to see that the change has been registered in ***popmemo.wps.***

The type of chart to be selected can be another style of bar chart. Click on the *Bar Chart* button on the toolbar as in Figure 24-9.

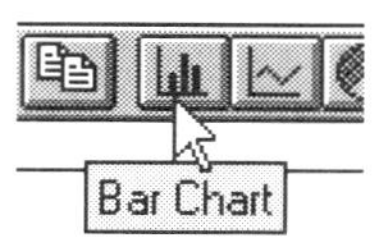

Figure 24-9. *Click on the Bar Chart button on the toolbar to choose a new style of chart.*

From the *Bar* dialog box, select option number 2, which is a stacked bar chart. Click on *OK* to return you to the charting screen to see the change. When you return to the word processor document using the **Window** menu, the chart is now a stacked bar, just as it is in the spreadsheet file, ***popsales.wks.*** Figure 24-10 shows the amended chart in ***popmemo.wps*** in its selected form.

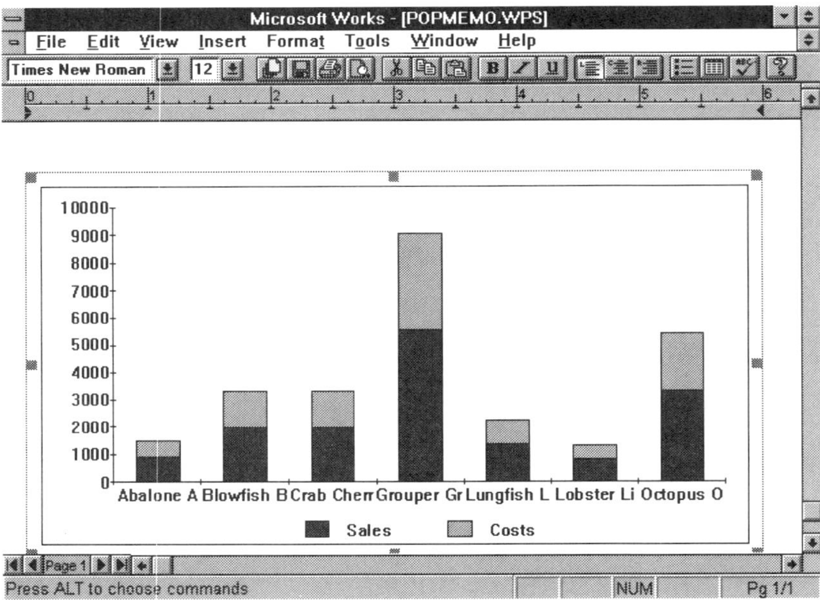

Figure 24-10. *The chart in the word processor document is changed to a stacked bar type, as it was changed to this form in the original spreadsheet chart file.*

Including Databases in a Word Processor Document

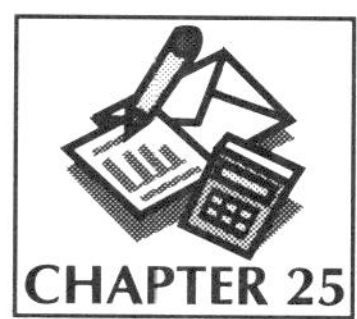

Works provides the facility to incorporate data from a database into a word processor file. Bringing data from a database into a word processor document is often called "mail merging."

Merging and mailing

One of the most common uses of the mail merge feature is a standard business letter. An identical business letter is usually sent to a number of people containing personal details of each client.

If this were to be done manually, the letters would be created individually and in each new letter the next client's name and address typed in. This is a very time-consuming process and can be avoided with Works.

Another common use of database information in the word processor is to create mailing labels or envelopes – usually to match the client list. Once again, creating these manually can be a very tedious task! This chapter shows you how to create form letters and mailing labels or envelopes in Works.

Before a form letter or a set of mailing labels can be developed, a database must be created. The database stores the information which will be inserted into the word processor document.

A database is made up of fields and records. The fields are labels for a type of information in the database. In a database for clients, names and addresses, the fields may be:

Name, Address, Suburb, City, State, Zip code.

One set of information – one client's details, for instance – makes up one record. To refresh your memory on database structure, refer to **Chapter 14, The Database Screen**. It is important to know how the database is made up, to use the mail merge facility most efficiently.

When a form letter or mailing labels are being created, you use placeholders for database fields. When the document is printed, field entries from each record are inserted into one copy of the form letter, or one mailing label.

The advantage of using database material in conjunction with a word processor document is that the database need be produced once only. Once created, it can be used again and again, for each new form letter or set of mailing labels required.

It is not necessary to insert all the fields from a database into a document. You can select only the ones which are relevant. It is also not essential that every record be used in the database. To select just a few records, perform a search or query on the database before the form letters or mailing labels are printed.

Creating a form letter

To create a form letter using database information, the database you will be using needs to be open. This chapter uses the database called ***address.wdb*** which is stored in the ***msworks.cbt*** subdirectory.

Open this file and examine the fields in the database. Figure 25-1 shows that the database contains the following fields: Name, Street, City, State, Zip, Career, Age, and Paid.

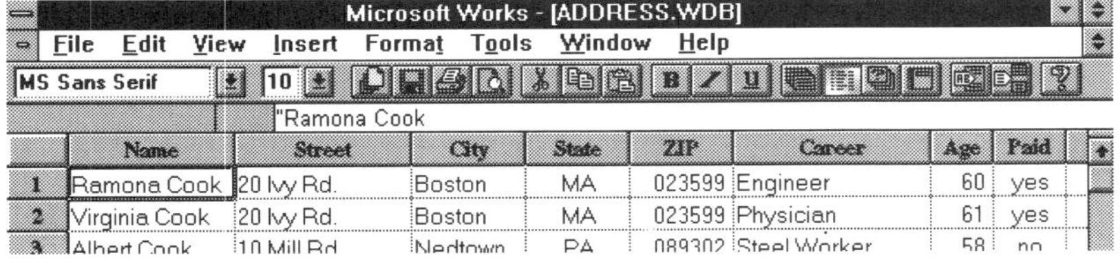

***Figure 25-1.** The **address.wdb** database.*

Some of these fields will be placed into the form letter in this example. Works places fields into a form letter as placeholders. A placeholder is the name of a database field enclosed by chevrons. For example, if the "Name" field was inserted into the form letter, it would appear as «Name» on the word processor document. When the form letter was printed, the placeholder would be replaced with a field entry from one of the records in the database.

Open a new word processor document now for your form letter.

Using the Database Field command

The *Database Field* command in the **Insert** menu (Figure 25-2) inserts database fields into the word processor form letter. Choose this command now to display the *Insert Field* dialog box.

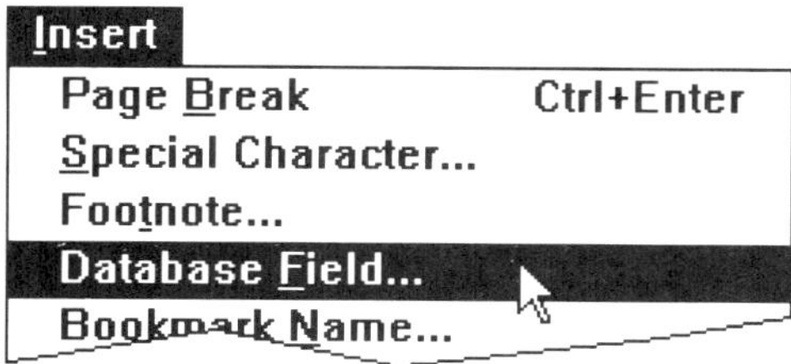

Figure 25-2. *Choose Database Field from the* ***Insert*** *menu.*

Selecting the database

You can choose the database whose field you want to insert at the insertion point in your letter. To do so, click on the *Database* button in the *Insert Field* dialog box (Figure 25-3).

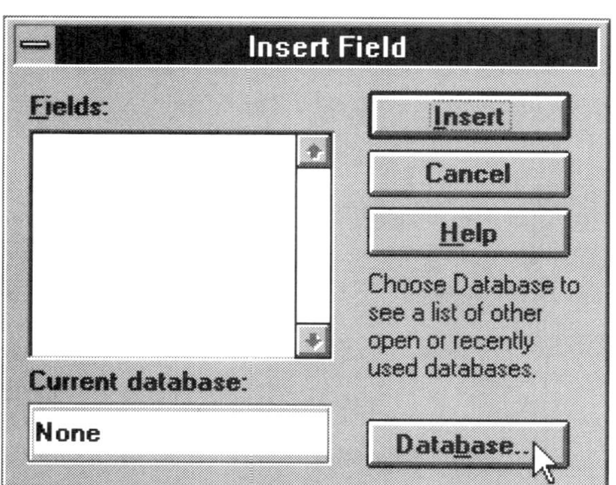

Figure 25-3. *Click on the Database button in the Insert Field dialog box.*

The databases you have used most recently are now listed in the *Choose Database* dialog box of Figure 25-4. At present one database only is open—***address.wdb***. Works indicates unopen databases using a filing cabinet icon. Click on the database whose fields you want to insert and then click on *OK*. In this case we want to select *ADDRESS.WDB*.

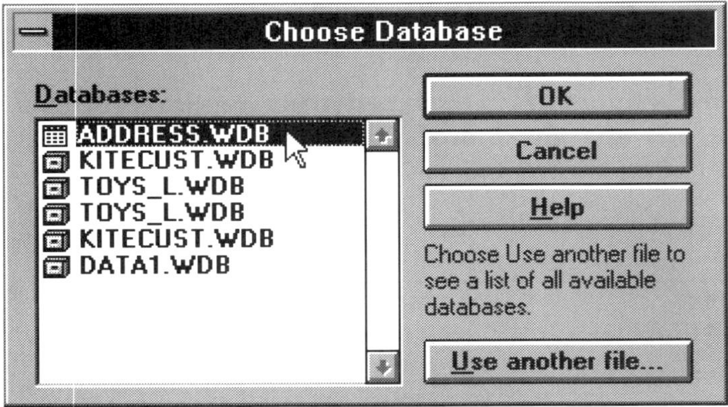

***Figure 25-4**. Click on ADDRESS.WDB and then on OK.*

SELECTING THE FIELDS

A list of the fields in a database is provided in the *Fields* list box when the appropriate database is selected (Figure 25-5). Only the fields required in the form letter need be inserted into the document. Placeholders for the fields are inserted by clicking on the field name in the *Fields* list box.

In this example, the form letter being created requires the address of the person receiving the letter, at the top of the page. The first field to be inserted, therefore, is "Street." Click on "Street" in the *Fields* list box and then on the *Insert* button as in Figure 25-5.

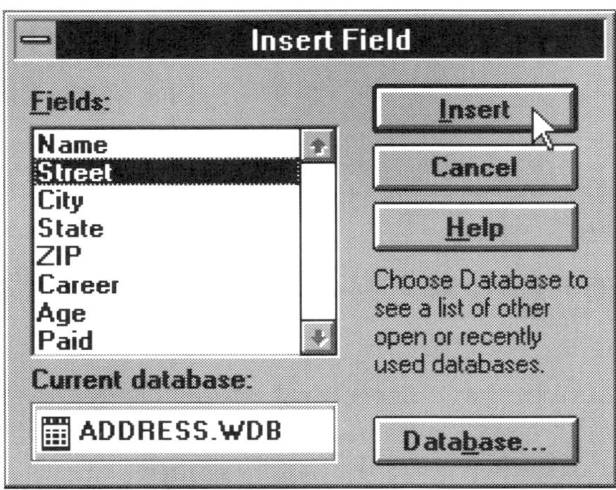

***Figure 25-5.** "Street" is being inserted into the form letter through the Insert Field dialog box.*

When you click on *Insert,* the *Cancel* button changes to *Close*. Click on *Close* to return to the document and you will see that a placeholder has been inserted into the form letter where the insertion point was located (Figure 25-6).

«Street»

Figure 25-6. *«Street» is the placeholder for the "Street" field from the database.*

ARRANGING THE FORM LETTER DOCUMENT

All fields are inserted into the form letter document in the same way. The arrangement of the form letter is completely up to you. For instance, a new placeholder can be placed on a new line, by pressing Enter. The placeholder can be inserted in the middle of a paragraph, surrounded by text. Placeholders can also be formatted, with bold or italic for example, depending on your requirements.

We will continue creating the form letter using some of these features. Press Enter to move to the next line and select *Database Field* from the **Insert** menu to display the *Insert Field* dialog box again.

The next field to be used is "City." Click on this field name and the *Insert* button to insert another placeholder. «City» is now on the line under «Street» as shown in Figure 25-7.

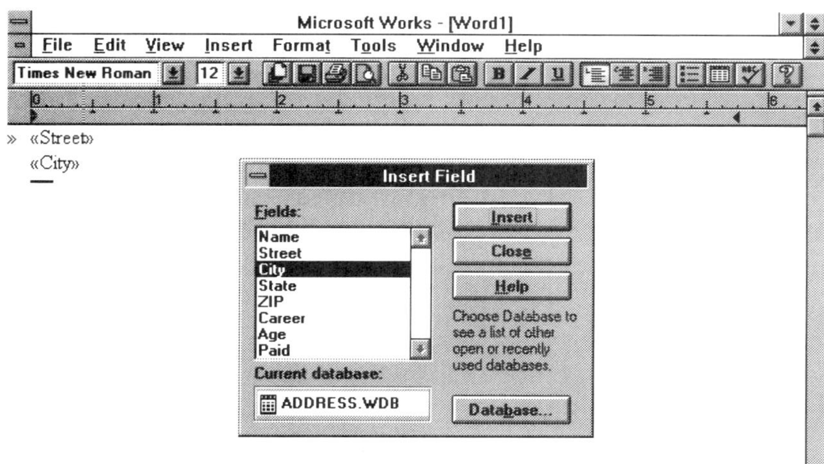

Figure 25-7. *The "City" field becomes part of the form letter document.*

You can insert a number of placeholders using the *Insert* button and then close the *Insert Field* dialog box. You can then rearrange the placeholders when you return to your document.

Insert placeholders for "State" and "ZIP" on the same line as «City». Works automatically includes a space between placeholders when you insert several fields without closing the *Insert Field* dialog box. Use the *Close* button to close the dialog box when you finish. The form letter looks like Figure 25-8 when these placeholders are in position.

«Street»
«City» «State» «ZIP»

Figure 25-8. *The placeholders for the address at the top of the page are in place.*

Placeholders can be inserted into the document while the letter is being typed. The placeholder becomes part of the text of the letter making it sound more personal. In this example, the remainder of the letter to be typed in is as follows:

Dear «Name»,

Congratulations on your membership.
We are pleased to have another «Career» as part of our organization.

The President.

Type the rest of this letter as shown. Be sure to leave spaces before and after the placeholders as necessary. Not leaving spaces leads to a cluttered form letter, with all of the words running into each other.

The final format of the form letter is illustrated in Figure 25-9.

«Street»
«City» «State» «ZIP»

Dear «Name»,

Congratulations on your membership.
We are pleased to have another «Career» as part of our organization.

The President.

Figure 25-9. *The completed form letter.*

Previewing the form letter

Mistakes can often occur in the fields which have been inserted into form letters, especially if the field names are somewhat cryptic. Form letters have been known to end up saying "Dear New York!"

It is particularly important, therefore, to view your form letter on the screen before it is printed. This reduces the chance of printing a large number of letters with one simple mistake in all of them.

The standard *Print Preview* command in the **File** menu of Figure 25-10 is used to view a form letter before it is printed.

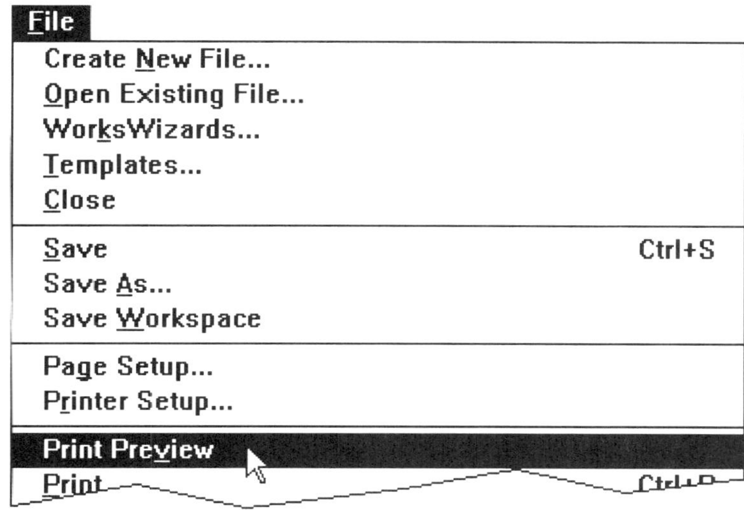

Figure 25-10. *The Print Preview command in the **File** menu.*

Choosing this command displays the *Choose Database* dialog box (Figure 25-11). The database being used in the form letters—***address.wdb***—needs to be selected from the *Databases* list box. To preview the form letters, click on the *OK* button.

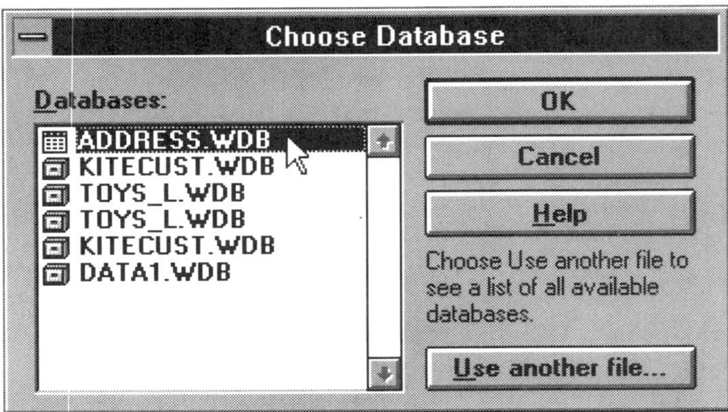

***Figure 25-11.** Ensure ADDRESS.WDB is selected and then click on OK.*

Works creates a new page for each record in the database. Each new page contains the standard letter with the corresponding information from the fields inserted into the placeholders. Figure 25-12 shows a zoomed view of the first page of the document which contains the data from record 1 of the database.

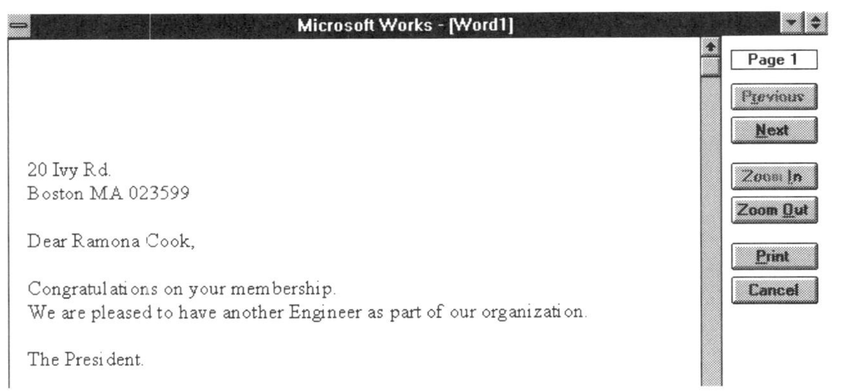

***Figure 25-12.** Page 1 in Print Preview showing the letter created for the first record in the database.*

PRINTING THE FORM LETTER

The form letter can be printed directly from the *Print Preview* screen by clicking on the *Print* button as shown in Figure 25-13.

Figure 25-13. The Print button in the Print Preview screen.

If you are not in the *Print Preview* screen, the *Print* command in the **File** menu is used to print the form letters (Figure 25-14).

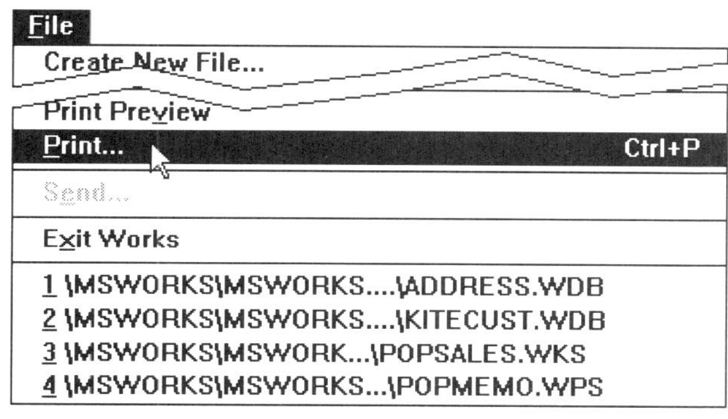

*Figure 25-14. The Print command in the **File** menu.*

Choosing the *Print* command from the **File** menu displays the *Print* dialog box. In this dialog box, the number of copies of each letter can be specified. You can also determine which pages of the document are to be printed. This option can be used to print a selection of records from the database. It is not as powerful as applying a query, but can be useful in some cases. Works also enables you to print in draft quality from the *Print* dialog box (Figure 25-15).

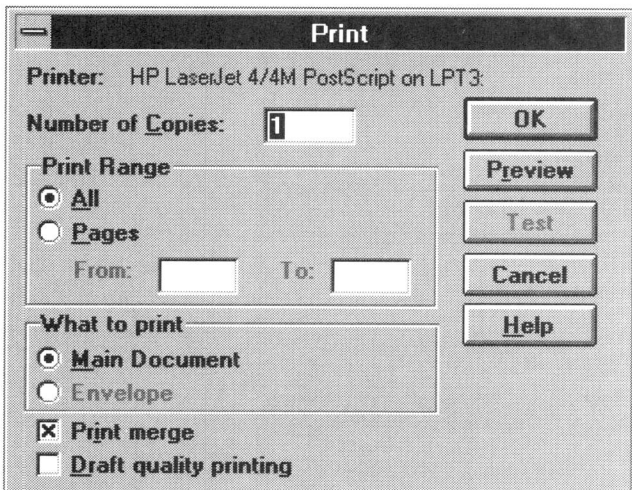

Figure 25-15. The Print dialog box.

Creating mailing labels

Mailing labels can be created in a word processor document using database information. The labels which are created can then be printed onto adhesive labels available from stationery suppliers.

Information from the database, used in the form letter, can be used again in the mailing labels. Creating labels in this way saves many hours of typing. It also leads to greater consistency and less chance of error.

Placeholders are inserted into a mailing label document in a similar way as into a form letter. Open a new word processor document, which will be called *Word2*, and leave ***address.wdb*** open as the database file.

Using the Envelopes and Labels command

A standard format for mailing labels consists of a name, street, city, state, and zip code. If these were inserted into a word processor document, the layout would be similar to Figure 25-16.

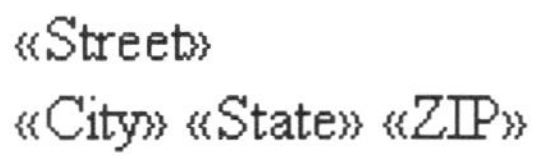

«Street»
«City» «State» «ZIP»

Figure 25-16. *The standard layout of the placeholders in mailing labels.*

To insert the field placeholders as shown, choose the *Envelopes and Labels* command from the **Tools** menu (Figure 25-17).

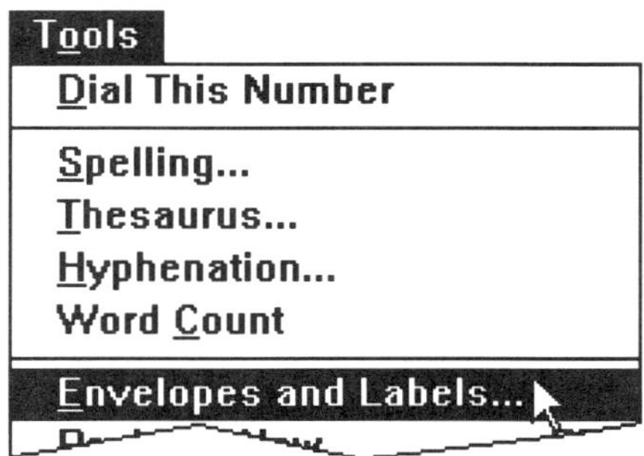

Figure 25-17. *The Envelopes and Labels command in the* ***Tools*** *menu.*

Selecting the database

Select the *Envelopes and Labels* command from the **Tools** menu and click on the *Mailing Labels* tab to display the dialog box shown in Figure 25-18.

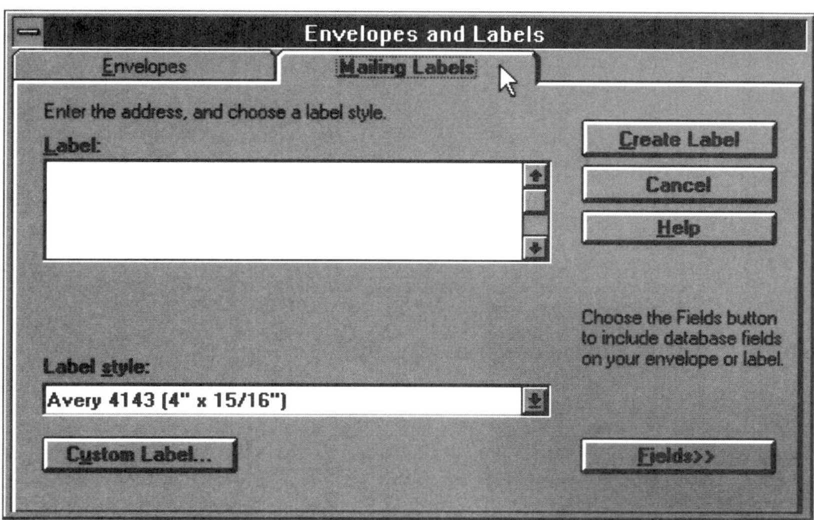

Figure 25-18. Click on the Mailing Labels tab in the Envelopes and Labels dialog box.

Click on the *Fields* button to expand the dialog box so that you can include placeholders for your Works data. The bottom of the *Envelopes and Labels* dialog box now looks like Figure 25-19.

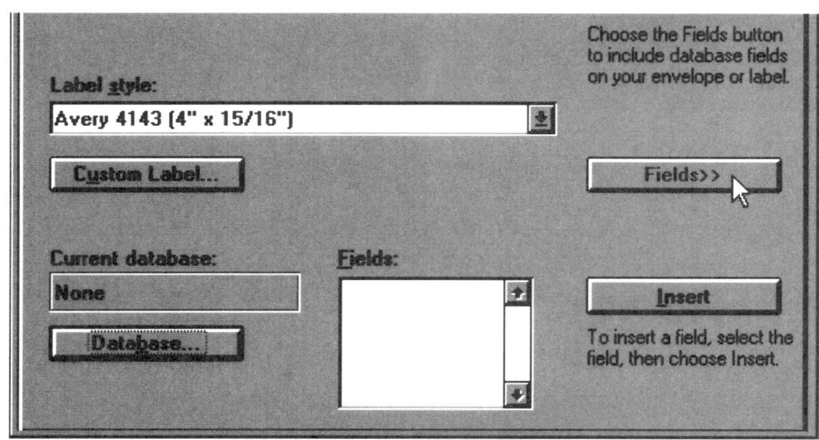

Figure 25-19. Click on the Fields button in the Envelopes and Labels dialog box.

The database on which the labels are based is selected using the *Database* button in this dialog box, in the same you did for your form letter. Refer back to the *Choose Database* dialog box in Figure 25-4 if you need help.

Continue to create your labels using the *Envelopes and Labels* dialog box as outlined below.

SELECTING THE FIELDS

Choosing the database filename and clicking on *OK* in the *Choose Database* dialog box displays a list of fields in the *Envelopes and Labels* dialog box. There are five fields required in the mailing label document.

The first placeholder needed in the labels is for the "Name" field. Click on this field name in the *Fields* list box (Figure 25-20).

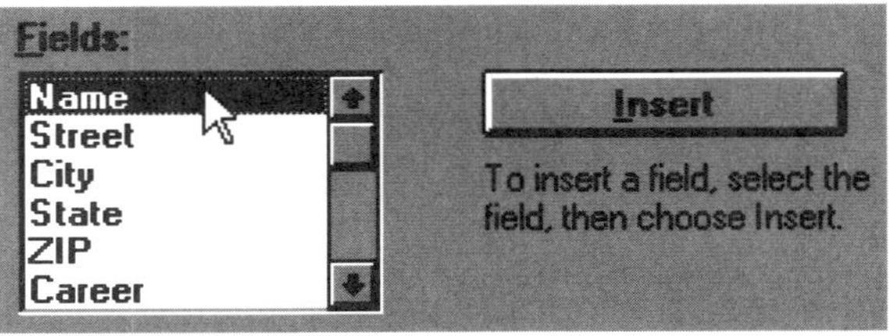

Figure 25-20. *Choose Name from the Fields list box.*

When you click on Insert, Works inserts a placeholder into the *Label* box enclosed in chevrons — «Name» — which is illustrated in Figure 25-21.

Figure 25-21. *A placeholder for the "Name" field is put into the Label box.*

ARRANGING THE FIELDS FOR THE ADDRESS LIST

The style of mailing labels usually places all the information together in a block, so it can fit neatly onto the adhesive labels.

Insert the remaining fields into the mailing label by choosing the next field you want and clicking on *Insert*. You can then move the placeholders to separate lines by pressing Enter between them, or along the line using the Spacebar or Tab keys as you can in your document, forming the layout illustrated in Figure 25-22.

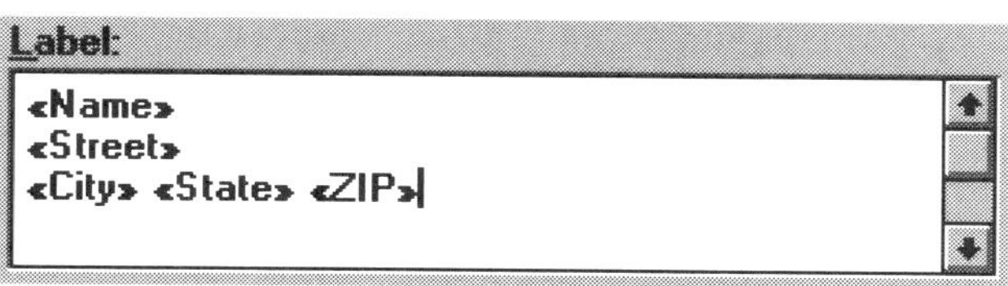

Figure 25-22. *The mailing label placeholders.*

ARRANGING LABELS TO BE PRINTED

The labels can be printed on prepurchased adhesive labels which come in a variety of dimensions. The size is determined by how many labels fit on the page — the number of rows and columns per page.

Printing labels depends on the printer you have connected and the type of labels being used. Choose the type of label stationery you have from the *Label style* drop-down list box shown in Figure 25-23.

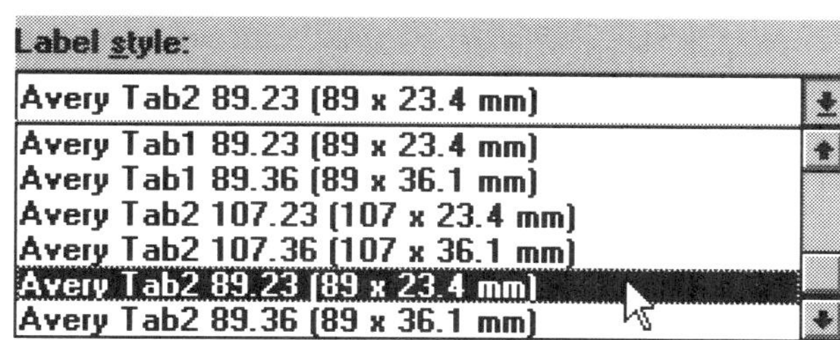

Figure 25-23. *Choose from the Label style drop-down list box to match your stationery.*

Once you choose a *Label style* click on the *Create Label* button to insert your label definition into your word processor document. This button is shown in Figure 25-24.

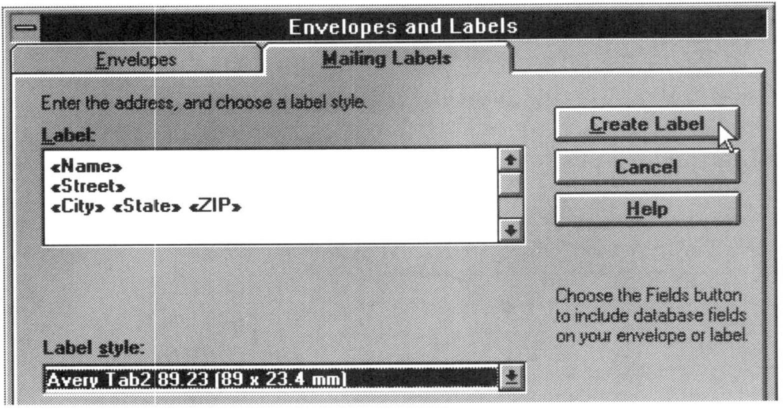

Figure 25-24. *Click on Create Label to close the Envelopes and Labels dialog box.*

Works copies your placeholders and inserts them into your document, followed by a page break (Figure 25-25).

» «Name»
«Street»
«City» «State» «ZIP»

»

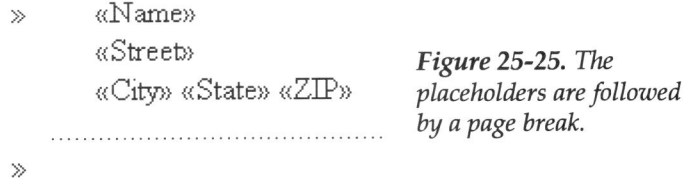

Figure 25-25. *The placeholders are followed by a page break.*

To print your labels choose the *Print* command from the **File** menu. This opens the *Print* dialog box. Select the *Mailing Labels* option in the *What to print* section if Works has not already selected this option (Figure 25-26).

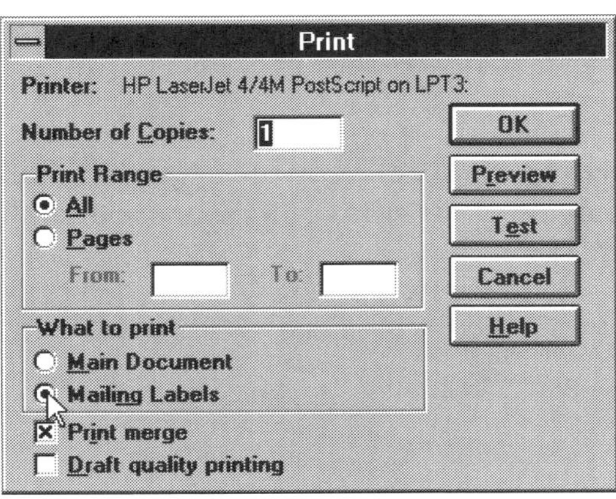

Figure 25-26. *Ensure the Mailing Labels option in the Print dialog box is selected.*

You can use two buttons in the *Print* dialog box to check how your labels will print. These buttons are the *Preview* and *Test* buttons. When you choose one of these buttons Works opens the *Choose Database* dialog box for you to identify the database whose data you want to print. Click on *ADDRESS.WDB* and then on *OK* to identify your database in this case (Figure 25-27).

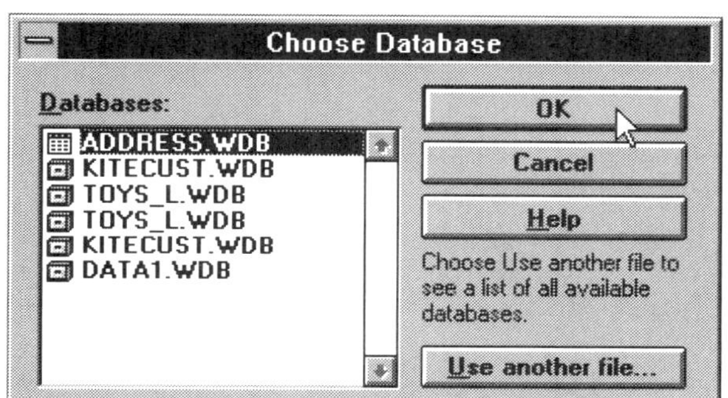

Figure 25-27. *The database to be used in the mailing labels –* ***address.wdb*** *– is selected.*

Click on the *Preview* button in the *Print* dialog box and complete the *Choose Database* dialog box to see an image of your labels on your screen, like that shown in Figure 25-28. See **Chapter 7, Printing Word Processed Documents** for details on using *Print Preview*.

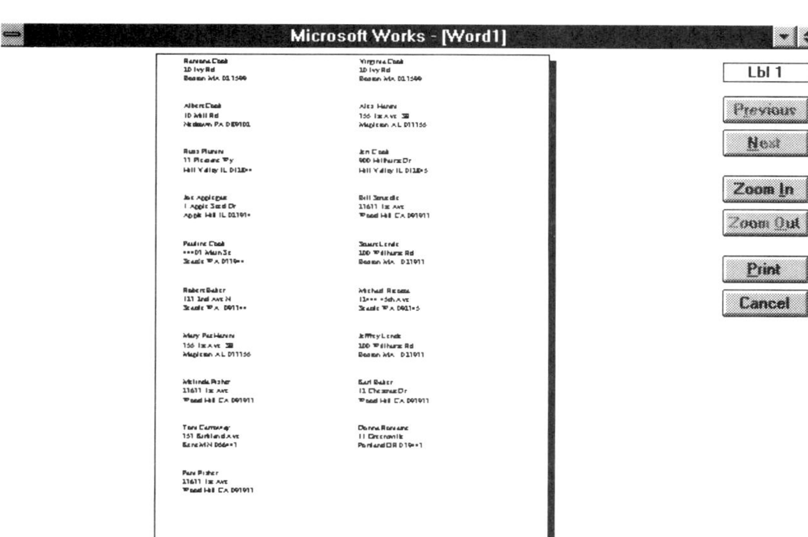

Figure 25-28. *The labels in Print Preview.*

If you choose the *Test* button from the *Print* dialog box and complete the *Choose Database* dialog box, Works prints the first two rows of your labels. This allows you to check the alignment of your stationery in your printer before printing all of your data. Once Works sends the test labels to the printer you see the *Test Label Printing* dialog box that Figure 25-29 illustrates. Click on *Print* in this dialog box if your stationery is correctly aligned, or on *Test* to repeat the test print. You can alter your label settings by clicking on *Adjust* or cancel the print operation by choosing *Cancel*.

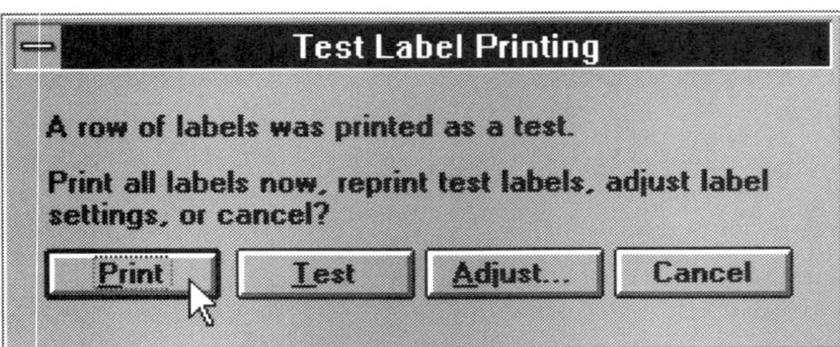

Figure 25-29. *The Test Label Printing dialog box.*

Creating envelope labels

You can create envelope addresses for printing on envelope stationery in a similar way to the way you created mailing labels above. Works provides these two features as alternatives. You therefore cannot create mailing labels and envelopes in the same document, so open a new word processor document by choosing *Create New File* from the **File** menu now.

In your new document choose the *Envelopes and Labels* command from the **Tools** menu and click on the *Envelopes* tab if it is not already on top (Figure 25-30).

You can expand this dialog box by clicking on the *Fields* button in the same way you did when creating mailing labels. You then click on the *Database* button to open the *Choose Database* dialog box as you did in Figure 25-3. When you complete the *Choose Database* dialog box you use the *Insert* button in the *Envelopes and Labels* dialog box to identify the fields for the *Address* on your envelopes. See Figures 25-3 to 25-4 if you need help on identifying your database and its fields.

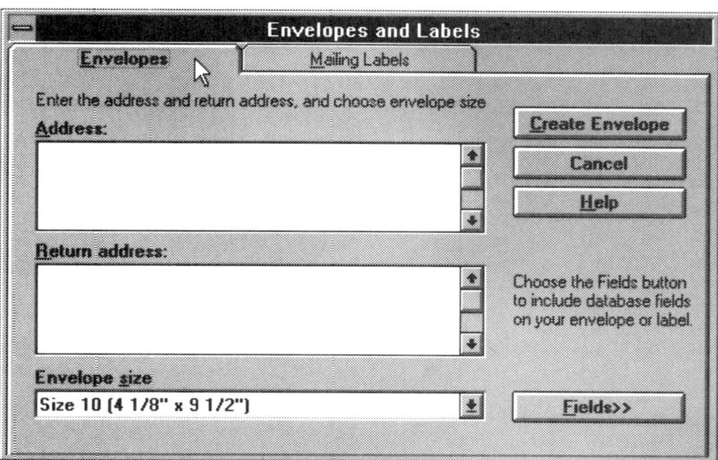

Figure 25-30. The Envelopes and Labels dialog box.

Once you complete the *Address* text box, you can type a *Return address* if your stationery is not preprinted. Works saves your address as the default for use on future envelopes.

Choose the size of your stationery from the *Envelope size* drop-down list box and click on *Create Envelope* as shown in Figure 25-31 to return to your document.

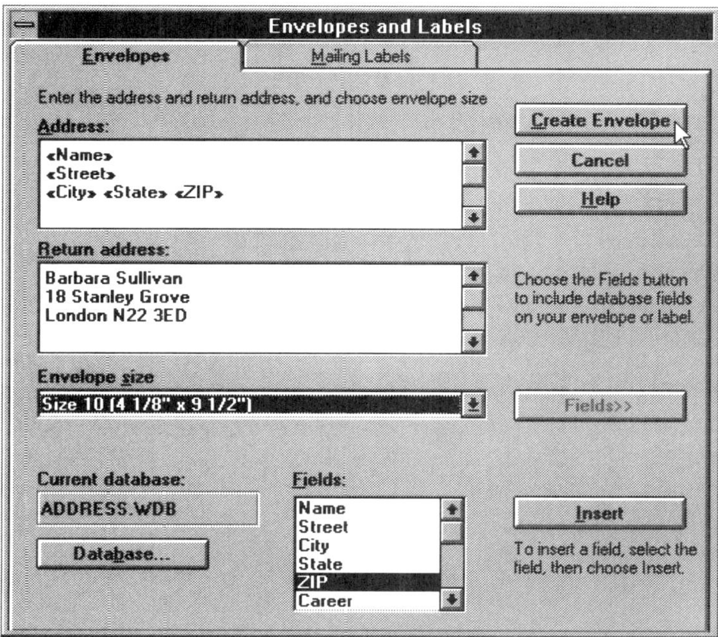

Figure 25-31. Complete the Envelopes and Labels dialog box and click on Create Envelope.

Works creates your envelope layout and follows it with a page break (Figure 25-32).

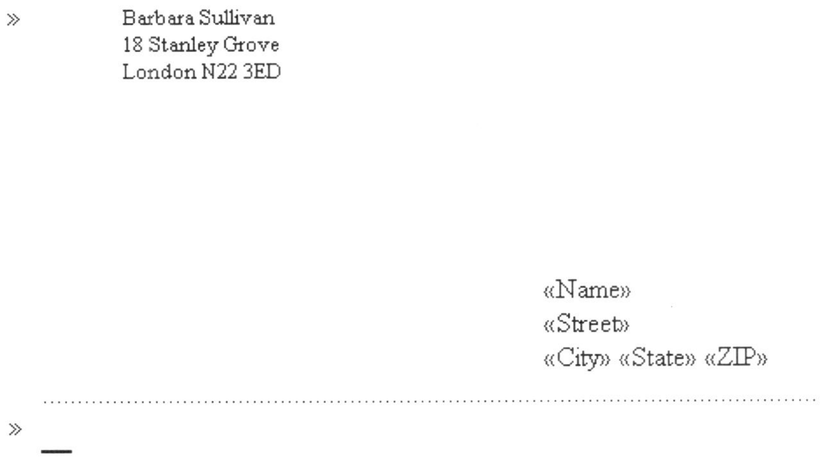

» Barbara Sullivan
18 Stanley Grove
London N22 3ED

«Name»
«Street»
«City» «State» «ZIP»

»

Figure 25-32. Works creates an envelope layout similar to this.

If your printer has an envelope feeder you can instruct Works to use the feeder when you print your envelopes. Choose *Options* from the **Tools** menu and select the *Printer's envelope feeder is installed* check box (Figure 25-33). Click on *OK* to return to your document.

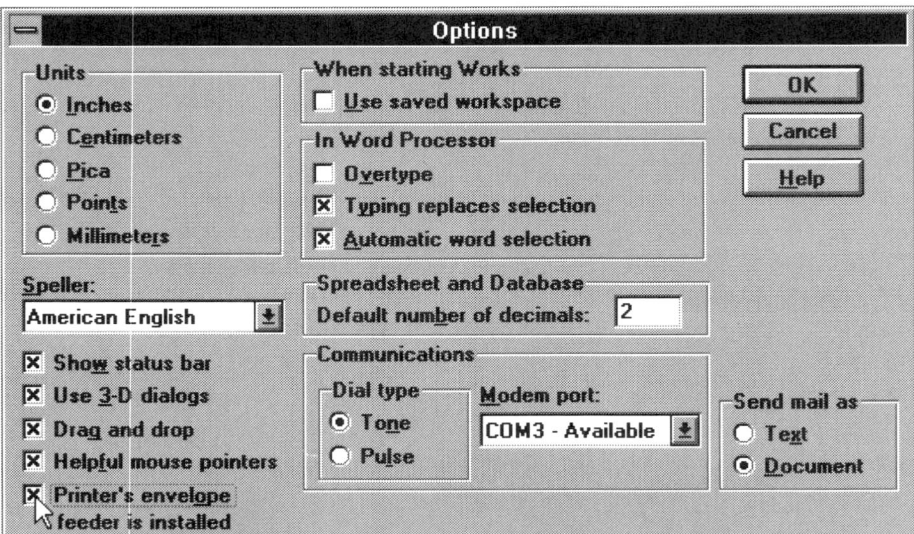

Figure 25-33. Choose the Printer's envelope feeder is installed check box in the Options dialog box.

To print your envelopes choose the *Print* command from the **File** menu. Ensure that the *Envelope* option is selected in the *What to print* section as it is in Figure 25-34. You can then choose *Preview* to view your envelope layout on the screen or click on *OK* to print your envelopes. Works uses the *Choose Database* dialog box as usual to identify your database when you choose either of these buttons.

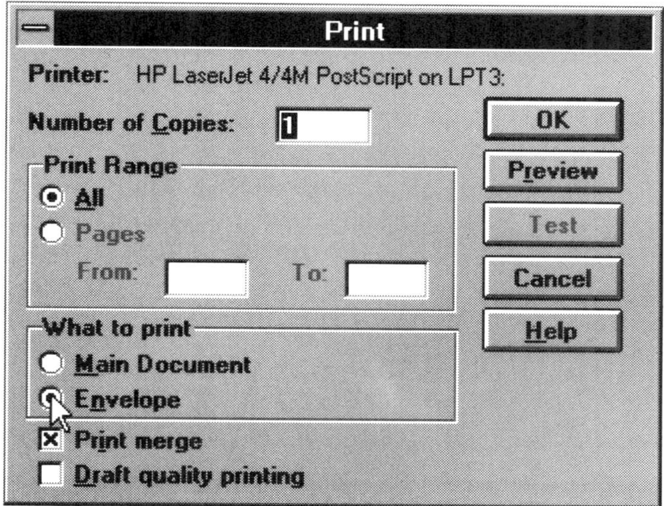

Figure 25-34. *Select the Envelope option in the Print dialog box if it is not already selected.*

Using WorksWizards and AutoStart Templates

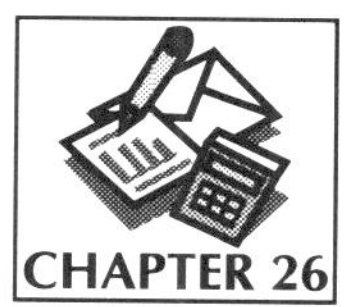

WorksWizards are like interactive helpers which can set up Works documents or organize your files for you. When you start a WorksWizard, Works asks you questions about the document you want to work with. The WorksWizard uses your answers to set up your document or organize your files for you.

AutoStart templates are like preformatted documents. You can use an AutoStart template as a basis for your own document, filling in details such as your address or the value of goods ordered in the spaces provided. Works provides an AutoStart template for many common documents like facsimile header sheets and financial statements.

WorksWizards and AutoStart templates are a standard part of Works and are loaded into your system at installation.

WorksWizards

Works provides twelve different WorksWizards. We use the *Address Book* WorksWizard as an example in this chapter, to familiarize you with WorksWizards.

You can start WorksWizards using the *Use A WorksWizard* button in the *Startup* dialog box. You can also choose the *WorksWizards* command from the **File** menu (Figure 26-1).

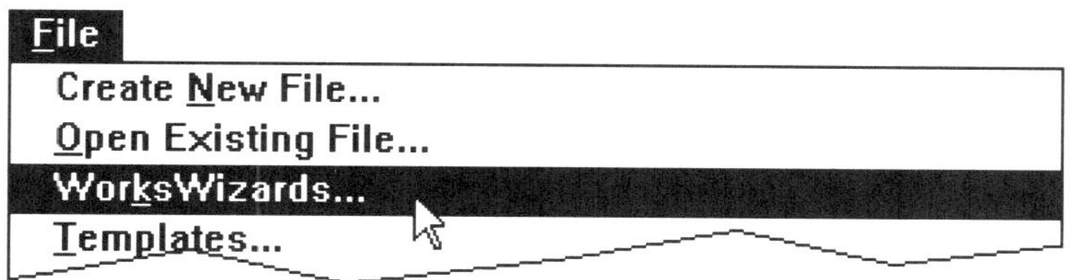

Figure 26-1. *Start WorksWizards from the Startup dialog box or the* ***File*** *menu.*

Figure 26-2 shows the *Startup* dialog box as it appears when you choose to start WorksWizards using either method.

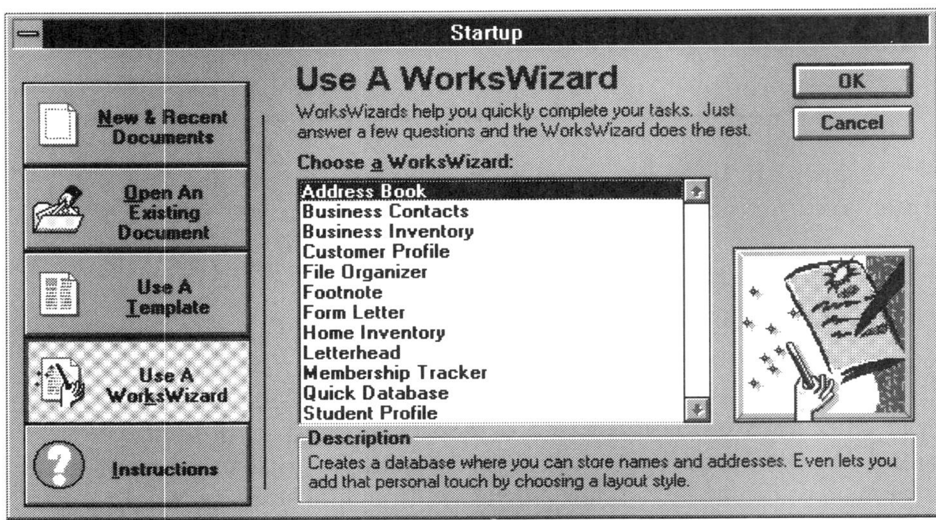

Figure 26-2. *You can choose which type of WorksWizard to use from this dialog box.*

The text in the *Description* box briefly explains about the WorksWizard selected in the *Choose a WorksWizard* list box. Currently the explanation is about the *Address Book* as that WorksWizard is selected. To view text for the other WorksWizards, click on the other options in the *Choose a WorksWizard* list box.

We will create an address book database as an example for you to follow in this chapter. To begin the *Address Book* WorksWizard make sure *Address Book* is selected in the *Startup* dialog box as in Figure 26-2 and click on *OK.*

Creating an address book

An address book is a database of names and addresses which you can use in form letters and mailing labels for example.

Works provides a number of screens which lead you through the creation of each of the WorksWizards. As you have chosen to design an *Address Book,* Works shows the welcome screen which Figure 26-3 illustrates.

There are four buttons which enable you to move through the WorksWizards screens. These are *Cancel, Begin, Back,* and *Next.*

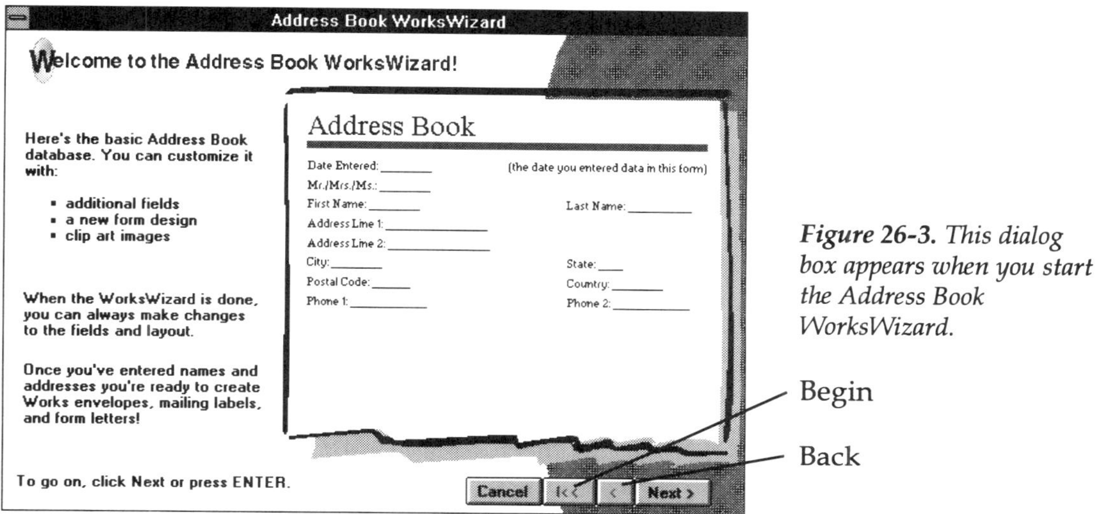

Figure 26-3. *This dialog box appears when you start the Address Book WorksWizard.*

The *Cancel* button lets you abandon your WorksWizard, while Begin returns you to the welcome screen for the WorksWizard you chose. At present, *Begin* is grayed as the screen you are viewing is the first. The *Back* button takes you to the previous screen of the WorksWizard. Again, Works has grayed this button. Finally, the *Next* button takes you to the next screen. Click on *Next* now.

The *Address Book* WorksWizard continues as shown in Figure 26-4. This screen lets you choose and preview additional fields to include in your address book. Any fields you choose are in addition to the standard selection that the WorksWizard provides.

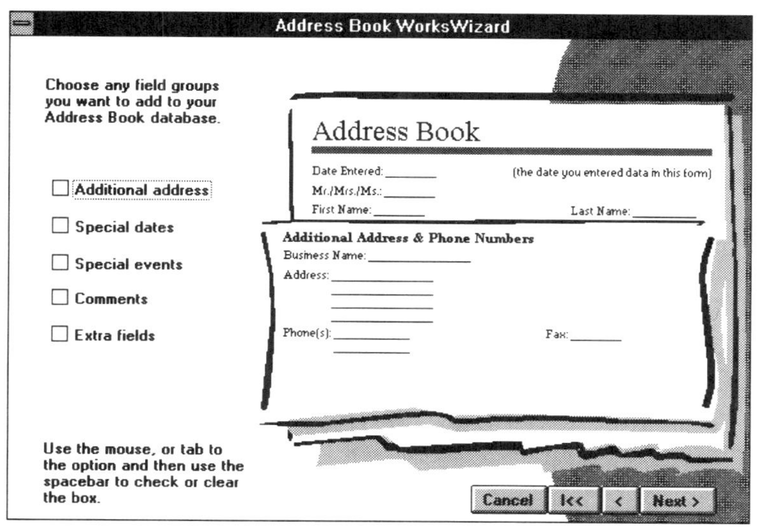

Figure 26-4. *You can choose additional fields using this screen.*

Click on *Next* to include only the standard fields in your address book.

Now Works asks what variety of address book you want to create, as you can see in Figure 26-5. Click on *Next* to accept the default of *Professional*.

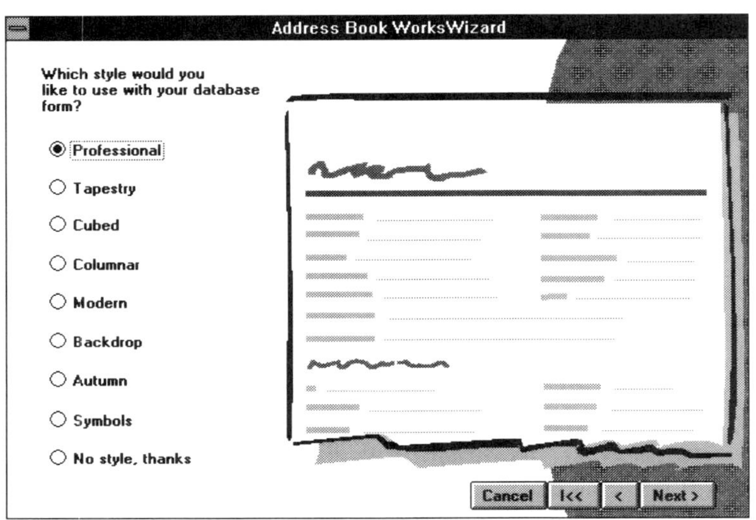

Figure 26-5. *Click on Next to accept a Professional style of address book.*

You can add clip art to your address book if you wish. Click on *No art, thanks* and then on *Next* to remove the suggested art (Figure 26-6).

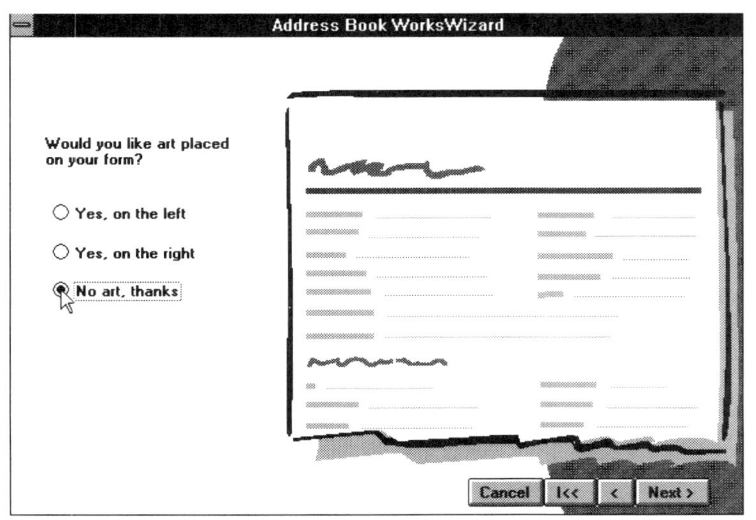

Figure 26-6. *Click on No art, thanks. Then click on Next to continue.*

The WorksWizard has now completed asking you for the specifications of your address book. Click on the *Create* button as shown in Figure 26-7 to have Works create your address book database structure.

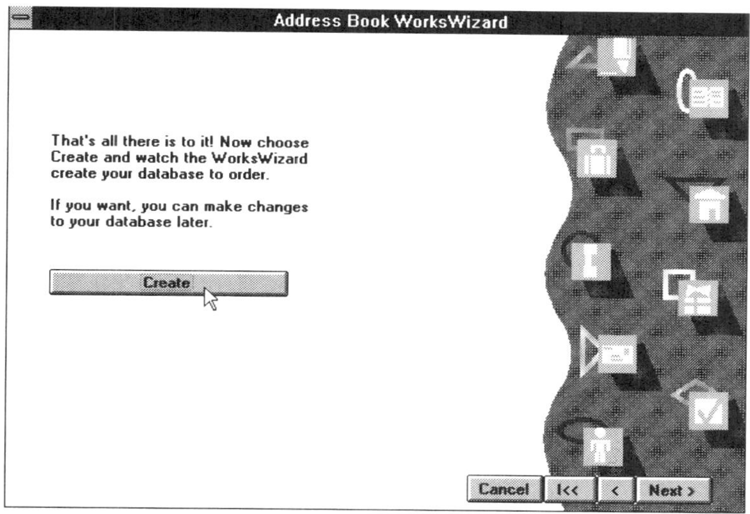

Figure 26-7. *Click on Create to confirm your WorksWizard options.*

Works now spends some time creating the database, inserting fields into Form view, which is similar to a form on a piece of paper. While creating your database fields, Works displays the dialog box shown in Figure 26-8.

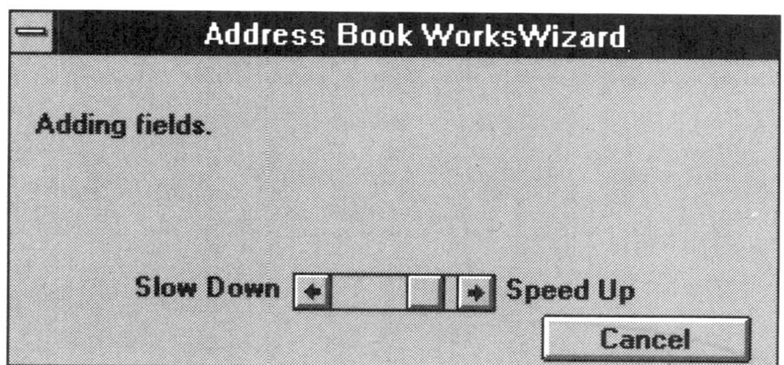

Figure 26-8. *Works displays this dialog box while creating your database.*

When it completes your database form Works displays the screen shown in Figure 26-9. Click on *OK* or press Enter to go to Form view in the Works database tool.

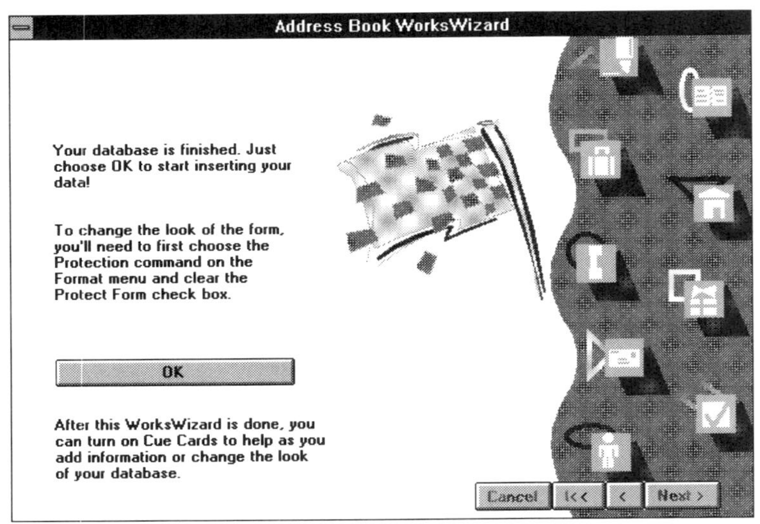

Figure 26-9. You see this WorksWizard screen when Works completes your database form.

You have now finished using the Database Designer WorksWizard. Your completed database form shown in Figure 26-10 is no different from any other Works database. You just simplified the form's creation by letting the WorksWizard issue the commands that you would choose to create this database yourself.

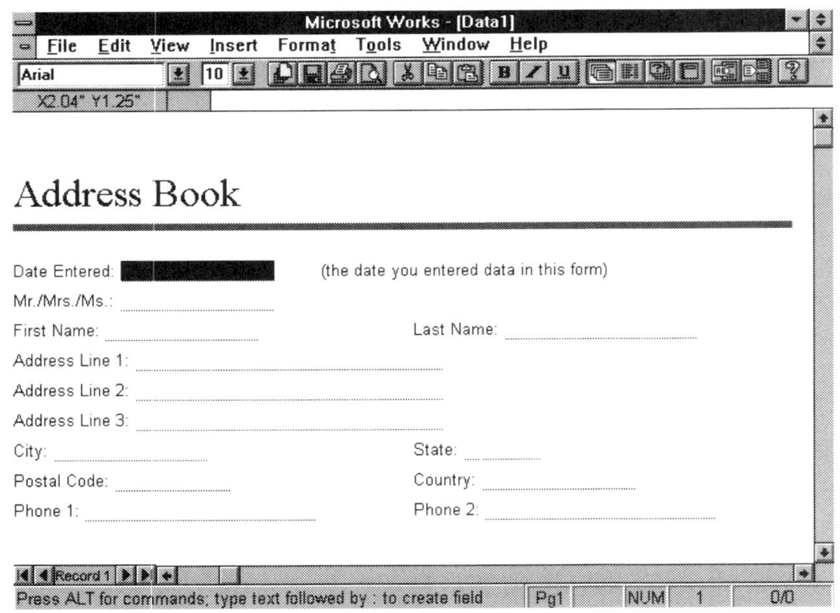

Figure 26-10. Your completed address book form looks like this.

Your address book at the moment has no data in it. You might like to save your file now as a ready-made address book form, as you would save any other Works database. Or you might choose to enter some address data, or abandon your form by closing it without saving. For more information on inserting data or saving your database, refer to **Chapter 15, Creating a Database**.

AutoStart templates

You can choose from many AutoStart templates provided by Works, giving you an outline for the document you want to create.

To create a document using an AutoStart template choose *Use A Template* from the *Startup* dialog box or *Templates* from the **File** menu (Figure 26-11).

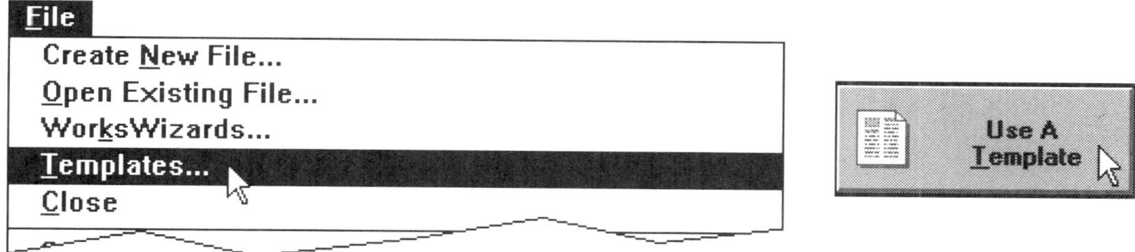

***Figure 26-11.** Start using a template from the Startup dialog box or the* **File** *menu.*

Whichever method you use displays the *Startup* dialog box as shown in Figure 26-12.

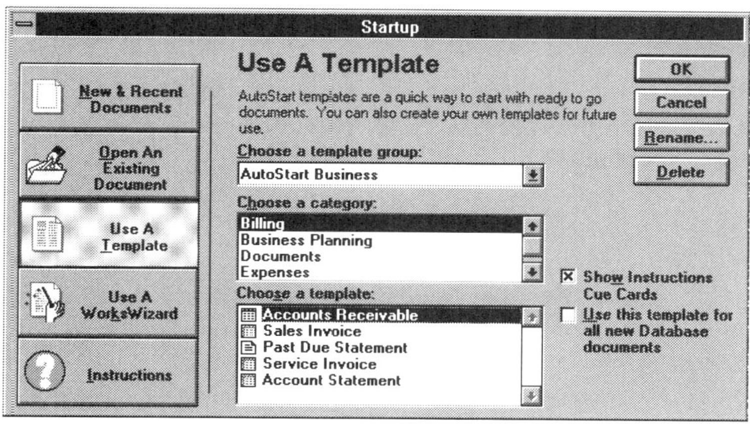

***Figure 26-12.** You can choose which type of AutoStart template to use from this dialog box.*

Because Works provides many AutoStart templates, the templates are organized into groups. Within the groups Works organizes the templates into categories. This makes it easier for you to find and choose the template appropriate to your needs. You can view the groups available by clicking on the arrow next to the *Choose a template group* drop-down list box.

Works shows in the *Choose a category* list box the categories in the group you choose. Similarly, Works displays in the *Choose a template* list box the templates for the current category. Figure 26-13 shows the templates in the *Billing* category of the *AutoStart Business* group.

As an example we use the *Sales Invoice* AutoStart template in this chapter. You can find this template in the *Billing* category of the *AutoStart Business* group. Click on *Sales Invoice* in the *Choose a template* list box as in Figure 26-13.

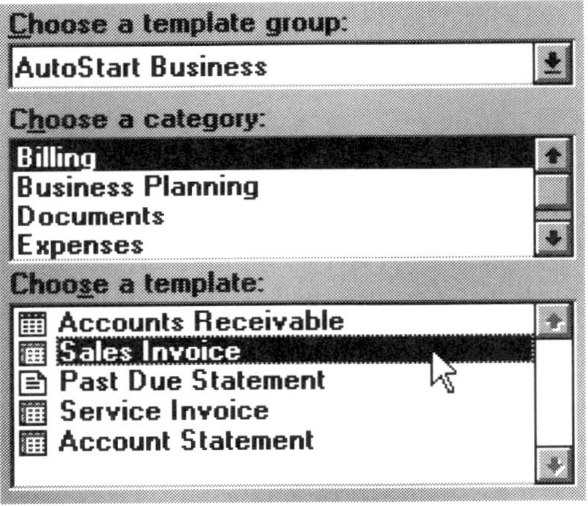

Figure 26-13. *Choose the Sales Invoice template from the Billing category of the AutoStart Business group.*

uses icons to represent the tool to which each AutoStart template corresponds, as shown in Figure 26-14. You can use templates for the database, spreadsheet and word processor tools.

Figure 26-14. *Works uses these icons to indicate the type of each template.*

AutoStart templates switch on cue cards by default. Recall from the Introduction in this book that cue cards are on-screen hints which remain visible as you work with your document. You can choose not to display cue cards by deselecting the *Show Instructions Cue Cards* check box shown in Figure 26-15 if you wish. Leave this check box selected for the moment to view the cue card specific to the template you choose.

You also have the chance to *Use this template for all new Spreadsheet documents* in Works. Selecting this check box causes Works to insert the contents of the template you have selected every time you create a new document using the spreadsheet tool. Works may call the check box *Use this template for all new Database documents* or *Use this template for all new Word Processor documents*, according to which tool corresponds to the template you choose. You may find this option useful if you usually use a particular Works tool to create only certain types of documents. Do not select this option just at the moment.

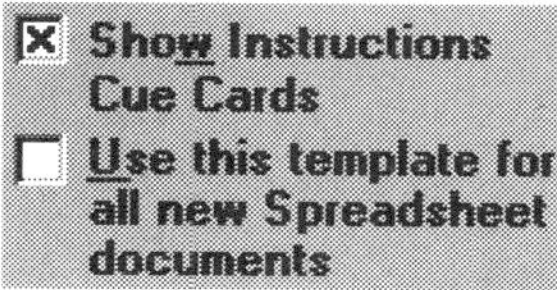

Figure 26-15. *You can choose whether to show instructions cue cards and whether to use this template for all new spreadsheet documents.*

Now that you have selected the *Sales Invoice* template and reviewed some of your options, click on *OK* to use the template to create a new spreadsheet document (Figure 26-16).

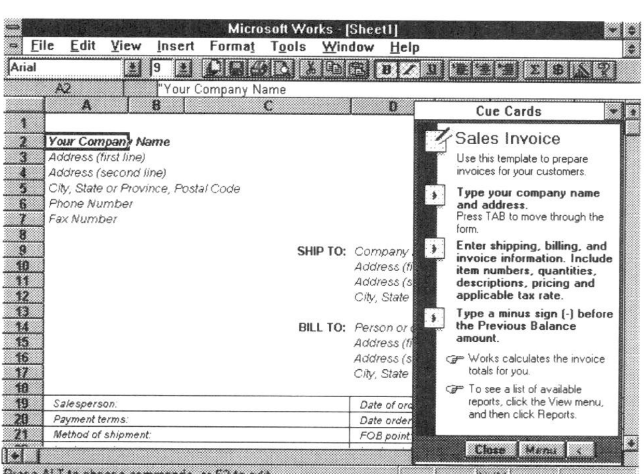

Figure 26-16. *Your screen looks similar to this when you click on OK to use the template.*

You can follow the instructions on the cue card to create an invoice in your new document. You fill in your company name, address, and all the other details for this particular invoice. Press the Tab key on your keyboard to move forward from one field to the next in your invoice. You can also press Shift-Tab to move backwards or use the mouse or arrow keys to move around as you would in any Works spreadsheet.

To switch off cue cards so that you can see more of your document, deselect *Cue Cards* in the **Help** menu as Figure 26-17 shows.

Figure 26-17. *Deselect cue cards in the* ***Help*** *menu.*

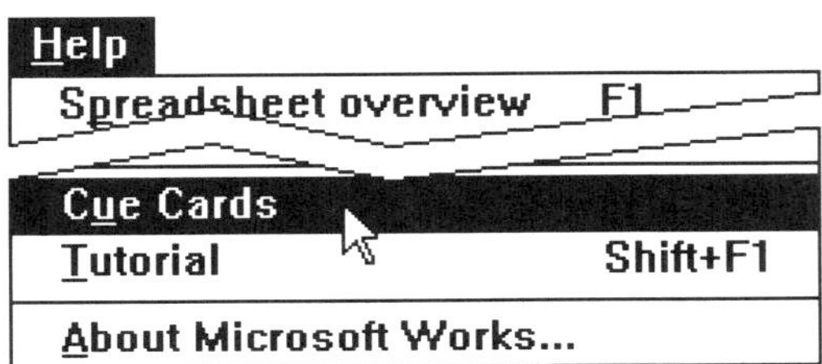

Figure 26-17. *Deselect cue cards in the Help menu.*

like to use *Print Preview* to view the entire invoice. Figure 26-18 shows what your screen looks like after you choose *Print Preview* from the **File** menu. Click on *Cancel* when you have finished using *Print Preview.*

Figure 26-18. *Choose Print Preview from the* ***File*** *menu to view the whole invoice.*

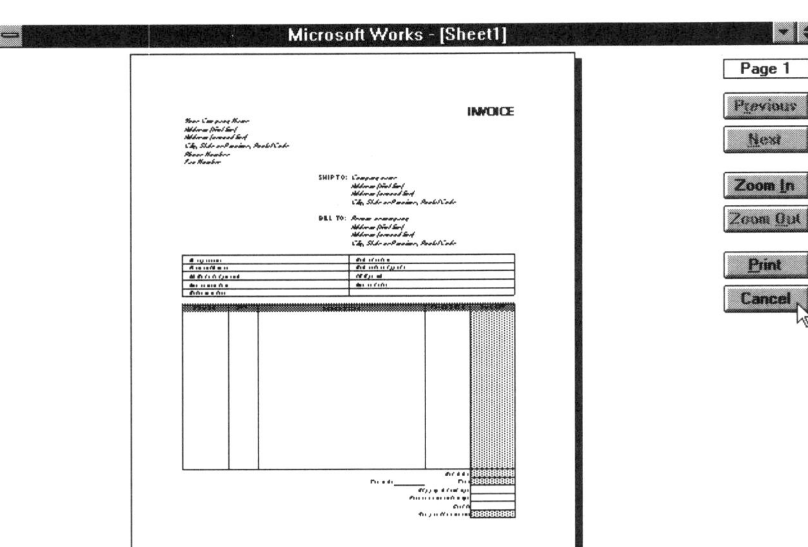

Figure 26-18. *Choose Print Preview from the File menu to view the whole invoice.*

save your invoice in the same way as you do with any spreadsheet in Works. For information on saving or printing your work see **Chapter 9, Entering Spreadsheet Data** and **Chapter 12, Formatting and Printing Spreadsheets**.

Exercise Section

Creating Documents — Exercise

In this exercise you will practise adding text, bookmarks, and using the *Go To* command.

People of all levels of expertise in Works can benefit from this exercise. If you like a challenge, complete the exercise using the Steps in Brief, listed below. This lists the exercise outline, with no hints.

If you need more assistance, refer to the Steps in Detail on the following pages. The Steps in Detail expand each step, listing details and hints that enable you to complete the exercise.

Steps in Brief

1. ***Open a new file in Works.***
2. ***Type in the following text:***

The audience
It is important to know what your readers are like, and what their needs and objectives are. Some planning and research is needed in the early phase, irrespective of whether you are creating a newsletter, brochure, or an advertisement.
Creating the wrong type of document for your intended market is very much a total waste of time.

---

3. ***Move to the word "audience" and insert "target" in front of it.***
4. ***Using Overtype mode, change the word "phase" to "stage." Turn Overtype off.***
5. ***Move to "planning" and insert a Bookmark.***
6. ***Return to the beginning of the document and use Go To to move to the "preparation" bookmark.***
7. ***Delete the word "important" then undo the last command.***
8. ***Save the file as audience.wps.***

Steps in Detail

1. *Open a new file in Works.*

Open Works by double-clicking on the Works Icon in the Program Manager (Figure 2x-1). Click on the *Word Processor* button in the *Startup* dialog box (Figure 2x-2). Your screen will now look like the one in Figure 2x-3. Maximize the document window by clicking on its maximize button.

Figure 2x-1. *Click on the Works icon in the Program Manager Window.*

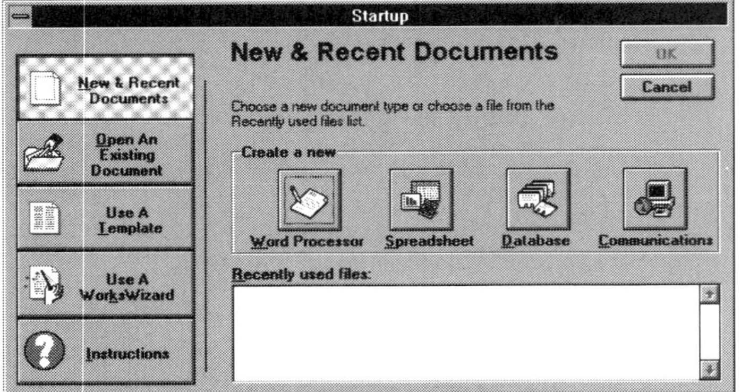

Figure 2x-2. *Click on the Word Processor button.*

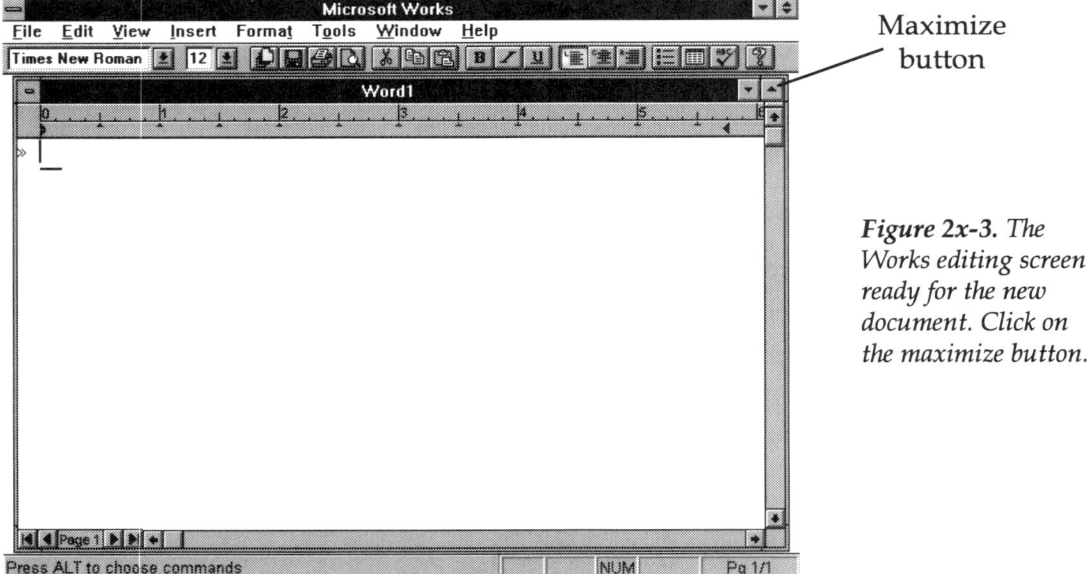

Figure 2x-3. *The Works editing screen ready for the new document. Click on the maximize button.*

2. *Type in the following text:*

The audience
It is important to know what your readers are like, and what their needs and objectives are. Some planning and research is needed in the early phase, irrespective of whether you are creating a newsletter, brochure, or an advertisement.
Creating the wrong type of document for your intended market is very much a total waste of time.

When you open a new document in Works, the insertion point will be positioned at the top left of the screen. All you do is start typing. The last character you type will appear to the left of the flashing cursor.

Note: *Use the Enter key to start a new paragraph only, as Works word-wraps automatically.*

Figure 2x-4 shows the screen after you have typed in the text. The exact position of the line breaks may be slightly different. If the words continue off the screen, then select the *Wrap For Window* command from the **Options** menu (**Chapter 1, The Word Processor Screen**).

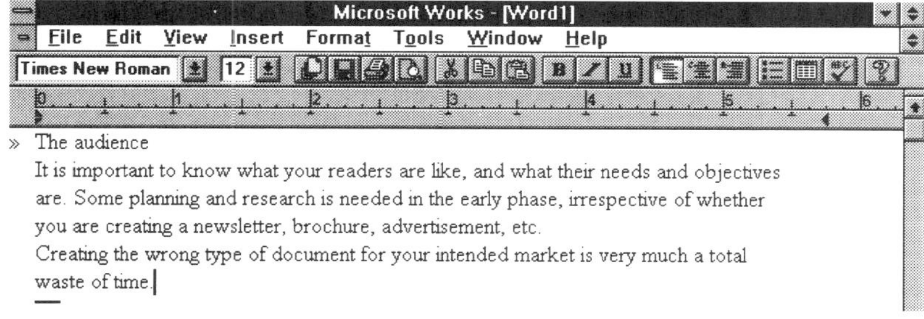

Figure 2x-4. *Start typing the text straight into Works. Don't worry too much about accuracy at this stage as you can easily edit the document with the Backspace and Delete keys.*

3. *Move to the word "audience" and insert "target" in front of it.*

Works, by default, will be in Insert mode. Moving the insertion point to the front of the word "audience" and typing in "target," will force the text to be pushed along the line. See Figures 2x-5 and 2x-6.

The audience
It is important to know v

Figure 2x-5. *Press Ctrl-Home to move to the beginning of the document, then Ctrl-Right arrow to move to the beginning of "audience."*

The target audience
It is important to know v
are. Some planning and

Figure 2x-6. *Type in the word "target" followed by a space which will be inserted into the first line. Your heading will now read "The target audience."*

4. *Using Overtype mode, change the word "phase" to "stage." Turn Overtype off.*

Press the Insert key to activate Overtype mode (see Figure 2x-7). Perform the additional steps as indicated in Figures 2x-8 and 2x-9. Be sure to turn *Overtype* off by pressing Insert when you have completed the steps.

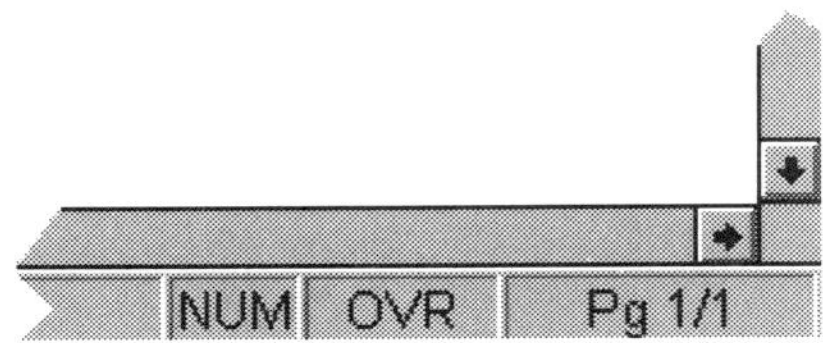

Figure 2x-7. *Check the status bar to see that Overtype was activated when you pressed the Insert key.*

our readers are like, and what their needs and objectives
ch is needed in the early phase, irrespective of whether
brochure, advertisement, etc.
cument for your intended market is very much a total

Figure 2x-8. *Click the mouse pointer at the beginning of the word "phase."*

our readers are like, and what their needs and objectives
ch is needed in the early stage, irrespective of whether
brochure, advertisement, etc.
cument for your intended market is very much a total

Figure 2x-9. *Type the word "stage" over "phase." The text, in Overtype mode, replaces the existing text to the right of the insertion point.*

5. *Move to "planning" and insert a bookmark.*

A bookmark is used to locate specific places in your document using the *Go To* command. You will create a bookmark to the reference made to the preparation required for your document. Follow the steps outlined with Figures 2x-10 through 2x-12.

The target audience
It is important to know
are. Some planning anc
are creating a newslette
Creating the wrong typ
waste of time.

Figure 2x-10. *Move your insertion point to the word "planning."*

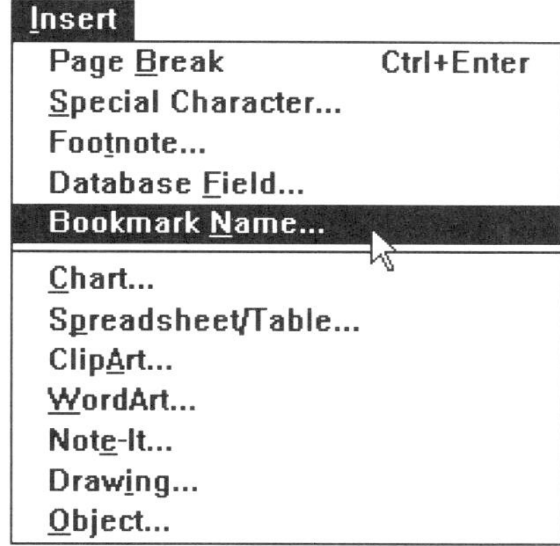

Figure 2x-11. *Select Bookmark Name from the* ***Insert*** *menu.*

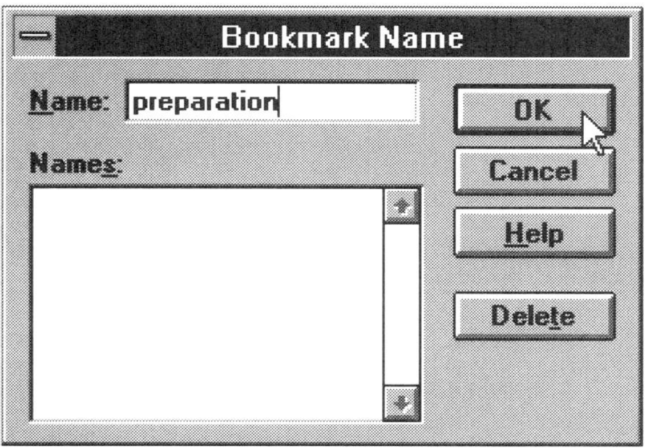

Figure 2x-12. *Type in "preparation" as the name of your bookmark. The insertion point will be in the Name text box, so you can simply type in "preparation." Click on OK.*

6. Return to the beginning of the document and use Go To to move to the "preparation" bookmark.

You can now test the bookmark (see Figure 2x-13). So that the insertion point actually moves to the required spot, return to the beginning of the document by pressing Ctrl-Home. Remember that you can also use *Go To* to move to a particular page.

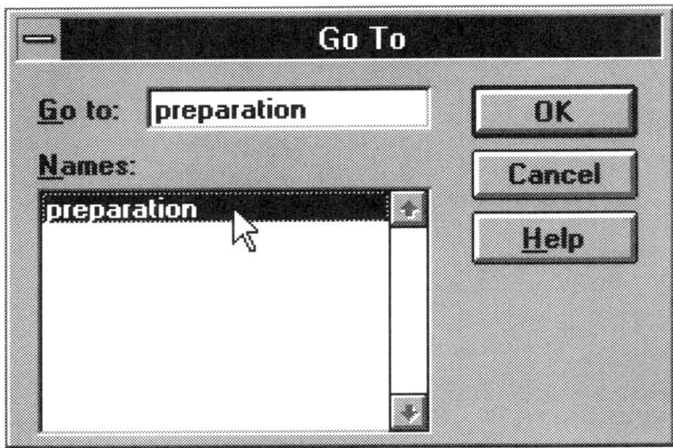

Figure 2x-13. *Access the Go To dialog box by pressing F5. Click the mouse pointer on the word "preparation" in the list box. Click on OK and the text pointer will move to the Bookmark – preparation.*

7. Delete the word "important" then undo the last command.

Move to the word "important" and delete it using the Delete key (see Figure 2x-14). Refer to Figure 2x-15 for additional steps.

The target audience
It is to know what your
planning and research i
creating a newsletter, b
Creating the wrong typ
waste of time.

Figure 2x-14. *The word "important" is deleted by moving to the beginning of this word and pressing the Delete key the required number of times.*

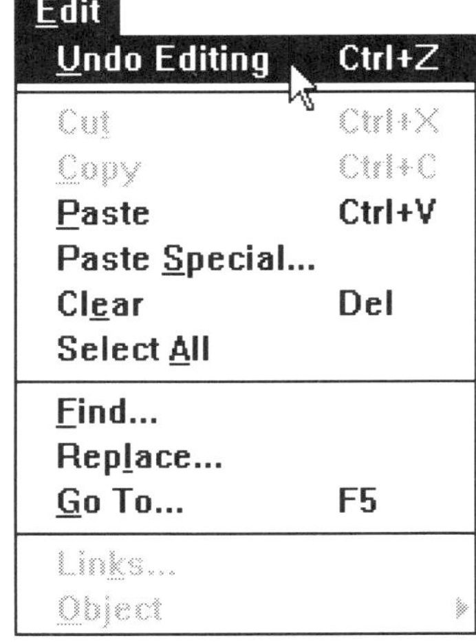

Figure 2x-15. *Choose Undo from the* **Edit** *menu and "important" appears on the screen again.*

8. Save the file as audience.wps.

Select the *Save* command from the **File** menu. As the file has not yet been saved, the *Save As* dialog box is activated. Type in the name of the file "audience" in the *File Name* text box and click on *OK*. For this exercise, the file is saved in the ***msworks*** subdirectory which is indicated by the open file in the *Directories* list box. You may save it in the directory you choose.

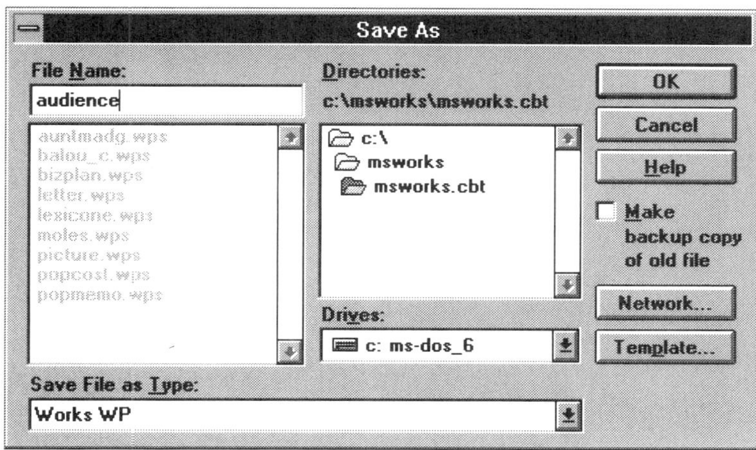

Figure 2x-16. *To save this document, select Save from the **File** menu to activate the Save As dialog box. In this dialog box, type in the name of the file, in this case "audience" (Works will automatically put on the extension) and select OK.*

Editing Documents — Exercise

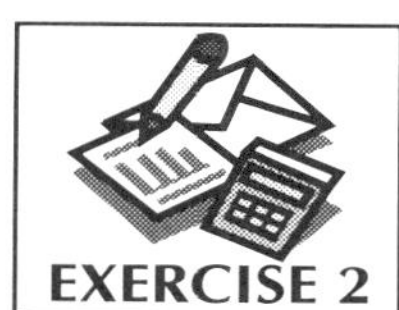

In this exercise you will practise using editing commands such as those to change the typeface, style, set tabs and indents, as well as copying and pasting.

People of all levels of expertise in Works can benefit from this exercise. If you like a challenge, complete the exercise using the Steps in Brief, listed below. This lists the exercise outline, with no hints.

If you need more assistance, refer to the Steps in Detail on the following pages. The Steps in Detail expand each step, listing details and hints that enable you to complete the exercise.

Steps in Brief

1. *Open the balou_c.wps file in the msworks.cbt subdirectory (within the msworks directory).*
2. *Use the Options dialog box to ensure that the "Typing replaces selection" option is enabled.*
3. *Highlight "July 10" and type "August 10" in its place.*
4. *Center the address at the top of the letter.*
5. *Change the font of the address to 16 point Helvetica.*
6. *Apply bold to "Sigmund Drafting Machine."*
7. *Indent to 1 in (2.5 cm) the first lines of the paragraphs beginning "BALOU has finally..." and "We will also...".*
8. *Set a decimal tab at 3 in (7.5 cm) for the prices in the last two paragraphs.*
9. *Type "Regards" at the bottom of the letter.*
10. *Copy "Art" from the first line and paste it under "Regards" on the last line.*
11. *Change the font of the word "Art," which was just pasted at the bottom of the document, to Script.*

Steps in Detail

1. ***Open the balou_c.wps file in the msworks.cbt subdirectory (within the msworks directory).***

Close any open files so you can follow Figures 3x-1 and 3x-2 to open the file ***balou_c.wps***. Depending on how your computer is setup, your ***msworks.cbt*** subdirectory may not be in exactly the same place as shown in Figure 3x-2.

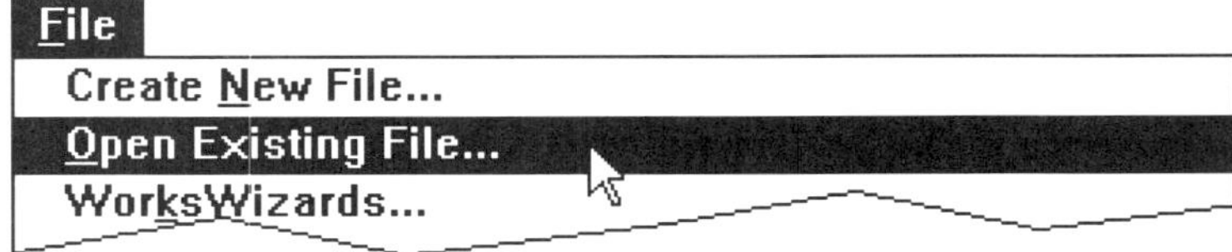

Figure 3x-1. *Select Open Existing File from the **File** menu to activate the Open dialog box.*

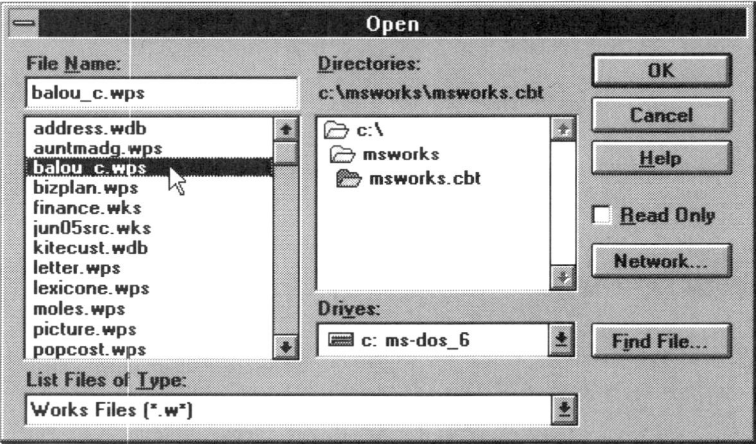

Figure 3x-2. *In this dialog box, find the file **balou_c.wps** from the **msworks.cbt** subdirectory, which is a subdirectory of **msworks**. Highlight the file name with the mouse and click on OK. Click on OK again if you receive the message "Cannot change: file is read-only."*

2. ***Use the Options dialog box to ensure that the "Typing replaces selection" option is enabled.***

When *Typing replaces selection* in the *Options* dialog box is active, you can highlight text to be replaced, start typing, and the new text will automatically replace the highlighted text. See Figures 3x-3 and Figure 3x-4 to see how to check this option.

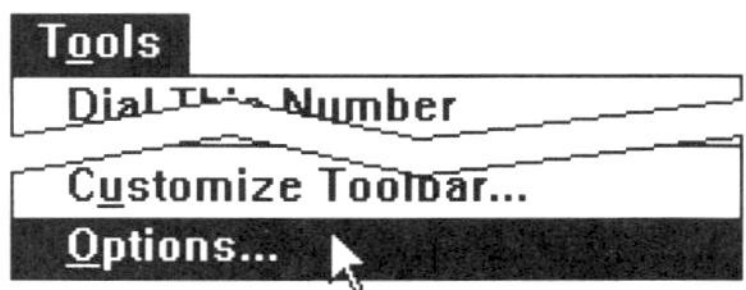

Figure 3x-3. *Choose Options from the **Tools** menu.*

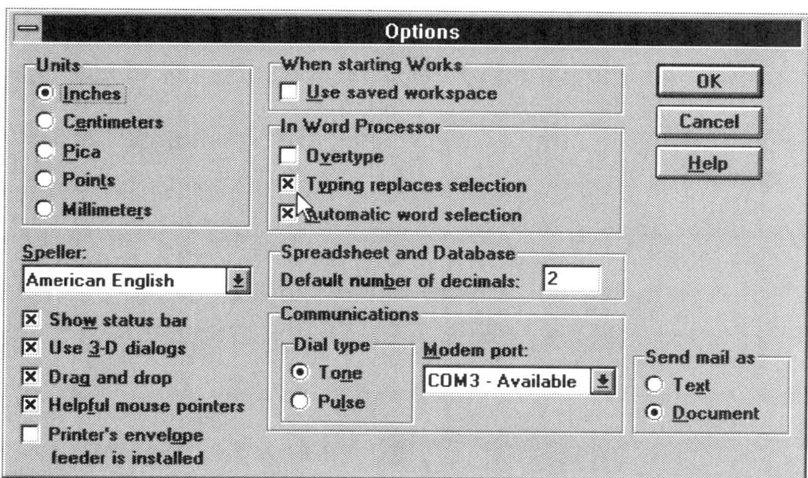

Figure 3x-4. *Ensure the Typing replaces selection check box has a cross in it in the Options dialog box.*

3. Highlight "July 10" and type "August 10" in its place.

With *Typing replaces selection* active, you can select "July 10" and replace it with "August 10" in one action.

Drag to highlight this text. Click so the insertion point is positioned just before the word "July." Hold down the left mouse button, move the insertion point to the right until both words are highlighted, and then release the mouse button (Figure 3x-5).

Machine with a 003X digital head. The following prices will be available to members until July 10, 1994:

Figure 3x-5. *Highlight the text by dragging with the mouse.*

Now that the text has been highlighted, all you need do is replace it by typing "August 10." Figure 3x-6 shows the result.

Machine with a 003X digital head. The following prices will be available to members until August 10, 1994:

Figure 3x-6. *This is how the text should look after "August 10" has been inserted.*

4. Center the address at the top of the letter.

To center more than one paragraph at once in Works, all of the paragraphs need to be highlighted before applying center align format. One way of highlighting a larger block of text is to use the "shift-click" method.

To highlight the address in this way, move to the beginning of the document—Ctrl-Home—hold down the Shift key, and click at the end of the address on the third line. Your screen should look like the one in Figure 3x-7. To center the address, see Figure 3x-8.

Art's Architectural Drawing Supplies
2358 W. 54th St.
North Haven, NH 34582

Figure 3x-7. *Highlight the address using the "shift-click" method of highlighting.*

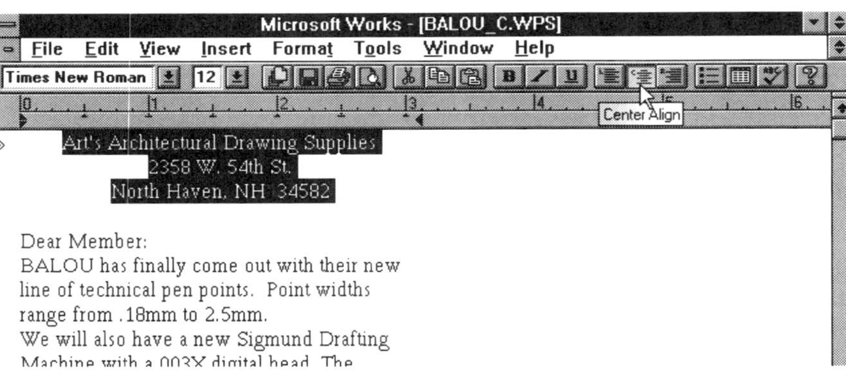

Figure 3x-8. *The easiest way to center text is to click on the Center Align button on the toolbar. You will notice that the text remains highlighted, which is useful when adding a number of formats to one piece of text. Keep it highlighted for the next part of the exercise.*

5. Change the font of the address to 16 point Helvetica.

As the text is still highlighted after applying centering, all you need do is select the different font from the *Font* submenu and a larger font size from the *Font Size* submenu on the toolbar. See Figure 3x-9 and 3x-10 for more details.

Figure 3x-9. *Open the Font submenu by clicking on the down arrow just to its right. Click on Helvetica from the list box. If you cannot see it, use the scroll bars to move through the list until it can be seen.*

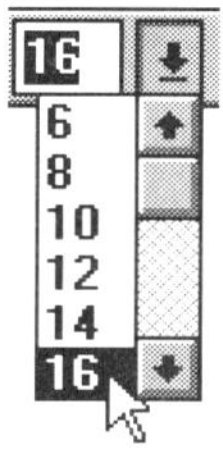

Figure 3x-10. *Open the Font Size submenu by clicking on the down arrow just to its right. If you can see 16 point, click on it now, otherwise you may need to scroll through the list box to find it.*

6. *Apply bold to "Sigmund Drafting Machine."*

Highlight "Sigmund Drafting Machine" in the second paragraph of the letter. To make it bold, just click on the *Bold* button on the toolbar as depicted in Figure 3x-11.

Figure 3x-11. *Click on the Bold button on the toolbar after "Sigmund Drafting Machine" has been selected to apply bold to the text.*

7. *Indent to 1 in (2.5 cm) the first lines of the paragraphs beginning "BALOU has finally..." and "We will also...".*

As you will be applying this format to the two main paragraphs, it is best to highlight them first and then apply the indent on the first line. Follow Figures 3x-12 through 3x-14 to achieve this.

Dear Member:

BALOU has finally come out with their new line of technical pen points. Point widths range from .18mm to 2.5mm.

We will also have a new **Sigmund Drafting Machine** with a 003X digital head. The following prices will be available to members until August 10, 1994:

Figure 3x-12. *Highlight the two paragraphs by dragging with the mouse.*

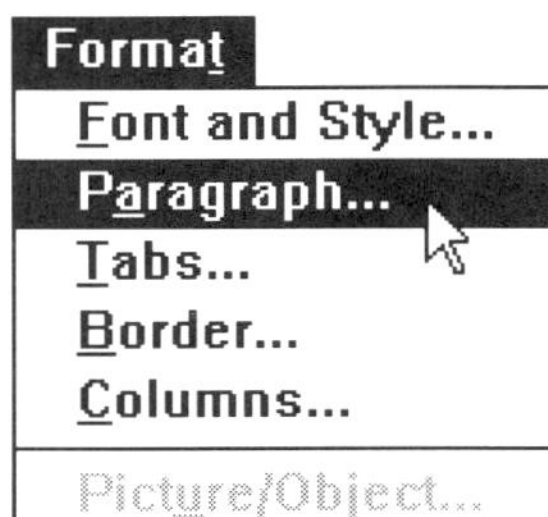

Figure 3x-13. *Choose the Paragraph command from the **Format** menu.*

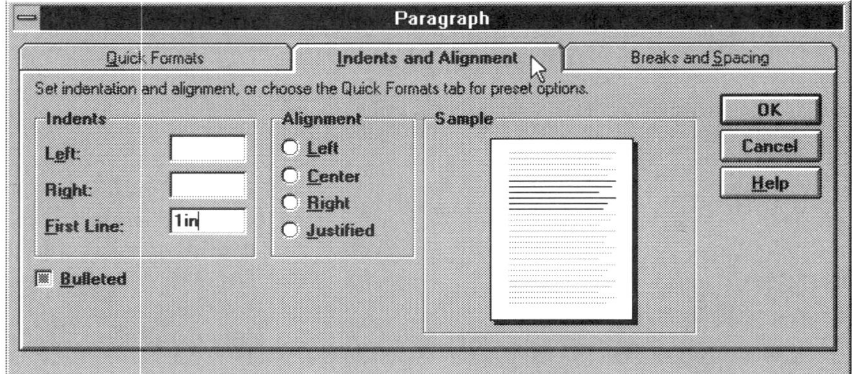

Figure 3x-14. *Click on the Indents and Alignment tab and type "1in" or "2.5cm" in the First Line text box. Click on OK to complete this step.*

8. ***Set a decimal tab at 3 in (7.5 cm) for the prices in the last two paragraphs.***

Once again, as you will be applying this paragraph format to two paragraphs, it is best to highlight them first (Figure 3x-15) and then apply the format.

Technical Pen Point $21.50
Sigmund Drafting Machine #340D $463.00

Figure 3x-15. *Highlight the two paragraphs using a highlighting technique of your choice.*

To insert a decimal tab, you need to access the *Tabs* dialog box either by double-clicking on the measuring scale of the ruler, or by choosing *Tabs* in the **Format** menu which is shown in Figure 3x-16. Figures 3x-17 through 3x-19 show how to add the decimal tab.

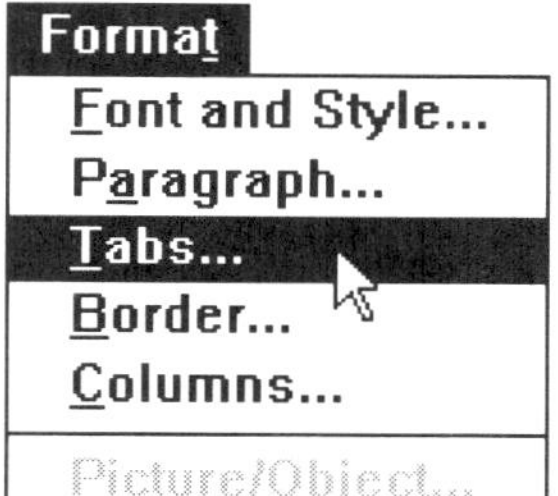

Figure 3x-16. *Choose Tabs from the* ***Format*** *menu to open the Tabs dialog box.*

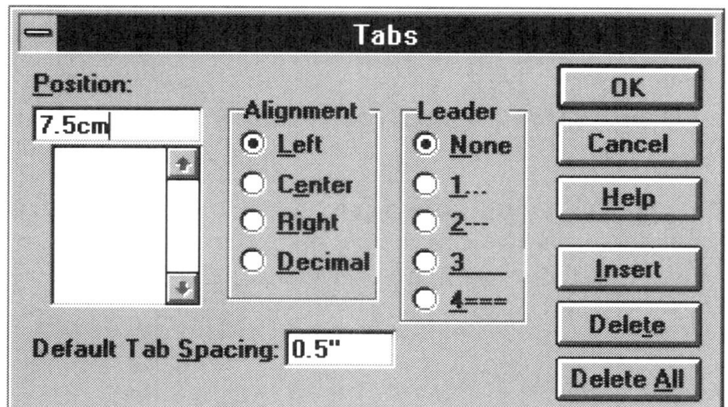

Figure 3x-17. *The insertion point will be flashing in the Position text box ready for you to insert the tab mark position. At this point type in "3in" or "7.5cm."*

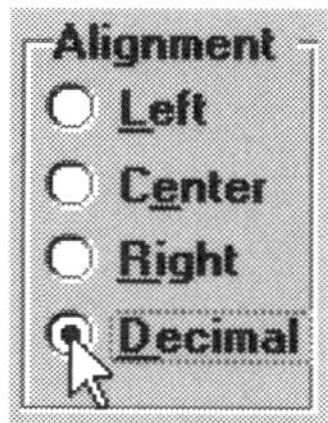

Figure 3x-18. *You are now ready to specify the type of tab you want in this position – decimal. Click on the Decimal option.*

Technical Pen Point $21.50
Sigmund Drafting Machine #340D $463.00

Figure 3x-19. Now click on OK to return to your document which should look like this. The figures went to the 3 inch mark automatically because the Tab key had been pressed before, but as no custom tabs had been set, they were sitting at the default tab marks.

9. Type "Regards" at the bottom of the letter.

To personalize the letter, you are going to close it "Regards Art." The first step is to move to the bottom of the document by pressing Ctrl-End and type in "Regards" as shown in Figure 3x-20. Make sure to press Enter after this to create a new line onto which you will put "Art."

Technical Pen Point $21.50
Sigmund Drafting Machine #340D $463.00

Regards

Figure 3x-20. Move to the bottom of the document by pressing Ctrl-End and type in "Regards."

10. Copy "Art" from the first line and paste it under "Regards" on the last line.

You do not need to type in "Art" again as it already exists in the document. Because of this you can copy it from the first line down to where it is required. Follow Figures 3x-21 through 3x-24 for instructions on how to copy and paste.

Art's Architectural Drawing
Supplies

Figure 3x-21. Highlight "Art" on the first line (only drag over the first three letters of "Art's").

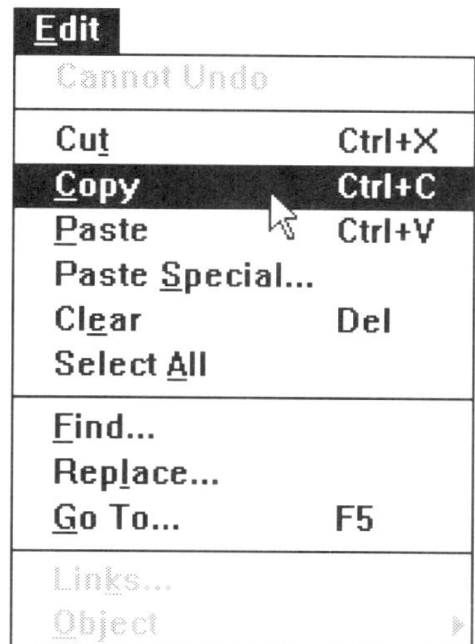

Figure 3x-22. Choose Copy from the **Edit** menu.

Technical Pen Point $21.50
Sigmund Drafting Machine #340D $463.00

Regards

Figure 3x-23. Move the insertion point to the end of the document by pressing Ctrl-End.

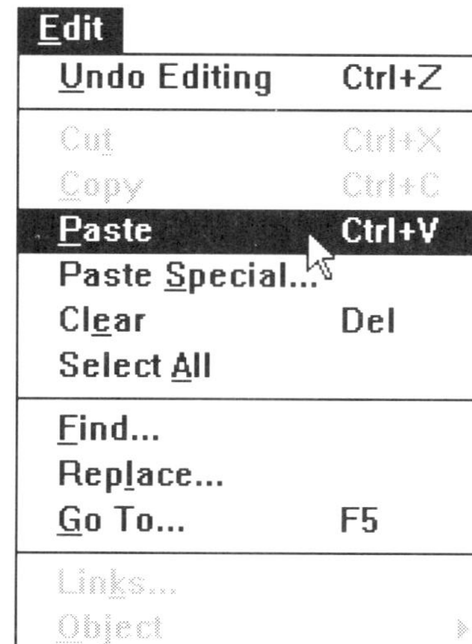

Figure 3x-24. Choose Paste from the **Edit** menu.

11. ***Change the font of the word "Art," which was just pasted at the bottom of the document, to Script.***

Highlight "Art" by dragging with the mouse, then follow Figures 3x-25 and 3x-26.

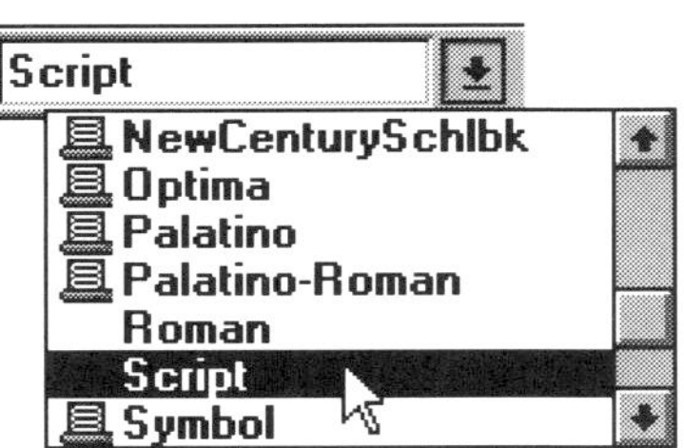

Figure 3x-25. *Open the Font submenu by clicking on the down arrow just to its right. Click on Script from the list box. If you cannot see it, use the scroll bars to move through the list until it can be seen.*

Technical Pen Point	$21.50
Sigmund Drafting Machine #340D	$463.00

Regards

Art

Figure 3x-26. *The end of your completed document should look like this.*

Advanced Document Editing — Exercise

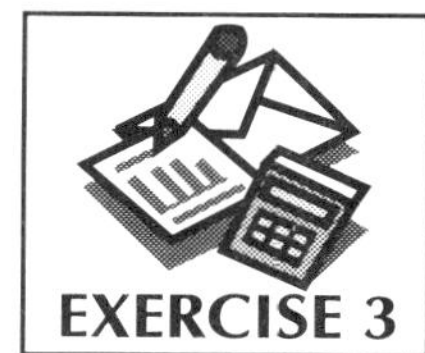

In this exercise you will practise editing page formatting, using commands to set margins; add a title, header, and footer; then search for and replace words.

People of all levels of expertise in Works can benefit from this exercise. If you like a challenge, complete the exercise using the Steps in Brief, listed below. This lists the exercise outline, with no hints.

If you need more assistance, refer to the Steps in Detail on the following pages. The Steps in Detail expand each step, listing details and hints that enable you to complete the exercise.

Steps in Brief

1. *Open the file bizplan.wps from the msworks.cbt subdirectory.*
2. *Insert a page break at the top of the document.*
3. *Move onto page one, type in the title "Business Plan for the Go Fly a Kite Company" and press Enter.*
4. *In the paragraph created in Step 3 only, increase the left and right margins by 2 in (5 cm) each.*
5. *Change the left margin for the document as a whole to 2 in (5 cm).*
6. *Put a double outline border around the title.*
7. *Insert a one-line header "Go Fly a Kite" and a one-line footer showing the page number. Ensure that these will not be seen on the title page.*
8. *Use the Replace command to replace "noiseless" with "silent" in your document.*

Steps in Detail

1. ***Open the file bizplan.wps from the msworks.cbt subdirectory.***

Close any files which may be open already by clicking on *Close* in the **File** menu. To open ***bizplan.wps***, follow the steps outlined in Figures 4x-1 and 4x-2. The exact location of ***bizplan.wps*** may vary, depending on how your machine has been set up.

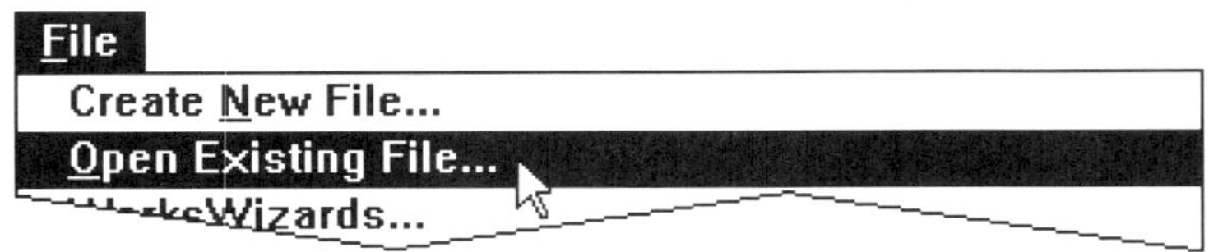

Figure 4x-1. *Select Open Existing File from the* ***File*** *menu.*

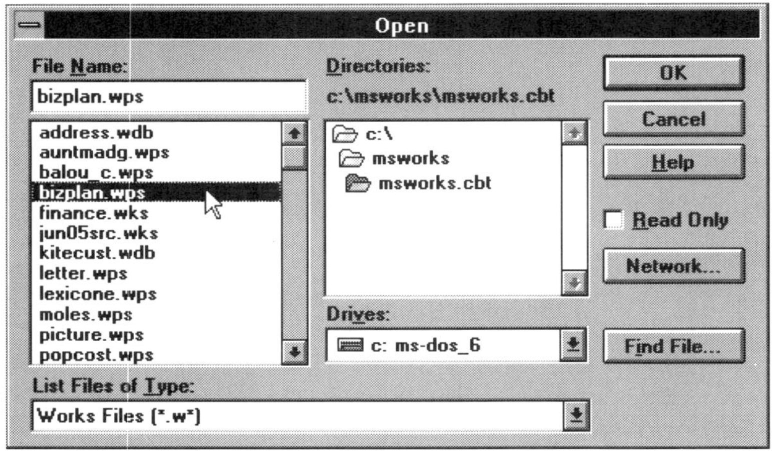

Figure 4x-2. *Move to the* ***msworks.cbt*** *subdirectory and double-click on the file* ***bizplan.wps*** *to open the file.*

2. ***Insert a page break at the top of the document.***

A page break is inserted into a document to the left of the insertion point. As you need to insert a page break at the very top of the document, move your insertion point in front of the first word as in Figure 4x-3.

Figure 4x-3. *Move the insertion point to the very top of the document to insert the page break in the correct position.*

There are two ways to insert a page break—through the menu or by using the keyboard shortcut. To use the menu, see Figure 4x-4. The keyboard shortcut for a page break is to press Ctrl-Enter simultaneously.

Figure 4x-4. *Select Page Break from the* ***Insert*** *menu to insert a page break using the menu.*

Works inserts a new beginning-of-page marker and a single broken line to indicate the new page break. Notice also in Figure 4x-5, that the page indicator on the status bar changes to allow for the new page.

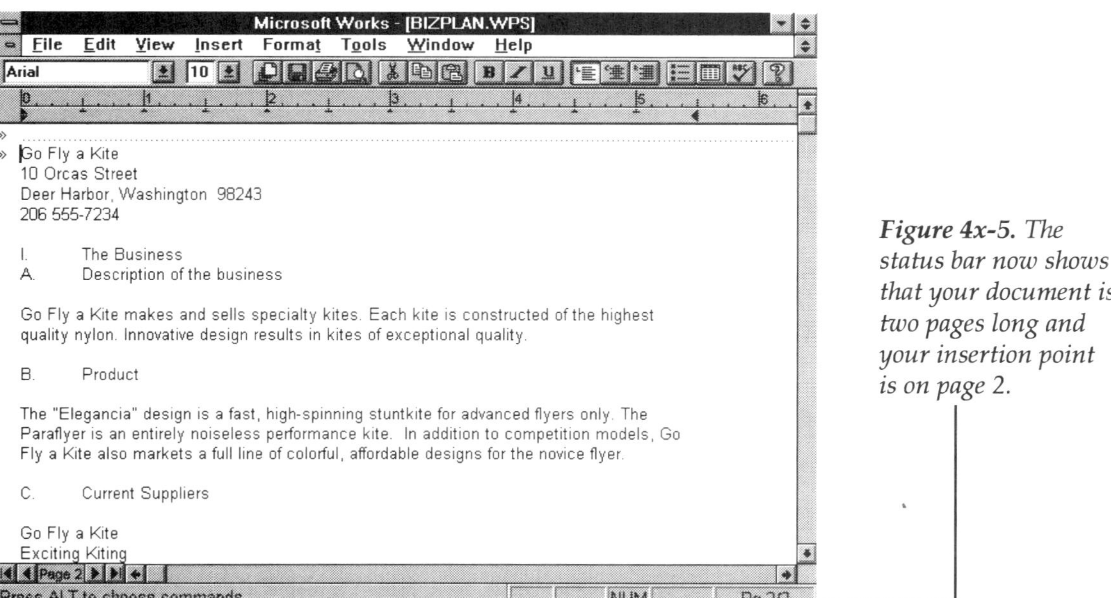

Figure 4x-5. *The status bar now shows that your document is two pages long and your insertion point is on page 2.*

3. *Move onto page one, type in the title "Business Plan for the Go Fly a Kite Company" and press Enter.*

To move your insertion point onto page one, press the up arrow key on the keyboard. The status bar will show that you are on page one as in Figure 4x-6. When you have typed in the above title and pressed Enter, your screen will look like the one in Figure 4x-6.

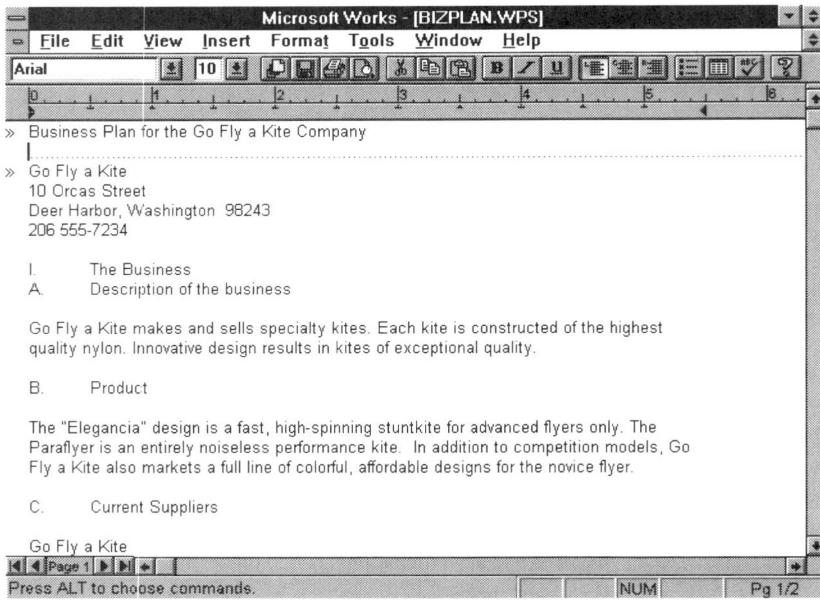

***Figure 4x-6.** The title has been typed in, ready to be formatted.*

4. ***In the paragraph created in Step 3 only, increase the left and right margins by 2 in (5 cm) each.***

As you want to change one paragraph only, put the insertion point within that paragraph first and then move the margin indicators along the ruler to the appropriate positions. Figures 4x-7 and 4x-8 give more details.

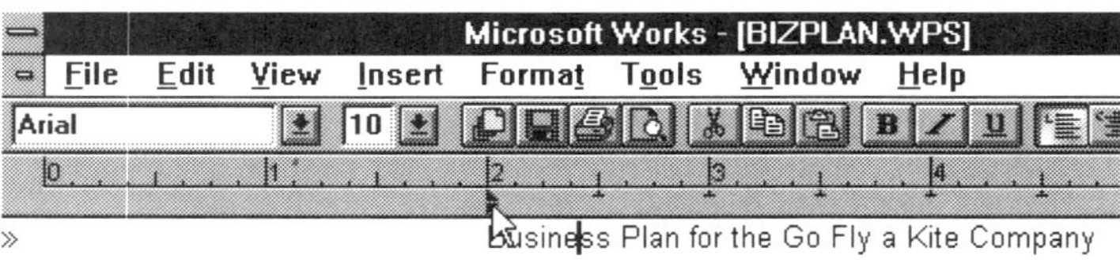

***Figure 4x-7.** To change the left margin of this paragraph, click in the paragraph and drag the left margin indicator from 0 to the 2 in (5 cm) mark.*

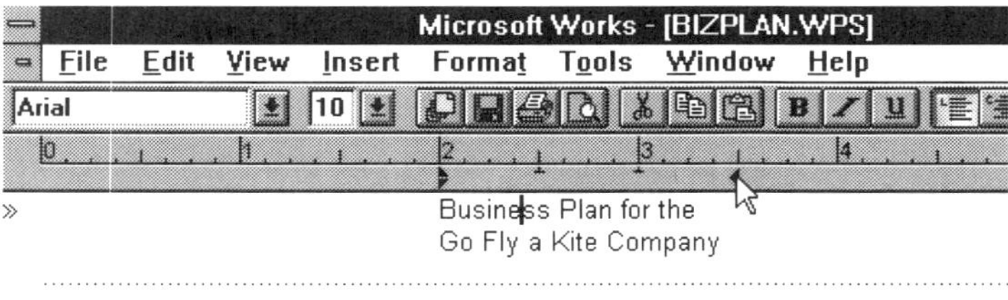

***Figure 4x-8.** To change the right margin, keep the insertion point in the paragraph and drag the right margin indicator to the 3.5 in (9 cm) mark.*

The margin *may* not alter the text on the screen. If this is the case, *Wrap for Window* may be checked in the **View** menu (**Chapter 1, The Word Processor Screen**). If it is active, uncheck it by choosing *Wrap for Window*.

5. ***Change the left margin for the document as a whole to 2 in (5 cm).***

You can change margins throughout your document by altering the dimensions in the *Page Setup* dialog box. Follow Figures 4x-9 through 4x-11 to complete this task.

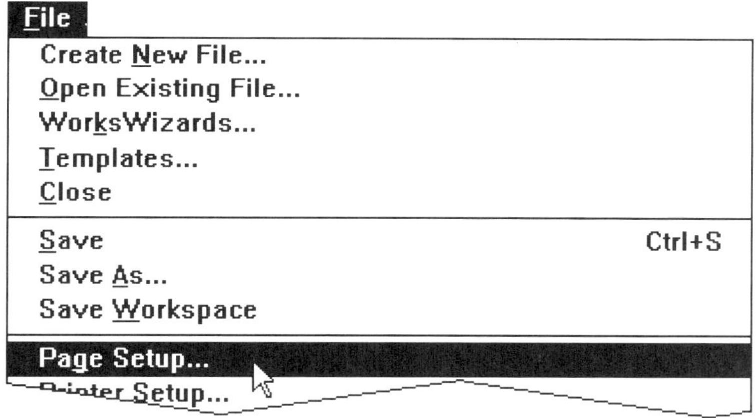

Figure 4x-9. *Choose Page Setup from the* ***File*** *menu.*

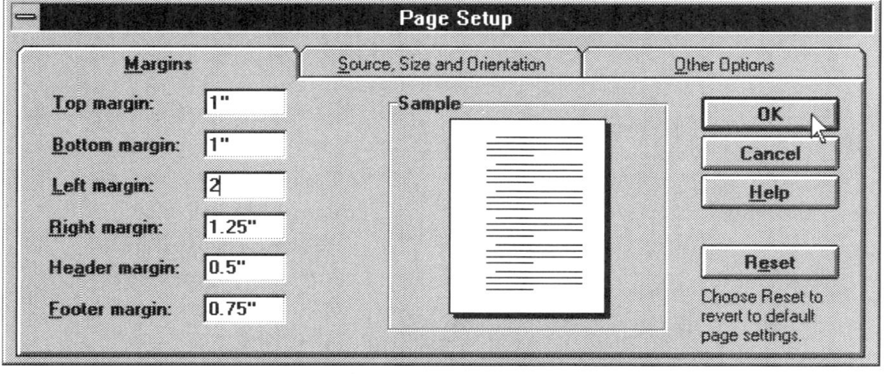

Figure 4x-10. *Change the left margin as shown here.*

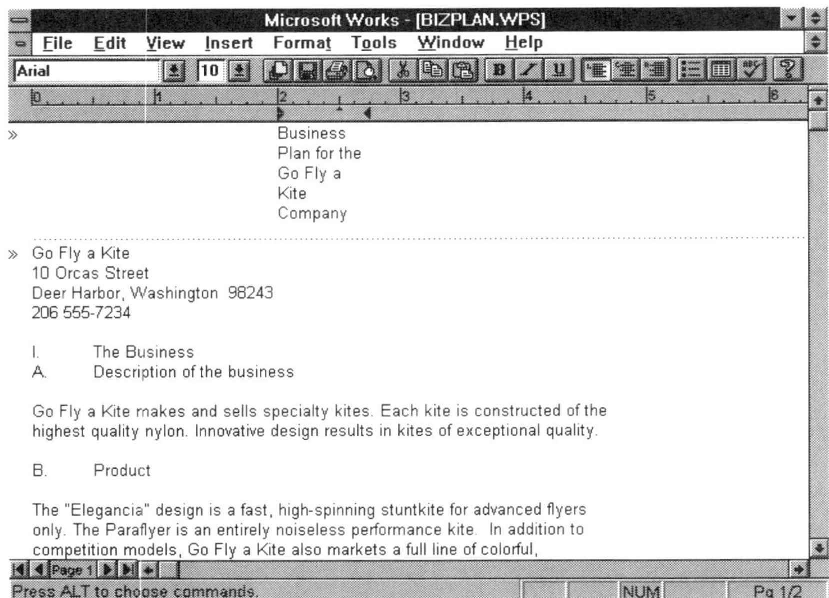

***Figure 4x-11.** Your screen should look similar to this after you click on OK in the Page Setup dialog box.*

6. *Put a double outline border around the title.*

A border is a good way of highlighting text—particularly headings and titles. The first step in putting a border around a paragraph is to move into that paragraph; so click in the title paragraph.

To complete putting a border around the title, see Figure 4x-12. The result is shown in Figure 4x-13.

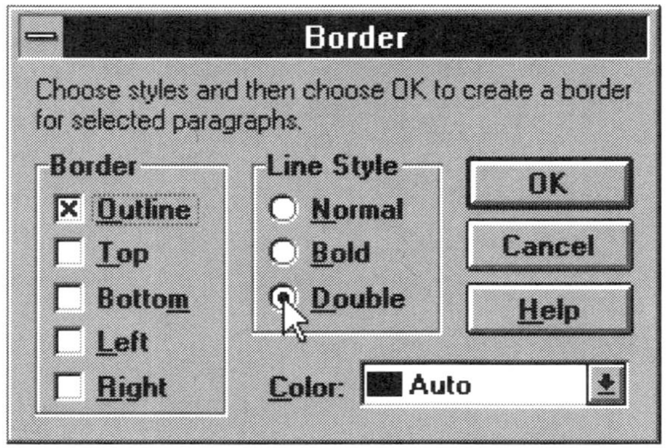

***Figure 4x-12.** Once the paragraph has been selected, choose Border from the **Format** menu and select the specifications of your choice. We have checked Double as the line style and Outline as the border.*

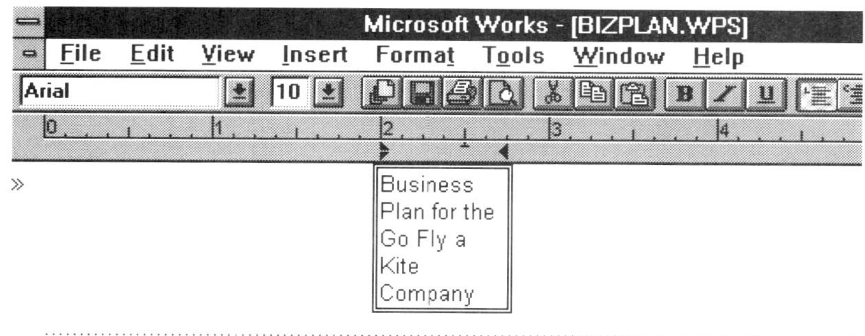

Figure 4x-13. *The title with the double line style and outline border.*

7. ***Insert a one-line header "Go Fly a Kite" and a one-line footer showing the page number. Ensure that these will not be seen on the title page.***

The insertion point can be in any position to insert headers and footers as they will affect the entire document. Now select the *Headers and Footers* command from the **View** menu to display the *Headers and Footers* dialog box. To place the header and footer outlined above, complete the text boxes as in Figures 4x-14, 4x-15, and 4x-16.

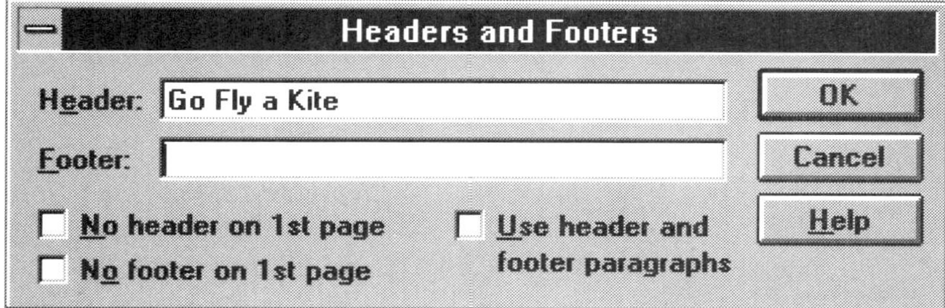

Figure 4x-14. *The text "Go Fly a Kite" is the header, so type this in the Header text box and press Tab to move to the Footer text box.*

Figure 4x-15. *The footer shows the word "Page" as well as the page number – type in "Page &p."*

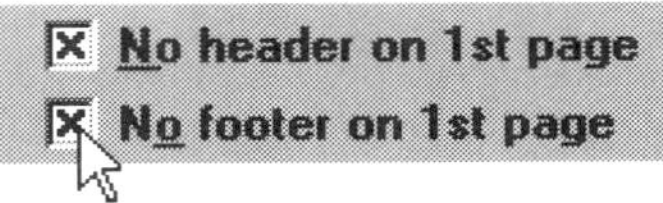

Figure 4x-16. So the headers and footers don't appear on the title page, select the options shown here.

8. ***Use the Replace command to replace "noiseless" with "silent" in your document.***

The *Replace* command in the **Edit** menu is a useful feature for finding and changing pieces of text in you document, as it saves you having to do it manually. To make the changes required, see Figures 4x-17 through 4x-19.

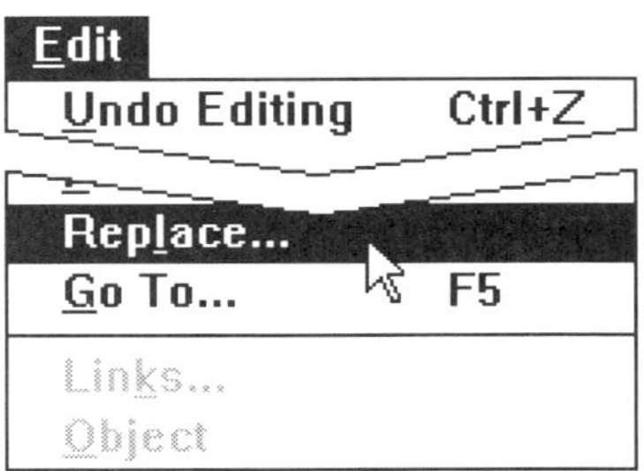

*Figure 4x-17. Move to the beginning of your document and choose Replace from the **Edit** menu.*

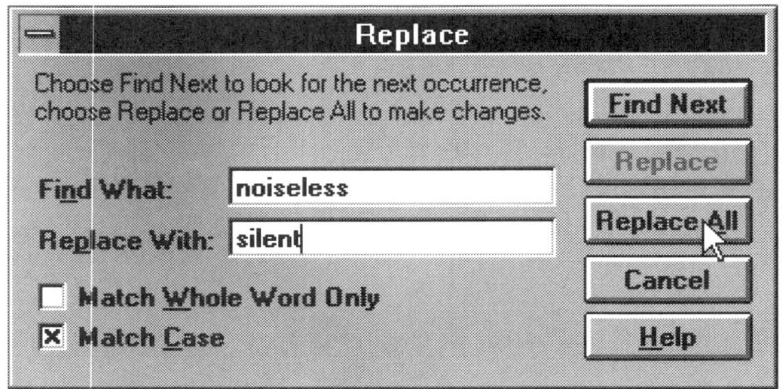

Figure 4x-18. Type "noiseless" in the Find What text box and "silent" in the Replace With text box. Now click on Replace All.

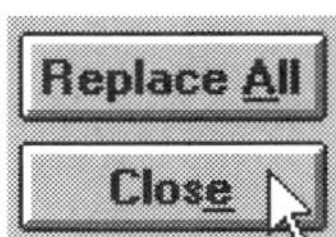

Figure 4x-19. Works changes the Cancel button to Close. Click on Close.

Your document is now complete. You may wish to save the file using *Save As* in the **File** menu and view the changes you have made through *Print Preview* in the **File** menu.

The Spell Checker and Thesaurus — Exercise

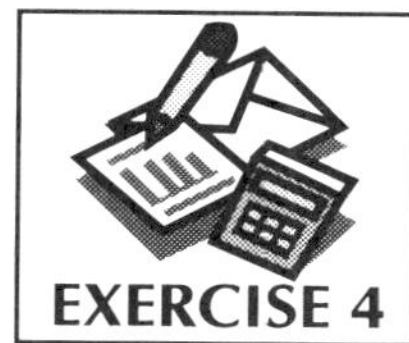

In this exercise you will practise using the spell checker and thesaurus features in Works.

People of all levels of expertise in Works can benefit from this exercise. If you like a challenge, complete the exercise using the Steps in Brief, listed below. This lists the exercise outline, with no hints.

If you need more assistance, refer to the Steps in Detail on the following pages. The Steps in Detail expand each step, listing details and hints that enable you to complete the exercise.

Steps in Brief

1. *Open a new document.*
2. *Type in the following text—don't forget the mistakes.*

   In order to fully understand design skills and and typography, a designer must first have a basic knowledg of reading patterns.
   When we are taught to read, weare told to start at the top left hand corner of the reading matter and work our way across and down, going from left to right again, until we reach the bottom of the document.
   From the Look'n'Good Design Co.

3. *Check the spelling in the document using the Spelling command.*
4. *Change "told" in the second paragraph to "instructed" using the thesaurus.*
5. *Count the number of words in the document using Word Count.*

Steps in Detail

1. Open a new document.

Before you open a new file in Works, be sure to close any files which may be open at present by selecting *Close* from the **File** menu. To open a new file at this point, choose *Create New File* from the **File** menu (Figure 5x-1). Click on the *Word Processor* button in the *Startup* dialog box to open a new word processor file. You are now ready to insert the information below.

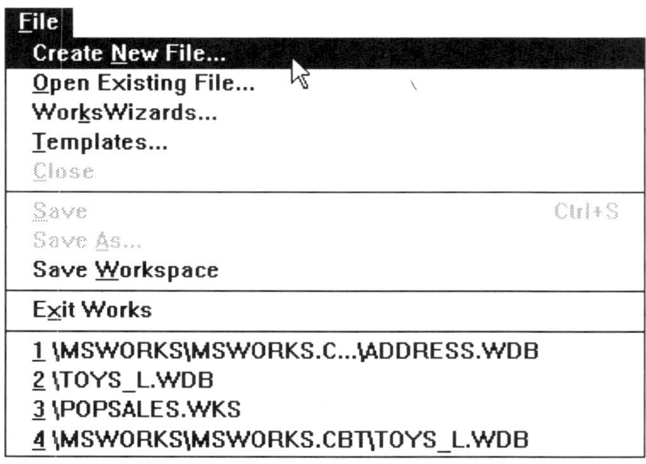

Figure 5x-1. *To open a new file, select Create New File from the **File** menu.*

2. Type in the following text—don't forget the mistakes.

Your insertion point will be flashing at the top of the new file, waiting for you to insert text. When the text has been typed in, your screen will look like that in Figure 5x-2.

> In order to fully understand design skills and and typography, a designer must first have a basic knowledg of reading patterns.
> When we are taught to read, weare told to start at the top left hand corner of the reading matter and work our way across and down, going from left to right again, until we reach the bottom of the document.
> From the Look'n'Good Design Co.

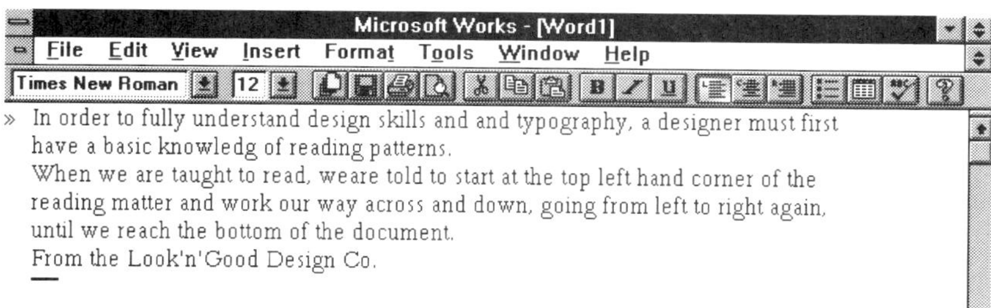

Figure 5x-2. *The text has now been typed into the document, including the spelling errors.*

3. Check the spelling in the document using the Spelling command.

To ensure the whole document is checked, move the insertion point to the beginning of the document by pressing Ctrl-Home.

The spelling checker starts when you choose *Spelling* from the **Tools** menu (Figure 5x-3) or by clicking on the *Spelling Checker* button on the toolbar (Figure 5x-4).

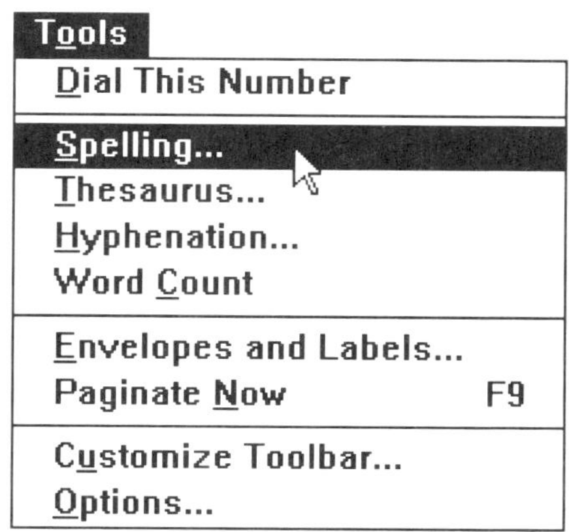

Figure 5x-3. *Selecting Spelling from the* ***Tools*** *menu starts the spell checker.*

Figure 5x-4. *Clicking on the Spelling Checker button on the toolbar also starts the spell checker.*

Start up the spell checker using the method you prefer. Follow Figures 5x-5 through 5x-8 to complete this task.

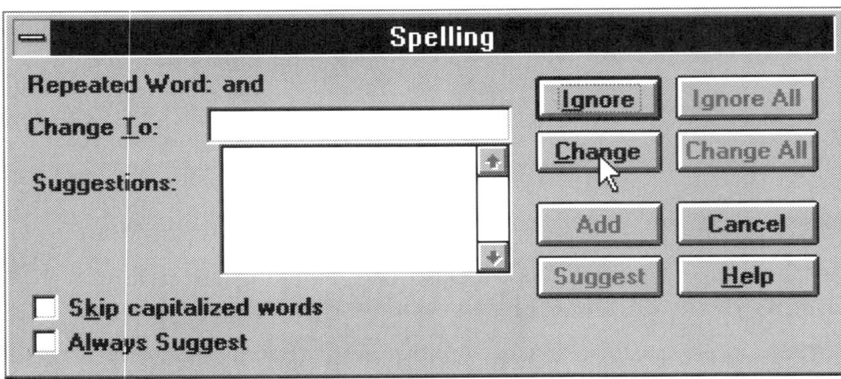

Figure 5x-5. *The first error it detects is the repeated word "and." Click on Change to delete one "and" and continue.*

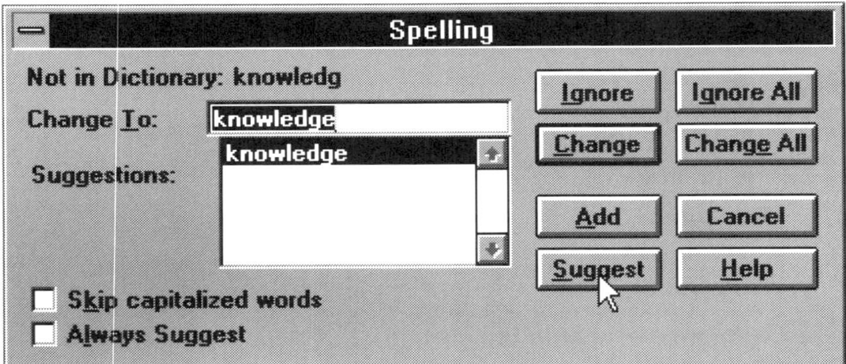

Figure 5x-6. *Works suggests alternative spellings for "knowledg" when you click on Suggest. The correct spelling of "knowledge" is selected, so click on Change.*

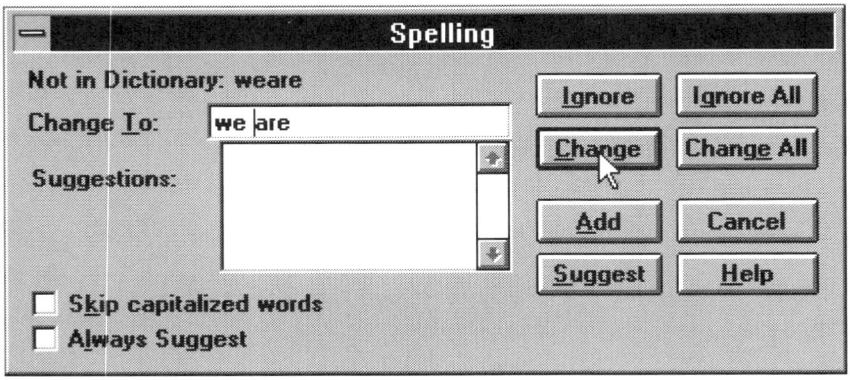

Figure 5x-7. *"weare" is the next error. Insert a space between "we are" in the Change To text box, then click on Change.*

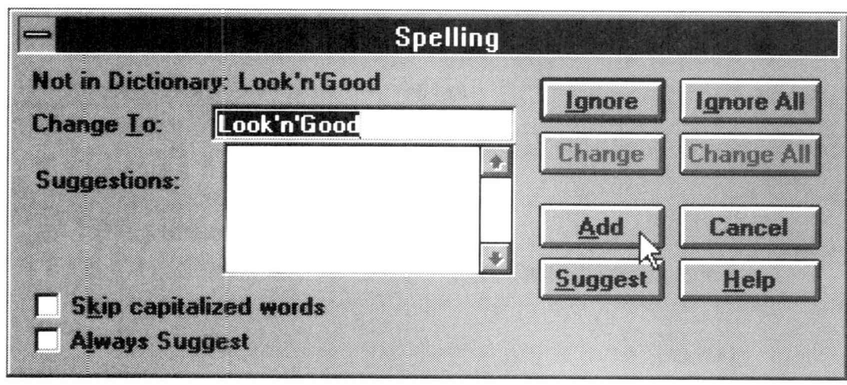

Figure 5x-8. *"Look'n'Good" is the name of a company. Click on Add to add it to the dictionary.*

You have now finished the spelling check, so click on *OK* in the dialog box of Figure 5x-9.

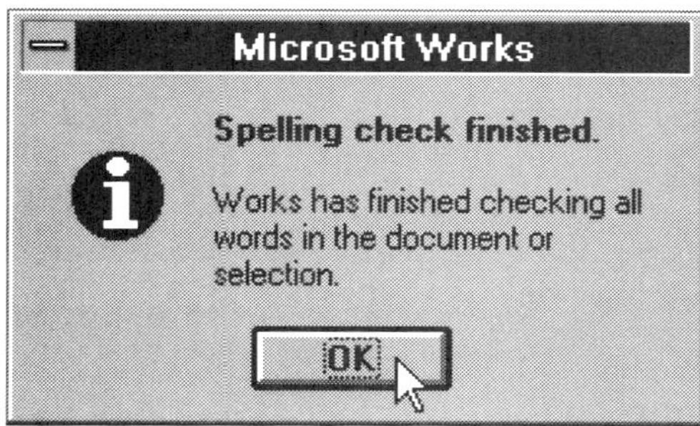

Figure 5x-9. *Works tells you that you have finished checking the document with this dialog box.*

4. *Change "told" in the second paragraph to "instructed" using the thesaurus.*

To find a synonym for a word, it must be highlighted before starting the thesaurus. Highlight "told" at this point or put the insertion point within the word. To start the thesaurus choose *Thesaurus* from the **Tools** menu (Figure 5x-10).

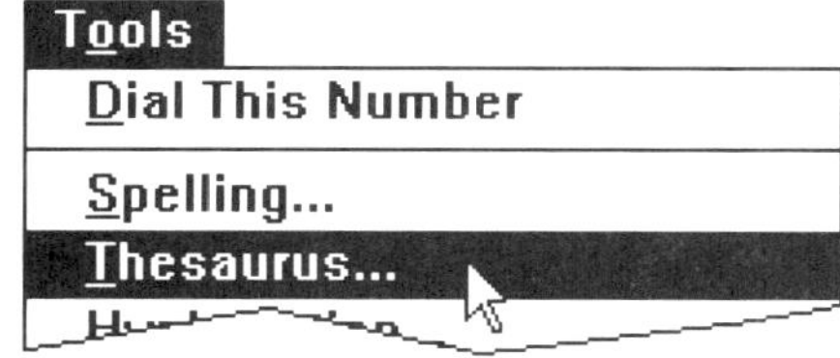

Figure 5x-10. *Selecting Thesaurus from the* **Tools** *menu starts the thesaurus.*

Once "instructed" is found, click on it and then on *Change* to make the change in your document (see Figure 5x-11).

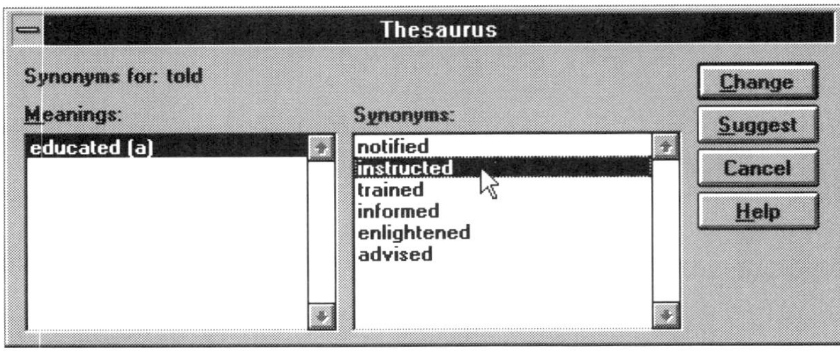

Figure 5x-11. *Click on "instructed" and then on Change.*

5. *Count the number of words in the document using* **Word Count.**

To count the number of words in a document, move the insertion point to deselect any selected text and choose *Word Count* from the **Tools** menu as in Figure 5x-12.

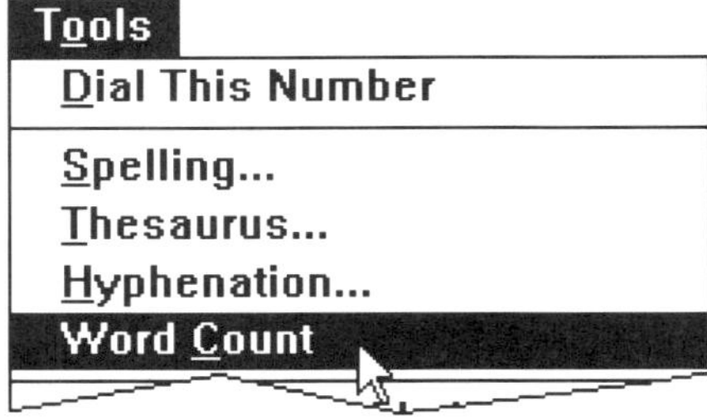

Figure 5x-12. *The Word Count command in the* ***Tools*** *menu.*

Works counts the number of words and displays the total in the dialog box of Figure 5x-13.

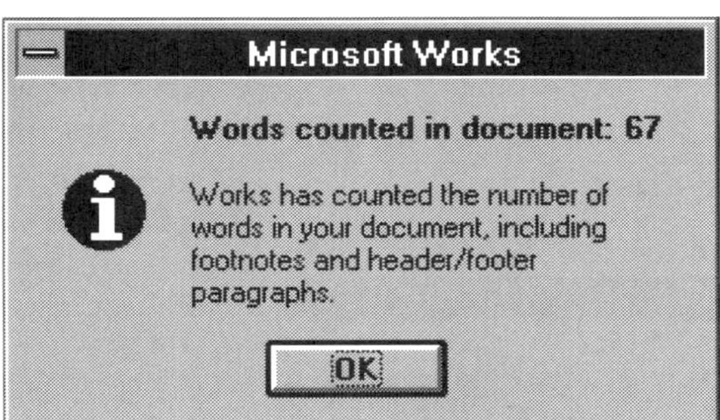

Figure 5x-13. *When the Word Count facility is complete, it will display this dialog box.*

The Drawing Program — Exercise

In this exercise you will practise starting the Draw package and adding graphics to a document.

People of all levels of expertise in Works can benefit from this exercise. If you like a challenge, complete the exercise using the Steps in Brief, listed below. This lists the exercise outline, with no hints.

If you need more assistance, refer to the Steps in Detail on the following pages. The Steps in Detail expand each step, listing details and hints that enable you to complete the exercise.

Steps in Brief

1. *Open the file lexicone.wps.*
2. *While the insertion point is at the beginning of the document, start the drawing program.*
3. *Draw a drop shadow box.*
4. *Type in the name of the bookshop: "New Earth Bookshop."*
5. *Change the font to Avant Garde, the point size to 14 point, and the style to bold.*
6. *Move the text into the drop shadow box and adjust the size of the object if necessary.*
7. *Import the graphic globe.wmf and move it into the box.*
8. *Adjust the objects so they fit comfortably in the shadow box.*
9. *Exit back to lexicone.wps to update the word processor file.*
10. *Edit the graphic, changing the color of the text to red.*
11. *Group the objects before exiting to the lexicone.wps document again.*

Steps in Detail

1. *Open the file lexicone.wps.*

Before you open the new file, make sure any files which were open are closed. Then follow Figures 6x-1 and 6x-2.

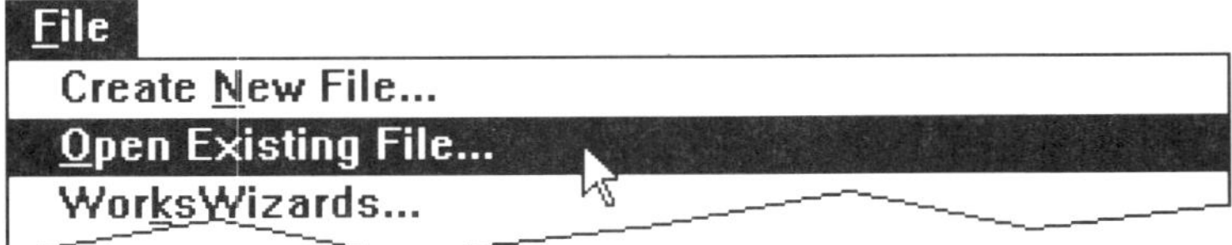

Figure 6x-1. *To open a file in Works, choose Open Existing File from the **File** menu.*

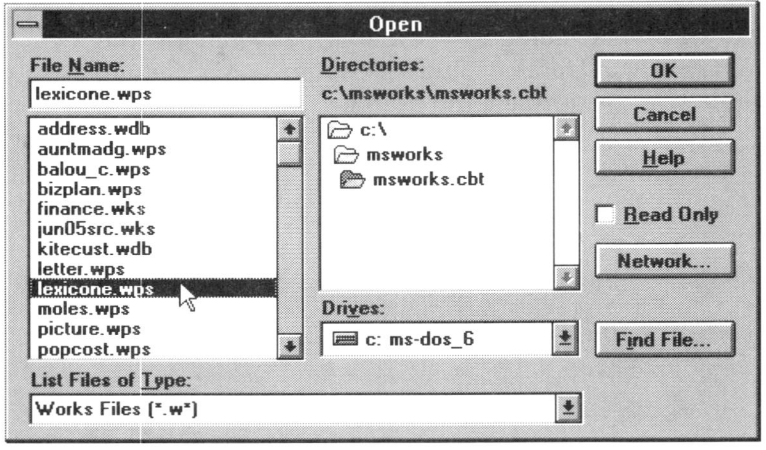

Figure 6x-2. *The file for this exercise – **lexicone.wps** – is in the **msworks.cbt** subdirectory.*

2. ***While the insertion point is at the beginning of the document, start the drawing program.***

Before you can put a drawing into your document, you need to load MS Draw into memory. This is done through the **Insert** menu, as Figure 6x-3 shows. The Draw screen is shown in Figure 6x-4.

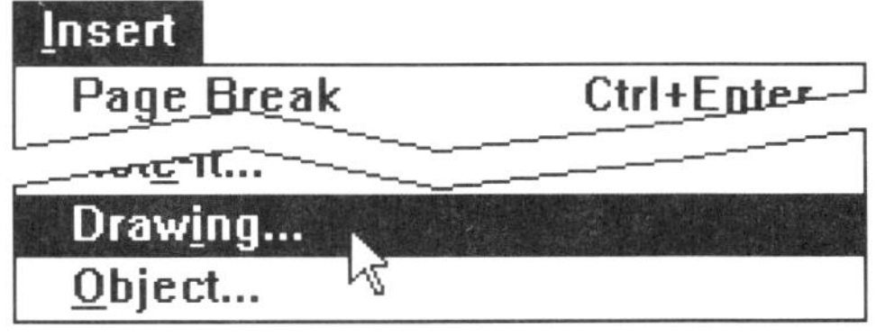

Figure 6x-3. *To load the drawing package – MS Draw – into memory, click on Drawing in the **Insert** menu.*

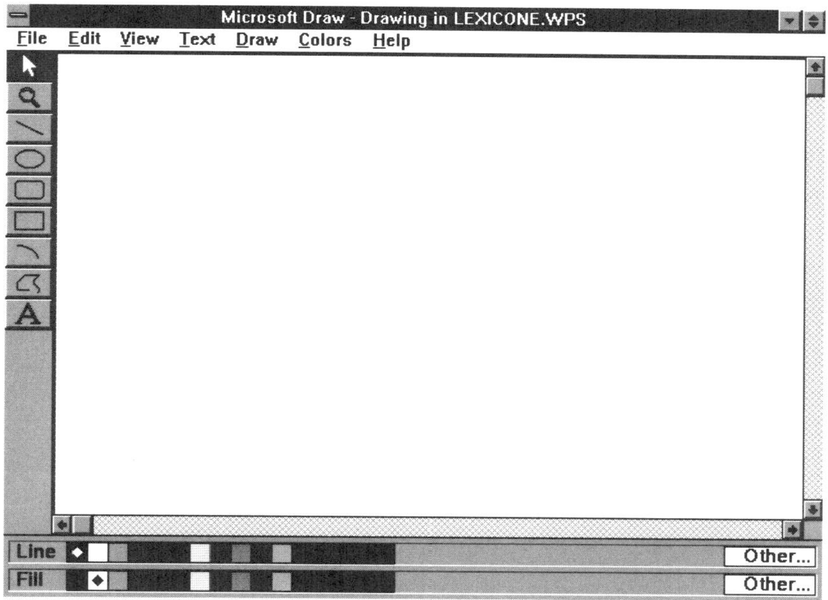

Figure 6x-4. *The screen in MS Draw.*

3. *Draw a drop shadow box.*

A drop shadow box is created in a number of steps. These initial steps are outlined in Figures 6x-5 and 6x-6.

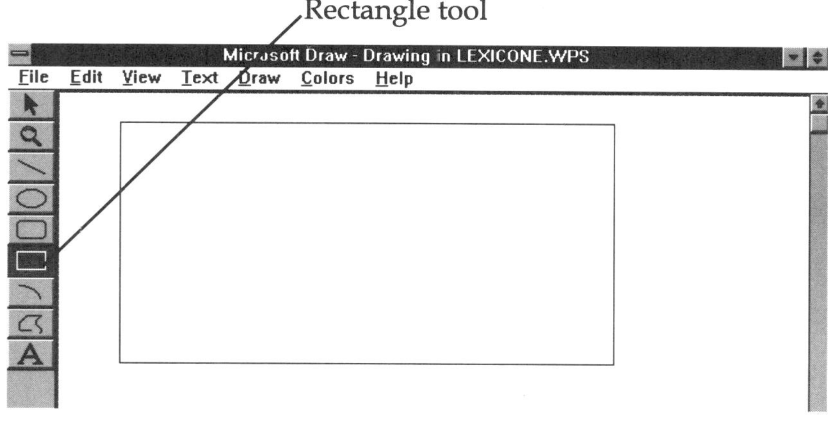

Figure 6x-5. *Choose the Rectangle tool from the toolbox and draw a rectangle like this one by dragging the pointer across the drawing area.*

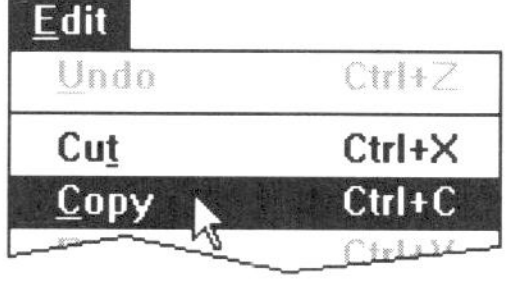

Figure 6x-6. *Copy the rectangle using the Copy command in the* ***Edit*** *menu while the rectangle is selected.*

The rectangle then needs to be pasted back onto the drawing screen through the *Paste* command in the **Edit** menu. While that new rectangle is selected, change the fill color to black (Figure 6x-7).

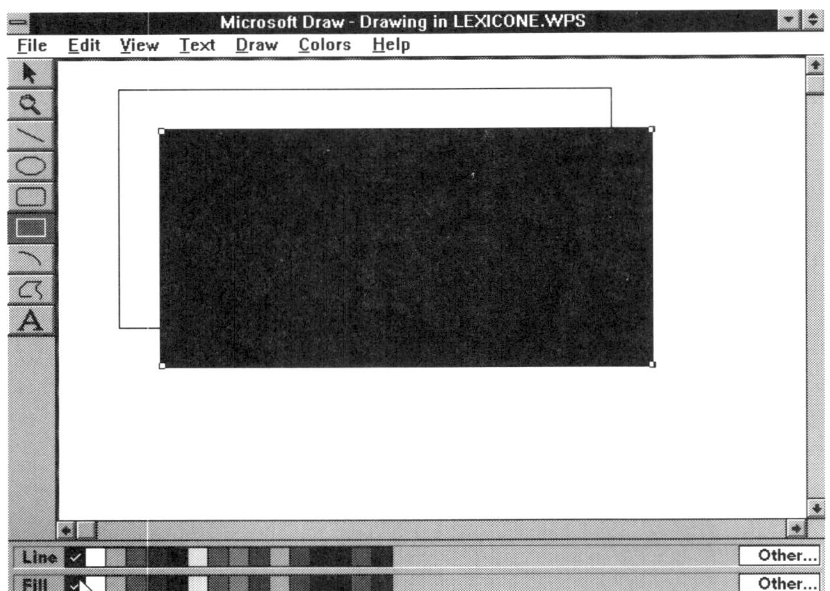

Figure 6x-7. **Figure 6x-7.** *Change the fill color of the new rectangle to black by clicking on the black fill square in the color palette. The check marks in the color palette appear as in this figure.*

To complete the drop shadow box, the two rectangles need to be brought closer together and the black rectangle then needs to be sent to the back. To move the black rectangle, select it with the Pointer tool, and drag it closer to the white rectangle. To continue with the box, see Figures 6x-8 and 6x-9.

Edit	
Undo	Ctrl+Z
Cut	Ctrl+X
Copy	Ctrl+C
Paste	Ctrl+V
Clear	Del
Select All	Ctrl+A
Bring to Front	Ctrl+=
Send to Back	Ctrl+-
Edit Object	Ctrl+E

Figure 6x-8. *Click on Send to Back in the* ***Edit*** *menu to move the black box behind the white one.*

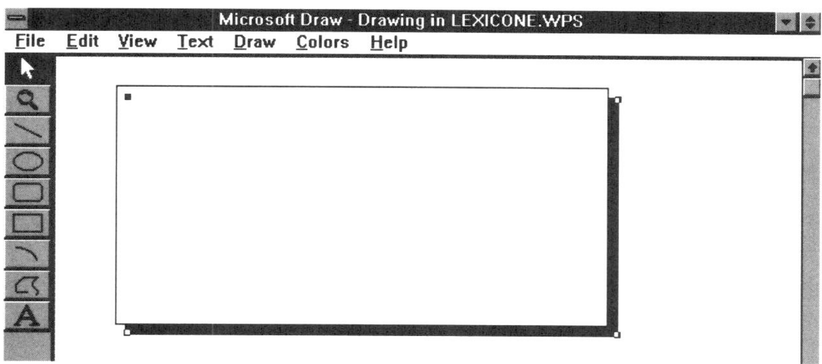

Figure 6x-9. *Your drawing screen should now look like this.*

4. *Type in the name of the bookshop: "New Earth Bookshop."*

To type text into MS Draw, the Text tool needs to be selected. The mouse pointer then becomes an insertion point which is clicked anywhere on the screen. Type in the text as in Figure 6x-10.

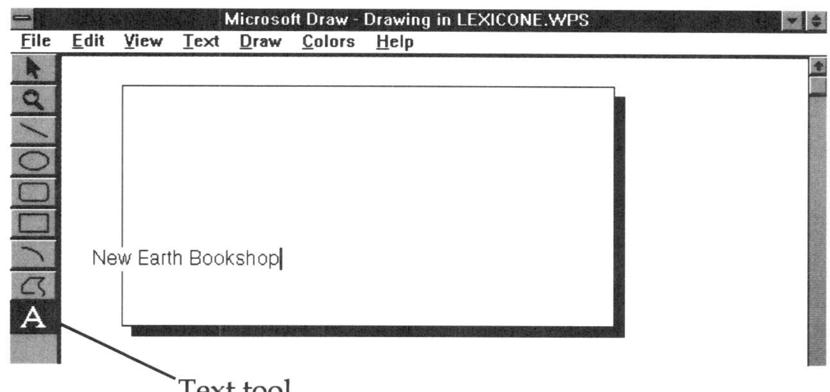

Figure 6x-10. *Select the Text tool and type in "New Earth Bookshop."*

5. *Change the font to Avant Garde, the point size to 14 point, and the style to bold.*

All of these changes are achieved through the **Text** menu. To change the text just typed, it must be selected as it is in Figure 6x-11, so click on the Pointer tool and then on the text. Change the font first by choosing *Font* and then *Avant Garde* from the **Text** menu, which is displayed in Figure 6x-11. Figures 6x-12 and 6x-13 show how to make the other changes.

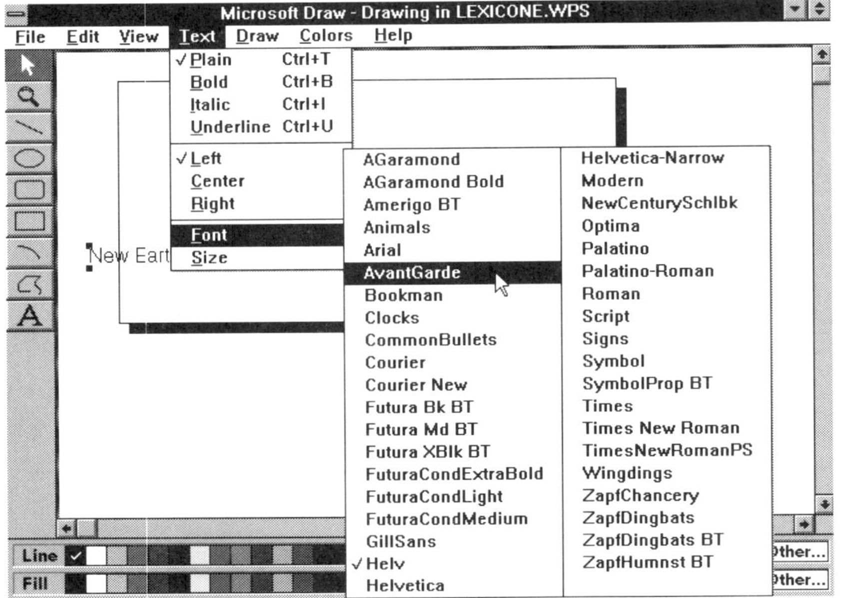

Figure 6x-11. *Choose Avant Garde from the Font submenu.*

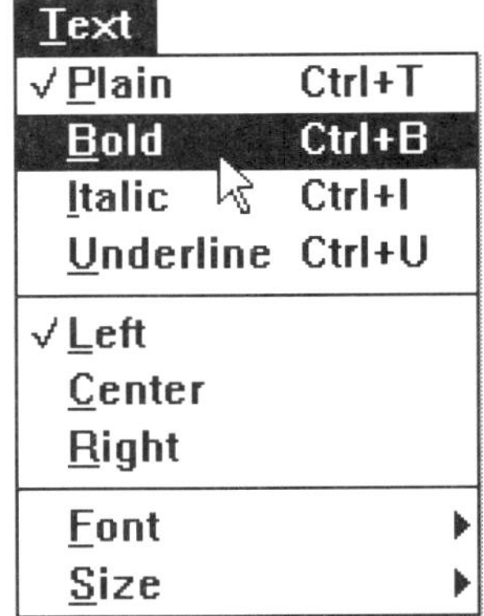

Figure 6x-12. *Choose Bold from the* ***Text*** *menu to change the type style to bold.*

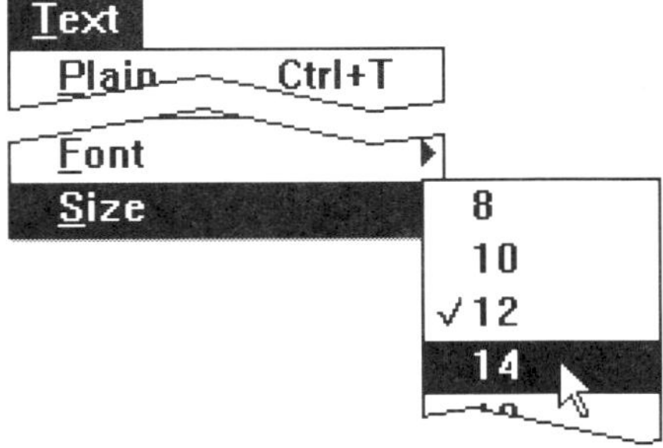

Figure 6x-13. *Choose 14 from the Size submenu to enlarge the text.*

6. ***Move the text into the drop shadow box and adjust the size of the object if necessary.***

To move the text, it must be selected, as in Figure 6x-14, and dragged to the new position. The rectangle looks like Figure 6x-14 when done.

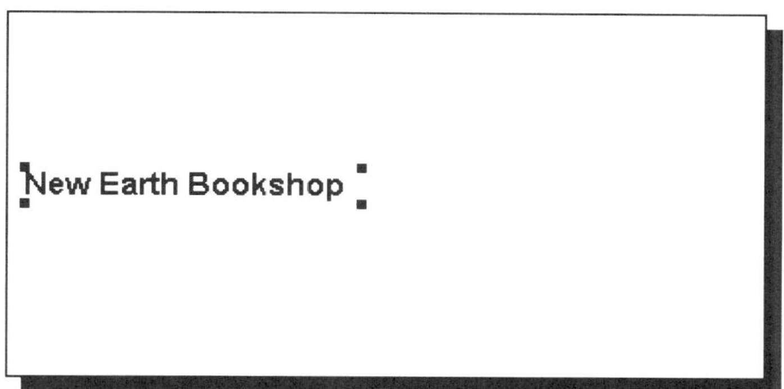

Figure 6x-14. *The text object is moved inside the drop shadow box by dragging it across the screen.*

7. ***Import the graphic globe.wmf and move it into the box.***

To complete this task, follow Figures 6x-15 and 6x-16.

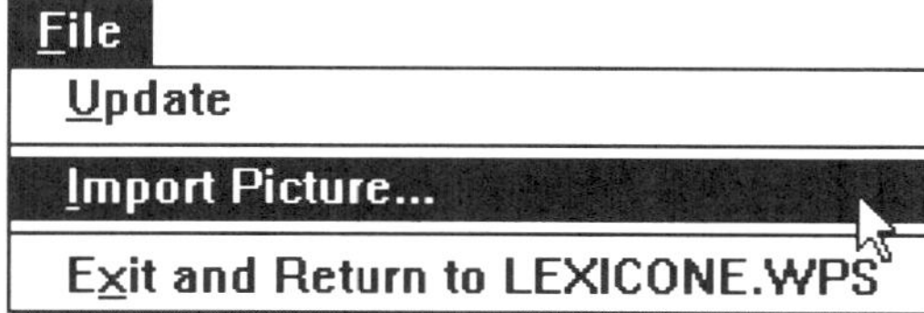

Figure 6x-15. *Select Import Picture from the File menu.*

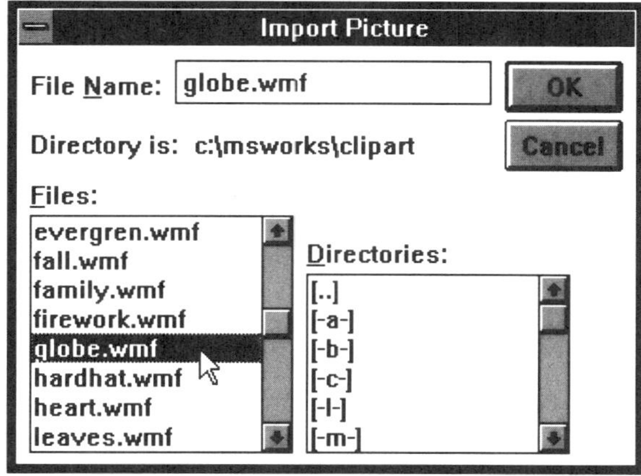

Figure 6x-16. *Select **globe.wmf** from the Import Picture dialog box. It is in the clip art subdirectory.*

8. Adjust the objects so they fit comfortably in the shadow box.

Drag the collection of objects that make up ***globe.wmf*** into the drop shadow box, as in Figure 6x-17. You may also want to drag the text caption to fit more comfortably in the box.

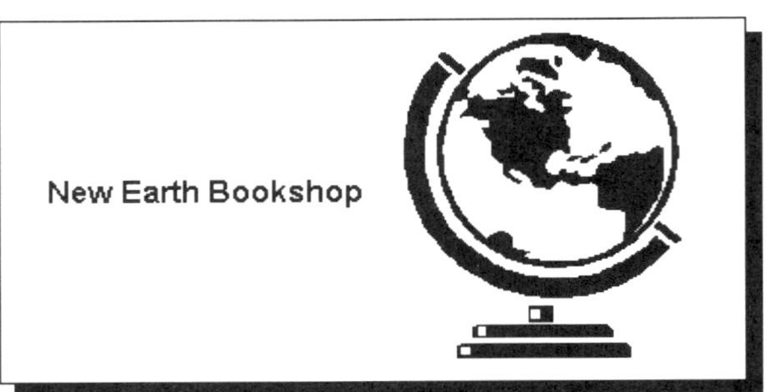

Figure 6x-17. *Move the picture inside the drop shadow box by dragging.*

9. Exit back to lexicone.wps to update the word processor file.

The graphic is now complete and ready to be imported into the file ***lexicone.wps.*** To do this, choose *Exit and Return to LEXICONE.WPS* from the **File** menu (Figure 6x-18).

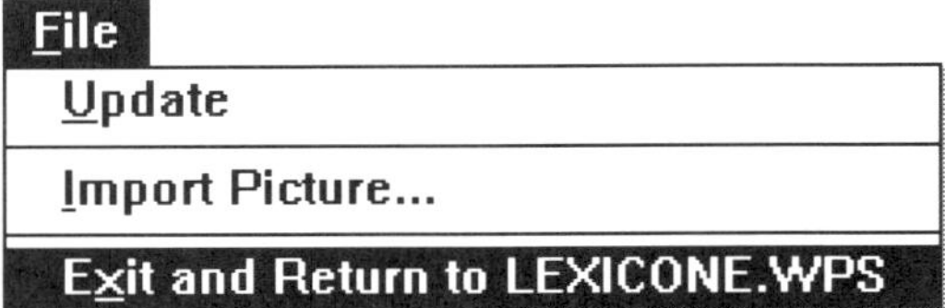

Figure 6x-18. *Select Exit and Return to LEXICONE.WPS from the **File** menu.*

Works asks you to confirm that the update is to take place in the *Update LEXICONE.WPS* dialog box. Click on *Yes* to continue. Your word processor document screen adjusts for the new picture and looks like Figure 6x-19.

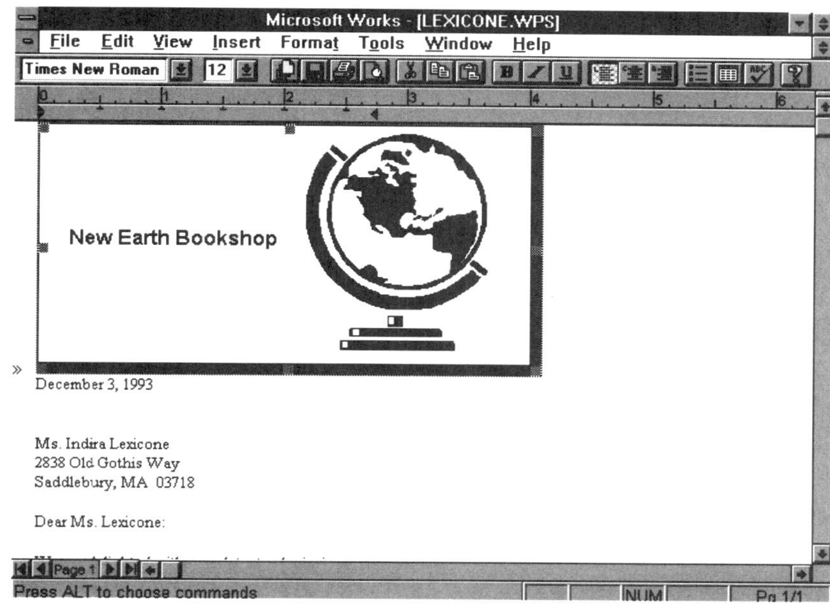

Figure 6x-19. The picture has been imported into the word processing screen.

10. Edit the graphic, changing the color of the text to red.

To edit a picture which has already been created in MS Draw, you need to select it and then access the Draw screen again. Figures 6x-20 and 6x-21 give you instructions on how to do this.

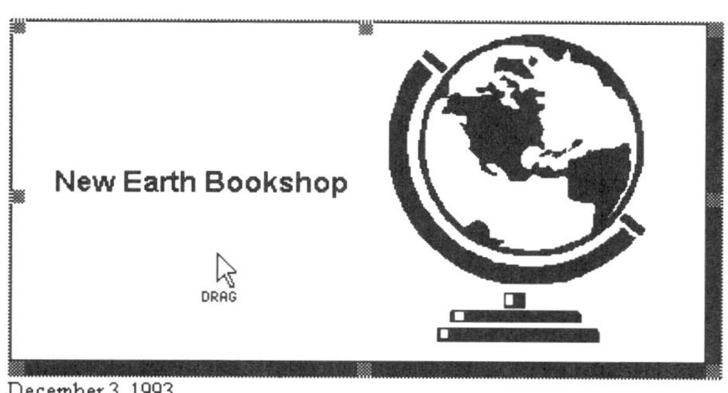

Figure 6x-20. *Select the picture in the word processing screen by clicking on it with the mouse.*

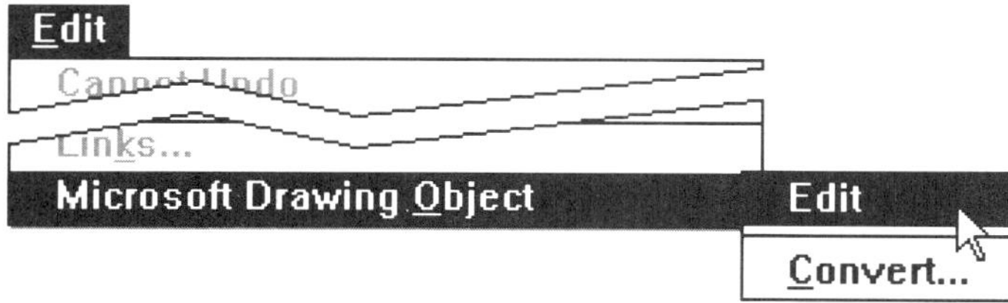

Figure 6x-21. *Select Edit from the Microsoft Drawing Object submenu of the* ***Edit*** *menu to reload MS Draw into memory.*

When the drawing program is initially reloaded, all objects which make up the logo are selected. Click anywhere on the drawing screen to deselect them. Now look at Figure 6x-22 to continue.

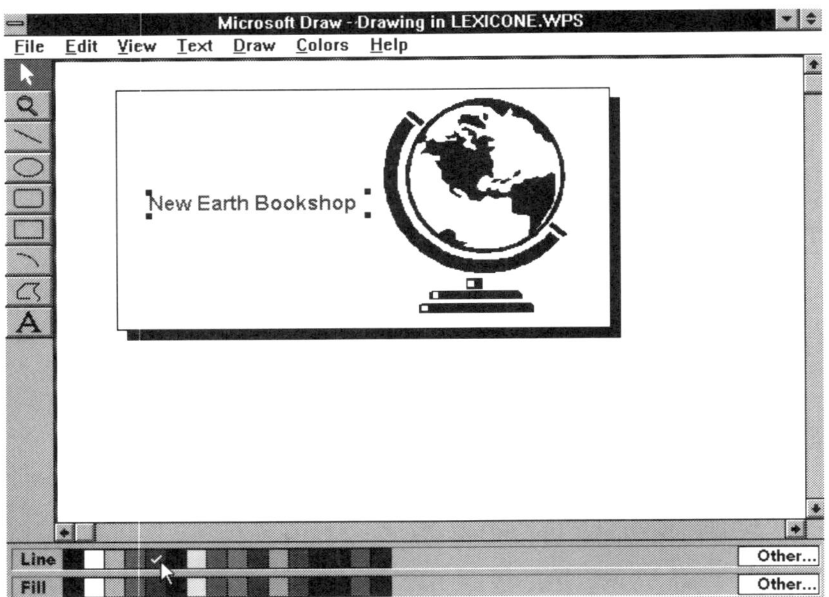

Figure 6x-22. Select the text object and choose the red box on the Line color palette to change the color. The color palette will put a tick in the red box whenever the text object is selected.

11. *Group the objects before exiting to the lexicone.wps document again.*

As all of the objects make up one logo, it is a good idea to group them into one object. They can be ungrouped for future editing, if necessary, but for the exercise, group all of them by following the instructions in Figures 6x-23 and 6x-24.

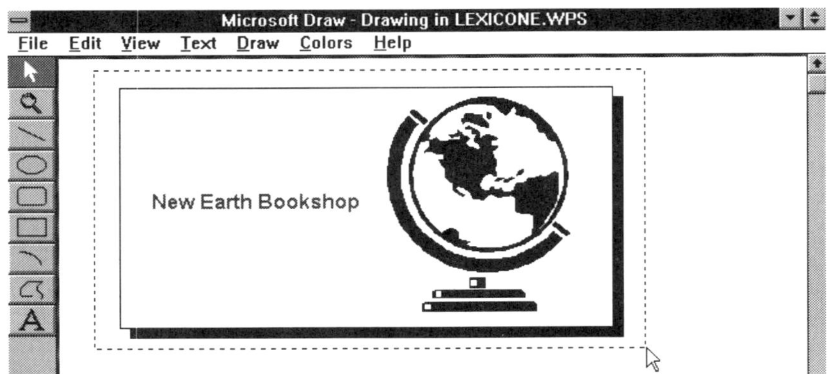

Figure 6x-23. You can select all of the objects by clicking on each of them while holding down the Shift key. It is easier to select them by dragging a rectangle around all objects using the Pointer tool.

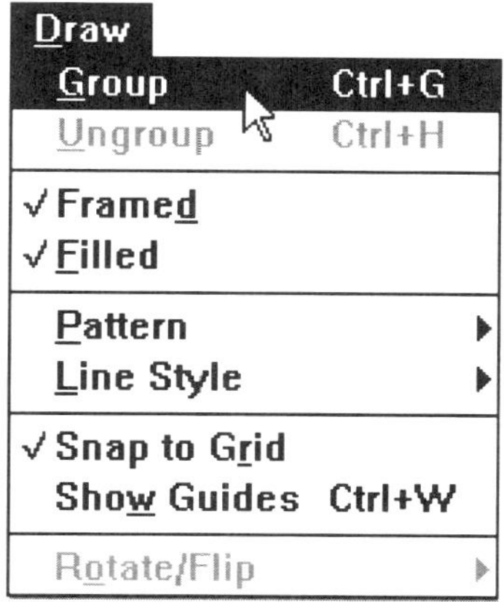

Figure 6x-24. *Choose Group from the **Draw** menu to group the objects into one. The logo has one set of handles only when it is grouped.*

Entering Spreadsheet Data — Exercise

This exercise gives you practice in entering data into the spreadsheet, as well as using formulas, protecting cells, and unlocking them.

People of all levels of expertise in Works can benefit from this exercise. If you like a challenge, complete the exercise using the Steps in Brief, listed below. This lists the exercise outline, with no hints.

If you need more assistance, refer to the Steps in Detail on the following pages. The Steps in Detail expand each step, listing details and hints that enable you to complete the exercise.

Steps in Brief

1. ***Enter the data as in Figure 9x-2.***
2. ***Insert a formula to calculate the total reels for "Gone With the Wind" in cell F3.***
3. ***Enter the formulas to calculate the total reels for "South Pacific," "Ben Hur," and "Showboat" in cells F4, F5, and F6 respectively.***
4. ***Use the Autosum button to calculate the number of total reels in cell F8.***
5. ***In cell D8, calculate the average number of reels using the AVG function.***
6. ***Unlock cells E3, E4, E5, and E6.***
7. ***Protect the entire spreadsheet, leaving cells E3 through E6 unlocked.***
8. ***Change the number of copies of "Showboat" in cell E6 to 12.***
9. ***Save the spreadsheet as "movies."***

Steps in Detail

1. *Enter the data as in Figure 9x-2.*

The data to be inserted into this spreadsheet is a combination of text and values. The pointer must be on the cell into which the data is to be inserted.

Click the mouse in cell A1 to begin with. The insertion point flashes in the formula bar when you type the first letter "O." Continue typing the text "Old Time Movie House - Inventory" as in Figure 9x-1 and press Enter. The text is shown in the cell as well as the formula bar.

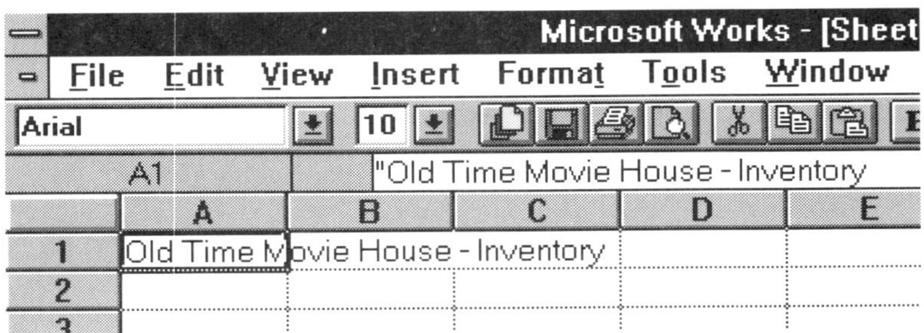

Figure 9x-1. *Begin data entry.*

Key in the rest of the data in the same way until all the data in Figure 9x-2 is entered.

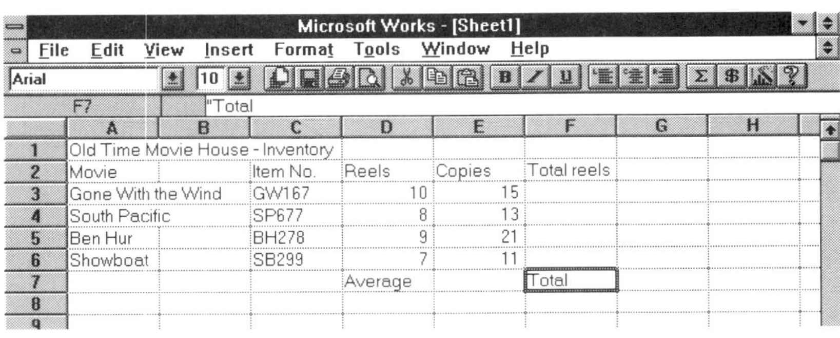

	A	B	C	D	E	F	G	H
1	Old Time Movie House - Inventory							
2	Movie		Item No.	Reels	Copies	Total reels		
3	Gone With the Wind		GW167	10	15			
4	South Pacific		SP677	8	13			
5	Ben Hur		BH278	9	21			
6	Showboat		SB299	7	11			
7				Average		Total		
8								

Figure 9x-2. *Enter the data in the spreadsheet as shown.*

2. ***Insert a formula to calculate the total reels for "Gone With the Wind" in cell F3.***

The total number of reels is calculated by multiplying D3 by E3, which is entered into F3. The pointer must be positioned on the cell where the formula is to be, so move the pointer to cell F3 using either the mouse or the cursor keys. To insert this formula from this point, follow Figures 9x-3 through 9x-7.

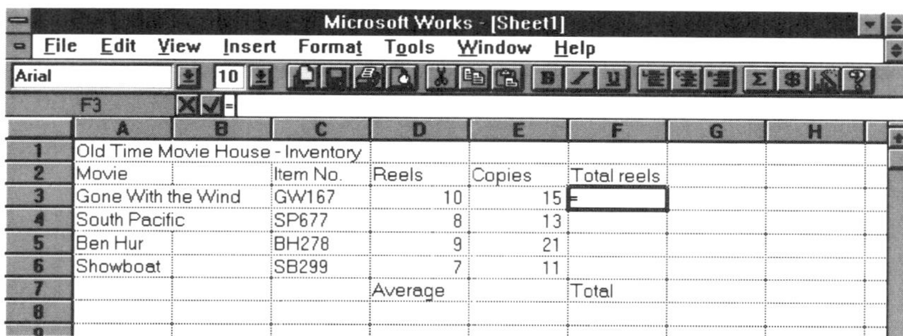

Figure 9x-3. Type in the equals sign (=) as the formula prefix.

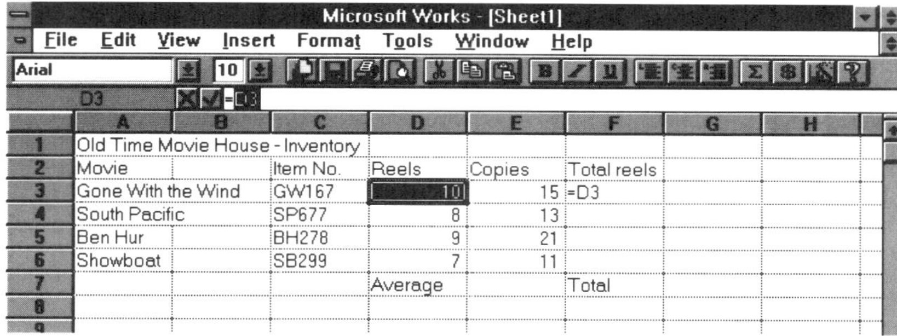

Figure 9x-4. Click on cell D3. The formula bar shows the formula as it is being entered.

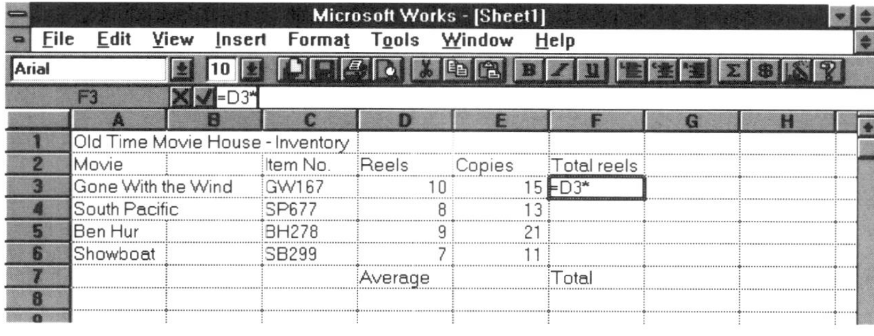

Figure 9x-5. Key in an asterisk (the multiplication sign). The pointer immediately returns to F3.

Microsoft Works - [Sheet1]
File Edit View Insert Format Tools Window Help
Arial 10
E3 =D3*E3
A B C D E F G H
1 Old Time Movie House - Inventory
2 Movie Item No. Reels Copies Total reels
3 Gone With the Wind GW167 10 15 =D3*E3
4 South Pacific SP677 8 13
5 Ben Hur BH278 9 21
6 Showboat SB299 7 11
7 Average Total

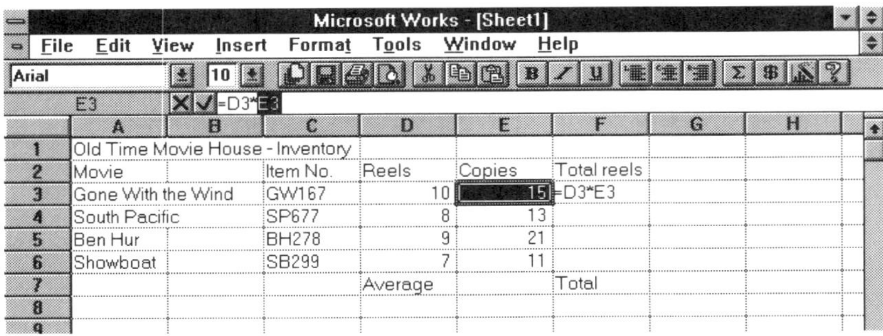

Figure 9x-6. *Click on cell E3 to continue the formula.*

Microsoft Works - [Sheet1]
File Edit View Insert Format Tools Window Help
Arial 10
F3 =D3*E3
A B C D E F G H
1 Old Time Movie House - Inventory
2 Movie Item No. Reels Copies Total reels
3 Gone With the Wind GW167 10 15 150
4 South Pacific SP677 8 13
5 Ben Hur BH278 9 21
6 Showboat SB299 7 11
7 Average Total

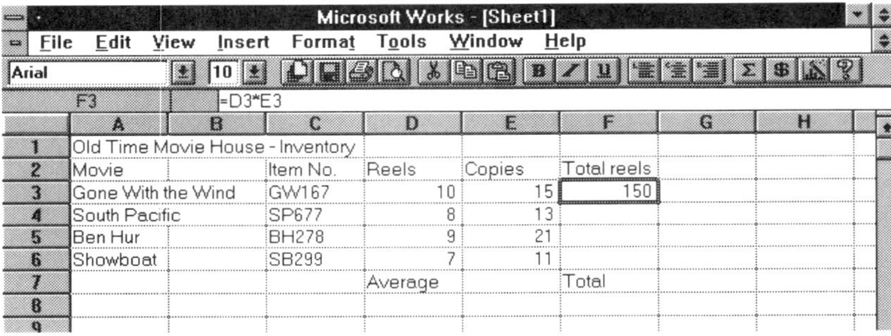

Figure 9x-7. *Press Enter and the answer is calculated and put into F3. The formula remains in the formula bar.*

3. ***Enter the formulas to calculate the total reels for "South Pacific," "Ben Hur," and "Showboat" in cells F4, F5, and F6 respectively.***

Move into the appropriate cell—F4 to start with—and repeat the steps outlined in step 2 of this exercise. When these formulas have been inserted, your spreadsheet should look like Figure 9x-8.

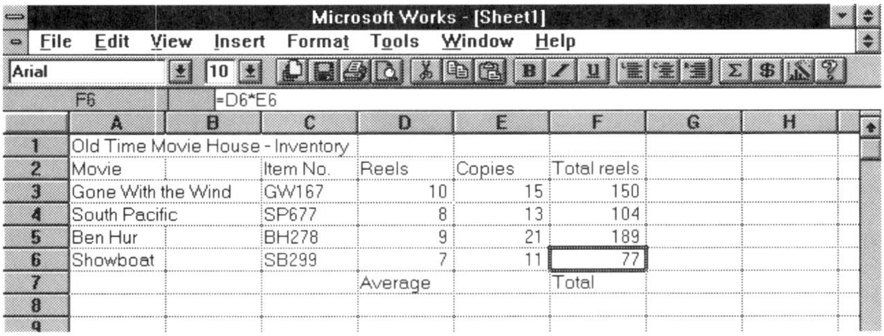

Microsoft Works - [Sheet1]
File Edit View Insert Format Tools Window Help
Arial 10
F6 =D6*E6
A B C D E F G H
1 Old Time Movie House - Inventory
2 Movie Item No. Reels Copies Total reels
3 Gone With the Wind GW167 10 15 150
4 South Pacific SP677 8 13 104
5 Ben Hur BH278 9 21 189
6 Showboat SB299 7 11 77
7 Average Total

Figure 9x-8. *The formulas are entered into F4, F5, and F6.*

4. *Use the Autosum button to calculate the number of total reels in cell F8.*

The *Autosum* button automatically inserts the function which adds a block of cells together. In this spreadsheet, cells F3 through F6 need to be added to obtain the number of total reels. The first step, as with inserting any formula, is to move to the cell where the formula is to go. Click on cell F8 and see Figure 9x-9 and 9x-10 to use this function button.

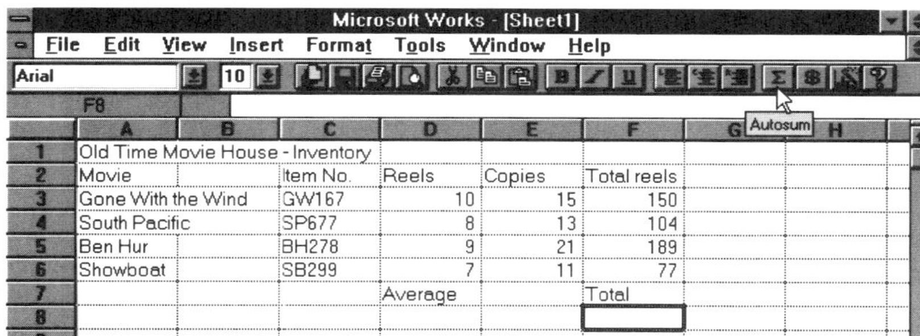

	A	B	C	D	E	F	G	H
1	Old Time Movie House - Inventory							
2	Movie		Item No.	Reels	Copies	Total reels		
3	Gone With the Wind		GW167	10	15	150		
4	South Pacific		SP677	8	13	104		
5	Ben Hur		BH278	9	21	189		
6	Showboat		SB299	7	11	77		
7				Average		Total		
8								

Figure 9x-9. Click on the Autosum button.

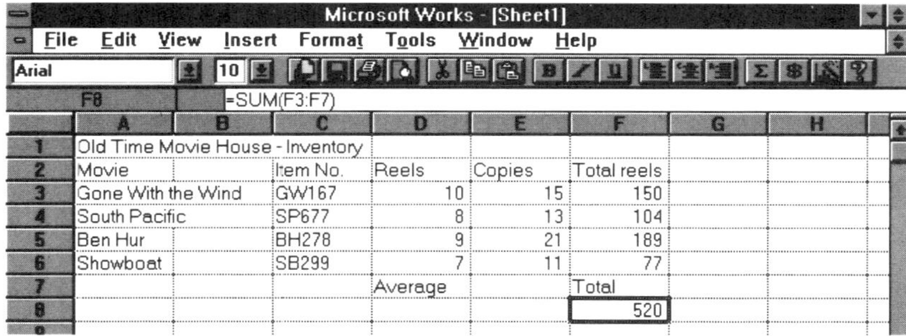

	A	B	C	D	E	F	G	H
1	Old Time Movie House - Inventory							
2	Movie		Item No.	Reels	Copies	Total reels		
3	Gone With the Wind		GW167	10	15	150		
4	South Pacific		SP677	8	13	104		
5	Ben Hur		BH278	9	21	189		
6	Showboat		SB299	7	11	77		
7				Average		Total		
8						520		

Figure 9x-10. Press Enter to enter this formula into F8.

5. *In cell D8, calculate the average number of reels using the AVG function.*

The average number of reels is calculated using another of Works' functions — AVG. The syntax of this is basically the same as the SUM function, in that it requires the name of the function followed by a block of cells. The block of cells to be averaged is D3 through D6, so move to cell D8 and see Figure 9x-11 for the first step.

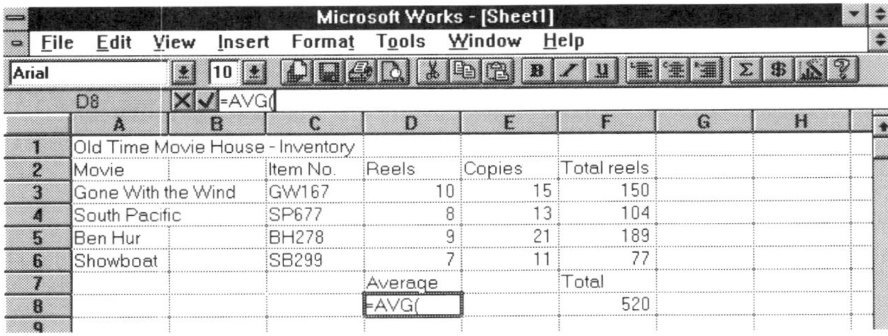

Figure 9x-11. *Key in the first part of the AVG function "=AVG(."*

The block of text now needs to be highlighted as in Figure 9x-12.

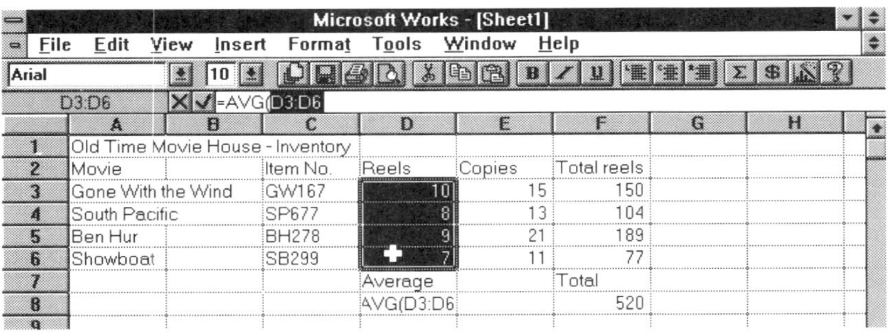

Figure 9x-12. *Using the mouse, click on cell D3 and drag down to D6. This is inserted into the formula bar.*

The formula is completed by keying in a right bracket ")" and pressing Enter, as in Figure 9x-13.

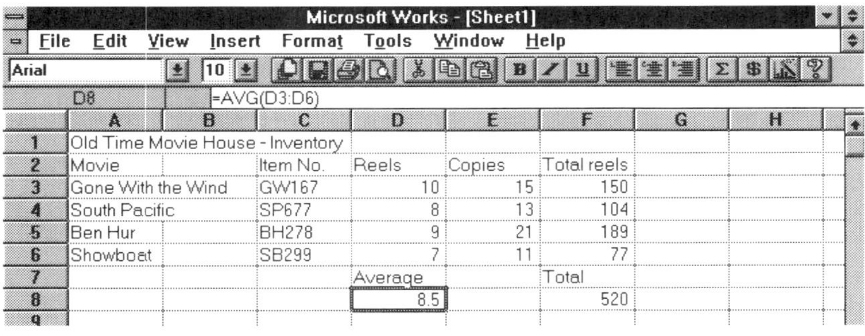

Figure 9x-13. *Close the brackets and press Enter for Works to calculate the formula.*

6. Unlock cells E3, E4, E5, and E6.

In Step 7, you protect the entire spreadsheet. Doing this, without unlocking cells, means that no cell can be changed. Assume, however, that the inventory is to be updated regularly and a new copy of "Showboat" is found.

Unlocking the cells where the number of copies are located, before the spreadsheet is protected, enables you to make alterations to the number of copies as you need to, leaving the formulas and standard data protected. To unprotect the required cells, follow Figures 9x-14 through 9x-16.

Figure 9x-14. *Highlight the cells E3 through E6 using the mouse.*

Figure 9x-15. *Select Protection from the* ***Format*** *menu.*

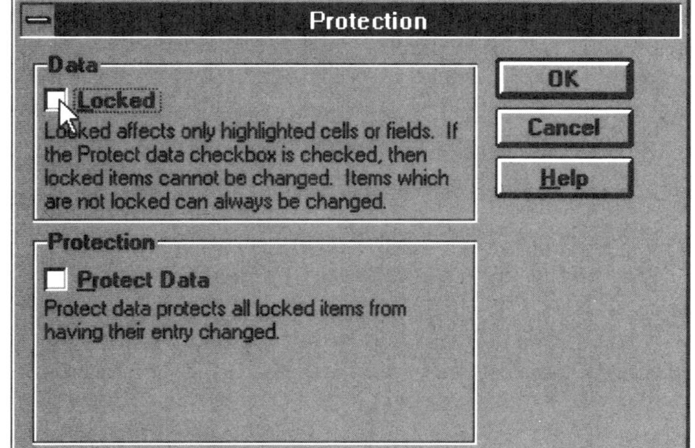

Figure 9x-16. *Deselect Locked in the Protection dialog box.*

7. Protect the entire spreadsheet, leaving cells E3 through E6 unlocked.

Now that the cells have been unlocked, the spreadsheet is ready to be protected. To protect the spreadsheet, choose *Protect Data* in the *Protection* dialog box (Figure 9x-17).

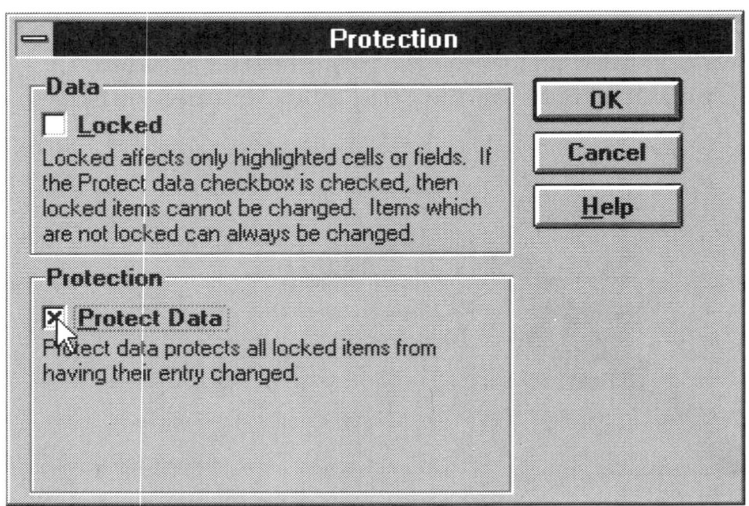

Figure 9x-17. *Protect the spreadsheet as shown.*

8. Change the number of copies of "Showboat" in cell E6 to 12.

You are able to change the contents of this cell because it is unlocked. Click on E6 and type in the new value of 12. Figure 9x-18 displays the refreshed screen.

Microsoft Works - [Sheet1]

File Edit View Insert Format Tools Window Help

Arial 10

E6 12

	A	B	C	D	E	F	G	H
1	Old Time Movie House - Inventory							
2	Movie		Item No.	Reels	Copies	Total reels		
3	Gone With the Wind		GW167	10	15	150		
4	South Pacific		SP677	8	13	104		
5	Ben Hur		BH278	9	21	189		
6	Showboat		SB299	7	12	84		
7				Average		Total		
8				8.5		527		

Figure 9x-18. *The number of copies is now 12 and has been entered into E6. Note that cells F6 and F8 have changed due to the new values in the equation.*

9. Save the spreadsheet as "movies."

To save the file, select *Save As* from the **File** menu as shown in Figure 9x-19.

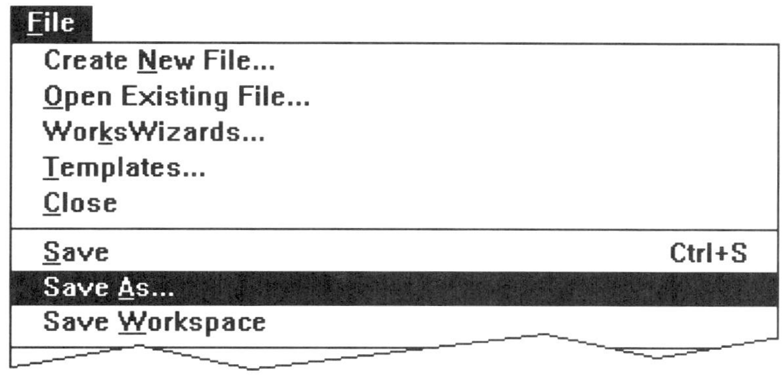

Figure 9x-19. *Choose Save As from the* ***File*** *menu.*

The *Save As* dialog box appears, into which you type the new name "movies" (Figure 9x-20). Click on *OK* to save the file.

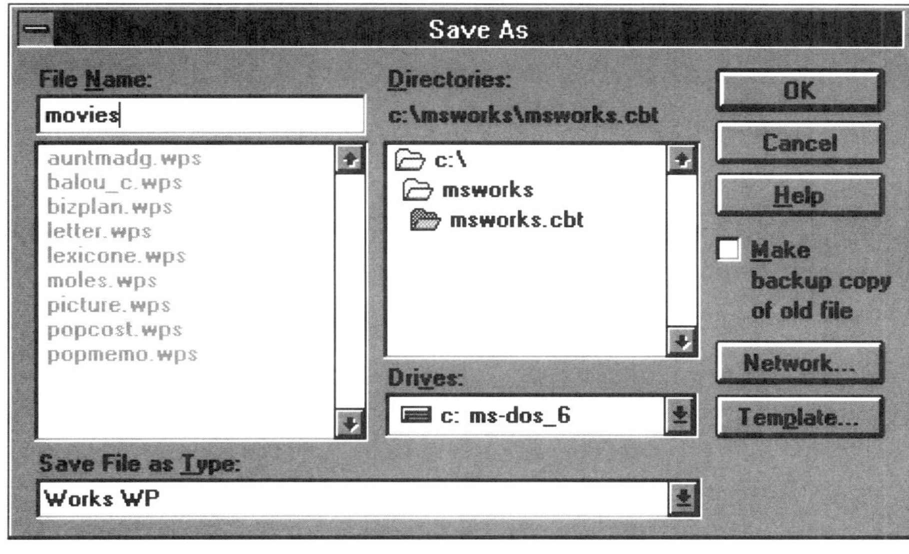

Figure 9x-20. *Type in the new name "movies" in the File Name text box.*

Editing Spreadsheets — Exercise

In this exercise you will practise editing what is in a spreadsheet. You'll learn how to name a range, change the number format of cells, and format the cells.

People of all levels of expertise in Works can benefit from this exercise. If you like a challenge, complete the exercise using the Steps in Brief, listed below. This lists the exercise outline, with no hints.

If you need more assistance, refer to the Steps in Detail on the following pages. The Steps in Detail expand each step, listing details and hints that enable you to complete the exercise.

Steps in Brief

1. ***Open popsales.wks from the msworks.cbt subdirectory.***
2. ***Apply the range name "Flavors" to cells A6 through A12.***
3. ***Edit cell A2 to read "Seabuddy Frozen Pops Inc."***
4. ***Change the numeric format of the values in columns B and C to Currency.***
5. ***Change the font of cell A2 to Helvetica.***
6. ***Remove bold and add italic in cell A2.***
7. ***Italicize the "Flavors" range.***
8. ***Center all the text in the block A6:A12.***
9. ***Change the width of column A to 16.***
10. ***Delete row 1.***

Steps in Detail

1. ***Open popsales.wks from the msworks.cbt subdirectory.***

   To access the *Open* dialog box (Figure 10x-1) select *Open Existing File* from the **File** menu. Double-click on the file to open it onto your screen.

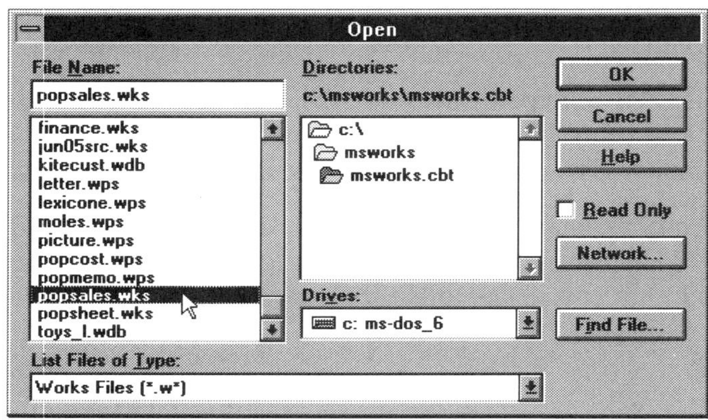

Figure 10x-1. ***Select*** ***popsales.wks*** *from the Open dialog box.*

2. ***Apply the range name "Flavors" to cells A6 through A12.***

   A range name is applied to a group of cells which are referred to frequently. The cells to be given the name need to be highlighted before the process of entering the name begins. Highlight the cells in Figure 10x-2 by clicking on cell A6 and dragging the mouse pointer down to A12.

6	Abalone Apricot
7	Blowfish Blueberry
8	Crab Cherry
9	Grouper Grape
10	Lungfish Lemon
11	Lobster Licorice
12	Octopus Orange

Figure 10x-2. *Highlight A6 through A12 by dragging over them with the mouse.*

The *Range Name* command is in the **Insert** menu (Figure 10x-3). Select it to get the *Range Name* dialog box of Figure 10x-4.

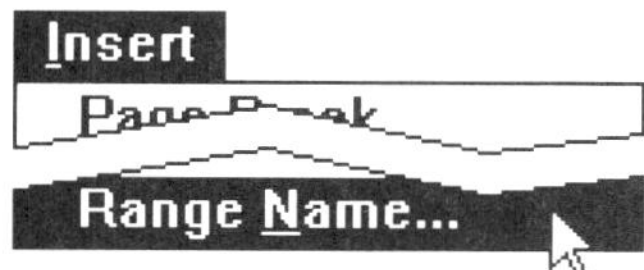

Figure 10x-3. *Select Range Name from the **Insert** menu.*

The *Range Name* dialog box inserts the text in the first cell into the Name text box—"Abalone Apricot." The name of this range is to be "Flavors" so key this into the *Name* text box, see Figure 10x-4, and click on *OK*.

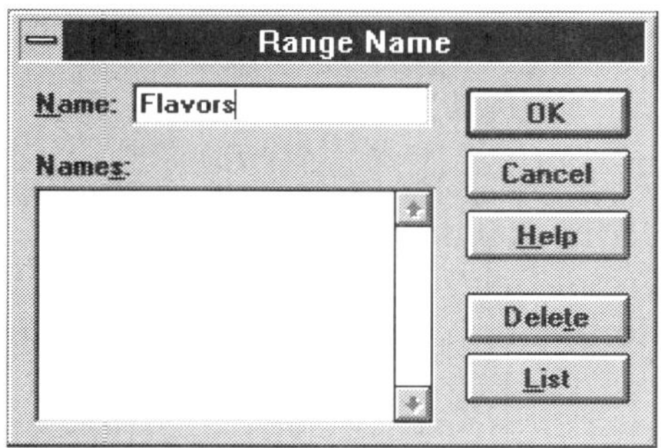

Figure 10x-4. *Type "Flavors" into the Name text box and click on OK.*

3. *Edit cell A2 to read "Seabuddy Frozen Pops Inc."*

To add the letters "Inc." to the end of this text, the insertion point needs to be reinserted back into the formula bar with cell A2 selected. The F2 key is a quick and easy way to edit a cell. Clicking the mouse in the formula bar would also work. Use either of these methods to edit the cell, and add the information as in Figure 10x-5. Press Enter when finished.

Figure 10x-5. *Type "Inc." into the formula bar while the insertion point is at the end of the text.*

4. Change the numeric format of the values in columns B and C to Currency.

The cells to be formatted must be highlighted before the format is applied. The easiest way to highlight the cells is to drag over them with the mouse as in Figure 10x-6.

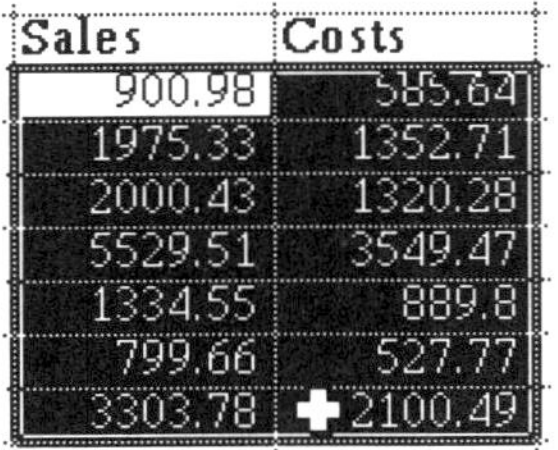

Figure 10x-6. *Use the mouse to select these cells.*

The Currency format is added to cells through the **Format** menu or by clicking on the *Currency* button in the toolbar. Use the toolbar to add the format to the highlighted cells (Figure 10x-7).

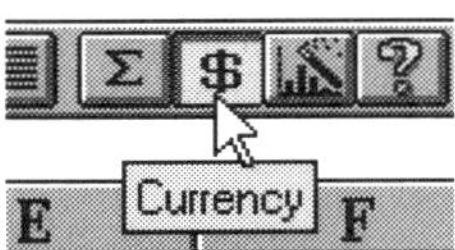

Figure 10x-7. *Click on the Currency button in the toolbar to change the format to Currency.*

5. Change the font of cell A2 to Helvetica.

The font attribute is changed through the **Format** menu or the *Font* submenu on the toolbar. To make the change in this example, use the *Font* command in the **Format** menu following Figures 10x-8 through 10x-10.

	A
1	
2	Seabuddy Frozen Pops Inc.
3	Sales by flavor for:

Figure 10x-8. *Move the cell pointer to cell A2.*

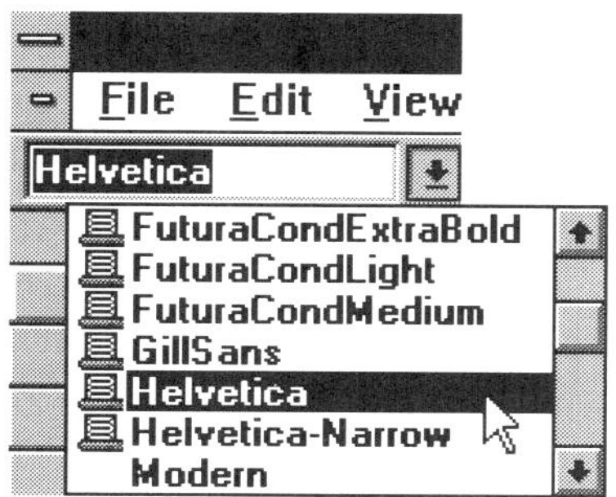

Figure 10x-9. *Select Helvetica from the Font submenu in the toolbar.*

Figure 10x-10. *Cell A2 looks like this after you click on Helvetica.*

6. *Remove bold and add italic in cell A2.*

The style of a cell is changed through the **Format** menu or using the toolbar. With the cell pointer in A2, use the toolbar to remove bold as in Figure 10x-11.

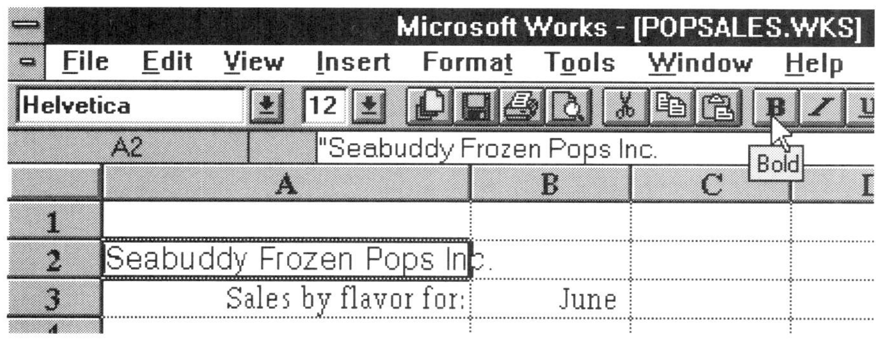

Figure 10x-11. *Click on the Bold button on the toolbar.*

The cell is made italic using the Italic button on the toolbar. Figure 10x-12 shows this button.

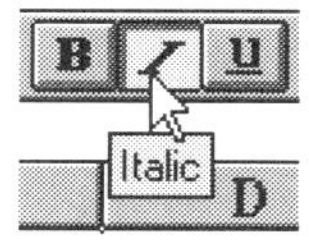

Figure 10x-12. *Click on the Italic button to italicize the cell.*

7. *Italicize the "Flavors" range.*

Earlier in this exercise, the *Range Name* "Flavors" was added to the cells A6:A12. In this part you can use that *Range Name* to quickly find and highlight the cells using the *Go To* feature. Press F5 and the *Go To* dialog box appears. To select this range, click on "Flavors (A6:A12)" in the *Names* list box (Figure 10x-13) and click on *OK*.

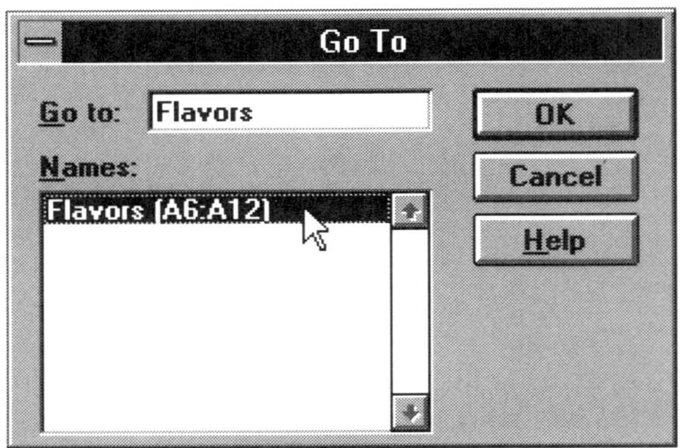

Figure 10x-13. *Click on "Flavors (A6:A12)" in the Go To dialog box.*

Once the cells are selected, an italic style is added in the same way as outlined previously (see Figure 10x-14).

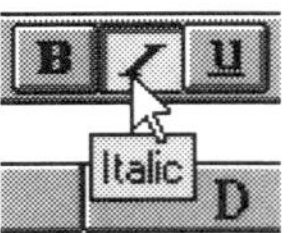

Figure 10x-14. *Click on the Italic button on the toolbar.*

8. *Center all the text in the block A6:A12.*

The cells A6:A12 should still be highlighted from the previous step. If you moved the cell pointer since then select the cells again using the mouse or the keyboard.

Alignment is changed using the toolbar or through the *Alignment* command in the **Format** menu. The latter method is used in Figures 10x-15 and 10x-16.

*Figure 10x-15. Select Alignment from the **Format** menu.*

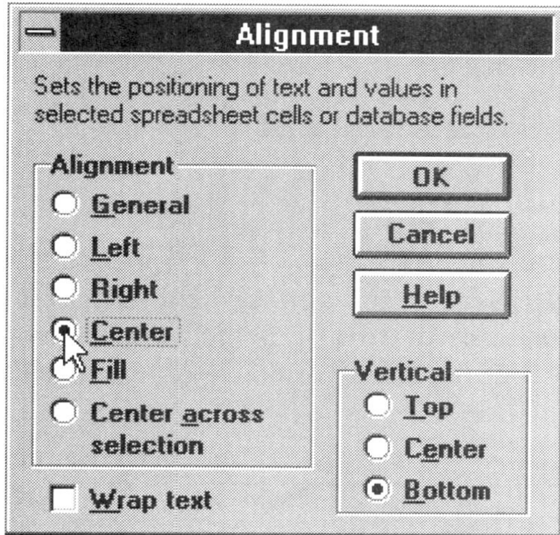

Figure 10x-16. Click on Center in the Alignment dialog box and then click on OK.

9. Change the width of column A to 16.

The insertion point must be sitting in column A to change its width. The width of one column is adjusted to a specific width through the *Column Width* command in the **Format** menu (Figure 10x-17).

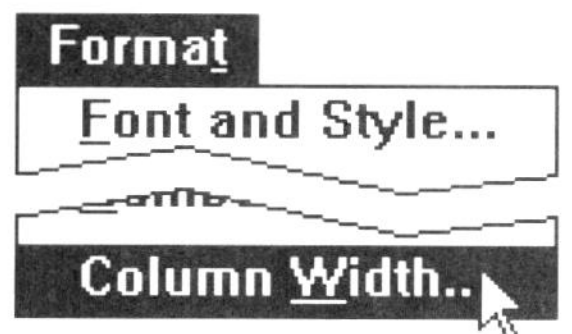

Figure 10x-17. Choose the Column Width command.

The *Column Width* dialog box appears with the preset width of 23 in the *Width* text box. Type 16 in this text box as in Figure 10x-18, and click on OK.

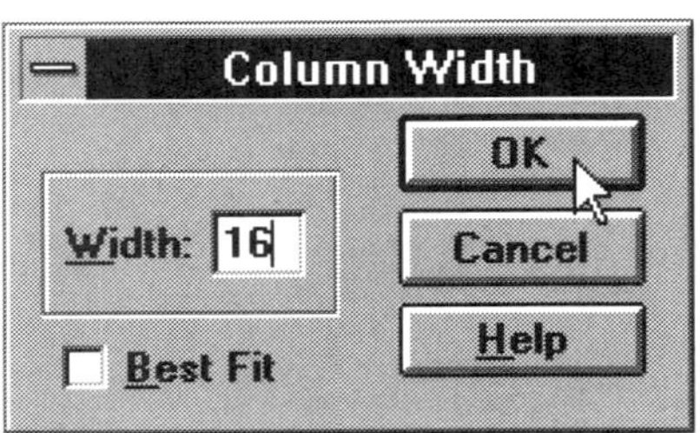

Figure 10x-18. *Enter 16 into the Width text box.*

10. Delete row 1.

Row 1 is not necessary in the spreadsheet so it can be deleted. Works deletes a column or row in which the insertion point is positioned. Follow Figures 10x-19 and 10x-20 to complete this task.

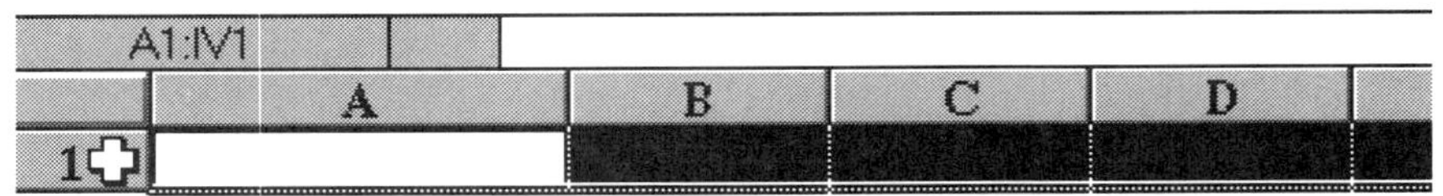

Figure 10x-19. *Select all of row 1 by clicking on the "1" in the worksheet frame.*

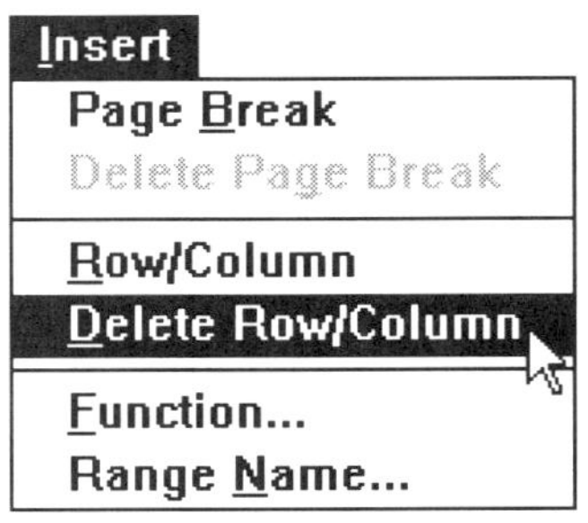

Figure 10x-20. *Choose Delete Row/ Column from the* ***Insert*** *menu.*

The exercise is now complete. You may wish to save the file under another name.

Moving, Copying, and Addressing Cells — Exercise

In this exercise you will practise how to move and copy the data in cells, as well as how to use cell addresses in formulas.

People of all levels of expertise in Works can benefit from this exercise. If you like a challenge, complete the exercise using the Steps in Brief, listed below. This lists the exercise outline, with no hints.

If you need more assistance, refer to the Steps in Detail on the following pages. The Steps in Detail expand each step, listing details and hints that enable you to complete the exercise.

Steps in Brief

1. *Create a new spreadsheet file.*
2. *Insert the data as shown in Figure 11x-3.*
3. *Move the heading in A1 across to C1.*
4. *Insert a formula to calculate the fee income in cell E4.*
5. *Use the Fill Down command to copy the fee income figures in column E.*
6. *Calculate the "commission to stars" figures as fee income multiplied by the commission rate.*
7. *Use the Fill Down command to copy the "commission to stars" figures in column F.*
8. *Sort the names into alphabetical order.*

Steps in Detail

1. ***Create a new spreadsheet file.***

A new spreadsheet file is created through the *Create New File* command in the **File** menu as Figure 11x-1 illustrates. The *Startup* dialog box appears on the screen. Click on the *Spreadsheet* button (Figure 11x-2) to open a blank spreadsheet.

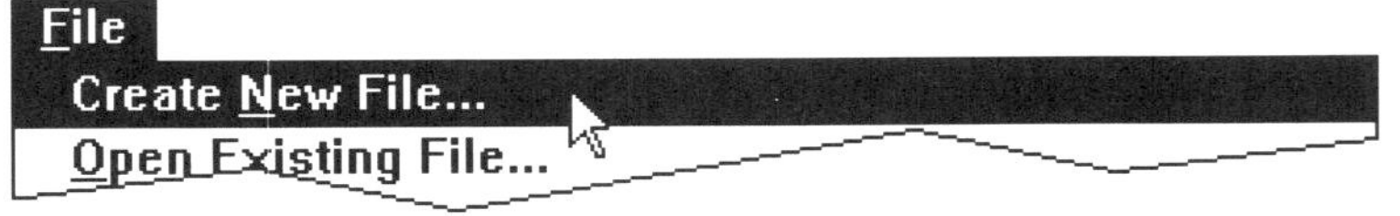

Figure 11x-1. *Click on Create New File.*

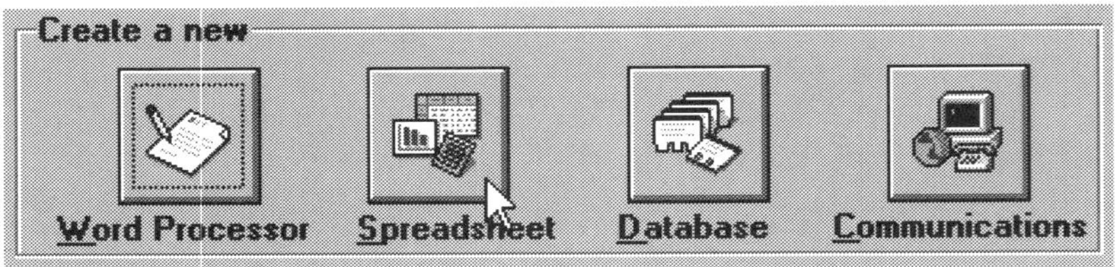

Figure 11x-2. *Click on the Spreadsheet button.*

2. ***Insert the data as shown in Figure 11x-3.***

Microsoft Works - [Sheet1]

File Edit View Insert Format Tools Window Help

Arial 10

F11 0.12

	A	B	C	D	E	F	G
1	Fifties Fan Club						
2							
3	Stars		No. of Fans	Memebership Fee	Fee Income	Commission to Star	
4	Sinatra	Frank	1,556,677	$25.50			
5	Domino	Fats	1,525,777	$22.00			
6	Richard	Little	767,688	$18.98			
7	Berry	Chuck	1,729,991	$30.00			
8	Laine	Frankie	455,666	$15.95			
9	Presley	Elvis	10,345,678	$35.99			
10						Commission Rate	
11						12.00%	

Figure 11x-3. *The data to be inserted.*

Various changes have been made to the format of the values and the size of columns in the spreadsheet. A summary of value formats is listed on the next page. The columns have been adjusted as necessary, using the column border on the frame. For more information on these changes, see **Chapter 10, Editing Spreadsheets**.

Cells C4:C9 — Comma, zero decimal places.

Cells D4:D9 — Currency, 2 decimal places.

Cell F11 — Percent, 2 decimal places.

Cells E4:E9 — Currency, 0 decimal places.

Cells F4:F9 — Currency, 0 decimal places.

3. *Move the heading in A1 across to C1.*

Moving the heading across the spreadsheet is an easy way of having a heading appear in the center of the data. Moving data can be done using the *Cut* and *Paste* commands in the **Edit** menu or by dragging. See Figures 11x-4 through 11x-5 for details on completing this step.

Figure 11x-4. *Click on cell A1.*

Figure 11x-5. *Move the mouse pointer onto the edge of the cell so that the pointer appears as shown.*

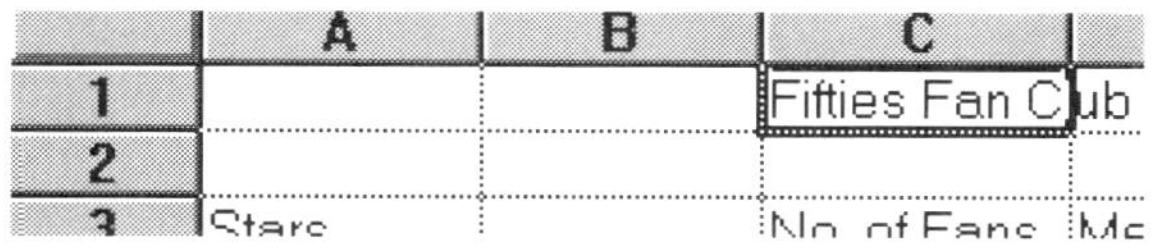

Figure 11x-6. *Drag the outline of the cell to cell C1 and release the mouse button to move the data.*

4. *Insert a formula to calculate the fee income in cell E4.*

The fee income is calculated using a formula which multiplies the number of fans in column C by the membership fee in column D. In E4, the formula is "=C4*D4." Move into cell E4 and type in a formula prefix (=) as in Figure 11x-7.

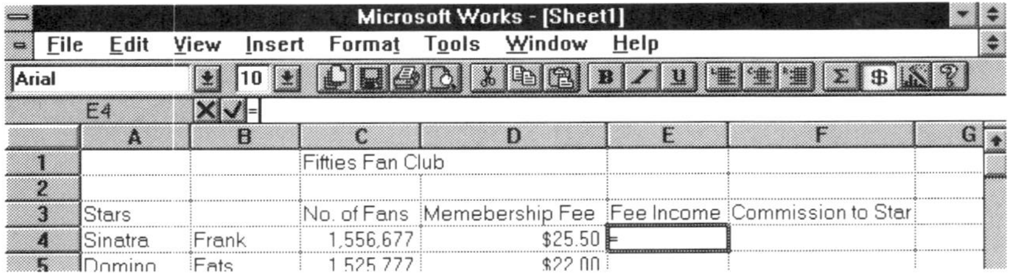

Figure 11x-7. Type in a formula prefix in cell E4.

You can create the rest of the formula using the pointing method outlined in Figures 11x-8 and 11x-9.

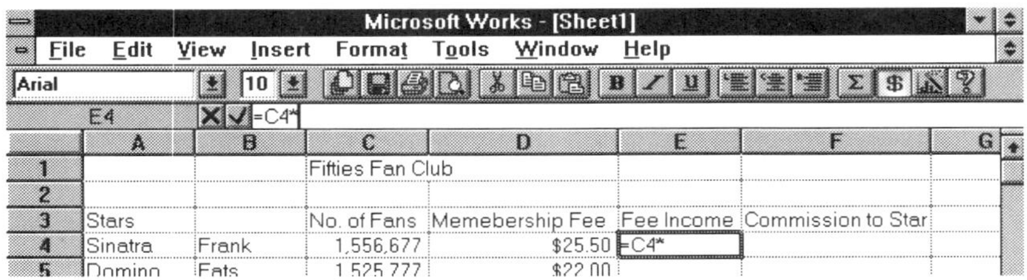

Figure 11x-8. Click on cell C4 and then type in a multiplication sign (*).

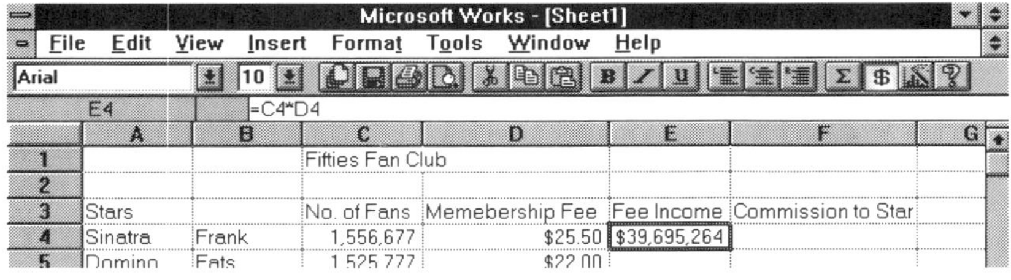

Figure 11x-9. Click on cell D4 and press Enter.

5. ***Use the Fill Down command to copy the fee income figures in column E.***

This basic formula is required in all the cells in column E. Instead of having to create the formula again, Works enables you to copy the formula into cells E5 to E9 using the *Fill Down* command in the **Edit** menu.

Highlight the block E4 to E9 which contains the cell being copied and the cells into which the data is being copied. See Figure 11x-10 for details.

Figure 11x-10. *Highlight E4:E9 to copy E4.*

The formula is copied relatively, when the *Fill Down* command is used in this case. This means that the formula in cell E5 calculates the fee income according to Fats Domino's number of fans and membership fee. Calculate the fee income for the remaining stars by selecting *Fill Down* from the **Edit** Menu (Figure 11x-11).

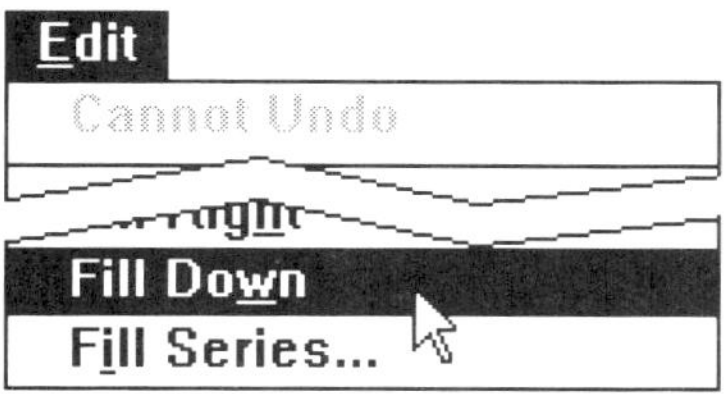

Figure 11x-11. *Select Fill Down from the* ***Edit*** *Menu.*

Adjust the width of column E if necessary. Your spreadsheet is now as shown in Figure 11x-12.

Figure 11x-12. *The completed figures.*

6. ***Calculate the "commission to stars" figures as fee income multiplied by the commission rate.***

This formula requires an absolute cell address for the commission rate as this is a constant figure referred to by a number of cells. The commission rate is in cell F11.

The complete formula for cell F4 is "=E4*F11." Move into F4 and insert "=" as the formula prefix. Figures 11x-13 and 11x-14 give details on completing this task.

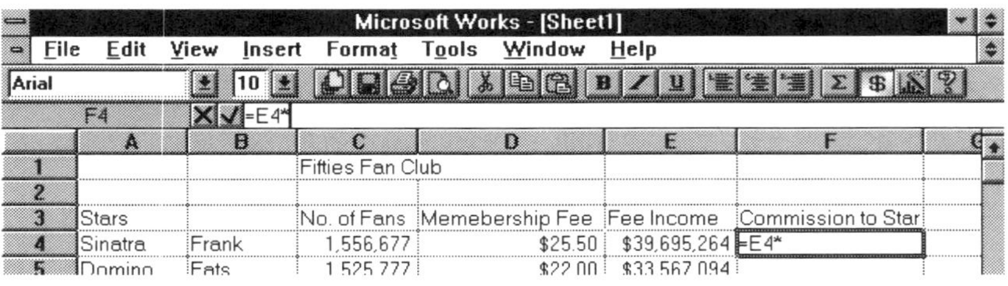

Figure 11x-13. Click on E4 and press the multiplication sign (*).

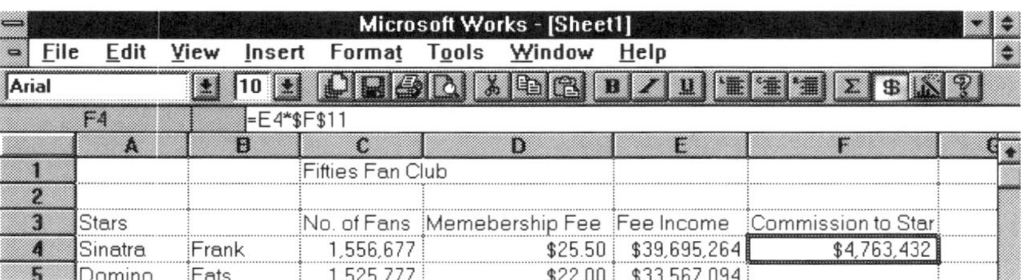

Figure 11x-14. Click on cell F11 and press the F4 key to make the cell address absolute. Press Enter.

7. ***Use the Fill Down command to copy the "commission to star" figures in column F.***

The formula in cell F4 is copied down the column using *Fill Down* in the **Edit** menu, as used in Step 5. Select cells F4:F9 and choose *Fill Down* so your spreadsheet is the same as Figure 11x-15.

Microsoft Works - [Sheet1]

File Edit View Insert Format Tools Window Help

Arial 10

F4:F9 =E4*F11

	A	B	C	D	E	F
1			Fifties Fan Club			
2						
3	Stars		No. of Fans	Memebership Fee	Fee Income	Commission to Star
4	Sinatra	Frank	1,556,677	$25.50	$39,695,264	$4,763,432
5	Domino	Fats	1,525,777	$22.00	$33,567,094	$4,028,051
6	Richard	Little	767,688	$18.98	$14,570,718	$1,748,486
7	Berry	Chuck	1,729,991	$30.00	$51,899,730	$6,227,968
8	Laine	Frankie	455,666	$15.95	$7,267,873	$872,145
9	Presley	Elvis	10,345,678	$35.99	$372,340,951	$44,680,914
10						Commission Rate
11						12.00%

*Figure 11x-15. The formula is copied down using the Fill Down command in the **Edit** menu.*

8. Sort the names into alphabetical order.

The names of the stars are not in alphabetical order and, using the *Sort Rows* command in the **Tools** menu, this is not difficult to achieve. The type of sort needs to determined first. In this case, column A is sorted in ascending alphabetical order. The rows to be sorted need to be selected as in Figure 11x-16.

3	Stars		No. of Fans	Memebership Fee	Fee Income	Commission to Star
4	Sinatra	Frank	1,556,677	$25.50	$39,695,264	$4,763,432
5	Domino	Fats	1,525,777	$22.00	$33,567,094	$4,028,051
6	Richard	Little	767,688	$18.98	$14,570,718	$1,748,486
7	Berry	Chuck	1,729,991	$30.00	$51,899,730	$6,227,968
8	Laine	Frankie	455,666	$15.95	$7,267,873	$872,145
9	Presley	Elvis	10,345,678	$35.99	$372,340,951	$44,680,914
10						Commission Rate
11						12.00%

Figure 11x-16. Highlight rows 4 through 9 by dragging the mouse pointer over the row labels on the frame.

The *Sort Rows* command in the **Tools** menu is used to sort the rows of the spreadsheet. Choose this now to display the *Sort Rows* dialog box. The dialog box is used the specify the sorting detail. The information in the *1st column* box is correct as it stands, Figure 11x-17.

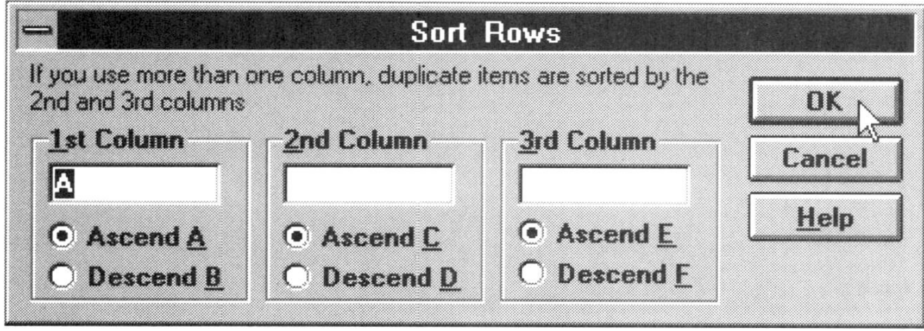

***Figure 11x-17.** The Sort Rows dialog box with the data used to sort the "Stars" into alphabetical order.*

Click on *OK* to sort the information; your spreadsheet then looks like Figure 11x-18.

3	Stars		No. of Fans	Memebership Fee	Fee Income	Commission to Star
4	Berry	Chuck	1,729,991	$30.00	$51,899,730	$6,227,968
5	Domino	Fats	1,525,777	$22.00	$33,567,094	$4,028,051
6	Laine	Frankie	455,666	$15.95	$7,267,873	$872,145
7	Presley	Elvis	10,345,678	$35.99	$372,340,951	$44,680,914
8	Richard	Little	767,688	$18.98	$14,570,718	$1,748,486
9	Sinatra	Frank	1,556,677	$25.50	$39,695,264	$4,763,432
10						Commission Rate

***Figure 11x-18.** The sorted spreadsheet.*

The exercise is now complete. You may wish to save the file using the *Save As* command in the **File** menu.

Creating Charts — Exercise

In this exercise you will practise how to create charts to make your data easier to interpret.

People of all levels of expertise in Works can benefit from this exercise. If you like a challenge, complete the exercise using the Steps in Brief, listed below. This lists the exercise outline, with no hints.

If you need more assistance, refer to the Steps in Detail on the following pages. The Steps in Detail expand each step, listing details and hints that enable you to complete the exercise.

Steps in Brief

1. *Open the file popsales.wks from the msworks.cbt subdirectory.*
2. *Create a new chart using cells A5:C9.*
3. *Enter the following titles:*
   Chart title: A2
   Subtitle: Selected Profits
   Y Axis title: US Dollars
4. *Change the font of the chart title to 20 point New Century Schoolbook. (Use Times if Schoolbook is not available.)*
5. *Change the second series color to dark blue.*
6. *Set the type of chart to a mixed line and bar chart, with the second series displaying a line.*
7. *Create a second chart using cells A5:B12 and change it to a pie chart.*
8. *Explode slice 3 to highlight the figures for "Crab Cherry."*
9. *Name the charts:*
   Chart1: Selected Profits
   Chart2: June Sales
10. *Change the paper orientation to landscape for "Selected Profits."*
11. *Preview chart "Selected Profits" in Print Preview.*
12. *Print the chart "Selected Profits."*

Steps in Detail

1. ***Open the file popsales.wks from the msworks.cbt subdirectory.***

The file ***popsales.wks*** is in the ***msworks.cbt*** subdirectory. Use the *Open Existing File* command in the **File** menu to display the *Open* dialog box. Double-click on ***popsales.wks*** (Figure 13x-1).

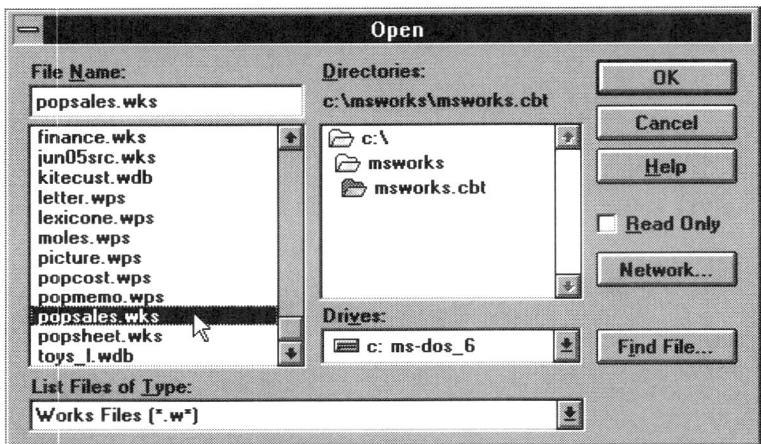

Figure 13x-1. Open popsales.wks.

2. ***Create a new chart using cells A5:C9.***

To create a new chart in Works, the cells which input the data into the chart—A5:C9—are selected first as in Figure 13x-2.

4			
5	Flavor	Sales	Costs
6	Abalone Apricot	900.98	585.64
7	Blowfish Blueberry	1975.33	1352.71
8	Crab Cherry	2000.43	1320.28
9	Grouper Grape	5529.51	3549.47
10	Lungfish Lemon	1334.55	889.8
11	Lobster Licorice	799.66	527.77
12	Octopus Orange	3303.78	2100.49
13			

Figure 13x-2. Cells A5:C9 are highlighted for the chart.

A chart is created using the *Create New Chart* command in the **Tools** menu, or by clicking on the *New Chart* button on the toolbar (Figure 13x-3). Use either of these methods to create the chart.

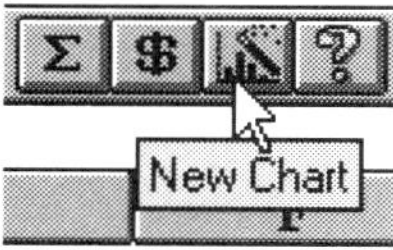

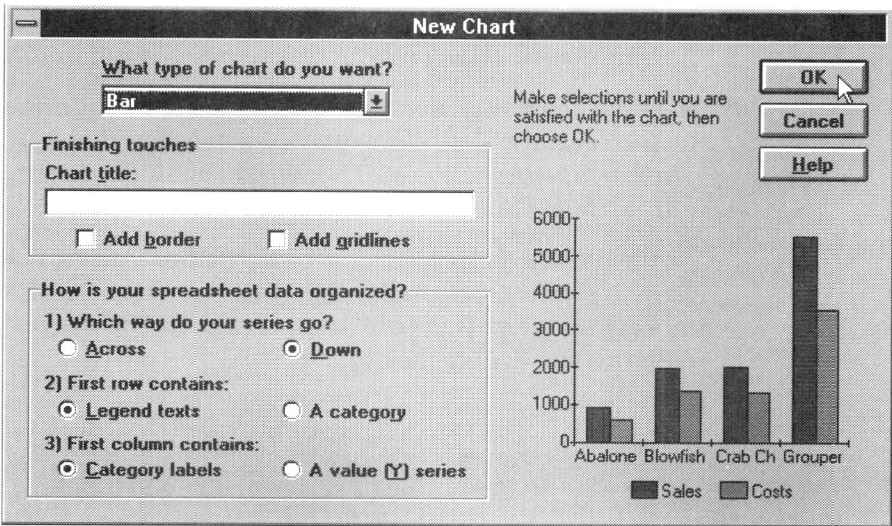

Figure 13x-3. Click on the New Chart button on the toolbar to open the New Chart dialog box. Click on OK to create the new chart.

3. ***Enter the following titles:***
   Chart title: ***A2***
   Subtitle: ***Selected Profits***
   Y Axis title: ***US Dollars***

Titles are entered through the *Titles* command in the **Edit** menu. The data for each title is then inserted into the appropriate text boxes in the *Titles* dialog box. Figure 13x-4 and 13x-5 give details.

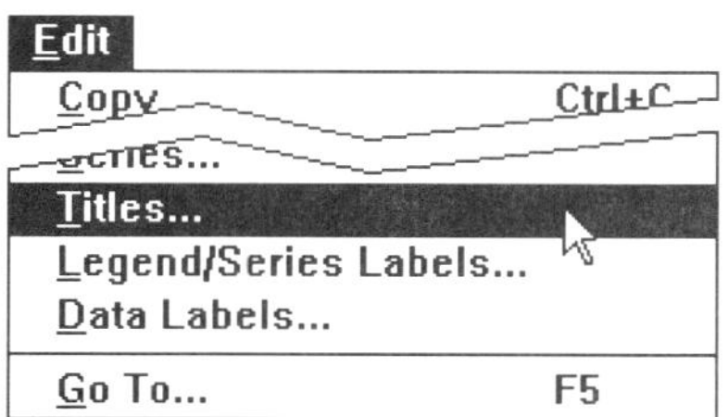

Figure 13x-4. *Choose Titles from the* ***Edit*** *menu.*

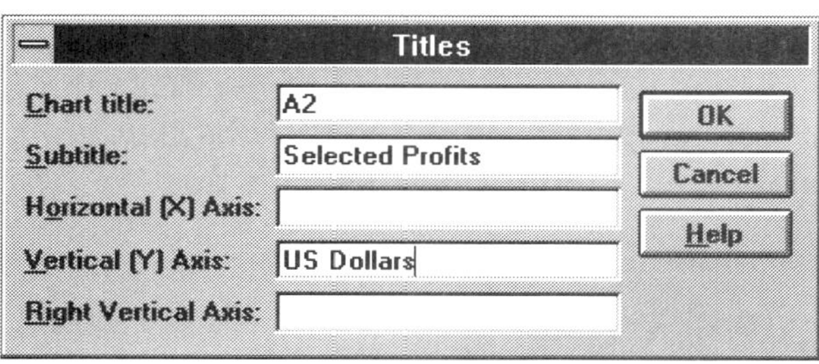

Figure 13x-5. *Type in the data in each text box as shown and click on OK.*

4. ***Change the font of the chart title to 20 point New Century Schoolbook. (Use Times if Schoolbook is not available.)***

As the chart title is important, it should be prominent. Changing the font and the size is one way of achieving this. We suggest New Century Schoolbook in a 20 point size, but if this is not available, any font, such as Times, can be used.

You need to select the chart title before you can change its font characteristics. Click on the chart title and choose *Font and Style* from the **Format** menu (Figure 13x-6). Complete the dialog box as shown in Figure 13x-7, and click on *OK*.

***Figure 13x-6.** Select your title and choose the Font and Style command from the **Format** menu.*

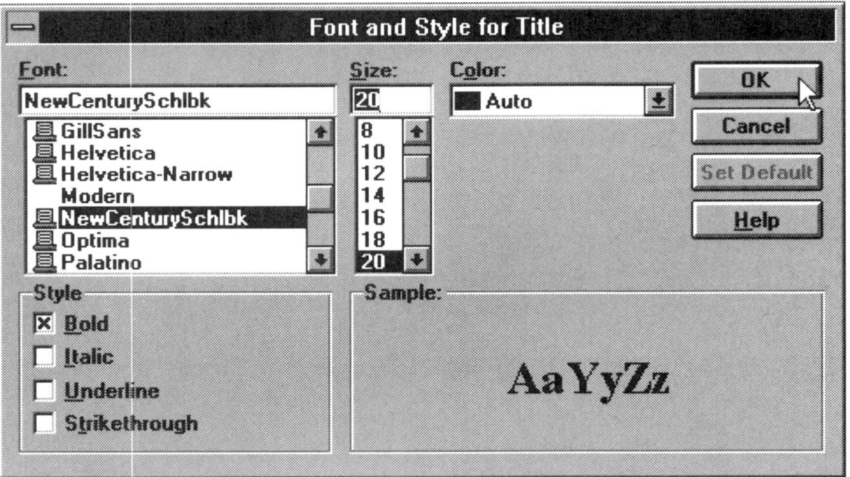

***Figure 13x-7.** Select New Century Schoolbook from the Font submenu and 20 from the Size submenu.*

5. ***Change the second series color to dark blue.***

At present, the second series is displayed as a green color on the screen. Colors can be changed through the *Patterns and Colors* command in the **Format** menu. Figure 13x-8 displays this.

Figure 13x-8. Choose the Patterns and Colors command in the **Format** menu.

In the *Patterns and Colors* dialog box, the series to be changed is selected before the change is made (Figure 13x-9).

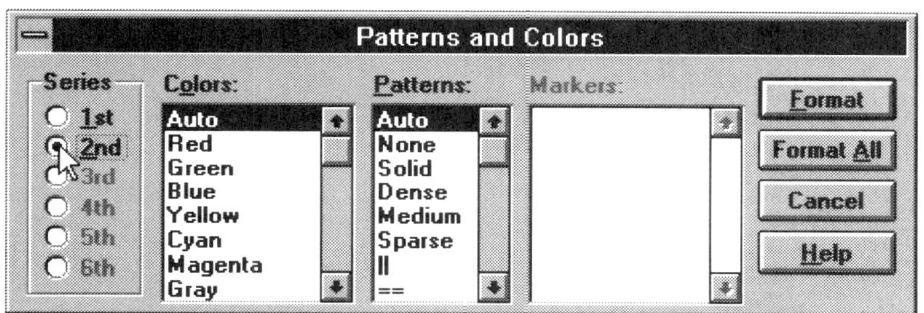

Figure 13x-9. Select 2nd from the Series section.

Once the series is selected, changes to the color and pattern are made. Figures 13x-10 and 13x-11 show details.

Figure 13x-10. Select Dark Blue from the Colors list.

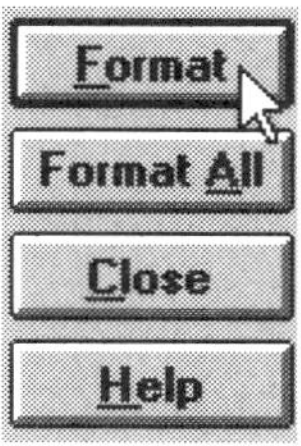

Figure 13x-11. Click on Format to set this color to the second series.

Before any changes were made, the third button in the dialog box said *Cancel*. The button automatically changes to *Close* once colors or patterns are altered. Click on *Close* to return to the chart.

6. ***Set the type of chart to a mixed line and bar chart, with the second series displaying a line.***

A Mixed Line and Bar type is used when a particular piece of information needs to be highlighted. In this case, the difference between the sales and costs figures are of great significance. Therefore, you can create a mixed chart, placing the costs figures on the line. Follow Figures 13x-12 and 13x-13 to create the chart in Figure 13x-14.

*Figure 13x-12. Select Mixed Line and Bar from the **Format** menu.*

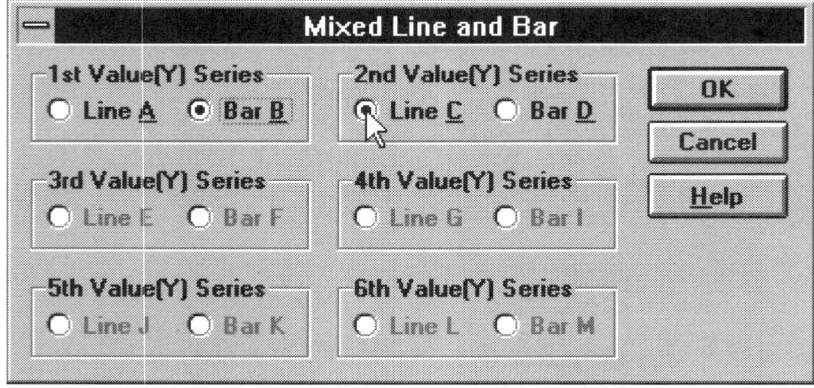

***Figure 13x-13.** Click on Line C in the 2nd Value (Y) Series section and then click on OK.*

The title can still be selected on your chart. Once you click on your chart outside of the title, the chart should look like that in Figure 13x-14.

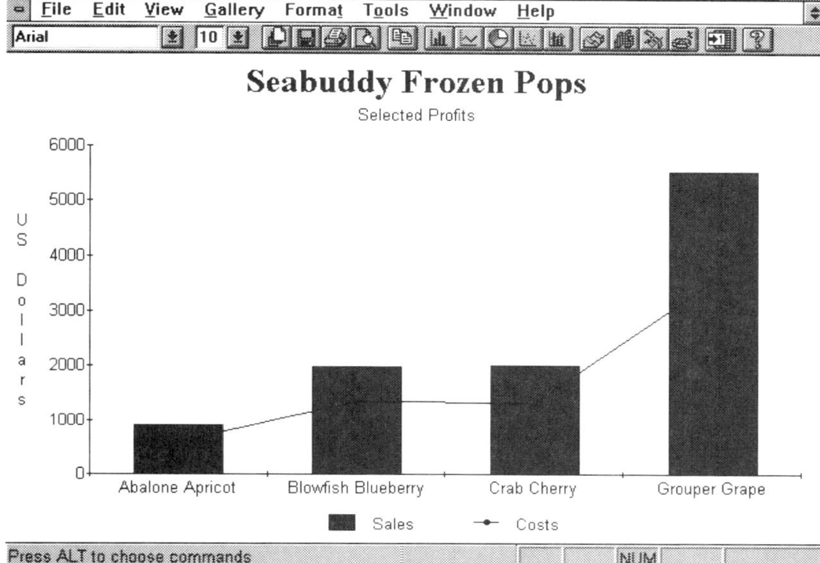

***Figure 13x-14.** The mixed line and bar chart.*

7. ***Create a second chart using cells A5:B12 and change it to a pie chart.***

A second chart can be created in the same spreadsheet. The second chart is created in the same way as outlined above. See Figures 13x-15 and 13x-16 for more details.

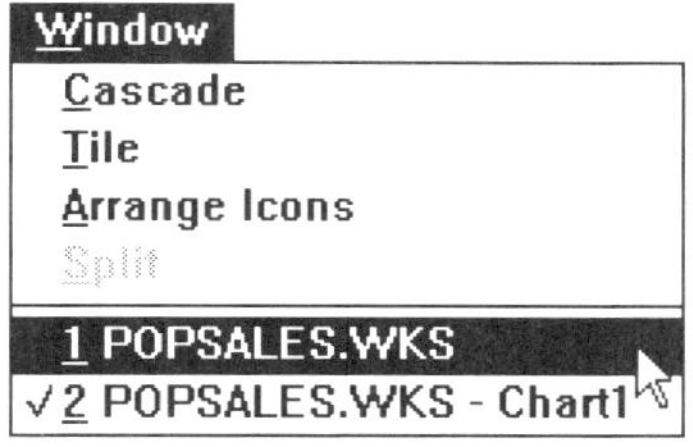

***Figure 13x-15.** Choose POPSALES.WKS from the **Window** menu to move back to the spreadsheet.*

5	Flavor	Sales
6	Abalone Apricot	900.98
7	Blowfish Blueberry	1975.33
8	Crab Cherry	2000.43
9	Grouper Grape	5529.51
10	Lungfish Lemon	1334.55
11	Lobster Licorice	799.66
12	Octopus Orange	[illegible]03.78

***Figure 13x-16.** Highlight cells A5:B12.*

Select *Create New Chart* from the **Tools** menu and click on *OK* in the *New chart* dialog box to create a bar chart which is the default chart type. To change the bar chart to a pie chart, see Figure 13x-17.

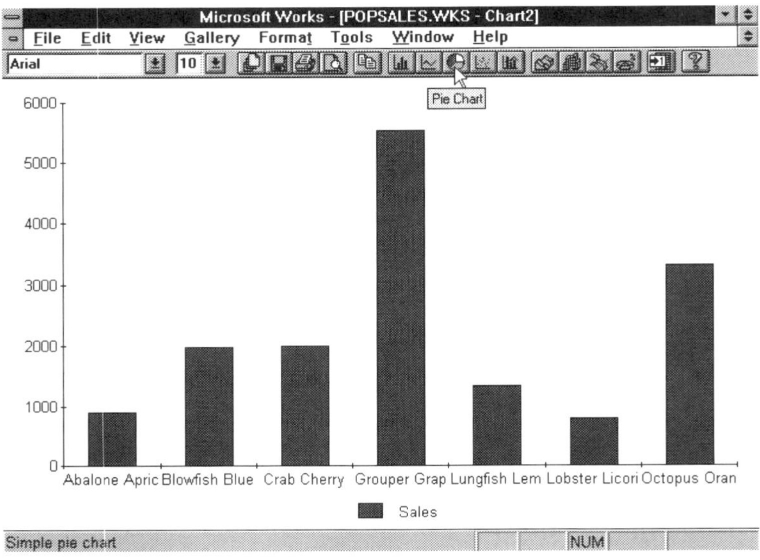

Figure 13x-17. *Click on the Pie chart button on the toolbar.*

The fourth type of pie chart in the *Pie* dialog box is suitable for this purpose. Click on it now and choose *OK* (Figure 13x-18) to return to your chart.

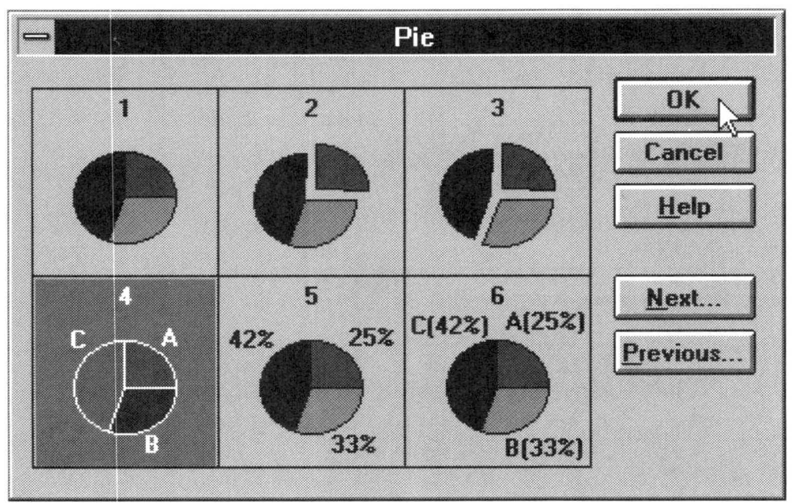

Figure 13x-18. *Choose the fourth option in the Pie dialog box.*

8. Explode slice 3 to highlight the figures for "Crab Cherry."

An exploded piece of "pie" draws attention to part of the pie. It is done through the *Patterns and Colors* dialog box which appears when a pie chart is active. Choose *Patterns and Colors* from the **Format** menu and see Figures 13x-19 and 13x-20 to explode the piece.

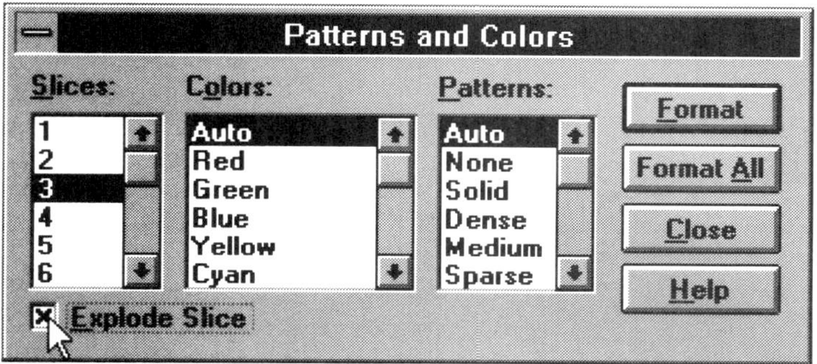

Figure 13x-19. *Click on 3 in the Slices section and then Explode Slice.*

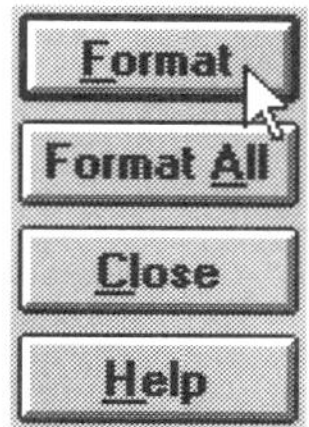

Figure 13x-20. *Click on Format to highlight slice 3.*

The *Patterns and Colors* dialog box is closed by clicking on *Close*. Do this now and your chart should look like the one in Figure 13x-21.

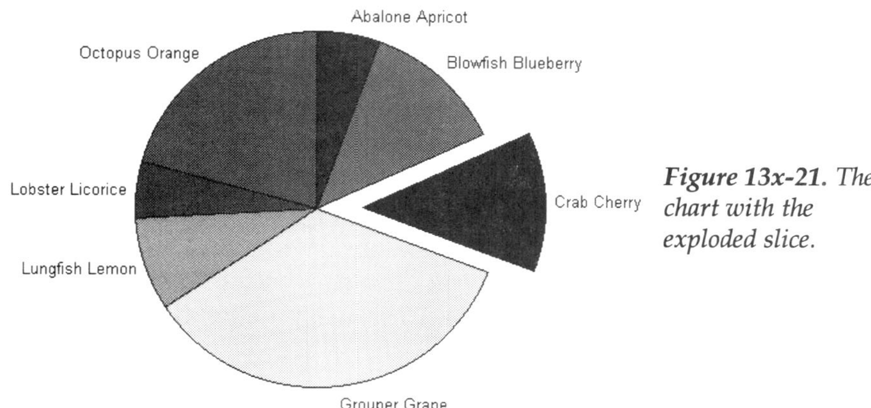

Figure 13x-21. *The chart with the exploded slice.*

9. *Name the charts:*
   Chart1: *Selected Profits*
   Chart2: *June Sales*

Spreadsheets which have more than one chart usually apply descriptive names to the charts to make them more distinguishable. ***Chart1*** is being called "Selected Profits" and this is applied through the **Tools** menu. Figures 13x-22 through 13x-24 show you how to apply names to your charts.

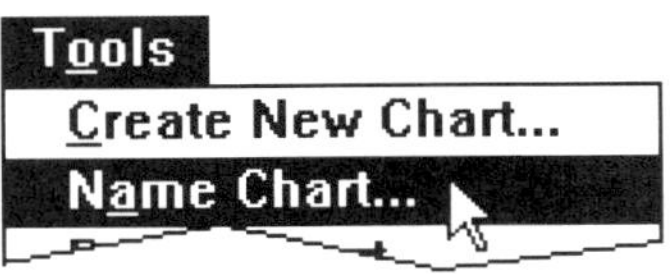

Figure 13x-22. *Select Name Chart from the* ***Tools*** *menu.*

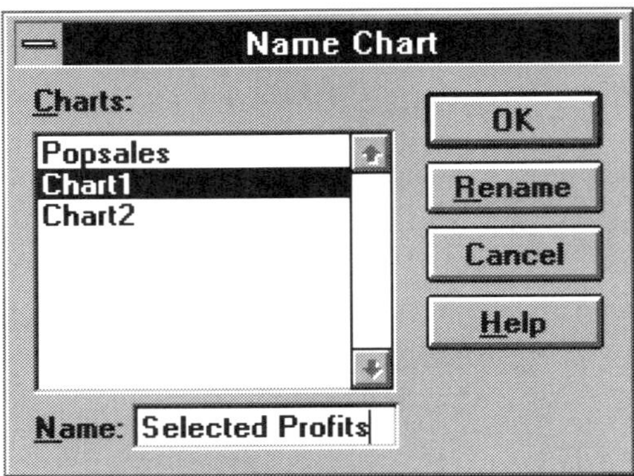

Figure 13x-23. *With* ***Chart1*** *selected, click in the Name text box, and type in "Selected Profits."*

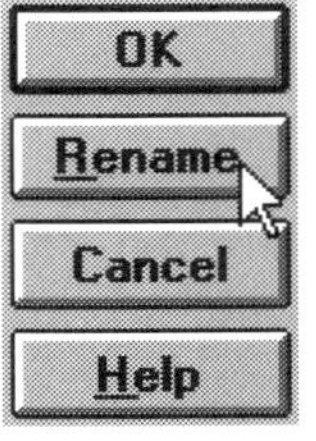

Figure 13x-24. *Click on the Rename button.*

A name is given to ***Chart2*** in the same way. The dialog box is still on the screen, so click on ***Chart2*** then click in the *Name* text box and type in "June Sales." Figure 13x-25 shows you the dialog box to give ***Chart2*** a name.

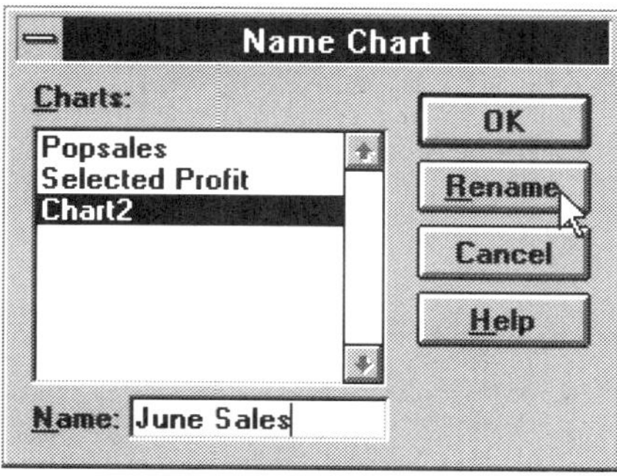

__Figure 13x-25.__ Click on Rename when "June Sales" is typed into the Name text box. Then click on OK.

10. Change the paper orientation to landscape for "Selected Profits."

Move back to this chart through the **Window** menu. Works stores the individual paper orientation you set for each chart. Changing the paper to landscape is a two-part process. The first step is to change the orientation in *Printer Setup*, which Figures 13x-26 and 13x-27 show.

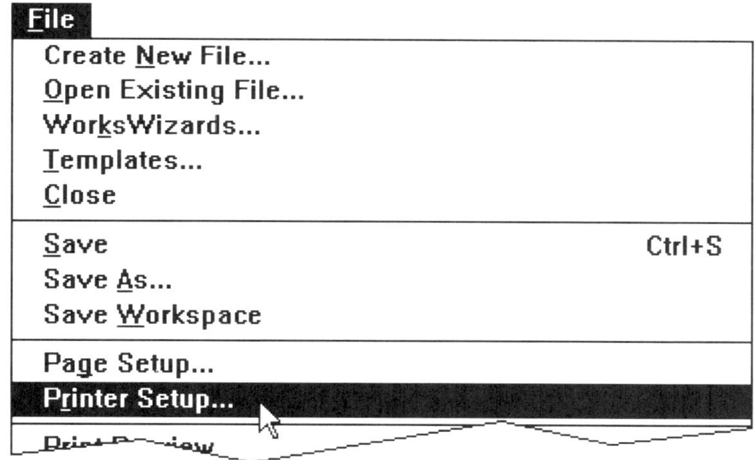

__Figure 13x-26.__ Choose Printer Setup from the __File__ menu.

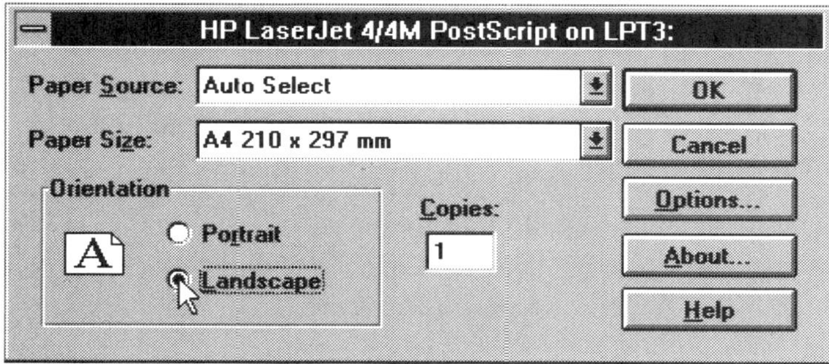

__Figure 13x-27.__ Click on the Setup button in the Printer Setup dialog box to open the dialog box for your printer. Click on Landscape as shown and click on OK until you return to your chart.

The paper size and type needs to be altered at this stage. This is done through the *Page Setup* dialog box which appears through the *Page Setup* command in the **File** menu. Click on the *Source, Size and Orientation* tab and then choose *Landscape* (Figure 13x-28).

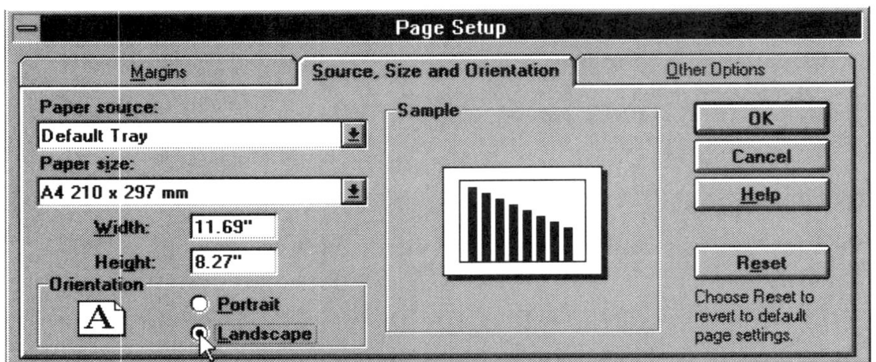

Figure 13x-28. *Choose Source, Size and Orientation. Then choose Landscape and click on OK.*

11. Preview chart "Selected Profits" in Print Preview.

To view the chart as it will print, click on the *Print Preview* button on the toolbar (Figure 13x-29). The screen is displayed in Figure 13x-30.

Figure 13x-29. *Activate Print Preview by clicking on the Print Preview button on the toolbar.*

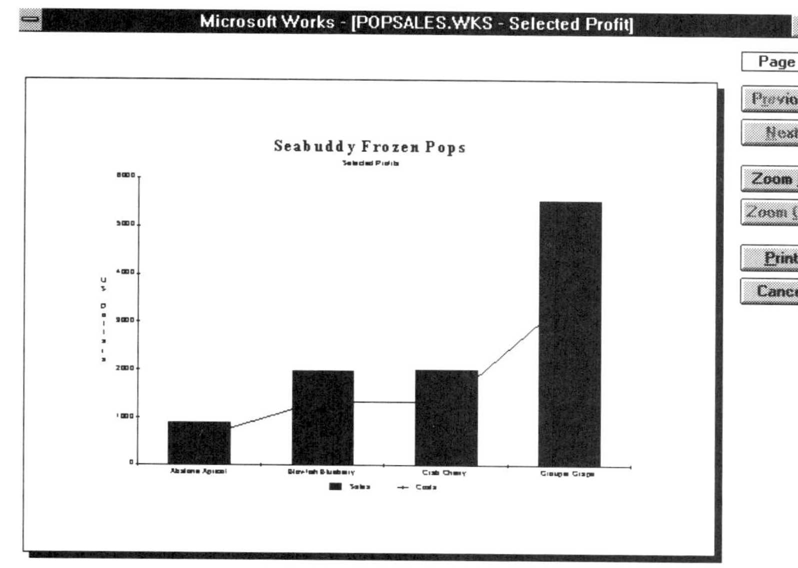

Figure 13x-30.
"Selected Profits" in Print Preview.

12. Print the chart "Selected Profits."

To print a single copy of your chart from *Print Preview,* click on the *Print* button (Figure 13x-31).

Figure 13x-31.
Click on the Print button in the Print Preview screen.

Creating a Database — Exercise

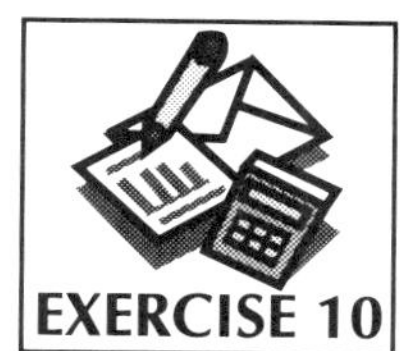

In this exercise you will learn how to create a database. You will create fields and then add data and a formula.

People of all levels of expertise in Works can benefit from this exercise. If you like a challenge, complete the exercise using the Steps in Brief, listed below. This lists the exercise outline, with no hints.

If you need more assistance, refer to the Steps in Detail on the following pages. The Steps in Detail expand each step, listing details and hints that enable you to complete the exercise.

Steps in Brief

1. *Open a new file.*
2. *Create the following fields with the corresponding lengths:*

   Record Name (20)
   Number in Stock (5)
   Shelf price (10)
   Total value (10)

3. *Insert the following text and values in the records:*

   Record Name: Swinging Sixties
   Number in Stock: 16
   Shelf price: $15

   Record Name: Twisting Fifties
   Number in Stock: 31
   Shelf price: $18

   Record Name: Jitterbugging Twenties
   Number in Stock: 9
   Shelf price: $26

4. *Insert a formula to calculate the "Total value" field.*

5. ***Insert a heading which says "Past Hits Record Store."***
6. ***Save the file as pasthits.wdb.***

Steps in Detail

1. ***Open a new file.***

To open a new database file, click on the *Database* button in the *Startup* dialog box as illustrated in Figure 15x-1. If the *Startup* dialog box does not appear on the screen when all the files are closed, double-click on the screen to display it.

Figure 15x-1. *Click on the Database button.*

The screen which is displayed is the Form view screen (Figure 15x-2). Later in the exercise, you change to List view to insert some field entries.

2. ***Create the following fields with the corresponding widths:***

Record Name (20)
Number in Stock (5)
Shelf price (10)
Total value (10)

To enter these fields in Form view, you need to position the insertion point in an appropriate place for the first field. As this exercise requires a heading on the form, move the insertion point down the form to the position shown in Figure 15x-2.

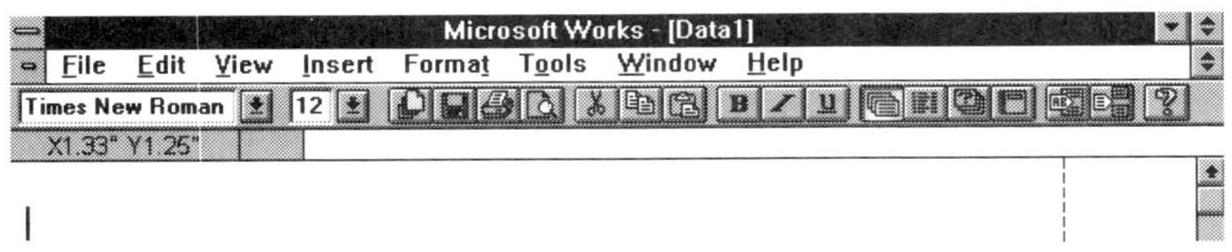

Figure 15x-2. *The Form view screen.*

A new field is inserted by typing in the name of the field, followed by a colon (:). Figure 15x-3 shows this being done for the first field which is "Record Name."

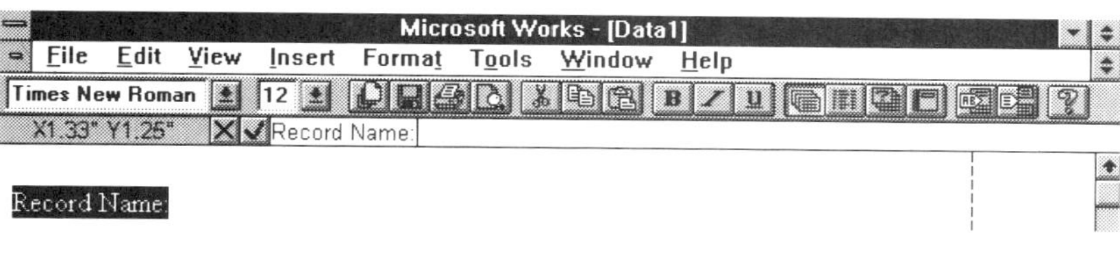

Figure 15x-3. *Type in the name of the first field "Record Name." Be sure to insert a colon at the end, before pressing Enter.*

The *Field Size* dialog box appears on the screen, into which you type the width of the field. The width of this field is 20 characters, which is the default. Click on *OK* to accept these specifications (Figure 15x-4).

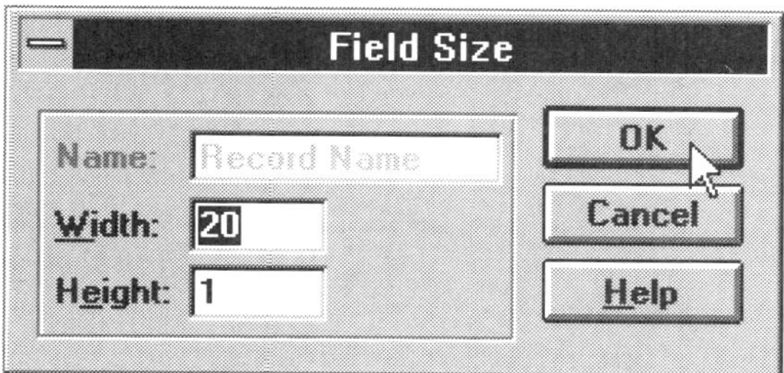

Figure 15x-4. *Click on OK.*

The first field appears on the Form view screen. You are now ready to enter the next field into your database. Notice how Works has conveniently placed the insertion point just under the "Record Name" field, just entered. Figure 15x-5 shows you the screen as it is currently.

Record Name:

Figure 15x-5. *The screen with the first field entered and the insertion point in the correct position for the next field.*

While the insertion point is in this position, type in "Number in Stock" followed by a colon. Figure 15x-6 shows what the formula bar should contain before pressing Enter.

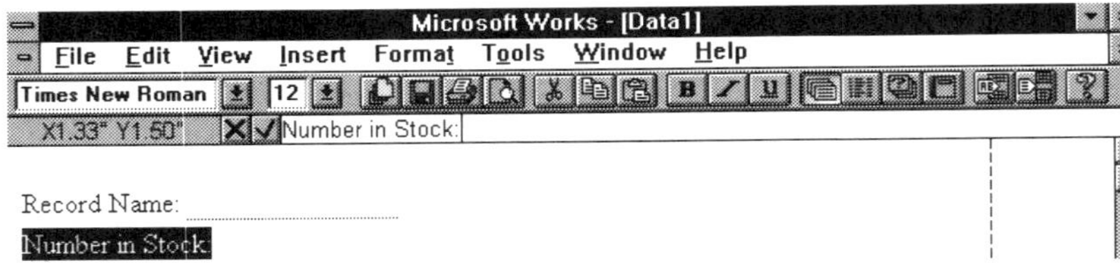

Figure 15x-6. *Type in "Number in Stock."*

The *Field Size* dialog box appears once Enter is pressed. This time the *Width* needs to be changed to 5 characters. See Figure 15x-7 for more details.

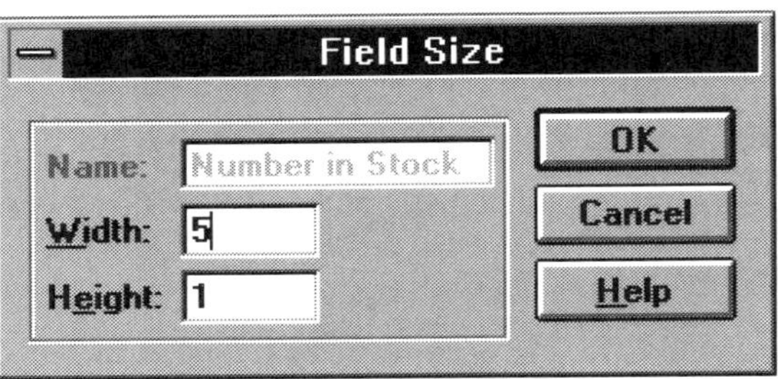

Figure 15x-7. *Type "5" into the Width text box to change the width of the second field to 5 characters and click on OK.*

Insert the next two fields in the same way—note the width of each. When done, the database in Form view should appear as in Figure 15x-8.

Record Name: ....

Number in Stock: ....

Shelf price: ....

Total value: ....

Figure 15x-8. *All four fields in the database have been entered.*

3. ***Insert the following text and values in the records.***

Record Name: Swinging Sixties
Number in Stock: 16
Shelf price: $15

Record Name:	Twisting Fifties
Number in Stock: 31	
Shelf price:	$18

Record Name:	Jitterbugging Twenties
Number in Stock: 9	
Shelf price:	$26

Each set of information outlined above makes up one record, excluding the "Total value" field, which is entered in Step 4 of this exercise. To insert this information into the database, the correct field must be highlighted. Click on the line to the right of the "Record Name" field to start entering the first field entry. Figure 15x-9 shows you the part of the screen to highlight.

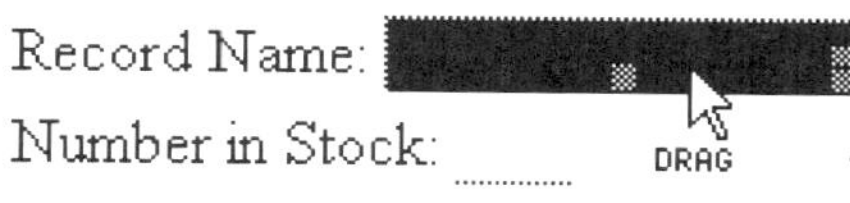

Figure 15x-9. *Highlight the field entry section of "Record Name."*

As soon as you start typing, the insertion point flashes in the formula bar. Insert the field entry "Swinging Sixties." See Figure 15x-10 for details.

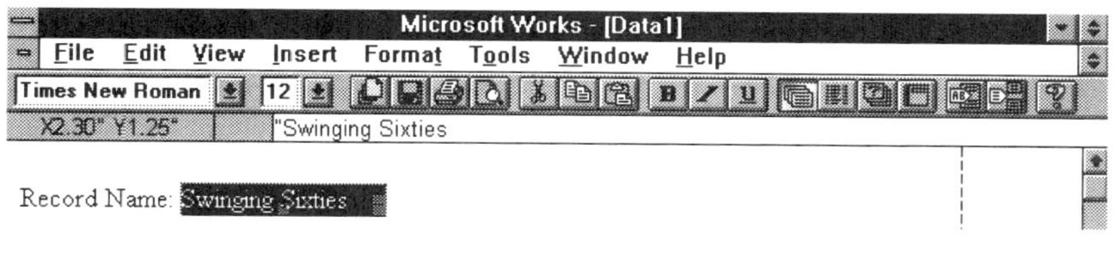

Figure 15x-10. *Type "Swinging Sixties" into the formula bar and press Enter. The text appears in the formula bar and on the Form view screen.*

To move to the next field quickly, press Tab. The next field is "Number in Stock." Type in the field entry as shown in Figure 15x-11.

Record Name: Swinging Sixties
Number in Stock: 16

Figure 15x-11. *Type in "16" as the "Number in Stock" figure for "Swinging Sixties."*

The next field entry is inserted in exactly the same way. Press Tab to move to "Shelf Price" and enter "$15." You can use the dollar sign, which does not interfere with the value when used in a formula.

When you press Tab again, the "Total value" field is highlighted. Adding the formula in this field is covered in the next part of the exercise. Press Tab once again to create a new blank record. The blank record has the same field names as the same as the first, but indicates that it is the second in the database on the status bar (Figure 15x-12).

Figure 15x-12. *The second record in the database appears when Tab is pressed on the last field.*

Insert the field entries for records 2 and 3. This is done in the same way as the data in record 1 was entered. Record 3 is displayed in Figure 15x-13.

Record Name: Jitterbugging Twenti
Number in Stock: 9
Shelf price: $26
Total value:

Figure 15x-13. *Record 3 in the database.*

4. *Insert a formula to calculate the "Total value" field.*

The "Total value" formula is used to determine the value of the stock, multiplying the number in stock by the shelf price. The exercise shows you how to complete this task in List view, although it could be done in Form view. Change to List view by pressing F9. The screen appears as shown in Figure 15x-14.

Microsoft Works - [Data1]
File Edit View Insert Format Tools Window Help
Arial 10
26

	Record Na	Number in	Shelf price	Total valu
1	Swinging Si	16	$15	
2	Twisting Fift	31	$18	
3	Jitterbuggin	9	$26	
4				

Figure 15x-14. *The database in the List view screen.*

Most of the columns are too narrow to read the field names and field entries clearly. These can be altered by adjusting the position of the column dividers on the frame. For each field, move the mouse pointer onto the frame and drag the column divider to the right until you can read the field (Figure 15x-15).

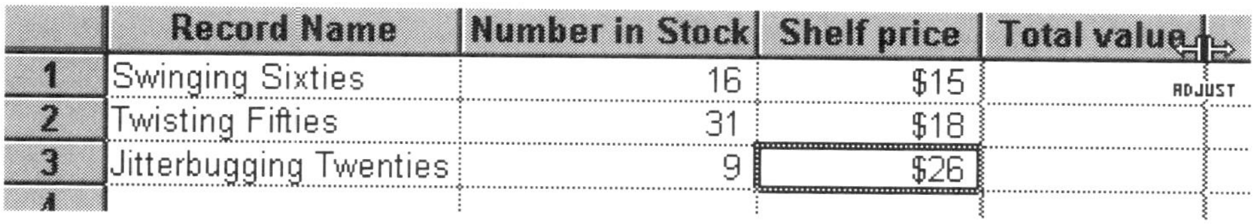

	Record Name	Number in Stock	Shelf price	Total value
1	Swinging Sixties	16	$15	
2	Twisting Fifties	31	$18	
3	Jitterbugging Twenties	9	$26	
4				

ADJUST

Figure 15x-15. *Adjust all the columns to fit the fields more comfortably.*

To calculate the total value in a record, multiply the number in stock by shelf price. The formula reads "=Number in Stock*Shelf price." This formula can be created by pointing as you are in List view. Follow Figures 15x-16 through 15x-18 to enter the formula in "Total value."

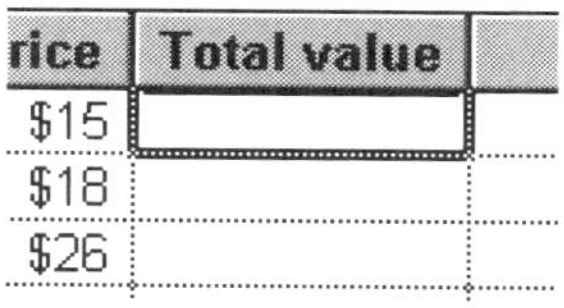

rice	Total value
$15	
$18	
$26	

Figure 15x-16. *Click in "Total value" of the first record.*

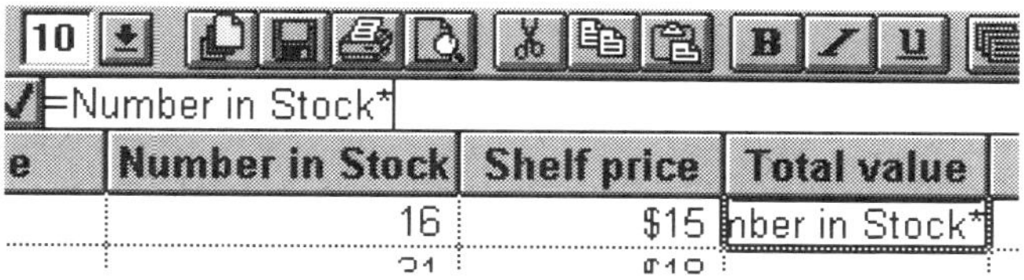

10

✓ =Number in Stock*

e	Number in Stock	Shelf price	Total value
	16	$15	nber in Stock*

Figure 15x-17. *Start the formula with "=," click on "Number in Stock," and type in "*" to multiply.*

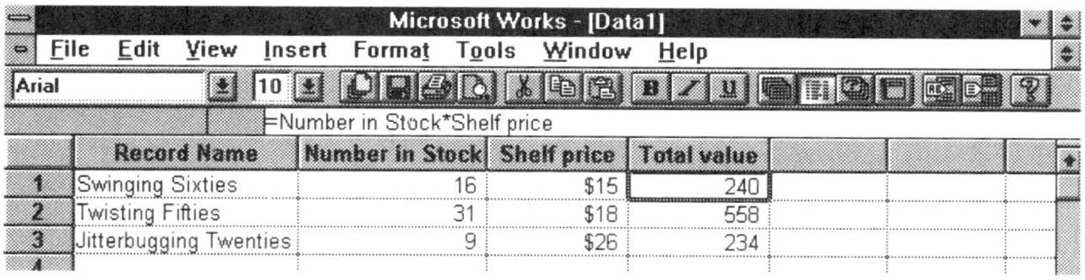

Microsoft Works - [Data1]

File Edit View Insert Format Tools Window Help

Arial 10

=Number in Stock*Shelf price

	Record Name	Number in Stock	Shelf price	Total value
1	Swinging Sixties	16	$15	240
2	Twisting Fifties	31	$18	558
3	Jitterbugging Twenties	9	$26	234
4				

Figure 15x-18. *Click on "Shelf price" and press Enter.*

The formula is entered into all "Total value" records. The formula is visible in the formula bar and the results are shown in the actual field entries (Figure 15x-18).

5. Insert a heading which says "Past Hits Record Store."

The database is almost complete. Move back to Form view by pressing F9. The formula entered in List view is displayed in Form view too (Figure 15x-19).

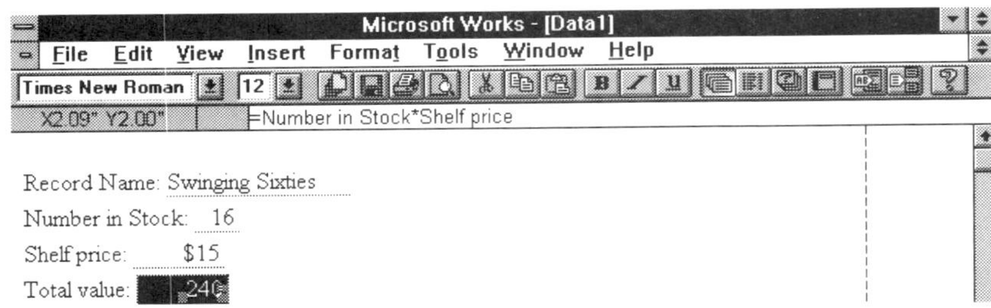

Figure 15x-19. The database in Form view.

You can insert a heading to add meaning to the database in Form view. Individual pieces of text are added in the same way as field names, except no colon is typed in at the end. See Figures 15x-20 and 15x-21 to add a heading to this form.

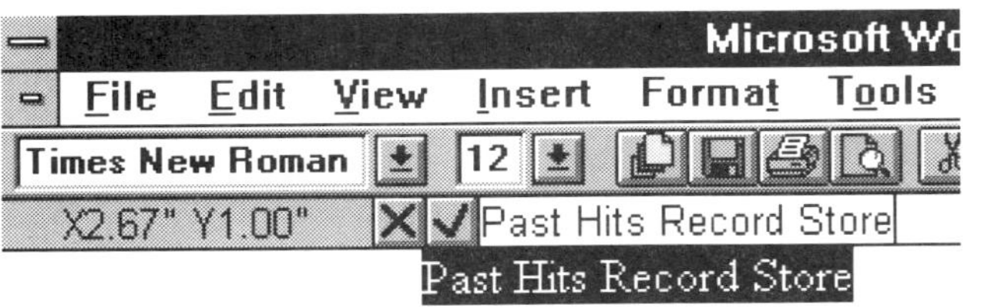

Figure 15x-20. Click at the top of the screen and type "Past Hits Record Store."

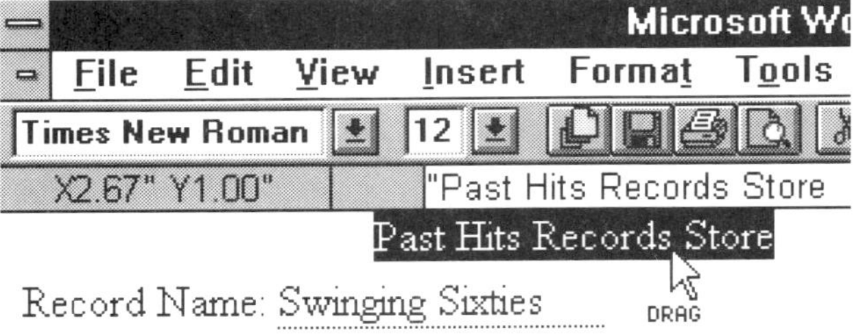

Figure 15x-21. Press Enter and the text becomes a "block" which can be moved around the screen.

6. Save the file as pasthits.wdb.

The file needs to be saved if you want to refer to it at a later stage. The *Save* command is in the **File** menu; choose this now as shown in Figure 15x-22.

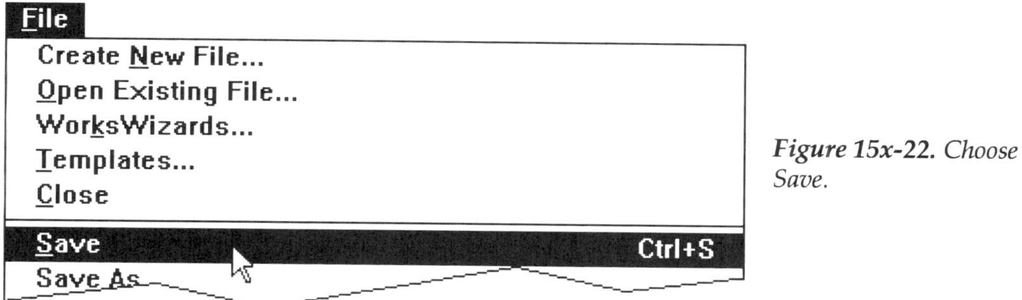

Figure 15x-22. Choose Save.

The *Save As* dialog box appears on the screen, into which you type the name of the file "pasthits," as illustrated in Figure 15x-23.

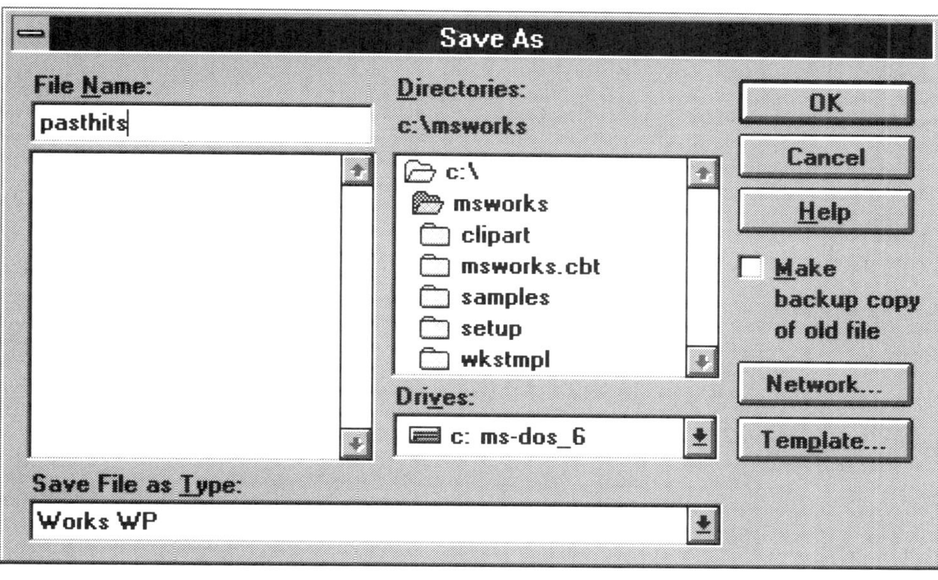

Figure 15x-23. Type "pasthits" into the Save As dialog box and click on OK.

Works automatically adds the *.wdb* extension.

Editing a Database — Exercise

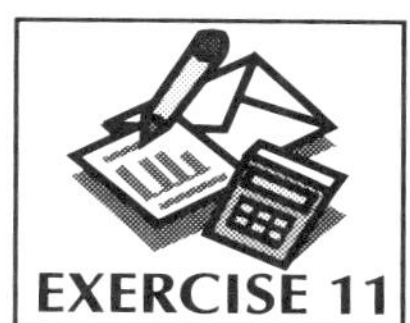

This exercise gives you practice in the process of editing a database.

People of all levels of expertise in Works can benefit from this exercise. If you like a challenge, complete the exercise using the Steps in Brief, listed below. This lists the exercise outline, with no hints.

If you need more assistance, refer to the Steps in Detail on the following pages. The Steps in Detail expand each step, listing details and hints that enable you to complete the exercise.

Steps in Brief

1. *Open the file toys_l.wdb from the msworks.cbt subdirectory.*
2. *Copy record 35 into record 36 and change the name of the new toy to "Rainbow Child."*
3. *Change the font of all field entries in Form view to Helvetica.*
4. *Change the label "Toy Stock" to bold.*
5. *Add a label saying "Low Season 1993."*
6. *Change the "Ordered" field entries to "month, day" format.*
7. *Protect the form.*

Steps in Detail

1. Open the file toys_l.wdb from the msworks.cbt subdirectory.

As no other files are used in this exercise, close any files which may be open and choose the *Open Existing File* command in the **File** menu. The *Open* dialog box appears on the screen, in which you can specify the directory and the type of files you need to see. Figure 16x-1 shows how to do this.

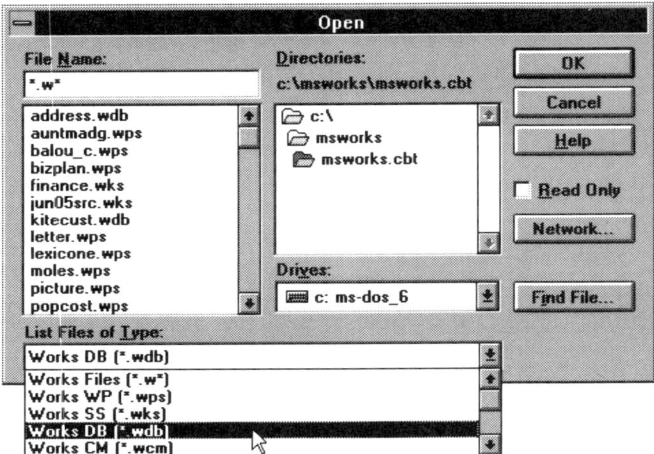

Figure 16x-1. *Choose* ***msworks.cbt*** *subdirectory from the Directories list box and Works DB (*.wdb) from the List Files of Type submenu.*

The *File Name* list box displays the database files only. Use the scroll bars to locate ***toys_l.wdb*** in the list box and double-click on the file name to open the sample file as in Figure 16x-2.

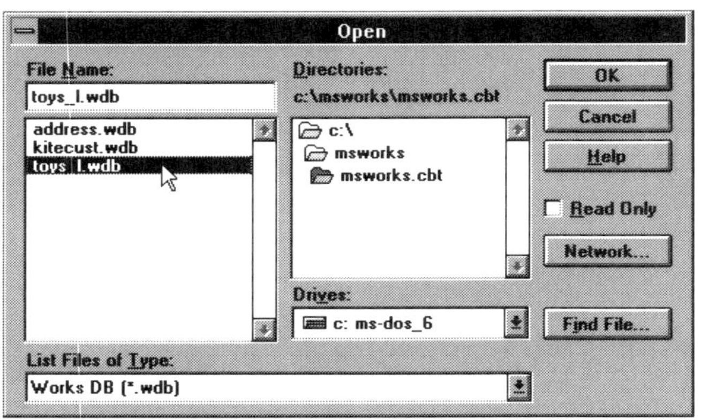

Figure 16x-2. *Open the* ***toys_l.wdb*** *file.*

2. ***Copy record 35 into record 36 and change the name of the new toy to "Rainbow Child."***

Instead of entering the same information twice, you can use the copy command. Switch to List view by pressing F9 if Works opened your file in Form view.

Scroll down to record 35 and select it by clicking on the record number on the frame as shown in Figure 16x-3.

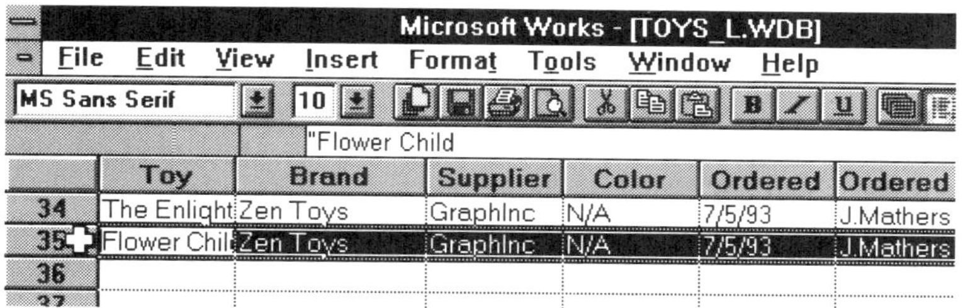

Figure 16x-3. *Highlight record 35 by clicking on the frame.*

The *Copy* command is in the **Edit** menu. Choose this now (Figure 16x-4).

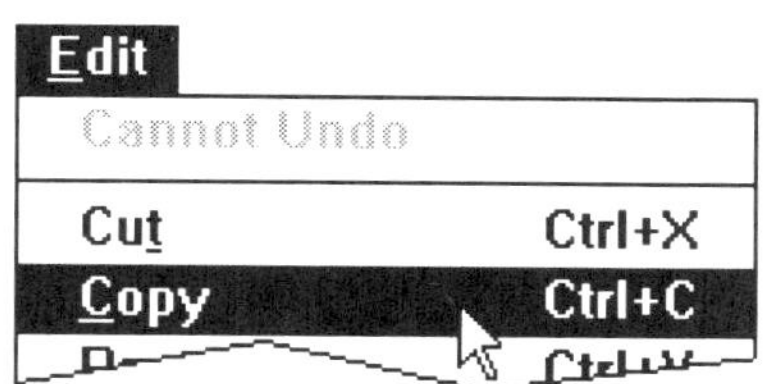

Figure 16x-4. *Choose Copy from the **Edit** menu.*

The new record is to be number 36. The insertion point must be in the first field of this record before the data can be pasted back into the database. See Figure 16x-5.

There is no need to highlight the entire record when pasting. Works has a copy of the whole of record 35 which was copied onto the Clipboard, and will be pasted where the insertion point is.

Figure 16x-5. *Move the insertion point into record 36.*

You can now use the *Paste* command to reinsert the data (Figure 16x-6).

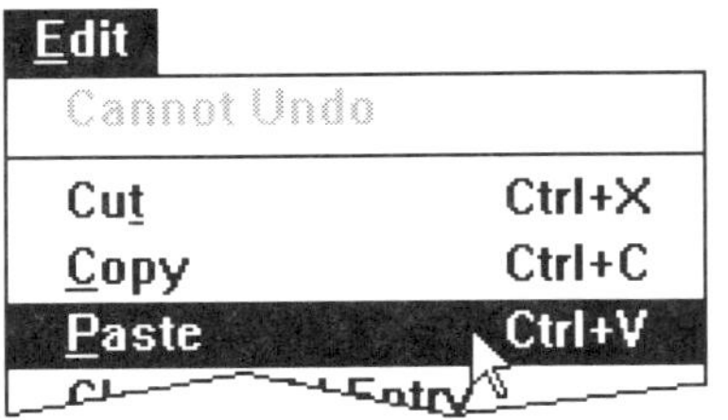

Figure 16x-6. *Choose Paste from the* ***Edit*** *menu.*

The contents of Record 35 and 36 are identical. Most of the entries remain unchanged, but the "Toy" field needs to be changed to "Rainbow Child." Figure 16x-7 shows how this is done.

Microsoft Works - [

File Edit View Insert Format Tools W

MS Sans Serif 10

Rainbow Child

	Toy	Brand	Supplier	Colo
34	The Enlight	Zen Toys	GraphInc	N/A
35	Flower Chil	Zen Toys	GraphInc	N/A
36	inbow Child	Zen Toys	GraphInc	N/A
37				

Figure 16x-7. *Highlight the "Toy" field and type in "Rainbow Child." Press Enter to enter in the different name.*

3. *Change the font of all field entries in Form view to Helvetica.*

Before the font is changed in Form view, Form view must be active. Changing to Form view can be done in a number of ways. One of these methods is shown in Figure 16x-8.

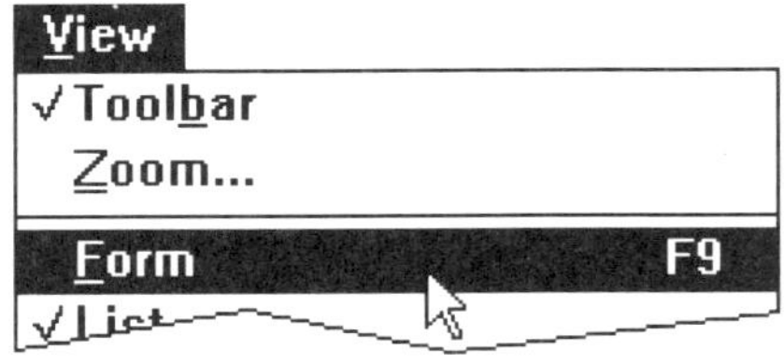

Figure 16x-8. *Select Form from the* ***View*** *menu.*

A font change in Form view affects your entire selection while you are in Form view, including any selected field names, field entries, and labels. Click on any field entry for the current record in Form view, then hold down the Ctrl key and click on the other field entries to select those also (Figure 16x-9). The font can be changed using the *Font* submenu on the toolbar, see Figure 16x-10.

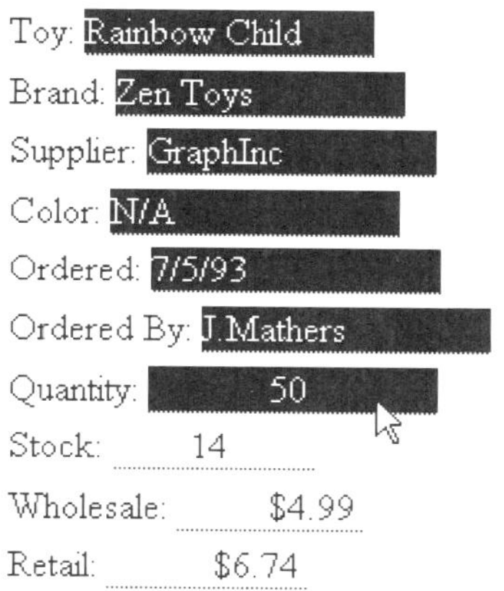

Figure 16x-9. *Select these field entries and the three remaining by using the Ctrl key and the mouse.*

Figure 16x-10. *Select Helvetica from the Font submenu. You may need to use the scroll bar to display it.*

4. *Change the label "Toy Stock" to bold.*

To add a text style to a label, it must be selected. Once selected, the style — bold — is applied. Figures 16x-11 and 16x-12 give details.

Figure 16x-11. *Select the label "Toy Stock" by clicking on it with the mouse.*

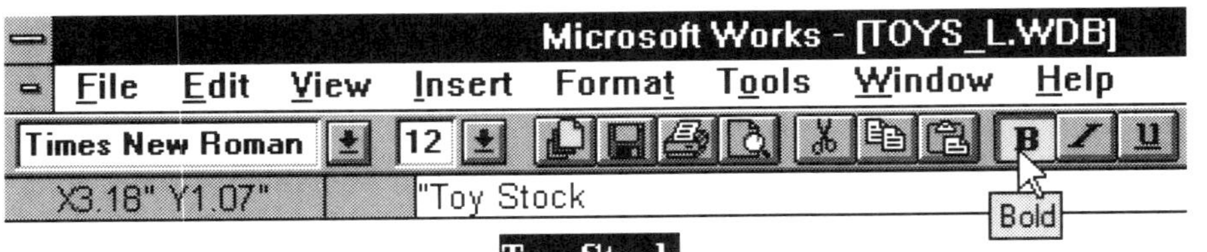

Figure 16x-12. Click on the Bold button on the toolbar.

5. Add a label saying "Low Season 1993."

A suitable place for this label is below the label to which you just applied bold. Click on your form in this position as illustrated in Figure 16x-13.

Figure 16x-13. *Click to position the insertion point.*

Type the text "Low Season 1993" for your label. Do this now and press Enter to confirm the change (Figure 16x-14).

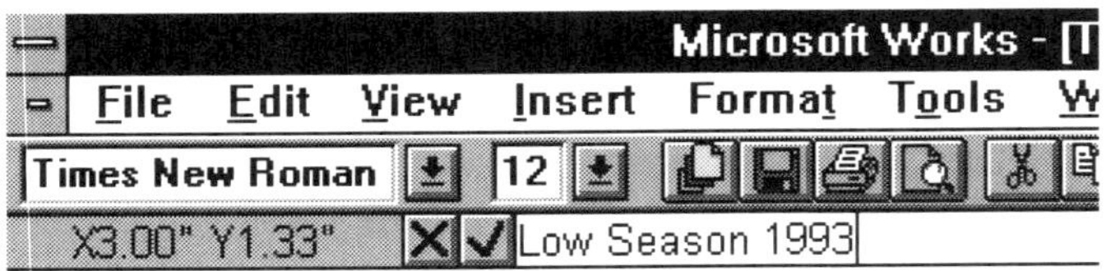

Figure 16x-14. *Type the text of your label.*

When you press Enter and click elsewhere, the top of your form should look similar to Figure 16x-15.

Toy Stock

Low Season 1993

Toy: Rainbow Child

Figure 16x-15. *The database in Form view at this stage.*

6. Change the "Ordered" field entries to "month, day" format.

The information in the "Ordered" field uses the value format of *month/day/year*. The *year* component is no longer necessary as 1993 appears in the label "Low Season 1993". This can be fixed simply by formatting the "Ordered" field with the *"month, day"* format which shows only the day and the month as the field entry.

The field to which the format is to be applied needs to be selected. Select the "Ordered" field entry in any record (Figure 16x-16).

Figure 16x-16. *Select an "Ordered" field entry.*

A value format is altered through the **Format** menu. In Figure 16x-17, the *Number* command is selected, which affects how values including dates and times appear in their fields.

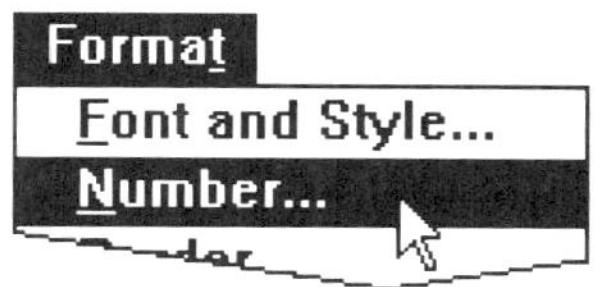

Figure 16x-17. *Choose the Number command from the* ***Format*** *menu.*

At this point, the *Number* dialog box is displayed. Select the *"month, day"* option as shown in Figure 16x-18, and click on *OK*.

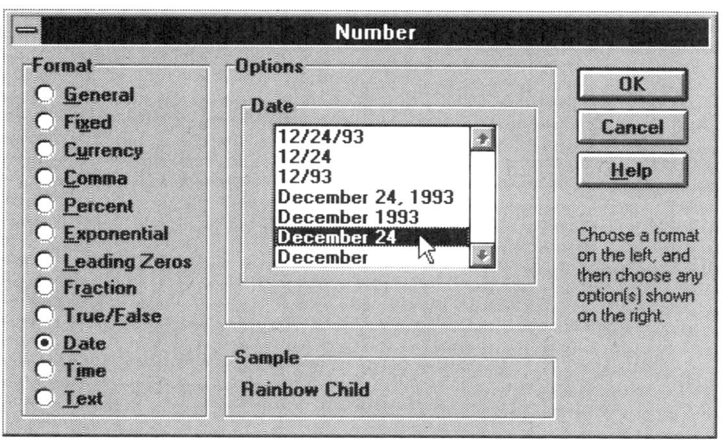

Figure 16x-18. *Change the format by choosing from the Options list box.*

The field entry is changed to the new format, where only the month and the day are visible. This is shown in Figure 16x-19.

Figure 16x-19. *The "Ordered" field entries appear in the format you chose.*

7. Protect the form.

To avoid any accidental changes to the layout of the Form, the *Protect Form* option can be selected. Choose the *Protection* command in the **Format** menu and then select *Protect Form* as in Figure 16x-20.

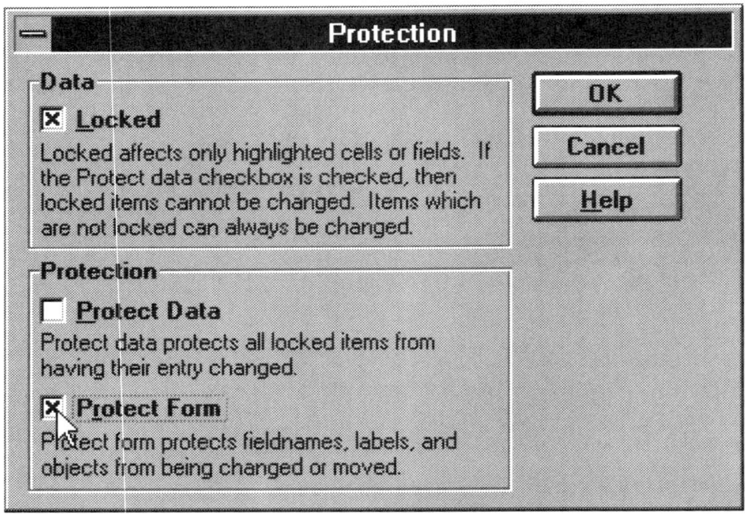

Figure 16x-20. *Choose Protect Form from the Protection dialog box.*

The exercise is now complete. You may wish to save the file under a different name using the *Save As* command in the **File** menu.

Viewing the Database — Exercise

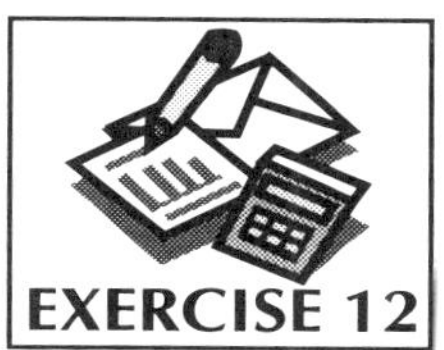

In this exercise you will practise how to query the database to retrieve information.

People of all levels of expertise in Works can benefit from this exercise. If you like a challenge, complete the exercise using the Steps in Brief, listed below. This lists the exercise outline, with no hints.

If you need more assistance, refer to the Steps in Detail on the following pages. The Steps in Detail expand each step, listing details and hints that enable you to complete the exercise.

Steps in Brief

1. ***Open the file address.wdb in the msworks.cbt subdirectory.***
2. ***Hide the field "Age."***
3. ***Sort the data using "City" as the first field and "Career" as the second. Both are to be in ascending order.***
4. ***Search for all the people who have paid, using the Find command.***
5. ***Rearrange the form in form view.***
6. ***Apply a query which looks for all people who are over 40 and live in Seattle.***

Steps in Detail

1. *Open the file address.wdb in the msworks.cbt subdirectory.*

Close any files which may be open and select *Open Existing File* from the **File** menu. From the *Open* dialog box, double-click on ***address.wdb*** in the ***msworks.cbt*** subdirectory (Figure 17x-1).

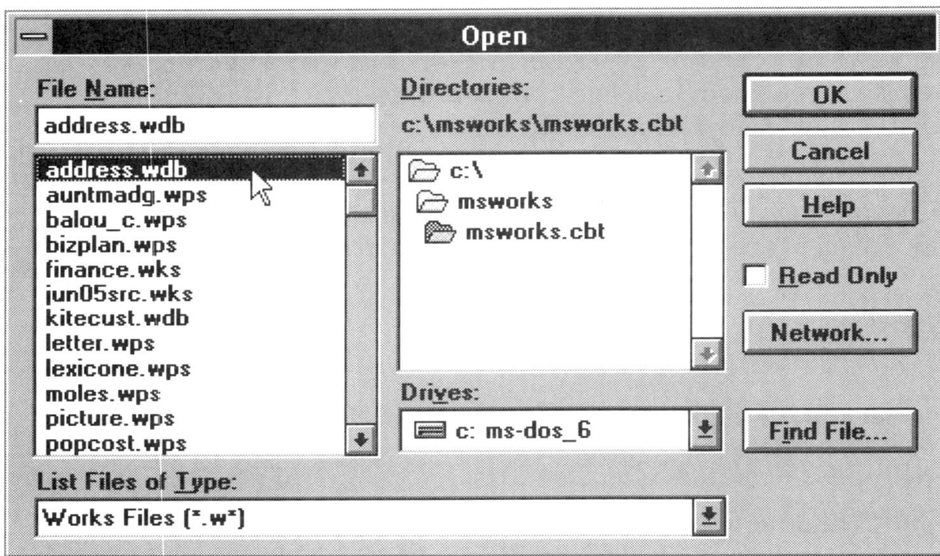

Figure 17x-1. *Open the **address.wdb** file.*

2. *Hide the field "Age."*

The file has previously been saved in List view, and therefore appears in List view on the screen. Stay in List view to hide the field in this part of the exercise. Move to the "Age" field, as this is the field to be hidden, and follow Figures 17x-2 and 17x-3 to complete this step.

Figure 17x-2. *Select Field Width from the **Format** menu.*

Figure 17x-3. *Type "0" in the Width text box and click on OK.*

3. ***Sort the data using "City" as the first field and "Career" as the second. Both are to be in ascending order.***

The *Sort Records* command is in the **Tools** menu. Choose this now to display the *Sort Records* dialog box. The sorting specifications are inserted into the *Sort Records* dialog box as in Figure 17x-4. The first field to be sorted is "City," and therefore is typed into *1st Field*. The *2nd Field* in the sort is "Career" as shown.

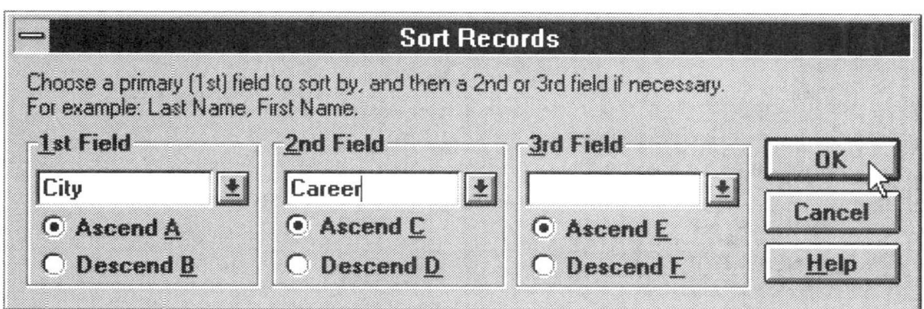

Figure 17x-4. *Type "City" into the 1st Field and "Career" into the 2nd Field.*

Microsoft Works - [ADDRESS.WDB]

File Edit View Insert Format Tools Window Help

Arial 10

23

	Name	Street	City	State	ZIP	Career	Paid
1	Joe Applegate	1 Apple Seed Dr	Apple Hill	IL	023934	Programmer	no
2	Jeffrey Lentle	200 Willhurst Rd	Boston	MA	023933	Child	yes
3	Ramona Cook	20 Ivy Rd.	Boston	MA	023599	Engineer	yes
4	Virginia Cook	20 Ivy Rd.	Boston	MA	023599	Physician	yes
5	Stuart Lentle	200 Willhurst Rd	Boston	MA	023933	Writer	no
6	Russ Plumm	33 Pleasant Wy	Hill Valley	IL	012844	Accountant	no
7	Jeri Cook	900 Hillhurst Dr.	Hill Valley	IL	012845	Designer	no
8	Tom Carroway	353 Kirkland Ave	Kent	MN	056443	Child	yes
9	Mary Pat Hamr	355 1st Ave. SE	Mapleton	AL	033355	Child	yes
10	Alex Hamm	355 1st Ave. SE	Mapleton	AL	033355	Nurse Practitioner	yes
11	Albert Cook	10 Mill Rd.	Nedtown	PA	089302	Steel Worker	no
12	Donna Romaine	11 Greensville	Portland	OR	039443	Company VP	yes
13	Robert Baker	123 2nd Ave N.	Seattle	WA	093344	Psychologist	no
14	Pauline Cook	44403 Main St.	Seattle	WA	033944	Retired	no
15	Michael Ricotta	12444 45th Ave.	Seattle	WA	092345	Teacher	yes
16	Melinda Fisher	23633 1st Ave.	Wood Hill	CA	093933	Child	yes

Figure 17x-5. *The database is sorted when you click on OK.*

4. Search for all the people who have paid, using the Find command.

To display a list of only the people who have paid, you can use the *Find* command and ask to see all the matching records. Choose *Find* from the **Edit** menu as in Figure 17x-6.

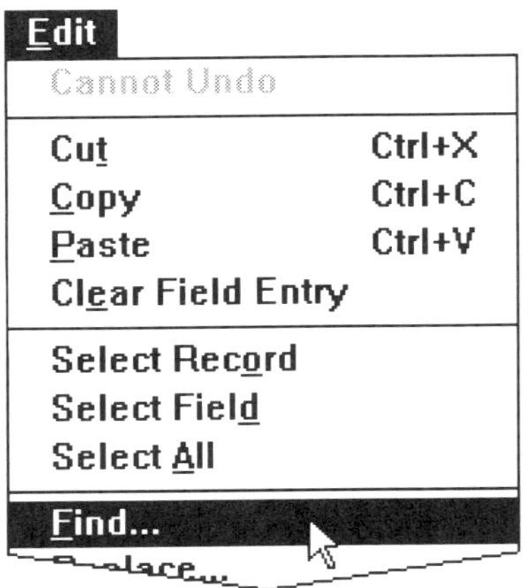

Figure 17x-6. *Click on Find in the* ***Edit*** *menu.*

The *Find* dialog box allows you to determine what is to be found and how it is displayed on the screen. Figure 17x-7 and 17x-8 show you how to do this.

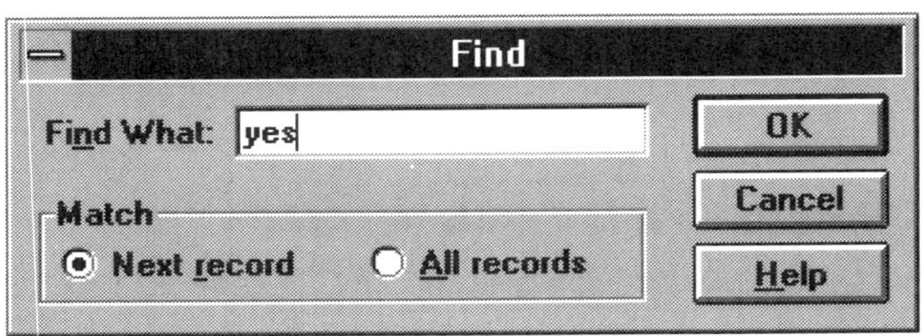

Figure 17x-7. *Type in "yes" in the Find What text box.*

Figure 17x-8. *Click on All records so all the records are shown simultaneously. Then, click on OK.*

When the search is complete, the screen looks like Figure 17x-9.

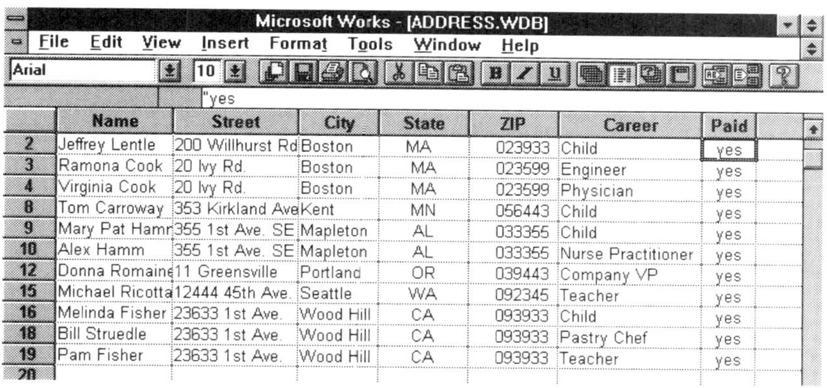

	Name	Street	City	State	ZIP	Career	Paid
2	Jeffrey Lentle	200 Willhurst Rd	Boston	MA	023933	Child	yes
3	Ramona Cook	20 Ivy Rd.	Boston	MA	023599	Engineer	yes
4	Virginia Cook	20 Ivy Rd.	Boston	MA	023599	Physician	yes
8	Tom Carroway	353 Kirkland Ave	Kent	MN	056443	Child	yes
9	Mary Pat Hamr	355 1st Ave. SE	Mapleton	AL	033355	Child	yes
10	Alex Hamm	355 1st Ave. SE	Mapleton	AL	033355	Nurse Practitioner	yes
12	Donna Romaine	11 Greensville	Portland	OR	039443	Company VP	yes
15	Michael Ricotta	12444 45th Ave.	Seattle	WA	092345	Teacher	yes
16	Melinda Fisher	23633 1st Ave.	Wood Hill	CA	093933	Child	yes
18	Bill Struedle	23633 1st Ave.	Wood Hill	CA	093933	Pastry Chef	yes
19	Pam Fisher	23633 1st Ave.	Wood Hill	CA	093933	Teacher	yes
20							

***Figure 17x-9.** A list of all the people who have paid appears on the screen.*

To redisplay all of the records, click on *Show All Records* in the **View** menu (Figure 17x-10).

***Figure 17x-10.** Choose Show All Records to redisplay the entire database.*

5. *Rearrange the form in form view.*

The form in this database has not been arranged previously. It is important to do it at this stage as the Form view reflects how it looks in Query view, which is used in the next step of this exercise.

Change to Form view now by pressing F9, and drag the fields around the screen (**Chapter 15, Creating a Database**), so all can be read. Figure 17x-11 gives you an example of how the form could look.

Name: Jeffrey Lentle

Street: 200 Willhurst Rd.

City: Boston

State: MA

ZIP: 023933

Paid: yes

Age: 5

Career: Child

***Figure 17x-11.** The screen in Form view is arranged more logically.*

6. ***Apply a query which looks for all people who are over 40 and live in Seattle.***

In Step 2 of this exercise, the "Age" field was hidden. In this step, you are to perform a query using that field. A query can be performed on a hidden field, so there is no reason to redisplay the field.

To start a query, you need to be in Query view. Figure 17x-12 shows you one way of doing this.

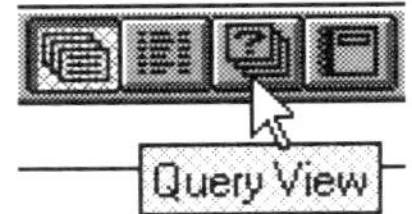

Figure 17x-12. *Click on the Query View button on the toolbar.*

The *New Query* dialog box is displayed, into which you can enter the query definition. The definition in this case requires two entries — one in "Age" and one in "City." Follow 17x-13 and Figure 17x-14 to insert the Query definition.

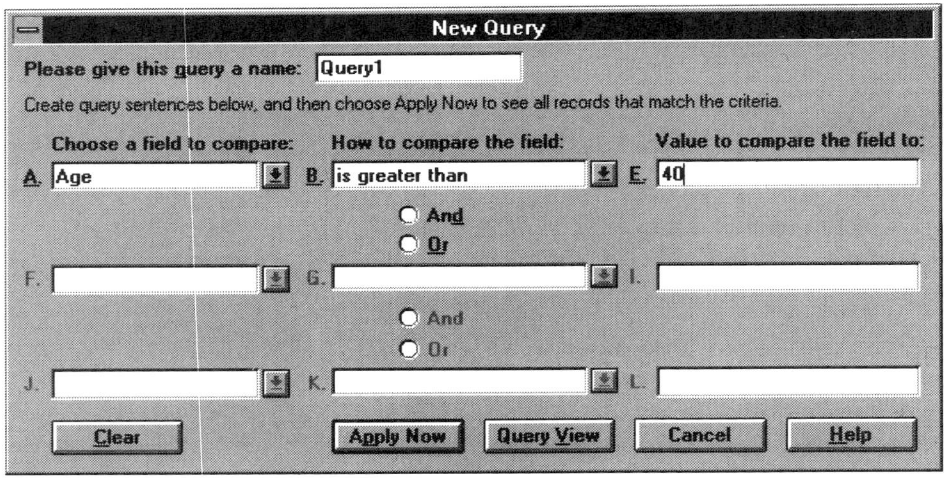

Figure 17x-13. *Choose "Age" and "is greater than" from drop-down list boxes A and B. Type "40" in text box E to complete the first part of the query criteria.*

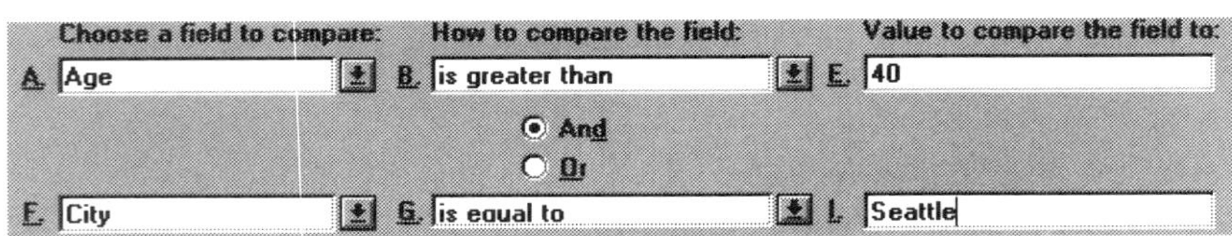

Figure 17x-14. *Click on the And option button, then choose "City" and "is equal to" as shown here. Type in "Seattle" and press Enter to complete your query.*

Pressing Enter activates the default *Apply Now* command button and closes the *New Query* dialog box. Click on the List view button to see the records which match your criteria.

The screen displays two records only as in Figure 17x-15.

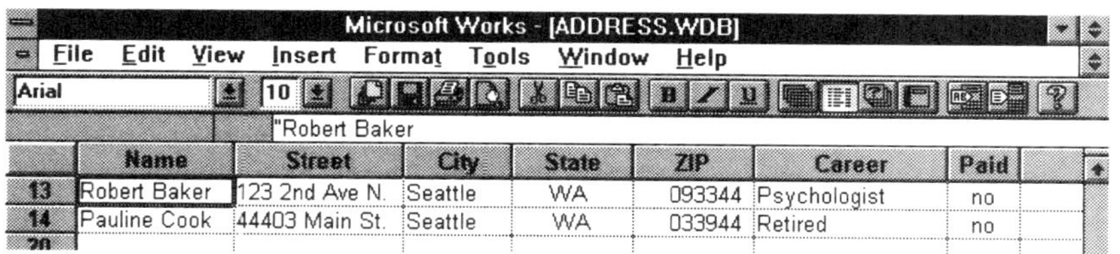

Figure 17x-15. *You can view the results of your query in List view.*

Creating Database Reports — Exercise

In this exercise you will practise the skills you need to create reports for your databases.

People of all levels of expertise in Works can benefit from this exercise. If you like a challenge, complete the exercise using the Steps in Brief, listed below. This lists the exercise outline, with no hints.

If you need more assistance, refer to the Steps in Detail on the following pages. The Steps in Detail expand each step, listing details and hints that enable you to complete the exercise.

Steps in Brief

1. *Open the file toys_l.wdb from the msworks.cbt subdirectory.*
2. *Create a new report with the title "Current Orders" using the fields: "Ordered," "Ordered By," "Quantity," and "Stock."*
3. *Add statistics to calculate the total number of toys ordered.*
4. *Italicize the heading and move it into column A in the same row.*
5. *Change the point size for the entire report to 12 point.*
6. *Name the report "Orders 1993."*
7. *View the report in Print Preview and print it to the printer.*

Steps in Detail

1. ***Open the file toys_l.wdb from the msworks.cbt subdirectory.***

Close any files which may be open at this stage using the *Close* command in the **File** menu. It is not essential to close the files, but helps to speed up your computer's processing time.

To open the file, select *Open Existing File* from the **File** menu. Figure 18x-1 shows the file being opened from the *Open* dialog box.

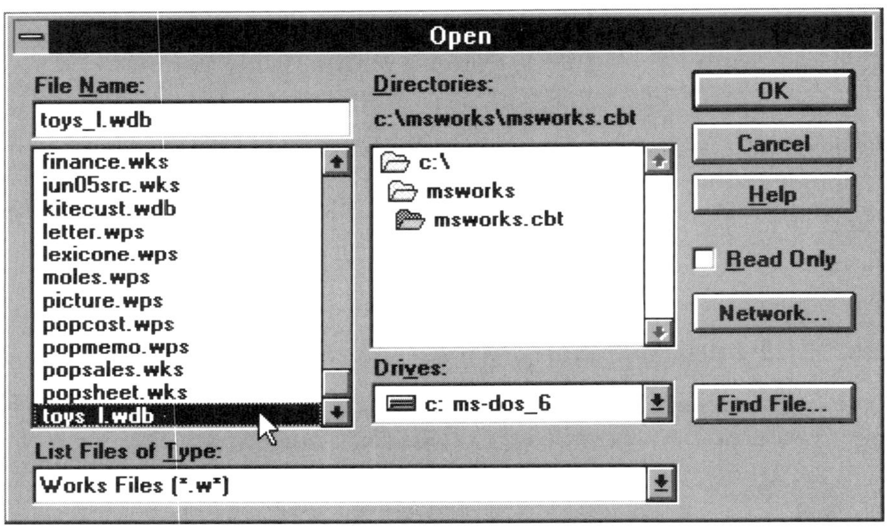

Figure 18x-1. *Open* ***toys_l.wdb*** *by double-clicking on it in the* ***msworks.cbt*** *subdirectory.*

2. ***Create a new report with the title "Current Orders" using the fields: "Ordered," "Ordered By," "Quantity," and "Stock."***

A new report needs to be defined first. To begin defining the report, click on *Create New Report* from the **Tools** menu (Figure 18x-2).

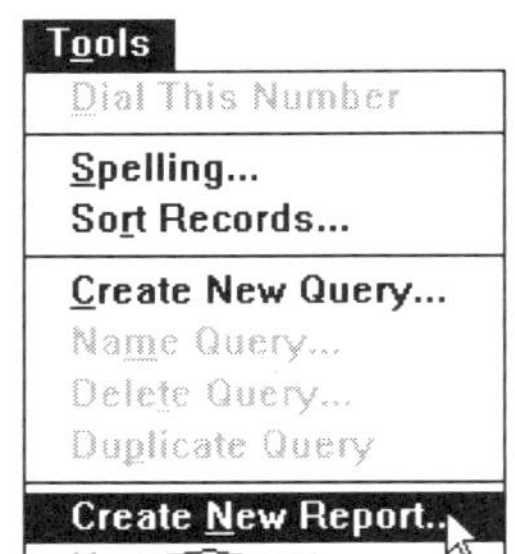

Figure 18x-2. *Select Create New Report.*

The *New Report* dialog box appears on the screen, in which you specify the title and fields to be included in the report.

The title to be used is "Current Orders" and is typed into the *Report Title* text box as in Figure 18x-3. The insertion point is positioned automatically in the *Report Title* text box when the *New Report* dialog box appears on the screen.

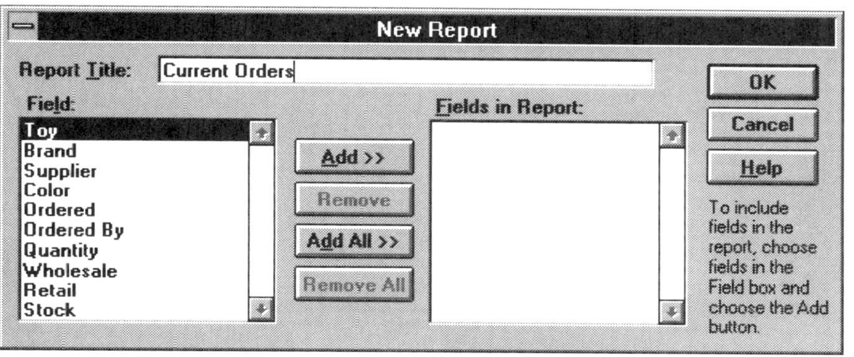

Figure 18x-3. *Type the title into the Report Title text box.*

The fields are added by selecting them from the list on the left of the dialog box and then clicking on the *Add* button. Follow Figures 18x-4 and 18x-5 to add the first field, which is the "Ordered" field.

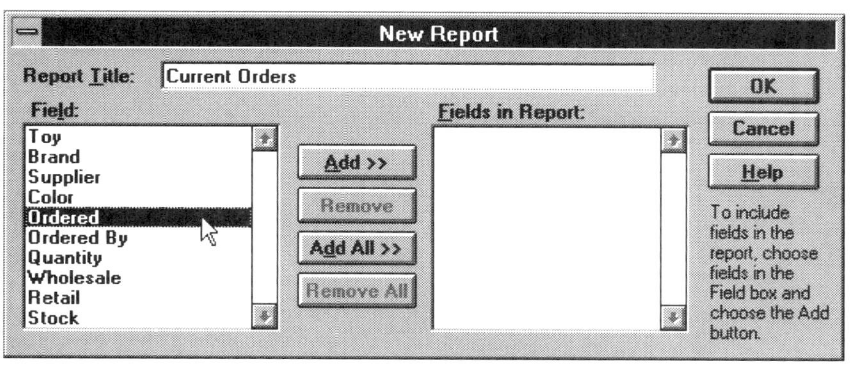

Figure 18x-4. *Click on "Ordered" in the New Report dialog box.*

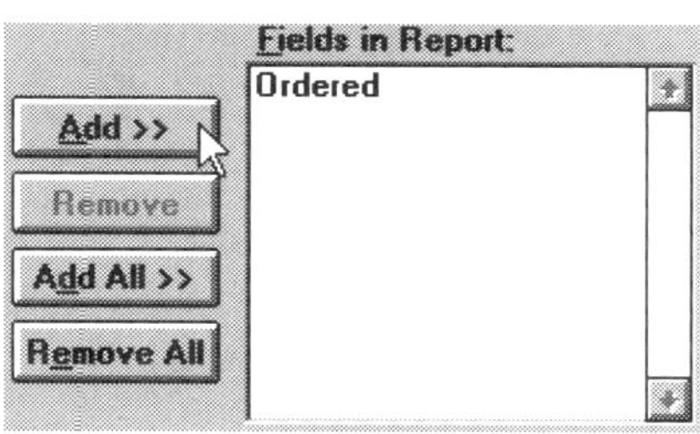

Figure 18x-5. *Click on the Add button to copy "Ordered" to the Fields in Report list box.*

The next field to be included is "Ordered By." Click on this field name and then on the *Add* button. Repeat this step for the "Quantity" and "Stock" fields. When complete the *New Report* dialog box should look like Figure 18x-6. Click on *OK* to confirm this part of the report definition.

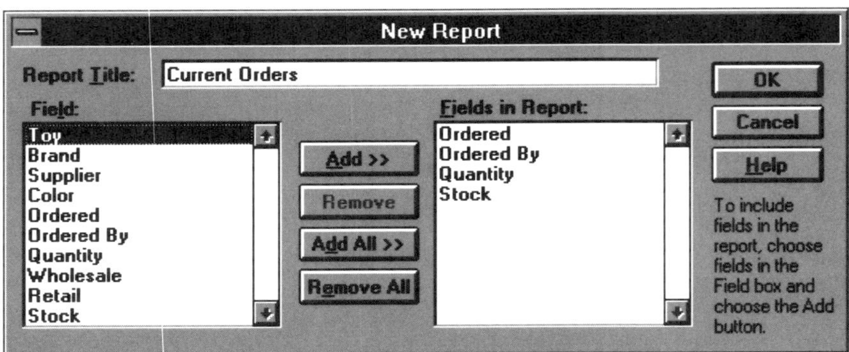

Figure 18x-6. *The fields have been added in the New Report dialog box using the Add button.*

3. *Add statistics to calculate the total number of toys ordered.*

The *Report Statistics* dialog box appears when *OK* is clicked in the *New Report* dialog box. The statistic to be used in this report calculates the total number of toys ordered. The field on which the statistic is based, therefore, is "Ordered." Highlight this field name in the *Report Statistics* dialog box as in Figure 18x-7.

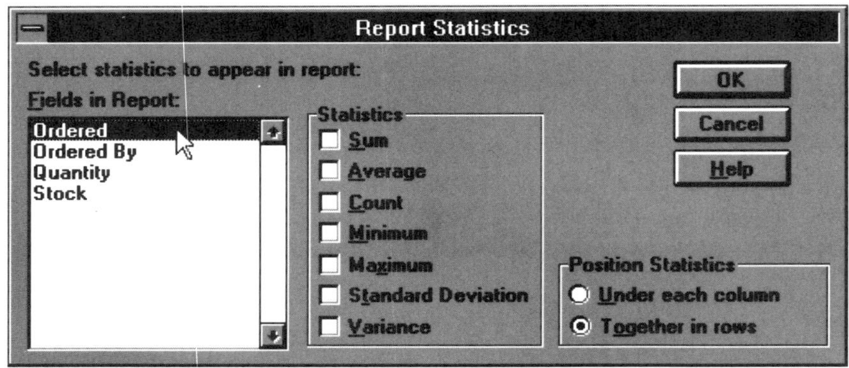

Figure 18x-7. *Highlight "Ordered" in the Fields in Report list box.*

The type of statistic applied to this field is the one which totals values in the field. SUM is used for this purpose, so the *Sum* check box needs to be selected. Figure 18x-8 shows this.

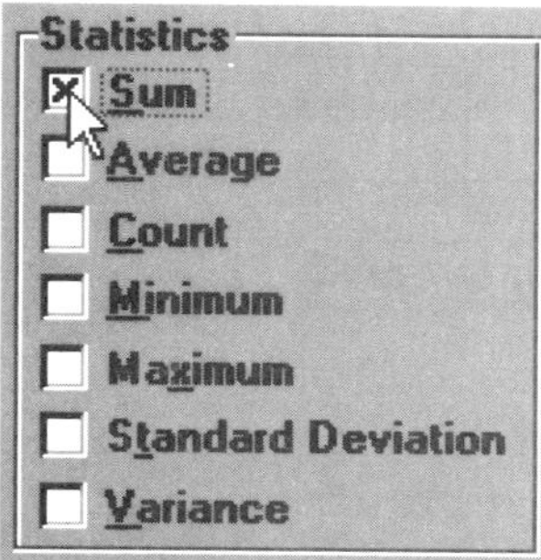

Figure 18x-8. *Select the Sum check box to calculate the total number of toys currently on order.*

Leave the *Together in rows* option checked in *Position Statistics* and click on *OK*. Works informs you that the report definition is complete and that the report can be viewed in *Print Preview* in the dialog box shown in Figure 18x-9.

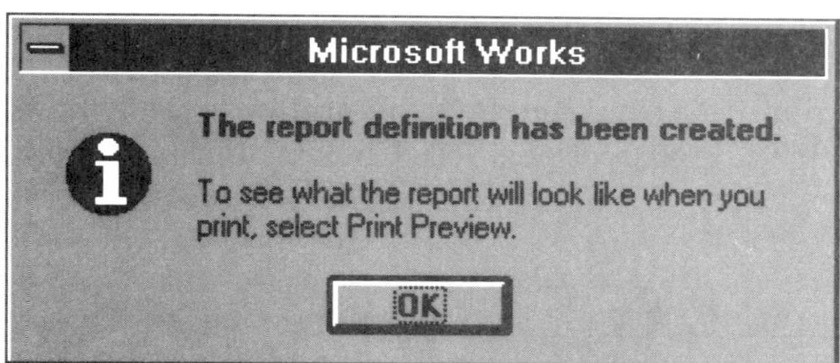

Figure 18x-9. *Click on OK in this dialog box to display the report definition screen.*

4. *Italicize the heading and move it into column A in the same row.*

The heading which was inserted in the *New Report* dialog box is located in the first title row in column E. It is bold by default and to change it to italic it must be selected first. Follow Figures 18x-10 and 18x-11 to complete this step.

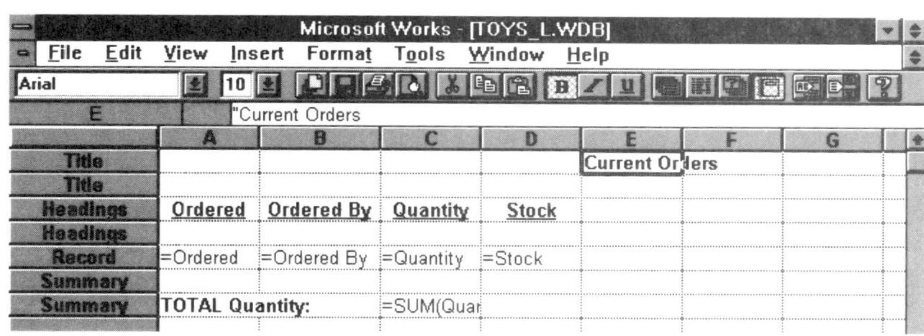

Figure 18x-10. *Click on the word "Current" in the title row in column E.*

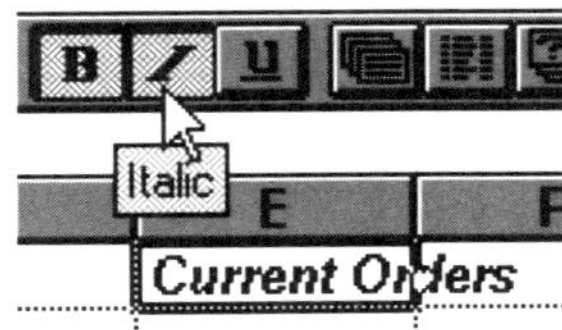

Figure 18x-11. Click on the Italic button on the toolbar.

The title is too far to the right of the report. To move it to column A, where it would look more appropriate, you can drag the title or use the *Cut* and *Paste* commands. Ensure that the title is highlighted as in Figure 18x-10 and choose *Cut* from the **Edit** menu or the toolbar (Figure 18x-12).

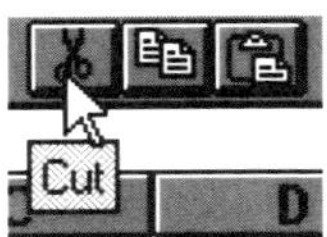

Figure 18x-12. Choose Cut.

The title is removed from the report definition screen and needs to be pasted back in the correct position. Click in column A in the same row and choose *Paste* from the **Edit** menu or from the toolbar as in Figure 18x-13.

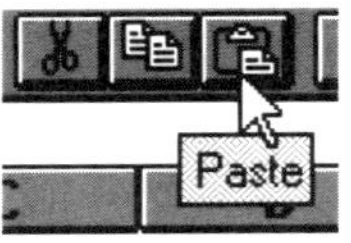

Figure 18x-13. Choose Paste.

The title appears in the new position as Figure 18x-14 shows.

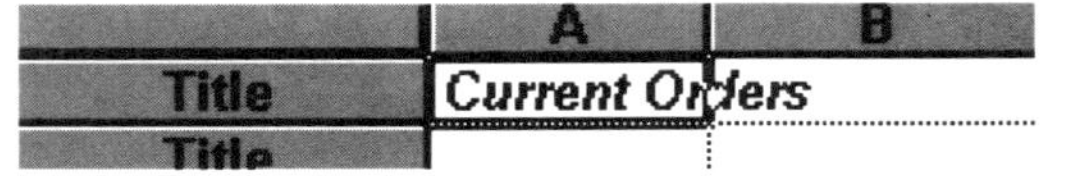

Figure 18x-14. The title is now in column A.

5. ***Change the point size for the entire report to 12 point.***

When the point size in a report is changed, it affects the contents of your current selection only. The size can be changed through the *Size* submenu on the toolbar or through the *Font and Style* command in the **Format** menu. The toolbar is used in Figures 18x-15 and 18x-16.

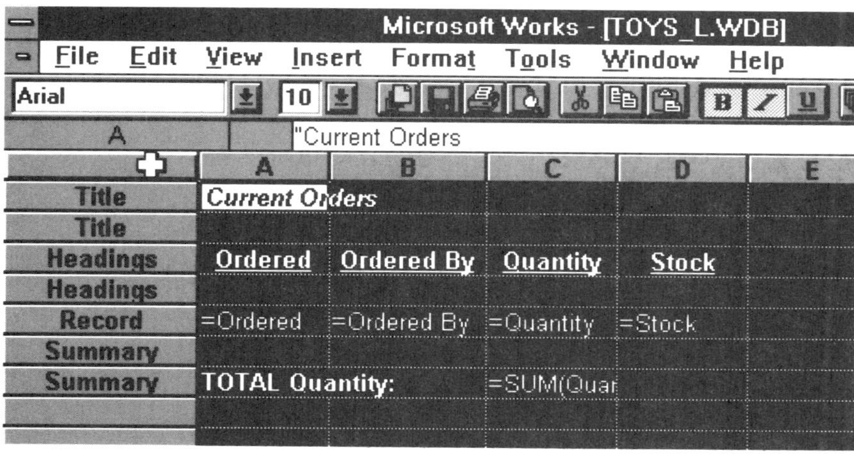

Figure 18x-15. *Click on the area above and to the left of your report title to select the entire report.*

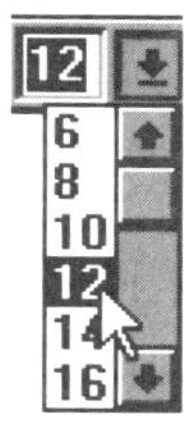

Figure 18x-16. *Select 12 from the Size submenu in the toolbar.*

Works changes the size to 12 point as Figure 18x-17 illustrates.

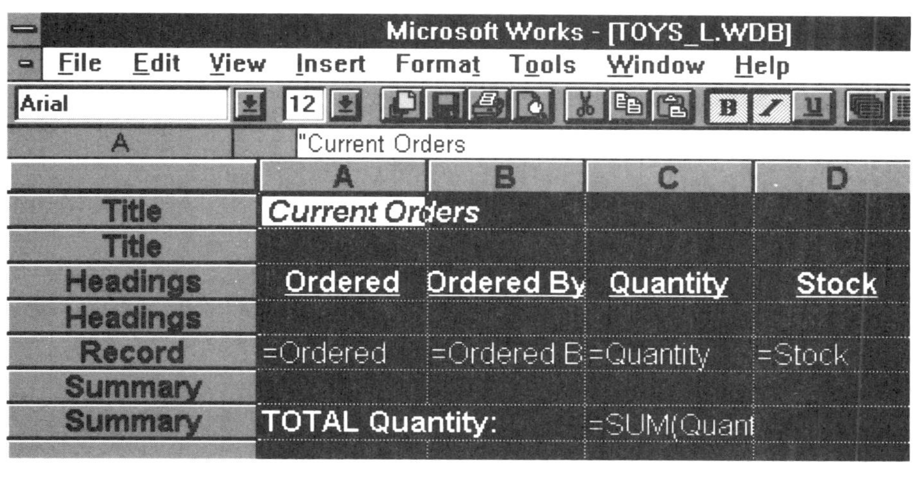

Figure 18x-17. *The size is 12 point.*

6. *Name the report "Orders 1993."*

A database can have more than one report attached to it. A more meaningful name is given to the report using the *Name Report* command in the **Tools** menu. Giving a report a name avoids confusion when many reports are added to the database. To add a name to this report, follow Figures 18x-18 through 18x-20.

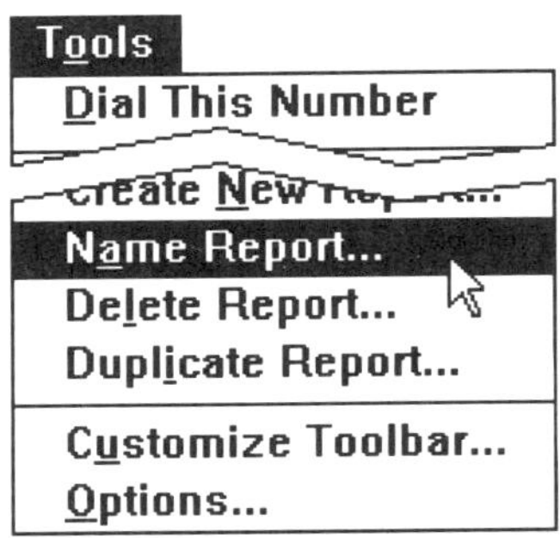

Figure 18x-18. *Choose Name Report from the* ***Tools*** *menu.*

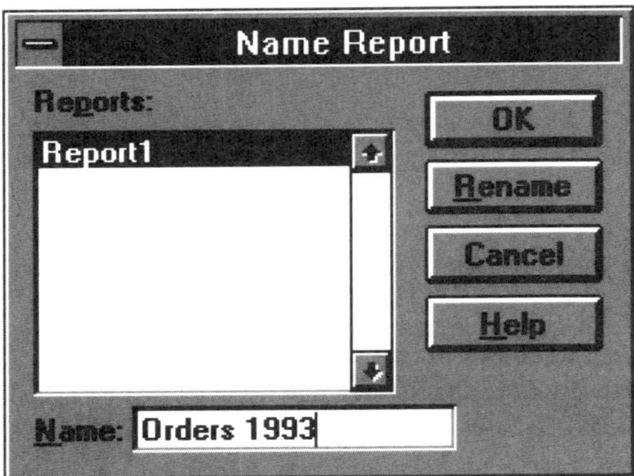

Figure 18x-19. *Report 1 is highlighted, so click in the Name text box and type in "Orders 1993."*

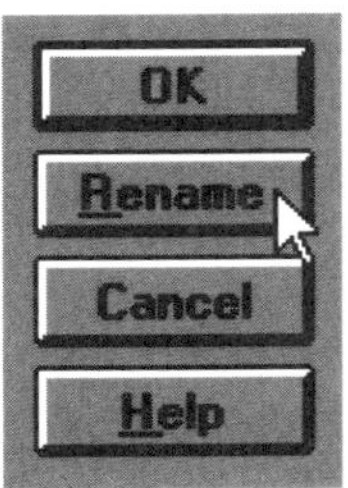

Figure 18x-20. *Click on Rename to change the name of the report.*

Click on *OK* to return to the report definition screen.

7. View the report in Print Preview and print it to the printer.

The quickest way to activate *Print Preview* is to click on the *Print Preview* button on the toolbar, as Figure 18x-21 shows.

Figure 18x-21. *Click on the Print Preview button on the toolbar.*

In the *Print Preview* screen you are shown how the report will appear on paper when it is printed. To print from this screen, click on the *Print* button (Figure 18x-22).

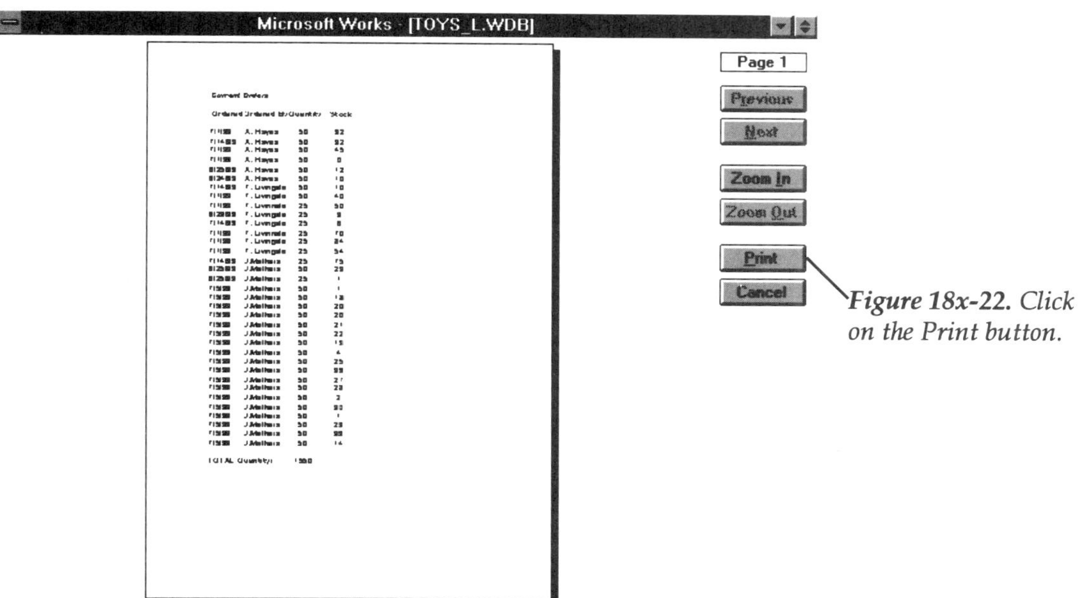

Figure 18x-22. *Click on the Print button.*

You have now completed this exercise. You may want to save your file under a different name using the *Save As* command in the **File** menu.

Index

D

E

F

G

H

Q

R

S